C000148857

Also published by Dunedin Academic Press:

Lainnir a' Bhùirn — The Gleaming Water: Essays on Modern Gaelic Literature
Edited by Emma Dymock and Wilson McLeod (2012)

Coimhearsnachd na Gàidhlig an-diugh — Gaelic Communities Today
Edited by Gillian Munro and Iain Mac an Tàilleir (2010)

Cànan & Cultur / Language and Culture: Rannsachadh na Gàidhlig 4
Edited by Gillian Munro and Richard A. V. Cox (2010)

Revitalising Gaelic in Scotland
Edited by Wilson McLeod (2006)

Cànan & Cultur / Language and Culture: Rannsachadh na Gàidhlig 3
Edited by Wilson McLeod, James E. Fraser and Anja Gunderloch (2006)

www.dunedinacademicpress.co.uk

BY POETIC AUTHORITY

The Rhetoric of Panegyric
in Gaelic Poetry of Scotland to *c.*1700

M. Pía Coira

DUNEDIN

Published by
Dunedin Academic Press Ltd
Hudson House
8 Albany Street
Edinburgh EH1 3QB
Scotland

ISBN 978-1-78046-003-1
© 2012 M. Pía Coira

The right of M. Pía Coira to be identified as the author of this book
has been asserted by her in accordance with sections 77 & 78 of the
Copyright, Designs and Patents Act 1988

All rights reserved.
No part of this publication may be reproduced or transmitted in any form or
by any means or stored in any retrieval system of any nature without prior
written permission, except for fair dealing under the Copyright, Designs and
Patents Act 1988 or in accordance with a licence issued by the publisher or
the Copyright Licensing Society in respect of photocopying or reprographic
reproduction. Full acknowledgment as to author, publisher and source must
be given. Application for permission for any other use of copyright material
should be made in writing to the publisher.

British Library Cataloguing in Publication Data
A catalogue record for this book is available from the British Library

Typeset by Makar Publishing Production
Printed by CPI Group (UK) Ltd., Croydon, CR0 4YY

Ós que estades lonxe, e ós que estades alén

Contents

Contents

Contents

Preface

In the preface to their anthology of Gaelic prose texts, *Ri Linn nan Linntean*, the editors state: 'Tro litreachas agus tro sheanchas, tron lagh agus tro smuaintean nan daoine fhèin, gheibh sinn dealbh air am beatha, air na bha iad a' dèanamh, a' smaoineachadh no a' creidsinn ann an iomadach cuspair, beag is mòr' ('Through literature and through history, through the law and through the thoughts of the people themselves, we obtain a picture of their life, of what they did, thought or believed about many topics, great and small', Cox and Ó Baoill (eds) 2005, p. ix). This is perhaps most true of medieval and early modern Gaelic poetry. While nowadays poetry is something chiefly available in books through individual reading, throughout the period covered in this work, when reading was generally a privilege of the élite classes, poetry was something mostly acquired and transmitted orally, and available in social gatherings at any level. And it is easy to see how oral transmission would facilitate dissemination as well as exchange of opinion. Different social levels had, of course, different types of poets and audiences, and therefore we have different types of poetry. Yet all the various categories were linked to each other by what John MacInnes, writing in the seventies, defined as the 'panegyric code', the set of conventions which can be found throughout Gaelic literature in all its genres and social categories. It is probably the fundamentally oral character of the transmission of poetry that provides the reason for this all-encompassing literary conformity, and this conformity, or consistency, must be seen as aiming to preserve social order and cohesion. And this is no surprise, for whether in the complex metrics of the professional *file* or in the accentual verse of the nurse to the household children, and even in the yet humbler waulking song, we find echoes of the principles for the government of society established in the ancient Gaelic laws.

There is an important social and political message, then, embedded in the poetry. Essential to the modern reader is the need to keep sight of the fact that this message is conveyed in codified diction, so that interpreting quite literally a poet's words can lead to serious error. The listing of allies so common in vernacular verse is one typical example: what we have here is rather the listing of potential allies, because this is a mere propaganda device. And so, while factual historical information can be found in Gaelic poetry, the reader must interpret the code before attempting to establish what constitutes a clean statement of fact. It should further be borne in mind that not infrequently poetic discourse is affected by metrical require-ments; thus a king-list may give some of the rulers in the wrong sequence in order to fit the rhyme. Another warning concerns the poetic recitation of genealogies. Here, as in the genealogical records proper, it is not uncom-mon to find gaps, often decided on for purely cost-saving reasons (the less important names in the pedigree being left out), although sometimes prob-ably because the information had simply been lost. None of these quirks would, however, detract from the key message that our sources intended to transmit. There is also the question of the veracity of genealogical claims of ancient noble origins, consistently reaching far back into pseudo-history or mythology, two 'historical' areas perfectly acceptable to the medieval and early modern mind. Above all, the guiding principle is that our poetry is concerned with the depiction of the subject praised as the ideal ruler — not what he is and has done, but what he ought to, and could, be and do — and the upholding of this claim through well-established themes and motifs. This concept was already highlighted in Gillies 1986, and the work of other scholars (for instance, McCaughey 1989, *Lasair*, or O Riordan 2007) shows the same key understanding of the necessity to interpret the code. The present work is offered as a fresh contribution to the study of Gaelic poetry, with focus on the rhetoric of panegyric of Scotland from the earliest extant compositions to the beginning of the eighteenth century. It is hoped that it will encourage further work on the less explored field of medieval and early modern Gaelic literary studies.

This book is the outcome of my work as a Research Fellow on a project funded by the University of Aberdeen. While I take sole responsibil-ity for the final production, I am indebted to a number of people who provided support, often in more than one way: Kath, Ronald and Máire Black, Steve Boardman, Angelo Forte, Marta Lara Coira, Michael Newton, Colm Ó Baoill, Richard Oram, the scholars who preceded me in the field, the anonymous reviewer, who provided very helpful commentary on an earlier draft, and all those who gave me time, space, and encouragement. My thanks also to the following: Aberdeen University's Queen Mother Library and Historic Collections, Edinburgh University Library, the National Library of Scotland, the Royal Irish Academy Library, Trinity College Dublin Library, Kerry Archaeological and Historical Society, Kerry Library, Tralee, and Dunedin Academic Press, with all of whom it has been a pleasure to work. And to David Dumville, who gave the project a start.

M Pía Coira, Drumlithie, October 2010

Spelling and nomenclature

Although most of the present work is concerned with the Gaelic Classical period (*c*.1200–*c*.1650), some of the poetic and other sources quoted are earlier, and therefore in a different spelling. Additionally, the Scottish Gaelic and Irish vernacular languages have their own spelling rules, which should be respected as much as their own grammatical forms. The spelling of Scottish Gaelic, however, can vary significantly between recent editions, which generally adhere to the Gaelic Orthographic Conventions 2005, and earlier printed material. While it is accepted that Gaelic spelling uniformity cannot be achieved in this work (and proposed, moreover, that it would be wrong to attempt to impose it), some general editorial method had to be adopted, and it is as follows:

Gaelic words are given in Classical Gaelic (e.g., *Gaoidheal*) except where they concern Scottish Gaelic vernacular poems or poets: so an Irish *bard* (the lower class of poet originally forming part of a *file*'s retinue), but a Scottish *bàrd* (like Iain Lom). *Gàidhealtachd* denotes Scottish Gaeldom. Personal names, surnames, and kindreds of any time within the period covered are normally given in the Classical language, except when quoted from sources where they are spelt otherwise, or when they are the names of vernacular poets. For instance: Eóin, Ailéan, Caimbéal, Mac Coinnigh, Clann Ghille Eóin; Iain mac Ailein, Caimbeul, MacCoinnich, Clann Ghilleathain. Occasionally a compromise has had to be made, as when a clan chief is also a vernacular poet; where the individual is best known as a poet, the name is given in vernacular spelling, e.g.: Donnchadh nam Pìos, Murchadh Mòr. As for a number of poets who composed syllabic verse for Clann Ghriogóir but may not have been *filidh* (see Chapter 5), their names are given in classical spelling on the grounds that their compositions do not belong to the 'sub-bardic' genre (see Chapter 2 for the classification of poets and poetry). The exception is Donnchadh, brother of the Dean of Lismore, who was definitely not a *file*, and whose surname is therefore spelled MacGriogair. Gaelic plurals are used for kindred names, as in Caimbéalaigh, Rósaigh, Mic Eóghain, Uí Néill. The royal lines are Bailliol, Brús, and Stiúbhart, but note 'Robert I', 'James II', 'Henry Stewart Lord Darnley' to avoid purism, while names of the kings from the Gaelic dynasties normally remain in Classical Gaelic (e.g., Maol Coluim III). *Mac* is capitalised when in a surname, otherwise *mac*. But where a Christian name is unknown it is capitalised, as in Mac Eachaigh; similarly NicGhillesheathanaich. Other names (e.g., English, Norse) are given in English. Females are listed in the index under the family patronymic (e.g., Mac Coirceadáil, Aithbhreac). Place-names are given in English unless in a Gaelic quotation.

Quotations from pre-classical and classical poems keep the spelling of the published source. In the case of manuscript material, the spelling has not been standardised, although contractions have been expanded. Quotations from vernacular poetry are in vernacular spelling (Scottish or Irish as appropriate) as given in the source, printed or unprinted. Translations are, unless otherwise indicated, as given in published sources (but normally I have kept *Gall* / *Goill* untranslated), except when quoting from *FFÉ* and *RC* when, as in the case of manuscript material, translations are my own.

'Scotland' is normally used meaning its current geographical extent. *Alba* is Britain in literature from earliest times (but Britain is *Breatain* in the later period), otherwise the name given to their kingdom by the Gaels of Dál Riada after they permanently overcame the Picts. The lords of the Isles are never the Lords of the Isles (except in the parliamentary honour given to Eóin mac Alasdair) since this was only a self-styling rather than a formal title. Sections from prose sources are indicated §, and similarly stanzas for poems. In the case of the latter, following letters indicate lines within the stanza. Numbers following 'MS 1467' denote the map number given by Ronald and Máire Black in their online publication.

Index of tables[1]

---

1 These tables represent the claims made in the genealogies, rather than historical accuracy.

Abbreviations

'Ane accompt'   'Ane Accompt of the Genealogie of the Campbells', *HP* ii, 72–111

'Craignish History' 'The Genealogical and Historicall Account of the Family of Craignish', ed. H. Campbell, in *Miscellany of the Scottish History Society*, Vol. 4 (1926), pp. 187–299

AC   *Annála Connacht: The Annals of Connacht (A.D. 1224–1544)*, ed. A. M. Freeman (Dublin: Dublin Institute for Advanced Studies, 1944)

ADD   *Aithdioghluim Dána*, ed. L. McKenna, 2 Vols, Irish Texts Society: Publications, 37, 40 (Dublin: Educational Company of Ireland, 1939–40)

AFOD   *Dánta do Chum Aonghus Fionn Ó Dálaigh*, ed. L. M'Kenna, (Dublin: Maunsel, 1919)

ALI   *Acts of the Lords of the Isles, 1336–1493*, ed. J. and R. W. Munro (Edinburgh: Scottish History Society, 1986)

Annales Hiberniae *Annales Hiberniae*, by J. Grace, ed. R. Butler (Dublin: Dublin University Press, 1842)

APS   *The Acts of the Parliaments of Scotland*, ed. T. Thomson and C. Innes, 12 Vols (Edinburgh, 1814–75)

ARÉ   *Annála Ríoghachta Éireann: Annals of the Kingdom of Ireland, from the Earliest Period to the Year 1606*, ed. J. O'Donovan (London: Hodges and Smith, 1851)

AU   *Annála Uladh: The Annals of Ulster, from the Earliest Times to the Year 1541*, ed. W. M. Hennessy, and B. MacCarthy (Dublin, 1829–89; repr. Blackrock: Éamonn de Búrca, 1998, with an introduction by N. Ó Muraíle)

Audacht Morainn *Audacht Morainn*, ed. F. Kelly (Dublin: Dublin Institute for Advanced Studies, 1976)

BAR   *Beatha Aodha Ruaidh Uí Dhomhnaill: The Life of Aodh Ruadh Ó Domhnaill*, comp. Lughaidh Ó Cléirigh, ed. Paul Walsh, 2 pts, Irish Texts Society: Publications, 42, 45 (Dublin: Educational Company of Ireland, 1948-57)

Berchán	*Prophecy of Berchán: Irish and Scottish High-kings of the Early Middle Ages*, by B. T. Hudson (Westport, CT: Greenwood, 1996)
BG	*Bàrdachd Ghàidhlig: Specimens of Gaelic Poetry 1550–1900*, ed. W. J. Watson (Inverness: Northern Counties, 1918; repr. Stirling: Learmonth, 1932)
BH	*The Blind Harper: The Songs of Roderick Morison and his Music*, ed. W. Matheson (Edinburgh: Scottish Gaelic Texts Society, 1970)
Black, *Catalogue*	*Catalogue of Gaelic Manuscripts in the National Library of Scotland*, by R. Black, 2 Vols [unpublished draft catalogue]
BL	*Na Bàird Leathanach: The Maclean Bards*, ed. A. M. Sinclair (Charlottetown: Haszard & Moore, 1898–1900)
BPD	*Bardic Poetry Database*, comp. Katharine Simms, http://bardic.celt.dias.ie/ (last accessed 1 September 2010)
BSC	*Bàrdachd Shìlis na Ceapaich: Poems and Songs by Sìleas MacDonald c.1660–c.1729*, ed. C. Ó Baoill (Edinburgh: Scottish Academic Press, 1972)
Celtic Studies	*Celtic Studies: Essays in Memory of Angus Matheson, 1912–1962*, ed. J. Carney and D. Greene (London: Routledge & K. Paul, 1968)
CGH	*Corpus Genealogiarum Hiberniae*, ed. M. A. O'Brien, Vol. 1 (Dublin: Dublin Institute for Advanced Studies, 1976)
Checklist	*Scottish Vernacular Verse to 1730: A Checklist*, comp. C. Ó Baoill and D. MacAulay, 2nd ed. (Aberdeen: Aberdeen University Department of Celtic, 1988, 2001)
Clan Donald	*The Clan Donald*, by A. J. and A. MacDonald, 3 Vols (Inverness: Northern Counties, 1896–1904)
CMCS	*Cambrian Medieval Celtic Studies*
Collectanea	*Collectanea de Rebus Albanicis*, ed. D. Gregory and W. F. Skene (Edinburgh: Iona Club, 1847)
Dán Dé	*Dán Dé: The Poems of Donnchadh Mór Ó Dálaigh, and the Religious Poems in the Duanaire of the Yellow Book of Lecan*, ed. L. McKenna (Dublin: Educational Co., 1922)
DC	*Duanaire Colach, 1537–1757*, ed. C. Ó Baoill (Obar Dheathain: An Clò Gàidhealach, 1997)
DD	*Dioghluim Dána*, ed. L. Mac Cionnaith (Dublin: Oifig an tSoláthair, 1938)
DIL	*Dictionary of the Irish Language: Based Mainly on Old and Middle Irish Materials. Compact Edition*, ed. E. G. Quin (Dublin: Royal Irish Academy, 1983)

DNB	*Dictionary of National Biography*, ed. H. C. G. Matthew and Brian Harrison, 60 Vols (2004)
DnBM	*Dán na mBráthar Mionúr*, ed. C. Mag Craith, 2 Vols (Dublin: Dublin Institute for Advanced Studies, 1980)
DnS	*Duanaire na Sracaire / Songbook of the Pillagers: Anthology of Gaelic Verse to 1600*, ed. W. McLeod and M. Bateman (Edinburgh: Birlinn, 2007)
Dispossessed	*An Duanaire, 1600–1900: Poems of the Dispossessed*, ed. S. Ó Tuama and T. Kinsella (Mountrath, Portlaoise: Dolmen, 1981)
DSL-DOST	*Dictionary of the Scots Language: Dictionar o the Scots Leid*, by V. Skretkowicz *et al.*, http://www.dsl.ac.uk/ (last accessed 1 September 2010)
E	*Comh-chruinneachidh Orannaigh Gaidhealach*, by Raonuill Macdomhnuill, Vol. 1 (Duneidiunn: Walter Ruddiman, 1776)
EB	*Eachann Bacach and Other Maclean Poets*, ed. C. Ó Baoill (Edinburgh: Scottish Academic Press, 1970)
EMWP	*Early Modern Women Poets (1520–1700): An Anthology*, ed. J. Stevenson and P. Davidson (Oxford: Oxford University Press, 2001)
EUL	Edinburgh University Library
FEMN	*Féil-sgríbhinn Eoin Mhic Néill: Essays and Studies Presented to Professor Eoin MacNeill, D.Litt., on the Occasion of his Seventieth Birthday*, ed. J. Ryan (Dublin: Three Candles, 1940)
FFCh	*Filí agus Filidheacht Chonnacht*, ed. Tomás Ó Raghallaigh (Baile Átha Cliath: Oifig an tSoláthair, 1938)
FFÉ	*Foras Feasa ar Éirinn: The History of Ireland*, by Seathrún Céitinn, ed. David Comyn and Patrick Dinneen, 4 Vols, Irish Texts Society: Publications, 4, 8–9, 15 (London: Nutt, 1902–14)
FMUB	*Féilscríbhinn Mháirtín Uí Bhriain*, ed. N. Mac Craith and P. Ó hÉalaí (Galway: Cló Iar-Chonnachta, 2007)
Foirm	*Foirm na n-Urrnuidheadh: John Carswell's Gaelic Translation of the Book of Common Order*, ed. R. L. Thomson (Edinburgh: Oliver and Boyd, 1970)
Fr. Annals	*Fragmentary Annals*, ed. J. N. Radner (Dublin: Dublin Institute for Advanced Studies, 1978)
GB	*The Gaelic Bards from 1411 to 1715*, ed. A. M. Sinclair (Charlottetown P. E. I. : Haszard & Moore, 1890)
GB2	*The Gaelic Bards from 1715 to 1765*, ed. A. M. Sinclair (Charlottetown: Haszard & Moore, 1892)
GC	*The Glenbard Collection of Gaelic Poetry* (Charlottetown: Haszard

& Moore, 1890)

Gleanings	*Gleanings from Irish Manuscripts*, ed. P. Walsh (Dublin: Three Candles, 1933)
GnC	*Gàir nan Clàrsach: The Harps' Cry*, ed. C. Ó Baoill and M. Bateman (Edinburgh: Birlinn, 1994)
GSMM	*Gaelic Songs of Mary McLeod: Òrain agus Luinneagan Gàidhlig le Màiri nighean Alasdair Ruaidh*, ed. J. C. Watson, Scottish Gaelic Texts, 9 (London; Glasgow: Blackie and son, 1934; repr. Edinburgh: Oliver and Boyd, 1965)
HMo	*The Highland Monthly*
HP	*Highland Papers*, ed. J. R. N. Macphail, Scottish History Society, 2nd series, Vols 5, 12, 20; 3rd series, Vol. 22, Edinburgh (1914–34)
IBP	*Irish Bardic Poetry: Texts and Translations together with an Introductory Lecture*, by O. Bergin, ed. D. Greene and F. Kelly (Dublin: Dublin Institute for Advanced Studies, 1970)
ID	*Iain Dubh: Òrain a Rinn Iain Dubh mac Iain mhic Ailein (c.1665–c.1725)*, ed. C. Ó Baoill (Obar Dheathain: An Clò Gàidhealach, 1994)
Irish Chiefs	*Irish Chiefs and Leaders*, by P. Walsh, ed C. Ó Lochlainn (Dublin: Three Candles, 1960)
JKHAS	*Journal of the Kerry Historical and Archaeological Association*
Laoide	*Alasdair mac Colla: Sain-eolus ar a Ghníomharthaibh Gaisge*, by S. Laoide (Baile Átha Cliath: Connradh na Gaedhilge, 1914)
Lasair	*An Lasair: Anthology of 18th-Century Gaelic Verse*, ed. R. Black (Edinburgh: Birlinn, 2001)
LB	*Leabhar Branach: The Book of the O'Byrnes*, ed. S. Mac Airt (Dublin: Dublin Institute for Advanced Studies, 1944)
LCAB	*Leabhar Cloinne Aodha Buidhe*, ed. Tadhg Ó Donnchadha (Baile Átha Cliath: Oifig an tSoláthair, 1931)
LCC	*Léachtaí Cholm Cille*
LCS	*Leabhar Chlainne Suibhne: An Account of the MacSweeney Families in Ireland, with Pedigrees*, ed. Paul Walsh (Dublin: Dollard, 1920)
LF	*Leabhar na Féinne*, ed. J. F. Campbell (London: Spottiswoode, 1872)
LMG	*Leabhar Mór na nGenealach: The Great Book of Irish Genealogies*, comp. D. Mac Firbhisigh, ed. N. Ó Muraíle, 5 Vols (Dublin: de Búrca, 2003–4)
LSMR	*Làimh-sgrìobhainn Mhic Rath*, ed. C. Mac Phàrlain (Dun-de: MacLeod, 1923)

Mac Cuarta	*Séamas Dall Mac Cuarta: Dánta*, ed. S. Ó Gallchóir (Baile Átha Cliath: An Clóchomhar, 1971)
Martin	*Curiosities of Art and Nature: The New Annotated and Illustrated Edition of Martin Martin's Classic* A Description of the Western Islands of Scotland, ed. M. Robson (Port of Ness, Isle of Lewis: Islands Book Trust, 2003)
MC	*The Macdonald Collection of Gaelic Poetry*, ed. A. and A. Macdonald (Inverness: Northern Counties, 1911)
Misc. K. Meyer	*Miscellanea Hibernica*, by K. Meyer (Urbana: University of Illinois, 1917)
ML	the MacLagan manuscripts in the Glasgow University Library, catalogued in Mackechnie 1973, pp. 412–452
MNL	*Mairghread Nighean Lachlainn: Song-maker of Mull*, ed. C. Ó Baoill, Scottish Gaelic Texts, 19 (Llandysul: Gwasg Gomer, 2009)
Monro	*Monro's Western Isles of Scotland*, ed. R. W. Munro (Edinburgh: Oliver and Boyd, 1961)
'MS 1467'	a fifteenth-century Scottish Gaelic manuscript now forming the first part of NLS Adv. 72.1.1
MT	*Mac-Talla*
MTT	*Mactalla nan Tùr*, ed. A. M. Sinclair (Sydney: Mac-Talla Pub. Co., 1901)
NLI	National Library of Ireland
NLS	National Library of Scotland
O'Grady	*Catalogue of Irish Manuscripts in the British Museum*, by S. H. O'Grady, 3 Vols (London: British Museum, 1926–53)
OIL	*Orain Iain Luim: Songs of John MacDonald, Bard of Keppoch*, ed. A. M. MacKenzie, Scottish Gaelic Texts, 8 (Edinburgh: Oliver and Boyd, 1964)
Onomasticon	*Onomasticon Goedelicum Locorum et Tribuum Hiberniae et Scotiae*, by Edmund Hogan (Dublin: Hodges, Figgis & Co., 1910)
PB	*Poems on the Butlers of Ormond, Cahir, and Dunboyne (A.D. 1400-1650)*, ed. J.Carney (Dublin: Dublin Institute for Advanced Studies, 1945)
PBA	*Proceedings (British Academy)*
PRIA	*Proceedings (Royal Irish Academy)*
RC	*Reliquiae Celticae: Texts, Papers and Studies in Gaelic Literature and Philology Left by the Late Rev. Alexander Cameron, LL.D.*, 2 Vols, ed. A. Mac Bain and J. Kennedy (Inverness: Northern Chronicle, 1892–4)

RIA   Royal Irish Academy

RPC   *Register of the Privy Council*, ed. J. H. Burton *et al.* (Edinburgh, 1877–1898)

Scotichronicon   *Scotichronicon: New Edition in Latin and English with Notes and Indexes*, ed. D. E. R. Watt (Aberdeen: Aberdeen University Press, 1987–1998)

SGS   *Scottish Gaelic Studies*

SHR   *Scottish Historical Review*

SO   *Sàr-obair nam Bàrd Gaelach*, ed. J. Mackenzie (Glasgow: Macgregor, Polson & Co., 1841; new ed. Edinburgh: N. Macleod, 1904)

SRE   *Songs Remembered in Exile: Traditional Gaelic Songs from Nova Scotia Recorded in Cape Breton and Antigonish County in 1937, with an Account of the Causes of Hebridean Emigration, 1790–1835*, ed. J. L. Campbell (Aberdeen: Aberdeen University Press, 1990)

Stewart 1880   *The Stewarts of Appin*, by J. H. J. Stewart (Glasgow: Maclachlan and Stewart, 1880)

SVBDL   *Scottish Verse from the Book of the Dean of Lismore*, ed. W. J. Watson, Scottish Gaelic Texts, Vol. 1 (Edinburgh: Oliver and Boyd, 1937)

TCD   Trinity College, Dublin

TD   *A bhFuil aguinn dar Chum Tadhg Dall Ó Huiginn (1550–1591)*, ed. Eleanor Knott, 2 Vols, Irish Texts Society: Publications, 22, 23 (London: Simpkin, 1922–6)

TGSI   *Transactions (Gaelic Society of Inverness)*

Other abbreviations

a.	*ante*, before
b.	born
br.	brother of
c.	*circa*
comp.	compiler, compiled by
d.	daughter of
grf.	grandfather of
grs.	grandson of
h.	husband of
m.	mother of
n.	niece of
p.	*post*, after
r.	*rí, rex*, ruled
s.	son of
sr.	sister of
trsl.	translation, translated by
w.	wife of

Iss e in coic(ed) gne in gnat[h]berla fogni do cac[h], (ar) asberad araili comad e in berla Feini fasaigi na filed, 7 conach berla fo leith *etir*.

(The fifth kind is the Usual Language which serves for every one; for others say of the *Bérla Féine* that it is the Commentaries of the Poets, and that it is not a separate language at all).

(*Auraicept na n-éces*, pp. 102–4).

Bha uair 's bu leamsa am fearann
eadar Sealtainn is Tuaidh.
An Dùn Èideann nan rìghrean
bhithinn cinnteach à duais.
Bhiodh teudan gan riaghladh
a chur rian dhomh air duain,
is gum freagradh gach balla
do dh'aicill is uaim.

(There was a time that mine was the land
between Shetland and Tweed.
In Edinburgh of the kings
my reward was assured.
Harpstrings would be tuned
to accompany my songs,
and every wall would echo
with word-rhyme and alliteration).

(Byrne, M. (ed.) 2000, pp. 324–5).

Chapter 1

Gaelic court poetry in Scotland:
historical background

A fourteenth-century Irish metrical tract preserves the following quatrain:

> Olc a n[dearna] mac Mael Colaim
> ar n-aimleas re hAlaxandair
> da-ní le gach mac righ romhainn
> foghail ar faras Albain.

> (It's bad, what Mael Coluim's son has done,
> dividing us from Alexander;
> he causes, like each king's son before,
> the plunder of stable Alba).[1]

The subject of this poetic attack was the future Scottish king David I, youngest brother of the current monarch, Alexander I, and the time of composition the early twelfth century.[2] We do not know who the poet was, but he was clearly the victim of discord between David and Alexander. This quatrain — perhaps part of a longer piece — is one witness that Gaelic men of learning were at the time operating in the area of modern Scotland that at the time was known as *Alba*. The existence of this and other Scottish-related medieval and early modern Gaelic poems raises questions on the purpose and the value of this particular literary genre in Scotland. We have a considerable amount of knowledge of the poet class

---

1   The sources of all poems quoted are given in Appendix 3.
2   Clancy (ed.) 1998, p. 184. See also below, chapter 7, p. 291.

responsible for the composition, preservation, and transmission of this type of literature. To draw a very brief sketch, obtained mostly from Irish sources, these men enjoyed an elevated status in society, as well as notable privileges, and by the later medieval period (from around 1200 onwards) were attached to noble patrons with whom they maintained a contractual relationship. They were a highly respected, and sometimes feared, class. As well as being engaged in literary composition, and in the education of their patrons' sons,[3] the *filidh* had a political role, as reflected in their activities as advisers and ambassadors to their patrons and as witnesses of their charters. What they had to say mattered, and their poems particularly so, since the persons these poems addressed paid elevated prices for their compositions.[4]

One important function attached to the Gaelic court poet was that of validator of political leadership. The *ollamh re dán* had an indispensable role at a chief's inauguration ceremony.[5] The panegyrics he composed were also validating devices in that they authoritatively invested the individual addressed with the credentials required of someone aspiring to become his people's leader.[6] Many of these credentials date back to pre-Christian times, and they match those found in the Gaelic law tracts; in that respect a panegyric may be regarded, as well as a political statement, as a sort of legal document verifying an individual's aptness and right to rule. In Scotland the nature of kingship changed considerably with the passage of time, adopting various aspects and elements of English and continental monarchy. One might have expected the ruler's traditional credentials to have become altered to adjust to the new ruling concepts and style, but in the main such adjustment did not take place. The qualifications required of the 'right ruler', the basis or bases of his entitlement to rule, and the visible signs of his good government, all remained very much the same. Very little

---

3 See below, chapter 2, p. 37.

4 Simms 1987, p. 60. Classic introductions to medieval Gaelic court poetry can be found, for instance, in Murphy 1940, Knott 1960, *TD* i, pp. xxxiii–xlv, Greene 1961, Carney 1967. For the contractual relationship between poet and patron see Breatnach 1983. For the poets as diplomats and political advisers see *ibid.*, pp. 51–60. For their educational role see below, chapter 2, pp. 37–8, 44.

5 Byrne 2001, pp. 15–16. In some cases this inaugural role was the prerogative of the *ollamh re seanchas*; see Simms 2000, p. 30.

6 Dewar 2006b, pp. 406, 418–19. See also Breatnach 2006, pp. 71, 72, 73–5.

has survived of panegyric poetry composed for the kings of Scots. The individuals addressed by *filidh* in the extant corpus of Scottish Gaelic praise poetry are almost exclusively vassals of the Scottish kings, or else Irish nobles. The key point is that as the nature of Scottish kingship changed, so did that of the kings' relationship with their vassals (feudalism being one important aspect), and yet very little of this is apparent in the poetry. In the new political context, therefore, the question of the purpose and validity of courtly panegyric, with its persistent adherence to its original rhetorical formulation, appears intriguing.

Validation of political leadership in medieval Gaelic panegyric was realised by means of a set of stock motifs of recognised resonance and meaning for the audience.[7] A literal reading of this type of poetry will lead the modern mind to erroneous interpretations. Historical fact, if present at all in a poem, will be found only after removing the various rhetorical devices which by convention must be present there.[8] To borrow the term first coined by John MacInnes, the stock motifs contained in the poetry constitute a 'panegyric code', found not only in the works of the professional court poets but indeed extending, albeit with variations, to all Gaelic literary genres.[9] While resiliently conservative — a characteristic perhaps nowhere best illustrated than in the poetic motif which portrays the subject 'ar lorg a shinnsear' ('like his ancestors', 'in his ancestors' footsteps') — this code was not completely petrified. Innovations were introduced on occasion, typically at critical points in time. One example is the convention that a poem's subject is suitable, or destined to become, high-king of Ireland. It has been suggested that it may have originated in the twelfth century when the Anglo-Norman incomers brought to an end the long period of the supposed high-kingship of Ireland.[10] Another is the depiction of the poem's subject as Catholic in religion; this first appeared,

---

7 *TD* i, pp. li–lxii; Watson 1914–19, pp. 209–14.

8 See Simms 1987, especially at pp. 60, 64, 70. See also McLeod 2002a, alerting historians to the dangers of a literal interpretation of Gaelic lordly titles; Dewar 2006b, which in cataloguing the rhetoric of political leadership detaches it from fact and factual claims; O Riordan 2007, a comparative study of medieval Gaelic panegyric and its continental counterpart which similarly notes the necessity for a rhetorical reading and interpretation of this genre (see especially pp. 16, 24–56, 61, 80, 115).

9 See generally MacInnes 2006b.

10 Ó Cuív 1963, pp. 253, 256.

again in Ireland, towards the end of the sixteenth century, when a sense of being Irish began to emerge which featured the tripartite make-up of Irish birth, Gaelic language, and Catholic religion.[11]

The credence and influence of the *filidh* are perhaps not easy for the modern mind to understand. Yet in Gaelic society the *filidh*'s verse was used by historians much as modern historians would use footnotes.[12] One of the duties of the chief poet was to record his patron's ancestry and noble deeds through such a medium, and chroniclers and annalists, even as late as the seventeenth century, would frequently underpin particular arguments in their narrative by appending a little closing note beginning 'mar adeir an file' — sometimes in Latin, perhaps for greater effect, 'ut dixit poeta' ('as the poet said') — followed by a quatrain or more which purported to carry the necessary authority.[13] The *filidh*'s learning was so extensive and so respected that whether the information given concerned an individual's lineage, a saint's miracles or the origin of a place-name, there was little doubt in the author's mind that his point would be accepted without reservation as long as it could be substantiated by poetic authority. Similarly, in classical poetry the same authority is conveyed by resorting to the 'written word' motif. Whether the poet is asserting the accuracy of his subject's genealogy, or defending one particular claim — for instance an individual's receipt of a royal charter confirming him in his territory — he often declares that he is speaking from his *seanrolla* ('ancient parchments'), *seinleabhair* ('ancient books'), 'do réiriúil an annálaigh' ('according to the information of the annals'), and so on.[14] Much has been made of the fundamentally oral character of medieval Gaelic culture, both in its form and its transmission. Yet at least at the highest levels of society the power and

---

11 The poem most explicitly proclaiming the 'faith and fatherland' ideology emerging in the late sixteenth century is perhaps Tuileagna Ó Maolchonaire's *Maith bhur bhfíor catha, a Chlann Róigh*, for Uaithne Ó Mórdha (†1600) , for which see Dewar 2006b, pp. 282–86. For the 'faith and fatherland' ideology see, for instance, Morgan 1995, pp. 15–16; Mac Craith 1996, p. 7.

12 Hudson 1996, p. 96.

13 See, for instance, Stokes (ed.) 1877, p. 112; O'Grady (ed.) 1988, p. 20; FFÉ ii, pp. 4–6, 46, 98, 144. See also generally Toner 2005.

14 See, for instance, *Leanam croinic clann nDálaigh*, for Aodh Ruadh Ó Domhnaill (†1602), at §§1b, 2c, 4b; *Ní dual gan chuimhne air cheart rígh*, for Conchobhar Ó Briain, third earl of Thomond (†1581), at §§5a, 10ab. See also below, chapter 4, p. 127, for an instance in Caimbéal poetry. On this point see McManus 2004, pp. 102–3.

weight of the written record were not lost to the professional men of learn-ing. This is particularly manifest not only in their frequent quotations from it, but also in their love for books and their unremitting efforts to preserve them by copying and re-copying them right through the middle ages and the early modern period.

'Lean an dùthchas bu chathair':[15] the poets and their patrons

The traditional belief is that the Gaels, led by Fearghus Mór mac Eirc, arrived in Scotland from Ireland, conquering and settling initially parts of the western seaboard *c.*500 AD, and later expanding eastwards.[16] Archaeologists have long puzzled over the apparent lack of material culture remains to sustain this view, although it has been eventually agreed, on the basis of linguistic evidence, that it must be the correct one.[17] Moreover, when attempting to establish the date of Gaelic settlement in Scotland, archaeologists now suggest that migration from Ireland into Scotland was not confined to that of Fearghus Mór and his companions, but rather took place over a very lengthy period.[18] The most recent scholarly conclusions, then, tell us little more than what has been available to us all along in medieval and early modern annals and chronicles. These texts show remarkably little change over time and, while as with with the court poetry but on quite different grounds, one should avoid their literal interpretation, they should not be too quickly dismissed as later fabrications.[19] The seventeenth-century Irish scholar Seathrún Céitinn, working from a variety of earlier material, tells us not only that there had been *Scuit* (that is, Gaels from Ireland) in Scotland

---

15 'Follow the tradition that was a birthright' (*Tha mulad, tha mulad*, §23e).
16 See especially Bannerman 1974. For an alternative suggestion, based on the almost total lack of material culture remains, see Campbell 2001.
17 Alcock 1993, p. 10.
18 *ibid.*; Nieke and Duncan 1988, pp. 8–11; Dumville 2002, p. 196.
19 The Gaelic genealogies (which are often included in the poetry and also form the backbone of historical narrative) tend to preserve the most authentic record material (Sellar1981, p. 110; see also Nicholls 1975, p. 258). This seems particularly true of Mac Domhnaill genealogies (see Ó Cuív 1984b, pp. 149–50). Sellar has also shown that much of the genealogical record can be verified against historical evidence; see, for instance, his 'The origins and ancestry of Somerled' (1966), and 'The earliest Campbells' (1973). Similarly, Gaelic historical writing, though unreliable in matters of detail, is usually correct in relating general trends of events (id. 1981, p. 124).

for centuries before Fearghus Mór 'mar aon ré Dál Riada' ('with the Dál Riada') settled there, but that throughout those centuries attempts had been made by the Irish Gaels from time to time to exact tribute from the *Cruithnigh* (Picts).[20] What seems to have been different about the events of *c*.500 is that, according to Céitinn, the current Dál Riada leader, Fearghus Mór mac Eirc, became the first to be styled *rí* of Dál Riada, his predecessors' title having been merely *taoiseach*. Precisely how this took place is not known, but there may be some significance in the claim that for his inauguration Fearghus Mór had *Lia Fáil* brought over from Ireland to Scotland, where it remained and would be used in royal inaugurations until the thirteenth century. To this day it is better known as the Stone of Destiny.[21] The 'Book of Ballymote', indeed, includes Fearghus in a list of Irish kings of Dál Riada.[22] Whatever the case, Fearghus perhaps first became a crucial ancestor to several main settler groups in the late seventh century, when the genealogical text *Cethri prímchenéla Dáil Riata* made all four contemporary principal kindreds the descendants of Fearghus Mór.[23]

Establishing the character and the date or dates of settlement is of considerably less importance to us than the consequences of settlement for the spread into Scotland of the Gaelic panegyric tradition. In other words, when did Gaelic poets from Ireland first come into Scotland, and when did Scottish-born Gaels begin to train as poets and to compose eulogy in the learned tradition? And who were the patrons of these poets? There are not for the time being, and there may never be, straightforward answers to

---

20 See, for instance, *FFÉ* ii, pp. 126, 236, 368, 372, 402, and especially pp. 382, 386. Niall Mac Muireadhaigh also acknowledges Gaelic movement across to Scotland previous to Fearghus Mór; see *RC* ii, p. 148. For an overview based chiefly on earlier sources see Watson 2004, pp. 213–24. The origin of the *Cruitheantuaith* (Picts) remains unclear. The version of *seanchas* is that they were a group, originally from Thracia, that was sent to *Alba* by Éireamhón when it became too powerful in Ireland; this might explain why the Irish kings expected tribute from them. See, for instance, Todd (ed.) 1848, pp. 120–4; *FFÉ* ii, pp. 114–15; *LMG* ii, §419.2, and iii, §§1156.2–1158.2, where it is clearly stated that the *Gaoidhil* of Ireland were overlords of the *Cruitheantuaith*. Modern scholarship can only establish that their language seems to be a form of British with some Gaelic influences; see Fraser 2009, pp. 51–3.

21 *FFÉ* i, pp. 206–8; iii, p. 8. See also below, chapter 5, p. 196.

22 Anderson (ed.) 1990, p. 153.

23 By making Cinéal Loairn and Cinéal nAonghusa segments of Dál Riada; see Fraser 2006, pp. 4–6.

these questions. In the first place, at the time by which we know with certainty of permanent Gaelic settlement in Scotland — around the early sixth century — the *filidh* were affiliated to monasteries rather than to particular secular noble families. It would not be until the poetic reorganisation of the twelfth century that the professional poets severed their ecclesiastical connexions, reorganised themselves into poetic families, and filled the patronage vacuum by attaching themselves to secular kin groups.[24] In connexion with this what first comes to mind is the foundation *c.*563 of the monastery of Iona by Colum Cille, who is traditionally credited, along with his companions and their successors, with the advancement of Christianity in Scotland. The Irish sources, including the poetry itself, present Colum Cille as a protector of the poet class.[25] One contemporary elegy for the saint has survived, composed by Dallán Forgaill, a poet from Ireland; but apart from it, there is very little Gaelic poetry, whether composed in Scotland or for individuals there, extant for the next six centuries or so after Colum Cille's time. The small corpus we do have is made up chiefly of religious poetry, with some secular verse, composed by monks or hermits, mostly in Latin.[26]

One problem is that the Gaelic survivals for this period are in the main isolated quatrains which were preserved as snippets inserted in annals or in grammatical tracts without any mention of authorship. Meagre as the extant corpus is, there are some conclusions we may derive from it. One is that there were poets composing in Gaelic for Scottish patrons from at least the early seventh century onwards.[27] Another is that their addressees were not only Gaelic nobles, but Pictish ones too. We have two poems on the Pictish king Bridei (†693), who defeated the Northumbrians at Dunnichen in Angus in 685, and a quatrain in praise of Aonghus mac

24 For these events see Mac Cana 1974, and below, p. 9.

25 *FFÉ* iii, p. 92–4; Sharpe (ed.) 1995, pp. 89–90.

26 But in the area roughly corresponding to modern Scotland there were other literary languages in use between the mid-sixth and mid-fourteenth centuries. To Latin and Gaelic must be added Welsh, Old English, Older Scots, and Norse; see the anthology in Clancy (ed.) 1998. For a recent edition of Colum Cille's elegy see Clancy and Márkus (eds) 1995, pp. 96–128.

27 The earliest specimens of poems composed in Gaelic given in Clancy (ed.) 1998, p. 113, are fragments of elegies for two different individuals who died in 622 and 625 respectively. See also below, chapter 7, p. 289.

Fearghusa (†761), king of the Eóghanachta of Magh Gheirrghinn.[28] That some of these poetic fragments deal with events of a local political character suggests that the authors may have been local too, although we cannot be entirely sure. That there was poet traffic between Scotland and Ireland from very early times — although its volume is impossible to determine — is well known. The extant elegy for Colum Cille, as we have mentioned, was the work of a poet from Ireland, as was a mid-eleventh century poem on the birth of Aodhán mac Gabhráin (†c.608),[29] although their authors' physical presence in Scotland cannot be proved. Céitinn, on the other hand, mentions one Labhán Draoi, a poet from Scotland contemporary with Colum Cille, who visited Ireland.[30] There is little doubt that poets other than visitors were at work in Scotland, since Iona, Colum Cille's foundation, quickly became a focal centre of learning. From the moment of their permanent settlement the leaders of the various migrant groups — such as the Uí Mhac Uais, Corca Riada, Cinéal nAonghusa, or Cinéal Loairn — would have needed an *ollamh* for their inauguration ceremonies, and the scholars affiliated to Iona and other monasteries probably fulfilled this function. Following this early practice, we still find the poet actively participating in Alexander III's inauguration in 1249, as indeed we find other features of the ceremony which have been identified as consistent with Gaelic inauguration tradition.[31]

It is only when the thirteenth century opens that the picture becomes much clearer. Enter Muireadhach Ó Dálaigh, better known as Muireadhach Albanach who, having made matters too hot for himself in Ireland, left for Scotland — whence his soubriquet — in search of new patrons.[32] In

28 See Clancy (ed.) 1998, p. 115, and below, chapter 5, pp. 185–6, 196.

29 *Ro bátar láeich do Laigneib*, for which see below, chapter 7, pp. 301–3.

30 *FFÉ* iii, p. 58. See also Black (ed.) 1981, p. 299, n. 6*b*.

31 For this identification see Bannerman 1989. See also below, p. 10. Uí Mhac Uais: ancestors of the Mac Domhnaill families of Scotland. Corca Riada: the descendants of Domhanghart Réite (i.e. Riada), ancestor of Cinéal nGabhráin and Cinéal Comhghaill; and the eponym of Dál Riada (see Fraser 2006). Another migrant group seems to have been a branch of Moccu Céin of southern Ireland, probable ancestors of Mic Ghille Moire (anglicised as Morison) of Ness; see Matheson 1976–8, pp. 65–6. Their eponymous ancestor, Cian, was the youngest son of Oilill Ólum, king of Munster.

32 For Muireadhach Albanach see, for instance, Thomson 1960–3, pp. 277–81. For the possibility of Muireadhach being a different individual from the Muireadhach Ó Dálaigh of Lios an Doill, with whom he has been traditionally identified, see Simms 2007. Lios an Doill: Lissadell, Co. Sligo.

this quest he was successful, for we find him attached to the hereditary *mormhaoir*, or earls, of Lennox. Muireadhach's choice of patrons may be of interest. Geography would have suggested that he first seek the patronage of the descendants of Colla Uais, either Raghnall or Dubhghall, the heirs of the great Somhairle (†1164) and rulers over Argyll and many of the Western Isles; yet he appears associated with the rulers of Lennox, which at the time corresponded to modern Dunbartonshire. Did Muireadhach approach Somhairle's sons but was refused as he had been by so many other nobles in Ireland? If this was the case, Raghnall's descendants would later reconsider, for according to tradition Muireadhach Albanach was the ancestor of the poetic family of Mac Muireadhaigh, who enjoyed consistent patronage from Clann Domhnaill.

Muireadhach was a poet in important respects very different from the ones we have encountered so far, as his secular patronage, for one thing, indicates.[33] In twelfth-century Ireland, in the wake both of ecclesiastical reform and of Anglo-Norman advance, a sort of revolution took place within the poet class. Until then, scholarly affiliations had been chiefly monastic. Now the poets severed their connexions with the church and proceeded to re-organise themselves. It would appear that the laicised personnel of the monasteries were, at least in a number of cases, allowed to keep their church lands, and that they turned them into poetic schools. Moreover, they now also began to arrange themselves into hereditary poet families — Muireadhach Albanach came from one of these. These 'new poets' also expanded their specialised fields of learning, for instance adding the discipline of *seanchas* — until then the specialism of the monastic scholar — to their own traditional repertoire of history, poetry (including *dinnsheanchas*), genealogy, metrics, and linguistics. Changes also took place in prosody and in the language of composition itself, as the new *filidh* set their own standard literary dialect, which would remain virtually static for some five centuries and has traditionally been known as Classical Gaelic. In their new milieu poets also had to find new sources of patronage, and it is from this point in time that we find them attached, in their hereditary office, to secular patrons (Ó Domhnaill of Tyrconnell in the case of Muireadhach Albanach's family, Uí Dhálaigh).

---

33 For what follows see Mac Cana 1974. See also Ó Cuív 1973.

Muireadhach Ó Dálaigh needs not be the first to have introduced this 'new poetry' into Scotland, for the Scottish poets either undertook their training or perfected it in the schools in Ireland. There is indeed evidence that other authors were composing poetry for Scottish patrons in the classical format in Muireadhach's time: one example is the poem *Domhnall mac Raghnaill rosg mall*, whose subject is the successor of Raghnall mentioned above and the eponym of Clann Domhnaill.[34] Because the author's name is unknown, there is of course a chance that this poem might have been the work of Muireadhach Albanach himself. However, that the new poetry, what we know as filidheacht na scol (in English commonly 'bardic poetry'), very soon spread beyond the island of Ireland is also shown by the existence of the eulogy *Baile suthach síth Eamhna*, composed for Raghnall mac Godhfhraidh (†1229), a king of Man with Scottish connexions, perhaps as early as the late twelfth century. A contemporary of Muireadhach Albanach was Giolla Brighde Albanach, apparently from Scotland but whose extant work was either composed in Ireland or for Irish patrons.[35] By around the mid-thirteenth century we find another unknown poet addressing the first Mac Domhnaill, Aonghus Mór (son and successor of Domhnall mac Raghnaill),[36] and yet another (whose family name may have been Mac Cimbaetha)[37] performing the traditional duties of the *ollamh* at the inauguration of King Alexander III in 1249. One Cathal mac Muireadhaigh who witnessed a document at Dunbarton in 1259 was probably Muireadhach Albanach's son and successor,[38] although no poetry composed by him is extant. In sum, the twelfth-century poetic reform carried out in Ireland was advanced to other Gaelic-speaking areas from very early on.[39] Ecclesiastical reform in Scotland, contemporary with that in Ireland, would have presented similar challenges to the Scottish poets and we may only speculate about their reaction and fate. In the face of imposed change we may imagine them following the same course of action as their

---

34 For this poem see below, chapter 3, pp. 62, 68–9.

35 See below, chapter 6, pp. 260–1, 278.

36 *Ceannaigh duain t'athar, a Aonghas,* for which see below, chapter 3, pp. 63–6 *passim*, 69 n. 78.

37 Bannerman 1989, pp. 139–142.

38 *ibid.,* p. 143.

39 A strong case has been made for the possibility that the Irish model was not adopted (or perhaps was adopted to various degrees) throughout Gaelic Scotland. See MacInnes 1975, p. 193; McLeod 2004, pp. 65–6.

colleagues in Ireland — the lay personnel would have detached themselves from the monasteries and attached themselves to secular patrons as their hereditary poets.[40] I have found no hard evidence of this, apart from that suggested by the case of Muireadhach Albanach (who, however, was an incomer) who founded, if tradition has it correctly, his own poetic family in Scotland. Most tantalisingly, we would very likely be illuminated by the classical panegyric of the later thirteenth and fourteenth centuries, but that period is almost a total blank: with one exception, no Gaelic poetry has survived for Scotland between the mid-thirteenth century and the early fifteenth. The exception is the well-known *Dál chabhlaigh ar Chaistéal Suibhne*, composed c.1310 for Eóin Mac Suibhne subsequently to the loss of his lands in Kintyre.[41] Unfortunately almost nothing is known about the author, Artúr Dall Mac Gurcaigh. Mac Gurcaigh has commonly been taken to be the poet's surname rather than his patronymic. If so, then it is almost certain that he belonged to a hereditary poetic family, but it is not known whether this family was Irish or Scottish.[42]

All we can state with certainty, then, is that by the beginning of the fifteenth century the manner of organisation of the Scottish *filidh* corresponds to that found in Ireland following the twelfth-century poetic reform, and that in their compositions the poets use the same language and metrics as their Irish counterparts. It is the learned panegyric of Scotland — whether of Scottish or Irish authorship — extant from earliest times down to the demise of the genre by the early eighteenth century that constitutes the main focus of the present study: from the establishement of Scottish Dál Riada through the rule of various royal Scottish dynasties in Scotland and later in Britain, reaching finally into the reigns of the new houses of Orange-Nassau and Hanover. We will consider the evidence from the literary works of those who for so long represented authority in

---

40 This seems to be taken for granted, for instance, in Thomson 1968, p. 70. In Scotland, however, a number of ecclesiastical foundations remained in the old style until the mid-thirteenth century; see Cowan and Easson (eds) 1976, pp. 446–7, 450–1; Broun 1999, p. 139.

41 See below, chapter 5, pp. 192–4.

42 Meek 1997, p. 6 suggests Irish authorship, while a Scottish provenance is favoured in Ó Mainnín 1999, pp. 28–9, n. 76. Surnames were coming into use in Scotland, in the context of royal administration, by the early twelfth century (see Black 1993, pp. xiii, xix). In Gaelic Ireland they had been in use from about a century earlier.

connexion with political leadership, focusing on the powerful legitimising rhetoric of their verse: the works of the court poets who composed in Gaelic and who with the passage of time witnessed the rise and then the decline of the Gaelic order as they knew it. We will also give attention to the work of a very different class of poets, known as 'vernacular poets'. The significance of these poets and the reasons for their inclusion in this study are laid out in the next chapter.[43] Last but not least, we will as appropriate refer to the extant material left by Gaelic genealogists and chroniclers, for these two classes and the *filidh*, as noted[44] and as we will see again, followed and supported each other with remarkable consistency. This mutual support was essential to invest the learned élite's claims with plausibility and authority.

'Wald thow in Poetrie thy mater wryte':[45] the later court poets

Despite his Gaelic affiliations, King Robert I of Scotland desired a royal inauguration in the contemporary 'European' style, that is with crowning and anointing, a desire that was achieved on the accession to the throne of his son, David II, in 1331.[46] It was the Brús dynasty, then, who abolished customary Gaelic royal inauguration. Surviving fragments of information show that until then the inaugurations of the kings of Scots continued to have if not all at least a number of elements essential in the Gaelic inaugural ceremony. The genealogy of David I (*r*.1124–1153) copied into the mid-twelfth century 'Book of Leinster' is no doubt in the format recited at his inauguration.[47] When John Balliol was deposed on 10 July 1296, he was compelled to hand over the wand of kingship to the English king Edward I.[48] This was *slat na ríghe* (a phrase that was also a classical panegyric code motif), another essential component of the inauguration rite. A third was the inauguration stone, and its significance can be gauged from the fact

---

43 See below, chapter 2, pp. 42–5. See also below, p. 16.

44 See above, pp. 4.

45 'Ane Ballat declaring the Nobill and Gude inclination of our King', printed in Cranstoun (ed.) 1891–33, i, pp. 31–8, at l. 215.

46 Bannerman 1989, pp. 137–8. The recitation of royal genealogy at coronations, however, would remain a part of the coronation ceremony of the kings of Scots until early-modern times. See Sellar 1989, p. 4.

47 *CGH*, §§162 c 44 – 162 d, pp. 328–9 and n. a.

48 Bannerman 1996, p. 32, from the evidence in the chronicles by Fordun and Wyntoun.

that in his quest for domination Edward I stole the Stone of Destiny, *Lia Fáil*, the inauguration stone of the kings of the Scots.[49] Whether the royal hereditary poetic family was permanently dismissed from service at the time when their *ollamh* was excluded by the Brús dynasty from the inauguration ceremony, or a little later, is impossible to tell. Their fate after their employment on a hereditary basis by the the kings of Scots is equally a matter for speculation. They may have been compelled to seek patronage elsewhere, in Scotland or Ireland, they may have been offered alternative employment in the royal household or, as would often be the case a few centuries later as a result of social change and the decline of Gaelic society generally, they may have entered the church.

The immediate question is whether the traditional inauguration rites survived, and for how long, among the Scottish kings' vassal lords. While we have evidence, in the extant corpus of classical panegyric, for at least a number of families keeping their hereditary poets until the early eighteenth century,[50] whether the poets continued to have a role in their patrons' inauguration ceremonies is less certain. Our evidence relates only to those who, increasingly since John of Fordun's time (late fourteenth century), came to be known as 'Highlanders' and to be viewed as 'wild' and culturally inferior. The Gaelic kindreds of southern and eastern Scotland — the 'Lowlanders' of modern terminology — would appear to have lost a number of their original customs by around the early fourteenth century; patronage of poets composing in Gaelic would be part of this loss, although it may simply be the case that the evidence has not survived for these areas.[51] Moreover, although we know that Gaelic inauguration survived until the close of the sixteenth century in Ireland,[52] whether all the Scottish Gaelic lords of the later medieval and early modern periods preserved this tradition, and for

---

49 For an overview of Gaelic inauguration rites see Simms 2000, pp. 21–40.

50 Niall Mac Muireadhaigh, hereditary poet to Clann Raghnaill, was still alive by 1725; see Thomson 1969–70, p. 283. For other hereditary poets and their patrons see McLeod 2004, pp. 70–8.

51 Skene (ed.) 1993, p. 38. Fordun's view of the Highlanders can hardly have been widespread since many contemporary Scottish families were of mixed Gaelic and non-Gaelic ethnicity; see 'The lost Gàidhealtachd', in Barrow 1992, pp. 105–26. For a suggestion that the view expressed by Fordun may have been held in some quarters at least a century earlier see Broun 2009, but note that his evidence is taken from foreign — French and English — commentators.

52 Nicholls 2003, pp. 31–2.

how long, is unknown. For the Mac Domhnaill family of the lords of the Isles we have sporadic but consistent inauguration evidence from authors writing between the mid-sixteenth century and the early eighteenth. Donald Monro (*fl.*1526–89), Archdeacon of the Isles, Martin Martin (*c.*1660–1719), tutor in the households of Mac Domhnaill of Sleat and Mac Leóid of Dunvegan, and Niall Mac Muireadhaigh (1636x39–*c.*1726), hereditary poet and historian to Mac Mhic Ailéin, the Mac Domhnaill chief of Clann Raghnaill, have all left witness.[53] When describing the inauguration ceremony, these authors are all speaking in the past tense. The lordship of the Isles was apparently forfeited by the government of James IV in 1493, and subsequently annexed to the crown, but there were further inaugurations, that of Domhnall Dubh (†1545) probably being the last.[54] Writing around 1567, Buchanan testified to the continuance of the traditional succession system 'among the clans in our own islands, and in Ireland'.[55] Apart from this witness, which gives no inauguration details, there is no evidence of maintenance of the customary inaugural rites of the various Mac Domhnaill cadet branches which at different times, from the mid-sixteenth century onwards, claimed Clann Domhnaill leadership.

We have also inauguration evidence for Clann Leóid. Eóin Borb (†*c.*1422) was inaugurated as Mac Leóid of Harris by Mac Leóid of Lewis by whom he was handed the sword of his predecessors as chiefs of Harris.[56] Further evidence shows that by the mid-sixteenth century Mac Leóid inaugurations continued to include the handing of the sword, the recitation of genealogy and the consent of the clan, and that the *ollamh* in poetry, who belonged to the Mac Gille Mhoire hereditary family, still retained a crucial role in the ceremony.[57] Clann Leóid were one of the principal families in the west, and their chiefs were among the principal members of the Council of the Isles.[58] The heads of Clann Ghille Eóin were of similar rank and also counsellors in the lordship, and it is reasonable to suppose that they, too, were inaugurated according to Gaelic custom. The poet's

---

53 *Monro*, pp. 56–7; *Martin*, pp. 240–1; *RC* ii, p. 160.
54 See below, chapter 3, p. 62 and n. 38. For the lack of evidence of an actual forfeiture see below, chapter 3, p. 73 and n. 97.
55 Buchanan 1579, p. 65; Bannerman 1977, pp. 221, 226.
56 Grant 1959, p. 46.
57 *ibid.*, p. 121.
58 See below, chapter 4, p. 155–6 and n. 159.

part in the ceremony, at least in the case of the chiefs of Duart, would have been the responsibility of the Ó Muirgheasáin *filidh*, who seem to have been under their patronage until the early seventeenth century.[59] It is likely that other chiefs of standing, like Mac Fionghuin or Mac Néill, as well as the heads of Mac Domhnaill cadet branches such as Mac Mhic Ailéin or Mac Eóin of Ardnamurchan were inaugurated in the same fashion. But for this there is no actual evidence, while for lesser kindreds, which probably maintained no *filidh* at all, as is discussed next, inauguration according to Gaelic custom may not have been a feature of succession.

It is uncertain that every chief would be financially able to maintain the expensive commodity of a poetic family.[60] While we have consistent evidence for Mac Domhnaill patronage of the Mac Muireadhaigh family until the early eighteenth century, much less is clear in the case of other patrons. We know that the Mic Eóghain were under Mac Dubhghaill patronage, and later under that of the Caimbéalaigh (although in the case of the latter the majority of the extant poetry is actually of anonymous authorship). The Mac Gille Mhoire family were, as noted, *filidh* to Mac Gille Eóin of Duart, while the Uí Mhuirgheasáin, some of whom were seemingly attached to Mac Gille Eóin's court in Mull in the role of historians, appear as poets to Mac Leóid of Dunvegan in the late seventeenth and early eighteenth centuries.[61] More obscure is the case of the Mac Marcuis family, who cannot be confidently associated with any one particular patron.[62] The statement of the writer of the seventeenth-century genealogical account known as the 'Craignish History' that 'Every considerable Family in the Highlands had their Bards and Shenachies', depending on what he means by 'considerable', may indicate that only a few major and very powerful kindreds maintained a hereditary poetic family.[63] There is a suggestion that the Scottish *bàrd* — a category which has no Irish equivalent — may have originated as an alternative to those chiefs who might not have been able to afford a *file*.[64]

---

59 See below, chapter 4, p. 159 and n. 172.
60 MacInnes 2006a, pp. 235–6.
61 Thomson 1968, p. 73.
62 See *id*. (ed.) 1994, p. 184; Ó Baoill 1976, pp. 183–93.
63 'Craignish History', p. 190.
64 See Thomson 1958, p. 4, and below, chapter 2, p. 37 and n. 50.

Although the *filidh* were deprived of their traditional part in the inaugurations of the kings of Scots, they seem to have continued to receive royal patronage from time to time until at least the reign of James IV (*r.*1488–1513).[65] As noted, it is not known when the Scottish kings ceased to keep a hereditary poetic family (perhaps in the early fourteenth century) but, along with the legal order, the *filidh* seem to have been among the first of the Gaelic learned classes to disappear from the royal court.[66] The Scottish monarchs, however, continued to receive praise from other, very different men of learning, and in languages other than Gaelic, and at this point we will briefly overview how the changing concept of the nature of government was viewed, not always favourably, in these other poets' works. The reason for this aside is that there were also Gaelic poets in our period, other than those fully qualified in their art at the schools, whose voices cannot be ignored. Frequently referred to as 'vernacular poets', they may be seen as the counterparts of those poets writing in Scots and in English who by the seventeenth century were employing their literary skills to debate political theory and to comment on current events.[67] By comparing their arguments with the contemporary non-Gaelic views of political leadership we can learn much, for one thing, about the socio-cultural split, actual and perceived, between 'Highlanders' and 'Lowlanders'. Neither group of poets (Gaelic or non-Gaelic) ever possessed the authority of the *file*, nor certainly his social standing, but both were well aware that poetry was an instrument of political power, and used it as such.[68]

Firstly, then, ecclesiastics continued to compose poetry in Latin, although the authors' names are generally unknown to us. What little has survived of their works comes chiefly from quotations by chroniclers like John of Fordun (†*c.*1384) and Walter Bower (†1449). Other fragments have been preserved in the works of chroniclers writing in Scots, like John Barbour (†1395) and Andrew Wyntoun (†1420) who, like those writing

---

65 Thomson 1986, p. 129.

66 See above, pp. 12–13. Royal hereditary physicians and musicians, for instance, survived for much longer. For the learned orders in medieval Scotland, including the period of their attachment to the courts of the Scottish kings, see generally Thomson 1968. See also below, chapter 2, p. 25 and n. 3.

67 See below, chapter 2, pp. 44–5.

68 For this awareness in poets composing in Latin and Scots see, for instance, Kratzmann 1991, pp. 428, 435.

in Latin, were churchmen.[69] A related genre, which flourished in Scotland in the fifteenth and sixteenth centuries, is that of the 'advice to princes' literature. This is one of the oldest literary genres of many cultures, including that of Gaelic Ireland, from whose tradition it may indeed have originally taken some inspiration.[70] But the advice on good government contained in the extant Latin and Scots works of this type is in many ways crucially different from that found in, for instance, *Tecosca Cormaic*. This is a ninth-century gnomic text containing a number of principles of good government many of which are found again and again in pre-classical as well as classical Gaelic panegyric.[71] The main difference between the Gaelic and the Latin and Scots traditions is perhaps the Christian centrality of the latter. Presented as God's steward on earth, and almost a deified figure himself, the king is to seek the common profit through good government achieved by implementing justice and submitting himself to good counsel. He is responsible to God only, and consequently warnings on eternal salvation and damnation are frequent. Other recurrent themes, equally absent from the counterpart Gaelic genre, are the issue of royal succession *versus* royal election, the necessity for the monarch to govern in accord with the three estates of Parliament (a reminder that royal power, though extensive, is not unlimited), and the reciprocal responsibilities of king and people.[72] Although often influenced by continental, especially French, political thought, the Scottish 'advice to princes' tradition nevertheless had its own distinctive features, such as its fundamentally pragmatic view of the monarchy, and its focus on law along with a conscious use of legal language.[73] Fourteenth- and fifteenth-century authors, whether writing in verse or prose, were nobles and churchmen, but only in a few cases were they attached to the royal court.[74]

69 For some instances see Clancy (ed.) 1998, pp. 286, 295–6, 297, 306–8.

70 Kelly (ed.) 1976, pp. xv–xvi. The recitation of a princely advice poem remained part of the inauguration ceremony at least until the time of Alexander III (*ibid.*, p. xiv).

71 Meyer (ed.) 1909. For another example see Smith (ed.)1928.

72 See generally Mapstone 1986.

73 *ibid.*, p. 5. Given that the rhetoric of Gaelic panegyric draws so heavily on ancient legal principles (see above, p. 2), the legal focus and language of this poetry are extremely interesting and worthy of research which is not within the scope of this study.

74 For contemporary and near-contemporary comment on fifteenth-century Scottish kings see, for instance, Skene (ed.) 1880, ii, p. 291; *Scotichronicon*, viii, pp. 300–21; Weiss (ed.) 1937; Connolly (ed.), 1992 (all on James I); Macdougall 1982, pp. 269–76

Sixteenth-century developments, when discussion of kingship was often incorporated into historical writing,[75] included the endorsement of elective, rather than hereditary, monarchy, and theories of resistance which ultimately sanctioned tyrannicide. Poetic criticism became now more rigorous, although in general the *speculum principis* genre remained conservative.[76] At the same time, from about the middle of the century, religious Reformation ideology became more and more inextricable from notions of monarchy. The poets of the reformed conviction commented on current events employing their own registers — the language of covenant and the language of commonweal, both connected with religious ideology.[77] Authors like Sir David Lyndsay, Richard Maitland, and Robert Sempill loudly articulated their views in poems which sometimes were sheer satire.[78] Mary Queen of Scots (*r*.1543–67), uniting in her person the conditions of womanhood and Catholicism, and suspected — and indeed accused — of involvement in the death of her husband, Henry Stewart Lord Darnley, was the most viciously attacked of all Stiúbhart monarchs.[79] Her son, James VI, was well aware of the increasing threats to the monarchy. Towards the close of the sixteenth century he wrote two political treatises in its defence, strongly arguing for its divine character. 'Basilicon Doron', in the format of princely advice to his first-born son and heir, was at the same time, like 'The Trew Law of Free Monarchies', James's response to the contemporary double threat: the Presbyterian model proposed by John Knox and Andrew Melville on the one hand, and on the other the king's own tutor, George Buchanan's, resistance and contract theory.[80] James VI's notion

---

on James III); id. 1997, pp. 283–306 (on James IV). The poem 'The Harp' (printed in Skene (ed.) 1880, ii, pp. 392–400), in the 'advice to princes' tradition, may have been addressed to James II; see Macdougall 1982, p. 274.

75 Such as the chronicles of John Mair (1467–1550), Hector Boece (1465–1536), and George Buchanan (1506–82). See, for instance, Burns 1996; Mason 1998.

76 For the poetry of the times of James V see, for instance, MacDonald 1996; Williams 1996b.

77 See Mason 1983.

78 See Kratzmann 1991.

79 Knox 1878. For a collection of Buchanan's criticisms of Mary, in English translation, see Gatherer (trsl. and ed.) 1958. Mary did have some supporters, such as the Catholic Bishop of Ross; see Leslie 1970.

80 See 'Basilicon Doron' and 'The Trew Law of Free Monarchies: or The Reciprock and

of divinely-ordained royal status permeates his political writings as well as parliamentary speeches. From his two earlier works to the addresses to the three estates in the years after he assumed also the English crown, James maintained that 'Kings are called Gods by the prophetical King David, because they sit upon GOD his Throne in the earth'.[81]

The theory of the divine right of monarchs developed from the political and religious tensions in much of reformed Western Europe, gathering momentum in Scotland — including Gaelic areas[82] — and England from the early seventeenth century. During the reign of Charles I, James VI and I's son and successor, politics would become confessional to such a degree that it was the king's attempt to force a new prayer book on the Scots that was ultimately the beginning of the road to civil war. In the ensuing struggle for supremacy between king and Parliament matters came to a head when Charles raised his standard against his own Parliament in 1642. The poetry of this period reflects the division and ill-feeling between 'Cavaliers' and 'Roundheads' (the supporters of the king and those of Parliament respectively). The former came from the Episcopalian nobility (but also from the peasantry), while the latter were made up of the emerging middle class and tradesmen of the Puritanical movement. The 'Roundheads' were perceived and condemned by their enemies as upstarts and subverters of the traditional order. In 1623 Richard Corbet, Dean of Christchurch (and a year later Bishop of Oxford), complained:

> A sad pressage to the danger of this land
> When lower strive to get the upper hand,
> When Prince and Peers to Peasants must obey,
> When laymen must their teachers teach the way.[83]

King Charles's enemies carried the day, but those who dared still complained about the new order of things and about

---

mutuall duetie betwixt a fre King, and his naturall Subjects', in Rhodes, Richards, and Marshall (eds) 2003, pp. 199–258 and 259–79 respectively.

81 Rhodes, Richards, and Marshall (eds) 2003, p. 261. For an example of the same concept in a speech to the Whitehall Parliament see Carrier 1998, p. 80.

82 See Findlay 2002.

83 'Against the opposing of the Duke in Parliament', Bennett and Trevor-Roper (eds) 1955, p. 82, quoted in Carlton 1983, p. 118.

the illgotten store
Of the upstart *Mushrooms* of our Nation.[84]

Thus Alexander Brome, a lawyer; but royal supporters came from various sectors of society. The Welsh physician Martin Lluelyn composed a consolation Christmas carol for the king in 1645, while Thomas Jordan, an unemployed actor following the suppression of the theatres in 1642, bitterly complained:

Lo here a Glorious *Realm* subverted stands...

Once *Europes Pride* and *Envy*, now their *Scoff*,
Since the base *Entrayles* cut the *Head* on't off...

Now all the *Limbs* are *Vassals* to the *Rump*,
Which...
Yields nothing but *stink* and *excrement*.[85]

In 1648 King Charles was put on trial for treason and declared guilty. After his execution in 1649, Oliver Cromwell took control of government, a 'succession' criticised by an anonymous poet:

Oliver, Oliver, take up thy Crown,
For now thou hast made three Kingdoms thine own...

We bow down, as cow'd down, to thee and thy Sword,
For now thou hast made thy self *Englands* sole Lord...
To *Charles* and his Kingdom thou art heir apparent.[86]

That same year Parliament declared that 'the people are, under God, the original of all just power', and that 'the Commons of England, in Parliament assembled ... have the supreme power in this nation':[87]

---

84 Davidson (ed.) 1998, p. 427.
85 *ibid.*, pp. 334, 379–80, 427–8.
86 *ibid.*, pp. 445–6.
87 Goldie 1997, p. 12.

subversion of traditional values was complete, although temporary. The monarchy was restored in 1660, although throughout the reign of Charles II and that of his brother and successor, James VII and II, the debate on the nature of kingship persisted. Tories — to use the term first coined in 1679 — like Francis Turner upheld the divine right of monarchs and stated that aristocracy and democracy (the classic alternative forms of government) were two 'political aberrations and deviations'.[88] Not only was a monarch's power absolute, but his subjects had an inviolable duty of obedience to him. Yet, despite his supreme, absolute power, a king remained subject to limitations. He needed good counsel; he was limited also by his own grants, promises, and coronation oath; if he became a tyrant he forfeited his right to rule; and descent and affinity of blood gave him no claim to the throne. The Whig counter-claim denied a monarch any special status, arguing that man's natural state was one of freedom and equality, though bound by divine and moral law. John Locke (1632–1704) viewed political rule as legitimate only when it came about by the voluntary consent of citizens; the people trusted its powers to government, but those powers reverted to the people if a breach of trust (tyranny) was committed, and retribution might require the execution of the tyrant. More radical theorists, like Algernon Sidney, even advocated a republic.[89]

We may note that these authors expressing their views on the nature of government in the seventeenth century were often socially far removed from their late medieval predecessors. If in any way connected to the church, they tended to hold important ecclesiastical office; otherwise these political theorists were by profession lawyers, notaries, academics, soldiers, and merchants, and some voices rose even from actors and journalists[90] — a far cry even from the literary circles attached to the courts of James V and James VI, and worlds away from the royal *ollamh* of the high middle ages and earlier. The model of government no longer was established and preserved by the authority of the king's poet or by his genealogists and chroniclers; more and more we find opinion emanating from almost every

---

88 *ibid.*, p. 21.

89 *ibid.*, pp. 24, 27–9, 29–31, 34.

90 Such as Marchamont Nedham (1620–78), a journalist who had no qualms in changing the nature of his political writing as circumstances changed too; see Davidson (ed.) 1998, p. 604.

sector of society, sometimes even denying the place and status accorded to a monarch in venerable tradition. In Scotland, which from the early seventeenth century formed part of the kingdom of Great Britain, regard for much of the ancestral culture had long been lost. Increasingly since the later fourteenth century the 'Highlanders' became a synonym for unruliness and barbarism.[91] Already by the mid-fifteenth century the Gaelic poet's recitation of genealogies had become the object of derision.[92] In the 1580s the Scottish poet Alexander Montgomerie (c.1550–98) probably provoked the hilarity of James VI and his court with his statement that 'the first Helandman, of God was maid, of ane horse turd'.[93] The desire to break with the Gaelic past was clear. Buchanan had already argued for a Pictish origin of the Scots, and in the seventeenth century the Stiúbhart origin legend was being reworked to make the British Arthur their ancestor.[94] The last of the Stiúbhart monarchs, Queen Anne (r.1702–14), was celebrated by the English poet Alexander Pope (1688–1744) as the one who rescued the nation from its ravisher, the 'foreign Master' William of Orange. In her reign, also, the union of the Scottish and English Parliaments took place. Pope unequivocally presented Anne as a 'British Queen', although at the same time he rejoiced that 'a STUART reigns'.[95] In Scotland a number of voices rose in complaint against the British Union, or else its terms, and an ancient Gaelic name was utilised in hot defence of the antiquity and the genealogical purity of the Scottish monarchs, the descendants of 'Fearghus [who] form'd our MONARCHY'.[96] In contrast, Queen Anne went to great lengths to present herself as a new Elizabeth, and to inspire continuity with the Tudor house rather than that of Stiúbhart. Her accession medal carried the legend 'Entirely English', which is also how she described herself in

---

91 See above, p. 13.

92 As in Sir Richard Holland's (fl.1450) 'The Buke of the Howlat' (Holland 1897, pp. 74–5). See Hudson 1991, p. 141.

93 Cranstoun (ed.) 1887, pp. 280–1. Perhaps incongruously in view of this mockery of ancient royal ancestors, Andrew Melville addressed James VI as the 'Greatest son of Fearghus'; see 'Introductory verses to Melville's "Gathelus" ', in McGinnis and Williamson (eds) 1995, at ll. 9–11, pp. 284–5.

94 Lynch 1994, pp. 131–32, 135.

95 Quotations Rogers 2005, pp. 100, 129.

96 See 'Writing the nation in 1707: Daniel Defoe, Lord Belhaven, and the "Vast Conjunction" of Britain" ', in Davis 1998, pp. 19–45 (quotation at p. 45).

her first address to Parliament[97] — her own blood precluded a break with the ethnic past, but public opinion might be shaped through imagery and political speeches.

Through the brief period of Orange rule, the temporary Stiúbhart return in the person of Anne, and the coming of the Hanover dynasty, in his home in South Uist Niall Mac Muireadhaigh continued to compose in *dán díreach*, for Clann Raghanill and for other patrons. His death around 1726 marked the extinction of the hereditary *filidh* of Scotland. The Stone of Destiny remained at Westminster Abbey. It was returned to Scotland on 3 July 1996, provision being made for its return to England when required for future coronations.

---

97 Rogers 2005, pp. 133, 141, 147.

Chapter 2

Gaelic court poetry in Scotland: literary background

Perhaps as early as the first half of the fourteenth century the Scottish kings had parted company with their Gaelic poets, and this presumably set a pattern for the nobility of what today we know as the Lowlands. The Highland and Isles lords, most if not all of whom had at least some non-Gaelic blood in their veins by the later medieval period, continued to provide poetic patronage until the eighteenth century. Some of them, like the Stiúbhairt or the Granndaigh, were of Norman origin but adopted the language of the Gaels and, at least to a degree, their customs. Others, like the Caimbéalaigh, whose original British ancestry is firmly maintained in Gaelic poetry and genealogies, even invented a Gaelic origin for themselves.[1] All of them, including the Mac Domhnaill lords of the Isles, recognised the official overlordship of the king of Scots, and were included in the kingdom's politics.[2] At the same time their culture and social customs were recognised as different by those inhabiting what is called the Lowlands in modern terminology, but not all the differences were perceived as negative. Gaelic musicians, for instance, remained the recipients of royal patronage for several centuries, while members of the Mac Beathadh medical family in the service of the lords of the Isles were physicians to the Scottish kings until the eighteenth century.[3] But when first French and then Scots replaced Gaelic as the language

---

1 See below, chapter 4, pp. 119–20.
2 Gregory 1881, p. 23; Grant 1988, pp. 119–20.
3 Evidence is extant for the appointment of royal harpers in the reigns of David II and Robert II (Bannerman 1996, pp. 32–3). For James IV see, for instance, Nicholson1974, p. 541. For the Mac Beathadh family see Bannerman 1986.

of the court, poets composing in Gaelic became redundant there.[4] In the Gaelic-speaking areas, however, they continued to represent a mark of prestige beyond the seventeenth century. George Buchanan, writing in 1579, tells us that in his time these poets, 'the name and function of whom are still preserved', still did very much what they had been doing since ancient times, as described by Lucan:

> Vos quoque, qui fortes animas, belloque peremptas,
> Laudibus in longum vates demittitis ævum,
> Plurima securi fudistis carmina BARDI.

> (The brave who fall in war, ye Poets, praise
> In strains that shall descend to distant times,
> And spread their fame, ye BARDS, in many songs).[5]

That was indeed the job of the Gaelic court poet — to compose praise for the warrior and to make it public in order to earn him lasting fame. As noted, the terms of praise were not arbitrary, but rather were taken from a collection of established motifs which, as used by the professional *file*, were authoritative endorsements of the praised individual's credentials and fitness to rule over his people.

Understanding the 'code'

In language, in metrical usage, and in the display of his knowledge of history, the *file* was expected to produce work of the highest standard. It is well known that the rules of classical Gaelic versification were extremely complex, and a poem in *dán díreach* is always a fascinating testimony of technical virtuosity. The poets themselves were proud of their skills and sometimes expressed their disdain for those who failed to attain less than prosodic perfection, or worse, who chose to compose in more demotic metres.[6] Apart from technical competence, the individual praised would also expect to be addressed in the terms of the established 'panegyric code'. In consequence, we find the same praise terms repeated in hundreds of

---

4 The rise of 'Inglis' (Scots) as the preferred language of aristocracy and government took place between 1350 and 1500; see, for instance, MacGregor 2009, p. 38.

5 Buchanan 1827, pp. 66, 99.

6 Introductions to composition in syllabic metres are given in Knott (ed.) 1934, pp. 1–20 and *BG*, pp. xxxvi–xliv. For accentual metres see *ibid.*, pp. xlvi–liii.

panegyrics. The modern reader may find this type of literature repetitive and predictable in much of its content, and indeed it must be so; to the medieval mind eulogy had to adhere to convention if its subject was to preserve his honour unmarred. It has been noted that 'sometimes [modern] critics have castigated this genre for being insincere, frigid, artificial, unoriginal, unnecessarily obscure, generally dead, and a massive squandering of talent'.[7] In the words of another scholar, this time focusing on the panegyric code as found in the work of the vernacular poets, 'such verse requires literary yardsticks other than style, balance, lyricism, originality, sincerity, realism, integrity. If the diction is codified we must understand the rhetoric... We must, in other words, "read the rhetoric" '.[8]

How, then, did the rhetorical code of classical Gaelic panegyric work? In very simple terms, the code was designed to present the subject of the poem as being, or destined or suitable to be, the 'right ruler'; the picture given was not intended to be an actual representation, but rather the model towards which the ruler should strive.[9] The attributes ascribed to the subject of the poem are generally well known, and a broad selection is given in Appendix 2 of this work.[10] But it is well to note at this point that among the most crucial of these conventional images is that of the individual as the one who can unite and lead his people, and as the protector of his people and territory. There is evidence that, when a chief falls short of certain standards and expectations, the poets tend to leave out that and other crucial motifs, concentrating on those that we could describe as non-controversial and non-committal — as custodians of the truth, the poets appear to make an effort to give sincere praise.[11] Those who were truly professional sometimes complained that there were some indeed who composed empty praise with the mere aim of prompting a reward, something that was punishable by law.[12] In religious poetry, some of the greatest

---

7 Gillies 1986, p. 108.

8 *Lasair*, p. xix. See also Ní Annracháin 2007, pp. 167, 174.

9 Mac Cana 1969, p. 38; Gillies 1986, pp. 113–15.

10 Eleanor Knott first produced a very substantial overview of these motifs; see *TD* i, pp. li–lxii. See also McCaughey 1989; Watson 1914–19, pp. 209–16; and *Lasair*, pp. xix–xxvii, 525–7 for the Scottish perspective. Dewar 2006b catalogues the classical panegyric code of Ireland of the period *c.*1400–*c.*1600.

11 Dewar 2006b, pp. 415–16.

12 *ibid.*, pp. 274–5 and nn. 457, 460.

poets have acknowledged *gné fhallsa m'ealathan* ('the falseness of my art'), resolving to focus on spiritual matters and praise God only.[13] Nevertheless, if the rhetoric of panegyric did not faithfully represent actual fact, it did the job it was created to do. This was to articulate the sanction, by those who had the necessary authority, of an individual's right to rule over his people. It is no mere coincidence that, as noted in the previous chapter, many of these established conventions replicate ancient legal principles, and would therefore invest poetic statements with all the weight and authority of the law.[14] And, as has been noted with reference to the depiction of the subject as the suitable partner for Ireland, the poetic rhetoric was no mere poetic fantasy or recitation of merely literary motifs: in it were encapsulated 'the traditional values and the ideological reference frame of the Gaels'.[15]

In a sense the praise terms easiest for us to understand are those that would appear the most absurd. One example is the assertion that nature endorses the right ruler with fertility and clement weather. There is no scientific basis to this, and yet the intended audience would understand it, as we must, as authentication that the right ruler was in place. Conversely, this motif, like the rest, could be reversed if the poet meant to express disapproval, as in satires. For instance, in his condemnation of Conchobhar Ó Briain, third Earl of Thomond (†1581), the poet Uilliam Mac an Bhaird stated that since Conchobhar had assumed the headship of Thomond,

> níor bhean fá iath an Fhorghais
> griangha le brataibh brughadh.

> (No ray of sunshine has touched the cloaks of the farmers throughout the land of the Fergus).[16]

---

13 *AFOD*, p. 2 (quotation). For other examples see Bateman 1990, pp. 7–8. This, however, deserves further exploration, since there is evidence that religious poetry was, like secular panegyric, composed on commission and for reward (see *Dán Dé*, p. xii), and therefore some moral may have been intended. For poets' defence of poetry see *ibid.*, p. 12, and *Mo-chean duit a Cholaim cháidh.*

14 See above, chapter 1, p. 2. See also Coira 2008a.

15 Ó Buachalla 1983, p. 86.

16 *Biaidh athroinn ar Inis Fáil*, §19bc. Forghas: the river Fergus in Clare, in the earl's territory.

The rhetoric of classical panegyric is often extended to historical writing. One example is the annalistic comment on Edward, brother of King Robert I. Edward, who was proclaimed king of Ireland by the Ulstermen in 1315, is reported to have caused utter destruction in Ireland, and then the annalist concludes: 'Uair tanicc go & gorta & dith daine re lind ar fodd Erenn ed tri mbliadan co leth, & do ithdais na daine cin amuras a cheli ar fod Erenn' ('For in this [Bruce's] time, for three years and a half, falsehood and famine and homicide filled the country, and undoubtedly men ate each other in Ireland').[17] The writer uses the images of lawlessness and disorder of society and of lack of plenty in the land — which in any case reflected actual circumstances — as caused by Edward's unjust rule, and as proof of his unsuitability to be his people's leader.

Sometimes we find echoes of the Gaelic panegyric code in early poetry in Scots. Wyntoun quotes from a song said to have been sung generally after the death of Alexander III. The dead king is portrayed as a protector of his people and as someone who had maintained law and order; other common conventions, like plenty and abundance, feasting in the ruler's lifetime, and the general distress ('perplexite', often *anbhuain* in Gaelic) after his departure, are also present:[18]

> Qwhen Alexander our kynge was dede,
> That Scotland lede in lauche and le,
> Away was sons of alle and brede,
> Off wyne and wax, of gamyn and gle.
> Our golde was changit in to lede.
> Christ, borne in virgynte,
> Succoure Scotlande, and ramede,
> That stade is in perplexite.

> (When Alexander our king was dead,
> who led Scotland in law and protection,
> gone was abundance of ale and bread,
> of wine and wax, of sport and enjoyment.
> Our gold turned into lead.

---

17 AC, p. 252.
18 Watson 1914–19, p. 213.

May Christ, born in virginity,
send succour and relief to Scotland
who is beset with distress).[19]

A Gaelic formulaic residuum seems to be detected similarly in some of the obituaries given by Walter Bower, who says of the third Earl of Douglas, Archibald 'the Grim' (†1400), that he 'in terrena prudencia fortitudine et audacia ... suo tempore Scotos quasi antecessit' ('surpassed almost all other Scots of his time in worldly wisdom, resolution and daring').[20] Compare the annalistic note of the death of Maghnus Ó Conchobhair (†1293), king of Connacht, where it is stated that he was 'fer cogthach conghalach bá moa gráin gaiscceadh, & rún oinigh do Ghaoidhelaibh Ereann i n-a aimsir' ('a warlike and valiant man, the most victorious, puissant, and hospitable of the Irish of his time'),[21] or that of Aodh Ruadh Ó Domhnaill (†1505), lord of Tyrconnell, 'fer bá mó grenn, & gaiscceadh, fer bá ferr ionnsaicchidh & anadh, fer rob ferr smacht, reacht, & riaghail baí i n-Erinn ina aimsir do Gaoidhealaibh' ('the most jovial and valiant, the most prudent in war and peace, and of the best jurisdiction, law, and rule, of all the Gaels in Ireland in his time').[22] Elsewhere Bower seems puzzled that during the reign of Robert III (r.1390-1406) nature had shown her approval through her fertility, despite the king's inability to maintain law and order: 'extitit in regno fertilitas victualium sed maxima discordia rixa et briga' ('there was an abundance of provisions in the kingdom, but a great deal of dissension, strife and brawling').[23] Of Robert Stewart, Duke of Albany (†c.1420), he says that he was an outstanding man, distinguished in bearing, mild, communicative and affable, 'a man of great expenses and munificent to strangers' — another obituary that would not have looked out of place in a Gaelic annalistic compilation.[24]

One of the praise terms or motifs that may need clarification is that of the individual eulogised as a raider. In contrast with the impossible literary

19 Printed in Clancy (ed.) 1998, p. 297; translation is my own.
20 *Scotichronicon* viii, p. 34.
21 *ARÉ*, iii, p. 458.
22 *ibid.*, v, p. 1282.
23 *Scotichronicon* viii, p. 62.
24 *ibid.*, p. 134.

claims such as nature's sanction, raiding is one of those motifs which must be handled more carefully, for as well as being part of the rhetoric of panegyric it may contain historical fact. Raiding in this context did not denote the unlawful plundering of one's neighbour. A successful raid was required of 'Every heir, or young Chieftain of a Tribe … before he was owned and declared Governour or Leader of his People'.[25] The damage caused would be repaired when the time came for the chief of those raided to perform the same feat.[26] Other raids were carried out to obtain the rent or tribute to which a chief was entitled, something that is directly connected with the poetic motif of exaction of tribute. The abundance of annalistic entries referring to 'hostings' have in the past led historians to imagine a state of perpetual warfare in Gaelic areas, while many of these 'hostings' were in fact no more than rent collections.[27] Many events described in the *caithréim* ('battle-roll') often included in a eulogy were actual successful raids performed by the individual praised.[28] It is here, in the *caithréim*, that we enter the historical realm, for many of the hostings they contained can be identified from other sources as having actually taken place. And it is here, also, that the poet must strictly adhere to the truth for, rhetoric aside, the individual praised must be prepared to be confronted by others about his claims.[29]

The panegyric code in Scottish poetry

For the purposes of this study, we define 'Scottish poetry', or 'poetry of Scotland', as the extant corpus of poems which in one way or another are of interest to Scotland. This approach includes the pieces addressed by Irish authors to Scottish patrons, and those addressed by Scottish authors to Irish patrons; these all may just as rightly be claimed to be Irish as Scottish, and indeed they are best classified as part of a wider literary culture transcending any 'national' boundaries. Where Gaelic was spoken and Gaelic social, cultural and political tradition understood at least to an extent, this

---

25 *Martin*, p. 101.

26 *ibid.*, p. 102.

27 Cunningham and Gillespie 2003, pp. 29–58. See also Simms 2000, chapter 9: 'The king's revenues', pp. 129–46, and Ó Riain 1973–4.

28 See, for instance, Tadhg Óg Ó hUiginn's *Toghaidh Dia neach 'n-a naoidhin*, for Uaitéar Búrc (†1440), at §§35–46.

29 Simms 1987, pp. 64, 65.

poetry could find its way, as is attested by some surviving verse for Pictish leaders and for Raghnall mac Godhfhraidh, king of Man.[30] Of Scottish interest are also considered pieces, almost certainly of Irish authorship, which may or may not have been composed for a Scottish patron; one example is *A éolcha Alban uile*, which may have been a teaching aid in use at poetic schools, and another *Ro bátar láeich do Laigneib*, a poetic version of a story found in Irish genealogies, tales and historical writing.[31] The interest for us of these poems of Irish and anonymous authorship which in one way or another connect with Scotland is the same as the interest provided by genealogies, tales and historical writing produced in Ireland: they provide additional information, factual or otherwise, but illuminating on Gaelic cultural values over the period covered here, and they allow us, to a great degree, to compare the Irish and the Scottish perspectives. As we will see, the general pattern is one of remarkable consistency of the various classes of professional men of learning, and of adherence to the earliest records; this applies just as much to key issues like genealogical claims, as it does to the poetic rhetoric, or panegyric code. Against this, some at least of the vernacular poets[32] appear more open to new fashions, normally origi- nating in Lowland Scotland, in England, or in Western Europe generally.

With the spread into Scotland of the literary culture of the Gaels, the poets faced new challenges. New place-names and personal names (through British, Pictish, Norse, and Norman intermarriage at various stages) had to be brought into their compositions to bind the leader to his territory and to his family, in the characteristic way of the genre. They also had to be linked to the various epithets and appellations of their stock-in- trade in order to achieve the effect — unifying, identifiable, and teeming with resonances — typical of their rhetorical systems.[33] There is also the intriguing question of the very limited use in Gaelic panegyric of Scotland of the motif depicting the chief as the spouse of his territory, the land being the goddess of sovereignty. This was an ancient literary representation

30 See above, chapter 1, pp. 7, 10.

31 For a discussion of the purpose of the composition of *A éolcha Alban uile* see Zumbuhl 2006, pp. 17–21. See also below, chapter 7, pp. 299–301, 301–3.

32 As defined below, see pp. 41–3.

33 For the sense of cultural identity and unity maintained through the rhetoric of the poets see MacInnes 2006d, pp. 28–9.

which acted as validator of the succession of a ruler.[34] In poetry for Irish leaders the ultimate goal or destiny associated with them went beyond the marriage partnership of a leader and his local territory: the highest term of praise was undoubtedly a poet's assertion of his patron's destiny to become the spouse of Banbha (to use one of various poetic names for Ireland), that is high-king of the whole of the island. In the extant Scottish material this motif is a rare occurrence, and where we do find it, it is virtually always in connexion with the Mac Domhnaill family, and with reference to the high-kingship of Ireland.[35] But a couple of modified versions of the 'spouse motif' are also present in panegyric for Scottish patrons. In these the reference is no longer to Ireland: in one poem Gilleasbaig Caimbéal, eighth Earl and Marquis of Argyll (†1661), is represented as the spouse of Britain, and in another Alún Mór, *mormhaor* of Lennox (†c.1200), is depicted as the spouse not of his territory, but of the river Lennox in it.[36]

After the kings of Scottish Dál Riada permanently united Scots (Gaels) and Picts under their own dominion, one would have expected some sort of 'kingship of *Alba*' motif to emerge in the poetry. Indeed these kings begin to be identified as *rí Alban* in the annals from the tenth century onwards.[37] Yet the kingship or high-kingship of *Alba* is never used in the extant poetic corpus in the way that the motif of the kingship of Ireland was regularly used. Suitability to become the high-king of Ireland, the highest possible praise motif, does appear mostly in poems for Irish nobles, but we also find it in some pieces for non-Irish subjects.[38] Anything of the kind appears elusive in the poetry of Scotland, even though *Alba* receives relatively frequent mention in the extant literature, sometimes in her literary designation, *Monadh*. It has been suggested that this might be due to the lack of stable boundaries of the *Gàidhealtachd* over time (first expanding, and then retreating north and west from about the thirteenth century), or perhaps to the early perception of *Alba* as a province of Ireland, rather

---

34 Herbert 1992, pp. 264–6.

35 Dewar 2006a, pp. 41–3. See also below, chapter 3, pp. 68–9, 82–3.

36 See below, chapter 4, pp. 138–9, and chapter 5, pp. 187–8.

37 *AU* i, p. 414; Anderson (ed.) 1990, i, p. 395. See also below, p. 48, and chapter 7, p. 302 n. 86.

38 As in *Baile suthach síth Eamhna* (§§10, 14ab), for Raghnall mac Godhfhraidh (†1229), king of Man.

than as a fully-fledged country.[39] Yet this does not fully explain the lack of poetic references during the classical period to some sort of high-kingship or supreme overlordship over the whole Scottish Gaelic community, over the kingdom of the Scots. The closest we come to a high-kingship motif in any form can be said to be found in the development of the motif of 'ceannas na nGaoidheal' but, strangely, such headship is not linked to any particular territory.[40] Nevertheless, as we will see in a later chapter, the concept of the kingship, or the high-kingship, of *Alba* also appears in an eleventh-century poem, raising questions on the possibility of the development of the motif.[41] One of the objects of this study is to tackle this conundrum in search of a plausible explanation of what might appear as a limited shelf-life of the high-kingship literary motif in poems composed for Scottish patrons.

The Scottish Gaels' connexions with Ireland are fondly remembered in classical panegyric. Irish place-names are common, particularly in poetry composed for members of Clann Domhnaill. Similarly, genealogical connexions with the great Gaelic heroes (historical and mythological) of the remote past are chiefly to be found in Mac Domhnaill, Mac Dubhghaill, and Caimbéal verse, with only very occasional presence in poems for members of the Mac Griogóir and Stiúbhart families, and a total absence from Clann Leóid poetry.[42] On reflection, this seems quite extraordinary given that in Gaelic records the lineages of the majority of the Gaelic kindreds of Scotland are taken back to important characters of Gaelic history and pseudo-history. A look at the extant genealogies, whether Irish or Scottish, reveals that most of the Gaels settled in Scotland claimed either Colla Uais, Corc mac Lughach, Niall Naoighiallach or Conaire Mór as their principal ancient progenitor. The exceptions are the Caimbéalaigh, Clann Mhic Neacail and Clann Leóid, whose ancestries — British in the case of the Caimbéalaigh and Norse in that of the other two — are traced back to the legendary Neimheadh (see Table 2.1).[43] These three kindreds became

---

39 Ó Baoill 1972–4, pp. 391–2; McLeod 2004, pp. 136–7.

40 See below, chapter 3, pp. 71, 97–9, and chapter 4, pp. 132–5.

41 See below, chapter 7, pp. 294–5, 301.

42 See below, chapters 3, pp. 65–6, 77, 80, 96; 4, pp. 126, 151–2; 5, pp. 199–200, 204; and 6, pp. 266–7. But note that possibly none of the extant syllabic poems for Clann Ghriogóir was the work of a *file* (see below, chapter 5, pp. 197–9).

43 See Skene 1876–80, iii, pp. 458–90. Skene conflated (thus often misleading later

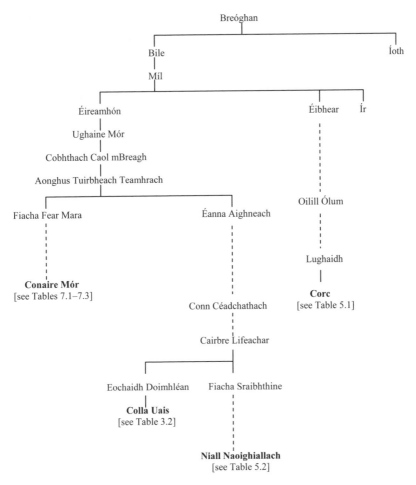

Table 2.1 Origins of the Gaels of Scotland
Source: LMG v.

— as did many later Norman incomers, and as did the medieval Norman settlers of Ireland — Gaelicised in speech and customs. The genealogical references we find in classical Gaelic panegyric, as will be seen, match their family lineages as proposed in the earlier genealogies. Later additions or modifications to pedigrees, notably in the case of the Caimbéalaigh, were

historians) the pedigrees found in 'MS 1467', Kilbride MS, and 'MacFirbis', for which see Sellar 1973, p. 117. Although genealogies often differ in matters of detail, the ultimate ancestors given for the Scots remain invariable.

disregarded by the *filidh*.[44] Since a venerable ancestor was 'the single most important source of prestige',[45] the fact that emphasis on Gaelic ancestry is only clearly paramount in Mac Domhnaill poetry poses questions on the self-view or sense of identity of other Scottish Gaelic kindreds and their poets, and on their perception of their place and role in both the Gaelic and the wider, Scottish and later British, settings.

Other features typical of Scottish Gaelic panegyric have been noted elsewhere, and will only be briefly mentioned here.[46] Scottish history or particular historical events or *Albanaigh* of the past are generally absent from the extant corpus. This is in sharp contrast to the poetry for Irish nobles, which abounds in references to great leaders, historical or mythological, and significant events of the past. Also notable is the lack of poetic names for specific places or regions of Scotland; generally they are given their actual name, and moreover they tend to stand bare, whereas in Irish panegyric place-names are commonly imbued with deep historical and mythological connotations. Similarly, the treatment of the landscape ignores the geographical differences between Scotland and Ireland — the depiction and the vocabulary remain firmly fixed on the Irish model.[47] The portrayal of the poet as his patron's lover is yet another undeveloped theme in classical panegyric of Scotland.[48] From the literary viewpoint, to sum up, classical panegyric very much defaulted on the original configurations of the poetic schools of Ireland. But there were some differences, and the main object of the present study is to examine the extant corpus of Scottish panegyric and establish its continuities and innovations in respect of the rhetoric of the 'right ruler' as originated in Ireland.

The classical poets of Scotland

While the professional *filidh* of Scotland were organised in the same manner and fulfilled the same tasks as their counterparts in Ireland, there are suggestions that the poetic system may have been more complex in

44 MacInnes 2006b, p. 271; Gillies 1976–8, p. 279.
45 McLeod 2004, pp. 115–16.
46 For what follows see McLeod 2004, pp. 124–6, 137–47. See also Ó Mainnín 1999.
47 This is further explored in McLeod 2003.
48 McLeod 2004, p. 137.

Scotland, with some extra layers of ranks of poets.[49] For instance, there seems to have been no Irish equivalent of the Scottish *bàrd*. The emergence of this category of poet may have been a consequence of limited economic means on the part of some chiefs. While the *file* was an expensive commodity, the *bàrd* belonged to a lower and less demanding order.[50] In early Ireland the *bard* was a poet of an inferior grade who normally formed part of the retinue of a *file*.[51] The Scottish *bàrd*, in contrast, could be employed on an independent basis as official poet to his patron, and in Scotland the word *bàrd* itself, in later times, seems to have been a generic term which included the *file*.[52] There are indications that overheads may have been further reduced in a number of cases by employing a poet to fulfil also the role of historian. According to the anonymous author of the 'Craignish History', 'The Bard was a Family Poet, and the Shenachie their prose writer, but very oft the Bard supply'd the place of both'.[53] The original *baird* came from the upper classes of society and seem to have had some training in a professional poetic school, but never to the high degree of the *filidh*.[54] In addition, there are instances of chiefs who simultaneously had in employment in their households both a *file* and a *bàrd*,[55] although the evidence is for the seventeenth century only. In the case of Scotland at least, to use the word 'bardic' in this context — as in 'bardic schools', or 'bardic poetry' — can be ambiguous and misleading.

As well as composing praise for their patrons, the court poets performed other functions directly connected with their learning. In Ireland they appear, until at least the later sixteenth century, in charge of the education of their patrons' young sons.[56] The arrangement seems to have been similar in Scotland, where the poets appear involved in the teaching, at least to a level, of Latin, a knowledge of which was a requirement for

---

49 MacAonghuis 2006, pp. 340–56; McLeod 2004, p. 67; *id.* 2010.

50 MacInnes 2006a, pp. 235–6.

51 Byrne 2001, p. 13.

52 Bannerman 1996, pp. 25–6.

53 'Craignish History', pp. 112–13.

54 Thomson 1958, pp. 5–6.

55 See, for instance, McLeod 2004, pp. 67–9, and below, p. 43 and n. 86.

56 For instance, Donnchadh Ó Briain, fourth Earl of Thomond (+1624), was fostered by Fionnghuala, sister of the poet and historian Tadhg mac Dáire Mhic Bhruaideadha until he was seven years of age, when Tadhg himself took charge of the supervision of the youth's studies. See McGrath 1943–4, p. 62; Ó Cuív (ed.) 1984, p. 89.

entry into universities.[57] By the sixteenth century Scots was increasingly replacing Latin as the written language of government in the Highlands, and again it is the poets who appear involved in the tutoring of the nobility in the Scots language.[58] Additionally, the *filidh* had the duty to expand and revitalise the adult nobles' education by relating to them historical and mythological stories. These had been learned by the poets themselves in the course of their professional training, and they formed an important part of their cultural heritage: 'primscéla hÉrend olchena fria naisneís do ríghaib 7 flaithib 7 dagdhoínib' ('and the *prím-scéla* of Ireland besides [are] to be narrated to kings and princes and nobles').[59] Knowledge of these tales was no mere knowledge for its own sake, for they contained information which might be useful in the defence of a particular political claim. Additionally, the poets would compose versified versions of these stories and then incorporate them into their panegyrics. Thus fifteenth-century Conchobhar, son of the Munster chief Diarmaid Ó Conchobhair Ciarraighe, was reminded by Tadhg Óg Ó hUiginn (†1448) that Ulster was *cairt a chinidh* ('his race's charter-land') on account of his descent from Fearghus mac Róigh, and was encouraged to wrest it from the Uí Néill.[60] Another example is provided by the same author's panegyric to Alasdair Mac Domhnaill, lord of the Isles (†1449), where Tadhg Óg pointed to Alasdair's right to the high-kingship of Ireland, on the basis of his descent from royal Colla Uais.[61] At times the political significance embodied in some of the stories needed to be interpreted and reformulated to suit changed circumstances; it was the professional poets, whose 'responsibility it was to conserve and to cultivate the whole wide range of traditional learning', who had the authority to do so.[62]

In Ireland the court poets were very much out of favour with its English administration. One main reason was that the poets sometimes composed incitements to battle, and were thus perceived as political agitators.[63] There

57 Bannerman 1983, pp. 221, 223.
58 *ibid.*, pp. 218, 223.
59 Quoted in Mac Cana 1980, p. 122.
60 *Fada ó Ultaibh a n-oidhre.*
61 See below, chapter 3, p. 67.
62 Mac Cana 1980, p. 7.
63 But, as noted by Eleanor Knott, the poets' political influence may have been overrated or misunderstood (*TD* i, p. xliv).

is not so much evidence for Scotland in this respect. As in Ireland, government passed legislation against the Gaelic poets from time to time, but for different reasons. In 1407 it was enacted 'that in all justice ayres the kingis justice tak inquisicione of sornaris, bardis, maisterful beggars or fenzeit fulys, and other banysh them the cuntry or send them to the kingis presone'.[64] Similar legislation enacted from time to time until the early seventeenth century suggests that what was being checked was the abuses of the *cliar sheanchain* or poets' band, who had no fixed abode and exploited the duty of hospitality among the population.[65] A 1449 act of parliament describes them as 'they [who] haue not qrupoun to leif of thair awin'.[66] The *filidh*, by contrast, were not only in employment but in very affluent circumstances too. Although some of them had an annual rent to pay to their patrons for the land allotted to them, others, like the Mac Muireadhaigh poets at least, continued to hold rent-free hereditary lands right up to the early eighteenth century.[67] As well as being paid for his literary compositions the *file* had various particular privileges, from a tribal circuit every quarter of the year to the entitlement, upon his patron's marriage, to the bridegroom's 'upper Garb, that is, the Plade and Bonnet'.[68] In sum, it is uncertain that the *filidh* were the objects of pieces of legislation such as those just quoted. The target of such legislation may rather have been the 'inferior sort' of the various kinds of 'bards' which are identified with 'beggers' in a seventeenth-century letter, and complained of in poetry.[69] Nor is it immediately apparent that the *filidh* were perceived as

---

64 Quoted in Watson 1914–19, p. 201. 'Maisterful': overbearing, strong-handed, especially of robbers or beggars (*DSL-DOST*, s.v., 1a).

65 Watson 1914–19, pp. 201–2. For the 'cliar sheanchain' see Gordon 1958, pp. 22–3.

66 Quotation Thomson 1958, p. 3, n. 2, from *APS* iii, 139.

67 *Martin*, p. 116. The Welsh scholar Edward Lhuyd noted in 1699 Niall Mac Muireadhaigh's presence in Uist, where 'He is an Heriditary Poet and holds lands'; see Campbell and Thomson 1963, p. 9. Niall, who probably died in 1726 (Thomson 1969–70, p. 283), was the last hereditary poet to Clanranald. An example of a different arrangement is that of the Mac Eóghain hereditary poets, who had their land in feu from the Caimbéalaigh; see below, chapter 4, p. 124 and n. 35.

68 A number of poetic privileges are listed in the poems *Mairg thréigios inn, a Amhlaoíbh* and in *T'aire riut, a Ghiolla-easbuig*. For evidence from the Irish side see, for instance, Breatnach 1983.

69 Gordon 1958, p. 22; *Mór an feidhm freagairt na bhfaighdheach; Duanaire na Sracaire*, §§1–3; *Ciallach duine fioruasal*, §1. The 'cliar sheanchain' are represented in oral tradition as a degenerate rabble (MacInnes 2006a, p. 238).

trouble-makers by the kings of Scots in the way that their counterparts in Ireland were perceived by the English monarchs. In fact it may be significant that, leaving aside the special case of the 'Harlaw brosnachadh', within the whole extant corpus of classical poems composed for Scottish patrons only three can be classified as incitement poems, and neither of them encourages an attack on the king or his forces. *Ar sliocht Gaoidheal ó Ghort Gréag* (1513) is an exhortation to the Earl of Argyll on the eve of the encounter with the English at Flodden; *Bi ad mhosgladh, a mheic Aonghais* (*c*.1600) and *Dual ollamh do thriall le toisg* (*c*.1595–1601) respectively urge Séamas Mac Domhnaill of Islay and the seventh earl of Argyll to give support to the Irish in their struggle against the English.[70]

The *filidh* seem to have died out in Scotland at around the same time as they did in Ireland, in the early eighteenth century.[71] But we find many signs of their decline long before that. In Ireland complaints by the *filidh* of the literary laxity of some fellow poets, or of the poetic pretensions of untrained individuals, sharply increased in the early seventeenth century.[72] Similar complaints are extant for seventeenth-century Scotland. In *Sona do cheird, a Chalbhaigh* (*c*.1640) Cathal Mac Muireadhaigh criticised an amateur for trading his clumsy verse for a place at the noblemen's tables.[73] Two late seventeenth-century poems, Niall Mac Muireadhaigh's *T'aire riut, a Ghiolla-easbuig* and the anonymous *Námha an cheird nach taithighthear*, attack the pretensions to knowledge of the poetic art by 'upstarts' without any qualifications, who are trying to supplant the *filidh*:

> cia ga rabha an ghairm ollaimh
> fuair tusa, a chromain chíordhuibh.

> (who had the title of Ollamh that you got,
> you black-tufted crow?).[74]

---

70 See below, chapter 3, pp. 82, 90, and chapter 4, pp. 128, 137.

71 Although in Ireland poetic schools may have been no longer operational by *c*.1641 (*IBP*, p. 159), poetry in the classical style continued to be composed. For early eighteenth-century Irish survivals, all of which are unpublished, see *BPD*.

72 Some examples are *Aonar dhamhsa eidir dhaoinibh, A mhic na meabhraigh éigse, Tairnig éigse fhuinn Ghaoidheal, Slán don droing da ndiongnainn dán.*

73 See especially §§1d, 2c, 3b, 5ab, 8, 9cd.

74 *T'aire riut, a Ghiolla-easbuig,* §11cd (see Thomson 1977, pp. 233–4 for some comment on

Maintaining the genre's quality was not the only challenge. The spread of print, according to one source, also worked against the traditional Gaelic men of learning. The last of the Mac Eóghain genealogists to the Caimbéalaigh was Niall mac Athairne (†1650). 'Printing of Hystorie becoming then more frequent, the necessity of maintaining these Annalists began to wear off', says the author of the 'Craignish History' to explain why no successor was appointed after Niall's death.[75] The decline of Gaelic learning in general is further illuminated by the same author's statement that 'there is [currently] no authentick histories extant in the Irish language in the Kingdome of Scotland'.[76] Writing in the eighteenth century, Dr Hector Maclean of Grulin (1703–1784) claimed that the Mac Gille Eóin family 'had their Shenachies and Bards … Yet they were so ungratefull to their Benefactors, or so negligent or ignorant as to have left Nothing upon Record worth Noticing preceding the Family's Settlement in the Island of Mull'.[77] According to Martin Martin the poets 'becoming insolent, lost ever since both the Profit, and Esteem which was formerly due to their Character; for neither their *Panegyricks* nor *Satyrs* are regarded to what they have been, and they are now allowed but a small Sallary'. He goes on to add that they had by then (the close of the seventeenth century) lost their entitlement to the bridegroom's upper garb, having now to be 'satisfied with what the Bridegroom pleases to give him'.[78] It is true that the *filidh* had always been an 'insolent' class, arrogant and demanding, but it is also true that financial debt was a widespread problem among Highlands and Islands chiefs, directly related to their increasing 'anglicisation'. It would seem, to sum up, that the demise of the poetic order was accelerated by a combination of adverse external circumstances, such as upstart encroachment, lack of patronage and the spread of print; Maclean of Grulin's complaint of poetic negligence, however, is questioned in a later chapter.[79] But the major single blow to the patronage of Gaelic learning had taken place earlier, with the forfeiture of the lords

---

this poem). *Námha an cheird nach taithighthear* is edited and translated in Appendix 1.
75 'Craignish History', pp. 190–1.
76 'Ane accompt', p. 72.
77 Macfarlane 1900, i, p. 118.
78 *Martin*, p. 116.
79 See below, chapter 5, p. 241–2.

of the Isles in 1493, soon after which many learned families who had held hereditary office for them became tenants of the crown.[80] It is significant that, as ever, Clann Domhnaill remained the immovable mainstay of traditional scholarship: Clann Raghnaill kept a hereditary poet family in the traditional contractual terms until the early eighteenth century and, interestingly, in a vernacular poem composed at that time they are noted as the only kindred who still maintain the traditional practices of hospitality and protection.[81]

The vernacular poets

In the first chapter I noted the 'vernacular' poets and their interest as commentators of social and political events. First of all, definitions must be given. By 'vernacular' we will understand here the term generally used for the everyday language as opposed to the standard literary language, or Classical Gaelic.[82] Within the term 'vernacular poets' we will incorporate various categories of poets active in the period considered in this work — those who ranked somewhere below the *file*, the amateurs from the nobility, and the folk poets or songsters.[83] The more popular literary genres encompassed within the term folk-song ('verse that was composed for singing and used styles popular with the non-learned … what we have left once we have abstracted the professional classical Gaelic or bardic verse … and the semi-bardic verse')[84] are not generally part of this study since they express personal emotion and had none of the perceived authority of the works of 'official' and 'semi-official' poets. We will rather focus on the work of those other categories of poets — often given the title *bàrd* or *aos-dàna* by the late seventeenth century[85] — who appear affiliated in various ways

---

80 See, for instance, Thomson 1960–3, pp. 288–9, 292.

81 See above, chapter 1, p. 13 and n. 50, and below, chapter 5, p. 222.

82 This usage, based on the differentiation between Latin and 'vernacular languages', is sensible since classical Gaelic stood with reference to 'everyday Gaelic' in the same position as Latin stood with reference to the 'everyday [romance] languages' of many European countries throughout the medieval and early modern periods. Classical Gaelic was the language of communication, not only of poets, but of all educated sections of Gaelic society. See Bannerman 1983, p. 226.

83 For an overview of these categories see, for instance, Thomson 1958, p. 2; *DnS*, pp. xli–xliv.

84 Thomson (ed.) 1994, pp. 77–8.

85 *ibid.*, p. 4.

to their patrons' courts where, as noted, a *file* might simultaneously be in employment.[86] Among these there is a considerable number of female poets, like Sìleas na Ceapaich, daughter of Gilleasbaig Mac Domhnaill, fourteenth chief of Keppoch (†1682), or Màiri nighean Alasdair Ruaidh, who was a nurse in the household of Mac Leóid of Dunvegan.[87] Women may have had access to the poetic schools, although no woman has ever been known to be *file* to a Gaelic chief.

Vernacular poetry, by definition, uses accentual rather than syllabic metres. However, establishing a clear-cut boundary between classical and vernacular poetry is not always straightforward. While the *filidh* chiefly composed in strict metre — syllabic *dán díreach* — they sometimes turned either to looser metrical forms, or to linguistic styles and metres proper to the vernacular language, or to both. On the other hand, the amateur poets from the nobility had some degree of training in classical composition, but they might employ the vernacular language or a mixture of classical and vernacular.[88] It is the work of these poets, therefore, that presents some difficulty in its classification; yet, since these authors were not qualified *filidh* and since they, and their poetry, were clearly differentiated by the *filidh* from their own, for the purposes of this study we will include them among the vernacular authors. Their poetry has been variously labelled 'semi-bardic', 'sub-bardic', 'sub-syllabic', and 'semi-classical'.[89] In terms of subject matter the work of these authors is generally less elevated than that of the *filidh*, while in the main their poems are in loose syllabic metres rather than in *dán díreach*. For instance, Donnchadh Caimbéal, second chief of Glenorchy (†1513), and Murchadh Mór Mac Coinnich, fourth chief of Achilty (†c.1689) have left us several instances of their classical skills, all of them in either the *óglácha* or the *brúilingeacht* styles.[90] These authors probably first became acquainted with classical versification under

---

86 An Clàrsair Dall was temporarily employed by Eóin Breac Mac Leóid both as poet and as harper, while the Dunvegan chiefs seem to have maintained hereditary *filidh* of the Ó Muirgheasáin family until at least the early eighteenth century. See Thomson 1994, p. 220, and below, chapter 4, pp. 158, 167.

87 *GSMM*, pp. xi–xii.

88 Thomson 1994, p. 301.

89 *id.*, 1990, p. 106; Gillies, 1976–8, p. 261; *id.*, 2006, p. 17.

90 Gillies (ed.) 1978, 1981; *id.* 2010, pp. 91–8. For Murchadh Mòr see below, chapter 5, pp. 233, 235. For this class of poets see also Thomson 1958, pp. 5–6.

the tutelage of their families' poets, who as noted were involved in the education of the young nobles. Again they may have received later on some more specialised training in a poetic school. Poetic gatherings in noble households, such as we read about in poems and in annals, would have provided further acquaintance with the genre.[91] That these amateurs could reach a high level of training in the poetic art is plain from some of their compositions but, at least in the case of Scottish authors, none seems to have achieved the metrical perfection of *dán díreach*.[92] Finally, it is worth noting that at least some of the 'strictly' vernacular poets, or vernacular poets 'proper' — those composing accentual verse in vernacular language — were sufficiently acquainted with classical verse to employ syllabic-based metres on occasion.[93]

Although the official role of legitimator of political leadership was exclusive to the *file*, the significance of the vernacular poets must be taken into account. They often enjoyed an official or at least semi-official poetic status, and to that extent would receive attention and respect from their audience, especially if their patrons did not maintain a *file*. For this reason and because of their close links with their chiefs they could shape public opinion, much as the *filidh* could, and as the ministers also did from the pulpit.[94] In addition, while the classical poets' central concern was the praise of the patron, much of the vernacular poets' work is commentary on contemporary events. The abolition of the lordship of the Isles gave way to a long period (*c.*1500 – *c.*1700) of general unsettledness in the Highlands and Islands known in Gaelic tradition as 'Linn nan Creach'. With central

---

91 An example from the annals is that of Mairghréad, daughter of Tadhg Ó Cearbhaill and wife of An Calbhach Ó Conchobhair Failghe, who in 1433 hosted a general gathering of the poets of Ireland and Scotland (*AU* iii, p. 128; *AC*, p. 472). On a less grand, and probably more frequent, scale is the case of one particular gathering at which Aodh Mág Uidhir (†1600) in his early youth extracted from the poet Eochaidh Ó hEódhusa the promise to dedicate him a quatrain in every poem he ever composed. The anecdote is found in Ó hEódhusa's poem *Connradh do cheanglas re hAodh*. Internal evidence from panegyrics also shows that the *filidh* were often visitors in the noble households. See, for instance, *A theachtaire théid bhu thuaidh*, §15abc; *Atáim i gcás eidir dhá chomhairle*, §§11–17. For some instances of evidence from Scottish vernacular poetry see below, chapter 4, p. 177; chapter 5, p. 212.

92 See especially below, chapter 5, pp. 198–9.

93 For example, Sìleas na Ceapaich; see *BSC*, p. lx. For another instance see below, chapter 5, p. 215, n. 132.

94 Findlay 2002, p. 249. See also below, chapter 3, pp. 107.

government control weak in those areas, and its attention to them only sporadic with the exception of a strong financial-return interest by the times of James VI, inter-clan feuding was frequent, and consequently much of the poetry of the period has a strong clan focus. In other instances the events in question are of a wider, national nature, such as the tug-of-war between Mac Domhnaill and the government for the earldom or Ross in the early fifteenth century, the mid- and later-seventeenth-century 'Wars of the Three Kingdoms' (including their religious component), or the matter of the Union of Parliaments in the early eighteenth century.[95] In general, the poems are concerned with the preservation of the cohesion of society at times of crisis, whether internal (for instance following a chief's death) or otherwise.[96]

Most of the extant vernacular poetry was composed from the sixteenth century onwards. From the mid-seventeenth century it shows a preoccupation with British national affairs.[97] Its main focus, like that of classical panegyric, is the celebration of the warrior aristocrat; to that extent it is no different from the Scottish literary tradition in Latin and Scots.[98] It also drew heavily on the rhetoric, themes, and imagery of classical tradition. Vernacular poems in themselves did not have the legitimating power of the compositions of the *filidh*, but the ornamental use of the classical panegyric rhetoric would be rich in echoes and resonances of established authority readily recognised by the audience. To give an example, Iain Lom's address to Domhnall Gorm Óg Mac Domhnaill of Sleat (†1643) as *A churaidh gun ghiamh* ('O hero without fault') would be immediately associated with the common motif of classical panegyric, drawn from venerable legal tradition, that the 'right ruler' must be without blemish, physical or otherwise.[99] Similarly, Murchadh MacCoinnich's depiction of Mac Domhnaill of Sleat's territory as 'Mar choll gun chnuasach gun mheas' ('like a hazel-tree without fruit, without growth') in his elegy for the same Domhnall

---

95 Thomson 1990, pp. 98, 116–17.

96 MacInnes 2006e, p. 169.

97 Thomson 1990, p. 106; *id.* (ed.) 1994, p. 296; MacInnes 2006a, pp. 235, 237.

98 See generally Edington 1998, where it is also noted that the Scots 'often viewed their entire history as one of protracted warfare' (p. 69).

99 *A Dhomhnaill an Dùin*, §5a. Compare 'Domhnall nar damh locht' ('Domhnall, free from fault'), from a classical quatrain quoted in the annals where the death of Domhnall Ó Briain (†1579) is recorded (*ARÉ* v, p. 1711).

Gorm Óg connects with the validating motif of the decay of nature after a chief's death.[100]

One recurrent theme in Scottish Gaelic vernacular poetry is the listing of the chief's friends and allies, actual or at least possible. This is one aspect of its characteristic clan focus, and the historian searching these poems for the establishment of political alliances must refrain from taking such listings at face value; the allies' names given did not necessarily represent a faithful reflection of political and military realities, for such lists were mere propagandistic appeals. The 'allies motif' was also borrowed from the classical genre, but its particular development in Scottish vernacular panegyric appears directly connected to actual historical circumstances.[101] Additionally, it seems to have often been employed to reinforce aristocratic connexions in poetry for kindreds of undemonstrable venerable noble ancestry.[102] Equally pervasive is the 'royalism motif', particularly from the mid-seventeenth century onwards. It has been noted that, despite the cultural affinity with Ireland so strongly reflected in their literature, and despite their disagreement with royal policies at various times, the Scottish Gaels had a strong sense of allegiance to the Stiúbhart kings, descendants of Maol Coluim III, as their sovereigns.[103] The vernacular poetry strongly supports this; if the seventeenth century wars also served to settle scores among clans, Gaelic aversion to the foreign blood that usurped the Stiúbhart throne is, perhaps most famously, represented in the words of Sìleas na Ceapaich:

'S e rìgh na muice
's na Cuigse Rìgh Deòrsa ...
rìgh fuadain nach buineadh dhuinn.

(King George is a swinish Whiggish king ... an alien king who has no place with us).[104]

---

100 *Sgeula leat, a ghaoth a deas*, §9c.
101 MacInnes 2006c, p. 169; id., 2006b, pp. 276–7.
102 See below, chapter 5, pp. 216–7, 233; chapter 6, pp. 272, 278.
103 MacInnes 2006b, p. 266. Maol Coluim Ceann Mór is traditionally identified with Maol Coluim III. For the suggestion that the appellative Ceann Mór might in fact be that of Maol Coluim IV see Duncan 2002, pp. 51–2, 74–5; Oram 2004, p. 17 and n. 1.
104 *A rìgh 's diombach mi 'n iomairt*, §6abm.

Sìleas was a Catholic, and Catholicism was at the time strongly associated with Jacobitism. However, Protestants could also favour the Jacobite cause, as in the case of the anonymous author of *Nac faic sibh, a dhaoine* (1693), a poem which includes a prayer for the return of 'Oighre Bhreatuinn' ('Britain's heir', §13h).[105] It is also the case that this sense of royalism is manifest in the poets whether or not they saw eye to eye with their patrons in the matter of political allegiances.[106] Clearly, and for all their Irish connexions — cultural, familial, and political — seventeenth-century Scottish Gaels had a fundamental sense of belonging not only in Scotland but in Britain too, and an interest in the wider British politics as well as an awareness of their natural right to participate in them. It would be at best simplistic to interpret their participation in national politics merely as an opportunistic manipulation of events to make them work for them within the context of inter-clan feuding. All this brings us to the all-important question of identities. There is a common view of medieval and early modern Gaelic Scotland and Ireland as one single 'cultural province' (a view put to the test and qualified in McLeod 2004). When to this view are added the patterns of fosterage, intermarriage, and Hebridean military service in Ireland, it might too readily be concluded that Irish links encouraged Scottish Gaelic political conduct independent from and rebellious against the Scottish, and later the British, government. Before proceeding to examine the poetry itself it is essential to reflect briefly on the question of self-perceived Scottish Gaelic identity.

Scottish Gaelic identities

Over the centuries between the earliest permanent Gaelic settlements in Scotland and the eighteenth century, the inhabitants of what is modern Scotland several times had to adjust their own perceptions of identity and sense of allegiance. The early settlers felt 'Irish' and viewed themselves as colonists in *Alba*.[107] Military expansion, intermarriage with Britons and Picts (and later Norwegians and Normans), and

---

105 Another Protestant poet who supported the Jacobite cause was Aonghus mac Alasdair Ruaidh MhicDhòmhnaill; see below, chapter 3, p. 104 and n. 233.

106 MacInnes 2006d, p. 30.

107 See below, chapter 7, p. 294.

above all a growing detachment from Irish overlordship, would have resulted in some adjustment to that original sense of identity in the following generations. One example is that of the Eóghanachta of Magh Gheirrghinn — their tribal name was Irish, as were the names of their kings even by the late eighth century, and indeed they claimed Irish ancestry, yet they appear in the sources as Picts.[108] The takeover of the Pictish kingdoms by the descendants of Cinéal nGabhráin and by their rivals, Cinéal Loairn, who came to occupy Moray, was accompanied by changes in royal titles. From the tenth century the rulers of Scottish Dál Riada — until then sometimes identified as kings of the Picts — begin to be given the designation *rí Alban* in the Irish annals.[109] By the time *Inglis* (the language of areas no longer Gaelic-speaking) became the language of government (*c*.1400), the literary term *Scoti*, meaning *Gaoidhil*, came to be used in *Inglis* to mean the people of the kingdom of Scotland (Scots). Interestingly, the title of the Scottish monarchs was 'king of Scots' ('queen of Scots' in Mary's case), retaining a very common Gaelic usage, that is the designation of a people rather than a territory, until the reign of James VI and I.[110] Similar adaptations are observed in the titles of the rulers of the Isles, whose lordly designations often reflect the Norse component in the blood of both the royal line and their people. Somhairle and his descendants appropriated for themselves the title *rí Innse Gall* (*rex insularum* in Latin sources), previously used by the Norse rulers of Man and the Western Isles.[111]

It has been shown by Dauvit Broun that it is possible to speak of the existence of 'a simple and self-contained Scottish identity as a country and a people defined by the kingdom itself' by the mid-thirteenth century'.[112] Broun also showed that also around the same time the concept emerged that every nation had a territory which had been divinely designated as their homeland, and for the Scots this homeland

---

108 See below, chapter 5, p. 185.

109 See above, p. 33 and n. 37. See also below, chapter 7, p. 296 n. 61.

110 For instance, An Calbhach Ó Conchobhair (†1458) is given the designation *rí Ua Failghe* in the annals; see *AC*, p. 454; *ARÉ* iv, p. 848.

111 There is some fluidity in the designations of these rulers; see Sellar 2000, and generally McLeod 2002a. See also below, chapter 3, pp. 54, 56, 58, 60, 61–3.

112 Broun 1998, p. 11.

was Scotland.[113] Modern historians have argued that a strong sense of Irishness was nevertheless preserved, at least by the educated élite, only beginning to suffer modification with the Wars of Independence: by the early fourteenth century the mythical Scota is said to have made Scotland, not Ireland, her final destination, rather than a much later colony of her descendants.[114] Religious Reformation would bring a split to the question of Scots identity, while developments including a notable increase in the creation of noble titles would spark off a surge of family-history writing and revision of pedigrees from the early seventeenth century onwards.[115] With the union of the Scottish and British crowns in the early seventeenth century, and again with the union of the two nations' parliaments in 1707, the issue of identity had to be revised once more, as Scots not only became British, but had to come to terms with the transformation in the concept of kingship itself.[116] Much modern scholarly work on the Scottish sense of identity is based on Latin and Scots writing and therefore represents the self-view of the Lowland educated élite. But as the cultural Highland-Lowland gap emerged and increased from at least the later fourteenth century, the 'Highlanders' more and more must be seen as a specific social group within the kingdom of Scots whose self-view presented a more complex pattern.

The 'Highlanders' of modern terminology and concept considered themselves *Albanaigh* since that label came to be used for them in the early tenth century.[117] In Ireland the term *Gaoidheal* began to acquire an ethnic connotation as a result of the Viking settlement there, and the Vikings themselves were called *Goill*, a word which originally meant 'Gauls' but by that time meant 'foreigners' generally.[118] In both Ireland and Scotland the ethnically-mixed descendants of the Vikings came to

---

113 *id.* 1999, p. 149.

114 *id.* 1998, p. 11. For the significance of the wars against the English in the development of a distinct sense of Scottish identity see Watson 1998.

115 See Lynch 1998. For other factors, including the decline of the Gaelic learned classes, related to the increase in genealogy and history at this time, see MacGregor 2002, pp. 217–18, 219–20.

116 See generally Lynch 1994. For the seventeenth century see also Brown 1998.

117 See above, p. 48 and n. 109.

118 Herbert 2000, p. 64.

be known as *Gallghaoidhil*. As *Alba* expanded, adding Norman groups to the already incorporated Gaelic, British, Pictish and Norse ones, the former would have been called *Goill* by the *Albanaigh*, in accordance with current linguistic use.[119] By the seventeenth century *Gall* was the common Scottish Gaelic term for 'a Lowlander', but matters of labelling are obscure in the previous centuries. We know that Domhnall Gallda (†1519), son of Alasdair of Lochalsh, obtained his soubriquet from his education at the royal court where he seems to have remained most of his life.[120] What this means is that by at least the later fifteenth century the Scottish court, once *Gaoidhealach*, had become so de-Gaelicised that to the Scots of the Gaelic-speaking areas it had become *Gallda*. In all likelihood this change in label came about as a result of both the cultural changes at the royal court and the influx into Scotland of English and Anglo-Norman nobles, churchmen, and merchants that took place in the twelfth and thirteenth centuries. In trying to solve this question one must firmly leave out the classical poetry and the later chronicle sources. In the latter the word *Gall* and its derivatives may be sometimes used anachronistically.[121] The poetry has even greater potential for misconception on account of its usage, or rather different usages, of the word *Gall*.[122]

If the Scottish Gaels perceived themselves as *Albanaigh* but also as *Gaoidhil* sharing *Alba* with *Goill*, we may wonder which identity came first, whether the linguistic and cultural, or the 'national', but this may be as pointless as wondering whether a person feels more racially white because they are blue- or brown-eyed. On the other hand, Scottish Gaelic ill-feeling for Lowlanders, together with a Gaelic sense of cultural superiority, only becomes apparent in the literature from the seventeenth century onwards, and even then the Gaels continued to feel Scottish, *Albanaigh*.[123] Much has been made of 'the Highland problem', although some historians have to an extent vindicated the Highlanders.

---

119 See below, chapter 3, p. 70 and n. 82.

120 Gregory 1881, p. 106.

121 For instance, Niall Mac Muireadhaigh, writing in the late-seventeenth century, uses the word 'Ghaltacht' [*sic*] when referring to events taking place two centuries earlier; see *RC* ii, p. 164.

122 See Coira 2008b, especially at pp. 141–58.

123 MacInnes 2006c, p. 39.

For instance, it has been noted that the traditionally-supposed medieval cultural and political distance between the royal court and the Gaelic lordships seems to have been overemphasised.[124] Central government did only occasionally give its full attention to the Highlands and Islands, but it is worth noting what the circumstances were when it did. One of the most serious conflicts was the battle of Harlaw (1411), a major confrontation stemming from the effort of Domhnall Mac Domhnaill, eighth lord of the Isles, to make good his legitimate claim to the earldom of Ross. The 1452 rebellion of Eóin mac Alasdair, tenth lord of the Isles, was apparently sparked off by James II's failure to keep his word to give him the keepership of Urquhart Castle.[125] The 1462 Treaty of Ardtornish, by which Eóin gave in to the approaches of Edward IV of England, belongs to the time of political chaos of the minority of James III. Similarly, the battle of Harlaw took place when James I was a minor and a captive in England, while Eóin's final forfeiture of 1493 was carried out, as Norman Macdougall noted, not by James IV himself but by his minority government.[126] To sum up, the only really serious conflicts of the fifteenth century were few and all took place when government was in the hands of factions; the significance of this may be of interest to the historian. The unrest that for so long scourged the Highlands and Islands after the abolition of the Gaelic lordship of the Isles was of course a direct consequence of Mac Domhnaill's forfeiture, and as for James VI's Highland policies, modern historians agree that much of 'the problem' was of the state's own making; in the words of one leading scholar, 'If there was a Highland problem, it was not the Highlands that caused it'.[127]

One recalls John of Fordun's statement that 'The highlanders and people of the islands... are ... faithful and obedient to their king and country, and easily made to submit to law, if properly governed'.[128] The words of Niall Mac Muireadhaigh also come to mind, where he explains

---

124 Boardman and Ross (eds) 2003, p. 21.

125 Eóin maintained that 'he had the kingis wryt and walx to haf the castell of wrquhart for iii zere' ('The Auchinleck Chronicle', printed in McGladdery 1990, pp. 160–73, at p. 169).

126 Macdougall 1997, pp. 175–6.

127 Lynch 2000, p. 215.

128 Skene (ed.) 1993, i, p. 38.

that he wrote his chronicle because 'do con*n*airc me gan iomrágh air bioth a*r* Ghaoidheal*uibh* ag na sgriobhnoiribh ata ag te*ch*t a*r* gnoidhibh na haimsire an mhui*nn*ti*r* do rin*n*e an tseirbhis uile' ('I saw that those who treated of the affairs of the time have made no mention at all of the Gael, the men who did all the service').[129] We sense the frustration and disillusionment of one speaking for all the 'dispossessed',[130] whose ancestors had first founded the kingdom, and whose service to it was now passed over in silence.

129 *RC* ii, p. 202.

130 For the sense of Gaelic 'dispossession' generally see MacInnes 2006d, p. 27; 2006c, p. 44; 2006b, p. 267.

Chapter 3

Mac Domhnaill and Mac Dubhghaill:
the descendants of Colla Uais

The seventeenth-century chronicler commonly known as 'Hugh of Sleat'[1] wrote that in the times of Alasdair Mac Domhnaill, ninth lord of the Isles (†1449), a Spanish visitor to Scotland had declared that the greatest wonder he had seen there was 'a grand man, called Macdonald, with a great train of men after him, and that he was called neither Duke nor Marquis'.[2] Whether the story is true or not, it illustrates the point that to the medieval Gaels — and perhaps also to those living, like the writer, in the seventeenth century — their own aristocratic titles were superior to any other, for although Alasdair was also Earl of Ross, it was not this title that caught the imagination of the Spaniard in the story. George Buchanan, writing in the later sixteenth century, stated that Eóin, Alasdair's son and successor, had, as his predecessors had also, usurped the royal title.[3] Buchanan — who was, according to the same Gaelic historian, a Gaelic speaker[4] — seems to have been misguided by Mac Domhnaill's territorial style 'rí Innse Gall'. The son of a Stirlingshire farmer, by age sixteen he was pursuing an education and a career on the continent, and on his return to Scotland he lived in the Lowlands. His Latin was much better than his Gaelic, for he translated *rí* as *rex*, clearly equating the Gaelic *ríghe* ('ruling; kingship, sovereignty') with feudal-style monarchy. Dean Monro was

---

1 Traditionally supposed to be a Mac Domhnaill historian, but for the possibility of the writer being one Aodh Mac Beathadh see Bannerman 1986, pp. 17–20.

2 *HP* i, p. 38.

3 'Regium enim nomen cum alii, tum non adeo pridem Ioannes e Donaldina familia usurpavit' ('for of late John, of the Mac Domhnaill family, as well as others before him, usurped the royal title', Buchanan 1582, i, 8v).

4 *HP* i, p. 11.

guilty of the same error.[5] Yet, in the Latin charters of the lords of the Isles it is not the style 'rex Insularum' that they give themselves, but 'dominus Insularum'.[6]

The Scottish lordship of the Isles originated, according to Gaelic tradition, with Somhairle (†1164), and came to an end with the death of Domhnall Dubh (†1545).[7] From Domhnall mac Raghnaill, Somhairle's grandson, the kindred was known as Clann Domhnaill. Over time Clann Domhnaill came to have numerous collateral branches, but the lords of the Isles, with the occasional early exception before primogeniture succession became established, came from the lineal descendants of Somhairle (see Table 3.1). We will see that the classical poetry composed for the main branch of Clann Domhnaill differs in a number of ways from that composed for its cadet branches. Since for the latter — with the exception of two Clann Raghnaill pieces — we have only poems composed from the later sixteenth century onwards, a chronological division between the two bodies of poetry happens almost naturally. In this chapter the later poetry is further subdivided into two sections separating Clann Eóin Mhóir panegyric from the verse composed for other Mac Domhnaill branches, for reasons which will shortly become apparent. The vernacular poems, on account of the different literary genre they constitute, are considered in the final section.

Early classical verse: the lords of the Isles

Titles: territory and ancestry

That there was some fluidity in the lordly styles of the ruling descendants of Somhairle mac Giolla Brighde has already been noted.[8] But their

---

5   'Alexander of *Ila* Earle of Rosse, and Lord of the Isles ore as the heighland men calls him king of the Iles' (*Monro*, p. 92). See also below, p. 54, n. 12.

6   *ALI*, p. xx. It is vital to bear in mind that *rí* does not necessarily equate with *rex* or 'king' in the medieval period (McLeod 2002, p. 34). In contemporary Ireland, in acknowledgement of the distinction between a Gaelic *rí* and the 'crowned kings' of the rest of Europe, *princeps* began to be used as the Latin for *rí*, while *rí* began to be replaced with *tighearna* (*dominus*); see Simms 2000, p. 38; McLeod 2006, p. 21. The Spanish ambassador Pedro de Ayala, who visited the Scottish court at the end of the fifteenth century, describes the lordship of the Isles as 'principatus insularum', held, like the *principatus* of Galloway, by the king; see Brown 1891, p. 45.

7   See below, pp. 57 and n. 18, 62 and n. 38.

8   See above, chapter 2, p. 43, n. 111.

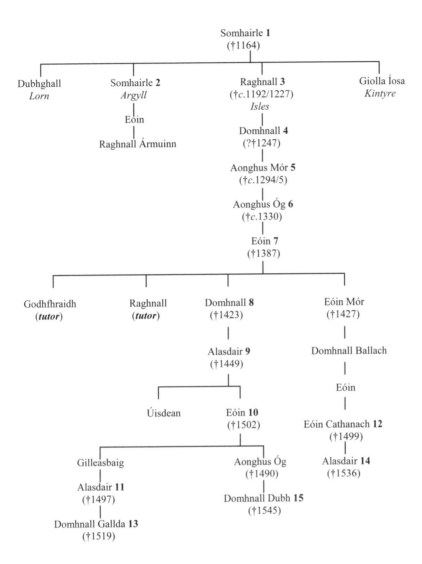

Table 3.1 The lords of the Isles.

Sources: 'MS 1467', nos. 30, 31; *RC* ii, pp. 154–60; Sellar 1966; McDonald 1997. 'MS 1467'
makes Dubhghall, the eponym of Clann Dubhghaill, the son of Raghnall mac Somhairle
rather than his brother. The 'Book of Ballymote' shows the same flaw. This has been some-
times as a deliberate genealogical manipulation (MacGregor 2000, p. 145), but may well have
been a mere scribal error transmitted from an earlier source; elsewhere (as in NLI G 2, the
'Great Book of Lecan' and later sources) the pedigree is given correctly. For the higher reli-
ability of 'Lecan' over 'Ballymote' see Woolf 2005, p. 200.

proper title was, as noted in the story about the fifteenth-century Spanish visitor, 'Mac Domhnaill'; this is the most common designation in Gaelic historical writing, 'na hAlba[n]' being often added in the Irish sources.⁹ 'Mac Domhnaill' is also the signature of Domhnall, lord of the Isles (†1423) in the only extant Gaelic charter; in their Latin charters the lords of the Isles style themselves 'dominus Insularum', the title 'comes Rossie' ('Earl of Ross') being added from at least 1432/3.¹⁰ Charter and chronicle entries also use the appellative 'de Ile' (Latin), 'of Ila' (English and Scots), 'a híle', in imitation of Anglo-Norman styles.¹¹ Irish annals and Scottish chronicles also give the territorial style 'rí Innse Gall', originally the title of the Norse kings of Man and the Hebrides, and later adopted by Somhairle's descendants.¹² Twelfth- and thirteenth-century non-Gaelic sources refer to the 'kingdom of the Isles', but this 'kingdom' should not be understood as a *ríoghacht* in the sense in which other contemporary kingdoms were.¹³ 'King (or lord) of the Isles' — the designation which Buchanan took as a usurpation — was in fact never more than a self-styling of the heads of Clann Domhnaill, rather than a formal title; and after Eóin mac Alasdair was forfeited in 1476 and allowed to hold his patrimony only as a lordship of parliament, the dignity 'Lord of the Isles' awarded him then by the Scottish king was 'at best a legal fiction'.¹⁴ We may note at this point that both Somhairle and his son and successor Raghnall are claimed to have introduced important social and legal changes. Somhairle seems to have regulated the status and contractual obligations of the poets, according to Niall Mac Muireadhaigh:

9   See, for instance, *RC* ii, pp. 162, 164, 166; *AU* iii, pp. 126, 350, 582, 608–9; *ARÉ* iv, p. 964.

10 *ALI*, §22, pp. 21–3, 36.

11 See, for instance, *ibid.* §19, §22; *RC* ii, pp. 160, 162, 210. Cf. Andrew de Moravia, William de Warenne, Robert de Brus.

12 See, for instance, *RC* ii, p. 156 (Raghnall, †c.1191–1227; for the date of death see McDonald 1997, pp. 78–9); *AU* i, p. 496 (Godhfhraidh, †989); *ibid.*, iii, 18 (Eóin,†1387); *AC*, pp. 252 (Mac Ruaidhrí, †1318), 604 (Eóin Mór, †1499). Raghnall mac Somhairle was 'callit in his time king of the Occident Iles' (*Monro*, p. 57). For this title in early charters see McDonald 1997, pp. 73–4.

13 McLeod 2002a, especially at p. 30.

14 *ibid.*, p. 33.

O Shomhairle chuaidh an chuing
oruinn re díol mar deirim:
ar ríomh is deachtadh ar ndán
fíor na chleachtadh re chonnbháil.

(The obligation was imposed by Somerled; it
was for us to repay it as I say: to retain, by
our metrics and the composing of our poems, the
true form of what was customary.)[15]

Raghnall mac Somhairle is credited with legal reform that was still effective in the times of the later lords of the Isles. When describing the composition of their council, Dean Monro states that Mac Domhnaill's councillors 'decernit, decreitit and gave suits furth upon all debaitable matters according to the Laws made be Renald McSomharle'.[16] These important changes introduced by both leaders suggest that in the century or so since their kindred had been displaced by the Norse much social disruption had taken place and that, on recovery of the family patrimony, the early leaders proceeded to re-organize it according to its original Gaelic tenets. Here it may be noted that, according to Gaelic historians, the lords of the Isles stood in opposition to the king of Scots after Mac Beathadh's murder of Donnchadh I in 1040, and were refused royal support against the Norse, a situation which persisted until the times of Domhnall III (r.1093–1097); Somhairle and his father sought the help of their kinsmen of Oriel, and it was with their military support that they succeeded in recovering their territories.[17] With Somhairle at the head of the regained patrimony (to which he also added Man and a number of the Western Isles) and re-establishing Gaelic custom, it is understandable that later Gaelic historical tradition should portray him as the banisher of the foreigners and the founder of the Scottish lordship of the Isles.[18] Its rulers were vassals of the Norse kings until 1266, when the

---

15 *Maith an sgéal do sgaoil 'nar measg*, §10 (trsl. Thomson 1977, p. 236).

16 *Monro*, p. 57.

17 *RC* ii, p. 154; *HP* i, p. 9.

18 For this tradition see *RC* ii, p. 154; *HP* i, pp. 5–11. Steer and Bannerman 1977, p. 201, notes that the first of Colla's descendants to have become 'rí Innse Gall' may well have been Godhfhraidh mac Fearghusa. For Somhairle's and Raghnall's careers see McDonald 1997, pp. 44–67, 73–80. According to the 'Manx Chronicle', it was the 1156

Isles were ceded to Scotland and their rulers' vassalage transferred to the kings of Scots: by the later thirteenth century they had become 'barons of the realm of Scotland'.[19] As noted,[20] through the later medieval period they received scant direct attention from central government, generally appearing on the historical record when they clashed with it. Yet there are also instances of Mac Domhnaill loyalty to their royal overlord, as in, for instance, their support on the battlefield at Bannockburn (1314) and at Flodden (1513).[21]

To return to the question of titles, the designation 'Mac Domhnaill' was of relatively recent creation. The family claimed descent from Colla Uais, whose original patrimony was in Oriel.[22] The ruling descendants of Colla Uais were originally styled Ó Colla,[23] although the title Ó Mearghaigh, after Mearghach, great-great-grandson of Godhfhraidh mac Fearghusa, is also noted in Irish sources, down to Eóin mac Aonghuis Óig (†1387) (see Table 3.2).[24] The eponym of Clann Domhnaill was Domhnall, son of Raghnall and grandson of Somhairle,[25] and the first Mac Domhnaill was his son and successor, Aonghus Mór (†c.1294/5). In his 'Geneologies of the Cheiff Clans of the Iles' Dean Monro informs us of the previous family designations. He states that from Godhfhraidh mac Fearghusa down to Somhairle

---

partition of the kingdom of the Isles between Somhairle and Godfrey (Godhfhraidh mac Amhlaoibh in Gaelic sources), king of Man, that was 'the cause of the downfall of the [Norse] kingdom of the islands, from the time when the sons of Somerled took possession of it' (Anderson (ed.) 1990, ii, p. 232; McDonald 1997, p. 41).

19 For this exchange see McDonald 1997, pp. 119–23 (quotation at p. 123). For the accompanying cultural change, which was underway even before 1266, see id., 1999.

20 See above, chapter 2, p. 51.

21 *Clan Donald*, i, 96–9, 317–18. For Mac Domhnaill participation in the Scottish Wars of Independence see McDonald 1997, chapter 6. For further evidence of Mac Domhnaill support of the crown, and indeed of an 'identification of the interests of the Gael with those of the Scottish king and the rest of the inhabitants of his realm', see Boardman 2012. I am grateful to Steve Boardman for allowing me access to this essay before its publication.

22 Annals, genealogies, poetry and tradition support each other concerning Somhairle's descent from the Northern Uí Mhac Uais of Oriel (see Sellar 1966, pp 135–51), a section of whom seems to have been settled in the Hebrides at least by the seventh century (Bannerman 1971a, pp. 263–5).

23 *RC* ii, pp. 152–4.

24 *LMG* ii, p. 88 ('Ua Meargaidhe'). Meargach ('Mearghach', 'Merghach') is given as great-grandson of Godhfhraidh mac Fearghusa in *RC* ii, p. 152.

25 *Monro*, p. 92.

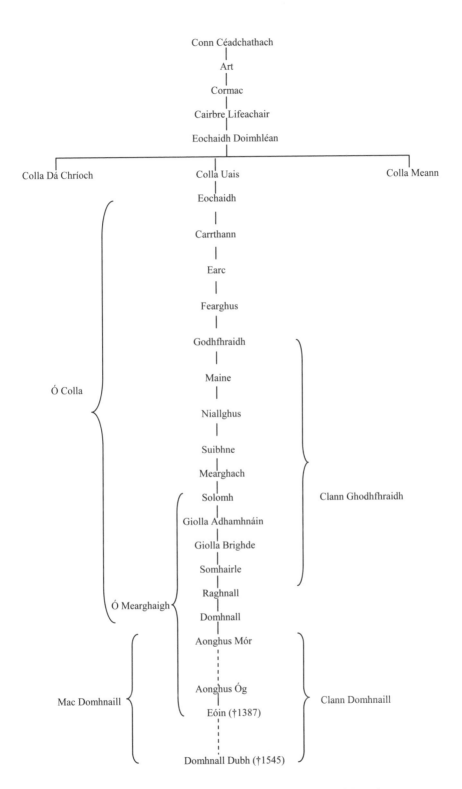

Table 3.2 Ancestry and titles of the Scottish lords of the Isles.
Sources: 'MS 1467', no. 35; *Monro; RC* ii; and as for Table 3.1.

mac Giolla Brighde the kindred were known as Clann Ghodhfhraidh.[26] The actual existence of this Godhfhraidh has been seriously questioned by one scholar, while another has proposed entirely different person, Godhfhraidh Crobhán — via an intermediate identification with another Godhfhraidh, son of Íomhar — who seized the kingship of Man in 1079 and died in 1095.[27] There are a number of issues with this identification, which was speculated on the basis that the misdating of Somhairle's death in *ARÉ* — a very late source — might be connected with the references to Godhfhraidh mac Fearghusa in the same annals. While the proposed amended chronology tallies, it is difficult to agree with the suggestion that Somhairle's descendants would be by the fourteenth century consciously rejecting their part-Norse ancestry and re-writing their pedigree by making Godhfhraidh the son of Fearghus mac Eirc, thus connecting themselves with the kings of Scots. In the first place, should this be the case the genealogists would have normally adopted the female-line approach, for instance they would have made Godhfhraidh the son of, or married him to, a female from the royal family of the kings of *Alba*. Proceeding otherwise would have left their claim open to challenge by their own learned class: as we will see, genealogical fabrications were not easily or at all accepted by the professional Gaelic orders.[28] Secondly, the disagreements among the various extant pedigrees concerning Godhfhraidh's ascent and descent strongly suggest that no direct agnatic connexion with the kings of *Alba* was ever intended. While in some sources Fearghus is given as son of Earc, in others he appears as Earc's grandson, and yet in others as son of Niallghus. Surely no Gaelic historian would have been ignorant of the paternity of Fearghus Mór of Dál Riada.[29] But most importantly, had early connexions with

---

26 *ibid.*, p. 93.

27 Hudson 1994, pp. 41–2, proposes a seventeenth-century fabrication; Woolf 2005 brings the fabrication theory up to the fourteenth century.

28 See, for instance, the poets' and historians' attitudes to late Caimbéal (chapter 4, p. 133), Mac Coinnigh (chapter 5, pp. 243–4), and even royal Stiúbhart (chapter 7, pp. 305–6) genealogical claims.

29 The earliest source is NLI G 2 (1344/5) (Woolf 2005, p. 200), with which the 'Great Book of Lecan' (RIA 23 P 2, *c.*1397–1418) and the Scottish 'MS 1467' (NLS 72.1.1, f. 1, 1467) and 'Book of Clanranald' (*RC* ii, pp. 148–309, late seventeenth century) agree closely. For other sources see Sellar 1966, pp. 125–6. Similarly Godhfhraidh variously appears as father, grandfather and grandson of Maine. Hesitations of this type are common in genealogical compilations.

the kings of *Alba* been claimed we would have doubtlessly found plenty of them in the extant literature, poetic, chronicle and annalistic. Clann Domhnaill consistently claim Irish ancestry (as do Clann Dubhghaill, also descended from Somhairle),[30] and even in the extant poetry composed subsequent to Eóin mac Aonghuis Óig's marriage to Mairghréad, daughter of Robert II, there is no attempt to highlight this female-line connexion with the kings of Scots, with one only, late — and Irish — exception.[31] It is true that references to Clann Domhnaill's Norse connexions are not attested in fifteenth-century poems (none is extant for the fourteenth). But they reappear in the sixteenth century, and are common, both in poetry and historical writing, right down to the end of our period; and they are never questioned by learned men.[32] Additionally, it must be noted that the annalists link Godhfhraidh mac Fearghusa to Oriel ('toiseach Oirghiall'), the patrimony of the three Collas and their descendants, rather than to Dál Riada or to the earlier Munster patrimony of the claimed ancestors of Fearghus mac Eirc.[33]

It is not known why Godhfhraidh, like Mearghach, originated a patronymic.[34] The most likely explanation is that at their particular points in time the original line split, and the new designations were created to distinguish their descendants from those of their brothers. Whichever the case, the designation 'Clann Ghodhfhraidh' changed after Somhairle's times, for 'fra [Somhairle] they wer for a quhyle named and called *Clansomerle*' [i.e. Clann Shomhairle].[35] Because, as noted, Somhairle is given by Gaelic historians as the founder of the Gaelic lordship of the Isles, the customary

---

30 See below, pp. 75, 77.

31 In the poem *Ainmigh ria ccách ceann a ccion*, for Raghnall Óg Mac Domhnaill, Marquis of Antrim (†1683). See below, p. 80 and n. 116.

32 See McLeod 2002, pp. 36–8; below, pp. 66, 74, 80, 96, and chapter 5, pp. 189–90 for a sixteenth-century reference to a thirteenth-century claim. For learned men's dismissal of, or reservation concerning, novel claims see further below, chapter 4, pp. 120, 126–7, and 6, pp. 265–6.

33 *ARÉ* i, p. 452. The designation 'toisech Innsi Gall' (*ibid.*, p. 486) is clearly given anachronistically, much in the same way as Céitinn once applied the title 'rí Alban' to Fearghus Mór mac Eirc (see below, chapter 5, p. 189). For the origins and ancestry of Fearghus mac Eirc see below, chapter 5, pp. 195–6.

34 But for a suggestion that it was on account of his increased sway as Dál Riada moved eastwards see Bannerman 1971b, p. 77; Steer and Bannerman 1977, p. 201.

35 *Monro*, p. 92. See also *Ceannaigh duain t'athar, a Aonghas*, §29a, and Steer and Bannerman 1977, p. 201, n. 12.

reference to Eóin mac Aonghuis Óig as 'first Lord of the Isles' (and to his three successors as second, third, and fourth) is inappropriate — he would have been rather the seventh from Somhairle (see Table 3.1).[36] Neither was Eóin mac Alasdair the last lord of the Isles on account of his apparent forfeiture in 1493,[37] for we have evidence for the proclamations of at least another three, and perhaps up to five, subsequent Clann Domhnaill leaders; the lack of governmental recognition of their title detracts nothing from the fact of their proclamations by their kindred.[38]

In the poetry, additionally, we find a variety of territorial designations, some merely complimentary, others reflecting the addressed individual's sway over particular areas, or his martial exploits in districts outwith his own dominions. In the eulogy *Domhnall mac Raghnaill rosg mall* the eponym of Clann Domhnaill is addressed as Ó Colla, and praised for his noble ancestry, Gaelic and Norse: he is not only a descendant of Colla and of Conn Céadchathach, but also of Amhlaoibh, king of Man, and of Godhfhraidh, who may be either the son of Fearghus or perhaps another Manx king (§§12a, 13a, 14b).[39] The reference to Domhnall's descent from Brian [Bóroimhe] (§13d) is probably through the maternal line. The poem contains allusions to 'Bé Bhionn' (§15c) and to 'Derbh-áil' (§16c), both of which names are attested among the Uí Bhriain of Thomond.[40]

---

36 Succession remains obscure at a couple of points in the early stages; in particular it is not clear whether Raghnall Ármuinn, who challenged the succession after the death of Aonghus Mór and effectively ruled during Aonghus Óg's minority, was ever inaugurated (see *HP* i, pp. 17–18). Tentatively, then, as it is given, this succession table is deemed much preferable to the alternative system making Eóin mac Aonghuis Óig the first lord of the Isles.

37 See below, p. 73.

38 Alasdair mac Gilleasbaig of Lochalsh (†1497) and his son Domhnall Gallda (†1519) (*RC* ii, p. 164; *HP* i, pp. 54–5, 58). Domhnall Gallda was a minor when his father died (*RC* ii, p. 164), and Eóin Cathanach of Islay (†1499) seems to have assumed the title 'rí Innsi-Gall' (*AU* iii, p. 442; *AC*, p. 604; see also Bannerman 1977, pp. 212–13). His son Alasdair (†1536) is called lord of the Isles in at least four Gaelic sources; see Nicholls 1991, pp. 12–13. Domhnall Dubh was the last lord of the Isles; that he was inaugurated may be inferred from the fact that he had a formal council, whose members signed the 1545 document requesting Henry VIII's aid; see, for instance, Mackenzie 1974, p. 141.

39 Domhnall's grandmother (Somhairle's wife) was Ragnhild, daughter of Amhlaoibh and therefore granddaughter of Godhfhraidh Crobhán (†1095) (McDonald 1997, p. 45).

40 For instance, Bé Bhionn was the name of the mother, a sister, and a daughter of Brian Bóroimhe; one Dearbháil (†1080) was Brian's granddaughter, and another, who died in 1116, was a great-granddaughter; see *FFÉ* iii, p. 256; *AU* ii, pp. 24, 84, 94; *ARÉ* ii, p. 914.

For Domhnall's successors who became leaders of Clann Domhnaill we have six classical poems: one for Aonghus Mór, fifth lord of the Isles from Somhairle and the first Mac Domhnaill; one for Alasdair, ninth chief; four for Eóin, tenth chief (who was forfeited by the government of James IV); and we also have two for the latter's son, Aonghus Óg (†1490).[41] In most of these poems the title given to the subject is Mac Domhnaill,[42] although this designation is absent from an eulogy for Eóin and from the two elegies for Aonghus Óg. In these poems the two men are identified as 'Eóin a h-Íle', and 'tighearna Íle' and 'rí Íle' respectively.[43] Because Alasdair is also acknowledged as 'Iarla Rois',[44] it may be that all the extant poems for Eóin, since they omit this title, were composed subsequent to his partial forfeiture in 1476, which deprived him of the earldom. The lack of the formal title 'Mac Domhnaill' in the poems for Aonghus Óg reflects the fact that he was never formally inaugurated; he stood in opposition to his father in the latter part of his rule, causing a division within Clann Domhnaill, 'an cinnedh ar taobh Aonghuis 7 na hármuinn ar thaobh Eoin' ('the tribe on the side of Aonghus and the nobility on the side of Eóin').[45] The appellations 'tighearna Íle' and 'rí Íle' in the elegies seem merely complimentary. They are perhaps given on account of the military defeat he inflicted on his father and the prominent part he took in the affairs of the lordship, but to Niall Mac Muireadhaigh he was merely 'oighre Eoin' ('John's heir').[46]

Other complimentary territorial styles given to the lords of the Isles are, for instance, 'fear Cola' ('ruler of Coll'), 'rí Leódhais' ('king of Lewis'), 'codhnach Chinn Tíre' ('lord of Kintyre'), 'flaith Íle' ('lord of Islay').[47]

---

41 *Ceannaigh duain t'athar, a Aonghas, Fuaras aisgidh gan iarraidh, Mór an feidhm freagairt na bhfaighdheach, Meisde nach éadmhar Éire, Ceannas Ghaoidheal do chlainn Colla, Fíor mo mholadh ar Mhac Domhnaill, Tháinig adhbhar mo thuirse, A chinn Diarmaid Uí Chairbre.*

42 *Ceannaigh duain t'athar, a Aonghas,* §§19c, 25a; *Fuaras aisgidh gan iarraidh,* §§7b, 23b, 30a; *Mór an feidhm freagairt na bhfaighdheach,* §22b; *Meisde nach éadmhar Éire,* §31b; *Fíor mo mholadh ar Mhac Domhnaill,* §1a.

43 *Ceannas Ghaoidheal do chlainn Colla,* §3b; *Tháinig adhbhar mo thuirse,* §9b; *A chinn Diarmaid Uí Chairbre,* §§4a, 5a.

44 *Fuaras aisgidh gan iarraidh,* §§3b, 4a.

45 *RC* ii, p. 162.

46 *ibid.*

47 *Ceannaigh duain t'athar, a Aonghas,* §§10b, 11b; *Fuaras aisgidh gan iarraidh,* §§5b, 10b, 17a.

While presented as lords over their Hebridean territory (Innse Gall),[48] the leaders of Clann Domhnaill are at the same time placed within the wider Scottish kingdom, the poetry containing numerous references to *Alba*.[49] Place-names are also employed in recollection of the family's Irish origins and connexions. Many of these are towns, rivers and mountains in Ulster, the homeland of Colla Uais[50] who, with his two brothers, acquired his territories, along with many other particular rights and privileges known as 'sochar síol gColla' ('the privileges of Colla's descendants'), through a pact whereby they recognised Muireadhach Tíreach as king of Ireland.[51] The poem for Aonghus Mór, however, contains a number of allusions to places in Connacht, possibly noting his ancestors' sway there, or perhaps the presence in that province of Aonghus's own kinsmen, who may have been his vassals; this is, incidentally, the only extant poem for a lord of the Isles which includes a *caithréim* ('battle-roll').[52] According to Niall Mac Muireadhaigh, 'do ghlachadar feín orlamhumus chúig ulad 7 oilltrian choigidh connocht 7 moran do shochruibh oile do lean re na sliochd na ndiaighe' ('[Colla Uais and his brothers] took possession of the province of Ulster and of the greater part of Connacht and of many other privileges that remained with their posterity after them').[53] Niall also states that Giolla Adhamhnáin, Somhairle's grandfather, was the founder of a monastery in Tír Fhiachrach, Co. Sligo, which suggests that the Connacht

---

48 *Ceannaigh duain t'athar, a Aonghas*, §§20d, 22b; *Fuaras aisgidh gan iarraidh*, §§5c; *Meisde nach éadmhar Éire*, §29c.

49 *Domhnall mac Raghnaill rosg mall*, §7a; *Ceannaigh duain t'athar, a Aonghas*, §§16c, 17c; *Fuaras aisgidh gan iarraidh*, §§4c, 12b, 14b, 16b, 18c, 20d, 23d, 27b; *Mór an feidhm freagairt na bhfaighdheach*, §§2b, 26a; *Meisde nach éadmhar Éire*, §§6b; 7b, 8b, 9c, 11d, 13a, 30b; *Ceannas Ghaoidheal do chlainn Colla*, §2a; *Tháinig adhbhar mo thuirse*, §§11d, 12d.

50 *Ceannaigh duain t'athar, a Aonghas*, §6b; *Fuaras aisgidh gan iarraidh*, §§8a, 30a; *Ceannas Ghaoidheal do chlainn Colla*, §7c; *Fíor mo mholadh ar Mhac Domhnaill*, §8a.

51 For a historical account see, for instance, *FFÉ* ii, pp. 358–60; 'Geinealach na gColladh', *LCAB*, pp. 48–51.

52 *Ceannaigh duain t'athar, a Aonghas*, §§7b, 8a, 22ac, 23abd, 24c, 28b. Aonghus Mór's *caithréim* is given in §§21–5.

53 *RC* ii, p. 152. For the territories and special privileges accorded to the three Collas by the king of Ireland see *TD* ii, pp. 228–9 (trsl. pp. 229–32). The *sochar* is often recited in poems for descendants of the Collas; see, for instance, *Éisd re seanchas síol gColla*, for Mac Marcuis of Knocknacloy, *Cuimhnigh sochar síol gColla*, for an unknown patron, or *Daoine saora síol gColla*, for Cú Chonnacht Mág Uidhir (†1589). For the story of the three Collas see *FFÉ* ii, pp. 356–64.

link was still strong by at least the early twelfth century.[54] As for the poet's mention of two districts in modern Co. Clare, it may be a reference to some expedition by Aonghus Mór which took him as far as Thomond, or they might simply be genealogical allusions.[55] Finally, references to Teamhair, Oileach, Fá[i]l, and Druim Caoin are used to mark the fact that Clann Domhnaill, as the descendants of Colla Uais, are the offspring of an Irish high-king.[56] The connexion with Tara, incidentally, is virtually exclusive to Clann Domhnaill in classical panegyric of Scotland.[57]

Colla Uais was undoubtedly, on account of both his accession to the high-kingship of Ireland and his establishment in Scotland, the most important famous ancestor of Clann Domhnaill. The family are also celebrated as being descendants of Conn Céadchathach,[58] of his great-grandson Cairbre Lifeachair,[59] of Eochaidh Doimhléan (son of Cairbre Lifeachair and father of Colla Uais),[60] of Godhfhraidh,[61] and of Somhairle.[62] Also noted is Clann Domhnaill's descent from 'rí Lochlainn', from Eóghan Mór (from whom descended the Uí Néill) and his father Niall Naoighiallach, and from Giolla Brighde, father of Somhairle.[63] These ancestors were not chosen at random by the poets. They all had

---

54 *RC* ii, p. 152.

55 *Ceannaigh duain t'athar, a Aonghas*, §24ab. For likely Mac Domhnaill kinship connexions with Thomond see above, pp. 62, 65.

56 *Ceannaigh duain t'athar, a Aonghas*, §§4d, 15b; *Fuaras aisgidh gan iarraidh*, §§8a, 23b, 30a; *Fíor mo mholadh ar Mhac Domhnaill*, §§12b, 16b. Druim Caoin is another name for Tara (*IBP*, p. 292 n. 1).

57 The only other Scottish kindred connected with Tara are the *mormhaoir* of Lennox; see below, chapter 5, p. 189. See also below, chapter 5, p. 204, for a misguided connexion of Clann Ghriogóir with Tara, by an amateur poet rather than a *file*.

58 *Domhnall mac Raghnaill rosg mall*, §13d; *Ceannaigh duain t'athar, a Aonghas*, §§17d, 27c; *Fuaras aisgidh gan iarraidh*, §§17c, 19a; *Mór an feidhm freagairt na bhfaighdheach*, §34b; *Meisde nach éadmhar Éire*, §§3c, 9a, 13c, 32bc.

59 *Ceannaigh duain t'athar, a Aonghas*, §27b.

60 *Meisde nach éadmhar Éire*, §33bc.

61 *Domhnall mac Raghnaill rosg mall*, §13a; *Ceannaigh duain t'athar, a Aonghas*, §29a. In the first of these two poems Godhfhraidh is made son of an Amhlaoibh. *DnS*, pp. 502 n. 45 and 503 n. 113, notes Woolf 2005's view that this is the Norse king Godhfhraidh Crobhán. For gaps in the genealogies between Godhfhraidh's father Fearghus and Colla Uais see Sellar 1966, p. 137.

62 *Ceannaigh duain t'athar, a Aonghas*, §29a.

63 *Mór an léan-sa ar aicme Íle*, §§9a, 10a, 14c. Descent from Eóghan and Niall came through the female line, by the marriage of Aonghus Óg to Áine, daughter of Cú Buidhe (Cú Muighe, probably more correctly, in *LMG* ii, §342.1) Ó Catháin (*RC* ii, p. 158).

some particular significance in the family history. Like Colla Uais, Conn Céadchathach and Cairbre Lifeachair became kings of Ireland; Eochaidh Doimhléan, by marrying Aileach, daughter of Udhaire, king of Alba,[64] had first made a royal Scottish connexion; Godhfhraidh's significance has already been noted as for some reason being considered the head of a new dynasty, and Somhairle's as the founder of the Scottish lordship of the Isles. The Norse connexion came from at least Somhairle's marriage to Ragnhild, while Godhfhraidh's mother may have been Norse.[65] Eóghan was, as noted, the founder of the Uí Néill dynasty, and Niall their eponym. Giolla Brighde, Somhairle's father, was credited with having obtained military support from his Oriel kinsmen which led to the recovery of Clann Ghodhfhraidh's patrimony, in which he himself played an important part.[66] Finally, there are occasional references to the period when the family also had possession of the Isle of Man.[67]

Themes and motifs

Most of the extant poems whose authors are known to be Irish are addressed to members of Clann Domhnaill, the principal Scottish branch of descendants of Colla Uais. Notably, however, the patrons are either the lords of the Isles or members of Clann Eóin Mhóir, the junior branch of Islay and Antrim; if Irish poets composed for other Clann Domhnaill cadet branches, their work has not survived.[68] Leaving aside Muireadhach Albanach Ó Dálaigh's two extant pieces for members of the family of the *mormhaoir* of Lennox and the two eulogies for James VI and I, the only other poem addressed to a Scottish patron and known with certainty to be of Irish authorship is *Dual ollamh do triall le toisg*, whose subject is the seventh earl of Argyll.[69] The overview of Clann Domhnaill classical verse offered here does not present poems of Irish authorship separately from those of Scottish authorship. For the purposes of this study that option is

---

64 *FFÉ* ii, p. 360.

65 Sellar 1966, p. 135.

66 He is in fact said to have been in command of the army (*RC* ii, p. 154).

67 *Ceannaigh duain t'athar, a Aonghas*, §25a; *Meisde nach éadmhar Éire*, §29d.

68 *Ceannas Gaoidheal do chlainn Colla* is attributed to a poet named as Ó hÉanna, who may have been of Irish origin; see Ó Mainnín 1999, p. 28 n. 74.

69 For these poems see below, chapters 4, pp. 128, 130, 135, 137; 5, pp. 186–90; 7, pp. 303–9.

unnecessary, for only two differences between the two sets appear observable. One is that only Irish authors employ the motif of the high-kingship (and connected motifs such as prophecy or the subject as the territory's spouse); the other is the usage of the *Gall* motif, discussed below. In everything else, leaving aside matters of individual style — for instance technical or imagery-related ornament — the rhetoric of panegyric applied by Irish poets composing for the lords of the Isles and Clann Eóin Mhóir is fundamentally the same as that of their Scottish counterparts.

In the poetry for the lords of the Isles we find most of the conventional motifs of the Irish 'panegyric code' — the individuals praised are celebrated for their martial prowess, their nobility of blood and of character, their generosity, their capacity to unite and to protect their people, their love of feasting, and so on. They are also noted for their seamanship or their ownership of fine boats.[70] The inclusion of *apalóga* is rare in the classical panegyric of Scotland (and where they are given they tend to be told more briefly than in Irish poetry), but the extant poems for the lords of the Isles do contain some. In his poem for Eóin mac Alasdair (†1502), the Irish poet Domhnall mac Briain Uí Uiginn relates the coming of the children of Míl from Spain to Ireland and the later arrival of the Gaels in Scotland.[71] The story of Cú Chulainn's grief after his son's death is retold by Giolla Coluim mac an Ollaimh to illustrate his own grief after the death of Aonghus Óg.[72] Brief references to *seanchas* are found in *Fíor mo mholadh ar Mhac Domhnaill* (§2c), where Eóin mac Alasdair is compared to Guaire, and in *Fuaras aisgidh gan iarraidh* (§§23–26). Here Tadhg Óg Ó hUiginn expresses his hope that Alasdair Mac Domhnaill will transfer to Ireland and become her high-king (a right inherited from Colla Uais), just as three illustrious Irishmen of old, Tuathal Teachtmhar, Lughaidh, and Colla Uais, all had at various times in history returned from *Alba* and obtained the high-kingship of Ireland. The offer of the Irish high-kingship is sometimes connected with the depiction of Clann Domhnaill as in temporary exile

---

70 *Ceannaigh duain t'athar, a Aonghas*, §21c; *Fuaras aisgidh gan iarraidh*, §29; *Fíor mo mholadh ar Mhac Domhnaill*, l. 8b.

71 *Meisde nach éadmhar Éire*, §§15–28.

72 *Tháinig adhbhar mo thuirse*. The *apalóg* is printed in *RC* i, pp. 58–63, and in M'Lauchlan (ed.) 1862, pp. 34–7. Meek 1982, p. 637 suggests that the use of this *apalóg* was 'veiled political comment' indicating that Aonghus Óg's father, Eóin mac Alasdair, lord of the Isles, had been involved in his son's murder (quoted in Ó Mainnín 2002, p. 408).

in *Alba*. As noted, this motif appears only in Mac Domhnaill panegyric of Irish authorship;[73] it almost certainly was developed from the historical account which describes the three Collas as entering into military service of the king of *Alba*.[74]

It should not be thought that any poetic statement that a certain patron is suitable to assume Irish sovereignty, or any invitation or encouragement to do so, was meant to be taken at face value. This is a literary motif — the highest praise motif — forming part of the rhetorical code of panegyric, from the language of authority lexicon used to legitimise an individual's fitness to rule; the *filidh* knew well that era of the high-kingship of Ireland was long passed.[75] While normally found in poems for Irish nobles, it sometimes appears in panegyric for other patrons with Gaelic connexions, such as Raghnall mac Godhfhraidh, king of Man.[76] In poetry for the Scottish lords of the Isles the earliest appearance of this motif is in the extant eulogy for Domhnall, eponym of Clann Domhnaill. Here the poet urges Ireland to cause Domhnall to return from Scotland to be her spouse, that is, the high-king of Ireland:

> A Bhanba, bean d'Albain é,
>> an fear do ghargaidh a gnaoi.
> Gan fhlaith i mBanbha na bí;
>> cá tarbha rí maith gan mhnaoi? ...

> A ghnúis ríogh [?] Teamhra na dtonn ...
> madh nacha bí craobh na crann
>> do-chí barr caomh ós do chionn.

> (Oh Banbha, remove him,
> the man who roughened her beauty, from Scotland.
> Do not be without a prince in Banbha.
> What is the profit in a good king without a wife? ...

73 McLeod 2004, p. 176. McLeod interprets this depiction as applying to all the Scottish Gaels.
74 See below, p. 88.
75 Ó Cuív 1963, pp. 253, 257.
76 See above, chapter 2, p. 33 and n. 38.

Oh countenance of royal Tara of the waves ...

a plain where no tree or branch

sees a gentle branch above your [Domhnall's] head.)[77]

The last couplet quoted embodies the convention that the right ruler is acknowledged by nature through her fertility — trees are so heavy with fruit that their branches bend low, not one of them hanging higher than Domhnall's head. Another instance of a Mac Domhnaill's right and suitability to become Ireland's spouse, and therefore her high-king, is found in *Meisde nach éadmhar Éire*, for Eóin, tenth lord of the Isles (§1–12).

Perhaps the most interesting feature of the poetry for the lords of the Isles is the fact that the motif of the struggle of the *Gaoidhil* against the *Goill* is completely absent from the extant compositions.[78] This motif originated in Ireland perhaps in the twelfth century,[79] but the word *Gall* was used with different meanings with the passing of time. During the Viking period it was applied to the Scandinavian invaders, including those who were of mixed Gaelic and Scandinavian ethnicity. Thus Domhnall mac Raghnaill is a *Gall*, 'na cheann gort goirmfhiadhach Gall' ('head of the Vikings' plain of splendid hunting-grounds'), followed from sea to sea by 'a ghallmhaoir' ('his Viking stewards'), Aonghus Mór is 'flath Gall' ('lord of Vikings').[80] From the twelfth century onwards *Gall* was commonly applied to the Anglo-Norman incomers who settled in Ireland and their descendants, as well as the *Sasanaigh* of England, and generally to 'a non-Gael'. The *Goill* fought by the *Gaoidhil* in the poetry were thus the Anglo-Normans and the English in Irish poetry throughout the classical period. In Scotland, however, the coming of the Anglo-Normans was by invitation and largely non-confrontational,[81]

---

77 *Domhnall mac Raghnaill rosg mall*, §§7, 9acd. For an alternative version see *DnS*, p. 79.

78 The word *Gall* appears in the poems for Domhnall mac Raghnaill (*Domhnall mac Raghnaill rosg mall*, §§11d, 13bc) and Aonghus Mór (*Ceannaigh duain t'athar, a Aonghas*, §15b), but in its meaning of 'Hebridean'. For this interpretation see *IBP*, p. 293, n. 6, and *DnS*, p. 79.

79 See above, chapter 1, p. 3 and n. 10.

80 *Domhnall mac Raghnaill rosg mall*, §§11d, 13bc; *Ceannaigh duain t'athar, a Aonghas*, §15b.

81 Stringer and Grant 1995, pp. 90–1; Bannerman 1989, pp. 147–8. See also below, chapter 6, p. 264.

which would have made the motif of the struggle against the *Goill* —
for this is undoubtedly what the Scottish Gaels would have termed the
Anglo-Normans[82] — hardly relevant in Scottish panegyric, where it is
generally rare. This may well have been the view of the authors of the
surviving poetry for the lords of the Isles, three of whom at least were
Irish.[83] There may have been *Gall* references in poems which have not
survived, but to judge from what is extant it would appear that the lords
of the Isles did not have a particular conflict with the *Goill*.

This appears singular indeed, given the traditional view of Clann
Domhnaill (and particularly the lords of the Isles) as troublesome
and rebellious, a view which historians may wish to re-assess. Even in a
poem composed not long after the abolition of the lordship of the Isles,
the author does not point the accusing finger, but merely praises Clann
Domhnaill in general conventional terms, depicting them as *Uaithne ána
Alban uaine* ('Brilliant pillars of green Alba'), that is, noting the loss that
their downfall represents for Scotland.[84] About half a century later, when
with the death of Domhnall Dubh the main line of the Mac Domhnaill
family became extinct, Giolla Coluim mac Giolla Brighde's *Mór an léan-sa
ar aicme Íle* again is silent in respect of the Scottish government's handling
of the lords of the Isles; the poet, who, like the author of the previous
poem, is a Mac Muireadhaigh, of the Mac Domhnaill hereditary *filidh*,
simply laments their *imtheacht* ('departure', §2a). Moreover, not only is the
conflict between *Gaoidhil* and *Goill* conspicuous by its absence, but almost
all of the poems are explicitly set within the context of *Alba* — Clann
Domhnaill belong in mainland *Alba* and her isles, and their following is

---

82 See MacInnes 2006f, p. 99; Coira 2008b, p. 141.

83 Tadhg Óg Ó hUiginn, Domhnall mac Briain Ó hUiginn and the anonymous author of
Ceannaigh duain t'athar, a Aonghas. For the likelihood of Ó hÉanna also being Irish, see
above, p. 66 n. 68.

84 *Ní h-éibhneas gan chlainn Domhnaill*, §5a. The statement 'Dobadh tréan gaoth ag tíorain
/ fán aicme chríonna chomhnairt' ('Mighty was the blast of tyrants against that tribe
wise and strong', §15ab) opens the last three quatrains, which have been added after the
dúnadh and might therefore be a later addition (a space was left between §14 and these,
and the ink is different for §§15–6; see *SVBDL*, p. 27). §15ab is clearly an elaboration
on the previous statement 'clann dárbh umhail na tíorain' ('a race to whom tyrants
bowed', §3c), which is almost certainly a general praise motif rather than a reference to
a particular conflict. The 'tyrants', at any rate, remain unidentified.

made up of *Albanaigh*.[85] One author, Ó hÉanna, complimented them as worthy holders of the *ceannas* ('headship') of the *Gaoidhil* of Ireland, but jointly with that of the *Gaoidhil* of *Alba*.[86] A further suggestion of Clann Domhnaill's sense of identity as *Albanaigh* is offered by the fact that their historians also recorded the history of the kings of Scots.[87]

Still in connexion with the absence of the *Goill* motif we may note two further literary items of interest. One is the annalistic entry noting the 1411 Battle of Harlaw, described as 'Maidm mór le Mac Domnaill na hAlpan for Gallaib Alpan' ('A great victory of Mac Domhnaill of Scotland over the *Goill* of Scotland').[88] The annalist clearly perceived the contest as one between *Gaoidhil* and *Goill*, but his perspective may be the Irish one, and it does not necessarily reflect the general contemporary viewpoint.[89] *Goill* was the contemporary term used in Gaelic Ireland to describe the descendants of the twelfth-century Anglo-Norman settlers. This brings us to the second item of interest, *A Chlanna Chuinn, cuimhnichibh*, commonly known as the 'Harlaw Brosnachadh'. This is a poem in vernacular language traditionally believed to have been composed by a Mac Muireadhaigh poet as an incitement to combat before the battle of Harlaw.[90] While the poem is addressed to 'clanna Chuinn' ('Conn's progenies', ll. 1, 40, 47, 48), a genealogical marker frequent in, though not exclusive to, poetry for Clann Domhnaill,[91] again no reference is made to the *Goill* (or to the *Gaoidhil* for that matter); indeed the enemy is not identified by the poet. To all this we may add the manner in which the conflict over the earldom of Ross in Domhnall mac Eóin's time is described by Niall Mac Muireadhaigh:

---

85 *Fuaras aisgidh gan iarraidh*, §§4c, 12b, 14b, 16b, 18c, 20d, 23d, 27b, 29b; *Mór an feidhm freagairt na bhfaidheach*, §2a; *Meisde nach éadmhar Éire*, §§6b, 7b, 8b, 9c, 11d, 13a, 30b; *Tháinig adhbhar mo thuirse*, §§11d, 12d.

86 *Ceannas Gaoidheal do chlainn Colla*, §2a. The context of the poem indicates that *ceannas* is that of the Gaels only, rather than a depiction of Mac Domhnaill as king of Scotland, or Ireland, or both.

87 Among the original contents of NLS 72.2.2 (seventeenth-eighteenth century) is noted 'the conclusion of a Gaelic chronicle of the kings of Scotland down to King Robert III', now missing (Black, *Catalogue*, p. 366).

88 *AC*, p. 410.

89 McLeod 2004, p. 26.

90 For the author see Thomson (ed.) 1968, pp. 148–9, 163–4, 166. For the view that it might have been composed at a later time see *DnS*, p. 229.

91 McLeod 2004, p. 117.

do phós [Domhnall] M*aire* inghen I*a*rla Rois 7 is *da* taoibh *sin* tainic I*a*rla*cht* Rois a*r* chloin Dom*naill* ... Do bhr*i*sd se cath caifech a*r* Dhiúc Murch*adh*ag sesa*mh* achi*o*rt fein *air* fa I*a*rrla*cht* Rois.

([Domhnall] married Máire, daughter of the Earl of Ross, and it is through her that the earldom of Ross came to Clann Domhnaill ... He fought the battle of Garioch [i.e. Harlaw] against Duke Murchadh in defence of his own claim to the earldom of Ross.)[92]

Niall correctly interprets the events within the framework of the Duke of Albany's designs, and there is nothing in his narrative to suggest that such events were perceived as a conflict between *Gaoidhil* and *Goill*. He also makes it clear that this was not an act of rebellion against royal authority, because he concludes the episode by describing how, once King James I had returned from English captivity, he proceeded to do justice, showing his goodwill towards the lord of the Isles and punishing the evil-doers:

a*r* te*cht* d*o*n chéad rí Semus ó braighden*as* riogh Sagsan fua*ir* Dom*nall* a hile toil 7 dain*g*hen a*n* ríogh a*r* Ros 7 a*r* a*n* chuid oile *da* inbhe 7 do cu*i*redh a*n* cen*n* do Diuibhge Murch*adh* 7 da m*ac*.

(After King James I returned from the captivity of the king of England, Domhnall of Islay obtained the king's goodwill and the security of Ross and of the rest of his patrimony, and Duke Murchadh and his sons were beheaded).[93]

The theme of conquest by the sword is equally absent from the extant poetry for the lords of the Isles, and indeed from the poetry of Scotland

---

92 *RC* ii, p. 160.

93 *ibid.*, 160. Mac Muireadhaigh confuses the dates and the lord of the Isles who was confirmed in the earldom; this was Domhnall's son and successor, Alasdair, and the earldom was probably confirmed to him in 1425; see Brown 1994, p. 58. The version of 'Hugh of Sleat' (*HP* i, pp. 27–32) is substantially the same as Mac Muireadhaigh's, with more detail on the struggle between Domhnall and Albany.

generally. This is a motif usually expressed by reference to the annexation of territory 'ar éigin' ('by force') or as 'cairt chloidhimh' ('swordland', literally 'the charter of the sword'). It is only found in two seventeenth-century poems, one for Coll Ciotach and the other for his son, Alasdair mac Colla, of the Mac Domhnaill cadet branch of Colonsay, with reference to the original acquisition of land in Scotland by the *Gaoidhil*, and to justify the Highlanders' position with respect to the Wars of the Three Kingdoms.[94] Otherwise, where *cairt* does appear it is in the sense of 'charter', a sub-class of the 'written word' motif (the other being the allusion to *seinleabhair*, 'ancient books') which is commonly employed to justify a claim.[95] As such we find it in Tadhg Dall Ó hUiginn's invitation to Alasdair, ninth lord of the Isles, to assume the kingship of Ireland:

> a chairte ciodh nach osglann
> cion ga aicme ar Alostrann.

> (do not his family papers tell Alastrann of the love which his own folk (in Éire) bear him?).[96]

The last two extant poems concerned with the lords of the Isles were composed some time after Eóin mac Alasdair was deprived of the lordship of the Isles in 1493. There is something shadowy about this forfeiture and the annexation of the lordship to the crown. Not only is there no official record of the forfeiture,[97] but it was on the basis of the 'legal fiction' of the 1476 bestowal of the title 'Lord of the Isles' on Eóin mac Alasdair that his 1493 forfeiture was carried out.[98] The Gaelic chronicles speak merely of a resignation by Eóin of his lands to the king,[99] and no comment on events is made in the surviving contemporary and near-contemporary poetry. In the last two extant poems, as noted, the poets

---

94 *Saoth liom do chor, a Cholla*, §5b, and *Mór mo mholadh ar mhac Colla*, §§4d, 6a. For these poems see below, pp. 84–5, 89.

95 See Appendix 2, *s.vv. cairt [chinnidh], seinleabhair, written word.*

96 *Fuaras aisgidh gan iarraidh*, §16cd. For an example of a later instance of *cairt* in this sense see below, p. 93.

97 *HP* i, p. 51 n. 2.

98 See above, p. 56 and n. 13.

99 *RC* ii, p. 162; *HP* i, p. 48.

lament Clann Domhnaill's departure, remembering brighter times in the conventional rhetoric of panegyric. Around 1500, after Eóin's forfeiture and his son Aonghus Óg's death, and with the heir — Domhnall Dubh, Aonghus Óg's son — securely restrained by the Earl of Argyll in the island of Inis Chonaill, Giolla Coluim mac an Ollaimh fell into pessimism and expressed the condition of Scottish Gaeldom as being joyless, a common elegiac motif. Without their protection, generosity, nobility of blood and character, love of justice, patronage of learning, and so on:

> Ni h-éibhneas gan Chlainn Domhnall ...
>
> Mairg ó rugadh an fheadhain,
> mairg fo dheadhail ré gcaidreabh;
> gan aonchlann mar Chlainn Domhnaill ...
>
> agus do bhí 'na ndeireadh
> feidhm is eineach is náire ...
>
> ní h-éibhneas gan Chlainn Domhnall.
>
> (It is no joy without Clan Donald ... Alas for those who have lost that company; alas for those who have parted from their society; for no race is as Clan Donald ... and in their rear were service and honour and self-respect ... it is no joy without Clan Donald).[100]

Some fifty years later, when the last lord of the Isles, Domhnall Dubh, was also dead, Giolla Coluim mac Giolla Brighde dejectedly lamented the passing of the house of Islay. His poem is mainly genealogical, devoting much praise to 'reimh na rosg mall' ('the dynasty of the stately eyes'),[101] including their great ancestors, Irish and Norse. It concludes with a prayer that, out of the few of their descendants who still remain, one may emerge who will restore the family's fortunes.[102]

---

100 *Ni h-éibhneas gan Chlainn Domhnaill*, §§1a, 11abc, 13cd, 14d.

101 *Mór an léan-sa ar aicme Íle*, §11a, perhaps an echo of *Domhnall mac Raghnaill rosg mall*, for the eponym of Clann Domhnaill, as above, p. 62.

102 *Mór an léan-sa ar aicme Íle*, §§16–17.

Later classical verse

Clann Dubhghaill

Before tracing the literary developments affecting the rhetoric of leadership in Mac Domhnaill poetry following the demise of the main line of the family and of the lordship of the Isles, we will consider the very small poetic survival for Clann Dubhghaill, who were also descendants of Colla Uais through Somhairle (see Table 3.3). This kindred had for their eponym Dubhghall, who may have been Somhairle's eldest son.[103] After Somhairle's death his territory was partitioned among his offspring, Dubhghall receiving the district of Lorn. Though originally a powerful lordship, Dubhghall's inheritance would only remain with the family for five generations. After the death of Eóin Mac Dubhghaill (†1316) without a male heir his patrimony was split between his daughters, who both married Stiúbhart nobles. While most of the original Mac Dubhghaill estate thus came into the possession of the Stiúbhairt, the headship of Clann Dubhghaill passed to the junior branch of Dunolly.[104] In the early fifteenth century a succession dispute arose which came to involve Clann Domhnaill as well as the Mac Cailéin and Stiúbhart chiefs. The contention prolonged itself until 1460, when it was resolved in favour of Eóin Ciar with the support of his cousin, Cailéan Caimbéal, first Earl of Argyll.[105]

It is this Eóin Ciar who is the subject of one of the two surviving poems composed for members of Clann Dubhghaill. *Do athruigh séan ar síol gCuinn* is an elegy ascribed to Eóghan mac Eóin mhic Eichthighearna, of the Mac Eóghain family who seem to have been hereditary poets to the Mac Dubhghaill chiefs and who came to be under Caimbéal patronage by the sixteenth century.[106] The name of the subject of the second poem, *A Mheic Dhubhghaill, tuar acáin*, is Donnchadh Carrach, but his identity remains obscure.[107] Eóin Ciar is identified as 'ceann Cloinne Dubhghaill' ('head of Clann Dubhghaill', §29b) and ascribed the usual attributes conventionally sanctioning the right ruler: his death has reversed the good omen (§§1a, 2a, 3c, 5d, 6c); it has not only caused general grief to people,

---

103 McDonald 1997, p. 71; Sellar 2000, p. 199.
104 Sellar 2000, pp. 217–19.
105 Boardman 2006, pp. 155–6, 172.
106 McLeod 2004, pp. 70–1.
107 *SVBDL*, p. 296.

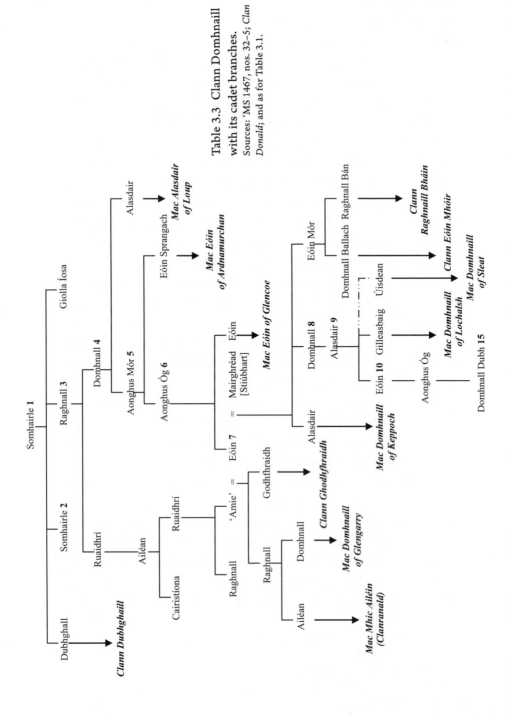

Table 3.3 Clann Domhnaill with its cadet branches.
Sources: 'MS 1467, nos. 32–5; *Clan Donald*; and as for Table 3.1.

but nature also mourns; Eóin's departure marks the end of raiding, of feasting, of prosperity, of peace, of the poets' honour.[108] He is celebrated as a descendant of Conn, Colla Uais, and Godhfhraidh,[109] and he is said to deserve a tomb of the magnificence of 'leacht gcéile gCruachan' ('the grave-slabs of the spouses of Cruacha', §14d). Cruacha is one of the poetic names for Ireland, a veiled implication of Eóin's standing as being equal to that of a high-king.

Donnchadh Carrach, the subject of the second poem, was not a chief. Therefore, although he is once addressed as 'son of Dubhghall' (§1a), we should not understand such form of address as the title 'Mac Dubhghaill', but rather as a reference to his descent from the founder of the family, perhaps in a manner similar to that used by genealogists when they shorten family trees by several generations.[110] That Donnchadh was not a chief is also attested by the fact that *A Mheic Dhubhghaill, tuar acáin* may be classed as an eulogy of the 'young-prince' type; not only is the subject described as a youth (§1), but the poet fails to depict him through the customary conventions used to sanction a chief's rule. Donnchadh is merely praised for his nobility of ancestry, his martial prowess, his hunting sorties, his fame, his intellectual achievements, and 'ceaird oile nach cualabhair' ('other arts that ye have not heard').[111]

Clann Eóin Mhóir

The forfeiture of the Gaelic lordship of the Isles had serious negative consequences for everyone in it, and in their train, unsurprisingly, for the Scottish government as well. With no figure of authority in the Highlands

---

108 *Do athruigh séan ar síol gCuinn,* §§1, 3d, 5c, 6ab, 8, 9d, 10, 11, 13cd, 14–15, 17, 18–20, 22, 23, 24cd, 26cd, 28d, 31.

109 *ibid.,* §§1a, 2b, 4c, 5a, 9c, 20b, 21b, 22a, 27a.

110 These gaps constitute one main reason why some historians reject Gaelic genealogies as fabrications but, as noted (above, chapter 1, p. 5 n. 19), Gaelic pedigrees, particularly the earlier ones, tend to be accurate in their general direction, even if they vary in detail. Where large genealogical gaps appear it is possible, if not likely, that the missing information had been lost, or perhaps was never recorded; it can hardly be a coincidence that the most complete genealogies are those of the most powerful families, who had the means to give patronage to historians, genealogists and scholars from other branches of learning.

111 *A Mheic Dhubhghaill, tuar acáin,* §§1, 3a, 5cd, 7ab, 9b (quotation), 9cd, 6bc, 9ab, 11ab. For some Irish examples of 'young-prince' poems see Dewar 2006b, pp. 119–22, 242–4, 292–3, 357–60.

and Isles (for royal government failed to effectively replace that of the lord of the Isles), the various kindreds until then under Mac Domhnaill sway, now unrestrained, broke loose and the era of bloody feuding began — the period known in Gaelic tradition as 'Linn nan Creach' ('the Age of Forays'), which so sharply contrasted with the previous 'Linn an Àigh' ('Age of Joy', or 'of Prosperity'). Those who had previously based their livelihoods on their positions as officials to the lords of the Isles, whether within the lordship itself or as administrative officers in the earldom of Ross, receiving from Mac Domhnaill grants of land in return for their services, now could only occupy land by receiving it in fee from the king.[112] The patronage of the arts received a severe blow, by which the Mac Muireadhaigh family of hereditary poets were particularly affected. Though initially found holding their Kintyre lands of the king, at some point in the later sixteenth century they sought, and were fortunate to find, a new source of patronage in Clann Raghnaill.[113]

For about half a century after the 1493 forfeiture, however, the larger part of Scottish Gaeldom actively sought to restore the lordship of the Isles. Of the various cadet branches of Clann Domhnaill (see Table 3.4), Mac Domhnaill of Lochalsh, Mac Domhnaill of Sleat and Mac Domhnaill of Islay at different times advanced their respective claims to the headship of Clann Domhnaill, and indeed succeeded in their endeavours.[114] But the lack of poetic survivals for this period is probably a reflection of the unsettled state of affairs. With the exception of two poems for members of Clann Raghnaill composed in the early sixteenth century, the next few survivals of Mac Domhnaill poetry belong to the later part of the same century, and they all have been preserved in Irish sources only. This is no doubt due to the Irish connexions of Clann Eóin Mhóir, for various of whose members these poems were composed. Poetry becomes more plentiful for the seventeenth century, mostly on account of Niall Mac Muireadhaigh's history, where a number of panegyrics, some of which we

---

112 For some examples see Bannerman 1977, p. 219; Thomson 1960–3, pp. 288–9, 291, 292.

113 Thomson 1960–3, pp. 295–96.

114 See above, p. 62 and n. 38. A partial success, however, for their acceptance as new heads was not necessarily unanimous: for instance, the encounter known as 'Blàr na Pàirc' ('the battle of Park') is described by Niall Mac Muireadhaigh as resulting from the opposition of Mac Coinnigh and 'cuid dferuibh an taobh túaigh' ('some of the men of the north') against the leadership of Alasdair of Lochalsh (RC ii, p. 163).

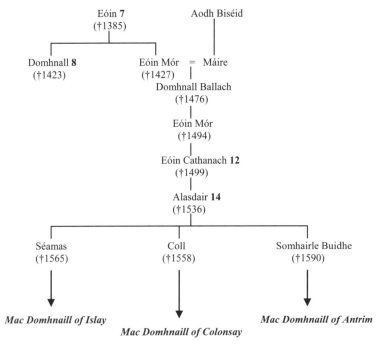

Table 3.4 Clann Eóin Mhóir.
Sources: *RC* ii, pp. 303–4; Hill 1993.

have already encountered, were included. Niall took care to preserve many pieces composed for his patrons, Clann Raghnaill, and for their ancestors, the lords of the Isles (as well as some for other persons), and thus was one principal cause of the imbalance in extant classical panegyric so favourable to Clann Domhnaill.

Of what extant poetry there is composed for the various cadet branches of Clann Domhnaill, the compositions for members of Clann Eóin Mhóir are, in terms of the conventional rhetoric of classical panegyric, closest to the earlier poems, and indeed to those composed for Irish patrons throughout the classical period. The family's original patrimony consisted of extensive lands in Islay and Kintyre; to these were added the Glens of Antrim through the marriage of the eponymous Eóin Mór — son and *tánaiste* of Eóin mac Aonghuis Óg, seventh lord of the Isles, and of Mairghréad, daughter of Robert II — to Máire Bhiséid, heiress of the Glens, in the early fifteenth century.[115] The family on either side of the channel

---

115 *RC* ii, p. 211.

would permanently split in 1595, but in the poetry for Clann Domhnaill of Antrim their Scottish origins continued to be proudly remembered along with their noble Irish ancestry: 'síol Domhnaill', 'roighne curadh chlann nDomhnuill' ('the best warrior of *Domhnall*'s race'), 'bile fréimhe Fearadhaigh' ('the warrior of the race of Fearadhach'). The connexion with Fearadhach (Fionn) was possible through the marriage of Eóin, seventh lord of the Isles, to Robert II's daughter.[116] Raghnall, first earl of Antrim (+1636), is termed 'ó Earca' ('Earc's descendant'), a reference, it seems, to the Scottish mother of an ancient Irish king, Muircheartach mac Muireadhaigh, who commonly appears in the sources as Muircheartach mac Earca.[117] *Do-dhéan craobhsgaoileadh na cColla*, an anonymous historical and genealogical poem for the first Earl of Antrim, notes that Colla Uais's mother was the daughter of a Scottish (that is, Pictish) king, and that his descendants sought new royal status 'aniath oilidh' ('in another land', that is in Scotland).[118] Poets also record Clann Eóin Mhóir's connexions with the earls of Ross — 'fir Rois', 'do ríoghroidh chródha Chláir Rois' ('of the valiant royal stock of Clár Rois'), 'flaith Rois', 'rígh Rois' — and with their remoter Norse ancestors, the *fionnlochlannaigh* or *fionnghaill*.[119] Pride in their Scottish ancestry is not unique to the Antrim branch of Clann Eóin Mhóir. The story the Collas' slaying of Fiacha Sraibhthine, their later banishment to Scotland, and Colla Uais's settlement there is a common theme in poetry for those of his descendants who re-settled in Ireland. One example is *Éisd re seanchas síol Colla*, for Mac Marcuis, chief of the Irish Mac Domhnaill sept of Knocknacloy, who claimed descent from Marcus, a younger son of Domhnall mac Eóin, lord of the Isles;

---

116 *Treisi an eagla ioná andsacht*, §§2d, 5d, 16a; *Do bheirim barr buadha is áigh*, §§2b, 3c, 6b; *Ainmnigh ria ccách ceann a ccionn*, §4d; *Fada cóir Fhódla ar Albain*, §17b. For the family split see Hill 1993. Fearadhach Fionn, a king of the line of Loarn Mór, father of the historical Fearchar Fada (+697) (Sellar 1981, p. 105).

117 *Díon tíre dá thighearna*, §§6c, 10d. Earc was the daughter of fifth-century Lodharnn (Loarn), 'rí Alban' (*LCAB*, p. 295). Siobhán, daughter of Conn Ó Néill of Clann Aodha Bhuidhe, a descendant of Muircheartach mac Earca, married Domhnall Ballach, son of Eóin Mór (*LMG* ii §342.3). Allusions to Earc are common in Clann Aodha Bhuidhe poetry. See, for instance, *LCAB*, pp. 78, 115–118, 196, 203, 238, and pp. 13–14 for Earc in the historical account 'An Leabhar Eoghanach'.

118 *Do-dhéan craobhsgaoileadh na cColla*, §§3–7, 13, 15.

119 *Treisi an eagla ioná andsacht*, §14c; *Do loiscceadh meisi sa Mhuaidh*, §21a; *An síth do rogha, a rígh Fionnghall*, §§1a, 6b, 8a, 9a, 20c; *Éireannaigh féin fionnLochlannaigh*, §1a; *Taisdil mhionca ór siabradh sionn*, §7d.

another is *Iad féin mhoras clann Colla*, for Feidhlim Mac Dubhghaill, of the *gallóglach* kindred of Connacht.[120] Tadhg Dall Ó hUiginn similarly recalled in *Fada cóir Fhódla ar Albain*, an eulogy for Somhairle Buidhe Mac Domhnaill (†1590), how of the three Collas, only Colla Uais had remained in Scotland (§§8–9). Tadhg Dall is also the author of *Mealladh iomlaoide ar Éirinn*, a poem in celebration of Somhairle Buidhe's marriage to Máire, daughter of Conn Ó Néill (†1559). In it he notes the 'iomlaoid egcothrom'('unequal exchange') between Scotland and Ireland, for no less than six great Irish high-kings had taken Scottish wives, whereas the reverse situation was unheard of. Now, however, Máire's marriage to a Scot has redressed the balance; not only is Somhairle Buidhe, as a *Gaoidheal*, entitled to a portion of Ireland but, as a descendant of Colla Uais, he has a claim to the high-kingship:

> Dlighidh fos mac Meic Domhnoill
> a cuid dÉirinn iobardhuinn
> > o tá ag roinn braonmoighi Breadh
> > re cloinn maordaidhe Mileadh
>
> Fuair an Colla or chin ar tús
> ceithre bliadna as e a iomthús
> > learga míne moighe Breadh
> > is righe thoighe Tailltean
>
> Ar chuid Cholla os é as oighre
> tiocfaidh do thaoibh Somhoirle
> > siol réaghCuinn duaim reroile
> > fa sdúaigh méarchuirr Mucroimhe

(Mac Domhnaill's son is entitled to his portion of Ireland darkened by yews, since Breagha of the dewy plains belongs to Míl's stately progeny. Colla, from whom he [i.e. Somhairle Buidhe] was originally descended, obtained for four years — such were the circumstances — the soft slopes of Breagha's

---

120 *Éisd re seanchas síol Colla*, §§9–18; *Iad féin mhoras clann Colla*, §§4–15.

Plain and the sovereignty of the house of Tailte [i.e. Ireland].
Since it is he who is the heir of Colla's share, to Somhairle's side
will come smooth Conn's race to be united under the prince of
Mucroimhe of peaks like fingers) (§§51–53).

This brings us back to the motif of the high-kingship of Ireland, which
Tadhg Dall here suggests awaits Somhairle. It is only the lords of the Isles
and members of Clann Eóin Mhóir, of all the kindreds of Scotland, who are
portrayed in classical poetry as suitable or destined to be kings of Ireland,
a motif that, as noted, is attested only in poems of Irish authorship.[121] *Bí ad
mhosgaladh, a mheic Aonghais*, composed around 1600, is an incitement to
Séamas Mac Domhnaill of Islay (who would succeed his father Aonghus in
the chiefship in 1614 and who died in 1626) to give military support to the
Irish in their rebellion against English rule known as the Nine Years' War.
The anonymous poet hints at Séamas's suitability to become high-king of
Ireland when he claims that

> Críoch Bhanbha na mbuinne líggeal,
>   is leath Alban, ní hiúl clé,
> do chairt ag labhra ar áon ortha,
>   a chráobh abhla Tholcha Té.

> (The land of Banbha of the white streams, and half of Scotland—
> 'tis no erroneous report — thy charter speaks of both of these,
> O branch of the apple tree of Tulach Té) (§29).[122]

In *Fada cóir Fhódla ar Albain* we find an interesting variation on the
customary poetic discourse justifying a patron's claim to the high-kingship
of Ireland. Here Tadhg Dall reverses the convention, instead portraying
Ireland as having a claim on Somhairle Buidhe:

---

121 I rectify my statement in Dewar 2006a, p. 42, that the motif of the high-kingship
appears only in poems for Clann Domhnaill of Antrim.

122 Tulach Té is used for Tara (*IBP*, p. 289 n. 18), and the 'apple tree' is therefore Séamas's
ancestor, Colla Uais, high-king of Ireland. For 'leath Alban' see below, pp. 87–9,
110–11.

Fada cóir Fhódla ar Albain ...

Créad an chóir nuaidhese aniodh
atá ag críoch cloinne Míliodh,
   má tá aguibh innis damh,
   fa n-aguir inis Alban? ...

Rogha leannáin Leasa Cuinn,
Somhairle mhac Meic Domhnuill.

(Long has Fódla had a claim upon Alba ... What new claim to-day
has the land of the Children of Míl, tell me if thou knowest —
whereby she sues the isle of Alba? ... The best-beloved of Conn's
Dwelling, Sorley, son of MacDonnell) (§§1a, 4, 13ab).

For this to take place, the ancient contract whereby the three Collas
and their posterity renounced the kingship of Ireland must be revoked,
and this will allow Banbha to take Somhairle as her spouse (§§41–43).[123]
This poem also contains one of the earliest known references to
the conflict with the foreigners in a panegyric for a member of Clann
Domhnaill of Scotland. The piece was composed in the later sixteenth
century, when the Tudor monarchs were tightening their grip on
Ireland through the imposition of reform at various levels — admin-
istrative, legal and socio-cultural — and through the implementation
of an aggressive military policy.[124] Its author, Tadhg Dall Ó hUiginn,
portrays Somhairle Buidhe as the suitable high-king of Ireland and as
the one who will banish the foreigners (*eachtranna*, §15b, *Danair*, §16c);
his assistance to Ireland will be like that of Caesar who liberated Rome
from oppressive barbarians (§§18–32). In an elegy for Domhnall Gorm
Mac Domhnaill, brother of Séamas, sixth chief of Islay (†1565), an Ó
Gnímh poet portrays his subject as 'ar bhfosccadh ar ghoimh na nGall'

123 For the conflict, and the contract which brought it to an end, see the references given
    above, p. 64 and nn. 51, 53. A further reference to the high-kingship of Ireland is found
    in the anonymous *Beid mar do bhádar roimhe* (§§3c, 11c), where Raghnall, second
    earl and marquis of Antrim (†1683), is said to be set to obtain the tribute of the five
    provinces (that is, of the whole of Ireland), and to be of the blood of the kings of Tara.
124 See, for instance, Lennon 1994, chapters 7–10.

('he who saved us from the fierceness of the Goill').[125]

Two more poems for members of Clann Domhnaill of Antrim make allusions to the conflict with the foreigners. In *Treisi an eagla ioná andsacht* the author — possibly the same Ó Gnímh poet — seeks reconciliation with the sons of Séamas, the sixth chief, his brother Somhairle Buidhe and the latter's son, explaining why he had temporarily sided with the English after being slighted by them (§§1–3, 7a, 8–9). In all these poems, therefore, the foreigners referred to are the English. We have noted the limited relevance of the motif of the foreigners in classical panegyric of Scotland;[126] it does make a strong appearance, however, in the vernacular poetry of the later part of our period, but it is then used with a different meaning and within a different context. This usage, which is further discussed below,[127] identifies the *Goill* with the Scottish Lowlanders but, interestingly, it is with this meaning that we find the term in the classical piece *Saoth liom do chor, a Cholla*, composed c.1623–4. Here Cathal Mac Muireadhaigh advises Coll Mac Domhnaill of Colonsay (†1647) — a sub-branch of Clann Eóin Mhóir — to refrain temporarily from attacking his Lowland enemies, for whom he uses the words *Goill* and *eachtrainn*.[128] The same usage is attested in *Mór mo mholadh ar mhac Colla*, for Colla's son, Alasdair, where the unknown Scottish author[129] uses *Goill* and 'fir Alban' to denote the Lowlanders, although we may note at this point that *Goill* was also used by vernacular poets as a label for the enemies of the house of Stiúbhart.[130] This is a bit of a revolution in classical panegyric, where the *Goill* had for the four previous centuries featured, if not as foreigners in a general way, as Englishmen. In all likelihood this usage came into the genre from the vernacular poetry which, reflecting everyday speech, used the word *Gall* to denote a Lowlander. Oddly, perhaps, this poem makes no reference to the fact that much of the information it contains concerns Alasdair mac Colla's part in the wider, national royalist struggle on behalf of King Charles I against his enemies; it reads rather like many contemporary

125 *Do loiscceadh meisi sa Mhuaidh*, §7c.
126 See above, p. 70.
127 See below, pp. 101–2.
128 §§4d, 7d, 9c, 12b, 17c, 18a.
129 There are several Scotticisms in this piece, as in §§2b, 13c; see Watson (ed.) 1927, pp. 76 n. 2b, 83 n. 13cd.
130 §§3a, 7a, 9c, 26a; first prose section, ll. 1, 34; second prose section, l. 68.

vernacular poems which depict the royalist cause as a Gaelic concern.[131]
The theme of royalism — the depiction of the subject as a loyal adherent
to the cause of the Stiúbhart monarchs — is a fresh development in Clann
Domhnaill poetry of the later period, as we will see in the next section of
this chapter. Yet this motif is absent from the extant poetry for the Clann
Eóin Mhóir main line. Even in *Beid mar do bhádar roimhe*, a poet's prayer
for the safety of his patron, Raghnall Mac Domhnaill, Marquis of Antrim,
as he sails from Ireland, the fact that he undertakes this journey in support
of King Charles is never mentioned.

Closely connected with the motif of the struggle against the foreign-
ers is that of the subject as the prophesied one who will banish them. In
the poetry of Ireland prophecy may be attributed to various ancient saints,
sages or legendary heroes, and the subject praised often said to be Aodh
Eanghach, the one who will fulfil the prophecy.[132] In Clann Domhnaill
poetry we have only three instances of this motif. In *Bí ad mhosgaladh, a
mheic Aonghais*, the incitement to Séamas Mac Domhnaill to support the
Irish against the English (*Danair*), the anonymous author evokes Fionn
mac Cumhaill's prophecy: the foreigners would be finally expelled from
Ireland by a descendant of Colla Uais. It is Séamas, the poet states with
confidence, who will fulfil the prophecy.[133] The other two references to
prophecy also come, like this one, from early-seventeenth-century poems.
Éireannaigh féin FionnLochlannaigh, for Raghnall Mac Domhnaill, first Earl
of Antrim, contains general praise in the usual terms; prophecy is one of
them, but here it is used vaguely, obviously in connexion with Raghnall,
but without reference to any particular events.[134] *Díon tíre dá thighearna*,
in praise of the same Raghnall and of his son Raghnall Óg, future Marquis
of Antrim, is a very similar piece, portraying the subjects through numer-
ous conventional praise motifs, among which prophecy once again is a

---

131 See below, pp. 108–9.

132 See generally Ó Buachalla 1989.

133 *Bí ad mhosgaladh, a mheic Aonghais*, §§10–23. Other prophets cited, including
Cathbhaidh (Conchobhar mac Neasa's druid) and Ciothruadh (Cormac mac Airt's
chief druid, see O'Curry 1873, ii, p. 213), are given in §§23–5.

134 'Do sgaoil d'fhádh snaidhm sean-tarngaireadh... | Tugar pár mín meamramrulla | ón
rígh do rádh tingheallranna' ('There has come from a seer a maze of old prophecies ...
| May I get the smooth parchment of vellum-roll | from the prince so as to recite the
prophecy' (§§18a, 19ab).

passing, as well a vague, reference — the two men guard the land against foreign attack, in fulfilment of prophecy (§12d).

The recitation of the subject's *caithréim* is rare in classical panegyric of Scotland. We mentioned one instance in the extant poetry for the lords of the Isles.[135] Another is found in *An síth do rogha, a rígh Fionnghall* (§§10–18), where an anonymous poet praises the martial prowess of Aonghus Mac Domhnaill of Islay (†1614) and his firm subjection of his territories, both in Scotland and Ireland; this poem, incidentally, contains an allusion to the special relationship between the poet and his patron, 'fear mo ghualann' (§7a).[136] The motif that depicts the poem's subject as his territory's lover or spouse is equally rare and, being as it is closely connected with the high-kingship, it is, like the latter, found only in poems for the lords of the Isles and Clann Eóin Mhóir of Antrim.[137] After its early appearance in the poem for Domhnall mac Raghnaill, and later in Domhnall Ó hUiginn's eulogy for Eóin, tenth lord of the Isles, it only surfaces again, and then briefly, in the late sixteenth century. We have only two instances, found in the two eulogies for Somhairle Buidhe. In the marriage poem the poet states:

> Fada ata Banba bean Floinn
> ag iarraidh fola Domnaill.

> (Long has Banbha, Flann's spouse, been seeking [to marry] Domhnall's blood).[138]

In *Fada cóir Fhódla ar Albain* Tadhg Dall states that, if Fódhla urges her claim on *Alba* and gets her rights, 'ní dóigh Éire i n-aontamha' ('it is not likely that Ireland will be left mateless', §1d). Later in the poem he reveals that Ireland's companion is to be Somhairle Buidhe,

> brath céile do Mhoigh Mhonaidh
> 's re bhfoil Éire ag anamhain.

---

135 See above, p. 64.
136 For *guala* and other terms reflecting this relationship see Breatnach 1983, pp. 45–6.
137 See above, p. 82 and n. 121.
138 *Mealladh iomlaoide ar Eirinn*, §42ab.

(the expected mate from *Monadh*'s Plain,
he for whom Ireland is waiting) (§13cd).

And again:

Do-bhéara Banbha, bean Chuinn …
 a fear féin ó Mhoigh Mhonaidh.

(*Banbha*, spouse of Conn … will bring her own man from the
Plain of *Monadh*) (§32ac).

There are two fresh developments in Clann Eóin Mhóir poetry. One
is the claim that Clann Domhnaill are entitled to 'baile (sometimes
taigh or *treabh*) is leath Alban' ('a house and a half of Scotland'). It is not
known exactly how this motif originated. It is found already as early as
the tale of Deirdre and the sons of Uisneach,[139] but it may be older. In a
poem by Niall Mac Muireadhaigh we read that Colla Uais had obtained
sway over 'urmhor ul*adh* … 7 leth oire*cht* alban' ('the greater part of
Ulster… and half of the inheritance of Alba').[140] To the poet who in
1588 composed *Éisd re seanchas síol gColla* (perhaps from the Ó Gnímh
hereditary poetic family)[141] for Mac Marcuis of Knocknacloy it was

---

139 *BG*, p. 281. The tale seems to have been composed in late eighth or early ninth century,
but it was reworked in the fourteenth or fifteenth centuries; see Mac Giolla Léith
(ed.) 1993, pp. 9, 13. It is said of Naoise 'gur chosain neart a láimhe féin treabh ar
leith Alban dó' ('[that] the strength of his arm gained for him a district in addition to
half of Scotland', see *ibid.*, pp. 88–89). For some discussion, including the possibility
of translating the expression as 'a separate district of Scotland', see *ibid.*, pp. 145–6;
Matheson (ed.) 1938, pp. 287–8; and Ó Murchú 2001, pp. 58–9 and n. 5'. Note also
that Thorstein the Red, a later-ninth-century Hebridean chieftain, is said in the sagas
to have received tribute from more than half of Scotland after his successful cam-
paigns in the mainland (*Collectanea*, p. 66). For the same idiom applied to Anradhán's
Scottish conquests see below, chapter 5, p. 190; and for a related expression concern-
ing Mac Gille Eóin's claim in Islay see below, chapter 5, p. 225.
140 *Labhradh Trían Chonguil go ciúin*, §18. For the same claim in an Irish source see *LCAB*,
p. 49. For the three Collas' conquest of territories in Ulster see above, p. 64 n. 53, and
further *RC* ii, p. 151, and *FFÉ* ii, pp. 360, 364.
141 'Bia*dh* misi ag mo m*h*uin*n*tir féin | clan*n* eo*ch*ui*dh* duas*bh*uig doib*h*léin' ('My own
people, the children of Eochaidh Doimhléan, have me [for their *ollamh*]' (§6ab).
For the claimed connexion of the Ó Gnímh and Mac Domhnaill families see Ó Cuív
1984b, pp. 152–4.

common knowledge that the three Collas' patrimony had been 'a house and a half of Scotland':

> Treb*h* is leat*h* albon uile
> m*a*r scaoileas gac*h* sceoluid*h*e.

> (A house and half of the whole of Scotland,
> as each story-teller makes known) (§16ab).

Seathrún Céitinn tells us of Colla Uais and his brothers that 'gabhaid fearann mór' ('they acquired large territories') in *Alba*.[142] When his two brothers eventually resettled in Ireland, it is likely that their lands in Scotland devolved on Colla Uais, whose own territory would thus have become very large indeed. We have no details of the early period concerning his and his descendants' expansion, but it may well be here that the claim to 'a house and half of Scotland' originated. In Irish tradition it is held that when the three Collas were banished to Alba, they arrived there with a host of three hundred, 'agus tug rí Alban cion mór agus agus buannacht dóibh' ('and the king of Alba received them with affection, and took them into military service').[143] This not only explains the poetic predisposition to portray Clann Domhnaill as being in Scotland merely on military service,[144] but also suggests that, if the Collas' mother was indeed a princess from *Alba*, they may have been accommodated territorially in a generous manner.

However that may be, the claim to 'leath Alban' appears sometimes in both classical and vernacular Clann Domhnaill poetry,[145] generally as a passing reference. As such we have seen it in a quotation from an eulogy

---

142 *FFÉ* ii, p. 382. The Isles, according to 'Hugh of Sleat', would have been added to the mainland patrimony of the descendants of Colla Uais in the early seventh century: 'As to the Isles, [Somhairle] had an undoubted right to them, his predecessors being possessed of them by the good will and consent of Eugenius the First, for obligations conferred upon him' (*HP* i, p. 9). Eugenius the First: Eochaidh Buidhe (†629), great-great-grandson of Fearghus mac Eirc.

143 *FFÉ* ii, p. 360.

144 See above, p. 68 and n. 73.

145 For examples in vernacular verse see below, p. 110.

for Séamas Mac Domhnaill Íle.[146] But, exceptionally, it is fully developed in *Mór mo mholadh ar mhac Colla*, for Alasdair mac Colla. This poem was probably composed shortly after the battle of Kilsyth, in 1645,[147] in which Montrose's forces defeated a numerically much superior Covenanting army. It is a celebration of the royalist victory, which the anonymous author portrays very much like a Gaelic enterprise against the Lowlanders, a particular viewpoint which, as noted, is common in vernacular verse.[148] But what is interesting in this classical poem is that the Kilsyth victory is presented as part of the process of the recovery by the *Gaoidhil*, led by Clann Domhnaill (§§3ab, 8–9), of their rightful inheritance in Alba: 'dúthchus do shíol Airt'('the birthright of Art's seed'), to which they are entitled by 'cairt an chloidhimh' ('the broadsword's charter'), that is the right acquired by conquest.[149] The allusion to the extent of the patrimony appears in §6, where 'úrleith Alban' ('the greater part of *Alba*') is used for 'baile is leath Alban':

> Cíos is cána ar úrleith Alban
> > aimsir oile,
> biaidh sin ag an droing mur dhlighe,
> > nó an roinn roimhe.

> (Tax and tribute over Alba's greater half once again those folk shall have as right).[150]

The motif of territorial division (*roinn, athroinn, roinn eile*) is well attested in classical poetry of Ireland — and not unknown in that of Scotland[151] — normally within the context of perceived threat of takeover by an enemy.[152] In the prose section of our poem the author links the ancient division motif to the contemporary struggle:

---

146 See above, p. 82.
147 Watson (ed.) 1927, p. 75.
148 See above, p. 84 and n. 127.
149 *Mór mo mholadh ar mhac Colla*, §4cd. See also §5ab.
150 For *úrleith* ('ar leth', 'the greater half') see Watson (ed.) 1927, p. 77, n. 6a; *EB*, p. 214.
151 See, for instance, *Domhnall mac Raghnaill rosg mall*, §6; *Ceannaigh duain t'athar, a Aonghas*, §3.
152 Coira 2008b, p. 153.

Agus ní roinn chomhthrom do-rinnedur Fir Alban eidir iad féin 7 armailte an rí(ogh) .i. do thairrngedur a sluaigh 7 a sochuidhe d'aontaobh chuca féin 7 nír fhágbhadur don leith eile acht fíorbhegán do shenfholuibh uaisle arda ionnarpach.

(And it was no fair division that the men of Alba [i.e., the Lowlanders] made between themselves and the king's army [i.e., the *Gaoidhil*]. They drew their hosts and their multitudes to one side toward themselves, and on the other side they left only some few of the ancient noble warlike stocks).[153]

Despite the numerical superiority of 'fir Alban', the Gaels had defeated them, as they had again and again in previous battles.[154] The author retells the tale of 'Belling the Cat', portraying the Lowlanders as the numerous mice none of whom dares to put the bell on the cat, Alasdair mac Colla.[155] Later in the poem 'fir Alban' are like 'an bethadhach beg baoth an damhán all*aidh*' ('that little silly creature the spider') who hopes to catch many insects in its web, only to have it destroyed by 'sran gaoithe' ('a blast of wind'), that is the Gaels.[156] The Lowlanders are further described as '[clanna] barún 7 bodach' ('the children of petty barons and churls'), 'lán do neimh 7 do námhadus 7 d'feirg' ('full of venom and of hostility and of wrath') towards the Gaels on account of the latter's 'uaisle 7 ... ardfholuidhecht'('nobility and high descent').[157] In the verse section the Lowlanders are further described as '[Goill] gruama' ('gloomy *Goill*', §10c), 'daorshluagh Gall le nert n-anbhann' ('pithless rabble of *Goill*', §11c), 'an bhuighen bholgmhor'('the big-paunched folk', §13a). This superior self-view of the Gaels and their description of the Lowlanders as an ignoble rabble, physically unattractive, is a theme of vernacular verse,[158] whence it seems to have come into this classical piece. The Scottish Gaels' noble blood is also clearly connected to their Irish origins:

---

153 *Mór mo mholadh ar mhac Colla,* prose section, p. 78.
154 *ibid.*, prose section, p. 80.
155 *ibid.*, pp. 78–80.
156 *ibid.*, p. 86.
157 *ibid.*
158 MacInnes 2006c, pp. 40–1.

Gaoidhil Éireann ocus Alban
  aimsir oile,
ionann a bfrémha is a bfine.

(The Gael of Alba and of Eire long ago were the same in origin
and in blood) (§14abc).[159]

The feeling in seventeenth- and eighteenth-century vernacular poetry that
the Scottish Gaels had been dispossessed of their rightful inheritance in
Scotland[160] and the allusions to the prophecy that the Gaels will come into
their own once again[161] are both undoubtedly connected with this ancient
claim of Clann Domhnaill's right to 'baile is leath Alban'.

The other development in Clann Eóin Mhóir poetry (though, again,
not exclusive to it) is the appearance of the title 'rí Fionnghall' ('king of the
Hebrideans'), as a variant of 'rí Innse Gall', again a usage of a complimen-
tary nature rather than a statement of an official title.[162] Concerning titles
we will note also that in *Díon tíre dá thighearna* the poet states that 'ainm i
Earca os iarladhuibh' ('the title Ó Earca is above earldoms', §6d). This type
of poetic claim appears from time to time in panegyrics for Gaelic nobles,
whether Scottish or Irish, who held also a non-Gaelic title.[163] The literary
vision of the superiority of a Gaelic title reminds us of the story of the
medieval Spanish traveller, in whose mind — or so the author would have
us believe — the grandeur of the lord of the Isles was associated with his
title Mac Domhnaill, and not with that of Earl of Ross.

Other Mac Domhnaill cadet branches

The poetry for the remainder of the cadet branches of Clann Domhnaill
shows significant differences in its choice of rhetoric of praise. Firstly, the
motifs of the high-kingship, of the chief as his territory's spouse, and of
the struggle of the *Gaoidhil* against the foreigners as understood so far are

159 See McLeod 2004, p. 195 for the possibility of a different reading which, however,
    would have no impact on the point made here.
160 See above, chapter 2, p. 52 and n. 130.
161 See below, p. 102.
162 *An síth do rogha, a rígh Fionnghall?*, §§1a, 8a; McLeod 2002a, pp. 36–7.
163 For an Irish example see *Mó iná iarla ainm Séamais*, for Séamas Buitléar, ninth Earl of
    Ormond (†1546). For a Scottish example see below, chapter 4, p. 135.

abandoned. We find a preference for other customary conventions such as the subject's martial prowess, his generosity and hospitality, his education, his character qualities, and his love of hunting, gaming and feasting.[164] Most of the extant corpus belongs to the seventeenth century, and only about a third of it is in classical metres — this is the period of decline of the classical poets and of dynamism of their vernacular counterparts, who as well as straightforward panegyric also composed verse which was rather commentary on social and political events of their time. At the same time, some of the traditional conceits are reshaped, while fresh themes and strands make their appearance. Scottish Gaelic society was seriously affected from the earlier part of the seventeenth century, following the promulgation of the so-called 'Statutes of Iona' in 1609 and especially of subsequent legislation along the same lines. By the mid-century the Scottish Gaels had become involved in the Wars of the Three Kingdoms, in which they threw their wholehearted support on the king's side,[165] and thereafter they continued to adhere to the Stiúbhart cause through the early Jacobite period of the later seventeenth and early eighteenth centuries. Like those writing in Scots and in English, the vernacular Gaelic poets — considered in the next section of this chapter — used their talent and their influence to reflect, to an extent, current opinion, but also largely to shape it.

Among the literary motifs reworked in the eventful seventeenth century is that of the struggle against the *Goill*, who now are almost invariably the Lowland Scots. There are very few instances, and they are found in classical poems only, of the common stock-phrase 'Gaoidhil is Goill'. This is used in both Gaelic classical panegyric and historical narrative, seemingly in a general complimentary way, aiming to place the individual in question above all others, Gael and non-Gael.[166] For instance, Cathal

---

164 For instance, *Fáilte d'ar n-Ailín nar Raghnallach, Deireadh do aoibhneas Innse Gall, Do ttuirlinn seasuimh síol cCuinn*, for members of Clann Raghnaill; *Níor ghlac cliath colg no gunna, Tuar doimheanma dul Raghnaill*, for members of Clann Domhnaill of Glengarry; *Mo-chean do-chonnarc a réir, Éireochthar fós le Clainn gColla*, for members of Clann Domhnaill of Sleat; *Clú oirbhirt úaislighes nech*, a poem in the 'young prince' style, that is presenting the subject as a promising young warrior suitable to attain to the chiefship, perhaps composed, to judge from internal evidence, for Gilleasbaig Mac Domhnaill, future eighth chief of Largie.

165 But for Caimbéal participation in these events see below, chapter 4, p. 139.

166 For some examples see *AU* ii, p. 386; *AC*, pp. 2, 7, 273; *ARÉ* v, pp. 1308, 1418, 1630, 1712.

Mac Muireadhaigh praised Domhnall Mac Domhnaill, twelfth chief of Clann Raghnaill (+1686), as 'mo thogha Ghaoidh*eal* is Ghall' ('My choice of *Gaoidhil* and *Goill*');[167] Raghnall Mac Domhnaill, tenth chief of Glengarry (+1705), is portrayed at the head of 'ghlans*luagh* Ghaoidh*eal* is Ghall' ('the bright host of *Gaoidhil* and *Goill*');[168] and the subject of *Clú oirbhirt úaislighes nech* — perhaps Gilleasbaig, future eighth chief of Clann Raghnaill Bháin, whose patrimony and main seat was in Largie[169] — is said to have the support of 'uaisle crú Gaoidheal is Gall' ('the nobility of the blood of *Gaoidhil* and *Goill*', §24a). But apart from this particular usage, in general the *Goill* in this period are no mere literary rhetoric, but real, flesh-and-blood Scottish Lowlanders, and generally the enemies of the house of Stiúbhart, as they are in vernacular verse. This, as we noted when discussing Clann Eóin Mhóir poetry, is a novelty in late Mac Domhnaill classical panegyric.[170] Even so, its entry into classical verse appears to be have been a somewhat reluctant one for, apart from the two Clann Eóin Mhóir poems noted above, we have no other instances of this usage. In *Éireóchthar fós le clainn gColla*, for Domhnall Gorm Óg Mac Domhnaill Sleat (+1643), first Baronet Sleat, a poem very similar to *Mór mo mholadh ar mhac Colla*, the Lowlanders are 'uaisle Alban' and 'fir Alban';[171] the latter term, as we have seen, was equated with *Goill* in two contemporary poems for members of Clann Domhnaill of Colonsay to denote the Lowland enemies of the Stiúbhairt.[172]

Perhaps the principal difference between the Colonsay poems and *Éireóchthar fós le clainn gColla* is that the latter overtly introduces the theme of royalism. This, also, was probably borrowed into classical panegyric from vernacular verse although, again, it can hardly be said to be pervasive. Domhnall Gorm is portrayed as 'cúirt*eoir* na ccairt le Cing Sérlus' ('courtier of charters with King Charles'), whose favour he enjoys, and as bravely

---

167 *Cóir fáilte re fear do sgéil*, §17b.
168 *Tuar doimheanma dul Raghnaill*, §28c.
169 See above, p. 92 n. 164.
170 See above, p. 84.
171 *Éireóchthar fós le clainn gColla*, §9a and first prose section, l. 2. Both poems are anonymous, structurally and thematically similar (both even retell the tale of 'Belling the cat'), and metrically *crosántachta*. *Éireóchthar* was composed *c*.1640 and *Mór mo mholadh* in 1645. They may be the work of the same author.
172 See above, p. 84.

fighting for his cause.[173] It is only in this poem that royalism is discussed at some length, but even so the author gives it a Gaelic slant. He presents Domhnall Gorm's support for the king as inspired by the ancient princely advice treaty, *Tecosca Cormaic*, the teachings of which 'fir Alban' had failed to understand: 'Ní rathm*hor* ríghe gan rígh 7 ní torrcharth*ach* tír gan tigh-*er*na' ('A kingdom without a king is not prosperous, and a land without a lord is not fruitful').[174] Elsewhere in Mac Domhnaill poetry royalism tends to consist of a brief note. For instance, Aonghus Óg Mac Domhnaill, ninth chief of Glengarry and Lord MacDonnell and Aros (†1680), is:

> Fer caidreabha ag cing Serlus ...
> sheasas a chúl is chongmhas,
> > foghnas d'a chrún no chaomhnas.

> (A man of King Charles's fellowship ...
> who sustains and supports him,
> serves and cherishes his crown).[175]

Domhnall Mac Domhnaill, twelfth chief of Clann Raghnaill (†1686) is in a similarly brief manner portrayed as fighting for his king.[176] Neither are denominational allusions common in later Mac Domhnaill poetry, even though at least some *filidh* engaged in the composition of religious verse; and when we do find them, they are not given within a clear political context, as noted below.[177] The theme of royalism, then, is almost never fully developed as it is in vernacular poetry. This is probably because discussion of the wider Scottish politics was no concern of classical panegyric, the business of which was rather the praise of the warrior in the familiar legitimating conventions of the age-old rhetorical code. But, exceptionally,

---

173 *Éireóchthar fós le clainn gColla*, §§5a (quotation), 6ab, 16–19.

174 For the same principle in another early princely-advice text see Kelly (ed.) 1976, §§12–21.

175 *Níor ghlac cliath colg no gunna*, §20acd.

176 *Deireadh do aoibhneas Innse Gall*, §9ab.

177 See, for instance, Cathal Mac Muireadhaigh's *Mairg chaomhnas a cholann*, and his consolation poems *A Sheónóid méadaigh meanma* and *Deimhin do shíol Ádhaimh éag*. Niall Mór Mac Muireadhaigh's *Dá lámh sínte le síoth nDé* does contain references to the cult of the Virgin Mary, thus giving away the author's religious confession.

in the poem *Dá chúis ag milleadh ar meamna*, probably the work of Niall Mac Muireadhaigh,[178] the author does engage in national politics. In doing this the Scottish poet was not unique, for his Irish counterparts have also left poems concerned with the national politics of Ireland at the time of serious English threat, and royalism as adherence to the house of Stiúbhart is well attested in seventeenth- and eighteenth-century Irish poetry.[179] Niall laments the exile of his patron, Raghnall, fifteenth chief of Clann Raghnaill (†1725), the Scottish nobility's loss of their patrimony, and the injustice of a king who has usurped the throne.[180] For the poet all that can be done now is pray in hope of help from God, who had helped Moses by splitting the Red Sea (§14–15).[181]

In vernacular poetry defence of the true faith is sometimes connected with political ideology.[182] There may be a hint of the same idea in some classical poems, but the few extant references to religion are not explicitly connected to the contemporary denominational conflict. The Catholic Raghnall Mac Domhnaill, second Earl and Marquis of Antrim, is portrayed by a classical poet as ever keen on 'díon creidmhe' ('protecting the faith').[183] Like him, Raghnall Mac Domhnaill of Glengarry (†1705) was a royalist, although a Protestant, of whom an unknown poet stated that 'a chreidimh 'na chloidhemh c[h]eart' ('his faith was his true sword').[184] Despite some allusions to royalism and the wider British politics, *Breatain* is almost non-existent, making an appearance only in *Éireochthar fós le Clainn gColla*, which notes Charles II as 'rígh Breatan' and 'airdrí Breatan' (§§5, 6, 9, prose section, ll. 3–4, and §16b). Most notable in this period, however, is the diminished appearance of *Alba*, so prominent in the poetry for the lords of the Isles, and even in an extant early sixteenth-century elegy for two Clann Raghnaill leaders.[185] By the seventeenth century *Alba* had become almost

---

178 Thomson 1969–70, pp. 293, 302–3.

179 See generally Ó Buachalla 1983; id., 1996; Caball 1998.

180 *Dá chúis ag milleadh ar meamna*, §§1–4.

181 For similar allusions to Moses and the Red Sea in vernacular poetry see below, p. 106. For Moses imagery in seventeenth-century classical Irish poetry see, for instance, Caball 1998, p. 111.

182 See below, p. 104.

183 *Taisdil mhionca ór siabhradh sionn*, §8ab.

184 *Tuar doimheanma dul Raghnaill*, §15c.

185 *Alba gan díon an diaigh Ailéin*.

an afterthought in classical — as well as in vernacular — poetry. We find only a few isolated allusions — a dead leader is mourned by *Alba*, his death is a loss to *Alba*, the battle of Sheriffmuir was 'gearradh aic*me* halban' ('the cutting of the men of Scotland').[186] Even more conspicuous by its absence is the motif of prophecy, which in contrast, as will be seen, became popular in vernacular verse.

Despite all the novelties of later Mac Domhnaill poetry, many of the traditional conventions are preserved in it. The individual portrayed is always presented as a brave warrior, a protector of his territory and people, a man of noble character, a generous patron of the poet class. His royal Gaelic ancestry is noted through references to Colla Uais, Eochaidh Doimhléan, Conn Céadchathach, Éanna, Art, Cobhthach Caol mBreagh; his ancient Norse connexions are remembered in the complimentary formula 'rí Fionnghall'.[187] His physical beauty, his hospitality and fame are celebrated, and nature is said to sanction his leadership through clement weather and fertility of the land. In *Mo-chean do-chonnarc a réir* Cathal Mac Muireadhaigh uses the convention of portraying himself as his patron's lover, this being the only instance of this conceit in classical poetry for Scottish subjects. In the same poem he also claims to have had his *guaille* ('shoulder') and *rún* ('confidence'), two of the special privileges to which an *ollamh* was entitled:[188]

> a ghualainn dúinn ós chionn cháigh ...

> do bhaidh go suairc a rún riom
>   's a chúl sliom ar chuairt 'am cheann.

> (he gave me the place by his shoulder before all others ...

> he of the smooth locks would come to visit me
>   and courteously give me his confidence) (§§6d, 13cd).

---

186 *Cumha ceathrair do mheasg mé*, §18c; *Do ttuirlinn seasuimh síol cCuinn*, §45d; *Mór mo mholadh ar mhac Colla*, §§2a, 26a; *Níor ghlac cliath colg no gunna*, §§11d, 12d.

187 Éanna [Aighneach], Cobhthach Caol mBreagh: ancestors of Conn Céadchathach (see Table 8.1).

188 For *rún* see Breatnach 1983, pp. 40–1.

Following the abolition of the Mac Domhnaill lordship of the Isles the rivalry between several of its main branches over the right to be recognised as head of Clann Domhnaill led to the emergence of a new literary theme: the later poetry sometimes displays the motif of 'ceannas na nGaoidheal' ('the headship of the Gaels') which, additionally, was contested in Caimbéal panegyric from the later sixteenth century onwards.[189] According to 'Hugh of Sleat', Mac Domhnaill of Sleat had in his possession a certain document in which the main Clann Domhnaill leaders recognised his leadership of the clan.[190] The historian was probably referring to an extant declaration to this effect[191] which, however, does not include the signature of Mac Domhnaill of Glengarry. The latter's pretensions to the leadership of Clann Domhnaill are noted by the Sleat historian,[192] and indeed Anghus Óg Mac Domhnaill (†1680), ninth chief of Glengarry and Lord McDonnell, often appears in Privy Council records as chief of Clann Domhnaill.[193] He is also termed 'ruire glic Gaoidheal' ('wise over-king of Gaels') in an extant elegy.[194] Yet it is possible that the claim to Clann Domhnaill leadership by a cadet branch was first put forward by a Clann Raghnaill chief, Raghnall Bán (†1509), who not only declined to join Domhnall Dubh's insurrection but was rewarded by the government for his help against the rebels with lands in North Uist resigned by Mac Domhnaill of Sleat.[195] He is, at any rate, said by a Mac Muireadhaigh poet to have assumed 'cennus Ghaoidheal'.[196] In later Clann Raghnaill poetry the phraseology is different; for example, the death of Domhnall, eleventh chief, in 1618 was said by Niall Mac Muireadhaigh to have been 'deireadh na riogh o ros' ('the end of the kings from Ross').[197] In a poem composed during the exile of Raghnall, fifteenth chief, the same author says:

---

189 See below, chapter 4, pp. 132–5.

190 *HP* ii, pp. 63–4.

191 Printed in *Clan Donald* iii, p. 654 (*HP* i, p. 64 n. 1).

192 *HP* i, p. 64.

193 *Clan Donald* ii, p. 640.

194 *Níor ghlac cliath colg no gunna*, §11a. For Glengarry leaders' claims to leadership of Clann Domhnaill in vernacular poetry see below, p. 110.

195 *Clan Donald*, ii, p. 240.

196 *Alba gan díon an diaigh Ailéin*, §4ab.

197 *Deireadh do aoibhneas Innse Gall*, §11b.

Ceann coimhéde ríoghfhuil Raghnaill
a n-easbhuidh seilbhe chrú Chuinn.

(The head of protection of Raghnall's royal blood
is lacking the patrimony of Conn's race).[198]

In poetry for the Mac Domhnaill of Sleat branch the claim to 'ceannas na nGaoidheal' appears in two seventeenth-century compositions, one for Séamas (†1678), ninth chief and second Baronet Sleat, and another, which uses the alternative wording 'codhnach cloinne Cholla' ('chief of Colla's children') for Domhnall Gorm Óg (†1643), eighth chief.[199] The expression itself is not used in a lament for the death of Caitirfhíona, daughter of Domhnall Gorm Óg, but is perhaps implied in the proclamation that this chief is 'aon damhna gill na nGaoidhiol' ('the one fit to have the supremacy of the Gaoidhil').[200] A statement by Niall Mac Muireadhaigh reflects the uncertainty over the settlement of the question, on which several Mac Domhnaill cadet branches all had a rightful claim — a conflict no doubt aggravated by the imposition of royal over Gaelic law. Following the extinction of the main line with the death of Domhnall Dubh, Niall muses:

ni bfuil fios agamsa cia da chinedh no da chairdibh is oighre dles-danach air, acht an cuiger mᶜsa Eoin mⁱᶜ aonghuis óig ... Raghnall 7 Gothfroigh ... 7 Domnall 7 Eoin mór 7 alasdair carrach.

(I do not know who of his kindred or friends is his lawful heir except these five sons of Eóin mac Aonghuis Óig ... Raghnall and Godhfhraidh ... and Domhnall and Eóin Mór and Alasdair Carrach).[201]

---

198 *Dá chúis ag milleadh ar meamna*, §8ab. Raghnall: Clann Raghnaill's eponym, son of Eóin, seventh lord of the Isles.

199 *Fuaras cara ar sgáth na sgéile*, §7b; *Éireochthar fós le cloinn gColla*, §40a. For similar references in vernacular verse see below, p. 110.

200 *Leasg linn gabháil go Gearrloch*, §32d.

201 *RC* ii, p. 210. Raghnall: eponym of Clann Raghnaill, and from whom sprang also the Glengarry branch. Godhfhraidh: eldest son of Eóin, seventh lord of the Isles, and ancestor of Clann Ghodhfhraidh; this cadet branch disappeared by the later fifteenth

The motif of 'ceannas na nGaoidheal' — which never appears linked to any territorial boundaries, and therefore seems purely ethnic — is, nonetheless, never anything more than a passing reference in extant Clann Domhnaill poetry, in contrast with the emphatic treatment given to it in more than one Caimbéal poem.[202] In a passing manner is also given the claim to 'baile is leath Alban' in Niall Mac Muireadhaigh's *Labhradh Trían Chonguil go ciúin*, it being the only instance of this motif in classical poetry for Mac Domhnaill cadet branches other than Clann Eóin Mhóir.

Labhradh Trían Chonguil go ciúin belongs to the poetic exchange known as the 'Red Hand Contention'. Poetic contentions were probably mere literary exercises in which participants displayed not only their literary skills but also their knowledge of history and genealogy, and their wit. The debate joined by Niall Mac Muireadhaigh was started in Ireland when some northern poets argued over which family was entitled to display the Red Hand emblem on their arms.[203] Niall's contribution was twofold. In his poem in reply to that in which Diarmaid Mac an Bhaird claimed the Red Hand for Clann Rudhraighe of Ulster, he reminded him that the latter had been defeated by Colla Uais, who had reigned over them;[204] in this way he had obtained the Red Hand, which was displayed in Somhairle's seal and had since remained with his line, Clann Domhnaill, being still 'nar mbréid mbratuighe' ('in our standard's cloth').[205] The Red Hand motif appears occasionally in Mac Domhnaill vernacular poetry of a very late date,[206] and was not exclusive to the main line of the family: it remained in the arms of the Montgomery earls of Eglinton, descendants of Eóin, seventh lord of the Isles, through the female line until the seventeenth century when one countess of Eglinton

---

century. Domhnall: eighth lord of the Isles and ancestor of Mac Domhnaill of Sleat. Eóin Mór and Alasdair Carrach: sons of the seventh lord of the Isles and the ancestors of Mac Domhnaill of Islay and Antrim and Mac Domhnaill of Keppoch respectively (see Table 3.3).

202 See below, chapter 4, pp. 132–5.

203 The extant poems on this debate are printed in *RC* ii, pp. 291–9. For some comment see Hughes 1990.

204 *Labhradh Trían Chonguil go ciúin*, §§6–8, 9cd. For the three Collas' conquest of territories in Ulster see *RC* ii, p. 152, and *FFÉ*, pp. 360, 364.

205 *Labhradh Trían Chonguil go ciúin*, §3d.

206 See below, pp. 111–12.

had it removed 'because it held a cross; she being a rigid Presbyterian'.[207]

Before closing the section on later classical verse, it is worth noting Niall Mac Muireadhaigh's second contribution to the Red Hand controversy. This is his reply to the Irish poet Eóghan Ó Donnghaile, who claimed the Red Hand for Ó Néill but also had the audacity to criticise Mac an Bhaird's scholarship along the way. Niall had little regard for Eóghan's 'oige óig'('young craft'),[208] and he condemned his poetry as the pitiful efforts of a buffoon.[209] He also rebuked him for his attack on the true professionals and lamented the scarcity of the latter following the demise of some and the exile in which many northern poets were forced to live on account of political circumstances.[210] He condemned upstarts like Eóghan (the Ó Donnghaile poets were indeed only a recently established poetic family):

> méla is eoga*n* na ughdar ...

> na olla*m*h riogh ro naire.

> (For shame that Eóghan is an author ...
> exceedingly shameful it is that he is a royal chief-poet).[211]

No doubt in a deliberate move to add insult to injury Niall, who had used impeccable *dán díreach* in his reply to Mac an Bhaird, addressed Ó Donnghaile (for whom he reckoned only *amhrán* was appropriate)[212] in *óglachas* style. Niall also used 'lower' metrics, approaching the vernacular, in the satire *T'aire riut, a Ghiolla-Easbuig*, as did Cathal Mac Muireadhaigh when satirising another amateur.[213] This seems to have been a favourite technique of the professional poets when they wished to insult those of lower letters or those composing, as Ó Donnghaile did, in looser styles.[214]

---

207 *HP* i, p. 27.

208 *Nár lém choisnes tu clú Chuinn*, §12a.

209 'ni glór abhloir ealadhain' ('art is not a buffoon's speech', *ibid.*, §12d).

210 *Nár lém choisnes tu clú Chuinn*, §§5, 13, 22a, 23ab.

211 *ibid.*, §§22d, 23d.

212 *ibid.*, §12c.

213 See above, chapter 2, pp. 40; Thomson 1977, p. 238; Black 1976–8, pp. 337–8.

214 Although most of his extant work is in *óglachas*, we have one instance of Ó Donnghaile's ability to compose *dán díreach* in the elegy *Ceist ar eólchuibh iath Banbha*, for an Ó

As the traditional social system collapsed around them, the classical poets thus deplored the new breed who appropriated the persona and the language of authority, for centuries their own sacrosanct jurisdiction.

Vernacular verse

In vernacular panegyric, which for Clann Domhnaill cadet branches survives from the later sixteenth century onwards and is almost entirely made up of accentual verse,[215] poets ascribe to their subjects many of the usual conventions of the classical panegyric code. The focus, however, tends to coincide with that noted for later classical verse: martial prowess, generosity, hospitality, education, character qualities, hunting, gaming and feasting are the preferred themes.[216] The vernacular poets, like their classical counterparts, introduce new themes and rework some old ones, although not always in the same fashion. Besides strict panegyric they have left us poetry which is not only commentary on the social and political events of their times, but a valuable source on contemporary views of kingship, its nature, and even its boundaries.

Among the literary motifs reworked in the eventful seventeenth century is that of the struggle against the *Goill*, who now are almost invariably the Lowland Scots, as noted above.[217] Màiri NicDhòmhnaill, daughter of Aonghus of Islay, in her vernacular elegy for her deceased husband, Domhnall Mac Domhnaill, eleventh chief of Clann Raghnaill (†1618), noted Domhnall's presence in Edinburgh, where you would expect to see a *Gall* rather than a *Gaoidheal*.[218] Another MacDhòmhnaill vernacular

---

Néill chief.

215 Exceptions are *Sgeula leat, a ghaoth a-deas* and *A chomhachag bhog na Sròine*, both composed in 'semi-classical' loose style, and four extant poems by Donnchadh MacRaoiridh: *Beir mise leat, a mhic Dè*, *Thàinig fath bròin air ar cridhe*, *Treun am Mac a thug ar leòn* and *Fada ta mis an-dèidh càich*. The first two are religious and the last two were composed for Cailéan Ruadh Mac Coinnigh, thirteenth chief and first Earl of Seaforth. Although officially a Mac Domhnaill poet, Donnchadh's work is all in 'semi-classical' style, and therefore he was not a *file*.

216 See, for instance, *Moch 's a mhaduinn 's mi 'g èiridh*, *Gur è naigheachd na Ciadain*, both for Clann Raghnaill chiefs; *Ach a nis on a liath mi*, for Aonghus Óg of Glengarry, Lord MacDonnell (†1680), and *Bíodh an uigheam-sa triall*, possibly for the same chief; *O! 's tuisleach an nochd a taim*, for Aonghus (†1661) of Largie; *An Nollaig air 'm bu ghreadhnach fion*, and *Sgeula leat, a ghaoth a-deas*, for Sleat chiefs.

217 See above, p. 84.

218 *Moch 'sa mhaduinn 's mi 'g èiridh*, §4ab. Similarly in the poem *Ho ró, gur fada |'s cian*

female poet, Sìleas na Ceapaich, lamented that Séamas Mac Domhnaill, thirteenth chief and sixth Baronet Sleat (†1720), had been buried by Goill.[219] The Goill are also the Lowland Scots in, for instance, Iain Lom MacDhòmhnaill's 1689 song for King James's army, in Aonghus mac Alasdair Ruaidh's political poem on the battle of Killiecrankie (1689), and in Murchadh MacMhathain's lament on the massacre of Glencoe (1692). Within the context of support for the Stiúbhairt, however, the term is often used to include their enemies, whether Scots or English.[220]

The motif of prophecy is also reworked in this later period. We have seen that the depiction of the subject as the prophesied deliverer who will expel the English — that is, the prophecy motif in its original classical Irish format — appears only in some poems for members of Clann Eóin Mhóir of Islay and Antrim. The prophets cited in Bí ad mhosgaladh, a mheic Aonghais are all Irish, as is customary in classical verse for Irish nobles.[221] But in the new prophecy motif of Scottish vernacular poetry we find several crucial differences. In the first place the prophet is always the same, the thirteenth-century Lowland laird Thomas Learmont of Erceldoune, better known as Thomas the Rhymer.[222] Secondly, the prophecy alluded to never refers to one particular individual, but to an event: the resurgence of the Gaoidhil in Scotland, their recovery of their Scottish patrimony. Thirdly, the foreign usurpers of the patrimony of the Gaoidhil are now the Lowland Scots, or else the latter and the English as one group. This motif is never found in a panegyric for an individual, but rather in poems dealing with contemporary political concerns, 'political poems' in the sense more familiar to us.[223] It is not to be found in classical panegyric.

---

fada gu leòr, whose subject, Aonghus Óg of Glengarry (†1680), died in Edinburgh.

219 Is coma leam fhèin na co-dhiù sin, §8c.

220 Is mithich dhuinn màrsadh as an tìr, §§4h, 10d; 'S e latha Raon Ruairidh, §§23f, 35ab ('luchd nam machraichean gallda'); Làmh Dhè leinn, a shaoghail, §11f.

221 See above, p. 85 and n. 133.

222 MacInnes 2006d, pp. 19–22. For a full study of Thomas in Gaelic tradition, and well beyond the period covered here, see Newton 2010; I am grateful to Michael Newton for giving me access to his article before its publication. Erceldoun: Modern Earlston, in Lauderdale, Berwickshire.

223 Soraidh do'n Ghràmach, §2gh; Mi ag amharc Srath Chuaiche, §13gd; An diugh chuala mi naidheachd, §22efgh; Dh'innsinn sgeula dhuibh le reusan, §9cd; Seo an aimsir 'n do dhearbhadh an targainteachd, §1ab. See also MacInnes 2006d, pp. 21–2; Lasair, pp. 379–80.

Of the several new themes appearing in the vernacular poetry the most prominent is that of royalism, and royalism understood as adherence to the house of Stiúbhart.[224] Royalism was also closely connected to the writing of genealogical histories which flourished among the Scottish Highlanders from the seventeenth century until the nineteenth.[225] There are many strands interlaced in Gaelic royalism, a number of them being substantially the same as those found in contemporary literature in Scots and English by authors of the same political inclinations.[226] Dynastic continuity is one; the accessions to the throne of William of Orange (1689) and of George of Hanover (1714) were rejected by Gaelic poets on the grounds of foreign usurpation. William is described by an unknown poet (who may or may not have been a MacDhòmhnaill) as 'rìgh fuadain' ('a foreign king');[227] he and Mary, Iain Lom accuses, have treacherously wrested a rightful inheritance without consent,[228] George is 'rìgh fuadain nach buineadh dhuinn' ('an alien king who has no place with us').[229] Around 1714, on hearing that James VIII was preparing to return from exile, Sìleas na Ceapaich encouraged him to recover his royal inheritance:

> Tha do chathair aig *Hanòver* ...
> do chrùn 's do chlaidheamh còrach.
>
> (Hanover has your throne ...
> your crown and your sword of justice).[230]

---

224 MacInnes 2006d, p. 10; 2006c, p. 44; 2006b, p. 272.

225 Genealogical history writing was a general contemporary European trend, but for the Scottish Gaels there were further reasons for the development of this genre, including the demise of the traditional learned classes; see MacGregor 2002, pp. 197, 219–20. They were not the work of professional *seanchaidhe* and, in contrast with them, these authors appear to a great degree influenced by Lowland historians, notably in the introduction of new, fashionable genealogical claims. See, for instance, below, chapters 4, p. 120; 5, pp. 199–200, 226, 228; 6, pp. 245–6, 256.

226 See above, chapter 1, pp. 18–22. The rhetoric of early Gaelic Jacobitism is explored in detail in Ní Suaird 1999.

227 *Mi am leabaidh air m' aon taobh*, §11g.

228 *An diugh chuala mi naidheachd*, §6abcd.

229 *A rìgh 's diombach mi 'n iomairt*, §6m. In *Gura fada mi am chadal*, (§§3gh, 4, 7d) Alasdair Dubh of Glengarry (†1721/4) is praised for having opposed King George, and his death said to be a loss to King James. See also *Alasdair a Gleanna Garadh*, §3h.

230 *'S binn an sgeul so tha 'd ag ràdhainn*, §4ac.

Divine right is added to the right given by heredity. Iain Lom hopes for the return of King James from exile:

> Rìgh Seumas 's a shìol
> A dh'òrdaich Dia dhuinn.

> (King James and his family
> whom God has ordained to protect us).[231]

Defence of the true faith becomes another weapon in the verse of Catholic poets. William and Mary's religion is 'sgeula gràin' ('hateful doctrine').[232] But not all royalists were Catholics. Aonghus mac Alasdair Ruaidh of Glencoe, a Protestant vernacular poet, was a most fervent defender the Jacobite cause;[233] similarly, an anonymous Protestant author put forward in 1693 strong arguments in support of the house of Stiùbhart, while deploring the condition of the times 'bho'n là mhurtadh Rìgh Seurlas' ('since the day King Charles was murdered').[234] Sometimes, however, denominational references are given without any link to the political context. Dòmhnall MacMharcais, who was probably a descendant of a hereditary family of *filidh*, addressed the Synod of Argyll in 1701 referring to its members as 'Cléir na fìrinn ... | Gan chlaonadh gan cháidh gan choir') ('the clergy of the truth ... | without falsification, blemish or sin'), and to the Church Moderator as 'ceann is rí na h-eaglais' ('the head and the King of the Church').[235]

William of Orange is also portrayed as a sinful, immoral king. He had allowed the marriage of his daughter and his sister's son, contrary to the teaching of Scripture; he had broken the fifth Commandment.[236]

---

231 *An ainm an àigh nì mi tùs*, §3ab. Divine right is sometimes associated to clan rulers: in *Bliadhna leuma d'ar milleadh*, §2c, Iain Dubh Mac Domhnaill states that Ailéan, fourteenth chief of Clann Raghnaill, had been ordained by God as a leader. For an Irish example in syllabic metre see *Toghaidh Dia neach 'n-a naoidhin*, §§1–14, where the motif is more fully developed.

232 *An diugh chuala mi naidheachd*, §6b (for the reference to Protestantism see *OIL*, p. 321). See also §8cd, 18abcd.

233 *'S e latha Raon Ruairidh*; MacInnes 2006e, p. 170.

234 *Nach faic sibh, a dhaoine*, §1g.

235 *Flaitheas saor le saoghal sean*, §§4d, 5bc. For the Mac Marcuis family see Thomson 1968, p. 73; Ó Baoill 1976; McLeod 2004, p. 78.

236 *An diugh chuala mi naidheachd*, §§6cdef. See also §5cd, and the anonymous *Mi am*

His seizing of the throne rightfully belonging to his uncle and father-in-law, James VII, was *mi-nadurr'* ('unnatural').[237] There are complaints that money is the mover and shaker of politics. In a poem condemning the 1707 Union, Iain Lom, expressing a common contemporary opinion,[238] criticised those who would wish to

> Toirt a' chrùin uainn le ceannach
> An ceart fhradharc ar sùilean.

> (Trade away from us before our very eyes our crown and sovereign rights).[239]

To Sìleas na Ceapaich, the government had robbed the Scots:

> 'Nuair thug iad air son òir uaibh
> Ur creideas is ur stòras,
> 'S nach eil e 'n diugh 'nur pòca.

> (since they have robbed you of your credit and your possessions in return for gold which is not in your pocket today).[240]

Only riches, she accused, had put the crown on King George's head, and he was now trying to lure the Scots with money.[241] Complaints about political lies are pervasive, among MacDhòmhnaill and other authors,[242] and poets reflect on the changeability and deceitfulness of the world.[243] Some poets perceived the troubled and sombre condition of the late

---

leabaidh air m'aon taobh, §7b.

237 'S e latha Raon Ruairidh, §29efgh.

238 *OIL*, p. 327.

239 *Ge bè dh'èireadh 'san lasair*, §12gh. The *OIL* editor attributed this poem to Iain Lom, but for the suggestion of an alternative authorship see Ó Baoill 1990.

240 'S binn an sgeul so tha 'd ag ràdhainn, §5efg.

241 *Dh'innsinn sgeula dhuibh le reusan*, §1ef; *A rìgh 's diombach mi 'n iomairt*, §4b.

242 'S e latha Raon Ruairidh, §§28f, 29e; *Nach faic sibh, a dhaoine*, §4cd; *Mi am leabaidh air m' aon taobh*, §5f; and the anonymous *Tha mulad cinnteach trom air m'inntinn*, §20f. See also below, chapters 4, p. 174; 5, pp. 218, 235; 6, pp. 257, 258.

243 *Làmh Dhè leinn, a shaoghail*, §1ab; *Nach faic sibh, a dhaoine*, §4cd. See also below, chapter 6, p. 258.

seventeenth century within a sin-and-punishment framework: William and Mary have behaved like Absolom, who turned against King David, his father; now King James is in exile, like Moses in Egypt, and his people are like the children of Israel.[244] The view that political evils were God's punishment for sin was common in seventeenth-century European literature, including classical Irish royalist poetry.[245] But although this view is sometimes found in Scottish Gaelic authors, it is not a widespread theme of Scottish Gaelic poetry; MacDhòmhnaill verse certainly focuses rather on anger (directed at *stàt* and '*committee*'), hope for a restoration of the Stiúbhart kingship, and a single-minded resolution that 'cha dèan sinn bonn clos gus an cosgar leinn Gall' ('we will not rest until the Lowlanders be slaughtered by us').[246]

The theme of the wheel of fortune is also exploited to bolster hope (when the wheel turns again justice and the natural order will be restored),[247] and poets pray for this to happen, for justice to be done, for the exiles to return, for God, who brought Moses from Egypt and split the sea, to keep injustice at bay.[248] There are also warnings against division, the anonymous author of *Nach faic sibh, a dhaoine* ominously quoting from the Bible:

Tigh an aghaidh a chéile
Chan fhaodar leis seasamh.

(A house divided cannot stand) (§17cd).[249]

---

244 *Tha mulad cinnteach trom air m'inntinn*, §§5h, 6; *An diugh chuala mi naidheachd*, §§13–14; *An ainm an àigh nì mi tùs*, §4c; *'S e latha Raon Ruairidh*, §31a. See also below, chapters 4, pp. 141, 146; 5, pp. 220, 223; 6, pp. 259, 273.

245 Thomas 1991, pp. 90–132; Worden 1985; Ó Buachalla 1983; Caball 1994; id. 1998, pp. 107–11.

246 *An ainm an àigh nì mi tùs*, §5bc (first quotation); *Is mithich dhuinn màrsadh as an tìr*, §4h (second quotation); *'S binn an sgeul so tha 'd ag ràdhainn*, §§1–3; *'S mi am shuidhe air a' chnocan*, §4. See also the anonymous *Mi am leabaidh air m' aon taobh*, at §13h.

247 *Mi am leabaidh air m' aon taobh*, §10. This theme entered Gaelic literature from Latin and Greek pagan religion; see Campbell (ed.) 1984, p. 3 n. 2.

248 *'S mi am shuidhe air a' chnocan*, §12ab; *Bliadhna leuma d'ar milleadh*, §15; *Tha mulad cinnteach trom air m'inntinn*, §§7efgh, 22gh; *Mi am leabaidh air m' aon taobh*, §3h; *Nach faic sibh, a dhaoine*, §13h.

249 From Lk 3:24–55: 'And if a kingdom be divided against itself, that kingdom cannot stand. And if a house be divided against itself, that house cannot stand'. For other

The same poem also notes the powerful influence that ministers could have, and how it was exerted to favour a political cause:

Tha luchd ar teagasig à pùpaid
air am mùineadh le *faction*.

(Those who teach us from the pulpit
are instructed by a faction).[250]

Similarly Sìleas na Ceapaich:

A liuthad cùbaid tha 'n dràsda
For chùram na gràisge,
    Agus easbuig fo àilgheas nam biast.

(there are now so many pulpits in the charge of rabble, and bishops at the mercy of beasts).[251]

As well as noting the use of the pulpit for political propaganda purposes, Sìleas is resenting the Presbyterian ministers' challenge to the traditionally-established episcopal authority. By using the 'rabble motif' on these subverters of values, religious as well as political, she joins the wider British literary throng. We noted the complaints in literature in English, from the reign of Charles I onwards, that royal power was being overridden by low-born upstarts, and how some political thinkers (known as Whigs from the late seventeenth century onwards) were further eroding the power of the traditional-style monarchy.[252] We find similar concerns in Gaelic poetry. An anonymous poet described James VII in 1693 as 'Ar éigneadh le prasgan' ('constrained by a mob').[253] To Iain Lom those who had calumniated King James to banish him were *ràbaill* ('a rabble') who produced only 'rucas is cealgan' ('arrogance and deceit').[254] Sìleas na Ceapaich had no kind words for either the Whigs or King George, 'rìgh

---

poets advising unity see *Seo an aimsir 'n do dhearbhadh*, §20; *'S binn an sgeul so tha 'd ag ràdhainn*, §5a.

250 *Nach faic sibh, a dhaoine*, §11ab. Cf. above, chapter 2, p. 44 and n. 94.

251 *Tha mulad, tha gruaim orm, tha bròn*, §13cde.

252 See above, chapter 1, pp. 18–22.

253 *Nach faic sibh, a dhaoine*, §2gh.

254 *An diugh chuala mi naidheachd*, §10ab.

na muice | 's na Cuigse' ('a swinish Whiggish king').[255] Iain Dubh also considered King William a *muc* who was contaminating the royal blood.[256] Other ignoble-animal imagery used by MacDhòmhnaill poets includes the depiction of the foreign monarchs as *clamhan* ('buzzard') and *sean-mhadadh-allaidh* ('an old wolf').[257]

Some poets directed violent literary attacks against the Caimbéalaigh, whose increasing aggrandisement and power was resented by many Highlanders, and particularly Clann Domhnaill, who had lost so much to them. In *Mi 'n so air m' uilinn* Iain Lom celebrated the Restoration of monarchy in 1660, but he also launched an attack on Argyll, whom the new circumstances had caused to fall from favour. The Caimbéalaigh, the poet accuses:

> Bha tarraing uainn ar cuid beartais,
> A chuir an Rìgh mach a *Whitehall* dhuinn.

> (were depriving us of our own wealth,
> which the King apportioned to us from Whitehall) (§24cd).

Among other invectives against them, Iain Lom has 'na farbhalaich bhreaca' ('the pock-marked foreigners', §24a), an unusual remark which probably intended to hurt to the bone, for the Caimbéalaigh, who comfortably straddled both the Gaelic and the Lowland worlds, went to great literary pains to assert their 'Gaelicness'.[258] An attack on the Caimbéalaigh for a different reason was the one launched by Aonghus mac Alasdair Ruaidh for their part in the 1692 massacre of Glencoe, when Clann Eóin of Glencoe had been 'gan riasladh' ('torn asunder'), their noble blood shed by 'na Duibhnich' ('the Caimbéalaigh').[259]

Poets sometimes seem to present their support for the Stiúbhart monarchs as if it were an exclusively Gaelic concern. The battle of

---

255 *A rìgh 's diombach mi 'n iomairt*, §6ab.
256 *Hei hò! Tha mulad air m' inntinn*, §6g; ID, p. 56.
257 *An diugh chuala mi naidheachd*, § 11e; *A rìgh 's diombach mi 'n iomairt*, §4g. For noble and ignoble animal imagery see McCaughey 1989, pp. 109–19.
258 See below, chapter 4, pp. 119–20, 132–5.
259 *'S mi am shuidhe air a' chnocan*, §§3ab, 6b.

Killiecrankie is portrayed by Aonghus mac Alasdair Ruaidh as a Gaelic confrontation with 'luchd nam machraichean gallda' ('the people of the Lowland plains') and 'luchd nan casagan ruadh' ('the red-cassocked folk').[260] Similarly, when she cites the prophecy of Thomas the Rhymer, Sìleas na Ceapaich is assured 'gur h-iad na Gàidheil a bhuidhneas buaidh' ('that it is the Gaels who will win the victory'),[261] while Iain Lom describes Viscount Dundee addressing the troops before the battle of Killiecrankie as 'A chlanna nan Gàidheal' ('oh kindreds of the Gaels').[262] In this way the poets proudly recorded and publicised the crucial part played by the Gaels in support of the Stiùbhart royal line. Yet they never lost sight of the nationwide character of the conflict: many political poems show an awareness of the interplay of the three kingdoms, Whitehall is specifically noted as the hub of high politics and government, and the king is 'Rìgh Bhreatuinn', he has a claim on 'Breatunn is Eirinn', prayers are said for the return from exile of 'Rìgh Seumas 's an t-éighre-s' a Bhreatuinn' ('King James and his heir to Britain').[263] The part played by royalist Lowlanders is also noted, and their brave loyal leaders are duly praised.[264] As was the case with classical verse, we find only a few isolated allusions to *Alba*: the death of Alasdair Dubh, eleventh chief of Glengarry (†1721/4), was a loss to the whole of *Alba*; the Marquis of Antrim, bringing support to the cause of Charles I, was welcome to *Alba*; Sìleas na Ceapaich, perceiving the Treaty of Union as a serious threat to the Scots, encouraged them to rise united against the English with the words: 'Alba, éiribh còmhla' ('Arise,

---

260 *'S e latha Raon Ruairidh*, §§19a, 23, 35h; see also §§35ab, 37gh. For references to the Lowlanders' form of dress see McCaughey 1989, pp. 105–6; MacInnes 2006c, pp. 40–1.

261 *Dh'innsinn sgeula dhuibh le reusan*, §9d.

262 *Is mithich dhuinn màrsadh as an tìr*, §5b.

263 *An diugh chuala mi naidheachd*, §8a; *'S binn an sgeul so tha 'd ag ràdhainn*, §7efg; *Mi am leabaidh air m'aon taobh*, §3c; *Tha mulad cinnteachd trom air m'inntinn*, §22gh. See also above, pp. 106, 109, and the anonymous *Nach faic sibh, a dhaoine*, §13h.

264 See, for instance, *Mhuire 's muladach a tha mi, Mi ag amharc Srath Chuaiche*, both praising Seoras Gordan, second Marquis of Huntly (†1649); *Soraidh do 'n Ghràmach, Mi gabhail Srath Dhruim-Uachdair*, for Séamas Grám, Marquis of Montrose (†1650); *Sgeul a thàinig an dràsda oirnn*, where John Lyon, fifth Earl of Strathmore and Kinghorne (†1715), is praised at §8; *Is mithich dhuinn màrsadh as an tìr*, where Eóin Grám, Viscount Dundee (†1689), is praised at §§2, 5.

Scotland, as one').[265]

The idiom 'ceannas na nGaoidheal' is absent from vernacular poetry, but the concept itself is found sometimes, albeit in different wording. It appears in Sìleas na Ceapaich's elegy for Séamas Mac Domhnaill, thirteenth chief and sixth baronet Sleat (†1720), as 'ceann mo stuic' ('head of my family').[266] One of Séamas's predecessors, Domhnall (†1695), was styled 'caiptean Chlann Dòmhnaill' by Iain Lom.[267] Leadership of Clann Domhnaill was also claimed several times for Mac Domhnaill of Glengarry in vernacular verse: Iain Lom defended the right of Aonghus Óg (†1680) to 'Iarlachd Rìgh Fionghall' ('the earldom of the King of the Hebrides'); Alasdair Dubh (†1721) was called 'oighre 'n Iarl Ilich' ('heir of the earl of Islay', that is of the lords of the Isles, earls of Ross), 'oighre dleasannach Ile' ('the rightful heir of Islay') and 'oighre dligheach Mhic Dhomhnuill' ('Mac Domhnaill's lawful heir').[268] This debate over the right to succeed to the leadership of Clann Domhnaill was, of course, merely academic, for both the lordship of the Isles and the earldom of Ross had long remained with the crown. For the Mac Domhnaill chiefs, however, the claim had all to do with the prestige attached to lawful descent from the greatest name in medieval Gaelic Scotland; the Sleat historian, for instance, took great pains to prove Mac Domhnaill of Sleat's case, including the thorny question of his natural descent.[269]

The claim to 'baile is leath Alban' emerges several times. In one poem it is mentioned in association with the 1411 Battle of Harlaw, and in another with the 1431 Battle of Inverlochy.[270] In a vernacular lament for Somhairle Mac Domhnaill, killed at the battle of Aughrim (1691), Séamas Dall Mac Cuarta remembers his ancestors:

---

265 *Fhuair mi sgeul moch Di-ciadain*, §5a; *Fàilt' a Mharcuis a dh' Alba*, §§1a, 2a, 5b; *'S binn an sgeul so tha 'd ag ràdhainn*, §5.

266 *Is coma leam fhèin na co-dhiù sin*, §6b.

267 *A bhean, leasaich an stòp dhuinn*, §1e.

268 *Is e mo chion an t-óg meanmnach*, §10c; *Mi 'g éiridh sa mhadainn*, §5c; *Gura fada mi am chadal*, §§1g, 5a.

269 *HP* i, pp. 63–5. Uisdean, ancestor of the house of Sleat, was a natural son of Alasdair, ninth lord of the Isles.

270 *A bhean, leasaich an stòp dhuinn*, §11; *Tapadh leat, a Dhomh'aill mhic Fhionnlaigh*, §14abc; MacInnes 2006d, p. 23.

... de shleachtaibh Mhic Dónaill,
Oidhre na dtalta ó Dhún Breatan go bóchna;
Leith Alban ba ceart dhóibh is Baile tré chróghacht.

(... of the families of Mac Domhnaill,
heirs of the territories from Dunbarton to the sea;
they had a claim on half and a house of Scotland on account of
[their] valour).[271]

The motif appears also in a eulogy for Domhnall Mac Domhnaill of
Sleat, eleventh chief and fourth Baronet Sleat (†1718), and in an elegy for
Alasdair Dubh of Glengarry.[272] All the same, it would seem that all these
allusions (both in classical and vernacular material) were simple recollec-
tions, proud, and perhaps nostalgic. There is no historical evidence that at
any time in our period Clann Domhnaill were in dispute with the Scottish,
or British, kings over their right to half of Scotland; even in the eulogy for
Alasdair mac Colla,[273] which might give a different impression on account
of its strongly Gaelic bias, the wider context is that of the struggle against
the Covenanters on behalf of the king of Britain.

The Red Hand motif, which we have come across in classical poetry,
is attested occasionally in MacDhòmhnaill vernacular verse of a very late
date. In his eulogy for Domhnall Mac Domhnaill of Sleat (†1695), tenth
chief and third Baronet Sleat, Iain Lom noted:

B'e do shuaicheantas taitneach ...
Làmh dhearg roimh na gaisgich nach tìom.

(Your brilliant emblem was ...
a red hand going forth in the van of fearless warriors).[274]

---

271 *Is in Eachroim an áir atáid ina gcónaí*, ll. 143–5. In *Is mairg nár chrean le maitheas
saoghalta* Dáibhí Ó Bruadair uses a similar expression: 'dá ngairminn baile is leath a
ngréithe-sean, | ba deacair 'na measc go mbainfeadh éara dhom' ('If I were to ask for
a village, with half its contents, | I'd find it hard to get a refusal among them', §3cd). I
am indebted to Colm Ó Baoill for these references. For another reference in an Irish
vernacular poem see Ó Murchú 2001, p. 59 n. 5.

272 *Tha ulaidh orm an uamharrachd*, §15e; *Gura fada mi am chadal*, §5ab. For some other
instances see McLeod 2002b, p. 19.

273 See above, pp. 84, 89.

274 *A bhean, leasaich an stòp dhuinn*, §13af.

In the 1715 'Song of the Clans' Iain Dubh mac Iain mhic Ailein praises Clann Domhnaill as

> Luchd sheasamh na còrach
> 'Gam b' òrdugh 'Làmh Dhearg'

> (Defenders of the right
> Whose signal was "Red Hand").[275]

Finally, in terms of plant and animal imagery to describe the patron, vernacular poets adhere to the conventional depictions employed by the classical authors. More interesting is the borrowing of the poet's reference to himself grieving for a deceased patron as Ó Maol Chiaráin had for his son Fearchar. Ó Maol Chiaráin — whose first name is not known — was a poet, apparently Scottish, who may have lived at any time during the fourteenth or fifteenth centuries and who dedicated to his deceased son a poignant elegy in *dán díreach*.[276] The grieving *file* makes a rare appearance in classical panegyric,[277] but the image seems to have captured the imagination of the vernacular poets and it is invoked by Máiri NicDhomhnaill in her elegy for her husband, Domhnall Gorm, *tánaiste* of Glengarry (†1689), and by Iain Dubh in a poem lamenting the deaths of various chiefs of Clann Raghnaill.[278] It was also used, as we will see, by poets composing for other kindreds.[279]

Conclusions

To summarise this chapter, we find two different models in the classical poets' praise of the descendants of Colla Uais. The poetry composed for the main Mac Domhnaill line (the lords of the Isles) and for Clann Eóin Mhóir, whether of Scottish or Irish authorship, presents a model much closer to the traditional Irish one. This includes the employment of motifs such as the high-kingship of Ireland and, closely related to this, prophecy

---

275 *Seo an aimsir 'n do dhearbhadh*, §4ef.
276 *Tugadh oirne easbhuidh mhór.*
277 *Tuar doimheanma dul Raghnaill*, §§32, 41.
278 *Chad d' fhuair mi an-raoir cadal*, §2b; *Gu bheil mulad air m' inntinn*, §12c.
279 See below, chapters 4, p. 180; 5, p. 224.

and the chief as his territory's spouse; these, however, are only attested in poems of Irish authorship. The motif of the struggle against the *Goill* is absent from the poetry for the lords of the Isles (including *A chlanna Chuinn cuimhnichibh*, the only extant vernacular poem of the period), who are at the same time proudly portrayed as belonging to the wider kingdom of Scotland. Moreover, no animosity against the Scottish kings, and no complaint against their treatment of the lords of the Isles — always proud *Albanaigh* — is registered in the extant poetry, or indeed in later Mac Domhnaill verse. In the panegyrics for the members of Clann Eóin Mhóir, whether of Islay or Antrim, the *Goill* do appear sometimes, and they do so in the Irish format of the motif: the foreigners are the English invaders of Ireland. The only exceptions are the two poems for Mac Domhnaill of Colonsay subjects (*Saoth liom do chor, a Cholla* and *Mór mo mholadh ar mhac Colla*, both of Scottish authorship), which are concerned with contemporary Scottish and British politics, and where the *Goill* are the Lowland Scots. In addition, in the compositions for the lords of the Isles historical references are always to the Irish past, while conversely the Antrim branch of Clann Eóin Mhóir regularly append allusions to their Scottish roots. Because we have only two extant poems composed for Mac Dubhghaill nobles it is not possible to establish a pattern in them. At any rate, they lack in *Gall* and prophecy allusions, and they contain one reference to the high-kingship, albeit rather opaque.

The second model is that found in the poetry for cadet Mac Domhnaill branches other than Clann Eóin Mhóir, and can be applied almost entirely to both classical and vernacular verse. In this model there is no mention of the motifs of high-kingship or the spouse-territory: in their use of the traditional poetic conceits validating an individual's fittingness to rule, we find the classical poets changing their emphasis. Their marked tendency is to focus on the warrior, education, character, feasting, hunting, and gaming motifs. But they also rework some of the earlier themes of classical panegyric, and they introduce new ones. The motifs given a new treatment are prophecy and the struggle against the *Goill*, and they often appear closely connected. The *Goill* are now the Scottish Lowlanders, although the English may sometimes be found forming part of the foreign enemy body. Prophecy shows a number of divergences from the conventional motif as normally found in classical panegyric. In the latter various Irish prophets may be invoked; in Scottish Gaelic poetry of the later period there is only one prophet, the Lowland Scot Thomas the Rhymer. The prophecy of classical panegyric concerns one individual who will banish the English; the new prophecy does not relate to any one individual, but to an event: the defeat of the Lowlanders and the Gaelic resurgence in Scotland which, nevertheless, does not aim at a Gaelic takeover of the Scottish kingdom. This type of prophecy is found in vernacular poetry only, and is not a feature of panegyrics for individuals.

The chief new theme of this second model is that of royalism which, like the reworked *Goill* motif, was probably borrowed into classical pan-egyric from vernacular verse. All the extant poems display support of the Stiúbhart cause. Among Catholic poets — which many MacDhòmhnaill authors were — the defence of the true faith is connected with the political struggle, but even Protestant authors appear as supporters of the Stiúbhairt. As well as sharing a number of concerns with contemporary non-Gaelic poets — dynastic continuity, the divine right of kings, rejection of a foreign royal line, and a deep aversion to upstarts in government[280] — all poets portray their support for the right king as a concerted effort which, though including Lowlanders and Englishmen, has the *Gaoidhil* as its pro-tagonists. At the same time the conflict is firmly placed within the wider kingdom of Britain, while allusions to *Alba*, so plentiful in the times of the lords of the Isles, are now negligible. Concern with the theme of political evils as God's punishment for sin is equally rare; in general, and even in the middle of disaster, the poetry reveals persistent hope and optimism that a Stiúbhart king will eventually occupy the British throne once again. The classical poets, although consistently presenting their subjects as loyal supporters of the Stiúbhairt, do not normally openly discuss politics as their vernacular counterparts do; the exceptions are two Colonsay poems and especially Niall Mac Muireadhaigh's *Dá chúis ag milleadh ar meanma*.

Three other new motifs appearing in later Mac Domhnaill poetry, both classical and vernacular, are 'ceannas na nGaoidheal', Clann Domhnaill's claim to 'baile is leath Alban', and the Red Hand. 'Ceannas na nGaoidheal' is mainly a concern of classical poetry; instead, the vernacular poems reflect the actual dispute over the right to succeed to the headship of

---

280 See above, chapter 1, pp. 18–22.

Clann Domhnaill, a theoretical dispute which had no bearing on actual titles or position. The other two new motifs are found in both classical and vernacular compositions. With one exception, none of the three is ever fully developed; they are only given as passing remarks. Neither do they seem to have had any connexion with actual contemporary events as, for instance, the royalism, prophecy, or *Gall* motifs did. The exception is the motif of the Red Hand as it appears in the two poems which Niall Mac Muireadhaigh contributed to the contention over the Red Hand which took place in his time; but even in Niall's poems, the motif is only discussed as part of a literary exercise, and there never seems to have been an actual dispute over the right to bear that emblem among the actual persons variously defended by the participating poets. The Red Hand motif, therefore, remains, like 'ceannas na nGaoidheal' and 'baile is leath Alban', a purely literary convention in Mac Domhnaill poetry.

The fact that we have Clann Domhnaill poetry covering pretty much the whole of the period here considered has allowed us to establish the existence of two clearly differentiated types of poetic rhetoric. These I have called the earlier and the later models, on the basis that more discernible departures from the rhetoric commonly found in poems by Irish authors for Irish subjects are found only in Mac Domhnaill verse composed from the sixteenth century onwards. Yet this classification must not be understood as purely chronological: as we have seen, the two surviving Clann Dubhghaill panegyrics date to the sixteenth century, and Clann Eóin Mhóir poetry is extant from the sixteenth century onwards, but both groups of poems are closer to the model observed in (earlier) poems for the lords of the Isles. The classification here proposed also gives us a framework against which to consider the extant poetry composed for other Scottish kindreds, and even the poems of Scottish authorship addressed to Irish subjects. This is not to suggest that the rest of the poetry of Scotland is, in terms of the panegyric code, in any way indebted to Clann Domhnaill. The classification of Mac Domhnaill verse advanced in this chapter is throughout this book employed as a working tool, not least because it just so happens that, allowing for peculiarities proper to each kindred, the rest of the Scottish poetry, as will be seen, also generally conforms to either one or the other of these models.

Chapter 4

Caimbéal and Mac Leóid:
the descendants of Neimheadh

In properly elucidating the origins of the Gaels, and generally the early history of settlement of Britain, 'The misfortune of our Historians and Criticks lay chiefly in their Ignorance of the Irish Language', wrote an anonymous seventeenth-century historian.[1] A contemporary made a similar complaint, noting that only a few fragments and traditions were extant, in his time, of the genealogical and historical records kept by great Highland families.[2] Both writers were dealing with the difficulty of establishing the origins of Clann Duibhne, the Caimbéal kindred. On this topic there seems to have existed some confusion by the seventeenth century, if not earlier. The two historians just quoted claimed an Irish origin for the Caimbéalaigh, the author of the 'Craignish History' citing the Irish author Seathrún Céitinn as one of his sources.[3] Another Irish historian, An Dubhaltach Mac Firbhisigh, took Mac Cailéin's genealogy, instead, back to the legendary Neimheadh.[4] Mac Firbhisigh reveals, nonetheless, some uncertainty, adding that 'Adeirid sgribhne ele gurob ar lorcc Fhathaidh, [cédna] mic Mec Con, ata Mac Ailín na hAlban' ('Other genealogies say that Mac Ailín of Scotland is descended from Fathadh, first son of Mac Con'), and speculating that the two genealogical claims might be explained by the existence of two separate families of the name Mac Cailéin.[5] Despite Mac Firbhisigh's hesitation, all earlier Gaelic genealogies

1   'Craignish History', p. 189.
2   See above, chapter 2, p. 41.
3   'Craignish History', p. 189. For Céitinn see below, p. 126.
4   *LMG* iii §§1007.2, 1007.4
5   *LMG* iii §1007.45. Fathadh: from Síol Luighdheach meic Íotha of south-west Munster (*ibid.* v, p. xiii). Caimbéal settlement in Ireland is well attested from at least the mid-sixteenth century, in the wake of the clan's involvement in Irish politics; see Campbell 2000–2, ii, 42. It may well be that the claim of descent from Fathadh was that favoured

117

claim for the Caimbéalaigh a British descent, ultimately from Neimheadh.[6] Neimheadh was the leader of a population group that *seanchas* gives as having invaded Ireland previous to the arrivals of the Tuatha Dé Danann and of the *Gaoidhil*. Neimheadh's grandson Briotán Maol settled in *Alba*, which from him came to be called Britain.[7] Gaelic genealogies also claim the Mac Leóid and Mac Neacail families of Scotland to be descendants of Neimheadh. These three kin-groups became fully integrated into Gaelic society, to the extent that they regarded themselves, and were regarded by those of Gaelic ancestry, as *Gaoidhil*. As we will see, however, the political developments of the later part of our period led Clann Duibhne's opponents to portray them as enemies of the *Gaoidhil*. The use of panegyric rhetoric of leadership in poetry composed for both kindreds of Nemedian origin is the subject of this chapter.

Clann Duibhne

Titles and ancestry

If by the seventeenth century there was some confusion concerning the origins of the Caimbéalaigh, little progress has been made by modern historians on the topic. This kindred first appears in the historical record in 1263, by which time they were attached to the Lochawe district in Argyll, also holding lands in Menstrie and Sauchen, in central Scotland.[8] The Caimbéalaigh were, however, incomers in Argyll, evidence suggesting that the Lennox may have been their original homeland.[9] By the mid-thirteenth century they had established marriage links with the Earls of Carrick, who were in turn similarly connected with the High Steward of Scotland and with the Brús family. But it is only in the early fourteenth century that the Caimbéalaigh first appear as powerful territorial lords. From then on they increasingly and steadily expanded their lands and their power and influence, while their loyal support of the Scottish kings was rewarded with important positions of power at the service of the crown. It has been proposed that the deliberate cultivation by the Caimbéalaigh of their crown

---

by these settlers. For Fathadh see also below, p. 126.

6　See 'MS 1467', no. 15, and below, pp. 119–22.

7　*FFÉ* i, p. 184.

8　Sellar 1973, p. 110.

9　*ibid.*, pp. 119–20.

affiliations partly aimed at self-protection against threats in the west, but was also linked with wider justifications of the place of the *Gaoidhil* in the history and in the future of the Scottish kingdom.[10] The Caimbéalaigh were also the first, and the most important, Gaelic kindred to embrace and promote religious Reformation in the sixteenth century: the first printed Gaelic Book, *Foirm na n-Urrnuidheadh* (1567), was a translation by Bishop Seon Carsuel (*c.*1522–1572) of the Book of Common Order, under the patronage of Gilleasbaig Donn, fifth Earl of Argyll.[11] Despite their loyalty to the crown, the Caimbéalaigh were not always on good terms with royal authority: in the sixteenth and seventeenth centuries, six consecutive earls of Argyll were, on charges of varying importance and for periods of varying length, declared rebel, imprisoned, or forfeited, and both the eighth and the ninth earls were executed.[12]

In contrast with the consistently unambiguous Mac Domhnaill genealogical tradition, Caimbéal pedigrees present important variations over time. According to the author of 'Ane Accompt of the Genealogie of the Campbells' the family 'assumed the surname Campbells in the days of Malcolm the third otherwayes called Malcolm Ceanmore, King of Scotland', that is in the eleventh century.[13] The earliest contemporary record, however, belongs to the later thirteenth century. It also identifies the Caimbéalaigh as the descendants of Duibhne, an individual who in all likelihood was historical.[14] Their chief was known as 'Ó Duibhne' or 'Mac Duibhne', and also as 'Mac Cailéin', from Cailéan Mór, who died around 1296. Duibhne in turn is presented in the earlier Gaelic genealogies as descending from one Artúr, who could have lived in the tenth century, and whom later genealogists coupled with the famed British King Arthur. By the mid-sixteenth century, however, Clann Duibhne felt the need to assert their place in the Gaelic world, as is attested in the poetry,[15] and fabricated an extraordinary pedigree which made Neimheadh a descendant

---

10 Boardman 2006, pp. 202–3.

11 *Foirm*, p. ix. For the spelling 'Seon Carsuel' see *ibid.*, p. 1.

12 See, for instance, Campbell 2000–2, ii, pp. 18, 60, 79, 83–5, 142, 272–5; iii, pp. 32–3, 51–52.

13 'Ane Accompt', p. 72.

14 Sellar 1973, p. 111; Boardman 2006, p. 11. For what follows see generally 'Ane Accompt', pp. 74–81; Sellar 1973; Gillies 1976–8; id., 1987.

15 See below, pp. 132–5.

of the ancient Gaoidheal, progenitor of all the Gaels.[16] In the late seven-
teenth century Caimbéal historians additionally claimed their patrons'
descent from William the Conqueror, through the marriage of an early
ancestor, who went to Normandy, to William's niece. This not only sup-
plied a further noble connexion but also explained the origins of the name
Caimbéal: this was said to derive from an original 'de Campo Bello', from
which the French name 'de Beauchamp' also derived. Another late claim
was that of descent from Diarmaid — the warrior who stole Gráinne from
Fionn mac Cumhaill, in whose service he was — who was inserted into
the Caimbéal pedigree as a son of Duibhne. This is a most unusual claim in
two important respects: firstly, Diarmaid was the hero of a romantic tale,
and secondly he was not an independent ruler, but stood in a subordinate
position as the king's guard.[17] These late claims, seemingly stemming from
some Caimbéal historians but never accepted by either the hereditary
seanchaidhe nor the *filidh*, appear sometimes in non-classical poetry from
the seventeenth century onwards, that is from the time of decline of clas-
sical verse.[18]

It has been suggested that these fluctuations in genealogical claims
(British, French, Irish) may have been the product of some 'cultural insta-
bility' on the part of the Caimbéalaigh.[19] Partly, however, their quest for
venerable royal ancestry, like their claims to the headship of the *Gaoidhil*,
stemmed from ideological rivalry, particularly with Clann Domhnaill.[20]
What seems evident is that Clann Duibhne had no clear knowledge of
their true origins. Their historians' complaints of unavailability of records
is mindful, and this may be no coincidence, of that of Dr Hector Maclean's,
who moreover blamed the lack on the poets and chroniclers themselves.[21]
The Mac Gille Eóin family, like the Caimbéalaigh, only came to the fore
relatively late in history.[22] It may well be that during their earlier and more
obscure period these families were not maintaining professional men of

16 *Collectanea*, p. 360.
17 Gillies 1987, pp. 58, 66.
18 id., 1976–8, p. 279; 1987, pp. 62, 66.
19 id., 1987, p. 72.
20 id., 1976–8, p. 283. For the motif of 'the headship of the Gael' in Caimbéal poetry see
below, pp. 132–5.
21 See above, chapter 2, p. 41.
22 See below, chapter 5, p. 209.

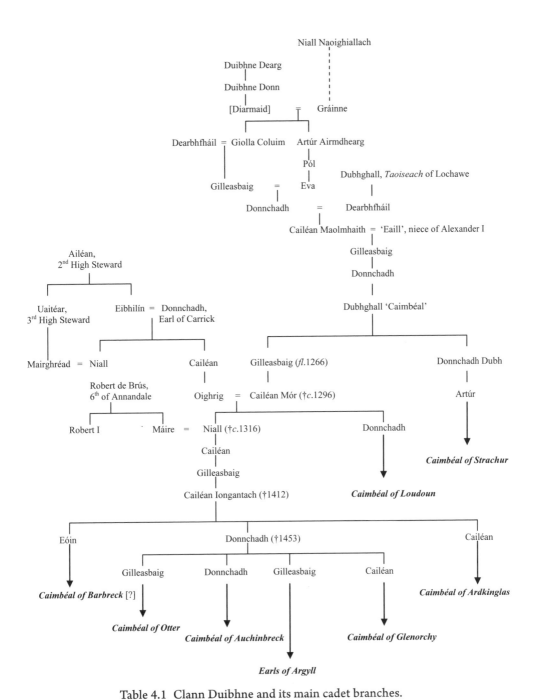

Table 4.1 Clann Duibhne and its main cadet branches.

Sources: 'MS 1467', no. 15 (omits the generations between Gilleasbaig son of Cailéan
Maolmhaith and Gille Coluim brother of Artúr Airmdhearg); Campbell 2000–2, i, pp. 9–42;
Sellar 1973; Boardman 2006. Diarmaid, and therefore the Irish connection, is not given
in 'MS 1467', where the generations between Gilleasbaig son of Cailéan Maolmhaith and
Gilleasbaig son of Gille Coluim are equally lacking.

learning in their service, only beginning to do so once they had acquired some standing and means, by which time no record had been preserved of the families' histories and origins. In connexion with this it may be noted that we have no poetry composed for Clann Duibhne before the early sixteenth century. For seventeenth-century Caimbéal historians the very real decline in Gaelic learning, and even the disinterest in the *Gaoidhil* by the otherwise admired George Buchanan, provided a plausible justification for the lack of information on the early history of their patrons and of other 'great [Gaelic] families, and their actings':[23]

> [Buchanan] gives a short specimen of such a Design in the introduction to his History, but being eager in the pursuit of his Countrey's Glory breaks it off unfinishd, an irreparable loss to posterity.[24]

While these historians made a valid point, the fact remains that Gaelic historical records did survive in Ireland, and in these the theory of Clann Duibhne's Gaelic ancestry cannot easily be disentangled from romantic fiction.

Classical poetry

Sgaoth aos ealadhna fhuinn Breatan
   bíd ag tionól teas is tuaith;
fir an chruinne ad theach ag teachta.

(A swarm of the learned of Britain's Isle gather from south to north; men of the round world come to thy house).[25]

This poetic address to the Marquis of Argyll acknowledges Caimbéal interest in, as well as patronage of, learning beyond the kindred's own hereditary *filidh* and *seanchaidhe*. It may also explain how the work of a sixteenth-century Spanish humanist and historian became available to the author of 'Ane Accompt of the Genealogie of the Campbells'. When

---

23 'Ane Accompt', p. 73.
24 'Craignish History', p. 190.
25 *Triath na nGaoidheal Giolla-Easbuig*, §24abc.

acknowledging his sources the anonymous historian states that these included 'some notes the writer gathered out of Pedro Mexia a Spaniard who writes of the original of diverse nations'.[26] One can only speculate on how this writer came to lay hands on Mexía's work, but the statement does add an international intellectual flavour to the patronage of learning extended by the Caimbéalaigh. Closer to home we find Eóghan Mac Gille Eóin, school master at Kilchenzie, in Kintyre, writing a collection of romantic tales for a Cailéin Caimbéal around 1691, as well as a book containing two metrical glossaries, some seven years later, for a certain Lachlann Caimbéal.[27] Another beneficiary was, as mentioned, Seon Carsuel, who employed his literary talent in response to the fifth Earl of Argyll's wish to promote religious Reformation.[28] Although he had some skills in classical versification (probably learned from the Mac Eóghain poets)[29] and was not averse to use them, Carsuel had little time for the *filidh* and *seanchaidhe* who were also patronised by Argyll and whom he antagonised.[30] His introduction to *Foirm na nUrrnuidheadh*, for instance, included a prefatory note to the reader in which he attacked 'lucht deachtaidh agas sgrīobhtha agas chumhdaigh na Gaoidheilge' ('composers and writers and preservers of Gaelic') for employing themselves in the preservation of 'eachtradha dīmhaoineacha buaidheartha brēgacha saoghalta' ('idle, wicked, false, worldly adventures') about the Tuatha Dé Danann, the sons of Míl, Fionn mac Cumhaill and so on, merely in pursuit of worldly reward.[31] Another, more subtle attack is contained in the little poem which he appended to his introduction where he names the intended readership of his book — generally the *Gaoidhil* of Scotland and Ireland but also, he qualifies:

---

26 'Ane Accompt', p. 96. Pedro Mexía's (*c*.1496–*c*.1552) encyclopaedic miscellany *Silva de Varia Lección* (1540), which became a European best-seller, is probably the work referred to here.

27 TCD 1362 (H.4.21) and TCD 1307 (H.2.12), No. 6, respectively. See Gwynn and Abbott 1921, pp. 85, 199.

28 See above, p. 119.

29 *Foirm*, p. 183.

30 *ibid.*, p. lxxxv. Carsuel's extant classical pieces (all in *óglachas* style) are *Gluais romhad, a leabhráin bhig*, and the religious poem *Seacht saighde atá ar mo thí. A cholann chugat an bás*, also a religious piece, is ascribed to Carsuel in NLI G 427 and in the Fernaig manuscript, but for other ascriptions see *BPD*, under poem first line.

31 *Foirm*, p. 11.

Gach seancha gan seanchus saobh,
    gach fear dáno nár aomh brég.

(Every historian without false history,
    every poet who has not yielded to lies).[32]

Carsuel's intention was, of course, to deflect the reader's attention from temporal matters and focus it on spiritual ones. Yet neither the fifth Earl of Argyll nor his successors for more than a century could be dissuaded from fostering Gaelic culture or from cultivating the prestige attached to the patronage of a hereditary poetic family. The Mac Eóghain family, who seem to have been hereditary genealogists and poets to Clann Dubhghaill at an earlier period,[33] may have enjoyed Caimbéal patronage since the early sixteenth century, and continued to do so until the mid-seventeenth.[34] As a note of interest, the Caimbéalaigh seem to have dispensed with certain privileges customarily bestowed on the *filidh*: while traditionally a chief's poet was entitled to rent-free land, there is evidence that from an early date Caimbéal chiefs were, instead, granting lands to their poets in feu.[35]

We have eight classical poems composed for members of various branches of the Caimbéal family in our period. In most cases it is not possible to ascertain the poet's identity, although in all probability the majority of the extant compositions are the work of Mac Eóghain poets. A number of features of Caimbéal poetry and poetic views of the Caimbéalaigh have been surveyed by William Gillies. Gillies noted that Clann Duibhne were perceived in the Scottish *Gàidhealtachd* simply as an important force in Highland politics until the mid-seventeenth century, when poets began to display a strong anti-Caimbéal feeling in their verse.[36] There was a number of factors leading to animosity against the Caimbéalaigh. This was probably not caused by their steady aggrandisement in itself, but may rather have owed much to the fact that to a very large extent it had taken place

---

32 *Gluais romhad, a leabhráin bhig*, §4ab.

33 *Foirm*, pp. 184–5. For the possible Irish origin of the Mac Eóghain family see *Foirm*, p. 186.

34 For the likelihood of Mac Eóghain poets being in Caimbéal employment by 1506 see MacGregor 2006, p. 56. For the last member of this family employed in a hereditary capacity see below, p. 140.

35 See Matheson 1953–9, pp. 200–1.

36 Gillies 1976–8, pp. 264–73.

at the expense of other clans: Clann Duibhne had benefited from the Mac Domhnaill fall and received royal grants in reward for their support against rebellious subjects generally. Although their holdings were also significantly increased through purchase and marriage, their steady policy of entering into bonds of manrent with other chiefs secured a position of advantage over them.[37] They had also kept Domhnall Dubh, heir to the lordship of the Isles, in their custody for some ten years, contributing to Clann Domhnaill disarray and internal dissension over the lordship's succession, and thus to general unrest. Ill feeling was exacerbated during the wars of the mid-seventeenth century, when Highland rivalries were connected with both the religious and the national political divides.[38] Although it is not apparent from the sources, the Caimbéal appropriation of their neighbours' professional learned families that accompanied their expansion is also likely to have contributed to such ill feeling. The Mac Eóghain poets and the Ó Conchobhair physicians, who were in the service of the earls of Argyll at least by the mid-sixteenth century, had previously been under Mac Dubhghaill patronage; similarly the Mac Pháil genealogists, also originally affiliated to Clann Dubhghaill, came to be attached to the Cawdor and Barbreck Caimbéal cadet branches.[39]

Hostility towards the Caimbéalaigh, nevertheless, is almost entirely confined to the vernacular poets. In the extant classical poetry it is found only once, in the mid-seventeenth century poem *Beid mar do bhádar roimhe*, composed for Raghnall Mac Domhnaill, Marquis of Antrim, at a time when the latter made an unsuccessful attempt to send supplies to Scotland:

> Claoidhfidh rea neart a námhuid
> beid na bhfuigheall fanámhuid
> Duibhnigh ... a ccloinne
> fa bharr doilghe is doghrainne.

> (His [i.e. Raghnall's] might shall overwhelm his foes, remnant of mockery shall they be, clan Campbell ... shall suffer the extreme agony of disaster) (§7).

---

37 Campbell 2000–2, ii, p. 5.
38 Gillies 1976–8, p. 268.
39 Campbell 2000–2, i, pp. 182–3, 186.

Yet the Caimbéalaigh are here simply presented as enemies: there is no insult or personal attack of the sort often found in vernacular poetry.[40]

As noted, the *filidh* ignored Caimbéal claims of French ancestry and of descent from Diarmaid.[41] Instead, they adhered to the Gaelic record, consistently referring to the Artúr in the Caimbéal pedigrees.[42] On account of their descent from this Artúr, Clann Duibhne are portrayed as British: 'd' fhéin Breatuin' ('of the British warrior-band'), 'tú as uaisle don fhuil Bhreatnuigh' ('thou art noblest of British blood').[43] One poet stated Mac Cailéin to be 'd' fhuil Artúir is Béine Briot' ('of the blood of Artúr and of Béinne Briot').[44] The source of this claim may be the same that led Céitinn to argue for an Irish origin of the Caimbéalaigh: 'téid Fathaidh [*sic*] Canann mac Mic Con i n-Albain gur ghabh fearann innte, gonadh da shliocht Mac Cailín go na ghabhlaibh geinealaigh' ('Fathadh Canann son of Mac Con went to Alba, and took possession of lands there, and from his posterity Mac Cailin and the correlative branches of that family have sprung').[45] Fathadh Canann was one of the three sons of Lughaidh Mac Con (*fl.* 250 BC), king of Ireland. Lughaidh's wife was a daughter of Béinne Briot, son of the king of Britain.[46] However, Béinne Briot appears in *Acallamh na Senórach* as father of one Artú(i)r and fighting in Fionn mac Cumhaill's warrior-band, and he also plays a part in other pieces of early Irish literature:[47] thus in our search for Caimbéal origins we are once again drawn into the realm of literary tale. It is perhaps for that reason that Mac Firbhisigh gave the claim to descent from Fathadh Canann only in the second place and without any discussion, stating merely, perhaps apologetically, that 'Ní fil aguinn a ngeneal*aigh* (?) acht a sgriobhadh mar légmuid, no mar adchímid, rér linn fén' ('We only have their genealogies

---

40 See above, chapter 3, p. 108, and below, pp. 147–8, for criticism of the Caimbéalaigh by vernacular poets.

41 See above, p. 120.

42 *Fhuaras rogha na n-óg mbríoghmhor*, §21d; *Maith an chairt ceannas na nGaoidheal*, §§26d, 45a; *Dual ollamh triall le toisg*, §§9d, 10b, 41b; *Mór an bróinsgél bás i Dhuibhne*, §§10a, 11b; *Mó iná ainm Iarrla Gaoidheal*, §6d; *Triath na nGaoidheal Giolla-Easbuig*, §§4b, 8a, 10a, 11-20, 21a, 22a, 23a, 25a.

43 *Maith an chairt ceannas na nGaoidheal*, §5d; *Triath na nGaoidheal Giolla-Easbuig*, §35a.

44 *Maith an chairt ceannas na nGaoidheal*, §16d.

45 FFÉ ii, p. 382.

46 Watson 2004, p. 216.

47 Gillies 1982, pp. 41, 70–1.

to write them as we read, or see, [them] in our own time').[48] Yet no hesitation is apparent in the fifteenth-century Scottish genealogical collection commonly known as 'MS 1467', where Caimbéal lineage is traced back to Artúr son of Iubhar (Uther [Pendragon]).[49] These ancient records — the written word — of the professional men of learning are, states one *filidh*, what contain the unpolluted Caimbéal family history:

> Ag sin duit do dhicheann seanchais,
>> slán croinice chur ar gcúl,
> ó bhéil suadh gan fhágbhál aoinfhir.

> (There thou hast thy history's peak, with warrant of record at its back, from the lips of doctors without one omission).[50]

The panegyric motifs most densely concentrated in Caimbéal poetry are those of the individual praised as a brave and skilled warrior, his nobility, liberality and patronage of learning. Depictions of the subject as the one who can unite his people and as their protector or defender, both important themes in the rhetoric of leadership, are also common. Of Gilleasbaig, the subject of *Maith an chairt ceannas na nGaoidheal* — who may have been the fourth, the fifth or the seventh Earl of Argyll — a poet claimed:

> Ceangluidh sé gan cheilg da chéile
>> curadh-uaisle Innsi Gall.

> (Without deceit he will bind together
> the warrior nobility of the Hebrides) (§44ab).[51]

Donnchadh Dubh Caimbéal (†1631), seventh chief of Glenorchy, was praised as 'táth gach tíre' ('[the] cement of every region') and as the one

---

48 *LMG* iii §1007.2.

49 'MS 1467', no. 15.

50 *Rug eadrain ar iath nAlban*, §34abc. *Slán croinice*: literally 'the warrant of a chronicle', cf. above, chapter 1, pp. 4–5.

51 For the likelihood of this poem's subject being the fourth earl see below, p. 129.

who 'd' fhóir … gach triobh san tír-si' ('… succoured each household in this region').[52] In *Ar sliocht Gaoidheal ó Ghort Gréag*, an incitement poem composed on the eve of the fateful encounter between the Scots and the English at Flodden in 1513,[53] Gilleasbaig, second earl of Argyll, is portrayed as the one who will defend the patrimony of the *Gaoidhil* against *Gall* threat (§§3, 7–9). Another Gilleasbaig, eighth Earl and Marquis of Argyll (†1661), was celebrated as:

> fear cabhra Gaoidheal is Gall …

> Ársaidh ar ccríoch do chosnamh …
>   ar ccrann fosgaidh fíneamhna …

> Fear ar ccoimhéid-ne a ccúirt ríogh …

> … a sgiath sgaoilte,
>   a thriath dhíona an Duibhnaicme.

> (he who helps Gael and Gall … He is a veteran to defend our bounds … he is our sheltering vine… He is our guardian in the king's court … thou wide-spread shield, thou lord that shelterest the race of Duibhne).[54]

Séamas Caimbéal, second chief of Lawers (†1561/2), was depicted, in a poem which probably was a celebration of his gallantry at Flodden, as bravely fighting the *Goill* and as 'díon daoine' ('the protection of men').[55] In *Dual ollamh do thriall le toisg* the seventh earl of Argyll is addressed as 'a liaigh luit bhionn muighe Breagh … a h-ionguire' ('oh physician of the wounding of the melodious plain of Breagha … oh shepherd').[56] Both images of the

---

52 *Mór an bróinsgél bás í Dhuibhne*, §§7c, 8c.

53 This is the traditional interpretation. For an alternative suggestion and dating see Ó Briain 2002, pp. 247–54. Coira 2008b and MacGregor 2010, working from different approaches, favour the earlier view.

54 *Rug eadrain ar iath nAlban*, §§1c, 2ad, 5a, 8cd.

55 *Fhuaras rogha na n-óg mbríoghmhor*, §18a. For this interpretation of the poem see Coira 2008b, pp. 154–8. See also MacGregor 2010, pp. 30–1.

56 §§4, 8cd. See also §§11b, 17ab, 18.

individual praised as the physician who will cure the ills of the land (often the whole island of Ireland) and as the shepherd guarding over it are common in panegyric composed for Irish nobles.[57]

The poetic motifs of submission and of exaction of tax and tribute are not particularly plentiful in poems for other Scottish patrons, including Clann Domhnaill, but they are are fairly frequent in Caimbéal classical verse. The second earl was reminded of his ancestors who had made no submission to foreigners; Donnchadh of Glenorchy submitted to none; the Marquis of Argyll received the submission of all.[58] The Marquis is noted for his capacity to exact *cíos* ('tax'), *cáin* ('tribute'), *comha* ('ransom', 'terms, conditions'), while the subject of *Maith an chairt ceannas na nGaoidheal* obtains 'cíos ó shluagh goirm-greanta Gaoidheal ... cruaidh an chíos ... ar achadh Airt' ('tax from the noble, graceful host of the Gaels ... grievous the tax ... over Art's plain').[59] I am tempted to find in the last of these references a suggestion that the subject of this poem is Gilleasbaig Ruadh, the fourth earl, who in 1555 secured a formal alliance with An Calbhach Ó Domhnaill of Tyrconnell. The terms of this alliance, based on already existing 'caimhnes agas p[h]airt' ('friendship and affection'), included the establishment of Mac Cailéin's superiority over the Irish chief and the latter's payment of tribute to the earl.[60] Although the agreement was renewed by the fifth earl, the generally celebratory tone of *Maith an chairt ceannas na nGaoidheal*, and its three references to tribute, particularly that of 'achadh Airt' (one of the poetic names for Ireland) strongly suggest that this poem was composed *c*.1555, in celebration of fresh Caimbéal progress, this time within the Irish Gaelic milieu. To this panegyric we will return shortly.[61]

While *apalóga* are not common in classical poetry of Scotland,[62] several are given in Caimbéal panegyric. The incitement poem for the second earl of Argyll retells the battle of Magh Tuireadh, by which Lugh put an end

57 See, for instance, *Diomdhach Éire d'fhuil Conuill*, §§5d, 16d, 13d; *Mairg atá tar éis Fhiacha*, §13d; *Mithigh cuairt a gceann Fhiacha*, §7c.

58 *Ar sliocht Gaodhal ó Ghort Gréag*, §18; *Mór an bróinsgél bás í Dhuibhne*, §8b; *Triath na nGaoidheal Giolla-Easbuig*, §§2d, 4a. See also *Fhuaras rogha na n-óg mbríoghmhor*, §23c.

59 *Rug eadrain ar iath nAlban*, §§19a, 20c, 21c; *Maith an chairt ceannas na nGaoidheal*, §§2c, 5b, 8d.

60 Mackechnie 1951; quotation at p. 97.

61 See below, pp. 133–4. For the treaty see also below, p. 145.

62 See above, chapter 3, p. 67.

to Ireland's oppression by Balar, leader of the invading Fómhoraigh: the poet hopes that Gilleasbaig will act likewise and end *Gall* oppression of the *Gaoidhil*.[63] In *Dual ollamh do triall le toisg* there are two *apalóga*. The first recalls the Biblical story in which the raven released by Noah never returned to the Ark; the second relates how Fionn and his warriors could not leave the fairy-palace of Bruigheann Caorthainn, unable to remove their feet from the magic soil of Innis Tile spread in it. The poet uses both stories to illustrate his own supposed inability to return to Ireland, seduced by Mac Cailéin's hospitality.[64] In *Triath na nGaoidheal Giolla-Easbuig* the poet describes the magnificent and hospitable court of King Arthur, with which the Marquis of Argyll's own court favourably compares (§§11–23). Finally, the author of *Mó iná ainm Iarrla Gaoidheal* turns to the Greek classics to compare the Marquis to Philip, father of Alexander the Great, who had had to face his son's envy (§§13–22).[65] Both the Marquis and his son are in fact claimed to excel Philip and Alexander, for the latter were heathens:

> *Fearr* tú iná Filib fuair geall …
> *fearr* t'oighre ná Alasdair …

> Alasdair do Chríost níor chreid
> nó *a* athair *d*arob ainm Filib.

> (You are better than Philip who obtained sovereignty …
> better is your heir than Alexander …

> Neither Alexander nor Philip, his father,
> believed in Christ).[66]

---

63 *Ar sliocht Gaodhal ó Ghort Gréag*, §§4–9. For the story see Stokes (ed.) 1891; Gray (ed.) 1982.

64 *Dual ollamh do triall le toisg*, §§21–9, 38–9; Watson 1914–19, pp. 199–200. For an Irish version of the story see Pearse (ed.) 1908. For a Scottish Gaelic text see *LF*, pp. 86–8. Innis Tile: an island north of Britain, probably mainland Shetland; see Watson 2004, pp. 6, 7, 8, 42–3.

65 In Greek tales it is claimed that as a young man Alexander complained that his father's great deeds would leave him nothing glorious to achieve; see Fox (ed.) 1978, p. 59.

66 *Mó iná ainm Iarrla Gaoidheal*, §§25ad, 26ab.

References to the patron's religion or to his piety are not particularly frequent in Caimbéal poetry. The Marquis is portrayed in a poem as 'triath chothuighthe a ccreidimh ... | go n-ardbhladh n-eaglasda' ('a lord who defends the faith ... | whose fame is high within the Church').[67] The subject's Protestant religion may be suggested by a reference to psalm-reading in an elegy for his slightly earlier contemporary, Donnchadh Dubh of Glenorchy, 'o Duibhne úr salmach súaghach' ('Duibhne's noble descendant who loved psalms and sages').[68] In his Gaelic translation of the Book of Common Order Seon Carsuel included a dedicatory epistle to his patron, the fifth Earl of Argyll which, though in prose, shows heavy influence of classical panegyric and which may be said to depict a new type of Gaelic leader: a promoter of the Reformed religion.[69] Carsuel, however, was not a *file*. The two poetic references to religion come from panegyrics the authorship of which cannot be established. If the authors were, as it is very possible, Mac Eóghain *filidh*, we may indeed be looking at a new development in the language of authority, that is in the rhetoric of leadership. This would be unique to Scotland, for the Irish *filidh* adhered to pre-Reformation religion, certainly at this time, and most of them for a long time afterwards. Carsuel, in fact, was not the only churchman to advocate the centrality of spiritual matters in a nobleman's make-up: John Knox advocated a 'godly nobility', and the role of the 'godly noble' was an important concern of ministers generally.[70] This view is sometimes reflected in poetry in Scots. The radical minister John Davidson celebrated the endeavours of Caimbéal of Kinzeancleuch, a small Ayrshire laird, in support of the Reformed religion:

> ... for the libertie,
> Of Christis Kirk and the Gospell.[71]

---

67 *Rug eadrain ar iath nAlban*, §6b. Ó Mainnín 1999, p. 46, interprets this reference as praise of Argyll as a defender of Reformed religion. This may be correct, but there are no allusions to denominational differences. A similar case is found in the poetry of Tadhg mac Dáire Mhic Bhruaideadha for his Protestant patron, Donnchadh Ó Briain, fourth Earl of Thomond (†1624). Tadhg was a Catholic, and so may deliberately have avoided any reference to religious denomination. Similar omissions are observable in the poetry for the also Protestant Tomás Buitléar, tenth Earl of Ormond (†1614); see Dewar 2006b, pp. 316, 321–2, 335.

68 *Mór an bróinsgél bás í Dhuibhne*, §11c.

69 *Foirm*, pp. 3–10; Meek 1998, pp. 42–3, 44–7, 55.

70 Dawson 1999, p. 211 and nn. 1 and 2, and p. 237.

71 Quoted *ibid.*, p. 222.

It may be, however, that we are reading too much into these references to psalm-reading. Attention to, or delight in, the psalms, while most marked in Clann Duibhne verse, is also attested elsewhere with reference to Gaelic subjects who in fact lived before the Reformation.[72]

But the truly prominent themes in Caimbéal classical panegyric are an insistence on their place in the Gaelic world, their leadership of it, and their role in the affairs of *Alba*. The word *Gaoidheal* — or any of its grammatical variants — is used almost obssessively in many poems, and appears in most.[73] What we have here is not merely the sense of 'Gaelic ambience' generally noted by Gillies in Caimbéal poetry;[74] it is rather as if the Caimbéalaigh felt a need to assert their place in Gaeldom, particularly from the late sixteenth century onwards. It is also from this date that we begin to find the claim of the headship of the *Gaoidhil* in Caimbéal poetry. Clann Duibhne had by then reached considerable standing in Scotland and were certainly the most powerful family in the west. But also with the death of Domhnall Dubh in 1545 the main line of the lords of the Isles had become extinguished; Mac Cailéin now advanced his claim to 'ceannas na nGaoidheal'. The appropriation of 'the headship of the Gaels' for the head of Clann Duibhne, that is for the earls of Argyll, is undoubtedly the boldest gesture in Caimbéal poetry. Such leadership had been in actual fact held by the lords of the Isles, and poetically claimed for various Mac Domhnaill cadet branches subsequent to the 1493 forfeiture of Eóin mac Alasdair.[75] It is around the same date that the poetry for Caimbéal nobles begins to display a clear consciousness of its subjects' increased status, within both the *Gàidhealtachd* and the kingdom of Scots: *Fhuaras rogha na n-óg mbríoghmhor* (*c.*1513)[76] contains several complimentary quatrains for Cailéan, third Earl of Argyll, whom the author styles 'rí fial uasal Gaodhal'

---

72 See *Créad í an long-sa ar Loch Inse*, §13d (where the motif is reversed, as this is a satire; the addressee is unknown), and below, p. 159 and n. 176.

73 *Ar sliocht Gaoidheal ó Ghort Gréag*, §§1ad, 3e, 7b, 10b, 11c, 19b; *Fhuaras rogha na n-óg mbríoghmhor*,§§33b, 35b; *Maith an chairt ceannas na nGaoidheal*, §§1a, 2ac, 3a, 4b, 5c, 7b, 8a, 9b, 16c, 28d, 29a, 41c; *Dual ollamh do triall le toisg*, §§5d, 6b, 12ad, 30d, 33a, 35d, 45b; *Mó iná ainm Iarrla Gaoidheal*, §§1a, 2b, 3a, 8d, 9d, 28ac, 37d; *Triath na nGaoidheal Giolla-Easbuig*, §§1a, 1b, 27b; *Rug eadrain ar iath nAlban*, §1c.

74 Gillies 1976–8, pp. 271–6. For a historian's defence of the sense of 'Gaelicness' of the Caimbéalaigh see Boardman 2006, pp. 158–9, 170.

75 See above, chapter 3, pp. 71, 97–9.

76 For the suggested date of composition see above, p. 128 and n. 55.

('the noble generous king of the Gael', §33b) and 'rí ós ríoghaibh' ('king above kings', §34d). A related rhetorical expression is 'iarla Gaoidheal', first attested, in the same poem, at a time when, subsequent to the forfeiture of the Mac Domhnaill earl of Ross and well before the new creations of the Seaforth and the MacDonnell and Aros earldoms (both seventeenth century), Mac Cailéin was the only Gaelic lord to hold the title of earl.[77] The same idea is expressed by phrases such as 'triath na nGaoidheal', 'codhnach Gaidheal', 'triath na ttalmhansoin thoir' ('lord of this western land').[78] Perhaps most mortifying for Clann Domhnaill was the poetic claim that Mac Cailéin was now in a position to overrun the Hebrides:

> Neart an fhéinnidh ó Ear Ghaoidheal
>   gébhuidh oilén Innsi Gall ...
>
> Gabhuidh leatsa, a mhic Mhic Cailín,
>   curuidh Fionnghall na n-eang sróil.
>
> (The might of the warrior from Argyll shall lay hold of Innse Gall ...
>
> Under thy banner, thou son of MacCailin, will go the heroes of the Isles with satin pennons).[79]

But it is in *Maith an chairt ceannas na nGaoidheal* that the Caimbéal claim to the headship of the *Gaoidhil* is fully developed. Having hinted that whoever holds the headship of the *Gaoidhil* is the receptor of their tribute (§2), the author continues:

> cia gá bfuil ó chóir a gceannas? ...
>
> Giolla-easbuig iarla Ghaoidheal
>   glacuis cairt ceannais an t-sluaigh.

---

77 *Fhuaras rogha na n-óg mbríoghmhor*, §35b. For some later instances see *Maith an chairt ceannas na nGaoidheal*, §§6a, 49c; *Dual ollamh do triall le toisg*, §§33a, 35d; *Triath na nGaoidheal Giolla-Easbuig*, §1b; *Mó iná ainm Iarrla Gaoidheal*, §§1a, 2b, 9d.

78 *Maith an chairt ceannas na nGaoidheal*, §9b; *Triath na nGaoidheal Giolla-Easbuig*, §1a; *Mó iná ainm Iarrla Gaoidheal*, §22c.

79 *Triath na nGaoidheal Giolla-Easbuig*, §§2ab, 36ab. For another instance see above, p. 127.

(Who has their headship by right? ...

Gilleasbaig, Earl of the Gaels, seized the charter of the headship of the people) (§§4c, 6ab).

He immediately proceeds to justify such claim: in the first place, Argyll is head of the *Gaoidhil* 'ó chóir a chartaigh' ('by right of his charter', §6c), a royal charter (§8b). In this he follows in the footsteps of his ancestors, whose own charters had obtained them 'sealbh na nGaoidheal' ('the patrimony of the Gaels', §7ab). This seems to refer to crown grants to the Caimbéalaigh of lands formerly held by the lords of the Isles, and perhaps also to the commissions of lieutenancy received at various times by several Mac Cailéin chiefs. But Argyll's right to 'ceannas na nGaoidheal', and therefore to their tribute,[80] stems also from his role as 'airdbreitheamh ós Albain' ('high law-giver above Scotland', §13a)[81] and his commitment to doing justice (§§13–15, 49), his martial prowess (§3c), his punishment of evil-doers, liberation of the oppressed, binding of the peace (§§14b, 15b, 42ab, 50). His following, which includes Clann Domhnaill, is listed in §§16–24. Finally he possesses 'na trí tréidhe is ferr ag flaith' ('the best three traits in a prince', §51b): the author is using here the legitimising motif of 'tréidhe tighearna' ('lordly traits'), or the qualities required in a chief.[82] For all these reasons, then, Argyll is entitled to 'Ceannas Ghaoidheal mhoighe Monuidh' ('the headship of the Gaels of the Plain of Monadh'), 'Ceannas Ghaoidheal oiléin Alba' ('the headship of the Gaels of the Isles of *Alba*'), 'ceannas gach cinnidh' ('headship of every kindred), 'Ceannas Ghaoidheal maicne Míledh' ('the headship of the Gaels of Míl's children') (§§2a, 3a, 43a). This claim (also variously formulated in the related expressions noted above)[83] is reproduced in three more poems, one for the seventh earl and

---

80 See above, p. 129.

81 The earls of Argyll held the hereditary post of Justice General of Scotland.

82 The motif appears also in *Rug eadrain ar iath nAlban*, §4d (' 's é go mbésuibh mbuan-flatha', 'he has the traits of a lasting prince'), and in *Triath na nGaoidheal Giolla-Easbuig*, §22ab ('Gach béas ríoghdha da raibh ag Artúr, | d' aithris a niú do ní sibh', 'Each royal trait possessed by Arthur thou dost repeat to-day'). This is a common poetic motif; see, for instance, *Do bhriseas bearnaidh ar Bhrian*, §39b; *Diomdhach Éire d'fhuil Conuill*, §11d. It is also found in annalistic and chronicle literature; see, for instance, *AC*, pp. 708–9; *BAR* i §193.

83 See above, p. 133.

two for his son and successor, the Marquis;[84] the latter is in *Rug eadrain ar iath nAlban* complimented as 'a chraobh óir na h-airdríghe' ('thou golden bough of the high-kingship', §25b), a reference, it would seem, to the Marquis's descent from King Arthur. 'Ceannas na nGaoidheal' is ascribed in Caimbéal poetry only to the earls of Argyll, never to any members of the cadet branches of Clann Duibhne.

Despite much celebration of Caimbéal status in the Gaelic milieu, poets give place of honour to their British ancestry. Not only is it Mac Cailéin who 'as uaisle don fhuil Bhreatnuigh' ('[is] noblest of British blood'),[85] but in *Mó iná ainm Iarrla Gaoidheal* his descent from King Arthur is presented as more prestigious than more recently-obtained titles and honours. Of these, the Gaelic 'Mac Cailéin' is given as greater than the non-Gaelic 'Earl of Argyll' (not a unique instance in learned panegyric),[86] while neither title has the standing of 'ríoghshloinneadh d'fhuil Artúir' ('the royal surname of Arthur's blood').[87] The author of *Dual ollamh do triall le toisg* claims moreover that Arthur had held sway in Ireland:

Do bhí a chíos ar Chruachaibh Aoi
's ar Bhóinn 's ar Gháille géasnaoi
    is ar lacht Bhuilleadh sing suthain:
    Cing Ardúir ór fhás[abhair].

(Crucha Aoi [seat of power in Connacht], the Boyne,
the swan-fresh Galey [Co. Sligo],
    the flow of the slender everlasting Boyle [Co. Roscommon]
    were under tribute to King Arthur, from whom you sprang).[88]

The claim of non-Gaelic superiority over the *Gaoidhil* is not really a departure from classical tradition. In his panegyrics a poet was expected to

---

84 *Dual ollamh do triall le toisg*, §§12b, 30d, 33a, 35d; *Mó iná ainm Iarrla Gaoidheal*, §§1a, 2b, 8b, 9d, 28a; *Triath na nGaoidheal Giolla-Easbuig*, §§1a, 1b, 5c.

85 *Triath na nGaoidheal Giolla-Easbuig*, §35a.

86 This poem's first line and its claim of the superiority of Gaelic titles echo *Mó iná iarla ainm Séamais*, composed by Uaithne mac Uilliam Uí Chobhthaigh for Séamas Buitléar, ninth Earl of Ormond (†1546). For some comment see Dewar 2006b, pp. 124–9, especially at p. 127.

87 *Mó iná ainm Iarrla Gaoidheal*, §§1–6 (quotation at §6d).

88 §9; trsl. and inserts McLeod 2004, p. 123.

give the foremost place to his patron — whether *Gaoidheal* or *Gall* — as Gofraidh Fionn Ó Dálaigh (†1387) reminded the offended Muiris Mac Gearailt (†1356), first Earl of Desmond, in a well-known quatrain:

> I ndán na nGall gealltar linn
> Gaoidhil d' ionnarba a hÉirinn;
>> Goill do shraoineadh tar sál sair
>> i ndán na nGaoidheal gealltair.

(In poetry for the English we promise that the Gael shall be banished from Ireland, while in poetry for the Gaels we promise that the English shall be hunted across the sea).[89]

One contrast with Clann Domhnaill panegyric is the relatively frequent presence of the *Gall* motif in Caimbéal verse. It is found in six of the eight extant classical poems, in two instances within the 'Gaoidhil is Goill' motif, a complimentary formula often used to present the subject as superior in general.[90] In *Maith an chairt ceannas na nGaoidheal* it is noted that Mac Cailéin's following is made up of 'gasruidh ghall' ('a *Gall* warrior-band', §16b, *Gall* here almost certainly meaning 'Lowlander') as well as of 'gairg fhir ó chrích ghairbh na nGaoidheal' ('fierce men from the Rough Bounds of the Gaels', §16c). More interesting are the remaining *Gall* references. Both *Ar sliocht Gaoidheal ó Ghort Gréag* and *Fhuaras rogha na n-óg mbríoghmhor* have as their main theme the struggle of the *Gaoidhil* against the *Goill*; Gilleasbaig, second earl of Argyll, and his cousin Séamas of Lawers, subjects of the poems, are portrayed as brave Gaelic warriors capable of keeping the foreigners at bay. As noted, both poems seem to refer to the early sixteenth-century frictions between the Scots and the English.[91] One forceful reason for this interpretation is the use,

---

89 *A Ghearóid, déana mo dháil*, §46; trsl. of this quatrain from *TD* i, p. xlvii.

90 *Triath na nGaoidheal Giolla-Easbuig*, §1c; *Rug eadrain ar iath nAlban*, §1c. It is also possible, however, to interpret in both cases the *Goill* as the Lowlanders (as is the case in the next quotation), among whom Gilleasbaig operated at a very high level on account of the various positions he held as a royal officer. For an Irish example see *Lá dá rabha ós ráith Luimnigh*, §7, where Domhnall Mac Bruaideadha includes *Goill* (here also the descendants of Anglo-Norman settlers) among those attending the inauguration of Conchobhar Ó Briain, third Earl of Thomond (†1580).

91 See above, p. 128 and nn. 53, 55.

in the eulogy for Séamas, of the the words *Danair* and *Dubhghaill* (§§10c, 22b, 16c), both employed to denote the English in classical panegyric of Ireland where, it is well to remember, Scottish *filidh* regularly trained. The *Goill* appear also in *Dual ollamh do thriall le toisg*, a request by Aodh Ruadh Ó Domhnaill's poet for the aid of the seventh Earl of Argyll against the English threat to the Irish:[92]

> táinic mise a Mhic Cailin ...
>> dod t'iarruidh siar tar sean lionn ...
>
> Soitheach gan sdiur Banbha Breagh
>> ó bhuaidhreadh Gall is Gaoidheal ...
>
> A Giolla-easbuig eachtuidh
>> foir ar Bhanbha ...
>
> (I have come, Mac Cailéin,
> to ask you west across the ancient water ...
>
> Breagha's Banbha is a a rudderless vessel
> on account of the trouble of English and Gaels ...
>
> Oh death-dealing Mac Cailéin,
> help Banbha, §§3bd, 6ab, 8ab).

We may note here that, for all their loyal service to the Scottish crown, the Caimbéalaigh had little hesitation in going against it by cultivating, from the times of the fourth earl of Argyll (1529–58) onwards, their links with the Irish by providing them with redshank support. Later earls, moreover, maintained direct connexions with Queen Elizabeth of England; the fifth earl accepted a pension from her, and the seventh felt so confident of

---

92 This poem is sometimes said to have been addressed by an envoy of An Calbhach Ó Domhnaill (†1566) to the fifth Earl of Argyll (see, for instance, Dawson 1988, p. 22 and n. 2; Ó Mainnín 1999, p. 37). Ronald Black, on internal evidence, noted that the addressee is in fact the seventh earl (Black, *Catalogue*, p. 358). Ó Domhnaill would, then, be Aodh Ruadh (†1602), and the context that of the Nine Years' War (1594–1603) between Irish and English.

Elizabeth's dependence on Caimbéal military support that he went as far as blackmailing her when she failed to reward his services.[93]

In the previous chapter we noted how *Alba* figures prominently in the poems composed for the lords of the Isles and for other Mac Domhnaill leaders of the earlier period, yet all but disappears from the second half of the sixteenth century onwards.[94] Here again Caimbéal poetry offers a contrast. Clann Duibhne nobles are consistently firmly placed within the context of *Alba*: to give some examples, the second Earl of Argyll will defend *Alba* against *Gall* attack; Mac Cailéin has a right to the headship of the *Gaoidhil* of *Alba*; he is 'airdbreithemah ós Albain' ('high-justice over Scotland'); the death of Donnchadh Dubh of Glenorchy, a warrior of *Alba*, is a great loss 'do iath Alban' ('to the island of *Alba*'); the seventh earl is 'os cionn Eireann is Alban' ('above Ireland and Scotland'), and has the support of *Alba*; the eighth earl is 'brath ceadala d' iath Alban' ('the expectation of combat of the land of Scotland'), he is 'Eachtair an fhuinn Albanuigh' ('the Hector of the land of Scotland'), his family have no counterpart in *Alba*.[95] Sometimes Scotland is given her poetic name, *Monadh*: Mac Cailéin is at the headship of the *Gaoidhil* of '[Magh] Monuidh' ('the Plain of Monadh'), he is a fruitful branch in '[Magh] Monaidh'.[96] After the union of the Scottish and English crowns the poets, while keeping the *Alba* motif, also ensured that the Caimbéalaigh were given their place in the wider kingdom of Britain: 'óig Breatan' ('Britain's young men') will do the will of the Marquis of Argyll; to his house, as we have seen, rally the learned men of Britain.[97] It was also the Marquis who received an extraordinary compliment from an unknown poet, who addressed him as 'a shearc bhraoinInnsi Breatan' ('oh love[r] of the dewy Isle of Britain').[98] This seems to be the only instance of a Scottish counterpart to the motif which in classical panegyric

---

93 Campbell 2000–2, ii, pp. 26, 122. For Caimbéal participation in Irish politics see generally Hayes-McCoy 1937, especially chapters 3–11.

94 See above, chapter 3, pp. 70–1, 95.

95 *Ar sliocht Gaoidheal ó Ghort Gréag*, §10d; *Maith an chairt ceannas na nGaoidheal*, §§1d, 8a, 13a; *Mór an bróinsgél bás í Dhuibhne*, §§2a, 12c; *Dual ollamh do triall le toisg*, §§14d, 19a; *Triath na nGaoidheal Giolla-Easbuig*, §10c; *Rug eadrain ar iath nAlban*, §3d. For *brath* see below, p. 141 and n. 104.

96 *Maith an chairt ceannas na nGaoidheal*, §2a; *Dual ollamh do triall le toisg*, §41c.

97 *Triath na nGaoidheal Giolla-Easbuig*, §8b, and see above, p. 122.

98 *Mó iná ainm Iarrla Gaoidheal*, §28d.

of Ireland depicts a subject — normally, but not exclusively, Irish[99] — as the spouse of the whole island. It is quite notable that the territory in this case is neither Ireland nor even *Alba*, but the wider British kingdom, the kingdom of Artúr, reputed ancestor of the Caimbéalaigh.

Caimbéal poetry is also interesting in that it does not follow the particular trends found in contemporary Clann Domhnaill verse: there is no marked partiality for the hunting, feasting and music motifs.[100] Additionally, and strange as it may appear in view of the important offices held by the Caimbéalaigh in the service of the crown, the motif of royalism is virtually absent. This is doubtless due to the fact that during the Wars of the Three Kingdoms Clann Duibhne fought on the Covenanters' side, while disagreement on questions of religion would later sour their relationship with the restored Stiúbhart monarchs. All in all, Clann Duibhne classical verse is certainly closer to the Irish model than is Mac Domhnaill poetry, if we except that composed for the lords of the Isles; from the latter, however, the *Gall* motif is absent whereas, as we have seen, it is relatively common in Caimbéal panegyric.[101] This impression of 'Irishness' is further reinforced by allusions to the *athardha* ('patrimony', 'fatherland', *'patria'*). This term became pervasive in classical Irish panegyric of the later sixteenth century, when Ireland was under severe English threat, and remained a frequent theme in early seventeenth-century poetry and prose.[102] In Clann Duibhne poetry it first appears in the early-sixteenth century *Ar sliocht Gaoidheal ó Ghort Gréag*, where the second earl of Argyll is encouraged to imitate the *Gaoidhil* of Ireland in their struggle against the *Goill*:

Is dú éirghe i n-aghaidh Gall ...

Ré Gallaibh adeirim ribh,
sul ghabhadar ar ndúthaigh;
ná léigmíd ar ndúthaigh dhínn ...

---

99   See above, chapter 3, p. 68.

100 See above chapter 3, p. 92.

101 See above, chapter 3, p. 69, and this chapter, pp. 136–7.

102 *Athardha* is, nonetheless, attested much earlier. See, for instance, *A-tá sunn seanchas Mu-Áin*, §9b (mid-thirteenth century); *Beir eolas dúinn, a Dhomhnuill*, §21b (mid-fourteenth century).

ar aithris Gaoidheal mBanbha,
caithris ar ar n-athardha.

(Meet it is to rise against Saxons ... Against Saxons, I say to
you, ere they have taken our country from us; let us not yield
up our native country ... let us, after the pattern of the Gael of
Banbha, watch over our fatherland, §§2a, 3abcef).

Another instance is found in *Rug eadrain ar iath nAlban*, a petition
to the Marquis to restore to the poet his patrimony. The author may well
be Niall Mac Eóghain, the last of the Mac Eóghain hereditary poets and
genealogists who were, according to the author of the 'Craignish History',
displaced by the proliferation of print.[103] The poet states that the Marquis
of Argyll's *ainm* ('title'), *inmhe* ('position') and *athardha* are all greater
even than Cú Chulainn's (§14). The extent of the *athardha* is not specified,
and in *Mó iná ainm Iarrla Gaoidheal* we find a similar ambiguity. In this
poem the author seems to reproach Gilleasbaig, eighth Earl of Argyll, for
not coming out in defence of his patrimony:

roibheag d'*fh*ior an dá ainma
cion d'oiread a atharrdha.

(For the man of the two titles there is too little
regard for the greatness of his heritage, §7cd).

Its extent is immediately given as encompassing the Hebrides:

Tug Giolla Easbuig folt fann
lámh ag ceann*us* fod Fionngha*ll*
coimhleantar don g*h*reim do ghabh
eirr goirmlecn*adh* [?Ghort] Gaoidheal.

(Giolla Easbaig, soft hair,
made an attempt for the headship of the plain of the Hebrides;
it was fulfilled because of the sway he took,
the chariot-fighter of the blue-sloped [?plain] of the *Gaoidhil*') (§8).

---

103 See above, chapter 2, p. 41, and *Foirm*, p. 185.

Here, since 'ceannas na nGaoidheal' is claimed for the same patron, the statement 'cion d'oiread a atharrdha' ('[he has won] the respect of his fatherland', §7d) seems to equate *athardha* with the *Gàidhealtachd*. Yet the poet also states that Argyll is 'bra*th* ceadala d'ia*th* Alba*n*' ('the expectation of battle of the land of Scotland', §10c), and so it may also be possible to understand *athardha* as referring to Scotland. The depiction of the subject as *brath* ('expectation, hope', sometimes *súil* with the same meaning) is, incidentally, common in Irish classical panegyric.[104]

One notable and almost complete absence is that of the motif of prophecy. It appears only once, in the eulogy *Mó iná ainm Iarrla Gaoidheal*, where the anonymous author declares to the eighth Earl of Argyll that 'tú an tí do tharrnguir Ciothruaigh' ('you are the one whom Ciothruadh prophesied', §30b).[105] The allusion is given without a context, embedded within a series of quatrains that compare Gilleasbaig to a number of heroes of the past, Biblical, Gaelic, and from Greek classical tradition. It may therefore be understood as merely complimentary rather than bearing any reference to actual historical circumstances; in any case it is given in the context of conflict in Ireland, not in Scotland. Complimentary comparisons to great figures, Gaelic, Latin and Greek, of the past are relatively frequent in Caimbéal classical verse. On the Gaelic side we have comparisons with Fionn, his grandson Osgar, Fearghus mac Róigh, Cú Chulainn, Conall Cearnach and Lugh Lámhfhada.[106] The heroes from Latin and Greek tradition include Hector of Troy, Alexander the Great and his father, Philip of Macedon, Jason, Aristotle, Pompey, Cato, and Caesar.[107] In addition, in line with the contemporary fashion, the figure of Moses[108] is invoked in *Mó iná ainm Iarrla Gaoidheal* (§30a).

---

104 See, for instance, *Mairidh teine i dteallach Gaoidheal*, §10a; *Maith ré sírleanmhain síol mBriain*, §16c; *Mór cóir cháich ar chrích Laighion*, §36c.

105 For Ciothruadh see above, chapter 3, p. 85 n. 133.

106 *Maith an chairt ceannas na nGaoidheal*, §37; *Rug eadrain ar iath nAlban*, §§2c, 5d, 26a; *Mó iná ainm Iarrla Gaoidheal*,§32d. The 'Fearghus' in *Maith an chairt ceannas na nGaoidheal*, §37c has to be to Fearghus mac Róigh, since the poet is comparing his subject's sword to various famous swords, and their owners, of the Gaelic past. For 'Caladbolg', Fearghus's sword, see MacKillop 1998, pp. 64–5.

107 *Maith an chairt ceannas na nGaoidheal*, §35b; *Mó iná ainm Iarrla Gaoidheal*, §§13–26, 31, 32; *Rug eadrain ar iath nAlban*, §§3d, 4abc, 26b. The name Jason is not given directly; he is referred to as the leader 'a luing airmleabhair Argo' ('in the slender battle-ship Argos', *Mó iná ainm Iarrla Gaoidheal*, §31d).

108 See above, chapter 3, p. 95, and p. 106 for some examples from vernacular verse.

Caimbéal classical verse is also notable in its abundant use of plant, animal and celestial-body imagery. Some examples are: 'gég thoraid' ('fruitful branch'), 'craobh dhoi-leónta' ('undamaged bough'), 'cnú ós crobhuing' ('the cluster's topmost nut'), 'a chaoir fhíona' ('thou wine-berry'), 'ar ccrann fosguidh fíneamhna' ('our sheltering vine'), 'a choillbhile is tiogh toradh' ('thou forest tree thick of fruit'); 'a eó bheóghoine anbhfann' ('thou vigorous salmon dealing mortal wounds'), 'leoghan lonn Locha Fíne' ('fierce lion of Loch Fíne'), 'seabhac luthmhor' ('vigorous hawk'), 'beithir cródha' ('brave bear'), 'Iolar móirmheanmnach' ('great-spirited eagle'); 'luan cneisgheal ághmhor armach' ('a white-skinned weaponed moon of prowess'), 'Tú an ré ghonta *agus* sí slán' ('You are the waning full moon').[109] In its rich use of these three categories of imagery Caimbéal panegyric has one counterpart in Clann Raghnaill verse, and is only surpassed by the poetry composed for Clann Domhnaill of Islay and Antrim. This is another feature that contributes to the overall 'Irishness' of Clann Duibhne poetry. In this context it is also worth noting the use of the motifs in *Maith an chairt ceannas na nGaoidheal* 'ar lorg a s[h]ean' ('on his ancestors' footsteps', §10d) and *mana, séan, tuar* ('an omen', §§29c, 30a, 38c, 47c, 48bd); and the expression 'fuidheall áir' ('survivors of slaughter') as well as the *athroinn* ('new division') *topos* in *Ar sliocht Gaoidheal ó Ghort Gréag* (§§19a, 10d). The last two motifs are sometimes exploited by Irish authors, always in connexion with a sense of threat, actual or perceived, to the *Gaoidhil* (or one particular kindred) or to the integrity of their patrimony.[110]

Vernacular poetry

As established in the second chapter, in this study we include among the vernacular poetry the various types of compositions in loose classical metres by authors who were not fully qualified, and did not fulfil the same role, as *filidh*, and whose work is sometimes known as, among other labels, 'semi-classical'.[111] Within the extant corpus of Caimbéal vernacular

---

109 *Dual ollamh do triall le toisg*, §§16c, 31b; *Triath na nGaoidheal Giolla-Easbuig*, §§3a, 22d; *Triath na nGaoidheal Giolla-Easbuig*, §§2d, 22c; *Ar sliocht Gaoidheal ó Ghort Gréag*, §14d; *Maith an chairt ceannas na nGaoidheal*, §33c (see also §§41b, 46a); *Dual ollamh do triall le toisg*, §§43a, 43b; *Fhuaras rogha na n-óg mbríoghmhor*, §11a; *Mó iná ainm Iarrla Gaoidheal*, §29a. For *gonta* as 'waning' see *DIL* G, 135: 71–5.

110 See, for instance, *Fuath gach fir fuidheall a thuaighe*, §§2d, 3d; *Mairg as bhráighe ar mhacraidh Murbhaigh*, §11d.

111 See above, chapter 2, p. 43.

verse a number of compositions are of this type.[112] As was the case with the classical poems, most of the authors' names are unknown to us. At least some of these poets, in contrast with the *filidh*, seem to have accepted the late Caimbéal claim of descent from Diarmaid. According to Am Bàrd MacShithich, composing around 1642:

> a sliochd Dhiarmaid
>> Mhic Ua Duibhne …
>
> O Dhiarmaid thàinig sibh uile.
>
> (Of the race of Diarmaid,
>> son of Ó Duibhne … From Diarmaid came you all).[113]

Similary the MacDhòmhnaill poet, Ian Dubh mac Iain mhic Ailein, who included Clann Duibhne in his 'Song of the Clans':

> Sann bho Dhiarmaid a shìolaich
>> Pòr lìonmhor nach gann.
>
> (From Diarmad are descended
> The large numerous clan).[114]

French descent, another claim ignored by the *filidh*, again is supported by some vernacular poets. An elegy for Gilleasbaig, ninth Earl of Argyll, notes his 'Fùil Francach is Bret'nach' ('French and British blood'),[115] and a similar claim is made in a poem for Dubhghall Óg Caimbéal of Auchinbreck (†1642), the anonymous author noting that his patron's blood is also 'Sagsonach', 'Spainneach' and 'Lochlannach'.[116] Allusions to

---

112 See especially Gillies 1976–8, p. 261.

113 *Tha sgeul agam dhuibh ri innseadh*, §18cd.

114 *Seo an aimsir 'n do dhearbhadh*, §16gh.

115 *'S truagh m' imtheachd o chùirt Mhic Cailéin*, §7c.

116 *'S uaigneach a-nochd cathair Dhubhghaill*, §4b. The English connexion is through the late claim of descent from William the Conqueror. The Spanish reference is to the ancestor of the Gaels, Míl Easbáinne. The Norwegian link was Dubhghall Óg's mother, Máire, the heiress of Uilliam Mac Leóid who was the ninth chief of Síol Tormoid and died in 1551 (see 'Genealogie of the family of Auchinbreck', *HP* iv, p. 65).

descent from Diarmaid and to French ancestry, however, are rare, indi-
cating perhaps that neither claim was of universal acceptance among the
vernacular poets.

At one level Caimbéal vernacular panegyric can be divided into two
categories: poems which are devoted to general praise, and poems directly
concerned with contemporary politics. Within the first category are found
all the 'semi-classical' panegyrics, that is those composed in loose imita-
tion of the classical style. Here the motifs favoured are generally those
found in classical poetry: the subject is celebrated for his martial prowess,
his generosity, hospitality, patronage of learning, his justice, the protection
of his people, his ability to obtain hostages, and so on.[117] One poet por-
trayed the ninth Earl of Argyll as a defender of the church, though without
any denominational specification; but he also described him as the pro-
moter of 'an creideamh cathardha' ('the civil faith').[118] To the reference to
psalm-reading noted in classical verse[119] we can add a couple more: one
appears in the eulogy 'S truagh m' imtheachd o Chùirt Mhic Cailéin (§§5a,
10a), and another in one of the two extant elegies for Dubhghall Óg of
Auchinbreck.[120]

Despite close Caimbéal involvement with monarch and government,
there is little emphasis on the subject's support for the crown. With the
exceptions of Version A of Triallaidh mi lem dhuanaig ullaimh, which
emphasises the third earl of Argyll's service to the king, and of a poet's
depiction of the ninth earl as 'buachail a chrun' ('the protector of the
crown'),[121] the motif of royalism is, as in Caimbéal classical panegyric,
non-existent. 'Ceannas na nGaoidheal' is not a theme with any of these
amateur gentleman poets, although the fourth and the ninth earls of Argyll
were described as 'rígh Ghaoidheal' and 'ceann-taic nan Gàidheal' ('head-
support of the Gaoidhil') respectively.[122] Caimbéal patronage of learning is

117 See generally Triallaidh mi lem dhuanaig ullaimh (especially [B]), O 's uaigneach a
nochd Clàr Ghiorra, 'S truagh m' imtheachd o chùirt Mhic Cailéin, Tha sgeul agam dhuibh
ri innseadh.

118 Tha sgeul agam dhuibh ri innseadh, §§3ab, 4ab.

119 See above, p. 131.

120 'S uaigneach a-nochd cathair Dhubhghaill, §1d.

121 Is maith mo leaba, is olc mo shuain, §1c. For some comment on the different outlooks
of Versions A and B of Triallaidh milem dhuanaig ullaimh see DnS, pp. 372–5.

122 Triallaidh mi lem dhuanaig ullaimh [A], §1b; Tha sgeul agam dhuibh ri innseadh, §1c.

not only acknowledged, but one poet also commented on the fourth Earl of Argyll 'as a shrewd and competent critic of poetry':[123]

Sgríobh go fiosach fíreólach
    a seanchas is a gcaithréim;
ná beir duan ar mhísheóladh
    go a léigheadh go Mac Cailéin.

(Write expertly, learnedly, their lore and their tuneful works; bring unto MacCailéin no poem lacking artistry to be read).[124]

The subject's capacity to exact tribute is noted in an elegy composed for Dubhghall Óg of Auchinbreck, and in Version B of *Triallaidh mi lem dhuanaig ullaimh*, for Gilleasbaig Ruadh, fourth Earl of Argyll.[125] In the latter poem the author states that the earl has the tribute of '[fir] Alban' (§17a) and, more interestingly, 'cíos Thíre Conaill' (§18a). The latter is a reference to the terms established by the 1555 treaty between Gilleasbaig Ruadh and An Calbhach Ó Domhnaill, lord of Tyrconnell, and renewed by Gilleasbaig Donn, the fifth earl, in 1560.[126] The treaty secured mutual support between Mac Cailéin and Ó Domhnaill but, as noted, its terms established Argyll's superiority: Ó Domhnaill and his descendants were to pay the earl and his posterity the annual amount of 400 Scots merks, 'mur chomhtharrtha umhlacht agas óglachais agas mur chís bhit(h)-bhuain coidhce' ('as a token of submission and service, and as a perpetual tribute').[127]

In terms of imagery, the 'semi-classical' poems resort to plant and animal motifs similar to those found in the classical compositions, but we also find a couple of interesting novel images. One is the comparison of Cailéan, third earl of Argyll, to William Wallace; this is so atypical that

---

123 *SVBDL*, p. xvii.
124 *Duanaire na Sracaire*, §7. Such is the translation of the editor of *SVBDL*. I prefer to interpret 'a seanchas is a gcaithréim' (rendered 'their rants and traditions' in *DnS*, p. 355) as 'their history and their battle-roll', accurately describing one of the principal duties of the court poet: to record his patron's venerable history and martial prowess, both the chief themes of most panegyrics.
125 *O 's uaigneach a nochd Clàr Ghiorra*, §4d; *Triallaidh mi lem dhuanaig ullaimh* [B], §17a.
126 See above, p. 129.
127 Mackechnie 1951, p. 98.

textual authenticity has been called into question.[128] The second is found in the anonymous *Tha sgeul agam dhuibh ri innseadh*, a despondent piece lamenting the execution in 1685 of Gilleasbaig, the ninth earl, whom the poet depicts as crucified like Jesus:

> Roghainn nan Albannach uile ...
>> Is beud a mhilleadh ...
>
> Fhuair an fhuil uasal a ceusadh
>> Mar fhuair Iosa.
>
> (The choice of all Scots ...
> His destruction is an evil deed ...
>
> His noble blood was crucified,
> as Jesus was') (§§6ad, 10ab).

The same poet makes use of the Moses image when he expresses his hope that God will send someone to rescue and lead Clann Duibhne just as He had sent Moses to rescue and lead the children of Israel (§30). Gilleasbaig himself left affairs in the hands of God in the poetic epitaph he composed for himself the night before his execution:

> More by friends' fraud my fall proceeded hath,
> Than foes: though now they thrice decreed my death.
> On my attempt though Providence did frown,
> His oppressed people God at length shall own.
> Another hand by more successful speed,
> Shall raise the remnant, bruise the serpent's head.[129]

The allusion to God's 'oppressed people' is undoubtedly an oblique reference to the story of the Israelites as narrated in the Bible. As for the use of the word 'remnant', it is tempting to see here an echo of the Gaelic *fuidheall* motif, skilfully connected with the Israelite plight.

---

128 *Triallaidh mi lem dhuanaig ullaimh* [A], §21a; see *DnS*, p. 518.
129 Quoted in Campbell 2000–2, iii, p. 53.

Of the strictly vernacular poems — those composed in accentual metres — three are praise pieces which develop very much the same themes and motifs found in the 'semi-classical' group.[130] One of them, Niall MacEalair's *Gur h-e sgeul an Iarl' Aora so*, composed in 1694, is of interest in that it uses the motif of 'deoch slàinte' (drinking the patron's toast, §6c), a theme which is attested already in an early-sixteenth-century Friseal poem and that became more common in the eighteenth century, particularly in Mac Coinnigh verse.[131] But in two other poems we do find direct allusions to, and a view of, contemporary politics.[132] Both are the work of Caimbéal women, the sister and the widow of Donnchadh, second Baronet Auchinbreck, whose Gaelic title was Mac Donnchaidh Ghlinne Faochainn. Donnchadh, son and successor of Dubhgall Óg for whom two elegies are extant,[133] was killed in 1645 at the battle of Inverlochy, where he led the Covenanting army. His sister, Fionnghal, was wife to Eóin Garbh, ninth chief of Coll. She laments the death of her brother and curses her own son, Eachann Ruadh (future ninth chief of Coll), who had fought on the royalist side at the battle.[134] In *Hò, gur mi tha air mo leònadh* Donnchadh's widow laments her husband's death as well as the slaying of other Caimbéalaigh in the same battle, and criticises the Marquis of Argyll for abandoning the field:

> Thug Mac Cailèin Mòr an linn' air,
> 'S leag e 'n sgrìob ud air a chinne!
>
> (Argyll took to the water
> and let that blow fall on his people!) (§4de).

Criticism of the Caimbéalaigh by their own, as in this female poet's case, is uncommon, but the wars of the mid-seventeenth century forced the Highlanders to take sides with one or the other of the contending

---

130 *'S uaigneach a-nochd cathair Dhubhghaill; Is math mo leaba, is olc mo shuain; Gur h-e sgeul an Iarl' Aora so.*

131 See below, chapter 5, pp. 239–40, and chapter 6, p. 277.

132 *Turas mo chreiche thug mi Chola; Hò, gur mi tha air mo leònadh.*

133 *'S uaigneach a-nochd cathair Dhubhghail* land the 'semi-classical' *O 's uaigneach a-nochd Clàr Ghiorra.*

134 *Turas mo chreiche thug mi Chola,* ll. 41–7; GnC, p. 112.

parties, and it is at this time that a strong feeling of antipathy towards Clann Duibhne is first evident among many vernacular poets.[135] One example is Iain Lom's 'N cuala sibh-se an tionndadh duineil. The poet, according to tradition, had been the royalist army's guide through the mountains in 1645, and seems to have witnessed the encounter at Inverlochy.[136] In this piece he celebrates the royalist victory, but also takes the opportunity to launch a vicious attack on the Caimbéalaigh, who fought on the opposing side. Their rout was 'sgeul a b'aite' ('more pleasing news', §7a) to the poet than the royalist victory itself. He describes them as 'Caimbeulaich nam beul sligneach' ('wry-mouthed Campbells'), 'pràbar an duilisg' ('dulse-eating rabble'), their limbs as spó[i]g, iongnan ('paws'), and their dead as manure on the battle-field.[137] Mockery of the Caimbéalaigh for physical blemish is inded common in poetic attacks against them.[138] Additionally, they are portrayed sometimes as not quite belonging among the Gaoidhil, or they are simply left out when listing allies.[139] MacDhòmhnaill poets were particularly antagonistic towards the Caimbéalaigh, but there are instances of similar hostility from other poets.[140] This contrasts with the more positive, earlier view, by which a subject's kinship connexions with Clann Duibhne, for instance, were as celebrated in poetry as were those with other important Gaelic families.[141]

Conclusions

The seventeenth-century Caimbéal historians' complaints of lack of Gaelic records, along with the fact that the earliest extant specimens of Caimbéal poetry coincide with the times of the early earls of Argyll, may indicate that Clann Duibhne only began to patronise Gaelic men of learning from perhaps the early sixteenth century. It is certainly from that time that Caimbéal patronage of poets, as well as of other hereditary Gaelic professional families, is attested. Caimbéal classical panegyric is very much in

---

135 See above, p. 124.
136 *GnC*, p. 106; Cowan 1997, p. 183.
137 *'N cuala sibh-se an tionndadh duineil*, §§7b, 9b, 11c, 19d, 20.
138 Gillies 1976–8, p. 271.
139 *ibid.*, pp. 269–71.
140 *ibid.*, pp. 264–5.
141 *ibid.*, pp. 263–4.

what we called 'the earlier model' in the previous chapter;[142] yet its principal overall feature is its even closer adherence to the Irish model. This is achieved through the poets' employment of most of the stock phrases or motifs found in panegyrics composed for Irish nobles. The depiction of the subject as the protector or defender of his people and territory, an important one in the genre, is frequent in Clann Duibhne verse, as is the *Gall* motif, which is absent from the extant poems for the lords of the Isles, and almost non-existent in those for later members of Clann Domhnaill. In poems dealing with actual contemporary conflict, whether of Scotland or Ireland — *Ar sliocht Gaoidheal ó Ghort Gréag, Fhuaras rogha na n-óg mbríoghmhor*, and *Dual ollamh do thriall le toisg* — the *Goill* are, as in the poetry of Ireland, the English. In the merely celebratory *Maith an chairt ceannas na nGaoidheal* the *Goill* are the Lowland Scots, who are portrayed as making up the subject's following, along with the *Gaoidhil*; this, too, parallels the Irish model, where the individual praised is sometimes presented as leading a composite host of *Gaoidhil* and *Goill*. Again in contrast with later Mac Domhnaill poetry, poets firmly place their subjects within *Alba*, which features prominently in Caimbéal panegyric. Neither do we find in the latter the new trend, distinctly favouring the warrior, education, character, feasting, hunting, and gaming motifs, typical of later Clann Domhnaill verse (and, as will be seen, of later verse composed for other kindreds). While *Alba* is a recurrent theme in the poetry for Clann Duibhne leaders, their place in the wider kingdom of Britain is also noted, sometimes neatly bound together with the claim of the kindred's descent from the British King Arthur. One poet went as far as portraying his Caimbéal subject as the lover of Britain, in which image we seem to find a unique Scottish counterpart to the Irish motif of the individual praised as the suitable spouse of his territory, ultimately the island of Ireland. The 'Irishness' of Clann Duibhne poetry is sometimes reinforced by the employment of the *athardha, fuidheall* and *athroinn* motifs.

All classical poets uphold Clann Duibhne's British origins, the earliest illustrious ancestors named being Artúr and Duibhne. The existence of a historical Duibhne is almost certain, from what can be inferred from documentary evidence. But this evidence stops at the mid-thirteenth

---

142 See above, chapter 3, pp. 112–13, 115.

century, and beyond that nothing can be said with certainty concerning Caimbéal origins and ancestry. Although in *Mó iná ainm Iarrla Gaoidheal* descent from Artúr is presented as paramount, the poetry is almost obsessive in its insistence on the place of Clann Duibhne in the Gaelic world and their leadership of it. The claim to 'ceannas na nGaoidheal' is, as in the case of Clann Domhnaill poetry, purely a literary convention, but its emergence in Clann Duibhne panegyric is connected with Caimbéal advancement, not only as royal officers and as powerful lords within the *Gàidhealtachd* of Scotland, but also as the recipients of tribute from the powerful Ó Domhnaill of Tyrconnell, in the *Gaeltacht* of Ireland. There are two great absentees from Caimbéal classical panegyric. One is the prophecy motif, which makes only one brief and vague appearance, seemingly merely complimentary, and certainly not connected with *Alba*. Royalism is equally absent, despite Caimbéal loyalty to the crown. Yet the absence of the royalism motif may be, quite simply, due to the Caimbéal poetry adherence to the Irish panegyric canon. References to religion are rare; one mention of psalm-reading seems to sanction the patron's Protestant faith, although a taste for psalm-reading is also attested twice concerning individuals who lived before the Reformation, one of whom at least was not a Caimbéal. Finally, it is important to note that in what we have extant of classical verse there is no mockery of the Caimbéalaigh or vicious attacks in the fashion found in vernacular poetry.

Most of the extant Caimbéal vernacular verse belongs to the amateur or 'semi-classical' genre. All authors employ many of the motifs commonly used by their classical counterparts — including references to psalm-reading — with the exception of that of 'ceannas na nGaoidheal'. This may be alluded to in a couple of instances, but failing in both to keep the phraseology. Some of these poets, following in the wake of later Caimbéal historians, upheld Caimbéal descent from Diarmaid and from the French nobility; yet, to judge from the moderate volume of allusions of this type, it would appear that such claims were not of universal acceptance even among the vernacular poets. Again in common with the *filidh*, amateur poets do not engage with the prophecy or royalism motifs. There is virtually no involvement in contemporary politics; this is only found in the only two extant accentual poems, both of which are elegies by bereaved Caimbéal women. They lack, however, the strong political focus found in the work of MacDhòmhnaill poets such as Iain Lom or Sìleas na Ceapaich: we have very little in the way of the Clann Duibhne vernacular poets' view of contemporary social and political conditions. If there were ever Caimbéal poets who discussed concepts of kingship, royal succession, or the suitability of upstarts for government, in the way other Gaelic poets as well as authors throughout Britain did, their work has not survived. The general impression is that the main concern of Caimbéal vernacular poets, like that of Caimbéal *filidh*, was to champion the cause of their patrons within the Gaelic world, their role within the Scottish and later the British kingdoms appearing as of secondary rank.

Clann Leóid

Titles and ancestry

Like the fluctuating Caimbéal genealogies, Mac Leóid pedigrees present some variations in their genealogical claims over time. The kindred's legendary origins, however, are traced in all genealogies back to Neimheadh through his grandson Lach Láidir, brother of Briotán, the reputed ancestor of Clann Duibhne and all the Britons.

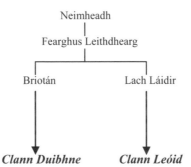

Table 4.2 Caimbéal and Mac Leóid descent from Neimheadh.
Sources: 'MS 1467', no. 15; *Collectanea*, p. 361; *LMG* iii, §§1365.3.

Clann Leóid's eponym was Leód, who lived in the later thirteenth century and whose own ancestry has been the subject of some scholarly debate. David Sellar has convincingly argued the case for Leód's descent from Sean Íomhar na mBreath, or Ivar Gamle, a tenth-century Norse king, through the latter's granddaughter, Helga, or Ealga in Gaelic sources.[143] We

---

143 See Sellar 1997–8, and Table 4.3.

do not have the name of the person she married, but this was certainly a Gael, for it is from this point onwards — with Ealga's son Giolla Muire — that we begin to find Gaelic names in the pedigree. He may have been a descendant of Fearghus mac Eirc: An Dubhaltach Mac Firbhisigh states that 'fós go n-abair nuai-shliocht ele mar so ... an da Mac-Leoid ... ar sliocht Conaire mec Edirsgeoil' ('moreover ... another new recension says as follows ... the two Mac Leóids ... are descended from Conaire s. Eidirscéal').[144] However, his statement has a tone of hesitation, and no such claim — linking Clann Leóid to the Scottish royal line — is to be found in either classical or vernacular verse. It was probably the result of changing fashions as much as a Mac Leóid desire to provide a noble Gaelic connexion for themselves, a desire already patent in the mid-sixteenth century when, like Clann Duibhne, they concocted a pedigree which made Neimheadh himself a descendant of 'Gathelus', though without any link as yet to Síol Conaire: such links would be the common aspiration of many kindreds in the seventeenth century.[145] It is rather Clann Leóid's royal Norse ancestry that is proudly noted in the poetry, despite the fact that the connexion was through the female line. This is not unique to Mac Leóid poetry: for instance, in the previous chapter we noted that Clann Aodha Bhuidhe verse commonly refers to the kindred's ancestor Muircheartach, king of Ireland, as 'mac Earca', Earc being his mother's name.[146] What is unusual is the lack of reference to a royal Gaelic lineage (that is, through agnatic descent) in Mac Leóid panegyric. We must not think that Ealga, the Norse princess, married much below her status and that this would be the reason for such lack. The answer to the puzzle is perhaps to be found in the fact that Clann Leóid remained vassals of the Norse kings until 1266, when the Western Isles were ceded to the king of Scots by the Treaty of Perth: early Mac Leóid chiefs would have naturally celebrated their kinship with their Norse overlord, and this would be preserved in the later poetry. All the same, the silence with respect to noble Gaelic descent remains difficult to explain.

---

144 *LMG* ii, §§411.1–411.2. For the descendants of Conaire see below, chapters 5, pp. 195–243, and 6, pp. 245–60.

145 *Collectanea*, p. 361. See below, chapter 5, pp. 199–200, 226–7; chapter 6, pp. 245, 256.

146 See above, chapter 3, p. 80 and n. 117. Another example is Fearghus mac Róigh, king of Ulster, Róch being his mother's name.

Leód's descendants split into two main branches. Síol Torcuil came to occupy territories in the Isle of Lewis (through marriage to a Mac Neacail heiress),[147] and in Assynt and Coigeach on the mainland. Síol Tormoid originally settled in Harris, although Dunvegan, in Skye, became their main seat, and held land also in the Glenelg peninsula. Although their immediate overlords were the Norse kings of Man and the Isles ('Innse Gall', the Hebrides), and ultimately the kings of Norway, Clann Leóid were briefly (1158–c.1164) the vassals of Somhairle, first Scottish lord of the Isles and Clann Domhnaill's ancestor, after he defeated and ousted his brother-in-law, Godhfhraidh son of Amhlaoibh (†1187).[148] Somhairle's immediate descendants were unable to retain the superiority of their newly-acquired island territories, but both Mac Leóid branches would later come to be vassals of their successors, the powerful Mac Domhnaill chiefs. When the Isles were ceded to the king of Scots in 1266, Lewis and Skye were granted to the Ó Beoláin earls of Ross.[149] In 1337 Eóin mac Aonghuis Óig, seventh lord of the Isles, was confirmed by King Edward Balliol in his territories, including both Skye and Lewis. Seven years later David II, king of Scots, also confirmed Eóin in his holdings, with the exception of Skye, which he regranted to Uilliam, Earl of Ross (†1372). Síol Torcuil, then, became vassals of the lords of the Isles in the mid-fourteenth century. Síol Tormoid would not come under Mac Domhnaill sway until about a century later, when Alasdair, ninth lord of the Isles, was recognised as Earl of Ross.[150]

Leód was also, according to An Dubhaltach Mac Firbhisigh, the ancestor of King Maol Coluim III, whom he gives as a descendant of Bran Beirbhe ('Bran of Bergen'), son of Leód (and therefore brother of Tormod, from whom Clann Leóid) (see Table 4.3). Leód's mother was Lára — 'agus as í táinig a sioth-broghaibh i riocht lára' ('she came from the fairy palaces in the guise of a mare')[151] — whose descent Mac Firbhisigh also traces back to Sean Íomhar, through Maghnus na Loinge Luaithe,

---

147 Matheson 1997–8, p. 324.
148 McDonald 1997, p. 70.
149 Grant 1959, p. 35.
150 ibid., pp. 38–9, 44.
151 LMG iii, §776.2. 'Lára' is the form of the name given by the editor of LMG. The nominative form is 'Láir' (DIL L, 32: 39–40).

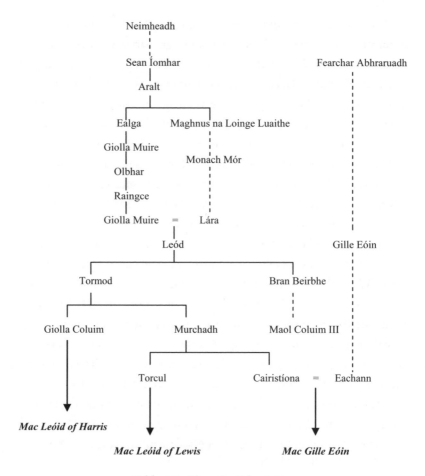

Table 4.3 Clann Leóid origins.
Sources: *LMG* ii, §406.9, iii, §§776.2; Sellar 1997–8.

brother of Ealga. Whatever the accuracy of Mac Firbhisigh's pedigree, it is worth noting that Maol Coluim III indeed had Norse connexions: his mother was a niece of Sigurd, Earl of Northumbria (†1055), perhaps the Sioghraidh named by Mac Firbhisigh.[152] What is interesting here, at any rate, is that one of the descendants of Maghnus na Loinge Luaithe is said to be Monach Mór, 'ó ráitear Dún Monaigh' ('from whom is named Dún

---

152 *LMG* ii, §776.2; iii, §§1365.3 (Síoghraidh in the index); Duncan 2002, p. 37. In an earlier king-list Maol Coluim's mother is called 'Suthen' (Anderson 1980, p. 284), which Duncan 2002, p. 37 says to be a Gaelic name.

Monaigh').[153] The location of Dún Monaidh is a matter for debate. One suggestion is that the term may have simply been used loosely to denote the seat of the Gaelic kings of Scotland;[154] this certainly would make sense if we read 'Dún Monaidh' as 'Monach's Fort' rather than interpret the expression as a purely tographical name. Mac Firbhisigh's records, then, give a Norse ancestry to the royal dynasty of Maol Coluim III through the maternal line, as well as to Clann Leóid, twice on the female side in the case of the latter.

The head of Síol Torcuil was styled Mac Leóid Leódhais ('of Lewis'). The territorial designation of the chief of Síol Tormoid was Mac Leóid na hAradh (or na hEaradh, 'of Harris'); this is also the preferred style in Gaelic sources, whether Irish or Scottish, although in English he is more commonly known as 'of Dunvegan', after the chiefs' main seat in Skye.[155] By the seventeenth century, after the destruction of Mac Leóid of Lewis, the head of Síol Tormoid was often referred to simply as 'Mac Leóid', and even as 'cenn ó Leóid' ('the head of Leód's descendants').[156] Both Mac Leóid branches were loyal supporters of their Mac Domhnaill overlords. Síol Tormoid already appear on their side even before that overlordship was royally confirmed around 1425: in 1411 they fought, along with Síol Torcuil, on the side of the lord of the Isles at the battle of Harlaw.[157] Eóin Borb, sixth chief of Harris and Dunvegan (†c.1442), acknowledged Mac Domhnaill's superiority in Skye, which Domhnall, lord of the Isles, claimed as Earl of Ross:[158] hence Síol Tormoid's allegiance to Clann Domhnaill at this time. But the Mac Leóid chiefs were no mere vassals of Mac Domhnaill: they were members of the Council of the Isles, and appear involved in the election of the lords of the Isles and witnessing a number of

---

153 *LMG* iii, §§776.2, 1365.3.

154 Watson 2004, pp. 394–5.

155 See, for instance, *RC* ii, p. 174; *ARÉ* vi, pp. 1950–1, 1974–5; *BAR* i, §§35, 55.

156 *Do ísligh onóir Gaoidheal*, §28a; see also §31b.

157 Grant 1959, p. 49. For 1425 as the probable date of the confirmation of Alasdair, lord othe Isles, in the earldom of Ross, see Brown 1994, p. 58. For Clann Leóid support of Mac Domhnaill at the two battles of Inverlochy, in 1427 and 1431, see Grant 1959, pp. 49–50. Friction between Síol Tormoid and the lord of the Isles flared up, however, when Eóin mac Alasdair Mhic Domhnaill granted Sleat, as well as lands in Uist, to his brother Uisdean (*ibid.*, p. 51).

158 Grant 1959, p. 47.

their charters.[159] To some, however, Clann Leóid were an upstart kindred who had thrived under the aegis of the later lords of the Isles. If the story related by 'Hugh of Sleat' is true, they were among those insulted at a feast given by Alasdair mac Domhnaill, lord of the Isles, at his mansion in Aros. It was Eóin Mac Domhnaill, tutor of Moydart, who caused them to leave the feast 'in a rage, and very much discontented' by having them, among others, be the last to be seated, stating that they were 'fellows who have raised up their heads of late, and are upstarts, whose pedigree we know not, nor even they themselves'.[160]

As well as adhering to their Mac Domhnaill direct overlords, Clann Leóid supported the crown by their presence, for instance, at Bannockburn in 1314.[161] By at least the later fifteenth century both Mac Leóid lords were participating in other affairs in the Lowlands: they were witnesses of a charter issued in Edinburgh in 1478, and Torcul, sixth chief of Lewis, 'made a great figure in the reigns of James II and III', at which time he may have been knighted.[162] Subsequent to the wane of the lordship of the Isles after 1493, Mac Leóid of Dunvegan passed to hold his estate of the crown. Mac Leóid of Lewis became principal in the protection of Domhnall Dubh, the young Mac Domhnaill heir, and in the struggle for the preservation of the Mac Domhnaill lordship. Torcul, the eighth chief, was forfeited in 1506, when his mainland territories were given to Mac Aoidh, while Lewis was to be let to suitable tenants for five years.[163] It was the beginning of the end of the Mac Leóid of Lewis lordship. Soon after the death of Domhnall Dubh in 1545, those who had been vassals of the lords of the Isles finally gave up in their efforts to restore the old lordship. The Mac Leóid of Lewis estate had been restored to the ninth chief in 1511; but the marriage of his successor, Ruaidhrí, to Seónaid, daughter of Eóin Mac Coinnigh, ninth chief of Kintail, Ruaidhrí's later repudiation of his wife, and his own new marriage, led to a feud with Clann Choinnigh which first gave the latter a foothold in Síol Torcuil's patrimony. In the struggle for the succession

159 *HP* i, pp. 57–8; *Monro*, p. 57; Grant 1959, pp. 50, 51, 74.
160 *HP* i, pp. 45–6.
161 Grant 1959, p. 36.
162 *ibid.*, p. 74.
163 *ibid.*, p. 101.

Torcul Conanach, Ruaidhrí's son by Seónaid, made Mac Coinnigh his heir, handing him over the title deeds. The lord of Kintail moved cunningly, taking advantage of the government's policy of dissolution of Síol Torcuil in order to bring the latter under his own subjection, something which was achieved in the seventeenth century.[164]

Síol Tormoid fared better, although it too underwent a succession crisis in the sixteenth century. This came about when Uilliam, ninth chief (†1551), named his only daughter, Máire, his heiress. Though female succession to the chiefship was not characteristic in traditional Gaelic society, Uilliam's step was not new in the Scottish *Gàidhealtachd*: Cairistíona, only lawful child of Ailéan, chief of Clann Ruaidhrí (†c.1295), was made her father's heiress; in 1346 'Amie' inherited the Clann Ruaidhrí lordship upon the death of her brother Raghnall; Eóghan Mac Dubhghaill of Lorn (†c.1388) left his estate to his two daughters. Two things are worth noting. Firstly, these heiresses never became chiefs: Cairistíona, who married a son of Donnchadh, first Earl of Mar (†1301), left the government of her Garmoran estates to her brother Ruaidhrí; 'Amie' was married to Eóin mac Aonghuis Óig, lord of the Isles, who incorporated the Clann Ruaidhrí estate to his own; and the Clann Dubhghaill patrimony, split between the two heiresses, was added to the Stiúbhart estate by the two sisters' marriages to members of the Stiúbhart family.[165] This brings us to the second point to be noted: the fact that female succession — which was possible under feudal law — tended to lead to the loss of patrimony by the original family. It may be for that reason that the succession of the Dunvegan heiress was contested not only by her father's brothers, but also by a more distant relative, Eóin a' Chúil Bháin, who usurped the chiefship at Uilliam's funeral, while the dead chief's brothers were absent. Both Uilliam's brothers would afterwards successively hold the chiefship of Síol Tormoid, while young Máire, a minor at the time, was removed from the scene and eventually married off to Donnchadh Caimbéal, Captain of Castleweem: she would become the mother of

---

164 *ibid.*, pp. 127–30, 185–96, 201–4, 217–8, 222. For a contemporary account see 'The Ewill Trowbles of the Lewes', in *HP* ii, pp. 265–79. For the fortunes of the kindred in the sixteenth century see MacCoinnich 2008; a fresh perspective on the view in many sources of Síol Torcuil as quarrelsome and blood-thirsty is offered in id. 2006. See also below, chapter 5, p. 229–30.

165 Gregory 1881, pp. 24, 27, 29; Sellar 2000, p. 218.

Dubhghall Óg, first Baronet Auchinbreck, whom we have come across as the subject of two extant panegyrics.[166]

Síol Tormoid, like other kindreds, became a prey to the Caimbéal policy of securing bonds of manrent from their neighbours.[167] One of these was obtained from Tormod, twelfth chief (†1585), in exchange for assistance in acquiring his patrimony; similarly Ruaidhrí Mór, fifteenth chief (†1626), agreed in his own hour of need to become Argyll's vassal for his lands in Glenelg.[168] Ruaidhrí Mór's son and successor, Eóin Mór (†1649), supported religious Reformation and declined to join Montrose's rising (1638) and later the First Bishops' War (1639). In contrast, the seventeenth chief, Ruaidhrí Mear, and his uncles Ruaidhrí of Talisker and Tormod of Berneray (two cadet branches of Síol Tormoid, see Table 4.4) were royalist supporters in the later Wars of the Three Kingdoms, during which they suffered heavy losses. Charles II's lack of gratitude after the Restoration was a disappointment to Síol Tormoid, whose support was permanently lost by the house of Stiúbhart.[169]

Classical poetry

We have about a dozen classical poems composed for members of Clann Leóid; the fact that only one of them is addressed to a member of Síol Torcuil is probably due to the loss of manuscripts and the end of patron-age which necessarily resulted from the decline in the family's fortunes. The earliest extant Mac Leóid panegyric was composed around 1420, the next one in chronological order is from about 1500, and the remainder all belong to the seventeenth and eighteenth centuries. Despite the gaps in the corpus of extant classical verse, the steady patronage of learned classes by Clann Leóid during our period is well attested. The Mac Gille Mhoire hereditary lawmen were established at Ness in Lewis by at least the mid-fourteenth century.[170] A branch of that family, who also went by

---

166 See Grant 1959, pp. 119–24, and above, pp. 143, 144, 145, 147.

167 See above, p. 125.

168 Grant 1959, pp. 133, 205.

169 *ibid.*, pp. 279, 289–306.

170 *BH*, p. 186. They probably were originally placed there by the lords of the Isles (extant evidence suggests that they had a judge 'in every Isle', see Bannerman 1977, p. 227), coming under Mac Leóid patronage after the destruction of the Mac Domhnaill lordship.

the patronymic Mac Muireadhaigh, were *filidh* to Síol Tormoid, for one of its members performed the *file*'s part at the inauguration of Eóin a' Chúil Bháin in 1551.[171] From about 1600 the Ó Muirgheasáin family — who may have previously been in the service of Mac Gille Eóin of Duart — were hereditary *filidh* to the Dunvegan chiefs.[172] They seem to have displaced the Mac Gille Mhoire poets, one of whose descendants, An Clàrsair Dall, was a tenant of Mac Leóid of Dunvegan, as well as an amateur harper and poet in the vernacular language.[173] Some of the Mac Muireadhaigh poets attached to Clann Raghnaill were also the recipients of Mac Leóid patronage.[174] A branch of the Mac Beathadh medical family were hereditary physicians to Mac Leóid of Dunvegan.[175] Alasdair Crotach, eighth chief of Síol Tormoid (†*c*.1547), 'had several harpers and Seanachies', and apparently translated a number of psalms into Gaelic.[176] He also distinguished himself by fostering piping; this musical tradition, which reached its peak in the early seventeenth century, had its main representatives in the Mac Cruimein hereditary family, who enjoyed Mac Leóid patronage and to whom members of other piping families went to complete their training.[177] In the later period, in changing times, Síol Tormoid extended their patronage of learning beyond the Gaelic milieu: Eóin Mór donated 100 merks to the University of Glasgow building fund, and later in the century three university students were assisted financially by Eóin Breac and Ruaidhrí Óg.[178]

The remote ancestors regularly recalled by the classical poets are the family's eponym, Leód, and his ancestor Olbhar, Ealga's grandson.[179]

---

171 Grant 1959, p. 121.

172 Matheson 1978, p. 24; McLeod 2004, p. 73.

173 Grant 1959, p. 370; *BH*, pp. 186–7.

174 *Sé h-oidhche dhamhsa san Dún* is the work of Niall Mór Mac Muireadhaigh, *Do ísligh onóir Gaoidheal* that of Cathal Mac Muireadhaigh, and Eóin Óg Ó Muirgheasáin is the author of *Creach Gaoidheal i reilig Rois*. Donnchadh Ó Muirgheasáin may have been the author of *Ar ttriall bhus ésguidh go Uilleam*, and *Do thuirn aoibhneas Innsi Gall* may have been composed by either Niall Mac Muireadhaigh (*RC* ii, p. 264) or an Ó Muirgheasáin author (McLeod 2004, p. 31 n. 47).

175 Grant 1959, p. 242.

176 *ibid.*, pp. 98, 164.

177 *ibid.*, pp. 244–5, 375–6.

178 *ibid.*, pp. 242, 359, 364.

179 See, for instance, *Sé h-oidhche dhamhsa san Dún*, §4a; *Do ísligh onóir Gaoidheal*, §§8a, 29a; *Creach Gaoidheal i reilig Rois*, §§3d, 4c, 33c, 46d, 47b; *Dual freasdal ar feirg flatha*,

There is also one reference to a Maghnus 'omhúr manúin*n*' ('from the castle of Man'),[180] probably Maghnus na Loinge Luaithe, who lived in the ninth century, or perhaps his father 'Magnus Aircin' ('Maghnus of Orkney'), or his son Maghnus Óg. The same individual is recalled in vernacular poetry.[181] The Norse connexion is further made through place-name references. Torcul, eighth chief of Lewis (who became Domhnall Dubh's main supporter and was forfeited in 1506) is said to be 'ó Charraig Bhoirbhe' ('from the Rock of Bergen'), Tormod of Berneray is 'Maighre ar dshroth na beirbe' ('A salmon of Bergen's noble line'), the city which replaced Trondheim as the Norse royal seat in 1217.[182] The latter's death is lamented 'ar fud laochruighe Lochl*uinn*' ('among Lochlainn's heroes').[183] In *Do ísligh onóir Gaoidheal* Cathal Mac Muireadhaigh laments the death of 'leóghuin Langa' ('the lion of Langa', §41a), Eóin Mór Mac Leóid.[184] Additionally, local territorial references are also common: 'rí Leódhuis' ('king of Lewis)', 'ríoghraidh Sgí' ('the royal line of Skye'), 'Ursa chothuighthe chláir Sgí' ('The supporting pillar of the land of Skye'), 'mil Mighinis' ('the warrior of Minginish'), 'fear finnEilge' ('the lord of fair Glenelg'), 'Fir dar chóir ceannas Chláir Sgí' ('Men to whom the headship of the plain of Skye rightly belonged').[185] Geographical references are nevertheless significantly inferior in number to the allusions to royal Norse descent.

We have noted already how there is, inexplicably, no mention at all of ancient noble Gaelic ancestry of Clann Leóid in classical verse. Yet the poets made their subjects' place within the Gaelic milieu very plain in their work. An elegy for Tormod of Berneray notes 'cru Do*m*nuill In*n*si Fion gall' ('the blood of Domhnall of the Hebrides', that is Domhnall mac

---

§§7a, 10a, 19a; *Mór a n-ainm a n-iath eile*, §§6b, 10a; *Ar ttriall bhus ésguidh go Uilliam*, §§5c, 23a; *Do thuirn aoibhneas Innsi Gall* §§7a, 42a; *Cubhuidh ttriall ar air tturus*, §§3a, 6d, 11b.

180 *Do thuirn aoibhneas Innsi Gall*, §30b.

181 Skene 1876–80, iii, p. 461. For this identification see *BG*, p. 315. Table 4.3, following *LMG*, gives Maghnus na Loinge Luaithe as son of Aralt, but for interevening generations see *Collectanea*, p. 361.

182 *Fhuaras mac mar an t-athair*, §7a; *Do thuirn aoibhneas Innsi Gall*, §33a.

183 *Do thuirn aoibhneas Innsi Gall*, §§30b, 33d.

184 For Langa as a Norse reference see Watson (ed.) 1940, p. 179.

185 *Fhuaras mac mar an t-athair*, §6d; *Creach Gaoidheal i reilig Rois*, §7a; *Do ísligh onóir Gaoidheal*, §10a; *Dual freasdal ar feirg flatha*, §§15b, 17d; *Mór a n-ainm a n-iath eile*, §3a.

Eóin, lord of the Isles) and 'Clann Giolleoin' (Clann Ghille Eóin) among the kinsmen and allies mourning the death of Tormod of Berneray.[186] Eóin Breac is 'éan goile ag Gaoidhealaibh' ('the wounding-bird of the Gaels'); Ruaidhrí Mór is presented as the leader of 'fóir Ghaoidheal' ('the troops of the Gaels'), and his death is said to be 'Creach Gaoidheal' ('the despoiling of the Gaels'); Cathal Mac Muireadhaigh similarly portrays the Gaoidhil as deprived of a leader following Eóin Mór's death in 1649.[187] Cathal's elegy is interesting in that it keeps up with contemporary rhetorical trends of panegyric composed for Irish chiefs, trends found also in Irish chronicle and annalistic writing. It shares much, for instance, with *Teasda Éire san Easbáinn*, Fearghal Óg Mac an Bhaird's elegy for Aodh Ruadh Ó Domhnaill (+1602), with Domhnall mac Eóghain Uí Dhálaigh's *San Sbáinn do toirneadh Teamhair*, for Domhnall Ó Súilleabháin Béara (+1618), and with Tadhg mac Dáire Mhic Bhruaideadha's *Eascar Gaoidheal éag aoinfhir*, for Donnchadh Ó Briain, fourth Earl of Thomond (+1624): all of these have in common a particular emphasis on the loss of honour to the Gaoidhil, their diminished strength, the certain takeover by foreigners, the end of peace and prosperity of the Gaoidhil.[188] More Irish flavour is added in Cathal's elegy by the use of the word *athardha*: Clann Leóid have been deprived of 'díon dob fherr 'gá n-athardha' ('the best defence of their fatherland', §9d). Yet, as in Caimbéal classical verse (with the exception of *Ar sliocht Gaoidheal ó Ghort Gréag*),[189] it is unclear exactly whether *athardha* is meant to be the Scottish Gàidhealtachd (Eóin Mór's death is represented to be a severe blow to the Gaoidhil) or rather Scotland ('iath nAlban'), all of which, the poet claims, is sorrowful on account of Eóin Mór's death (§32a). Another instance of *athardha* is

---

186 *Do thuirn aoibhneas Innsi Gall*, §§28–29. The Mac Domhnaill connexion is through the female line: Tormod's mother was a daughter of Mac Domhnaill of Sleat (*GSMM*, p. 126), and therefore a descendant of Uisdean, illegitimate son of Alasdair, lord of the Isles and Earl of Ross, and grandson of Domhnall mac Eóin, the individual referred to here. For the same connexion in vernacular verse see below, p. 170. Tormod's grandmother was Síleas, daughter of Eachann Mór MacGille Eóin; see Pine (ed.) 1952, p. 1656.

187 *Dual freasdal ar feirg flatha*, §20b; *Creach Gaoidheal i reilig Rois*, §§1a, 2d; *Do ísligh onóir Gaoidheal*, §§1cd, 5, 6.

188 *Do ísligh onóir Gaoidheal*, §§1–7. For an example of this style of rhetoric in historical writing see *BAR* i §188; *ARÉ* vi, pp. 2296–8.

189 See above, pp. 139–41.

found in an eulogy for Uilliam of Luskintyre, son of Tormod of Bernera. The unknown author speaks of the fittingness of visiting Uilliam in the north, the poet's own *athardha*. The word seems here to merely indicate the poet's native land.[190]

Sometimes Clann Leóid are also connected with the Gaelic environment through the subject's comparison to great Gaelic heroes of the past, although these references are less plentiful than one would expect. Torcul, eighth chief of Lewis, is compared to Guaire, his horse to Cú Chulainn's and Conall Cearnach's horses; the death of Eóin Mór, sixteenth chief of Dunvegan, causes grief comparable to that caused by the death of Cormac mac Airt; the sorrow for the passing of Tormod of Berneray (†1706) is like the sorrow after the deaths of Conn and Conaire.[191] If this type of reference is scarce, there is a complete lack of allusions to classical Latin or Greek heroes. Neither the paucity of references to heroes from *seanchas* nor the lack of comparisons to those from continental classical traditions can be supposed to reflect lack of education, Gaelic or otherwise, in Clann Leóid nobles. Families who maintained hereditary poetic families had direct access to education, part of which at least they received from their *filidh*.[192] Whatever else a chief's library contained, as late as the early eighteenth century that of Mac Leóid of Dunvegan included a number of Gaelic manuscripts.[193] If the author of the 'Bannatyne Manuscript' is to be believed in his statement that Alasdair Crotach translated Biblical psalms into Gaelic, then this chief was fluent in Latin. Later chiefs are known to have attended university,[194] a requirement for entry to which again was Latin fluency. As for Biblical references, an *apalóg* is given in *Do ísligh onóir Gaoidheal* (§§33–8) to equate the sorrow felt after Eóin Mór's death with the Flood, while in *Do thuirn aoibhneas Innsi Gall* (§§19–20) the affliction of the Hebrides after Tormod of Berneray's passing is like 'Maoith na baibhioloine ambroid' ('The weeping of Babylon in bondage', §19a).

---

190 *Cubhuidh ttriall ar air tturus*, §1.

191 *Fhuaras mac mar an t-athair*, §§4d, 10ab, 11a; *Do ísligh onóir Gaoidheal*, §27; *Do thuirn aoibhneas Innsi Gall*, §§21, 30a. There is a third reference to Guaire in *Ar ttriall bhus ésguidh go Uilliam*, §16c.

192 See above, chapter 2, pp. 37–8.

193 Grant 1959, p. 371.

194 *ibid.*, pp. 240–1, 249, 364.

In matters of common praise terms Mac Leóid classical verse differs from both Mac Domhnaill and Caimbéal poetry. The motifs found in most dense concentration are those of the individual's royal blood and fame, followed by his beauty, character qualities and martial prowess.[195] There is no marked partiality for the motifs favoured in later Clann Domhnaill panegyric (although feasting and hospitality are more abundant in pieces for the Berneray chiefs),[196] and no necessity to assert Clann Leóid's place on the Gaelic scene, as we found to be characteristic of Caimbéal poems.[197] Mac Leóid patronage of learning, and particularly of poetry, is frequently noted in extant panegyrics for members of both the Dunvegan and Berneray houses, although perhaps no more than is the norm in the genre.[198]*Alba*, while found a few times, receives no particular emphasis: Eóin Mór is 'coillbhile ós Chlár Monaidh' ('the hazel-tree above the Plain of Scotland'); his death is mourned by nature: 'do sgé minnlinnte Monuidh' ('Monadh's clear lakes have belched forth'); it is a blow to '[N] a Gaoidhilsi fhóid Alban' ('These Gaels of Alba's land'); it is bewailed by 'slógh oilén na hAlban' ('the folk of Alba's islands'),[199] and also:

... tar iath caithfhréimhe Cuinn ...

Tuirsi Eóin fá iath nAlban,
brón nach éidir d'iomardadh;
    mar tá ag Gaoidhealaibh 'na ghoimh
    atá ag saoirfheruibh Sagsan.

---

195 An interesting martial prowess allusion is found in the Caimbéal eulogy *Maith a chairt ceannas na nGaoidheal*, at §22a: 'Fine Leóid na mbratach mbodhbha' ('Leóid's race of the warlike [or deadly] banners'), a phrase best known from the first line of the only extant Mac Gille Eóin panegyric, rather a fragment (for which see below, chapter 5, pp. 213–14); if my suggested dating for *Maith a chairt ceannas na nGaoidheal* is correct (see above, p. 129), the two pieces would be contemporary with each other, and one of the two would echo the other.

196 *Rug an fheibhe a terme as teach*, §§1a, 9d; *Ar ttriall bhus ésguidh go Uilliam*, §§1cd, 2, 8b; *Do thuirn aoibhneas Innsi Gall*, §§3abc, 4, 27.

197 See above, pp. 119, 132–5.

198 *Creach Gaoidheal i reilig Rois*, §§3b, 10cd, 44cd, 47a, 48ab, 52ab, 53ab, 54; *Do íslgh onóir Gaoidheal*, §§4cd, 38a; *Do thuirn aoibhneas Innsi Gall*, §§34–37; *Rug an fheibhe a terme as teach*, §§15b, 16a; *Ar ttriall bhus ésguidh go Uilliam*, §§9, 24.

199 *Dual freasdal ar feirg flatha*, §9c; *Do íslgh onóir Gaoidheal*, §§6a, 27d, 41d.

(... beyond the region of the warrior-stock of Conn ...
Sorrow for Eóin covers the land of Alba, grief that cannot be
surmounted; as among the Gael it is an anguish, even so is it
among the Saxon nobles).[200]

The anonymous author of *Mór a n-ainm a n-iath eile* states that the deaths
of Eóin Breac (†1693) and his son, Ruaidhrí Óg (†1699), had filled with
sorrow 'Fir Alban o muir go muir' ('the men of Scotland from sea to sea',
§6a), causing 'Alba ar gach taoibh' ('Alba everywhere', §7b) to be in dis-
tress. Clann Leóid's grief, and generally that of the Hebrides, after the
passing away of Tormod Mac Leóid of Berneray surpasses that of 'slogh
oile dalbannchuibh' ('any other Scottish host'), is felt by the whole of 'Fine
Conaire' ('Conaire's descendants', that is the majority of the Scots).[201]
Britain is even less of a concern in Clann Leóid poetry, with one solitary
appearance where Cathal Mac Muireadhaigh claims that the death of Eóin
Mór was lamented by the *Gaoidhil* 'fá iath braoininnsi Breatan' ('through
the land of Britain's dewy island').[202] Indeed the geographical references
are mostly to 'Innse Gall', sometimes to *Fionnghall*.[203]

The *Gall* motif is similarly exceptional. Eóin Breac and Ruaidhrí Óg
were claimed to be:

slata 's a ngráin ag Gall*uibh*
gan bhaig o eachtrannuibh.

(champions, hated by *Goill*
and having no affection from foreigners).[204]

There is no reason to suspect here any actual connexion with contem-
porary affairs. This is an isolated statement in the middle of many other
ordinary praise motifs, and therefore as a mere motif (that of the subject
as capable of keeping strangers at bay) must it be taken. The same is to be

200 *Do ísligh onóir Gaoidheal*, §§31c, 32.
201 *Do thuirn aoibhneas Innsi Gall*, §§1, 2d (quotation), 3, 16ab (see also §8b); *Creach Gaoidheal i reilig Rois*, §21c.
202 *Do ísligh onóir Gaoidheal*, §4d.
203 See, for instance, *Rug an fheibhe a terme as teach*, §§7ab, 9d; *Do thuirn aoibhneas Innsi Gall*, §§1a, 2a, 16b, 20a; *Creach Gaoidheal i reilig Rois*, §§24c, 38b, 55d, 65a.
204 *Mór a n-ainm a n-iath eile*, §9c.

said of the statement, in another poem, that after Eóin Mór's death the *Gaoidhil* are without a protector and 'umhal d'f[h]oirinn allmharrdha' ('subject to a foreign people').[205] Finally, the *Goill* appear in the complimentary set expression 'Gaoidhil is Goill' in an elegy where it is stated that after the death of Tormod of Berneray there is no one left to challenge either *Gaoidheal* or *Gall*.[206] Equally conspicuous by their absence are the prophecy and royalism motifs, which the *filidh* left entirely out of their work despite Clann Leóid's loyal service to the crown in the seventeenth-century wars. There is little involvement with the religious question, and certainly no reference to denominational politics. Tormod of Berneray was said to have been 'aoinfhear go seacht subhailcibh' ('a man who had the Seven Virtues'), and his death to be lamented by 'lucht eagluise' ('churchmen'); Eóin Mór surely was in Heaven, since he was 'gan fhios uilc nó iomarbhuis' ('knowing no evil or transgression').[207] There seems to be a hint of characteristic early seventeenth-century Providentialism (presenting contemporary evils as a consequence of sin)[208] in Cathal Mac Muireadhaigh's elegy for Ruaidhrí Mór of Dunvegan when, in the middle of his description of the usual devastating consequences following a chief's death, he then states:

> Mór is éigean d'aiseag uainn
> aithreach an t-éigeart 'gat fhéin.

> (We must make much restitution; your soldiers repent of the wrongs inflicted).[209]

A little later in the poem, in the section where he gives Ruaidhrí Mór's *caithréim*, Cathal seems to be struck by the sudden and ominous thought that Mac Leóid's death may have come about in punishment for his reiving career in Ireland:

---

205 *Do ísligh onóir Gaoidheal*, §5b.
206 *Do thuirn aoibhneas Innsi Gall*, §10c. This expression also appears in *Cubhuidh ttriall ar air tturus* (§5c), but unfortunately most of the quatrain is illegible.
207 *Rug an fheibhe a terme as teach*, §3d; *Do ísligh onóir Gaoidheal*, §46b; *Do thuirn aoibhneas Innsi Gall*, §26b.
208 See above, chapter 3, p. 106 and n. 245.
209 *Do ísligh onóir Gaoidheal*, §25ab.

Tús dá fhoghlaidh i n-iath Ír,

  — ná ba foghlaidh Dia 'na dhiaidh —

do bhíodh ós cách in gach céim.

(He began his career of reiving in Ireland — May it not be that God's vengeance follows thereon — He was leader in every foray).[210]

Mac Leóid poetry contains a number of motifs which, though appearing perhaps only once or twice, are interesting in that they show the persistence of the ancient praise rhetoric of the *filidh* at a time when already traditional society was much changed. The 'lordly traits' motif is used by Cathal Mac Muireadhaigh in his elegy for Eóin Mór: 'do lenadh d'airrdhibh airdríogh' ('he followed the attributes of high-kings').[211] The *fuidheall* ('remnant') motif is employed in *Do thuirn aoibhneas Innsi Gall*, when after the death of Tormod of Berneray the poet notes in shock that Mac Leóid chiefships are of short duration, the clan leaders being too quickly snatched by death which is, alas, not even by combat: what is left now is but 'Fuiglech áir aicmha olbhuir' ('The remnant of the slaughter of Olbhar's race', §10a). One would almost have expected the poet to connect with the contemporary Providentialist approach, and blame this condition on general sinfulness; but here again involvement in social or religious matters is shunned. There are two instances of the word *muirn*, generally meaning 'affection' but also denoting the special affection owed contractually by the patron to his poet.[212] It is possible that this is what was invoked by the author of *Do thuirn aoibhneas Innsi Gall* when he recalled 'a méd muirne' ('so much affection', §25c) he had received from Tormod Mac Leóid of Berneray, and by Eóin Óg Ó Muirgheasáin's similar remark on 'Mo ramhuirn-se ó ríoghraidh Sgí' ('The great tenderness I received from the lords of Skye').[213] Another recollection of the *file's* customary privileges, this time his right to share his patron's bed, is found in *Dual freasdal ar feirg flatha*, a warning poem by an anonymous author whose skills had been mocked by Eóin Breac, his sons and other relatives:

---

210 *ibid.*, §40abc.

211 *ibid.*, §28b.

212 See Breatnach 1983, pp. 44–5.

213 *Creach Gaoidheal i reilig Rois*, §7a.

Nó má thogras ó nOlbhair
mo chogadh mar chomhairle
   ciodh má nobainn luighe leis
   más obair dhuine dhílis.

(Or, if Olbhar's descendant's
chosen counsel is to fight me,
what if I decline to lie with him,
[even] if that is the duty of a loyal man?) (§10).

The poet's favourite threat is, as ever, to stop singing the offending patron's praise, and therefore to deprive him of everlasting fame: he needs neither lance nor gun for this fight (§19) — a reminder of the dreadful power of the words from the mouth of an antagonised *file*.[214] This is an example of the self-confidence and arrogance of the Scottish *filidh* even by the late seventeenth century when, despite the increasing decline in patronage of classical poets, they still felt able to threaten with satire.

Vernacular poetry

We have about twice as many vernacular poems composed for Clann Leóid as we have classical ones, and we have also most of the names of the authors, who all lived between the mid-seventeenth century and the early to mid-eighteenth. Two were MacGhilleathain poets: Fionnghal nighean Alasdair Ruaidh, and Iain mac Ailein mhic Iain mhic Eoghain. We have two poems by Lachlann mac Theàrlaich Òig, a MacFhionghuin poet, and various pieces by authors bearing the surname MacLeòid: Pòl Crùbach, Fear Chontalaich (whose given name was Iain), NicGhillechaluim and Màiri nighean Alasdair Ruaidh. There is also Ruairidh MacGhillemhoire, or MacMhuireadhaigh, known as An Clàrsair Dall ('The Blind Harper'), a descendant of the previous family of *filidh* to Mac Leóid of Dunvegan, a harper and amateur *bàrd* who was temporarily attached to Eóin Breac's court.[215] There is even an eulogy sent by an Irish poet to the head of

---

214 For the same idea see the threat of satire to Eóin Stiúbhart of Garth, below, chapter 6, p. 271.

215 See above, p. 159 and n. 173.

Dunvegan.[216] Most of the extant vernacular poems were composed for the Dunvegan chiefs, and a number of them for heads of the Berneray and Talisker cadet branches of Síol Tormoid. There is no extant vernacular poetry for the main branch of Síol Torcuil in our period, although three pieces have survived which were composed for a chief of one of its cadet branches, often known as Mac Leóid of Raasay, but whose Gaelic patronymic was Mac Gille Choluim. Of Raasay, and neighbouring Rona, Archdeacon Monro wrote in the mid-sixteenth century that they belonged 'to Mᶜgillichallum of Raarsay be the sword, and ... to the Bischop of the Iles in heretage', an expression strongly reminiscent of the Gaelic 'cairt chloidhimh' ('charter by the sword') and 'cairt chinnidh' ('the race's charter-land') which are one common topic of classical verse.[217] In 1611, when there was no hope of restoring the Lewis chiefship, Mac Gille Choluim became vassal of Mac Coinnigh of Kintail.[218]

By far the most densely concentrated motifs in Mac Leóid vernacular poetry (all of which is accentual, with no extant 'semi-classical' instances) are those of the patron's generosity, hospitality, fame, patronage of poets, and lavish feasting. Prominent is also the depiction of the subject as a brave warrior, but as a whole the extant vernacular verse is principally concerned with the celebration of social life in the Mac Leóid court as sponsored by its chiefs. The picture is one of merry entertainment: hunting, drinking, gaming, music, dance, song, storytelling, are the treat of guests, among whom are of course the poets themselves.[219] The poets also celebrate their subjects' physical beauty and character qualities and their ownership of fine boats.[220]

---

216 *A theachtaire téid i ccéin go talamh Mhic Leóid.*

217 *Monro*, p. 70. For an example of the use of both terms see *Fada ó Ultaibh a n-oidhre*, §18.

218 Grant 1959, p. 258.

219 *Gur muladach thà mi*, §§2, 3, 7–11, 15ab, 16abc; *An naidheachd so an dé*, §§5b, 8bcdef; *Is mi am shuidhe air an tulaich*, §§12efgh, 13–14; *Is i so iorram na truaighe*, §8e; *Mo chràdhghal bhochd*, §§14a, 18; *Mo bheud is mo chràdh*, §§3abd, 4; *Tha do mhìolchoin air iallain*, §7; *Soraidh no dhá le dùrachd uam*, §5a; *Tha móran móran mulaid*, §4gh; *Théid mi le m'dheoin*, §§10a, 16ab, 10b, 12b; *Cha sùrd cadail*, §§8d, 11–12; *Ri fuaim an taibh*, §§2a, 6b.

220 *Théid mi le m'dheoin*, §§5c, 13–15; *Soraidh no dhá le dùrachd uam*, §3cd; *Chasùrd cadail*, §§4cd, 5h, 7d, 9af, 13; *Gur muladach thà mi*, §§5c, 6c; *Is i so iorram na truaighe*, §§8b, 10h; *Tha móran móran mulaid*, §4f; *Mo chràdhghal bhochd*, §4a; *Is mi am shuidhe air an tulaich*, §§3, 6cd, 8c, 9abcd, 14efgh; *Ri fuaim an taibh*, §§11, 12abc, 15d, 16c, 17c; *Mo bheud is mo chràdh*, §§2bcd, 5bcd, 6cd.

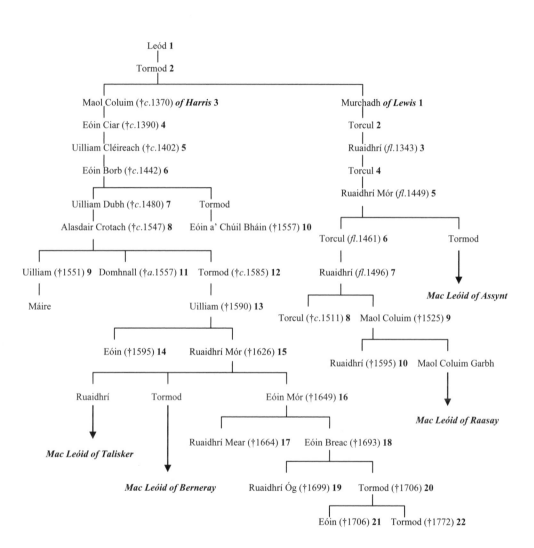

Table 4.4 Clann Leóid and its main branches.
Sources: Grant 1959; Matheson 1978–80a and 1978–80b; Sellar 1997–8; MacCoinnich 2008.

Noble descent from the ancient kings of Norway is also an important
theme in Mac Leóid vernacular poetry: Clann Leóid are of 'fuil nan rìghrean
mòr … | fuil chlann rìgh á Lochlann' ('the blood of the great kings … | the
blood of the descendants of the king from Lochlainn'), 'De shloinneadh
nan rìghrean | Leis na chìosaicheadh Manainn' ('from a line of kings who
laid Man under tribute'), 'Lochlannaich threun' ('mighty *Lochlannaich*),
'O bhaile na Boirbhe' ('from the city of Bergen').[221] Leód, Olbhar (Olghar
in the vernacular language) and Maghnus are the only ancient noble ances-
tors noted, aside from Torcul and Tormod, the eponyms of the two main
branches of Clann Leóid.[222] Máiri nighean Alasdair Ruaidh also refers to
Ruaidhrí Mear as from 'sliochd … Ochraidh', a reference which remains
obscure.[223] Like the classical authors, the *bàird* make no reference to ancient
Gaelic noble ancestors of Clann Leóid; however, they do note their kinship
connexions with, and their friends and allies among, contemporary Gaelic
families. Màiri nighean Alasdair Ruaidh noted Mac Leóid of Dunvegan's
descent from 'Iarla Ìle 7 Rois' ('the earl of Islay and of Ross'), his kinship
with 'sìol Cholla … Bho chóigeamh Chonnacht' ('the race of Colla …
from the province of Connacht');[224] an unknown poet noted Ruaidhrí
Mór's kinship with the Mac Gille Eóin, Caimbéal of Auchinbreck, Mac
Domhnaill of Islay and Mac Néill of Barra families;[225] NicGhillechaluim,
in her lament for Eóin Garbh, sixth chief of Raasay (†1671), named 'Iarla
Cheann Tàile' ('the Earl of Kintail', that is Coinneach Mór Mac Coinnich,
third Earl of Seaforth and Mac Gille Choluim's overlord) as one of those

---

221 *Soraidh no dhà le dùrachd bhuam*, §§5d, 6a; *Ri fuaim an taibh*, §23a; *Gur e an naid-
heachd so fhuair mi*, §§11gh, 12cd. See also *Is mi am shuidhe air an tulaich*, §4cd.

222 See, for instance, *Thèid mi le m'dheoin*, §§6a, 9a; *Gur e an naidheachd so fhuair mi*,
§12b; *Ri fuaim an taibh*, §23c; *Cha sùrd cadail*, §13a; *Shìl Olaghair gun ainnis*, §1a;
Seall a-mach an e an latha e, l. 9.

223 One Eachraidh is mentioned as a leader of one of the pre-Gaelic population groups
in Ireland; see *LMG* i §49.2. Perhaps this line should read 'sliochd Olghair Ochraich',
instead of 'sliochd Olghair is Ochraidh'? 'Ochrach' is attested as associating an indi-
vidual with a place-name (Ochair in the nominative singular). The place-name Echar
(Echuir) is attested between the rivers Suir and Barrow (*Onomasticon, s.vv.* 'ochrach'
and 'echar').

224 *Gur e an naidheachd so fhuair mi*, §12gh; *Cha sùrd cadail*, 15b. For the kinship connex-
ion see above, p. 161 n. 186. For the Connacht origin of Clann Domhnaill see above,
chapter 3, p. 64 and n. 53.

225 *Soraidh no dhà le dùrachd bhuam*, §§6c, 7d, 9c, 10c.

mourning her subject's death.[226] Additionally, in a eulogy for Tormod Mac Leóid of Berneray, Màiri nighean Alasdair Ruaidh celebrated her patron's connexions 'ris gach Iarla tha an Albainn, | Is ri h-uaislean na h-Eireann' ('with every earl that is in Scotland, and with the nobles of Ireland').[227]

In general, Mac Leóid vernacular poetry, like its classical counterpart, remains very localised. Place-name references, which however are not particularly plentiful, are to Skye and Harris and specific locations in them, such as Dunvegan, Aros or Ullinish.[228] Exceptionally, Pòl Crùbach described the death of Eóin Mór as a great ebbing-tide coming on 'fir Innse Gall' ('the men of the Hebrides').[229] Allusions to *Alba* are rare. One is found in NicGhillechaluim's elegy for her brother Eóin Garbh of Raasay:

> Cha'n 'eil ait' ann an Alba
> Nach cual' ainm air do spionnadh.

> (There is no place in Scotland
> that has not heard the fame of your mettle).[230]

To Màiri nighean Alasdair Ruaidh, Eóin Garbh was 'Albannach treun' ('a mighty man of Alba'), and Tormod, future twentieth chief of Dunvegan, excelled in wisdom 'gach Ridir bha an Albainn' ('every one of Scotland's knights').[231]

The *Goill* appear occasionally. The formulaic 'Gaoidhil is Goill' is borrowed in *Ri fuaim an taimh* (§22ab), in praise of Tormod of Berneray:

> Slàn Ghàidheil no Ghoill
> Gun d'fhuaras oirbh foill.

> (Gael or *Gall* I defy to show that deceit was found in you).

---

226 *Seall a-mach an e an latha e*, l. 16; *GnC*, p. 150.

227 *Is mi am shuidhe air an tulaich*, §4efg.

228 *Is muladach mi, hì ó*, ll. 11, 33; *Théid mi le m'dheoin*, §§12a, 16a; *A' cheud Di-luain de'n ràithe*, §5ch; *Tha mulad, tha mulad*, §7fg; *A Choinnnich, cuiream le chéile*, §8a.

229 *Is i so iorram na truaighe*, §7ab.

230 *Tha do mhìolchoin air iallain*, §3ab.

231 *Mo bheud is mo chràdh*, §4d; *Is mi am shuidhe air an tulaich*, §5f.

In a poem addressed perhaps to the same Tormod while he was in exile in France[232] in the late 1650s, Màiri nighean Alasdair Ruaidh expressed her concern for his friends and followers:

> Iad a thachairt gun cheann
> Fo chasaibh nan Gall.

(they are without a leader under the *Goill*'s foot).[233]

The *Goill* here are no doubt the English, for this was the time of the Cromwellian occupation of Scotland. Yet some twenty years later An Clàrsair Dall used the same word to indicate the Scottish Lowlanders, and presented Eóin Breac's place among them as an honourable achievement:

> ach thu bhith faoilidh ann,
>   on fhuair mi gu h-ùr éibhinn thu
> 'n Dùn-éideann a measg Ghall.

(you were, truth to tell, open-hearted in your station, since I found you in Edinburgh, youthful and genial, among southron strangers).[234]

Ruairidh Dall again referred to the *Goill* — otherwise 'luchd cleòc' ('the cassocked-folk') — to denote the Lowlanders[235] in *Miad a' mhulaid tha'm thadhal*, but this time to criticise Eóin Breac's successor, Ruaidhrí Óg, for his absenteeism from Dunvegan and for his adoption of an expensive Lowland lifestyle:

---

232 *An naidheachd so an dé*, §22f.

233 *ibid.*, §22c. The editor of *GSMM* takes the subject of this poem to be Tormod, future twentieth chief of Dunvegan (†1706) (*GSMM*, pp. 127–8). Yet this stanza clearly places the subject in exile in France (see previous note), where Tormod and others, having been excepted from Cromwell's 1655 pardons, joined Charles II. The evidence for either position remains contradictory and unresolved, as discussed in the forthcoming revised edition of *GSMM* by Colm Ó Baoill, to whom I am grateful for allowing me a sneak preview.

234 *Tha móran móran mulaid*, §2efgh.

235 For similar idiom in Mac Domhnaill vernacular verse see above, chapter 3, p. 109 and n. 260.

Chan fhaca mi féin bho thùs
    ri fad mo chuimhne-sa riamh
gun taighteir, gun triath an Dùn ...

... [Tha Mac Leòid]
    ann an daor chùirt nan Gall ...

miad an déidh air cùirt Ghall cha sguir.

(from the beginning, in the whole of my recollection, I never saw [Dunvegan] Castle a useless stance without tutor or lord ...

[... Mac Leóid is] leading an expensive life at court among southron strangers ...

their fondness for court life among southron strangers is unabated) (§§13fgh, 16e, 17d).

We noted Màiri nighean Alasdair Ruaidh's mention of Tormod of Berneray's exile in France. Màiri's work contains some more specific references to contemporary politics. In *Ri fuaim an taibh* (§21) she celebrated Tormod of Berneray's loyal service to King Charles:

Bha fios có sìbh
Ann an iomartas rìgh,
An uair bu mhuladach strì Theàrlaich.

(All knew what you were in the conflicts of a king, when the wars of Charles were vexing us).

She also commented on the injustice committed in her time against some members of Clann Leóid, whose support of King Charles had eventually resulted in their exile:

Gur rò bheag a shaoil mi
    Ri mo shaoghal gun éisd'mid,

Gun cluinneamaid Leòdaich
   Bhith 'gam fògradh á'n oighreachd,
Is á'n còraichean glana
   Is á'm fearainn gun déidh air.

(How little I ever dreamed that in my lifetime we should hear
of the MacLeods' exile from their heritage and from their clear
rights, and that against their will).[236]

A MacGhilleathain poet, Iain mac Ailein, also noted the royalism of
Domhnall Mac Leóid, third chief of Talisker (†c.1743), who in the early
eighteenth century was living in exile at the French court on account of
his affection 'do rìgh Tearlach'.[237] But it is in the work of An Clàrsair Dall
that we find a louder and more extended treatment of current political
affairs, in the style of MacDhòmhnaill poets such as Iain Lom or Sìleas na
Ceapaich. In 1689 Ruairidh Dall composed a poem in which he attacked
those who had forsaken 'an rìgh dleasdanach' ('their rightful king'),
condemned political lies, and expressed his hope that James VII would
return to his country, ''s a dh'èighear e 'na chòir' ('and is proclaimed in his
heritage').[238] Like other Gaelic poets and in common with other authors
from the wider British kingdom,[239] he attacked the upstarts who were
subverting the traditional values:

an chomunn chealgach mhasgalach
bhuail bas air bharr na h-uails'.

(the deceitful, fawning clique whose palms struck a blow at
nobility in the highest place).[240]

He similarly took up the theme of 'cuibhle 'n fhortain' ('the wheel of
fortune'), warning those who currently had the upper hand that it would
eventually turn, and that their certain fate was to be:

---

236 *Gur e an naidheachd so fhuair mi*, §8abcdef.
237 *Air sgiath na maidne as luaithe*, §4mnop.
238 *Sèid na builg sin, ghille, dhomh*, §§3–6, 10b, 12cd.
239 See above, chapter 1, pp. 18–21, chapter 3, p. 114, and below, chapter 5, pp. 218, 235.
240 *Sèid na builg sin, ghille, dhomh*, §12cd.

... nan cùis ghàire
do na Gàidhealaibh 's glan beus.

(a laughing stock to Gaels of true principle).[241]

With his depiction of the *Gaoidhil* as the eventual victors Ruairidh
Dall subscribes to the vision of other poets of royalism as a fundamentally
Gaelic affair within the wider British kingdom.[242] However, neither the
motif of prophecy nor that of Moses, both commonly associated with
that of royalism, is found among the vernacular poets composing for Mac
Leóid chiefs.

An Clàrsair Dall's outspoken political poetry may well have prompted
his dismissal by Eóin Breac from Dunvegan, where he had been admit-
ted, though not officially appointed either harper or *bàrd*, by a special
arrangement with that chief. Eóin Breac had remained neutral during
the events usually called 'the Glorious Revolution' and, perhaps finding
Ruairidh Dall's political poems an embarrassment, he sent him over to
the mainland, giving him a farm in his Glenelg estate.[243] On this account
he was criticised by the poet,[244] while there is little doubt that the latter's
condemnation of the absenteeism and extravagance of Ruaidhrí Óg, Eóin
Breac's son and successor, was at least partly fuelled by the disappoint-
ment and helplessness of his own fallen state. Ruairidh Dall seems further
affronted by the aggrandisement of Mac Leóid's personal servant, who
now behaves like an upstart:

glé stràiceil air each 's e triall —
    is co ard e 'na bheachd
ris an àrmann a chleachd bhi fial;
    cha ghlacar leis crann,
cas-chaibe 'na làimh cha b'fhiach,
    's e cho spaideal ri diùc,
ged bha athair ri bùrach riamh.

---

241 *ibid.* §§7a, 15ab.
242 See above, chapter 3, p. 108.
243 *BH*, pp. xlviii–xlix, lviii–lix.
244 *A' cheud Di-luain de'n ràithe*, §5.

(very much the grand gentleman as he sets off on horseback, of as high degree to his own mind as the chief who made a practice of liberality. He will not touch a plough, while a spade in his hand would be beneath his dignity. The man is as elegant as a duke, though his father laboured the soil all his days).[245]

An Clàrsair Dall's criticism of social upstarts is similar to the criticism of poet upstarts by the anonymous author of *Námha an cheird nach taithighthear*. In both cases the individuals attacked are reminded of the baseness of their status: they were born to labour the soil, the occupation of a churl.[246]

References to the subject's devoutness or protection of the church are negligible in Clann Leòid vernacular poetry — one is contained in *Air sgiath na maidne as luaithe* (§21), an eulogy for Domhnall mac Eóin, third chief of Talisker — and there is no involvement with denominational issues. What we do find is a concern by various late seventeenth- and early eighteenth-century poets with the decline of Gaelic ways, and particularly of poetic patronage. An Clàrsair Dall's unusually strong admonition to Ruaidhrí Óg, nineteenth chief of Dunvegan, to 'lean an dùthchas bu chathair' ('follow the tradition that was a birthright') certainly placed much emphasis on the liberality of the young chief's ancestors.[247] In the poem where Ruairidh Dall severely criticised the same chief for his adoption of Lowland ways and for being absent from his patrimony, he depicted Dunvegan as glum and dejected:

> Tha Mac-alla fo ghruaim
> anns an talla 'm biodh fuaim a' cheòil
>   'n ionad tathaich nan cliar,
>   gun aighear, gun mhiadh, gun phòit ...
>   gun chuirm, gun phailteas ri dàimh.

(Echo is dejected in the hall where music was wont to sound, in the place resorted to by poet-bands, now without mirth, or

---

245 *Miad a' mhulaid tha 'm thadhal*, §26.
246 See Appendix 1. For the scorn of the noble class for manual work see MacInnes 2006d, pp. 27–8.
247 *Tha mulad, tha mulad*, §§18–23 (quotation at §22c).

pleasure, or drinking ... without feasting, without liberality to men of learning).[248]

The poet was of course exaggerating — resentful of his dismissal from Dunvegan — for poetic patronage of the Ó Muirgheasáin *filidh* by Mac Leóid of Dunvegan remained uninterrupted for at least another twelve years, and Ruaidhrí Óg is known to have been generous to poorer clansmen and pipers as well as to poets.[249] Continued patronage of both classical and vernacular poets is also well attested for Mac Leóid of Berneray. Màiri nighean Alasdair Ruaidh celebrated Tormod's house as:

> ... innis nam bàrd
> Is nam filidh ri dàn
> Far am bu mhinig an tàmh.

> (the resting-place of *bàird* and of *filidh* of poetry, where often they reposed).[250]

Elsewhere Màiri again substantiates the enduring good relations between Tormod and the *filidh*:

> Thog na filidh ort sgeul
> Fhad 's a dh'imich an ceum
> Nach fhaca iad na b'fhéile gnùis.

> (The *filidh* have spread a report of thee, far as their steps have led, that a countenance more liberal they never saw).[251]

But truly conditions were declining for the poets in general (in Gaelic Scotland as in Ireland),[252] and we find the development of a new motif

---

248 *Miad a' mhulaid tha 'm thadhal*, §3abcdfg.
249 See Grant 1959, p. 173, and for the record of payment to 'Duncan McIldonich McLeod's Irish poet' in 1706 see *ibid.*, p. 371.
250 *An naidheachd so an dé*, §7bc.
251 *Mo chràdhghal bochd*, §9.
252 For an instance of a complaint about the decline of patronage in contemporary Irish vernacular poetry see above, chapter 3, p. 111 n. 271.

which we might call 'poet's poverty'. Iain mac Ailein lamented the chang-
ing times for Clann Leóid and the loss of 'cleachdadh nan sean daoine'
('the practice of the ancient')[253] leading to his own weakened condition.
He used to be the recipient of the hospitality and liberality of Olbhar's
descendants, yet he now wears 'brat air a chuladh' ('a patched mantle'), he
is in 'uireasbhaidh fhuathach' ('hateful need').[254] Ruairidh Dall employed
the 'poet's poverty' device in his criticism of Eóin Breac for dismissing him
from Dunvegan:

> fàth mo ghearain a bhith falamh
>   's mi tamall o d' làimh.

> (The cause of my complaint is that I am destitute at a distance
> from your hand).[255]

He resorts to depicting himself receiving charity from his neighbours, who
speaking to each other note:

> tha e falamh …

> Fhaic thu 'n t-uan gun mhàthair,
>   an clàrsair gun chruit;
> an leabhair gun leughair …
> 's ro-mhath 'n airidh
>   ghlaine seo thoirt dhuit.

> (he is destitute …

> See the lamb without a mother, the harper without a harp;
> the book without a reader … it is very proper to give you this
> glass).[256]

The decline of traditional Gaelic ways in general was illustrated by
Lachlann mac Theàrlaich Òig, a MacFhionghuin poet, through a dramatic

---

253 *Shìl Olaghair gun ainnis*, §1k.
254 *ibid.*, §§1op, 3pq.
255 *A' cheud Di-luain de'n ràithe*, §4kl.
256 *ibid.*, §§2i, 3cdeij.

allegory which directly attacked the loss of three core attributes of a Gaelic chief: 'Iochd, is Gràdh, is Fiùghantas' ('Mercy, Love, and Generosity'). These are personified as children whom the poets finds wandering lost and crying. They describe themselves as 'Clann dhaoin' uaisle cùramach' ('Offspring of responsible gentlemen').[257] When 'an Fhéile' ('hospitality') was lost, they were entrusted to 'maithibh Innse Gall' ('the good men of the Isles'), and were kindly welcomed and nurtured by the Mac Leóid chiefs of Berneray and Dunvegan, as well as by other Gaelic chiefs, all of whom are now dead.[258] The personification of Mercy, Generosity and Love is alien to the Gaelic panegyric code: it is a new development which may have been borrowed from contemporary English verse.[259] Despite these innovations, the vernacular poets composing for Mac Leóid nobles clung tenaciously to the traditional praise motifs borrowed from classical verse, an adherence which accounts in a very large measure for the persistence of so much of the ancient panegyric code long after he demise of classical poetry. Thus we find the 'lordly traits' motif, albeit in revised wording ('cleachdainn mhic rìgh', 'the practice of a king's son'), in Màiri nighean Alasdair Ruaidh's *Ri fuaim an taibh* (§14a), while Pòl Crùbach resorted to two motifs commonly employed to describe the effects of the subject's death — the darkness brought on by a shower or by an extinguished candle:

Mar gum biodh fras ann
    A chaisgeadh uainn soillse nan speur,
No coinneal d'a mùchadh.

(As if a shower
were blocking the firmament's brightness,
or like a candle had been extinguished).[260]

---

257 *Marbhfhaisg air a' mhulad sin*, §4ac.

258 *ibid.*, §§4efgh, 5–15.

259 *Lasair*, p. 376.

260 *Is i so iorraim na truaighe*, §12efg. Cf. *Creach Gaoidheal i reilig Rois*, §30cd: 'do neól cumhadh ós clár Sgí | dubhadh do-ní i lá an laoi' ('the cloud of sorrow for you that veils the land of Skye causes darkness at mid-day'). For *coinneal* representing the subject see *TD* i, p. liv, and for examples of the use of this imagery in Irish poetry see *Dá bhrághaid uaim i nInis*, §20b; *Máthair chogaidh críoch Bhanbha*, §48d.

Finally, there may be also an indication of the traditional classical motif that states that a subject's youth is no impediment to his attaining to the chiefship, in Ruairidh Dall's words to Ruaidhrí Óg of Dunvegan:

> na bi faoin ann am barail
> ged tha car aig an òg ort.

> (do not be shallow in judgment, though youth handicaps you).[261]

The same poem contains an instance of the image of the grieving Ó Maol Chiaráin which we already encountered in Mac Domhnaill verse, both classical and vernacular.[262] It was used by An Clàrsair Dall in his elegy for Eóin Breac, although the poet confuses deceased and mourner, mistakenly referring to Fearchar as lamenting his father's death.[263]

Conclusions

As with the also Nemedian Clann Duibhne, we find some discrepancies between Clann Leóid pedigrees of various times, as well as a desire, from at least the sixteenth century onwards, to give themselves an ancient and noble Gaelic origin. Classical and vernacular poets as well as historians — including those writing in English — are all in agreement concerning the kindred's royal Norse origin. Although this was via the female line, through the marriage of Ealga to an unnamed *Gaoidheal* who may have been a Dál Riada nobleman, the literature preserves no references to Clann Leóid's noble Gaelic ancestors, with two late exceptions. One is the sixteenth-century linking of the Mac Leóid Norse forbears to the legendary Gaoidheal, and the other Mac Firbhisigh's uncertain statement in the seventeenth century.[264] The lack of allusions to ancient noble progenitors in panegyric is uncharacteristic, and so far remains unexplained. This lack is, nonetheless, no obstacle to a Mac Leóid self-view of belonging in Gaeldom, as attested in the poetry, although without the insistence found in Caimbéal verse.

---

261 *Tha mulad, tha mulad,* §21cd.
262 See above, chapter 3, p. 112.
263 *Tha mulad, tha mulad,* §15cd.
264 See above, p. 152.

The main themes in classical verse are, as well as Clann Leóid's royal Norse lineage, their martial prowess, physical beauty, character qualities and fame. The poetry gives a very localised, self-contained general impression: mentions of *Alba* and of 'Innse Gall' are rare, and Britain is virtually non-existent. The motifs of royalism and religion are absent, and there is little involvement in social, political or religious matters. In all this the extant Mac Leóid panegyric conforms to the canons of the genre, a conformity reinforced by the occasional employment of other conventional motifs such as *athardha* (with the same ambiguity of geographical extent noted in Caimbéal poetry), *fuidheall*, *muirn* and 'tréidhe tighearna'. In common with the poetry composed for Scottish patrons in general — the Caimbéalaigh being an important exception, and Clann Eóin Mhóir another though to a much lesser degree — there is no exploitation of the *Gall* motif. Mac Leóid classical panegyric departs from the norm in yet other ways: references to *seanchas* are scarce, and there are no comparisons to great heroes from the classical Latin and Greek traditions. Neither do we find a tendency to follow the new trends observed in later Mac Domhnaill poetry, and this includes a complete absence of the motifs of royalism and prophecy. Mac Leóid classical verse, though in many ways closer to the earlier rather than the later models established for Clann Domhnaill panegyric,[265] thus has its own particular flavour.

Vernacular poetry is mainly concerned with the celebration of courtly social life under Mac Leóid patronage, and reads, in general, as localised (through mostly local place-names) and detached from the wider kingdom and national politics as the classical corpus. The rank of royal Norse Clann Leóid among the *Gaoidhil* is buttressed through resort to the 'friends and allies' motif, presenting the subject as well-connected, by blood and by way of alliances, to some of the great families in the Scottish Gaeldom. Vernacular poets, as was the case with those composing for the other kindreds considered so far, continue to preserve the panegyric code by borrowing classical motifs. The *Gall* motif makes some appearances, sometimes to denote the English, sometimes indicating the Scottish Lowlanders, and once as part of the merely formulaic 'Gaoidhil is Goill' motif. It does not always have a negative connotation: being part of the *Gall*

---

265 See above, chapter 3, pp. 112–15.

court at Edinburgh is rather a motive of pride. Although allusions to *Alba* are rare and Britain is invisible, sometimes poets comment on contemporary national politics to note their subjects' royalism and to complain of its lack of reward. However, one author does engage wholeheartedly in discussion of events: Ruairidh MacGhillemhoire, An Clàrsair Dall, joins MacDhòmhnaill and other poets in their support of the rightful king, denunciation of upstarts, depiction of royalism as a Gaelic affair, and use of the wheel of fortune rhetoric. Topics missing from his political poetry are those of prophecy, the Moses or Israelite rhetoric, and denominational politics, that is the role of true religion in the political contest. Ruairidh Dall and other poets eulogising Clann Leóid also lament the decline of traditional Gaelic ways, and in poems dealing with this issue we find two innovations: the motif that we may call 'poet's poverty' — portraying the poet as unwanted, hungry, or clad in rags — and the personification of virtues, the latter possibly being a borrowing from contemporary English poetry.

Chapter 5

Other patrons:
from the Lennox to the Mearns;
Mac Griogóir, Mac Gille Eóin, and Mac Coinnigh

The two previous chapters explored the praise rhetoric of the *filidh* (or the language of authority of classical panegyric) and of the *bàird* (whose own verse could be so powerful both in voicing public opinion and in shaping it) as found in the extant corpus of poetry for the descendants of Colla Uais and for the descendants of Neimheadh. Most of the surviving classical poetry of Scotland is concerned with those two kin groups. The remaining Highland kindreds may be divided into Gaelic and Norman (*Gall*) although, like those descending from Colla Uais and from Neimheadh, most of them, if not all, through intermarriage came to be of mixed ethnicity. Many of the descendants of the medieval Norman settlers became Gaelicised: they adopted the Gaelic language and customs, including a Gaelic-style form of the title of the head of the clan.[1] There is some difficulty, therefore, in drawing a clearly cut line between Gaelic and non-Gaelic families. For the purposes of the present study the differentiation between *Gaoidheal* and *Gall* (Norman, whether French or English) is made according to each kindred's genealogical claims. In this approach we take as a guide the earlier rather than the later Gaelic genealogies: the manipulations of the pedigrees by seventeenth-century historians (such as we noted for Clann Duibhne)[2] are no more than a reflection of changing tastes and social patterns.

In this chapter and the following two we will first consider the surviving poetry concerned with the remaining Gaelic kindreds of Scotland, and

1   See below, p. 232 and n. 224, and chapter 6, p. 265.
2   See above, chapter 4, pp. 119–20.

next that concerned with those of *Gall* origin. We will also examine the extant verse of Scottish authorship composed for Irish patrons. Last of all we will review, as a very special case study, the extant poetry composed by *filidh* for the kings of Scotland and Britain, and summarise the opinion on monarchs and monarchy pronounced by *bàird*, which unavoidably emerges as we deal with vernacular poets attached to the various kindreds. Leaving aside the descendants of Colla Uais and the Gaelicised offspring of Neimheadh, the *Gaoidhil* of Scotland claimed descent from either Corc mac Lughach, Niall Naoighiallach or Conaire Mór. The Scottish offspring of Corc, king of Munster, were the Leamhnaigh, from whom the Lennox disctrict received its name and for whom two poems are extant, and the Eóghanachta of the Mearns, for whom there is left only one single and very early quatrain.[3] The Mac Lochlainn, Mac Laghmainn, Mac Suibhne, Mac Néill and a few more kin groups who originally settled in Cowal and Knapdale were said to descend ultimately from Niall Naoighiallach, king of Ireland.[4] Only two poems composed for Niall's Scottish offspring have survived, while the bulk of the extant corpus is concerned with the descendants of Conaire Mór, the kindreds who claimed to stem from the people of Dál Riada, and more specifically from either Fearghus Mór or his brother Loarn Mór, whom most sources from at least the seventh century onwards make the sons of Earc. Only the royal line of the kings of Scots is shown in the extant genealogies, chronicles and poetry to descend from Fearghus Mór, the first Dál Riada leader to be, according to Gaelic sources, rí rather than taoiseach.[5]

The descendants of Corc

Corc mac Lughach was a contemporary of Niall Naoighiallach, whose death is given in the annals under the year 405.[6] He belonged to the Eóghanachta, one of the two great ruling families of Munster; the other was Dál gCais, who shared with the Eóghanachta the same illustrious

---

3   See below, pp. 185–6. For the descendants of Corc see 'MS 1467', no. 21; *LMG* ii, §§411.5–421.5; Skene 1876–80, iii, pp. 475–6.
4   'MS 1467', nos. 21, 27, 29; Sellar 1971 (which notes the uncertainty of the Mac Néill pedigree).
5   See above, chapter 1, p. 6.
6   *ARÉ* i, p. 126.

ancestor, Oilill Ólum, king of Munster.[7] There are several versions of the story of the settlement of Corc's progeny in *Alba*. In some it is stated that Corc left Ireland to escape the affections of his stepmother, while in others it is two of his sons, Cairbre Cruithneachán and Maine Leamhna, who went to *Alba* to take possession of their Pictish mother's hereditary lands. Their mother was said to be the daughter of Fearadhach Fionn, 'rí Alban', and her name was Moingfhionn, or alternatively Leamhain.[8] There is a problem of chronology with this claim, however, since Fearadhach Fionn (otherwise known as Fionnchormac) lived much later, in the later seventh century. Earlier sources state, probably more correctly, that Moingfhionn was the daughter of Fearadhach Fionn Feachtnach, king of *Cruitheantuath* or *Alba*.[9] It is possible that the equation in later times of Fearadhach Fionn Feachtnach with the Fearadhach Fionn of the tribe of Loarn Mór was a fabrication aimed to give the descendants of Corc a kinship connexion with the royal rulers of Dál Riada. This fabrication, if not simple confusion, seems to be what has led some modern historians to give the settlement of this kin group in the Lennox as having taken place subsequently to that of Dál Riada.[10]

Corc's son Cairbre Cruithneachán settled in the Mearns in Kincardineshire, and his people were known as the Eóghanachta of Magh Gheirrghinn (the Gaelic name of the Mearns) (see Table 5. 1). Maine Leamhna occupied the area of the Lennox as head of the Leamhnaigh.[11] All we have left of poetry for Cairbre's descendants is one quatrain in praise of Aonghus mac Fearghusa (†761). Aonghus, the founder of an important eighth- and ninth-century royal dynasty, became overlord of the Pictish groups south of the Grampians, and a serious threat to Dál Riada.[12] The surviving quatrain eulogising him — preserved in the 'Book of Leinster' — was probably part of a longer poem celebrating his military victories:

---

7 Watson 2004, p. 218. For the origins of the Eóghanachta see Sproule 1984.

8 'MS 1467', no. 20; *LMG* ii, §§410.5, 411.5–412.5; *FFÉ* ii, pp. 382–4. Watson 2004, p. 221 states that Maine was the grandson, not the son, of Corc. See also Sproule 1985, pp. 15–17.

9 Watson 2004, p. 219; *FFÉ* ii, pp. 234, 384; Skene 1876–80, iii, p. 475.

10 See, for instance, Brown 2003, p. 202.

11 *LMG* ii, §§411.6, 412A.1; *FFÉ* ii, pp. 384–6.

12 Hudson 1994, pp. 26–8.

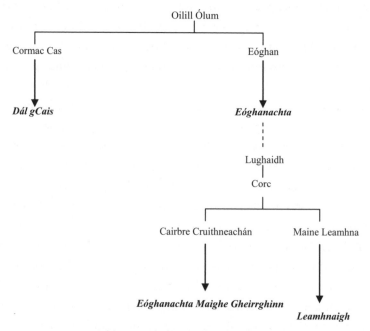

Oilill Ólum

Cormac Cas   Eóghan

Dál gCais   *Eóghanachta*

Lughaidh

Corc

Cairbre Cruithneachán   Maine Leamhna

Eóghanachta Maighe Gheirrghinn

Leamhnaigh

Table 5.1 The descendants of Corc.
Sources: 'MS 1467', no. 21; *LMG* ii, §§411.5–421.5.

Fó sén dia ngaib Oengus Albain
Albu thulchach trethantriathach;
ruc do chathrachaib costud clárach
cossach, lámach, lethansciathach.

(Good the day when Óengus took Alba,
hilly Alba, with its strong chiefs.
He brought battle to towns, with boards,
with feet and hands, and with broad shields).[13]

For the descendants of Maine Leamhna, however, we have two com-
plete poems composed in the early classical period, *Saor do leannán, a
Leamhain* and *Mairg thréigios inn, a Amhlaoíbh*. We have also the first
name — Donnchadh Mór — of a poet designated as 'ó Leamhnacht'
('from Lennox'), but whether he belonged to the Leamhnaigh or to some

13 Quoted in Katherine Forsyth 2000, p. 28; trsl. Clancy (ed.) 1998, p. 144.

of the other kin groups also established in the Lennox area is not known. His only surviving work is an undatable satire.[14] The early history of the Leamhnaigh is a complete blank until the later twelfth century, when their chief emerges as *mormhaor* of Lennox, in East Dunbartonshire. Alún Mór son of Muireadhach (†c.1200), for whom the first of the two poems was composed and who is traditionally regarded as the first Earl of Lennox, was the head of the kindred in the later twelfth century. In 1178 his territory was granted as a crown fief to David of Huntingdon, brother of King William I, but in the early thirteenth century it was restored to Alún Mór's son and successor, Alún Óg (†1217), who was recognised by the crown as *mormhaor* or *comes* of Lennox.[15] The earldom remained with the family until the mid-fifteenth century, when all four sons of Eisibéal, Countess of Lennox (and Duchess of Albany through her marriage to Murchadh Stiúbhart) died without legitimate issue. Thereafter it passed to the Stiúbhart family.[16] The Leamhnaigh were loyal subjects of the kings of Scots, although disinclined, it seems, to accommodate the Norman influx of the time. During the Wars of Independence they became staunch Bruce supporters, but their relations with the Stiúbhart monarchs were less smooth, eventually inducing Donnchadh, the eighth earl (†1425) and Eisibéal's father, to form an alliance with the Duke of Albany which would lead to his own downfall and execution.[17]

Both extant poems for the Leamhnaigh are attributed to Muireadhach Ó Dálaigh, the Irish poet who sought shelter and new patronage in Scotland and was reputedly the founder of the Mac Muireadhaigh family of *filidh* of Scotland.[18] Alún Mór, the first earl, is the subject of the earlier of the two poems, an eulogy in which the conventional motif presenting the subject as his territory's lover or spouse is given what is, I believe, an unprecedented twist. Alún Mór is presented not as the spouse of his territory, but of the river Leamhain (modern Leven or Lennox) in it:

---

14 *Mairg duine do chaill a ghuth*, in *óglláchas* of *rannaigheacht mhór*. For other kindreds established in the district see Brown 2003, p. 210, and below, p. 206.

15 Brown 2003, p. 203; Neville 2005, pp. 14–15.

16 Brown 2003, p. 205.

17 id. 2003, pp. 214–20. The family pedigree in 'MS 1467' ends with this Donnchadh; see 'MS 1467', no. 20.

18 See above, chapter 1, pp. 8–9.

Sáor do leannán, a Leamhain,
Alún Óg mac Muireadhaigh,
a chúl druimneach gan duibhe,
ua Luighdheach o Liathmhuine.

Maith do chonách giolladh ngeal
o do charais do chédfhear;
a rí Bealaigh do bhí a ndán
gurb' í Leamhain do leannan.

(Noble was your lover, o Leamhain,
Alún Óg son of Muireadhach,
whose hair was wavy and bright,
the descendant of Lughaidh from Liathmhuine.

Great has been the good fortune of the bright youths
since you loved your first spouse;
o king of Bealach, it was fated
that Leamhain would be your lover).[19]

This treatment of the spouse motif might perhaps be seen as a synec-doche, a figure of speech which names a part to stand for the whole. The poem incorporates a little story from *seanchas* which explains how the river, originally called Gearrabhainn ('Short River'), came to be called Leamhain: this was the name of Corc's wife — the mother of Maine from whom the Leamhnaigh stemmed[20] — who was drowned in the river. Fr McKenna noted that Leamhain is also the name of a river in Kerry, said to be originally called Garbhabha na bhFian.[21] Additionally, from this poem we learn that the mother of Alún Mór was '[inghean] Ailín' (§13b); this probably explains the introduction of the name Alún in the family, and suggests that Alún Mór's mother may have been of Northumbrian Saxon origin.[22]

---

19 *Saor do leannán, a Leamhain,* (§§1–2). Liathmhuine: the plain later covered by Lough Neagh, in northern Ireland, but generally an ornamental epithet (*ADD* ii, p. 241). Bealach: 'Balloch at the foot of Loch Lomond, the ancient seat of the Earls of Lennox' (Watson 2004, p. 483).

20 See above, p. 185.

21 *ADD* i, p. 172.

22 She may have been the daughter of an eleventh-century Northumbrian, 'Alwynn, son of a Saxon, Arkill' (*ibid.*).

Mairg thréigios inn, a Amhlaoíbh, on the other hand, is a complaint addressed to an individual named Amhlaoíbh, who might be a son of Alún, second Earl of Lennox.[23] The poet accuses Amhlaoíbh of having failed to grant him his rights, some of which he enumerates: 'Fiche loilghioch … searraigh urlomha Alban … rogha gach fóid' ('Twenty milch-cows … swift Scottish foals … choice land', §2abc)[24] and, more intriguingly (§4cd):

> cuid don chill do dhligh duine,
> a ghil fhinn, dá almhuire.

These two lines are translated tentatively by the editor of the poem as 'one has become entitled to a portion of the church-land (?), oh fair bright one, by virtue of what he has brought from over-seas (?)' (that is, in return for the poetic art he has brought from Ireland).[25] Could the poet be referring to the relatively recent poetic re-organisation by which in Ireland some poets at least were allowed to keep their church lands, which they turned into schools?[26]

Both poems contain allusions to the Leamhnaigh's venerable ancestors, Corc, his father Lughaidh, and their remoter ancestor, Oilill Ólum.[27] *Mairg thréigios inn, a Amhlaoíbh* additionally makes a reference to another son of Leamhain, 'Corc mór … | cathuidhe na claoinTeamhra' ('the great Corc …| the warrior of sloping Tara', §15a), who also went by the name Crónán, according to Mac Firbhisigh.[28] It also recalls 'Clann … Chonghail' and 'clann Ghofraidh' (§13ac), no doubt Amhlaoíbh's ancestors on the maternal side, for they are given, in a quatrain separate from others which all refer to ancestors in the male line, in the section which the poet closes with the statement (§18ab):

> <M>uinntior h'athar aithnidh damh
> is muinntior mhaith do mháthar.
>
> (I am acquainted with your father's people
> and with your mother's good people).

23 Ó Cuív (ed.) 1968, p. 93.
24 See also Quiggin 1911, p. 112.
25 Ó Cuív 1968, p. 97. *Cell*: in a number of examples, 'monastic settlement or foundation, collection of ecclesiastical buildings' (*DIL* C, 110: 30–2).
26 See above, chapter 1, p. 9.
27 *Saor do leannán, a Leamhain*, §§1d, 11b, 12bc; *Mairg thréigios inn, a Amhlaoíbh*, §§14bc.
28 *LMG* ii, §411.6–421.2.

If this interpretation is correct then 'clann Ghofraidh' strongly points to kinship connexions with the descendants of Godhfhraidh mac Fearghusa, claimed ancestor of Somhairle and of Clann Domhnaill.[29] The allusion to 'Clann ... Chonghail', admittedly, remains obscure, and of course the eponym involved might be either Scottish or Irish in origin. The royal blood of the Leamhnaigh — on the Munster as well as the *Alba* side — is particularly celebrated in *Saor do leannán, a Leamhain* (§§3b, 4ab, 6ab, 12b), and their chief's rank as 'mormhaor Leamhna' is noted in both.[30] In the poem for Alún Mór, additionally, we read that 'Dob annamh céim catha Gall' ('Unknown was the tramp of the troop of *Goill*') around the banks of the river Leamhain. It is tempting to see here a reference to the apparently uneasy relationship of the *mormhaoir* of Lennox with the Norman settlers, but we might be reading too much into the poet's words. Merely a passing reference, this statement is probably best seen as the conventional motif which presents a chief as capable of keeping strangers out of his territory.

The descendants of Niall

The Scottish families who claimed descent from Niall Naoighiallach occupied lands in Cowal and Knapdale. Their common ancestor was said to be Anradhán, who would have settled in Scotland in the early eleventh century, having left Ireland in a great rage after losing the kingship of Aileach to his brother Domhnall, ancestor of the later Ó Néill chiefs.[31] According to 'Leabhar Chlainne Suibhne', a sixteenth-century Irish chronicle, Anradhán conquered by the sword 'baile 7 leth Alban' — an expression which we have encountered as a Clann Domhnaill poetry stock phrase — and eventually made his peace with 'rí Alban', whose daughter he married.[32] Whether there actually was such a marriage we cannot know, but those who claimed descent from Anradhán certainly were marrying into the principal families of Gaelic Scotland and Ireland from at least the late twelfth century

---

29 See above, chapter 3, pp. 58, 60.

30 *Saor do leannán, a Leamhain*, §§13a; *Mairg thréigios inn, a Amhlaoíbh*, §§8b, 12b.

31 *LCS*, §1, p. 2; Sellar 1971, pp. 25, 27.

32 *LCS*, §2, p. 4. See above, chapter 3, pp. 87–9, 99, 110–11. The pattern of the story itself is very similar to that claimed for Colla Uais: loss of the kingship, conquest of land in Scotland, marriage to a Scottish princess.

onwards.[33] Clann tSuibhne's eponym, Suibhne, who according to tradition built Castle Sween in Knapdale, was a great-grandson of Anradhán.[34] By the mid-thirteenth century Clann tSuibhne had become a powerful kindred not only in Knapdale but also in Kintyre, where they held Skipness Castle.[35] Around that time their expansion clashed with the Stiúbhart family's own expansionism. How Clann tSuibhne came to leave Scotland and settle in Ireland is not clear. Traditionally it has been believed that they lost their lands to the crown, although this is not immediately evident.[36] The version in 'Leabhar Chlainne Suibhne' is that a Mac Suibhne chief, Eóin an Eangnamha ('of the Prowess'), having killed the *mormhaor* of Mar in a dispute, was banished by the king of Scots and subsequently displaced Ó Breisléin of Fánad (Donegal), who had insulted him during a previous visit.[37] Whatever happened, Clann tSuibhne were established in Fánad by the 1260s, and for about four centuries they remained attached to the Ó Domhnaill chiefs as their *gallóglaigh*. We may note that, again according to 'Leabhar Chlainne Suibhne', Eóin an Eangnamha was a foster-son of 'Mac Gofraga na nOiléin' ('Mac Godhfhraidh of the Isles').[38] This is not altogether improbable. Clann Ghodhfhraidh was the name given to Clann Domhnaill's ancestors until Somhairle's time.[39] As noted, there were kinship connexions between Anradhán's and Somhairle's descendants from at least the later twelfth century,[40] and this type of connexion was often reinforced through fosterage agreements. If the 'Leabhar Chlainne Suibhne' pedigree is accurate, Eóin an Eangnamha would have been roughly contemporary with Somhairle. The problem here is, as usual, the chronology, for there is a century gap between Somhairle's time and the time when Clann tSuibhne would have begun their settlement in Ireland. But it is possible that there are gaps also in the genealogy, or perhaps that it was not this Eóin but a descendant who settled back in Ireland in the mid-thirteenth century after coming into conflict with the crown. Suibhne's line, at any rate, had a short

---

33 Sellar 1971, pp. 30–1.

34 *LCS*, §3, p. 4.

35 Meek (ed.) 1997, pp. 9–10.

36 *ibid.*, pp. 10–11.

37 *LCS*, §13, p. 16.

38 *ibid.*, §9, p. 11.

39 See above, chapter 3, pp. 58, 60.

40 See especially Sellar 1971, p. 31.

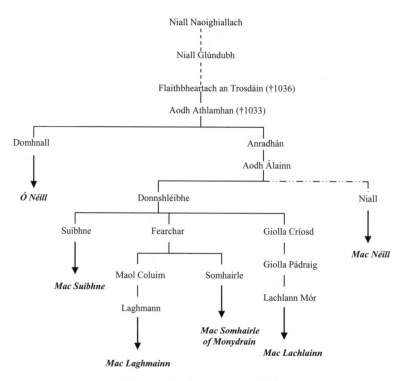

Table 5.2 The descendants of Niall.
Sources: 'MS 1467', nos. 21, 27, 29; Sellar 1971.

stay in Scotland before returning to Ireland. Some, however, did remain in Scotland and became vassals of the Caimbéalaigh.[41]

It is for a Mac Suibhne chief that one of the two extant panegyrics for Niall's descendants was composed. The subject of Artúr Dall Mac Gurcaigh's *Dál chabhlaigh ar Chaistéal Suibhne* is generally believed to be Eóin Mac Suibhne (*fl.*1310).[42] The poet encourages Eóin to recover his patrimony in Scotland, but whether this is an actual incitement or a mere poetic eulogistic device is a matter of debate. We must be particularly wary of attaching actual significance to those statements that appear quite impossible or contrary to actual circumstances, as would be the case here.

---

41 *SVBDL*, p. 258. Note also that the *LCS* mention of a visit by Eóin an Eangnamha to Fánad previous to his exile (above, p. 191) may suggest much earlier contact and perhaps settlement there.

42 For the historical background see Meek (ed.) 1997, pp. 7–12.

The object of Gaelic classical poetry is to present the individual praised as the ideal ruler, and this includes naming the things that he is capable of doing; it does not follow that he will actually do them. One example of this literary device is *Beir eolas dúinn, a Dhomhnaill*, Gofraidh Fionn Ó Dálaigh's incitement to Domhnall Mac Cárrthaigh (†c.1391), heir of a Desmond chief, to recover his ancestors' original patrimony in Munster.[43] Further instances are the invitations to Scottish Mac Domhnaill nobles to assume the high-kingship of Ireland.[44] In none of these cases can the poet's exhortation be taken at face value. *Dál chabhlaigh ar Chaistéal Suibhne* may well be yet another example of this literary device: most of the poem deals with the description of a sea-voyage and the rest depicts Eóin Mac Suibhne as happily reinstalled in his Scottish patrimony, while no actual incitement, or even identification of the enemy, is given. The *Goill*, it is true, are mentioned once:

> caol c[h]laidheamh ó ghreis uí Ghuaire,
> maolaighthear leis guailne Gall.

> ([when] a slender sword [is used] in an attack by the descendant of Guaire [i.e. Eóin], limbs are lopped from *Goill's* shoulders by it).[45]

While the *Goill* may here be the Stiúbhairt, Norman in origin and at the time encroaching on Mac Suibhne territory, the word appears as an isolated reference and therefore is probably used as a mere motif. It is in fact given within a section which lists other conventional attributes of the right ruler:[46] Eóin is portrayed as a skilled warrior, he is praised for his physical beauty, his generosity, his patronage of the poet class, his gentleness except to his enemies, and nature is depicted as welcoming him back to Scotland, where the people, including the poets, will equally welcome him (§§14d, 17c, 18ab, 19–20, 21, 22cd, 28d).

There are in the poem three references to Scotland (*Alba, Sliabh*

---

43 O Riordan 2007, pp. 57–73, especially at p. 61.
44 See above, chapter 3, pp. 68–9.
45 *Dál chabhlaigh ar Chaistéal Suibhne*, §24cd.
46 Coira 2008b, p. 144.

Monaidh), attaching Eóin to his patrimonial land, while his current resi-
dence in Ireland is noted by his depiction as 'leathchrann sgorach codach
Cuinn' ('one of the two piercing lances of the region of Conn', §14d). Of
interest is Mac Gurcaigh's description of 'the arming and departure of
the fleet'. It is highly similar to descriptions of this type found in medi-
eval Norse and Danish literature, probably reflecting the mixed Gaelic-
Norse culture of the Scottish Western seaboard at the time.[47] Indeed
Eóin and his warriors are described as *Lochlannaigh* (§3d). Since by
this time Clann tSuibhne probably had kinship connexions with Clann
Ghodhfhraidh[48] — whose Norse associations are sometimes recalled
in poetry[49] — the term here is likely to be a reference to their ancestry
through the female line. Mac Suibhne is also given royal Gaelic ancestry:
he is said to be '[ua] Ghuaire' (§24c), that is, a descendant of the ancient
king of Connacht who was most renowned for his boundless liberality.
Eóin's ancestor Maolmhuire an Sparáin had married Beanmhidhe, daugh-
ter of Toirrdhealbhach Ó Conchobhair (†1156), a twelfth-century king
of Connacht.[50] However, Toirrdhealbhach belonged to Uí Bhriúin, the
progeny of Brión, son of Eochaidh Muighmheadhón and brother of Niall
Naoighiallach, while Guaire was of Uí Fhiachrach, the descendants of
Fiachra, Brión and Niall's brother.[51] If Mac Gurcaigh is correct in naming
Guaire as Mac Suibhne's ancestor, the connexion between the two kin-
dreds could only have come about through an Uí Fhiachrach marriage to
an Uí Bhriúin female. No other noble ancestors of Eóin Mac Suibhne are
named in the poem.

The only other extant poem for a descendant of Niall is *A phaidrín do
dhúisg mo dhéar*, an elegy by Aithbhreac Nic Coirceadáil for her deceased
husband, Niall Óg Mac Néill, a chief of Gigha and constable of Castle
Sween who flourished in 1455. Aithbhreac composed this poem in syl-
labic metre, but in the simpler *óglachas* style. Her thoughts are with her
beloved's generosity and hospitality (§§1c, 5c, 6cd), his nobility of blood
and character qualities (§5c), and the grief that his departure has brought

47 Meek (ed.) 1997, pp. 13–15.
48 See above, p. 191 and n. 40.
49 See above, chapter 3, pp. 74, 80.
50 Sellar 1971, p. 30.
51 Byrne 2001, pp. 233–51 (pp. 239–46 for Guaire).

to her and to those in his territories (§§2–3, 8–10, 15). She particularly notes his generous patronage of the poet class, which according to her had attracted poets from various locations in Ireland (§§6–7). She makes no reference to ancient noble ancestors — other than identifying Niall Óg's kindred as 'Clann Néill', 'sliocht na Niall' (§§9b, 13b) — or to their original homeland. Place-names are used to bind the subject to his territories (§10ab) and also, more abundantly, in the author's rich use of noble animal imagery, always within the span of the Western Isles: 'leómhan Muile' ('lion of Mull', §4c), 'seabhag Íle' ('hawk of Islay', §4d), 'Seabhag seangglan Sléibhe Gaoil' ('Slim bright hawk of Sliabh Gaoil', §7a), 'dreagan Leódhuis' ('dragon of Lewis', §7c), 'éigne Sanais' ('salmon of Sanas', §7d).[52] Aithbhreac also uses a common plant imagery motif, portraying her subject as 'Cnú mhullaigh a mogaill féin' ('the topmost nut of their cluster', §13a). Quite exceptionally, she makes no allusions to his warrior skills. Equally absent are references to *Alba*, the regional character of the place-names giving a localised, self-contained impression in what is fundamentally a personal poem.

The descendants of Conaire (I): Dál Riada of *Alba*

The lineage of Fearghus mac Eirc, reputed first *rí* of Dál Riada of Scotland, is traced back to Cairbre Riada (or Rioghfhada), son of Conaire Caomh, a second-century king of Ireland and a descendant of another high-king, Conaire Mór mac Eidirsceóil.[53] According to *seanchas*, Cairbre Riada and some of his people moved from Munster to Ulster, where they settled and were known as Dál Riada, at the end of the second century or the beginning of the third. From there they began their settlement in *Alba* — where Cairbre himself is said to have been — under a leading *taoiseach*. This leader's subordinate position with respect to the portion of Dál Riada in Ireland and with the Irish kings remains an unresolved matter, as does the exact point in time when Dál Riada's portion in *Alba* became fully independent. All we can say is that from the eleventh century onwards *seanchas* tradition portrays 'Scottish Dál Riada' as still subordinate to Irish leaders

---

52 Sliabh Gaoil: in South Knapdale; Sanas: Machriehanish, near Campbeltown (*SVBDL*, p. 272).

53 'MS 1467', no. 1; *LMG* ii, §§400.2–400.3; *FFÉ* ii, pp. 268–70.

by the sixth century at least, and Fearghus mac Eirc as the first *taoiseach* of this territory to adopt the title *rí*.[54]

The descendants of Cairbre were, therefore, as Gaelic sources have it, established in western Scotland (Oirthear Ghaoidheal, 'the East-land of the Gaels', roughly modern Argyll) well before Fearghus Mór's time (*c*.500), though they were not the first population group from Ireland to settle in Britain.[55] Little is available from Gaelic sources concerning their early contacts and relations with Picts, Britons or other Gaelic kindreds in *Alba*. Céitinn — quoting the German Jesuit scholar Nicolaus Serarius (†1609) — states that in the times of Niall Naoighiallach the men of Scottish Dál Riada routed the Picts and expanded into northern *Alba*. He also records, after Bede, their defeat, in alliance with the Picts, by the Saxons in 684, and a later defeat of Dál Riada by the Picts under Aonghus mac Fearghusa, king of the Eóghanachta of the Mearns. In their conflicts with their neighbours Cairbre Riada's Scottish descendants seem to have been supported by the kings of Ireland.[56] Céitinn connects the claim of Fearghus Mór mac Eirc as the first *Gaoidheal* to become 'rí Alban', previously the title of Pictish kings, with the *Lia Fáil*, or the Stone of Destiny: this, he says, was sent to him from Ireland for his inauguration in Scotland, where it remained until it was seized by Edward I of England.[57] However, as we will see, the first 'rí Alban' is Cionaoth mac Ailpín, not Fearghus Mór, in the poetry. Céitinn uses *Alba* anachronistically: we should understand his statement as referring to the kingship of Dál Riada rather than of *Alba*.

Sketching a genealogical tree of the descendants of Fearghus Mór mac Eirc is no easy task, since different pedigrees sometimes conflict with each other. For instance, the lineage of Airbheartach (father of Cormac from whom no fewer than ten fifteenth-century kin-groups claimed descent) is in 'MS 1467' often, but not always, abbreviated, so that in many places

---

54 The eleventh-century version (the 'Preface' to *Amra Choluim Cille*) refers to the sixth-century convention of Druim Ceat as including the regulation of the exaction of tribute from Dál Riada in Scotland by the high-kings of Ireland. For some discussion see Fraser 2007, pp. 318–22. For the survival of this tradition in later Gaelic historians see *FFÉ* i, p. 208; *ibid*. iii, pp. 94–6, 382; *LMG* ii, §§407.7, 418.2–418.3.

55 See above, chapter 1, p. 6 and n. 20.

56 *FFÉ* ii, pp. 330, 378; iii, pp. 138–40, 148.

57 *FFÉ* i, pp. 206–8.

he appears as son of Fearadhach Fionn,[58] while in Irish sources it is much fuller but significantly different.[59] Another example is the strange mixture of addition and transposition noted below for the pedigree of Clann Ghille Eóin.[60] What all sources do point to is the descent of most clans from Loarn Mór, son of Earc, the exception being the line of Cionaoth mac Ailpín, which is given to stem from Loarn Mór's brother, Fearghus Mór. The kingship of the Scottish descendants of Conaire alternated initially between these two groups, until the royal line of Loarn Mór — the last two monarchs of which were Mac Beathadh and Lulach — was forever displaced by their rivals following their defeat at Stracathro in 1130.[61] In the extant verse for Fearghus Mór's descendants we have only poems composed for monarchs of Dál Riada, *Alba*, or Britain, which are reviewed in chapter 7's section dealing with the poetry composed for kings. In the rest of the present chapter we explore the poetry composed for various reputed descendants of Loarn, an overview completed in chapter 8, which closes with the study of the extant poems composed for Irish patrons and for subjects of Norman ancestry.

Clann Ghriogóir

It is to the compilers of the 'Book of the Dean of Lismore', themselves of Clann Ghriogóir, that we are indebted for the preservation of nine poems in classical style for Mac Griogóir chiefs. The fact that so many panegyrics for a relatively minor chief are in existence (and there may well have been more which have not come down to us) would suggest that perhaps it was not only the major chiefs — Mac Domhnaill, Mac Cailéin, and Mac Leóid, subjects of most of the extant classical verse of Scotland — who patronised *filidh*. But whether the Mac Griogóir chiefs maintained a hereditary poetic family is a different matter. Indeed, it is not entirely clear that the authors of these poems were *filidh*. Of the extant Mac Griogóir syllabic poems *Parrthas toraidh an Díseart* was composed for Donnchadh, keeper of the castle of Glenorchy (†1518),

---

58 'MS 1467' nos. 7, 14, 17; cf. no. 6 (where Fearchar Abhraruadh is given in error for Fearchar Fada).

59 Compare 'MS 1467', no. 6 and *LMG* ii, §406.11.

60 See below, pp. 206, 209.

61 Hudson 1994, p. 146.

and *Ríoghacht ghaisgidh oighreacht Eoin* for Eóin mac Pádraig, sixth chief
(†1519). The first of these poems is ascribed to An Giolla Glas Mac an
Táilliúir, and the second to Dubhghall mac An Ghiolla Ghlais, who may
have been the former poet's son: if so, it is possible, though by no means
certain, that a hereditary family of *filidh* of the surname Mac an Táilliuir
was in the employment of the Clann Ghriogóir chiefs. On the other hand
we have four poems, all for Eóin mac Pádraig, composed by Fionnlagh,
An Bard Ruadh: two are in the looser *óglách* style, and the other two
in *brúilingeacht*, a style also allowing simpler forms of rime than that of
dán díreach.[62] Fionnlagh was also the author of a malevolent satire — so
malevolent that it might in fact be a mock-satire — addressed to Ailéan
Mac Domhnaill, fourth chief of Clann Raghnaill, but this one also falls
short of the metrical perfection required by *dán díreach*.[63]

Was Fionnlagh a *file*? Although he is called *bard* — a title never given
to a *file* in Ireland — this term came to be used in Scotland to designate the
various types of poets generally.[64] Yet it would be unusual for a *file* to be
named without reference to his surname: it is the vernacular poets (includ-
ing the noble amateurs replicating classical metres) who are often desig-
nated in a similar way to 'An Bard Ruadh'; thus Am Bàrd MacMhathain,
Am Bàrd MacShithich, or Am Bàrd Mucanach. The fact that Fionnlagh
Ruadh was a visitor to the Mac Diarmada chief of Moylurg in Connacht
might suggest that he was indeed a *file*, but cannot be taken as conclusive
evidence since the cultural exchange between Scotland and Ireland does
not seem to have been limited to that of the *filidh*.[65] A similar case is pre-
sented by An Bard Mac an tSaoir, a contemporary of An Bard Ruadh, by
whom we have two extant syllabic compositions, neither of which, again,
is in *dán díreach*.[66] The three remaining poems are by An Fear Dána Mac
Giolla Fhionntóg, whose poetic styling suggests that he was not a *file*, by

---

62 *Fada atáim gan bhogha, Gealladh gach saoi don each odhar* and *Fhuaras mo rogha theach mhór* respectively.

63 *Theast aon diabhal na nGaoidheal.*

64 See above, chapter 2, p. 37 and n. 52.

65 For instance, the lament *An taobh tuath ud cha tèid mi*, for Eóin Molach Mac Coinnigh of Applecross, is ascribed to an Irish *bard*, and Eóin Molach is said to have been celebrated by the Earl of Antrim's harper; see *GnC*, p. 174.

66 *Créad í an long-sa ar Loch Inse* and *Tánaig long ar Loch Raithneach*, both satires perhaps directed at members of the Caimbéal kindred.

Donnchadh MacGriogair, brother of the Dean of Lismore, who certainly was not one, and by a certain Fionnlagh Mac an Aba. When we look at the whole of the Mac Griogóir poems we realise that not one of them complies entirely with the rules of *dán díreach*. It may be the case that these authors were all either amateur poets from the nobility, as Donnchadh MacGriogair certainly was, or poets of a category different from that of *file* (an expensive commodity which perhaps the kindred could not afford), and if so it would be the case that all of the extant Clann Ghriogóir poetry should be classified as vernacular.[67]

Clann Ghriogóir are said to take their name from Griogór (†1360), commonly known as 'na srian n-óir' ('of the Golden Bridles').[68] The fifteenth-century collection of pedigrees contained in 'MS 1467' places him seven generations down from Cormac mac Airbheartaigh, thus making him a descendant of Loarn.[69] But there are discrepancies between the genealogies given in 'MS 1467' and those contained in the poetry. The earliest of the extant classical Clann Ghriogóir poems is *Buaidh thighearna ar thóiseachaibh*, an eulogy composed by An Fear Dána Mac Giolla Fhionntóg for Maol Coluim, a chief who died in 1440. The poet only traces his patron's genealogy back to Donnchadh Beag, first lord of Glenorchy and Griogór's father.[70] The author of *Aithris fhréimhe ruanaidh Eoin*, Donnchadh MacGriogair (brother of the Dean of Lismore) goes beyond that, continuing the pedigree back to 'Ailpín oighre Dubhghaill' (§§10d, 13d). But when Donnchadh composed this poem — an eulogy for Eóin mac Pádraig — he was probably influenced by his contemporary Hector Boece's speculations on the origins of Clann Ghriogóir. Boece's view was that the eponymous Griogór was either a brother or a son of Cionaoth mac Ailpín, and therefore a descendant of Fearghus mac Eirc; Donnchadh MacGriogair followed him in this, but that he was uncertain how to make

67 It has been noted that poems by Scottish authors known to have been *filidh* are remarkably few in number in the 'Book of the Dean of Lismore' (Ó Mainnín 2002, p. 409). The individuals principally responsible for its compilation, a number of whom were also the authors of poems included in it, were not *filidh*; the latter do not seem to have been formally involved in the project (*ibid.*, p. 414). Meek sees the work as 'much indebted to the heritage of the Lordship of the Isles' (Meek 1996, p. 268); for the view that the debt is rather to the Caimbéalaigh see Ó Mainnín 2002.

68 As in *Ríoghacht ghaisgidh oighreacht Eoin*, §10b.

69 'MS 1467', no. 7.

70 *SVBDL*, p. 262.

the genealogical connexion is suggested in that he skipped the details of the earlier generations leading up to Ailpín, merely stating:

> Fear ar fhichid is tú a dhíth,
> ó Eoin Dubh nach dubh cridhe,
> do cheart sheanchas is é soin
> go Fearghus mac Earc ághmhoir.

> (A score and one, excluding thee, from John the Black, who was not black of heart; such is thy history aright, up to Fergus son of Erc the warlike) (§11).[71]

Donnchadh MacGriogair, it is well to remember, was not a *file*: the *filidh*, like their colleagues the professional *seanchaidhe*, were notoriously impervious to new-fangled claims and shifts in fashion tastes. To Boece and those who adhered to his opinion it was more reputable to have connexions with the contemporary Scottish royal line, descendants of Fearghus mac Eirc. The Irish sources are no help: no record of Clann Ghriogóir is found even in Mac Firbhisigh's great genealogical collection. Neither is Clann Ghriogóir descent from Fearghus Mór claimed in 'MS 1467', where the lineage is traced back to Cormac mac Airbheartaigh, and therefore to the royal line of Lorn (see Table 5.3).

Originally Clann Ghriogóir occupied lands stretching from Glenorchy in eastern Argyll across to Glenlochy in northern Perthshire. From what probably was their earliest seat their chiefs took the denomination 'of Orchy'.[72] This is also the territorial style used in classical poetry, although there are also allusions to their lands in Glenstrae and Glenlyon.[73] One Eóin of Orchy, 'Magnates Scotiae', is on record in the later thirteenth century, and one 'Hugh of Orchy' is similarly historically documented; the latter is probably the Aodh Urcháidh named by Donnchadh MacGriogair, again erroneously, as an ancestor of his poem's subject.[74] Neither Eóin nor Aodh of Orchy is mentioned in

---

71 For Boece's view and its influence see Sellar 1981, pp. 109–10.

72 Gregory 1831, pp. 5–7. For Clann Ghriogóir history see Macgregor 1898–1901, and especially MacGregor 1989.

73 *Aithris fhréimhe ruanaidh Eoin*, §3b; *Parrthas toraidh an Díseart*, §9d; *Buaidh thighearna ar thóiseachaibh*, §6c; *Ríoghacht ghaisgidh oighreacht Eoin*, §§11a, 21d.

74 Gregory 1831, p. 6; *Aithris fhréimhe ruanaidh Eoin*, §8d.

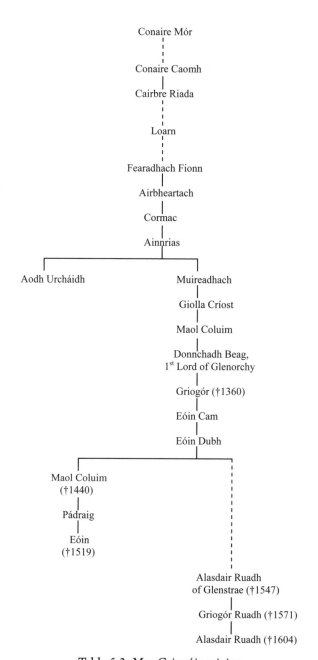

Table 5.3 Mac Griogóir origins.
Sources: *Buaidh thighearna ar thóiseachaibh*; 'MS 1467', no. 7; *SVBDL*, p. 262.

the earlier *Buaidh thighearna ar thóiseachaibh*, and they are equally absent from the 'MS 1467' pedigree, probably because they were not direct ancestors of the current chiefs, as suggested for Aodh in Table 5.3. In non-Gaelic sources the first chief recorded as 'lord of Glenorchy' was Donnchadh Beag, Griogór's father.[75] On account of their connexions with the lords of Lorn, Clann Ghriogóir were adversely affected by Mac Dubhghaill's forfeiture by Robert Bruce.[76] In 1306 Glenorchy was granted to Donnchadh Caimbéal in reward for his services to King Robert I, although the Caimbéalaigh would not obtain a legal title to the estate until *c.*1329, during the reign of David II. For some time Clann Ghriogóir resisted Caimbéal overlordship. From 1358 onwards three consecutive Mac Griogóir heiresses married into the Caimbéal family. The third and most important of these marriages was that of Mairghréad to Mac Cailéin (Cailéan Iongantach, †1412), whose grandson Cailéan became the first Caimbéal lord of Glenorchy. For a while relations between Clann Duibhne and Clann Ghriogóir were friendly, and sometimes reinforced through fosterage agreements.[77] In 1513 members of Clann Ghriogóir, like their overlords, fought at Flodden.[78] Indeed, up to the 1550s Clann Duibhne and Clann Ghriogóir enjoyed a close relationship as both kindreds expanded in tandem.[79] In 1554 Cailéan Caimbéal of Glenorchy purchased the superiority of the Glenstrae lands, Clann Ghriogóir remaining in the service of the earls of Argyll as well as, from then on, of Caimbéal of Glenorchy. Yet Clann Ghriogóir showed themselves capable of acting quite independently, something that soured their relationship with their overlords. In the late sixteenth century they became involved in a long and bitter feud with Clann Duibhne which ended with Clann Ghriogóir's destruction by the Caimbéalaigh, and with their dispossession and proscription in the seventeenth century, when James VI and I made the mere bearing of the surname Mac Griogóir a capital offence.

All nine extant Mac Griogóir syllabic poems were preserved by the

---

75 *SVBDL*, p. 262. The late (and highly unreliable, see above, pp. 199–200, and below, p. 204) *Aithris fhréimhe ruanaidh Eoin*, inserts one Giolla Faoláin between Donnchadh Beag and Aodh Urcháidh, and gives one Conán as the latter's father (§§8ab, 9ab).

76 Gregory 1831, p. 8. For what follows see Campbell of Airds 2000–2, i, pp. 101–2.

77 One fosterage contract is given in full — reproduced from Innes (ed.) 1855 — in Macgregor 1898–1901, i, p. 90.

78 Macgregor 1898–1901, p. 90.

79 MacGregor 1989, p. 406.

early sixteenth-century compilers of the 'Book of the Dean of Lismore', and thus belong to the period when the kindred's star was still in its rising. Indeed they were still taking pride in their Caimbéal connexions: Eóin mac Pádraig, the chief who died in 1519, could boast 'Fuil Artúir' ('the blood of Arthur') in his veins; Mac Cailéin was a fitting critic for the project of a *duanaire* which Seamus MacGriogair, Dean of Lismore, and his team had in hand.[80] Mac Griogóir classical verse is in the earlier rather than the later Scottish model,[81] and therefore retains much of the original 'Irish flavour'. This includes the unequivocal placing of Clann Ghriogóir within the Gaelic milieu while at the same time firmly locating this milieu within the wider kingdom of *Alba*, though without the Mac Domhnaill emphasis on the clan as the paramount defenders of the Scottish kingdom.[82] But in contrast with the earlier model as found in Clann Domhnaill verse, the classical panegyric for Mac Griogóir chiefs, like Caimbéal poetry, includes *Gall* references. These seem to be in every case disconnected from any actual events, that is, they are used merely as the conventional motif depicting the right ruler as the one able to safeguard his people and territory against foreigners: Clann Ghriogóir have obtained the foremost place of honour 'ó Ghallaibh'('on account of their victories over the *Goill*'), 'Ní mó leó Gaoidhil ná Goill' ('Of Gael they reck no more than of *Gall*'), Eóin mac Pádraig is 'fear chuireas argain ar Ghallaibh' ('a man who ravages *Goill*').[83]

Poets composing for Mac Griogóir nobles are fond of comparing their subjects to the great Gaelic heroes of the past. Eóin mac Pádraig is like Osgar and like Fionn, his horses are like Cú Chulainn's; Maol Coluim mac Eóin Duibh (†1440) has the hunting rights of the whole of *Alba* just as Fionn had had those of the whole of 'Éireann ... ó Chiarraigh go Carn Bhalair' ('Ireland ... from Kerry to Balar's Cairn').[84] The story of Fionn's

---

80 *Aithris fhréimhe ruanaidh Eoin*, §16ab; *Duanaire na sracaire*, §7.

81 See above, chapter 3, pp. 112–5.

82 *Buaidh thighearna ar thóiseachaibh*, §§5a, 14c; *Fhuaras mo rogha theach mhór*, §§2b, 14d, 17c; *Fada atáim gan bhogha*, §2c; *Gabh rém chomraigh, a mheic Ghriogoir*, §§10c, 11c; *Ríoghacht ghaisgidh oighreacht Eoin*, §§3a, 9a; *Parrthas toraidh an Díseart*, §18a; *Gealladh gach saoi don each odhar*, §13d.

83 *Buaidh thighearna ar thóiseachaibh*, §7b; *Ríoghacht ghaisgidh oighreacht Eoin*, §9a; *Gealladh gach saoi don each odhar*, §13e. For a detailed overview see Coira 2008b, pp. 146–8.

84 *Ríoghacht ghaisgidh oighreacht Eoin*, §§11c, 13d–20; *Buaidh thighearna ar thóiseachaibh*, §§8–15; *Gealladh gach saoi don each odhar*, §§4,12. Carn Bhalair: somewhere in the far

hunting rights is one of the three *apalóga* found in Clann Ghriogóir poetry. A second is contained in *Gabh rém chomraigh, a mheic Ghriogóir*, where Fionnlagh Ruadh seeks Eóin mac Pádraig's forgiveness for some unknown offence: the poet would like to make his peace with him just as Conall Clogach of old had with his foster-father, Conchobhar mac Neasa (§§6–8). The third *apalóg* is found in *Fhuaras mo rogha theach mhór*, where Fionnlagh Ruadh tells the story of the old hag whom Mac Diarmada (probably the chief of Moylurg in Connacht) allowed into his house; there she slept for a whole year, at the end of which she awoke transformed into a lovely young maiden (§§8–12). Other points of interest in Mac Griogóir classical verse are the preservation of the 'lordly traits' motif ('buaidh thighearna', 'tréidhe tighearna')[85] and, perhaps more interestingly, the praiseterm 'oide dámh', 'instructor of poets' or perhaps 'foster-father of poets'. Both translations of *oide* are closely related: we read in the ninth-century glossary *Sanas Cormaic* that 'is i n-ace bis an deiscipal acind aiti' ('the pupil is always in fosterage with the teacher').[86] Donnchadh Mac Griogóir, keeper of Glenorchy Castle, was celebrated by An Giolla Glas Mac an Táilliuir as 'oididhe dámh', 'oide na n-éigeas' ('instructor of poets'), '[m'] oide' ('my instructor').[87] Oddly, there is an almost total lack of references to illustrious ancient ancestors, or their territories, in Clann Ghriogóir panegyric. We noted Donnchadh MacGriogair's Boece-inspired claim of the kindred's descent from Fearghus mac Eirc, whose remote ancestor was Conaire. Aside from this, the only ancient forebears to be named are Conall and Conn, given in the same poem (§16c). These seem to be Conall Gulban and his ancestor Conn Céadchathach but, if so, then this is an equally unlikely claim, for Clann Ghriogóir could not possibly stem from both Conn and Conaire, unless there had been at least one earlier Mac Griogóir marriage to a Mac Domhnaill, for instance, of which there is no mention in any sources. The connexion with Tara (§6d), made on account of either genealogical claim, is therefore flawed.

The strictly vernacular (accentual) poetry for Clann Ghriogóir focuses on the subject's martial deeds, generosity, hospitality and love of hunting

---

north of Ireland (Watson 2004, p. 65 and n. 1). See also *Onomasticon, s.v. c[arn] bhaile*.

85 *Buaidh thighearna ar thóiseachaibh*, §§1a, 7c.

86 *DIL* A, 251:12–13.

87 *Parrthas toraidh an Díseart*, §§2a, 9b, 11c.

and feasting. But it also reflects the troubled conditions of the clan from the late sixteenth century onwards: their hounding by the Caimbéalaigh and the loss of their patrimony. *Moch madainn air latha Lùnast'* (popularly known as *Griogal Cridhe*), a syllabic-based lament for Griogór Ruadh of Glenstrae, was composed by his widow, 'Marion' (Mòr), daughter of Donnchadh Caimbéal of Glenlyon (†1578),[88] and is another instance of a Caimbéal woman turning against her own kin.[89] Young Griogór Ruadh had, on his coming of age in 1562, rebelled against his overlord, Caimbéal of Glenorchy, who would allow him to keep his patrimony only under insulting conditions. A bitter feud ensued, culminating in 1571 when the young chief was captured and executed by Glenorchy.[90] 'Marion' notes that her beloved's capture had been 'le foill' ('by treachery'), and curses her own father and grandfather as well as the Caimbéalaigh in general (§§6–7). There is also a series of poems, all of anonymous authorship, concerned with the battle of Glenfruin in the Lennox (1603), where Griogór Ruadh's son and successor, Alasdair Ruadh (†1604), routed a royal army commanded by Alasdair Mac a' Chombaich of Luss. The defeated are the *Goill*, here no mere poetic motif but the Lowlander enemy: at Glenfruin Clann Ghriogóir had slain *Gallbhodaich*, there had been 'pudhar nan Gall' ('the wounding of the Lowlanders'), 'luchd cleòchd' ('the cloaked people'), 'clann nan Gall' ('the children of the Lowlanders') had been destroyed.[91] Just as perplexingly as in the classical poems, there is a lack of reference to venerable ancient ancestors.

Clann Ghille Eóin

We have noted the frustration of Dr. Hector Maclean of Grulin, who lived in the eighteenth century, concerning the loss of Gaelic historical records, which he blamed on the ungratefulness or the negligence of 'Shenachies and Bards'.[92] 'All that remains', he continued, 'is a bare Catalogue of Names from Gillean [Gille Eóin na Tuaighe] upwards to Inighisteurteamher [Aonghus Tuirbheach Teamhrach] who is said to have reigned in Ireland

---

88 *BG*, p. 328.

89 See above, chapter 4, p. 147.

90 See MacGregor 1999, pp. 120–1.

91 *A mhic an fhir ruaidh*, §22c; *Is beag mo mhulad 's mi am fràmh*, §§5c, 6a; *An saoil sibh féin nach foghainnteach*, l. 18. See also *Tha mo chiabhan air glasadh*, §§3c, 4c.

92 See above, chapter 2, p. 41.

Five Generations before Fergus the First King of Scotland'.[93] This 'catalogue' was in the possession of the Rev. Eóin Mac Beathadh (*c*.1640–1715), the last of the Mac Beathadh medical family, and its contents, Maclean affirms, were not only in agreement with another 'catalogue' kept by the chief of Coll but also very much with the version of 'Dr Kennedy', apparently a contemporary scholar with genealogical interests.[94] Maclean's frustration is the more understandable in view of the fabrications of later historians. Yet, scarce as his sources — which included a classical poem[95] — were, he convincingly dismissed as one such fabrication the claim that the Mac Gille Eóin and Mac Coinnigh families shared a common ancestor. More recently David Sellar has proved him correct.[96]

Clann Ghille Eóin took their name from Gille Eóin Mór mac Mhic Raith, also known as Gille Eóin na Tuaighe ('of the Battle-axes'), who may have lived in the early thirteenth century. Before him the kindred was known as Clann Chon Duiligh, from Cú Duiligh, one of three sons of Raingce and grandson of Sean Dubhghall Scóinne ('of Scone'), who in turn was claimed to be a son of Fearchar Abhraruadh, of the royal line of Loarn (see Table 5.4). Sean Dubhghall would have lived in the early twelfth century, and may have been a judge.[97] The descendants of the two other sons of Raingce, Cú Catha and Cú Síthe, came to settle in the Lennox and in Fife respectively. Clann Ghille Eóin's lineage beyond Sean Dubhghall, however, presents serious obstacles. Our earliest Scottish source, 'MS 1467', shows some major discrepancies when the pedigree is set against those of other kindreds claiming descent from Loarn Mór. It places five generations which in Lulach's pedigree appear immediately down from Fearchar Fada, immediately down from Eochaidh Muinreamhar, and five generations above Fearchar Fada in Lulach's pedigree, immediately before Fearchar Abhraruadh.[98] In common with Irish

---

93 Macfarlane 1900, i, p. 118.

94 *ibid.*, p. 119.

95 *Clann Ghille Eóin na mbratach badhbha*, for which see below, pp. 212–14.

96 Sellar 1981, pp. 110–13. See also below, pp. 226 n. 203, 228 n. 208.

97 'MS 1467', nos. 2, 24.

98 It also substitutes Leathán for Buadhán, perhaps in an attempt to explain the later denomination 'Leathanaich' for Clann Ghille Eóin; see Black's note to 'MS 1467', no. 24. These, however, may be errors by the scribe, who seems to have been working in a hurried manner. See below, chapter 6, p. 250 and n. 13.

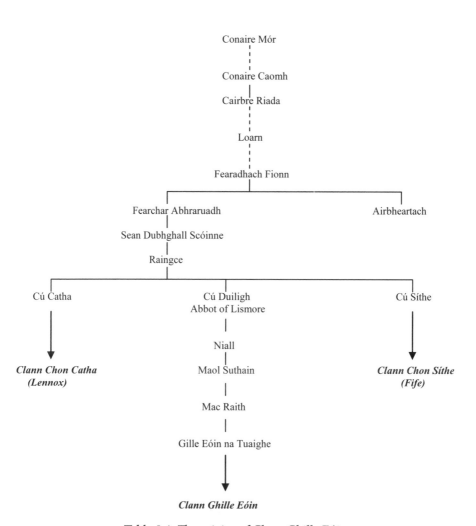

Table 5.4 The origins of Clann Ghille Eóin.
Sources: 'MS 1467', no. 24; *LMG* ii, §§405.9–406.9; iii, §§1153.3–4; Macfarlane 1900, p. 120. For sources making Ceallach, son of Raingce, Abbot of Lismore, see Maclean-Bristol 1995, p. 163 n. 3.

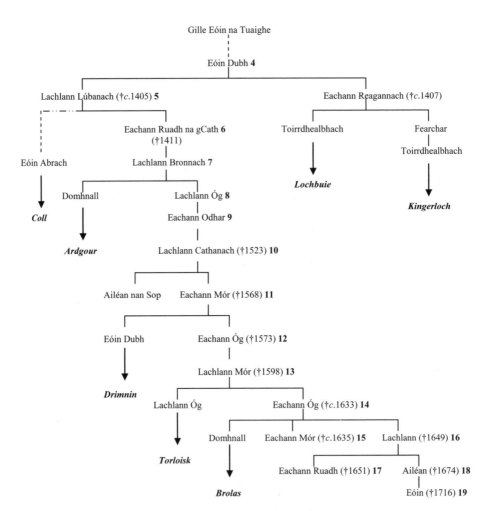

Table 5.5 Clann Ghille Eóin cadet branches.
Sources: *DC*, p. xvi; Maclean-Bristol 1995, pp. 158–98.

sources, however, 'MS 1467' makes Clann Ghille Eóin a descendant of Loarn Mór through Fearchar Abhraruadh, while Mac Firbhisigh notes a more recent version connecting the clan to Conaire Mór.[99] Most suspiciously, no other Scottish kindred traces its descent through Fearchar Abhraruadh; was this person a late-medieval fabrication designed to give Clann Ghille Eóin a reputable origin once they became important figures in the Gaelic world? It may be no coincidence that they were among those insulted by the tutor of Moydart at Mac Domhnaill's feast in the early to mid-fifteenth century.[100]

Similarly uncertain is where the original patrimony of Cú Duiligh's progeny, the future Clan Ghille Eóin, lay. Skene speculated that the kindred may have moved from north Moray to the Lorn district in the twelfth century, something not entirely improbable.[101] But their earliest historical appearances belong to the fourteenth century, when they were occupying Ballachuan, a farm in the isle of Seil — ten miles south of Oban, in the Firth of Lorn — and possibly also lands by Loch Tarbert.[102] According to 'Hugh of Sleat' the land in Seil was a grant by Eóin of Lorn, by which the kindred became Mac Dubhghaill's vassals.[103] By the time the last Mac Dubhgaill lord of Lorn died in 1316, Gille Eóin's descendants seem to have been an established kindred, and could boast some important kinship connexions: the eponym's grandson, Giolla Coluim, is said in Gaelic sources to have married 'Rioghnach, ingean Gamhail, mormair Cairrge' ('Ríoghnach, daughter of Gamhal, *mormhaor* of Carrick').[104] This marriage connected Giolla Coluim and his successors with the earls of Carrick, who were in turn linked by marriage with the High Steward of Scotland.[105]

But most importantly for Clann Ghille Eóin's rising fortunes, a marriage was arranged between Lachlann Lúbanach (†c.1405), progenitor of the Duart branch, and Máire, daughter of Eóin mac Aonghuis Óig, seventh

---

99 'MS 1467', nos. 2, 24 and link to readings in other manuscripts; *LMG* ii, §§405.3, 405.7–405.9, 410.6–411.2. See also below, p. 226.

100 *HP* i, pp. 45–6. Cf. above, chapter 4, p. 156.

101 Skene 1878–90, iii, p. 343; Maclean-Bristol 1995, p. 2.

102 Maclean-Bristol 1995, pp. 11, 13.

103 *HP* i, p. 21.

104 *LMG* ii, §406.4; iii, §1153.6; Skene 1878–90, iii, p. 481. Gamhal may rather have been a *mormhaor*'s son (Maclean-Bristol 1995, p. 9).

105 See Table 4.1.

lord of the Isles. While this union earned the lord of the Isles a strong ally, for Clann Ghille Eóin it led to greatly increased social standing and to major territorial expansion during the fifteenth century, and on a more reduced scale in the sixteenth. Lachlann Lúbanach was appointed chamberlain (steward of the household) to his brother-in-law, Domhnall, eighth lord of the Isles; his grandson Lachlann Bronnach appears in company of Domhnall's successor, Alasdair — if we are to believe 'Hugh of Sleat' — socialising in Edinburgh with the Earl of Orkney.[106] The Duart and Lochbuie chiefs were members of the Council of the Isles, and along with the heads of other main Clann Ghille Eóin branches they witnessed charters of the lords of the Isles.[107] Their new social rank is reflected also in the burial in Iona of Mac Gille Eóin chiefs related by blood to the lords of the Isles.[108] Subsequent grants to the heads of various branches of Clann Ghille Eóin included lands in Mull, Tiree, Coll, and on the mainland Morvern, Ardgour and Lochiel.[109] There is evidence that the charters they received from Mac Domhnaill were subsequently confirmed by the kings of Scots, whose vassals the lords of the Isles were.[110] As they expanded territorially the kindred founded new family groups. The main two were the descendants of Lachlann Lúbanach and of his brother, Eachann Reagannach. From the former stemmed the houses of Duart, Coll and Ardgour on the western shore of Loch Linnhe, and later those of Boreray in North Uist, Drimnin on the north-east shore of the Sound of Mull, and Torloisk in north-west Mull. Eachann Reagannach was the progenitor of the main families of Lochbuie in Mull and Clann Toirrdhealbhaigh (later known as Mac Gille Eóin of Kingerloch), as well as those of Urquhart in Morayshire, Dochgarroch near Inverness, and Knock in Mull. The main Clann Ghille Eóin families seem to have been independent from each other. In the later period Mac Gille Eóin of Duart, who had become the most powerful of them, began to claim, without any factual historical foundation, leadership of the whole clan. In reality each Mac Gille Eóin chief was a direct vassal of

---

106 *HP* i, pp. 22–3, 36.

107 *Monro*, p. 57; *HP* i, p. 24; Bannerman 1977, p. 222.

108 *Monro*, p. 63; Maclean-Bristol 1995, pp. 47, 58; Steer and Bannerman 1977, pp. 129–31.

109 *HP* i, pp. 36–7, 46–7; Bannerman 1977, p. 217.

110 Maclean-Bristol 1995, p. 44.

the lord of the Isles, and after the latter's forfeiture in 1493 they passed to hold their patrimonies of the crown.[111]

In the late fourteenth century Clann Ghille Eóin joined Eóin Mór of Islay (†1427), who showed his discontent concerning his portion of the heritage by rebelling against his brother and chief, Alasdair, ninth lord of the Isles. Mac Gille Eóin of Duart was the foster-father of Eóin Mór's son, Domhnall Ballach, which probably explains[112] his support of the rebellion. This seems to have been the only instance of Clann Ghille Eóin's rebellious behaviour. Their otherwise steady support of the lords of the Isles brought them into conflict with royal government on more than one occasion: at Harlaw in 1411 they fought for Clann Domhnaill,[113] and in the early sixteenth century they backed Domhnall Gallda of Lochalsh in his effort to succeed to the lordship of the Isles. But confrontation between Mac Domhnaill and royal government, such as that which led to the encounter at Harlaw, was rare,[114] and thus Clann Ghille Eóin were able most of the time to give loyal service to the kings: Gille Eóin Mór's son and successor Maol Íosa is said to have fought the Norse at Largs in 1263, and in 1407 Eachann na gCath — who four years later would be killed at Harlaw — was granted a safe-conduct to visit the captive king James I in England.[115] In the sixteenth century Duart continued to be the most powerful chief of Clann Ghille Eóin and became an ally of Argyll. Probably under the latter's influence the Duart chiefs converted to Protestantism, and at the battle of Glenlivet (1594) the current chief fought on Argyll's side against the forces led by the Catholic Seoras Gordan, second Marquis of Huntly, and Francis Hay, ninth Earl of Errol. That would be, however, the last time a Mac Gille Eóin chief — with the exception of the head of Torloisk during the Montrose wars[116] — sided with Argyll. Throughout the mid-century Wars of the Three Kingdoms and beyond, Clann Ghille Eóin remained steadfast supporters of the Stiúbhart kings. But their zenith was behind them. Plagued by financial debt they became

---

111 *ibid.*, pp. 89, 146.

112 *HP* i, p. 32.

113 Maclean-Bristol 1995, pp. 84–5.

114 See above, chapter 2, p. 51.

115 Maclean-Bristol 1995, p. 32.

116 id. 1988, p. 86.

easy prey to the expansionist Caimbéalaigh, and in 1680 their patrimony was granted by the king to Argyll.[117]

It seems strange that only one classical poem, or rather a fragment of one, composed for Clann Ghille Eóin has survived. It begins *Clann Ghille Eóin na mbratach badhbha* and was appended by Dr. Hector Maclean, in a Scots-based rather than Gaelic orthography, at the end of his genealogical history of Clann Ghille Eóin.[118] In the few quatrains preserved there is one reference to Mac Gille Eóin martial prowess in Ireland. If Dr. Maclean's ascription of the poem to a Mac Muireadhaigh author is correct, then it might have been composed in the times of Eachann Mór (†1568), eleventh chief of Duart: in 1532 he was sent by the king to fight in Ireland, on Ó Domhnaill's side and against Ó Néill and the English,[119] while the Mac Muireadhaigh connexion may have been provided by Eachann's wife, Máire, daughter of Alasdair Mac Domhnaill of Islay.[120] If Eachann Mór is the subject of the poem, then Niall Mór Mac Muireadhaigh, who was roughly contemporary with him, might be its author.[121] What, then, happened to the rest of Mac Gille Eóin classical verse?[122] According to Mairghread nighean Lachlainn, a vernacular poet, both 'bàird agus filidh' would be found in the household of Sir Eóin Mac Gille Eóin, nineteenth chief of Duart (†1716).[123] This may of course refer merely to visiting poets enjoying Duart's hospitality. There is also an allusion by Eachann Bacach to 'Mac Mhuirich, Mac Fhearghais'; but, again, this does not necessarily imply that hereditary learned men of this name, or names, were in Mac Gille Eóin employment.[124] It is thought

---

117 *EB*, p. xlii.

118 Macfarlane 1900, i, p. 142; rep. with a Classical Gaelic transcription in Campbell 1961, pp. 90–1.

119 Maclean-Bristol 1995, p. 99.

120 Theirs was the only marriage of a Duart chief to a Clann Domhnaill woman since that of Lachlann Lúbanach to the daughter of the lord of the Isles in the later fourteenth century.

121 For other suggestions concerning the poem's dating and authorship see *EB*, pp. 170–1.

122 If only for reasons of prestige, it is almost inconceivable that, once they came to prominence, they would not have patronised *filidh*, or that the latter would not sought their patronage.

123 *Is goirt leam gaoir nam ban Muileach*, §12ef.

124 *Thriall bhur bunadh gu Phàro*, §1c. It is not clear whether one or two surnames are involved here. For some discussion see *EB*, pp. 170–3.

that until the early seventeenth century, when they appear attached to Mac Leóid of Dunvegan, the Ó Muirgheasáin family were hereditary *filidh* to Mac Gille Eóin of Duart.[125] By that time the Duart family were already under financial strain, which had started accruing through their involvement in the Irish wars,[126] the same wars which, ironically, had earned them poetic praise. By 1617 the Duart estate had been placed in the hands of trustees. It seems probable that the financial pressures forced the Duart chiefs to dismiss their *filidh*, who then found patronage under Mac Leóid. But the question still lingers of what happened to Mac Gille Eóin classical poetry, if any of it was preserved for them in writing. Were their books and records destroyed by the earls of Argyll after they obtained the Duart patrimony in 1680? Were they taken by their *filidh* when they left Duart's employment? We will probably never have an answer. At any rate the Duart chiefs were able to retain a *bàrd* in their employment: Eachann Bacach, 'an t-Aosdana Mac Illeathain' (*fl.*1650), was 'am fear mo dheireadh do na baird Mhuileach aig an robh duais, bho cheann chinneadh airson a bhi na bhard' ('the last of the Mull *baird* who had a wage from his chief for his being a poet').[127]

The surviving fragment of *Clann Ghille Eóin na mbratach badhbha* is all about the martial prowess of Clann Ghille Eóin, but embedded in it we do find various other conventional praise motifs. They are hardy raiders (§3a) and the receptors of 'cluain na cleire' ('poetic flattery', §3c), and:

> 'S mairg don tsluagh ar feadh na Fodla
> 'gan dail diomdha.
>
> (Woe to the host throughout Ireland
> that would give them dissatisfaction) (§1c).

As noted, this may well be a reference to the exploits of Eachann Mór and his redshanks in Ireland, where they were sent by James V. All the same, this may be no more than a common eulogistic device. In our fragment, indeed, the ambience remains Gaelic: Clann Ghille Eóin are noted

---

125 See above, chapter 4, p. 159 and n. 172.
126 Maclean-Bristol 1988, p. 81.
127 Quoted *EB*, p. xliv. See also *ibid.*, p. xlv.

as 'gasraidh gleusda Ghaoidheal' ('a warrior-band of Gaels ready for action',
§2a), rather than Scots. There is also an allusion to Cú Raoi mac Dáire
(§4d), but within a sentence that at present is far from clear. The quat-
rain is problematic. One of its lines contains an extra syllable, which my
indicate textual corruption, and the word spelled *cuini* (using Scots-based
orthography) by Dr Maclean of Grulin, to whom we owe the preservation
of the fragment, is of uncertain meaning:

> Si ghivigh i ghuoig o righi gin dialtari
> Sinin dar crou is dar cuini sdi Churi mac Dari.

Further, the preposition do ('dar crou ... dar cuini ... sdi Churi mac
Dari'), might convey the meaning 'the same to' rather than 'the same as'.[128]
Perhaps the poet is saying that whatever royal awards Mac Gille Eóin is
made, 'it is the same to our blood and to our champions [descending]
from Cú Raoi mac Dáire', where 'our blood' and 'our champions' would
mean the poet himself and his own kindred.[129] However, if the author was
a Mac Muireadhaigh, a reputed descendant of the Ulster Ó Dálaigh poetic
family, he could not be claiming descent from Cú Raoi, whose homeland
was Munster. From extant genealogies we can place Cú Raoi in relation
to Mac Gille Eóin's ancestors as shown in Table 5.6: Clann Ghille Eóin's
lineage is not traced back to Cú Raoi. If the poet is referring to his own
lineage, he is claiming descent from Síol Luighdheach (also Dáirfhine,
the descendants of Cú Raoi, son of Dáire) and therefore kinship with Síol
nÉibhir (also Deirgtheine, Iar's descendants, among whom were Dál Riada
and therefore Clann Ghille Eóin), both population groups being known
as Clanna Deaghaidh. Dr. Maclean was aware of this genealogical connex-
ion, as shown by his transcription of two separate Gaelic pedigrees and his
quotation of Dr. Kennedy, a contemporary scholar.[130]

---

128 *DIL* I, 294: 56–7; 295: 1–5.

129 *cuini*: perhaps, corrupted during oral transmission, for *cuingidhibh*, from *cuingid*
('champion, warrior'); see *DIL* C, 595: 67–8, 78. This would add yet another syllable
to the line, but as we have it is already corrupted. It might also be possible to translate
cuini as 'the equal of' (*DIL* C, 594: 73–6), but this option, too, has its own problems.
For an alternative translation see *DnS*, p. 165.

130 Macfarlane 1900, i, p. 119. For Cú Raoi see *FFÉ* i, p. 122, ii, pp. 220–2.

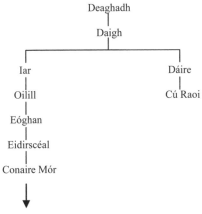

Dál Riada of Ireland and Scotland

Table 5.6 Relationship of Cú Raoi and Clann Ghille Eóin.
Source: *LMG* ii, §§602.6, 1140.6, 1141.2–4.

The remainder of the poem might have contained further genealogical references, but that material has been lost forever. What we do have is a considerable corpus of vernacular verse (about sixty poems), but here we encounter a strange silence on the matter of noble ancestry. Gille Eóin na Tuaighe is mentioned once;[131] elsewhere the poets — who are chiefly Mac Gille Eóin gentry and generally compose in accentual metres[132] — merely refer to the Gaelic tradition of Egyptian origins, through Míl Easbáinne, Gaoidheal and Scota, back to Pharo himself.[133] Their ancestors' settlement in Ireland is also remembered, and Éireamhón noted in one poem as the progenitor of Clann Ghille Eóin.[134] Éireamhón, however, was the claimed ancestor of most Scottish *Gaoidhil*, including the descendants of Colla Uais. In brief, apart from the one reference to the eponym, Gille Eóin, and the occasional allusion to Éireamhón, Mac Gille Eóin poetry fails to evoke venerable noble ancestors in the way that Colla Uais, Artúr and Olbhar,

---

131 *Ge grianachan latha*, §9a.

132 Two love poems by Maighstir Seathan (*EB*, nos. 18 and 20) are in 'semi-classical' style. Some poems, like *Marbhaisg air an t-saoghal chruaidh* or *Thriall bhur bunadh gu Phàro*, are variants of syllabic forms.

133 *Ge grianach an latha*, §22bc; *Tha mi am chadal 's gur tìm dhomh dùsgadh*, §§4–6; *Iomchair mo bheannachd*, §§3–4; *Thriall bhur bunadh gu Phàro*, §1a; *Tha iongnadh air an Dreòllain*, §6ab.

134 *Tha mi am chadal 's gur tìm dhomh dùsgadh*, §7 (reference to Éireamhón); *Iomchair mo bheannachd*, §3nop.

for instance, are evoked in Mac Domhnaill, Caimbéal and Mac Leóid panegyric respectively. One consequence of this genealogical blank is that Clann Ghille Eóin verse similarly lacks geographical references connecting the poems' subjects with their early ancestors' original territories. There are many place-names in Clann Domhnaill poetry, for instance, recalling the kindred's ancestral territories in Ulster and even in Connacht, while the Caimbéalaigh celebrate Artúr's kingship of Britain, and Clann Leóid name Norway and places there. There is nothing of the kind in Mac Gille Eóin verse, where geographical references are related to the territories they currently occupy: Duart, Aros, An Dreòllain (a name for Mull), Loch Cumhainn:[135] The lack of mention of ancient noble ancestors and their original homeland may be related to Clann Ghille Eóin's relatively late rise. As noted, they are derided as upstarts in 'Hugh of Sleat's' narrative, reflecting, if not a fifteenth-century view, at least the author's.[136] Elsewhere the same writer states that 'they never had a rigg of land but what they received from Macdonald'.[137] The Sleat historian has been criticised for his attacks on Clann Ghille Eóin,[138] but his resentment of their betrayal of Clann Domhnaill in their time of need is understandable: Mac Gille Eóin progress had come about through their Mac Domhnaill overlords, and so he decried their ungratefulness when later, 'when the Macdonalds were in adversity … [Clann Ghille Eóin] became their mortal enemies'.[139]

The dearth of references to ancient noble ancestors, however, is counterbalanced in two ways. Firstly poets are particularly fond of remembering the sixth chief of Duart, Eachann na gCath, who commanded Mac Domhnaill's right wing at the battle of Harlaw and was killed in the encounter along with six hundred of his men.[140] Secondly we find a profuse employment of the 'friends and allies' motif, within which may

---

135 *Gura h-oil leam an sgeul seo*, §15cd; *Tha mi am chadal 's gur tim dhomh dùsgadh*, §8. For An Dreòllainn see *EB*, pp. 233–4. Loch Cumhainn: in the north of Mull (*EB*, p. 210).

136 See above, p. 209.

137 *HP* i, p. 23.

138 Maclean-Bristol 1995, p. 16.

139 *HP* i, p. 23.

140 *Thriall bhur bunadh gu Phàro*, §1f; *Is goirt leam gaoir nam ban Muileach*, §6g; *Tha mi am chadal 's gur tim dhomh dùsgadh*, §§9–10; *Gura h-oil leam an sgeul seo*, §§9efgh, 10 (for the reference in the last see *EB*, pp. 204–6); *HP* i, p. 29; Mair 1892 [1521], Bk. vi, p. 348.

be included the celebration of aristocratic kinship connexions: Iain mac Ailein's *Iomchair mo bheannachd*, an elegy for Sir Eóin, nineteenth chief of Duart (†1716), recalls the marriage of Lachlann Lúbanach to the daughter of the lord of the Isles:

> Ciad nighean Mhic-Domhnuill,
> Mar mhairiste pòsda.
>
> (Mac Domhnaill's first daughter
> as [his] wedded wife) (§4ijk).

In an eulogy for Sir Eachann, seventeenth chief (†1651), the same poet notes his subject's connexion with the Marquis of Hamilton, and seems to hint at a love affair between Sir Eachann and Argyll's daughter. Màiri NicGhilleathain notes a Caimbéal connexion in a poem for Lachlann, ninth chief of Coll, also mentioned in an anonymous elegy for Eachann Ruadh, seventeenth of Duart.[141] Mac Leóid, Mac Coinnigh, various branches of Clann Domhnaill, Camshrón, Mac Néill, and Mac Fionghuin are included among the following, and the various Mac Gille Eóin branches will support one another.[142] While the 'friends and allies' motif is common in Scottish Gaelic vernacular poetry, its abundance in Mac Gille Eóin verse seems partly connected with the clan's dire circumstances, particularly under their heavy debts to Argyll in the seventeenth century.[143] By listing allies the poet would provide much-needed hope and encouragement. Much of Clann Ghille Eóin poetry is indeed concerned with 'dol sìos Chloinn Ghill-Eathain' ('the decline of Clann Ghille Eóin'), principally lamenting their changed circumstances, but also sometimes expressing hope that the clan's fortunes will be restored.[144]

---

141 *Gura h-oil leam an sgeul seo*, §§9ef, 12abcd; *'S ann Di-Satharn a chualas*, §8ef; *Ach ga grianach an latha*, §12e. For these allusions see *EB*, pp. 204, 207–8, and *DC*, pp. 65–6.

142 *Mhic Móire na gréine*, §16; *Cuid de adhbhar mo ghearain*, §§3–6, 8; *Gur bochd nàidheachd do dhùthcha*, §9ab; *Ach ga grianach an latha*, §10abc; *Iomchair mo bheannachd*, §§9, 11–14; *'S ann Di-Satharn a chualas*, §8abcd; *Mo cheist an Leathanach mòdhar*, §5abcd.

143 See *OIL*, p. 251.

144 *'S ann Di-ciadain an là, Uam-s' tha ràitinn, Tha iongnadh air an Dreòllain, Cha choma leam fhèin no co-dhiù sin, An tùs an t-samhraidh seo bhà, Cuid de adhbhar mo ghearain* (*EB*, p. xxxix). See also *'Dheagh Mhic-Coinnigh a Brathainn*.

The allies motif is sometimes used within the context of royalism, one important theme in Mac Gille Eóin verse. Here we find a number of the same motif-components found in Clann Domhnaill and Clann Leóid vernacular poems.[145] Genealogical continuity of the royal line, against the intrusion of the foreign William of Orange, is upheld by Maighstir Seathan in *Ge grianach an latha*:

O nach maireann rìgh Teàrlach
Na Seumas a bhràthair,
'S nach e 'n sliochd na 'n luchd phàirt tha 'nan lorg,

'S olc a' chòir a th' aig Uilleam
O *Hòlland* nan currac
Air còmhnadh le duine d'ar seòrs ...

Ar leam bu chòra do dh'Albainn
A' chathair rìoghail a dh'earbsa
Ri fear de shliochd Fhearghas nan còrn.

(Since neither King Charles nor his brother James is alive, and since it is not their kindred or supporters who have succeeded them, William, from Holland of the bonnets, has a poor claim for support on such as us ... In my view, Scotland ought rather to have entrusted the royal throne to one of the race of Fearghas [mac Eirc] of the drinking horns) (§§17–18, 21).

Iain mac Ailein similarly distinguishes between 'a' chraobh thorach' ('the fruitful branch', that is, King James), and 'a' chraobh ùr' ('the new branch', or King William), the upstart king.[146] He notes the arrogance and deceit of political traitors, whom Mac Domhnaill poets associated with the upstart rabble:[147] it was 'luchd na foille 's an ardain' ('deceitful and arrogant folk') who beheaded King Charles and sent James wandering,

---

145 See above, chapters 3, pp. 102–9; 4, pp. 173–5.
146 *Mun sgeul so chualas*, §3ce; *BL*, p. 97.
147 See above, chapter 3, p. 107. For other poets complaining of deceit see p. 105 n. 243.

substituting William and Mary.[148] Iain mac Ailein also hopes for the ful-
filling of 'tairgineachd' ('prophecy'), presumably that uttered by Thomas
the Rhymer.[149] The motif of the wheel of fortune is also used several times
by Mac Gille Eóin poets, Maighstir Seathan giving it a spiritual slant: it is
God, 'A nì ìosal is àrd neach' ('who humbles and exalts a man') who turns
the wheel of fortune, and if Clann Ghille Eóin have been lowered now,
surely they will rise again.[150] Indeed poets express their trust that divine
Providence will set things right, both Clann Ghille Eóin's fortunes and
the national political crisis.[151] Iain mac Ailein hopes that the current hard
circumstances are merely:

> ach leasan
> Thun ar teagasg na's fhearr.
>
> (but a lesson
> for our better teaching).[152]

It is only Ian mac Ailein who truly engages, in some poems, with the
wider contemporary British politics. In a piece celebrating the valour of
the men of Mull at Killiecrankie he attacks those whom King James had
treated right but who then forsook him:

> Re àm a fheuma, Sasann thrèig e,
> Alba is Eirinn còmhla.
>
> (in the time of his need England forsook him,
> Scotland and Ireland together).[153]

He rejects King William, 'an t-eun [coimheach]' ('the foreign bird'),[154]
as a stranger placed on the throne by those disloyal to Stiúbhart line:

---

148 *Mun sgeul-sa tha aca*, §14.
149 *Nam faicinn gum b' fhìor*, §2cd. See above, chapter 3, pp. 102, 109.
150 *Ge grianachan latha*, §§29–33 (quotation at §29b).
151 *'N Raon Ruairidh seo bha ann*, §4ef; *Tha iongnadh air an Dreòllain*, §§8–12.
152 *Nan tiocfadh, nan tiocfadh, nan tiocfadh do sgeul*, §11gh.
153 *'N àm dhol sìos*, §3cd.
154 *Cha labhair mi táireil*, §2c.

Ach facal soitheamh duirt neach roimhe
Gum bi gach nodha rò gheal.

(but a wise saying long since uttered
tells that anything new seems brighter).[155]

He complains of political deceit,[156] and takes up the contemporary strand condemning the turning of the son against the father:[157]

Am mac a' gabhail brath air athair
Leis a' chlaidheamh chòmhraig.

(The son taking advantage of the father
with the sword of combat).[158]

Finally, he upholds the divine right of kings:

Ge b'e tì dhe'n dèan Dia rìgh
Gur còir bhith strìocadh dhò-san.

(whoever the man God makes king,
to submit to him is proper).[159]

Both Iain MacBheathadh and Iain mac Ailein present the current adverse circumstances (Clann Ghille Eóin's poverty, debt, gloom and their leader's exile, as well as the wider political events leading to the usurpation of the throne) as divine punishment for sin.[160] The Caimbéalaigh are noted to be on the enemy side,[161] and are attacked by Iain Lom with his usual viciousness in two poems in praise of Duart chiefs.[162] Sometimes we

---

155 ibid., §3gh.
156 'N àm dhol sìos, §6e.
157 See chapter 3, p. 112.
158 'N àm dhol sìos, §5ef.
159 ibid., §7cd.
160 Tha iongnadh air an Dreòllain, §11cd; Mun sgeul-sa tha aca, §10b.
161 Thriall bhur bunadh gu Phàro, §13h; Gur bochd nàidheachd do dhùthcha, §10.
162 Cuid de adhbhar mo ghearain, §§9, 13; Mur bhith 'n abhainn air fàs oirnn, §§5c, 6a, 7a.

can detect a note of bitterness in the poets' voices, seemingly wondering whether Clann Ghille Eóin's gallant fight for the Stiúbhart cause was worth it at all: there are several complaints about the price that they paid for their royalism, and Mairghread nighean Lachlainn bluntly laments their unwavering loyalty to the king; better, she adds, to be crafty and deceitful 'mar bha an nàimhdean miorúnach' ('as the spiteful enemy was').[163] 'Mìo-rùn [mòr] nan Gall' ('the [great] hate, or spite, of the Lowlanders') became a common theme in eighteenth-century Gaelic poetry, but the *Goill* as the Lowland enemies are already present in Mac Gille Eóin poetry, as in that for other kindreds,[164] in the seventeenth century. The *Goill* are the English in *Gura h-oil leam an sgeul seo* (§6h), a lament for Eachann Ruadh, seventeenth chief of Duart, who was killed at the battle of Inverkeithing (1651), fighting John Lambert's English parliamentarian army.

Elsewhere, however, the *Goill* are the Lowland Scots, though not always with a negative connotation: Lachlann Mac Gille Eóin, ninth chief of Coll (†1687), is celebrated for his socialising in 'bailtean nan Gall' ('the Lowlanders' towns').[165] The poem *San Dreòllain thà air iomadh fàth*, perhaps composed aorund 1692 when Duart lost his estate to Argyll, notes the *dù-Ghaill* (§8d) drinking in the hall where Mac Gille Eóin himself used to feast. In addition, three different poems refer to the Lowlanders as 'luchd Beurla' ('English-speakers').[166] Elsewhere Iain mac Ailein notes, like other contemporary poets and historians,[167] the decline in Gaelic culture and custom: he criticises those who would rather become *Gallta* ('Lowlandised'),[168] who spend their time socialising in Edinburgh, use only the English language, and follow Lowland fashions in clothing, food and drink.[169] In another poem he recalls a happier time when he stayed at Mac Gille Eóin's residence in Aros, whence he continued on a circuit to

---

See also *Cha choma leam fhèin no co-dhiù sin*, §§1d, 4a, 5d; *Dheagh Mhic Coinnigh à Brathann*, §7; *Ge grianach an latha*, §13.

163 *Fhuair mi sgeul's chan àicheam e*, §§4, 5ab.

164 See above, chapter 3, pp. 101–2; chapter 4, pp. 171–3.

165 *Mun sgeul-sa tha aca*, §6g; *'S ann Di-Sathan a chualas*, §6h (quotation).

166 *Is beag adhbhar mo shùgraidh*, §5a; *Gura h-oil leam an sgeul seo*, §6a; *'N àm dhol sìos*, §10h.

167 See above, chapter 4, pp. 122, 177–80.

168 *Beir an t-soraidh-sa uam-s'*, §12b.

169 *ibid., passim.*

enjoy Sleat's hospitality, then Mac Leóid's. Currently only Mac Mhic Ailéin (Mac Domhnaill of Clann Raghnaill) remains unchanged in the traditional practices of hospitality and protection.[170] Here we may also mention two poems composed partly to counteract the criticisms of the work of the Celtic scholar Edward Lhuyd.[171] In them Maighstir Seathan and Anndra mac an Easbaig praised Lhuyd's efforts to save Gaelic, Maighstir Seathan noting that this had been the language of the court for a thousand years, as well as the language of religion, and of 'gach eoladhain sháor' ('every noble art'). It had been sold in court for a new, recent language, 'caint Dhúbhghall' ('the speech of southrons'), and the *Gaoidhil* had become ashamed of their own tongue.[172] But Lhuyd's work, the poet continues, had awakened Gaelic from its grave, stopping the threat of forgetfulness by the *Gaoidhil* of their own history, and also making it possible for them to be taught the Word of God in their own language.[173]

'Fir Alban', on the other hand, never has any negative associations in Mac Gille Eóin poetry; the term seems to be used as an alternative to *Albanaich*, which Clann Ghille Eóin, like other Scottish Gaels, were proud to be if the poetry is anything to go by.[174] Thus Lachlann, sixteenth chief of Duart (†1649) was the noblest of 'fir Alba', and Eachann Ruadh, seventeenth chief, king above the top branches of 'fir Alban'.[175] Elsewhere the latter is described as ''na threun-fhear Albanach' ('a Scottish champion').[176] *Alba* herself receives some poetic attention: Duart's ancestors were 'Craobh ... | Fhreumaich bun ann an Albain' ('A tree which ... put down roots in Scotland'),[177] and Iain mac Ailein laments Scotland's condition following William of Orange's accession to the throne:

> Ach Alba bheag dhona
> Bha gun onair fo 'n ghrein aic'.

---

170 *Thoir fios bhuam gu Anndra*, §§9–11.
171 *Ar teachd on Spáin do shliochd an Gháoidhil ghlais* and *Ordheirc an gniomh saor bhur comhluin; EB*, p. 245.
172 *Ar teachd on Spáin do shliochd an Gháoidhil ghlais*, ll. 6–12, 15–18, 27–8.
173 ibid., ll. 29–30, 37–8, 41–2.
174 See above, chapter 3, pp. 70–1, 109; chapter 4, pp. 138, 163–4, 171.
175 *Cuid de adhbhar mo ghearain*, §2b; *Ach ga grianach an latha*, §5f.
176 *Nam faicinn gum b' fhior*, §3d.
177 *Thriall bhur bunadh gu Phàro*, §1e.

(But poor little Scotland,

without honour under the sun).[178]

The poetry, then, gives Clann Ghille Eóin a Scottish identity, even though their belonging in that smaller circle of the *Gaoidhil* receives just as much, if not more, emphasis: Eachann Ruadh, seventeenth chief, is 'grianan nan Gaidheal' ('the sun of the Gaels') and his park is 'Ionad lubh-ghort nan Gàidheal' ('the site of the gardens of the Gael'); Ailéan, eighteenth chief, was 'iuchair nan Gaidheal' ('the guide of the Gaels'), and his death represented the loss of 'cruadal is misneach nan Gàidheal' ('the courage and grit of the Gael').[179] Britain receives no mention at all, although it clearly is implied in Mairghread nighean Lachlainn's lament for Sir Eóin, nineteenth of Duart, a staunch Jacobite whose departing is a loss to the *rìoghachd* ('kingdom').[180]

Mac Gille Eóin vernacular verse contains many conventional pan-egyric code motifs, apparently better balanced than we find them in its Mac Domhnaill and Mac Leóid counterparts, the former focusing on the warrior, education, character, feasting, hunting, and gaming motifs, and the latter on the celebration of social life at the chief's court.[181] Noteworthy, however, is the abundance of the motif of the subject as the protector or defender of his people and territory. Mairghread nighean Lachlainn described Sir Eóin as coming to his people 'le còmhnadh' ('with help'), and to Iain mac Ailein he was 'Mar thaice ri 'r cùl' ('like support behind us'); his exile had left his people like a flock without a shepherd, 'gun righ, gun cheann-cinnidh, gun duthaich … gun fhear gleidhidh, no faire, no stiuiridh' ('without a king, without a chief, without a patrimony … without a guardian, without a watchman, without guidance'), like the people in Egypt (that is, the Israelites) tyrannised by Pharo, wounded, scattered, and plundered.[182] After Sir Eóin's death Mairghread nighean Lachlainn portrayed his people as exposed to attack, a motif common in

---

178 *Mun sgeul so chualas*, §5ef.

179 *Cuid de adhbhar mo ghearain*, §2a; *Gura h-oil leam an sgeul seo*, §16ab; *Ge de stoc mi an dèidh 'n crìonaidh*, §3g; *Is goirt leam gaoir nam ban Muileach*, §16h.

180 *Is goirt leam gaoir nam ban Muileach*, §7gh.

181 See above, chapter 3, p. 92, and chapter 4, p. 168.

182 *'S mi gun chadal aig smaointean*, §7d; *Nam faicinn gum b' fhìor*, §4a; *Mun sgeul-sa tha aca*, §§7g, 8dfg, 9g, 10cde.

classical elegies.[183] Iain Lom slightly twisted the motif of the subject as protector, trying to goad Clann Ghille Eóin into action against Caimbéal encroachment by claiming that they were no longer brave defenders, and by recalling their past leaders who would not have allowed 'uachdranach Mhuile' ('the supremacy of Mull') to be taken from them.[184] Mac Gille Eóin of Duart's ruin may have deprived him of his *filidh*, but there was no lack of vernacular poets to take over, in a fashion, the role of political legiti-mators, resorting to crucial panegyric code motifs to give them, and their people, encouragement and hope. The promise of land and people again becoming fertile upon the return of the exiled chief was used by these poets to the same effect,[185] along with the already noted motifs of divine Providence and the wheel of fortune.[186]

Clann Ghille Eóin vernacular verse contains no allusions to ancient classical Latin or Greek heroes. There is a Biblical reference in Eachann Bacach's lament for Eachann Ruadh, who died without an heir. By remind-ing his audience that after Job lost his seven sons he was given another seven, the poet reassures them that they will lack no new leader.[187] The motif describing the poet's grief as comparable to that of Ó Maol Chiaráin on his son's death is employed by Mairghread nighean Lachlainn in her elegy for Sir Ailéan of Duart.[188] In her lament for Sir Eóin she matches her grief to that of Oisein over the passing of Fionn and his followers.[189] Both Ó Maol Chiaráin and Oisein are invoked to the same effect by Anndra mac an Easbaig in his elegy for his brother Alasdair Mac Gille Eóin of Otter.[190] Clann Ghille Eóin poetry is not particularly plentiful in animal or plant imagery describing the patron, but it does preserve some other conven-tional images of the classical panegyric code. Sir Lachlann, sixteenth of Duart (†1649), is 'ursann cath' ('a pillar of combat'); Domhnall, tenth of Coll (†1729), is noted for his fine taste in Spanish wine and brandy.[191]

---

183 *Is goirt leam gaoir nam ban Muileach*, §4efg.
184 *Mur bhith 'n abhainn air fàs oirnn*, §§8–10.
185 *Nam faicinn gum b' fhìor*, §§12, 14–15.
186 See above, p. 219.
187 *Gura h-oil leam an sgeul seo*, §17abcd; *EB*, p. 210.
188 *Is goirt leam gaoir nam ban Muileach*, §12d.
189 *Cha choma leam fhèin no co-dhiù sin*, §2b. For the Oisein reference see *EB*, p. 239.
190 *'S bochd an sgeula seo thàinig*, §5ab.
191 *A Lachainn Òig gun innsinn ort*, §3g; *Soraidh gu Breacachadh bhuam*, §§5h, 6h, 7f.

The motif of the subject's kindness to friends and harshness to enemies is preserved in Anndra mac an Easbaig's lament for his brothers.[192] Eachann Ruadh was praised as *comh-dhalta* ('foster-brother') of an anonymous author, a reminder, as in a similar instance in Mac Griogóir poetry, of the close relationship between poet and patron.[193] The *fuidheall* motif may be seen surviving in Mairghread nighean Lachlainn's words on Clann Ghille Eóin 'Nach fhàgadh fuigheall spùinnidh dhiubh' ('that none of them have survived the plundering').[194] The expression 'taigh is leath', commonly found in Clann Domhnaill poetry, is used by Eachann Bacach to denote Mac Gille Eóin property in Islay.[195] But as well as many time-honoured turns of phrase we find a new development. Eachann Bacach points to the leniency of Lachlann, sixteenth chief of Duart, concerning the rents owed to him by his tenants.[196] This form of discourse, alien to the medieval panegyric code, illustrates the new status of the chiefs of the later period as landlords over their people.[197]

Clann Choinnigh

Like Clann Duibhne and Clann Ghille Eóin, Clann Choinnigh only became an important kindred relatively late in history and, beyond a rather late date, similarly lack a clear genealogical line. Their eponym, Coinneach, lived around 1400, and the surname Mac Coinnigh is first attested in 1480.[198] By the later medieval period they were attached to

---

For examples of wine-drinking in classical poems see, for instance, the Irish *Briathra cogaid con cath Laighneach*, l. 68; *Cia ré gcuirfinn séd suirghe*, §13b; *Branuigh ar chlú ós cloinn Néill*, §24cd; *Ní leis fhéin a bhfaghann Aodh*, §§24, 30; and the Scottish *A chinn Diarmaid Uí Chairbre*, §4b; *Ríoghacht ghaisgidh oighreacht Eoin*, §7b; *Fhuaras mo rogha theach mhór*, §6a; *Sé h-oidhche dhamhsa san Dún*, §1d.

192 *Gur cràiteach an othail*, §10.

193 *Ach ga grianach an latha*, §8a. See above, p. 204.

194 *Mo rùn an t-Ailein*, §5h.

195 'taigh is leth Íle' (*Gur bochd nàidheachd do dhùthcha*, §11a). For the editor's translation as 'More than half of Islay' see *EB*, pp. 213–4. For 'taigh is leath' in Clann Domhnaill verse see above, chapter 3, pp. 87–9, 110–11.

196 *Thriall bhur bunadh gu Phàro*, §7d. For another, slightly later example see below, chapter 6, p. 256.

197 For the process of this transformation see Dodgshon 1998. This new motif is included by Ronald Black in the section that discusses the much older one of the chief as the protector of widows, orphans and the poor generally; see *Lasair*, pp. xxxii–xxxv.

198 Matheson 1942–50, pp. 192, 199. For an overview of the emergence of this kindred see MacCoinnich 2003.

Kinlochewe in Wester Ross, but even the earliest extant clan histories, compiled in the later seventeenth century, show confusion in respect of the kindred's original patrimony.[199] In the fifteenth-century 'MS 1467' their genealogy can be traced back, through Gille Eóin na hAirde, to Cormac mac Airbheartach and therefore to the royal line of Loarn.[200]

Some seventeenth-century historians, infected by the new taste for Norman ancestors, inserted into the Mac Coinnigh pedigree a Cailéan, of the Anglo-Irish Mac Gearailt (or FitzGerald) family. He was said to have supported the Scots against the Norse at the battle of Largs (1262), and thereafter 'married The Daughter of McMahon Heritor of The Half of Kintail', Mac Mathghamhna's heiress.[201] Cailéan was made to be the father of Coinneach, the kindred's eponym, whom 'The Highlanders called Mac Chainichs taking The Patronymick from The Mac Mahon rather than from Colin whom they esteemed a Stranger'.[202] This late fabrication would serve to explain how Cailéan's descendants obtained territory in Scotland, but Cailéan did not exist. He represents Gille Eóin na hAirde himself, who belonged to the del Ard family, apparently of Gaelic origin. Indeed the Mac Coinnigh and Mac Mathghamhna families were two separate lines stemming from this Gille Eóin.[203] At some point Gille Eóin was made a descendant of Cormac mac Airbheartaigh, but Mac Firbhisigh notes with caution that this is according to 'nuaishliocht ele' ('another new recension').[204] By the seventeenth century Clann Choinnigh were claiming common ancestry with Clann Ghille Eóin. Niall Mac Muireadhaigh, clearly aware of this variant version, expressed an uncertainty similar to Mac Firbhisigh's when the latter tried to make sense of conflicting late Caimbéal genealogical claims.[205] Having first given the Clann Ghille Eóin pedigree back to their eponym, Gille Eóin Mór, Niall then adds:

---

199 *ibid.*, p. 211. The earliest history is Sir Robert Gordon's (†1656) (see Gordon 1813). For later sources see MacGregor 2008, p. 367.
200 'MS 1467', nos. 11, 12, 14.
201 *HP* ii, pp. 6–7; Macfarlane 1900, i, p. 56.
202 Macfarlane 1900, i, p. 57.
203 Sellar 1981, pp. 107, 111–13.
204 *LMG* ii, §411.2.
205 See above, chapter 4, p. 117.

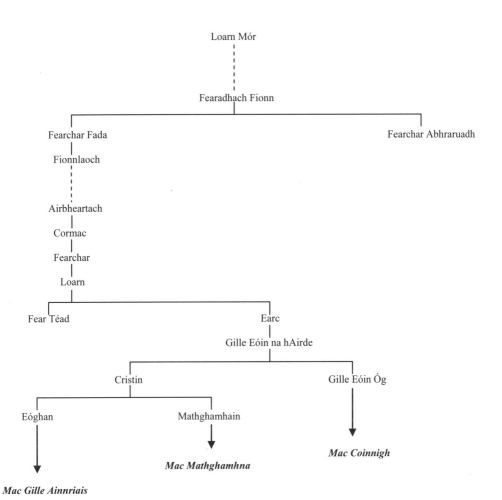

Table 5.7 The origins of Clann Choinnigh.

Sources: 'MS 1467', no. 11; Sellar 1981, pp. 111–13. For a warning that descent from Cormac mac Airbheartaigh is from a new recension see chapter 5, p. 226.

7 dir cuid occ *gur* on Ghioll eoin mhóir so a tan*n*ig c*lann* choin*n*-
digh a*r* a nadhb*ar* go roibh birt m^c aigi .i. Maolisa o bhfuillid
c*lann* Giollaeaoin, 7 Coin*n*dech o bhfuillid c*lann* Choin*n*digh.

(and some say that it is from this Gille Eóin Mór that Clann
Choinnigh came, for the reason that he had two sons, namely
Maol Íosa, from whom are Clann Ghille Eóin, and Coinneach,
from whom Clann Choinnigh).[206]

He then gives Clann Choinnigh's genealogy according to this claim,
which is merely a very awkward insertion of the pedigree into that of
Clann Ghille Eóin resulting in two Gille Eóins: Gille Eóin Mór (son of
Mac Raith and Clann Ghille Eóin's eponym) and Gille Eóin na hAirde,
who is turned into Mac Raith's son in order to continue the genealogy,
via Fearchar Abhraruadh, all the way back to 'Ferch[a]r fada rígh alban'.
This is at odds with 'MS 1467' (and with Irish sources), where Clann
Choinnigh's pedigree is traced back to Fearchar Fada (through Cormac
mac Airbheartaigh), and Clann Ghille Eóin's to Fearchar Abhraruadh.[207]
The absurdity of all this was plain to Niall, who did not fail to note the
improbability of the Mac Gille Eóin connexion.[208] There may even be a
hint of cynicism in his closing statement which names the various clans
claiming descent from Fearchar Fada and then adds, 'm*ar* adir cuid mh*ór*
aoca' ('as many of them say').[209]

Whatever their origins, by the early fourteenth century Clann
Choinnigh appear as vassal tenants of the Ó Beoláin earls of Ross,
and afterwards of the lords of the Isles when the latter obtained that
earldom.[210] Their relationship with both overlords was an uneasy one,
particularly in the aftermath of the Wars of Independence, when Clann
Choinnigh refused to join the Earl of Ross in support of Brús. On account
of this they were expelled from their territory and deprived of the con-
stableship of Eilean Donain Castle, which they had held hereditarily for

---

206 *RC* ii, p. 300.
207 See above, p. 226 and n. 200; *LMG* ii, §405.9; *ibid.* iii, §1153.39.
208 *RC* ii, p. 300; Sellar 1981, pp. 111–12.
209 *RC* ii, p. 300.
210 Matheson 1942–50, pp. 201, 209; *HP* i, p. 33.

some time. It was probably during their years in exile that they came to occupy land by Loch Kinellan, near Strathpeffer in Easter Ross.[211] It would be at least a century and a half before Clann Choinnigh managed to return to Kinlochewe; this may have been facilitated by the marriage of Coinneach a' Bhláir (†1491) to Mairghréad, daughter of Eóin, tenth lord of the Isles.[212] But Clann Choinnigh had been disloyal to their Mac Domhnaill overlords before this marriage, and they would continue to be. They refused to support Domhnall, eighth lord of the Isles, at Harlaw and later, and in Gaelic *seanchas* they, along with a daughter of the displaced tutor of Lewis, are made responsible for the murder of Aonghus Óg Mac Domhnaill in 1490.[213] They also opposed both Alasdair of Lochalsh and Domhnall Gorm of Sleat in their respective efforts to restore and lead the Mac Domhnaill lordship of the Isles.[214] Clann Choinnigh opposition to Mac Domhnaill went hand in hand with their loyal service to the crown. There was no repeat of their fourteenth-century conflict with the king, and a reward granted to Coinneach Mór in 1414 seems to have acknowledged his refusal to support Mac Domhnaill at Harlaw.[215] Clann Choinnigh received grants of land in Ross (to be held directly of the king) after Mac Domhnaill forfeited it in 1476, and the Earl of Sutherland, new Earl of Ross, appointed Alasdair Ionraic (†1488) his deputy in the management of the earldom.[216] Coinneach a' Bhláir, notorious for his defeat of Clann Domhnaill at the battle of Park (*c*.1491), was knighted by James IV, and his son Eóin (†1561), the first of the clan's chiefs to become a privy councillor, supported the king at Flodden.[217]

Clann Choinnigh's rise to prominence, well on its way by the sixteenth century, reached its zenith in the seventeenth, both in terms of territorial expansion and social advancement. The writer of 'The Ewill Trowbles of the Lewes' was in no doubt of the Mac Coinnigh chiefs' greed and

211 Matheson 1942–50, pp. 201, 205, 209, 211.

212 *ibid.*, pp. 212, 214. 'Hugh of Sleat' mistakenly gives Eóin mac Aonghuis for Eóin mac Alasdair as the lord of the Isles in question (*HP* i, p. 27). For the possibility of earlier Mac Coinnigh blood links with Clann Domhnaill see MacCoinnich 2003, pp. 187–8.

213 Mackenzie 1894, p. 65; Matheson 1942–50, p. 212; *HP* i, pp. 51–2.

214 *Clan Donald* ii, 381; Mackenzie 1894, p. 99.

215 Matheson 1942–50, p. 212.

216 Mackenzie 1894, pp. 75, 80.

217 *ibid.*, pp. 108, 131, 133.

their determination to take possession of Lewis by exploiting dissension within Clann Leóid. He also noted their double-dealings at the time when James VI ordered the colonisation of the island by Lowland adventurers and their harsh persecution of Clann Leóid.[218] In 1614 Lewis was finally granted to Coinneach an Áigh (†1611), who also succeded in obtaining the superiority of the possessions of Mac Domhnaill of Glengarry. His son and successor, Cailéan Ruadh (†1633), entered into a law suit with Argyll, which he won and with it the superiority of Arisaig and Morar.[219] In the later sixteenth century the Mac Coinnigh chiefs were, like the Caimbéal earls of Argyll and the Gordan earls of Huntly, the main means employed by government to exert control in the Highlands.[220] Royal favour was particularly marked by the bestowal of the title Lord Kintail on Coinneach an Áigh in 1609 and by the creation of Cailéan Ruadh as first earl of Seaforth in 1623. The sixteenth-century Mac Coinnigh chiefs were loyal supporters of Queen Mary, but their successors took the Protestant side, Cailéan Cam (†1594) acting against Catholics in the 1580s.[221] Although Seoras, second earl of Seaforth (†1651), wavered between supporting covenanters and royalists, he ultimately died in exile where he had followed Charles II. His successors, the third, fourth and fifth earls, were all royalists. The fifth earl, Uilliam Dubh (†1740), was attainted and forfeited and, though he returned from exile and received a royal pardon in 1726, he was never restored. The earldom of Seaforth was re-created on his grandson, Coinneach (†1781), the peerage becoming extinct after the latter's death without issue.[222]

While a large part of Clann Choinnigh's interests — particularly in terms of territorial expansion — remained firmly attached to the western Highlands and Isles, in several ways a turn to the eastern Highlands and the Lowlands is detected from the later fifteenth century. Earlier Mac Coinnigh chiefs had married into the Mac Dubhghaill, Mac Leóid, and Mac Domhnaill families. The last of these marriages was that of Coinneach a' Bhláir to the daughter of Eóin, tenth lord of the Isles, a short-lived union by which Mac Domhnaill probably hoped to secure Clann Choinnigh's

218 *HP* ii, pp. 268, 271, 276–9.
219 MacKenzie 1894, pp. 218, 221, 231, 241–2.
220 Grant 1959, p. 94.
221 MacKenzie 1894, pp. 138, 145, 170.
222 *ibid.*, pp. 277, 283–7, 292–7.

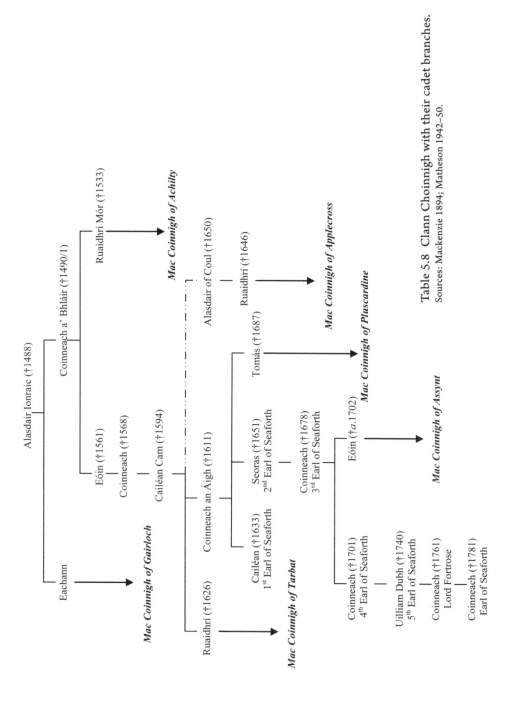

Table 5.8 Clann Choinnigh with their cadet branches.
Sources: Mackenzie 1894; Matheson 1942–50.

elusive loyalty.[223] Subsequent chiefs chose their marriage partners from within the neighbouring Grannd and Friseal families, as well as from those of Stiúbhart of Atholl and Mac Gille Buidhe (Ogilvie) and Foirbeis (Forbes) of Aberdeenshire.[224] The fourth and fifth earls of Seaforth, Coinneach Óg (†1701) and Uilliam Dubh, chose English wives.[225] On the other hand, sixteenth-century and later Clann Choinnigh chiefs were regularly educated in the Lowlands, and were privy councillors and popular figures at the royal court.[226]

There is no extant classical poetry for members of Clann Choinnigh, and no indication that their chiefs may have ever had a family of *filidh* in their employment. The poems most closely resembling those of the classical poets are two compositions by Donnchadh MacRaoiridh for Cailéan, first Earl of Seaforth, but these belong to the 'lower', 'semi-classical' type.[227] The only poet known to have been attached to a Mac Coinnigh chief was Murchadh MacMhathain, a lineal descendant of a fifteenth-century Mac Mathghamhna chief. Murchadh is described as *aos-dàna* to the fifth earl of Seaforth, of whom he held lands until 1719.[228] There is also a lament for Ruaidhrí, first of Applecross (†1646), by Màiri nighean Alasdair Ruaidh, who is said to have been nurse to two Applecross chiefs.[229] An anonymous Irish '*bàrd*' is the author of another lament for an Applecross chief, Eóin Molach (†c.1685), and we have an elegy by Brian, 'Am Bàrd Assainteach', for a Mac Coinnigh of Suddie.[230] Aside from some compositions of unknown authorship, the rest of the extant Clann Choinnigh verse is the work of members of the clan itself. Little is known of Iain MacCoinnich or of Cailean Dubh MacCoinnich, although we do know that the latter was raised in the household of the first earl of Seaforth.[231] Finally, at least

---

223 See above, p. 229 and n. 212; MacKenzie 1894, pp. 84–7.

224 For the Gaelic title of the Ogilvie chiefs, and for Síol Gille Chríost as the clan's name, see Dwelly 1977, p. 1024.

225 For all marriages see MacKenzie 1894.

226 See, for instance, Macfarlane 1900, i, pp. 62, 63; MacKenzie 1894, pp. 129, 146, 149, 182, 242.

227 *Treun am Mac a thug ar leòn* and *Fada ta mis an-dèidh càich*.

228 Thomson (ed.) 1994, p. 5.

229 *Tha mise ar leaghadh le bròn*; MacDonald 1984–6, p. 414.

230 *An taobh tuath ud cha tèid mi*; *Tha mulad, tha sgìos orm*.

231 *GC*, p. 365.

two of the heads of the Achilty branch were also poets: Alasdair mac
Mhurchaidh, fourth chief (†c.1643), and his son and successor, Murchadh
Mòr (†c.1689),[232] both of whom were able to compose in the 'semi-clas-
sical' style. Alasdair has left mostly religious verse, as well as the lament
Tuirseach dhúinne ri port, discussed below,[233] while of Murchadh Mór we
have an assortment of love, religious, panegyric and political works.

There is no extant Clann Choinnigh poetry composed before the
seventeenth century. Most of the surviving corpus was composed for
members of the main line of the family, but we also have some pieces for
various chiefs of the Gairloch, Applecross, and Suddie cadet branches. The
poetic rhetoric focuses on the subject as a skilled warrior, on his generosity
and hospitality, his love of music and feasting, and his character qualities.[234]
Also frequent is the praise of the subject's fame and of his seamanship or
ownership of fine boats.[235] As was the case with Mac Griogóir and Mac
Gille Eóin poetry, Mac Coinnigh panegyric fails to name ancient noble
ancestors. Màiri nighean Alasdair Ruaidh, for instance, merely makes a
vague reference to '[sliochd] nam fear mór' ('seed of great men').[236] Once
more this lack is counterbalanced by noting the subjects' numerous fol-
lowing. Sometimes these allusions are of a general nature, as in Murchadh
MacMhathain's statement that Uilliam Dubh had the loyalty of the nobil-
ity as well as of the poor, or Iain MacCoinnich's that Eóin Molach had a
great following.[237] But more frequently the subject's friends and allies are
named; these include Mac Leóid of Dunvegan, Mac Domhnaill of Sleat,

---

232 Maclean 1951–2, p. 133.

233 See below, p. 238.

234 See, for instance, *Gur tric teachdair bhon eug*, §§5–6, 7–9, 10; *Tha mise ar leaghadh
le bròn*, §§1bcde, 2de, 3abc, 4cd, 6, 7c8cd, 13abe; *Creach as truime na gach creach*,
§§4ab, 7, 13ab, 14; *Deoch slàinte an Iarla Thuathaich*, §§3cdef, 5, 7d, 11def; *Deoch-
slàinte chabair fèidh seo*, passim; *'S math b' aithne dhomh-sa t' armachd*, §§1–5, 7, 8efgh;
An-diugh do Gheàrrloch cha tèid mi, §§1de, 4; *Tha mulad, tha sgìos orm*, §§7–9; *Mo
chridhe-sa ta fo chràdh*, §§2k, 3de, 4befghik, 6bhij, 9f, 11aj; *An taobh tuath ud cha tèid
mi*, §§1efghi, 3cefg, 5eghi.

235 *Gur tric teachdair bhon eug*, §13; *Creach as truime na gach creach*, §5a; *Deoch slàinte an
Iarla Thuathaich*, §7cdef; *Tha mise ar leaghadh le bròn*, §4f; *'S math b' aithne dhomh-
sa t' armachd*, §2h; *Mo chridhe-sa ta fo chràdh*, §§7b, 11b; *Tha mulad, tha sgìos orm*,
§§10efgh, 12cd; *An taobh tuath ud cha tèid mi*, §2.

236 *Tha mise air leaghadh le bròn*, §2d.

237 *Deoch slàinte an Iarla Thuathaich*, §6defg; *Mo chridhe-sa ta fo chràdh*, §11i.

Mac Fionghuin, Mac Shimidh, Grannd, and the earl of Antrim.[238] There are only three instances of the motif of the subject as his people and territory's protector or defender. They are contained in three elegies, two for Applecross chiefs, and the third for Mac Coinnigh of Suddie, and they are mere passing references in every case.[239] Other motifs include hunting, the subject's education and patronage of poets, and his nobility. There are two references to the subject's royal lineage: Cailéan Ruadh, first earl of Seaforth, is 'slat fhoghainteach rìgh' ('a portly royal scion'), and Ruaidhrí, first chief of Applecross, has 'càirdeas rìgh anns gach ball' ('kinship with kings [...] in thine every member').[240] Both allusions to royal blood are of a vague nature, since they fail to name any ancestors who had actually been kings. Territorial references are always local to Clann Choinnigh: subjects are connected, for instance, to Brahan, Eilean Donain, Seaforth, Stornoway, Gairloch, and A' Chomraich (Applecross).[241] Plant and animal imagery is limited.

Of several important lacks, in terms of the panegyric code, perhaps the most notable in Clann Choinnigh poetry is the almost total failure to identify the poems' subjects as *Gaoidhil*. In the extant poems only one instance is found, in *Raoir a chunnaic mi bruadar*, where the fifth earl is praised as 'iuchair nan Gàidheal' ('the guide of the Gaels', §9h), the same image we have met in a poem for Eóin, nineteenth chief of Duart.[242] The theme of royalism is almost completely absent too, despite the long Mac Coinnigh history of loyalty and service to the crown. Even in a poem by Coinneach MacRaith of Ardelve lamenting the Jacobite defeat at Sheriffmuir all we find is praise of the martial bravery of various Clann Choinnigh and other nobles and a concern with their current predicament: the actual cause they had fought for is not mentioned.[243] But a couple of political

---

238 *Deoch slàinte an Iarla Thuathaich*, §9cdef; *Deoch slàinte chabair fèidh seo*, §§11–13; *Raoir a chunnaic mi bruadar*, §§3–8.

239 *Tha mise ar leaghadh le bròn*, §10e; *Mo chridhe-sa ta fo chràdh*, §9g; *Tha mulad, tha sgios orm*, §2c.

240 *Gur tric teachdair bhon eug*, §8a; *Tha mise ar leaghadh le bròn*, §3c.

241 *Tha mise ar leaghadh le bròn*, §§1a, 8d, 9d, 10d; *Deoch slàinte an Iarla Thuathaich*, §§8bd, 9b; *An-diugh do Gheàrrloch cha tèid mi*, §1a; *An taobh tuath ud cha tèid mi*, §4c.

242 See above, p. 223.

243 *Tha Uilleam cliuiteach an diugh fo chàs*. But the author does describe the opponents of the Jacobites at Sheriffmuir as '[a'] ghràisg' ('the rabble') at §15d, in contemporary fashion.

poems by Murchadh Mòr MacCoinnich of Achilty (†c.1689) make the exception to this general pattern. Murchadh Mòr is the only author within the extant corpus of Clann Choinnigh poetry to engage fully with contemporary political affairs. In two pieces composed around 1689 he introduces a number of the themes common in similar early Jacobite poems. Providentialism, if not the divine right of kings, is upheld in his statement that 'Le threis taghar gach rìgh' ('Every king is chosen by his [i.e. God's] strength').[244] Cromwell's government is portrayed as a crowd of greedy upstarts, and their ways as malicious and deceitful:

Dìon T' fhìor-eun bho'n ealta bhorb
　　Tha sreap, le mìorun 's le ceilg,
　　Nar corun ri dibhearg.

(Protect Thy eagle from the barbaric flock that is vindictively climbing, with malice and deceit, into our crown).[245]

It is presumably Cromwell himself, the wretch who 'Bhuail ... ploc 'san uailse' ('struck a blow at the nobility') — an expression almost identical to that of An Clàrsair Dall in a 1689 poem — and seized power and authority, who is meant by Murchadh Mòr as 'Iudas fallsa' ('False Judas').[246] Other themes, such as the deceitfulness of the world, its fickleness, political treachery, the betrayal of the king for money, and the sin of pride as the cause of the current evils, all found in Murchadh Mòr's work, were common in Gaelic vernacular poetry from the mid-seventeenth century onwards.[247]

Apart from Murchadh Mòr's political poems, there is next to no cultivation at all of the theme of royalism in the surviving Clann Choinnigh verse. This is most puzzling in the case of *Raoir a chunnaic mi bruadar* and *Deoch slàinte chabair fèidh seo*, dated 1716 and 1719 respectively. Although both pieces deal with events related to the activities of Uilliam Dubh in

---

244　*Is deas duinn cobhair Mhic Dhé*, §1b.

245　*ibid.*, §3abc.

246　*Olc an t-adhbhar uabhair*, §§9c, 10abc. See above, chapter 4, p. 174.

247　*Olc an t-adhbhar uabhair*, §§1a, 4bcd, 8cd; *Is deas duinn cobhair Mhic Dhé*, §6a. See above, chapter 3, pp. 102–6.

support of the Stiúbhart cause, there is little actual indication of it, perhaps on account of his less than heroic conduct at Sheriffmuir.[248] The only clear reference is the statement in *Raoir a chunnaic mi bruadar* that 'bu tu nàmhaid na Muice' ('you were the sow's enemy', §9h), a reference to King George.[249] Both poems are in fact in the style of, for instance, Iain Dubh's 'Song of the Clans' (*Seo an aimsir 'n do dhearbhadh*) in that they portray the various Highland kindreds united in a common cause, but without Iain Dubh's emphasis on 'seirbheis a' chrùin' ('the service of the crown', §1h) and without any of the motifs — such as divine right, descent, prophecy, wheel of fortune, and so on — commonly found in contemporary royalist poetry.[250] There is one single allusion by the author of *Deoch-slàinte chabair fèidh seo* to the fickleness of the world:

> Faire, faire, 'shaoghail —
>> Gur caochlaideach carach thu!
>
> (So that's how it is, O world —
> How fickle and changeable you are!) (§11ab).[251]

Comment on Clann Choinnigh is sometimes found in the more sharply political production of MacDhòmhnaill poets, who do not hesitate to criticise them if they deem it appropriate. Thus they are among those praised by Iain Dubh in his 'Song of the Clans', but castigated by Sìleas na Ceapaich for their cowardice at Sheriffmuir (1715) and attacked by Iain Lom for their support of the Union of Crowns.[252] Some time before that, Clann Choinnigh seem to have disappointed those whom they boasted to be their friends and allies. Following Argyll's invasion of Mull in 1692 an anonymous author reproached Coinneach Óg, fourth Earl of Seaforth (†1701), for his failure to rise in support of Clann Ghille Eóin:

---

248 See *EB*, p. 140, for an account of Uilliam Dubh's part at the battle, and for the bad repu-tation it earned him, and below, pp. 236–7, for criticism by MacDhòmhnaill poets.

249 Cf. above, chapter 3, p. 107. For the background of *Deoch-slàinte chabair fèidh seo* see *Lasair*, pp. 412–16.

250 See above, chapter 3, pp. 102–9; chapter 4, pp. 174–5.

251 Cf. above, chapter 3, p. 105. For a discussion on the possible authorship of this poem see *Lasair*, pp. 412–5.

252 *Seo an aimsir 'n do dhearbhadh*, §10; *Mhic Coinnigh bhon Tràigh*, §1; *Ge bè dh' èireadh 'san lasair*, §14.

'Dheagh Mhic-Coinnigh a Brathainn,
'S cian 's gur fad' 'tha thu 'd laighe,
'S nach do dh-eirich thu fhathast,
'Chur le deagh Mhac Gilleain.

(Oh good Mac Coinnigh from Brahan,
it is a very long time you have been lying,
not having yet risen
to take the part of good Mac Gille Eóin).[253]

Yet another lack in Clann Choinnigh verse is the poets' failure to portray their subjects as supportive members of the wider kingdom of Britain. *Breatain* appears only once in the extant poetry, where Murchadh MacMhathain describes the joy of 'iomadh diùc a tha 'm Breatainn' ('many a duke in Britain') upon Uilliam Dubh's homecoming in 1719.[254] *Alba*, too, receives negligible attention: Mac Coinnigh of Suddie is celebrated for his fame in *Alba*, Uilliam Dubh for his reputation ''n cùirt na 'n Albannach' ('at the Scots' court') and also, as a result of his military victories over the Lowland enemies, for having received *urram searbhant* ('a servant's respect') from the nobility of *Alba* throughout the kingdom.[255] There are some instances of the motif of the struggle against *Goill*, a term which generally seems to indicate the Lowlanders, but sometimes, as in one of the elegies for Cailéan Ruadh, first earl of Seaforth, is applied to the English.[256] The Lowland Scots are *Dubhghaill* whom Uilliam Dubh fights in *Deoch slàinte chabar fèidh seo* (§4gh). They are 'fir chleòc' in an anonymous lament for Coinneach Mac Coinnigh, sixth of Gairloch (†1669), where the subject is celebrated for his struggle against them and for his stance 'gun taing do luchd bèurla, no chleòc' ('in defiance of English speakers and Lowlanders').[257] The 'mìorùn mòr nan Gall' motif makes an early appearance in a mid-seventeenth-century political poem by Murchadh Mòr of

253 *'Dheagh Mhic Coinnigh à Brathainn*, §1abcd. The Mac Néill chief is similarly rebuked in §2.

254 *Raoir a chunnaic mi bruadar*, §2efg.

255 *Tha mulad, tha sgìos orm*, §12cd; *Deoch slàinte an Iarla Thuathaich*, §7c; *Gum beannaicheadh mo Dhia dùileach*, §5gh.

256 *Gur tric teachdair bhon eug*, §§3, 8c, 9a.

257 *An-diugh do Gheàrrloch cha tèid mi*, §§4e, 5e.

Achilty, as quoted above,[258] and also in a piece celebrating the pardon and return home of the fifth earl of Seaforth in 1726, where Murchadh MacMhathain refers to 'luchd mìorùin' twice.[259]

Mac Coinnigh vernacular poetry contains two instances of what seems to be a survival of the old *muirn* motif of the classical poets. In his elegy for Coinneach, third earl of Seaforth (†1678), Iain MacCoinnich ponders: 'Ce 'm feasd bho'm faighinn-s' mùirn?' ('From whom will I receive affection now?'),[260] and Alasdair mac Mhurchaidh laments the death of Mac Coinnigh of Fairburn in these terms:

Smuainmid air cheannard an Tùir,
    Bho'n d'fhuaras mùirn is mì òg.

(We reflect on the chief of the Tower [of Fairburn],
    from whom I received affection when I was young).[261]

This poem is highly reminiscent of other extant contemporary pieces lamenting the passing of a number of Gaelic nobles who had patronised poets and complaining of poetic penury. Having reflected on the death of various Mac Coinnigh, Mac Leóid, and Mac Domhnaill patrons, Alasdair mac Mhurchaidh muses:

Iomadh caraid do chaidh bhuam
    Bho'm faighinn-se cuairt is lòn,
Ged tharla mì a nochd gun chuirm:
    Mo dheoch is è burn ri òl.

(Many a friend has departed from me
    from whom I would get a circuit and dining,
    though tonight I find myself without an invitation:
    water is my drink).[262]

---

258 See above, p. 221.
259 *Gum beannaicheadh mo Dhia dùileach*, §4hl.
260 *Creach as truime na gach creach*, §2c.
261 *Tuirseach dhúinne ri port*, §6ab.
262 ibid., §14.

He continues to decry his 'làmh lom' ('bare hand') and his being 'Gun chosnadh air muir no tìr' ('without employment on land or sea'), although he also expresses his confidence that he will still enjoy the hospitality of Seoras, second earl of Seaforth (§§15b, 16b, 18). Alasdair's depiction of himself as destitute is probably no more than an adoption of the 'poetic poverty' motif, because as chief of Achilty he was unlikely to depend on patronage for his sustenance.

Clann Choinnigh poetry is almost devoid of comparisons of the subjects praised with great heroes of the past, Gaelic or otherwise. A reference to Fionn is found in *Tha Uilleam cliuiteach an diugh fo chàs*, where Coinneach MacRaith states of the Kintail champions that 'Cha robh an àicheadh fo bhrataich Finn' ('They would not be refused under Fionn's banner', §2b). The Oisein motif appears once, where Alasdair of Achilty claims to feel, after the deaths of so many Highland and Island leaders, 'Mar Oisin an déidh nam Fiann' ('like Oisein after the Fianna').[263] There are only two Biblical allusions. The first one is in the early-seventeenth-century consolation poem *Treun am Mac a thug ar leòn*, addressed by Donnchadh MacRaoiridh to Cailéan Ruadh after the death of the latter's only son. MacRaoiridh exhorts Cailéan Ruadh to be like Abraham, who was prepared to offer his only son, Isaac, as a sacrifice to God (§3ab). The second Biblical allusion appears in Murchadh MacMhathain's welcome home to Uilliam Dubh in 1726, where the earl is portrayed victorious over the Lowland 'luchd mìorùin':[264]

> mar chuir Rìgh Dàbhaidh le slungag làidir
> 'na smàl Goilìath.

> (as David extinguished Goliath
> with a strong little sling).[265]

Finally, the toasting ('deoch slàinte') of the fifth earl of Seaforth seems a favourite topic with Murchadh MacMhathain, who employed it in

263 *ibid.*, §1d.
264 See above, pp. 221, 237–8.
265 *Gum beannaicheadh mo Dhia dùileach*, §5cd.

Deoch slàinte an Iarla Thuathaich, Deoch-slàinte chabair fèidh seo,[266] *Raoir a chunnaic mi bruadar* (§2a), and *Gum beannaicheadh mo Dhia dùileach.* This motif is not unique to Mac Coinnigh verse: it is found also in a seventeenth-century Caimbéal poem,[267] and in a panegyric by the Glencoe poet Aonghus Mac Domhnaill for Colla Mac Domhnaill, sixteenth chief of Keppoch, composed, like those for Mac Coinnigh, in or shortly after 1715.[268]

Conclusions

The present chapter surveyed the extant poetry concerned with the Scottish Gaelic kindreds claiming descent from Corc mac Lughach and from Niall Naoighiallach, and that composed for three of the kindreds stemming from Conaire. Very little of either classical or vernacular verse has survived for either of the first two groups. Along with a number of the conventional motifs of classical panegyric, the two thirteenth-century poems for members of the Leamhnaigh also contain information on poetic privileges, and an unusual twist of the 'spouse' motif by which Muireadhach Albanach portrays the river Lennox, rather than the whole district, as the subject's lover. There are no references to *Alba*, although the Scottish royal lineage of the Leamhnaigh is celebrated as much as their Irish one. Their forebears on the maternal side are named as Conghal and Godhfhraidh. The former's identity remains obscure; he may have been either Scottish or Irish. Godhfhraidh is almost certainly the progenitor of Clann Ghodhfhraidh and therefore of the future Clann Domhnaill. Corc and remoter ancestors are noted on the Irish side, and Munster is mentioned as their ancient patrimony. In contrast, the two extant poems for descendants of Niall are almost entirely devoid of allusions to ancient noble ancestors: Niall himself is named in the elegy for a Mac Néill chief, and the Mac Suibhne poem contains only an obscure reference to Guaire, suggesting perhaps a link through the female line. In the latter poem the subject, Eóin Mac Suibhne, is unequivocally identified as belonging to *Alba*, where his original patrimony lay. The *Goill* appear in this poem, as they also do in the eulogy for Alún Mór of Lennox, but in both cases as

---

266 If indeed he was this poem's author; see above, p. 236 n. 251.

267 See above, chapter 4, p. 147.

268 *Deoch slàinte Mhic 'ic Raonuill.*

the conventional motif by which the ideal ruler is capable of guarding his territory against foreign threat. All in all, then, the extant poetry for the descendants of Corc and of Niall is in the earlier rather than the later of the models identified for Mac Domhnaill panegyric.[269]

Of the three kindreds claiming descent from Conaire considered in this chapter — Clan Ghille Eóin, Clann Ghriogóir and Clann Choinnigh — only the first can be confidently attached to an ancient noble ancestor, but our sources are genealogical rather than poetic, with only one vernacular piece asserting Mac Gille Eóin descent from Éireamhón.[270] The garbled version of the Mac Gille Eóin pedigree in 'MS 1467' appears suspicious, suggesting a late medieval fabrication, and perhaps that the kindred were indeed the 'upstarts' which 'Hugh of Sleat' makes them to be. The claim of descent from Conaire through Loarn Mór and Fearchar Abhraruadh is supported by Irish sources, but not without reservation.[271] Clann Ghriogóir and Clann Choinnigh are made in the fifteenth-century 'MS 1467' the descendants of Conaire through Loarn Mór and Fearchar Fada, but again these claims are never sustained in the extant poetry. The later Clann Ghriogóir claim of descent from Fearghus Mór is first attested in an early sixteenth-century poem, whose author, Donnchadh MacGriogair, was not a *file*, and was probably influenced by Boece. The later Clann Choinnigh claim of shared ancestry with Clann Ghille Eóin led to an impossible clan pedigree in the 'Book of Clanranald', which met with the scepticism of the writer, Niall Mac Muireadhaigh. Significantly, the extant poetry for the three kindreds has in common a general lack of references to ancient noble ancestors and, consequently, to an original homeland. It would appear that when in the eighteenth century Maclean of Grulin blamed the lack of early records on the ungratefulness or negligence of *filidh* and *seanchaidhe* he was misguided. Clann Ghille Eóin probably only began to employ hereditary learned men (and therefore to maintain genealogical records) in the later fourteenth century, when they came to prominence through their association with the lords of the Isles. Similarly, Clann Ghriogóir and Clann Choinnigh may not have initially,

269 See above, chapter 3, pp. 112–15.
270 See above, p. 215.
271 See above, pp. 209, 228, 246.

as was suggested for Clann Duibhne,[272] patronised learned families who would have recorded their origins and ancestry. It is probably no coincidence that modern scholars have not been able to establish the historical veracity of the genealogical records beyond the thirteenth century at most.

Although Clann Ghriogóir flourished only until the mid-sixteenth century, their resistance to Caimbéal encroachment subsequently leading to their downfall, yet it is for them that we have a substantial body of poems in classical style. These are in the earlier model, and therefore closer to the Irish one, and include, unlike the poetry for the lords of the Isles, references to the *Goill*. These are always mere motifs, that is, unconnected with any actual enemy of the *Gaoidhil*. Additionally, Mac Griogóir classical panegyric contains a number of references to ancient Gaelic heroes, and has preserved three *apalóga*, all from Irish tradition, and the motif of 'tréidhe tighearna', the lordly traits expected in the right ruler. For all its Irish flavour, Clann Ghriogóir verse unequivocally portrays its subjects as belonging in *Alba*. The same emphasis is displayed through Mac Gille Eóin vernacular poetry (but is not found in the extant classical fragment), while allusions to *Alba* are much less frequent for Clann Choinnigh.

Strictly vernacular poetry (that is, accentual and in the vernacular language) reflects the current fortunes and misfortunes of each kindred. Adversity has caught up with Clann Ghriogóir and Clann Ghille Eóin, and the part played by the Caimbéalaigh in the turn of events is noted by the poets, a Caimbéal woman once more turning against her own. Clann Ghille Eóin verse links these events, and links also the wider British political crisis, to a turn in the wheel of fortune, and hopes for divine Providence to restore balance. If much of the material is concerned with 'dol sìos Chloinn Ghill-Eathain', there is also room for discussion of national politics in support of the Stiúbhairt. Here the Jacobite rhetoric contains the same elements found in poetry for other kindreds: divine right, prophecy, genealogical continuity, condemnation of upstarts and political traitors, the current misfortunes as punishment for sin, and so on. There is a certain pessimism, however, as poets become disappointed with the Stiúbhart dynasty and wonder whether Clann Ghille Eóin's support of the royal cause had been worth it. Royalism is much less a theme of Clann Choinnigh

---

272 See above, chapter 4, pp. 120, 122.

verse, which otherwise is in the late poetic model as established for Mac Domhnaill poetry. It lacks, however, the usual emphasis on the subjects as *Gaoidhil*. Aside from that, Mac Gille Eóin and Mac Coinnigh poetry have in common a number of characteristics. The dearth of allusions to ancient venerable ancestors and to an original patrimonial land, probably due to their late rise, is counterbalanced by frequent resort to the 'friends and allies' motif, which also serves in Clann Ghille Eóin's case to provide encouragement and hope in their hour of difficulty. References to *Alba* are limited, particularly in Mac Coinnigh poetry, and *Breatainn* is almost non-existent. There are no comparisons of the subjects praised to great heroes of the past, whether Gaelic or from the classical Latin or Greek traditions, and only isolated Biblical references. Ó Maol Chiaráin and Oisein are recalled to describe the poet's own grief. The expression 'taigh is leth Íle' in a Mac Gille Eóin poem is reminiscent of the Mac Domhnaill claim to 'taigh is leth Alban'. The classical theme of the *muirn* received by the poet from his patron seems preserved in some Mac Coinnigh poems. The *Goill* are present in the poetry for all three kindreds. In most cases they are Lowlanders and enemies, and described as 'fir chleòc' and 'luchd Beurla', while 'míorún nan Gall', an idiom which would become a widespread theme in the eighteenth century, appears in two mid-seventeenth century Mac Coinnigh poems. At other times the *Gall* reference lacks any negative connotations, typically when noting the patron's status through allusions to his socialising in Lowland towns. Finally, Mac Gille Eóin poets show concern for the decline of Gaelic ways and celebrate Edward Lhuyd's efforts on behalf of the preservation of Gaelic culture and language.

Chapter 6

Other Gaelic patrons,
and patrons of Norman descent

The descendants of Conaire (II): Other Gaelic kindreds
Origins and historical background

In the previous chapter we noted that by the fifteenth century, according to 'MS 1467', Clann Ghille Eóin, Clann Ghriogóir, and Clann Choinnigh were claiming descent from the royal line of Loarn (and therefore from Conaire): Clann Ghille Eóin through King Fearadhach Fionn's son Fearchar Abhraruadh, and the other two through the same king's son Fearchar Fada. We also noted that by the seventeenth century Clann Ghriogóir and Clann Choinnigh were revising their pedigrees. The latter linked themselves to Clann Ghille Eóin, while in the case of Clann Ghriogóir — for whom variations to genealogical claims can be traced back, through the poetry, to the early sixteenth century — lineal descent from Cinéal nGabhráin became preferable to that from Cinéal Loairn given in 'MS 1467'.[1] 'MS 1467' also makes Loarn the ancestor of various other Scottish kindreds, many of which similarly re-invented their pedigrees in later times. Clann Mhic Fhionghuin, for instance, were by the seventeenth century alleging descent from the same Ailpín supposed by Boece to be a remote ancestor of Clann Ghriogóir, and a similar tradition developed among Clann Ghuaire.[2] Such an assertion, while preserving these kindreds' Gaelic origins, gave them an affinity with Cinéal nGabhráin, the line of the contemporary kings of Scots, rather than with the early rival royal house of Cinéal Loairn as recorded by earlier professional Gaelic historians, whose version remained unchanged

---

1 See above, chapter 5, pp. 199–200, 206, 226, 228.
2 MacKinnon 1931, pp. 4, 5; Skene 1902, pp. 345, 418. See also below, pp. 256 and 274 n. 45 for some references in vernacular poetry.

in later times.[3] 'MS 1467', however, does not list all of the clans, and for those not named there our earliest Gaelic sources are the seventeenth-century historians Niall mac Muireadhaigh and 'Hugh of Sleat'. Where relevant information appears in their writings it tends to be given as a passing comment or by-road (for both historians were concerned principally with Clann Domhnaill history), for instance where the author wishes to amend some contemporary claim which differs from, or is not contained in, his own records. To give some examples, we are informed that the ancestors of the Rothaigh and the Rósaigh were of the Uí Néill, having come to Scotland in the early thirteenth century as part of the dowry of Áine, daughter of Ó Catháin, on her marriage to Aonghus Óg, sixth lord of the Isles. The Mac Beathadh family, who later became hereditary physicians to the lords of the Isles, as well as physicians to the kings of the Scots until the eighteenth century, arrived in the same manner and were of the same origin, while Clann Mhic an Phearsáin and the 'Butikes' (Budges) of Caithness were of the sept of Ó Dochartaigh, themselves also of the Uí Néill.[4] Clann Mhic Raith, according to a seventeenth-century genealogical historian writing in English, were also said to be of Irish ancestry, while the origin of Clann Mhic Aoidh of Strathnaver remains obscure to our day. They are generally thought to have come from Ireland and for that reason they are included in this section.[5]

When we turn to the Irish pedigrees to compare them with those in 'MS 1467' the first thing to come to our attention is the lack of information on many Scottish kindreds. Of all those given descent from the kings of Dál Riada in 'MS 1467' only a few are given such origin by An Dubhaltach Mac Firbhisigh. Mac Firbhisigh based his great collection on older records but he also reproduced variant versions, sometimes discussing them and their validity, and not infrequently citing his sources. The information he supplied on the Scottish descendants of Cairbre Riada can be summarised and drawn into a family tree (Table 6.1) according to which the descendants of Loarn came to split into three branches: Clann Ghille

---

3 'MS 1467', nos. 25, 26; *LMG* ii, §406.13.

4 *RC* ii, p. 158; *HP* i, p. 20, where Áine is named 'Margaret', but see McLeod 2004, p. 43. For the Mac Beathadh royal physicians see above, chapter 2, p. 25 and n. 3.

5 Mackay 1829, pp. 27–49; Skene 1902, pp. 361–2. For the Mac Raith tradition of a common origin with Clann Ghille Eóin and Clann Choinnigh see *HP* i, pp. 198–9; Macrae 1899, pp. 4, 331–2.

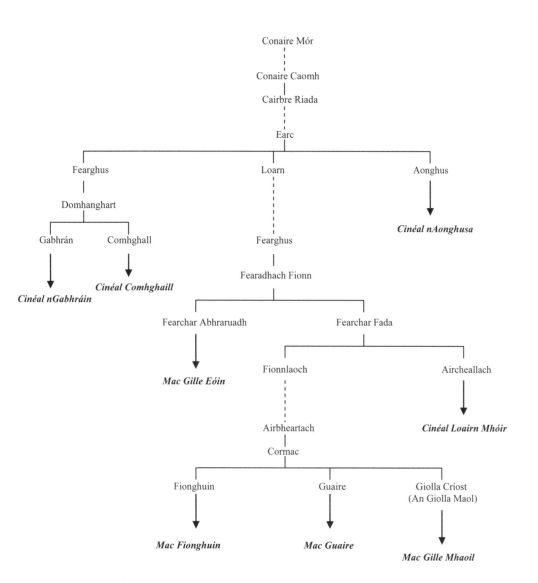

Table 6.1 The Scots of Dál Riada from Mac Firbhisigh.
Source: LMG ii, §§400.1–407.3.

Eóin, stemming from Fearchar Abhraruadh; Cinéal Loairn proper — the royal house of Moray — descending from Aircheallach, son of Fearchar Abhraruadh's brother Fearchar Fada;[6] and finally the descendants of Aircheallach's brother, Fionnlaoch, through Cormac mac Airbheartaigh. Only three kindreds — Clann Mhic Fhionghuin, Clann Ghuaire, and Clann Mhic Ghiolla Mhaoil — are named by Mac Firbhisigh as the offspring of Cormac mac Airbheartaigh.

If we similarly draw a family tree according to the 'MS 1467' pedigrees, and then compare it with the tree as supplied by Mac Firbhisigh, the picture becomes crowded. Here the information obtained from Irish sources remains the same, but we find that many other names of established kindreds are given as descending from Loarn. Fearadhach Fionn is given a third son, Domhnall Donn, thus accounting for the ancestry of Clann Aoidh of Ugadale in Kintyre and of another kindred which may be Clann Labhartaigh.[7] Fearchar Fada is given two more sons who become the ancestors of the Mac an Tóisigh and Mac Neachtain families respectively, and similarly two more sons are named for Cormac mac Airbheartaigh, providing a royal lineage for several other kindreds (see Table 6.2). Dubhghall Albanach, who in 1467 copied these pedigrees from an original thought to have been compiled around 1400, was a Scot.[8] Did he have information on Scottish families not accessible to their Irish counterparts? It is not unlikely, but the fact that so many kindreds are so tightly packed together, particularly in the case of the issue of Cormac mac Airbheartaigh, appears highly suspicious. Of Airbheartach, Mac Firbhisigh merely says that 'do aitreabh da trebh dég i f Fionnlochlannuibh (?) ... Muil<e>, agus Tír ... Aodha, agus Cruibhinis' ('[he] settled twelve households in Fionnlochlainn [i.e., the Hebrides] ... Mull, and Tiree, and Craoibhinis').[9] Clann Mhic Fhionguin were certainly associated in early times with both Mull and Iona, and Clann Ghuaire's patrimony was part of Mull as well as the adjacent isle of Ulva,[10] but it does

---

6 Aircheallach is also given as the son of Fearchar Fada in the poem *A éolcha Alban uile*, for which see below, chapter 7, pp. 299–301.

7 'Labhartaigh' given tentatively in 'MS 1467', no. 10.

8 Black, *Catalogue*, pp. 14, 15; Ó Baoill 1988, pp. 122–5.

9 *LMG* ii, §406.12. Craoibhinis: a name for Iona (Skene 1876–80, iii, p. 489 n. 59).

10 Mackinnon 1931, pp. 5, 6; Skene 1902, p. 345.

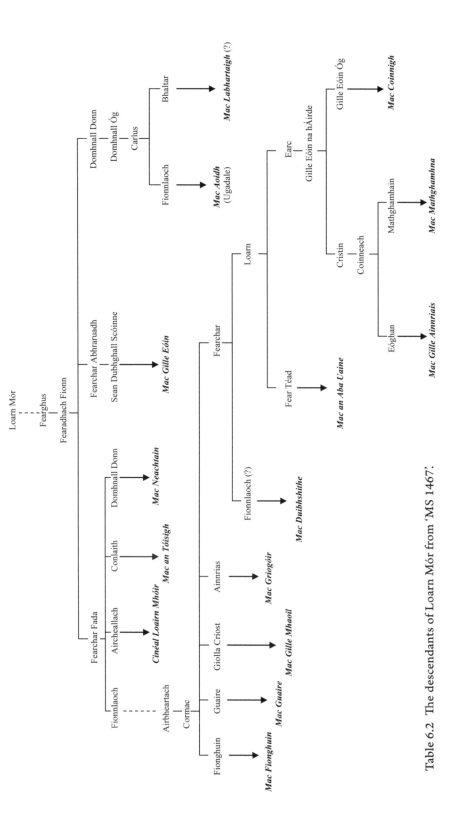

Table 6.2 The descendants of Loarn Mór from 'MS 1467'.

not necessarily follow that from Airbheartach's twelve households, and through his son Cormac, had sprung all the kindreds listed as of such descent in 'MS 1467'.

Were these pedigrees, then, fabricated by their original compiler? It has been suggested that the compilation (as we have it, a copy from a text from c.1400) shows the sway of the contemporary lord of the Isles, by listing his vassal clans.[11] Yet there is something counter-intuitive about this suggestion, for not all the clans subject to the lords of the Isles are listed, while the Caimbéalaigh for instance are, although they were never Mac Domhnaill's vassals. When we look at the general lay-out of the pedigrees, it is very noticeable that the lineages of the two royal lines of Cinéal nGabhráin and Cinéal Loairn are given first; then those of other kindreds claiming descent from Cinéal Loairn and of kindreds claiming descent from Niall, from Corc mac Lughach, and from non-Gaelic ancestors (such as the British Caimbéalaigh or the Norse Clann Mhic Neacail); and finally the genealogy of Clann Dubhghaill and Clann Domhnaill, descendants of Colla Uais. If the author had meant to produce a 'Mac Domhnaill-sway map', he would probably have given the Clann Domhnaill genealogy either in the first place, or immediately after the pedigrees of the royal lines of Scotland. He seems rather to have aimed to give a 'map' of the ancestry of the various Scottish kindreds, even if they are not all included and even if they are listed sometimes in what seems a slightly haphazard manner — for instance, he failed to group Anradhán's descendants together.[12] This may well be due to the fact that he was probably writing the pedigrees in a hurried manner as suggested by Ronald Black.[13] He may have been, then, simply writing a genealogical history of the *Albanaigh* of his time, since his completed collection looks not unlike many Irish wider genealogical compilations such as were often included in learned tracts, religious or lay or of a mixed nature. But whichever was Dubhgall Albanach's aim when he inserted the pedigrees into the manuscript, he was reproducing an older source and he accepted it as reliable: he shows no hesitation, or even outright dismissal, such as we have noted in *seanchaidhe* and *filidh* when dealing with genealogical claims differing from those kept in their ancient

11 Steer and Bannerman 1977, p. 205; MacGregor 2000, p. 143.
12 'MS 1467', nos 9, 21, 27.
13 Black, *Catalogue*, p. 14.

books, or absent from them. This in itself is extremely interesting, suggesting that if the pedigrees in 'MS 1467' reflected a fabrication, then its origin must have been much earlier than the fifteenth century, by which time they were accepted as genuine by the Gaelic learned men.

Generally the Gaelic kindreds considered in this chapter come to light in the historical record by the early fourteenth century. Most of them did not have direct participation in the higher politics of the kingdom. Although friction between them and the crown is sometimes recorded, by and large they appear on the king's side and against his enemies in all major conflicts. For instance, members of the Camshrón, Mac an Tóisigh, Mac Aoidh, and Mac Raith families are named among the supporters of the Scottish crown at Bannockburn (1314), Halidon Hill (1333), Flodden (1513), or Pinkie (1547). For some of them, additionally, tradition claims support of the fight against the Moray rebels (1163) and against the Norse at Largs (1263).[14] Against this pattern of royal support stands, quite strikingly, the exception of Harlaw (1411), when most of these clans backed the lord of the Isles.[15] This battle, however, was not the result of conflict with the crown, but rather Mac Domhnaill's attempt to obtain a legitimate claim against the greedy designs of a regent.[16] Otherwise those clans which were vassals of the lords of the Isles — and a large number of them were in the fifteenth century, when the Mac Domhnaill lordship was at its zenith — generally managed to combine their service to the crown with support of their immediate overlord. The Camshrón chiefs, for instance, regularly took the side of the lords of the Isles in the latter's feuds, and Clann Fhionghuin support went beyond Eóin mac Alasdair's 1493 forfeiture, for they backed the various subsequent efforts to restore the Mac Domhnaill lordship.[17] Clann Mhic Raith, on the other hand, had by the fifteenth century become Mac Coinnigh's vassals and opposed Clann Domhnaill at

---

14 Macrae 1884, pp. 11, 12, 43; Macfarlane 1900, i, pp. 36–40, 159, 165, 167–8, 235; Mackay 1829, pp. 28, 63, 64, 130; Mackay 1906, pp. 39, 42–3, 76, 90; MacKinnon 1931, p. 6; *HP* i, p. 199; Skene 1902, p. 314.

15 *HP* i, pp. 29–30; Mackenzie 1884, p. 25; Macfarlane 1900, i, p. 147. But for Mac Aoidh opposition to Clann Domhnaill just before Harlaw see Mackay 1906, p. 55.

16 See above, chapter 3, pp. 71–2.

17 MacKenzie 1884, pp. 40, 45; MacKinnon 1931, p. 12. As an exception Clann Chamshróin, along with Clann Mhic an Tóisigh, opposed Clann Domhnaill at the battle of Inverlochy (1431) (*HP* i, pp. 39–40).

the battle of Park (*c*.1491).[18] The Rothach chief, having made his submission to James IV in 1495, helped quell the 1497 rebellion led by Alasdair of Lochalsh, eleventh lord of the Isles.[19]

For the later period the general pattern is one of support for the royal house of Stiúbhart, from the Wars of the Three Kingdoms in the mid-seventeenth century right through to the battle of Sheriffmuir in 1715 and indeed beyond, into the second part of the Jacobite conflict which is outwith the scope of this study. Religious divergence was not incompatible with loyalty to the Stiúbhairt. Highland leaders who, like Mac Fionghuin, converted to the Reformed religion, fought on the same side as Catholics such as the Clann Raghnaill chiefs or the Gordan earls of Huntly.[20] One exception to the pattern of continued Stiúbhart support is that of Clann Mhic Aoidh of Strathnaver, whose chiefs changed sides in 1689, becoming supporters of William of Orange, and later of George of Hanover.[21] The Rothaich similarly opposed the royalists. The anti-Jacobite stance in the case of these two clans might well be connected to the absence of their leaders from their patrimonial lands: both the Mac Aoidh and Rothach chiefs spent prolonged periods lending military service on the continent through the seventeenth century.[22] This view would seem to be confirmed by documented internal clan divisions: the Rothaigh of the cadet branches of Coul, Bearcrofts, and Newmore, for instance, all gave their support to Charles I and Charles II.[23] Good relations between the Gaelic clans and the crown could be marked, at any time in our period, by placing clan chiefs in positions of power or responsibility and by bestowing on them titles. To give some instances, Mac an Tòisigh chiefs were from the later twelfth century and until the later fifteenth hereditary constables of Inverness Castle. Domhnall, sixteenth Mac Aoidh chief (†1649), was knighted by the king in London in 1616, created a Baronet of Nova Scotia in 1627, and raised to the peerage as Lord Reay in 1628. The Rothaigh were barons of Foulis since the later

---

18 Macrae 1899, pp. 14–19.
19 Gregory 1881, pp. 92–3.
20 MacKinnon 1931, pp. 20, 22.
21 Skene 1902, pp. 364–5.
22 *ibid.*, pp. 315, 364.
23 Fraser 1954, pp. 26–8.

twelfth century. Uilliam, twelfth baron (+1505), was knighted by James IV and received from him a commissionary of justice within the shire of Inverness; Roibéard Mór, fifteenth baron (+1588), was principal baillie to James VI in Ross and Ardmannoch; and Eachann (+1635) was created Baronet of Foulis by Charles I.[24]

Typically, although not in all cases, the clan chiefs were styled after the founder of their kindred. Thus the titles of the heads of Clann Mhic Fhionguin and Clann Mhic an Tóisigh were Mac Fionghuin and Mac an Tóisigh respectively. Mac Aoidh, the chief of Clann Mhic Aoidh, is sometimes referred to as *ceann ar Mhorgannachaibh* ('chief over the Morgannaigh'), *Morgannaigh* being another name for his clan, after their fourteenth-century ancestor Morgann, grandfather of the eponymous Aodh.[25] Mac Duibhshithe, Mac Neachdain, and Mac Guaire are some other instances of chiefly titles in the same fashion. Mac Gille Chamshróin may have been the original denomination of the chiefs of Clann Chamshróin, but if so then it seems to have fallen into disuse. From around the mid-fifteenth century the title of the kindred's head was Mac Domhnaill Duibh, after Domhnall Dubh, the eleventh chief, who at Harlaw fought on the side of the lord of the Isles.[26] He is *uachtaran ar chloinn chámshroin* ('chief over Clann Chamshróin') in Niall Mac Muireadhaigh's historical narrative, while territorial references in the poetry include those to Eóghan Beag, fourteenth chief (*fl.c.*1550), as 'ceann-Lochiall 'us Druim-na-Saille' ('head of Lochiel and Drumsallie'), and to Eóghan mac Ailéin, seventeenth chief (+1719) as 'Eòghain òig Tòrr a' Chaisteil' ('Young Ewen of Tor Castle').[27] Other clan heads seem to have had only a territorial style, as in 'Fear Fòlais', the designation of the chief of the Rothaigh, from Foulis, north of Dingwall, in Ross-shire.[28]

---

24 Macfarlane 1900, i, pp. 156, 159, 160, 186. Ardmannoch: for Ardmeanach, the Gaelic name of the Black Isle; see Beaton 1882–3, p. 477 and n. 1.

25 *RC* ii, p. 176; Skene 1902, p. 361.

26 Mackenzie 1884, pp. 7, 25, 31.

27 *RC* ii, p. 174; *B' fheàrr leam gun sgrìbhteadh dhuit fearann*, l. 10; *Cha b'e tùirneal a' chnatain*, §15a. Drumsallie: west of Kinlocheil, Inverness-shire. Tòrr a' Chaisteil: a castle built by Eóghain mac Ailéin near Fort William, on the banks of the river Lochy (*OIL*, p. 305).

28 *Deoch-slàinte chabair fèidh seo*, §2a.

The poetry

Within the extant corpus of poetry for members of the Scottish Gaelic kin-dreds considered in this chapter only one piece can confidently be taken to be the work of a *file*. This is *Adhbhur tuirsi ag fuil Fhionghuin*, an anony-mous elegy in *dán díreach*, for Eóin Óg (†1682), son and heir of Lochlann Mór, sixteenth chief of Clann Mhic Fhionghuin.[29] It is not clear whether the Mac Fionghuin chiefs had their own *filidh*. Like the Mac Leóid and Mac Gille Eóin chiefs, they too were counsellors to the lords of the Isles, and additionally seem to have been their original hereditary stewards. In this office, as well as in their Mull lands, they were however displaced by Clann Ghille Eóin; instead they were made marshalls of the army of the lord of the Isles, and received from the latter a new grant of lands in Mull.[30] That Clann Mhic Fhionghuin were acknowledged to belong among the most ancient and noble families in the lordship is suggested by the story of the tutor of Moydart's insult to the 'upstart guests' at the Aros feast: Mac Fionghuin was, along with Mac Guaire, among the first to be invited to be seated.[31] Yet they may not have had the means to support a hereditary family of *filidh*; according to Dean Monro, they were 'thanes of les living and estate'.[32] They seem to have had a connexion with Iona: their alterna-tive chiefly title is given in 'MS 1467' as Mac Coluim [Cille], and Monro has it that they were buried at Reilig Orain, the graveyard at the chapel of St Oran's in Iona.[33]

The elegy for Eóin Óg Mac Fionghuin, the second half of which eulo-gises his father, Lochlann Mór, contains many of the motifs of classical panegyric. Both subjects are noted for their nobility of blood, martial prowess, generosity, hospitality, patronage of poets, hunting skills and love of music, feasting and gaming, and nature is depicted as mourning Eóin Óg's death.[34] An *apalóg* is incorporated to compare the general grief (of the whole kindred, of the Hebrides, and of the whole of Scotland)[35] to that

---

29 Heir: from internal evidence (§14d).
30 *HP* i, pp. 23, 33.
31 *ibid.*, p. 45.
32 *Monro*, p. 57.
33 'MS 1467', no. 26; *Monro*, p. 63.
34 *Adhbhur tuirsi ag fuil Fhionghuin*, §§5cd, 7b, 8ab, 15, 17, 20, 24d, 25cd, 30ab.
35 *ibid.*, §§1a, 3cd, 14a, 15b.

caused by the death of Naoise (§§9–13). The author is in no doubt of his subjects' ancient noble origins: they are of 'sliocht Chairbre réidh Rídhfhoda' ('the race of smooth Cairbre Rioghfhada'), '[fuil] Feraghaigh' ('the blood of Fearadhach [Fionn]'), and therefore of the royal line of Loarn, consistent with the genealogy given in 'MS 1467'.[36] Neither is he in any doubt of their identity as Scots: as well as the unequivoval statement that Clann Mhic Fhionghuin are of 'seanfhuil on fhonn Albanach' ('the ancient blood of the land of *Alba*', §6d), the elegy contains several allusions to either *Alba* or the *Albanaigh*, who lament Eóin Óg's death.[37] The place-names used also connect the subjects to their Scottish patrimony: 'féinnidh Mhoigh Muile' ('the hero of the plain of Mull'), 'ceann na ccuradh a Sgíth' ('the head of the warrior-band from Skye'), '[marbhthair] bhric Bláthbheinne' ('slayer of the trouts of Blaven'), '[marcach] Sratha Suardail' ('knight of Strathordle').[38] Finally, imagery includes the representation of the subject as a candle ('A choinnle Chill Moruibhe', 'O candle of Kilmaree') and of his kindred as the remnant of a glorious race, in this case 'iarsma fola Feraghaigh' ('a remnant of Fearadhach [Fionn]'s blood').[39]

We do have another syllabic composition, *Fada dhomh an laighese*, a personal poem composed by 'an Barún Eóghan Mac Combaigh' in the late-fifteenth or early-sixteenth century. But the combined facts that the author is a titled individual, perhaps from a branch of the Stiúbhart family, and that the piece is in very loose metre, strongly suggest that the author was an amateur rather than a *file*, and if so then, consistent with the parameters set for this study, the piece should be classed as vernacular.[40] The poem contains little in the way of panegyric code rhetoric. The author laments having been in his sick-bed for a long time, and states that he would pay 'Táin bó Cuailnge' ('The cattle-drove of Cuailnge'), 'ga bolga Chon Chulainn' ('the spear of Cú Chulainn'), ' Ór Éibhir is Éireamhóin'

---

36 *ibid.*, §§4b, 6b. See 'MS 1467', no. 26.

37 *Adhbhur tuirsi ag fuil Fhionghuin*, §§13d, 14a, 15d.

38 *Ibid.*, §§7ac, 25d, 26d. Blaven: a mountain in Skye. Strathordle: part of Clann Mhic Fhionghuin's patrimony, in north-west Skye, from which later chiefs took the designation 'of Strathordle'. See MacKinnon 1931, p. 8.

39 *Adhbhur tuirsi ag fuil Fhionghuin*, §§6b, 26a. Kilmaree / Kilmarie: Cill Ma Ruibhe, west of the Sleat peninsula, in Skye.

40 See above, chapter 2, pp. 42–3. For the likelihood of the Stiúbhart connexion see *SVBDL*, p. 297.

('The gold of Éibhear and of Éireamhón'), and so on, 'i luach leaghais' ('as fee for healing') (§§2–5). Finally he expresses his confidence that a visit by Alasdair Mac an Tóisigh (an unidentified individual) would surely restore him his health (§6). This closing statement is indeed the only one in the poem which can be said to be a classical panegyric code motif, since it seems to relate to that which depicts the subject as a curative influence, often comparing him to a healing herb.[41]

The extant vernacular verse includes a poem addressed by Iain Lom to Lochlann Mór Mac Fionghuin, father of Eóin Óg, the subject of *Adhbhur tuirsi ag fuil Fhionghuin*. Lochlann Mór succeeded to the chiefship in 1664, was a supporter of King Charles and is said to have been knighted by him on the battlefield at Worcester (1651).[42] The poem is in the general style of vernacular panegyric, focusing on the subject's warrior skills, liberality and love of feasting, and including a list of allies.[43] Iain Lom also notes that Lochlann Mór did not adopt ' 'm fasan bh'aig càch' ('the habit of others') who were 'smachdail mu'n mhàl air tuaith' ('severe with the tenantry over rent', §8). We found a similar reference in a Mac Gille Eóin poem, also composed in the seventeenth century, and noted that this is a new development in the panegyric code, now depicting the chief as a landlord and his people as his tenants.[44] Another point of interest is Iain Lom's reference, under influence of new contemporary genealogical claims, to Mac Fionghuin as a descendant of the royal house of Cinéal nGabhráin (§7ab), rather than that of Cinéal Loairn as upheld in the surviving classical Mac Fionghuin poem and in all Gaelic genealogical records. The differing genealogical claims in the two extant Mac Fionghuin poems, the one classical and the other vernacular, and both composed in the later seventeenth century during Lochlann Mór's lifetime, constitute yet another illustration of the *filidh*'s dogged refusal to accept new-fangled versions of history, and the vernacular poets' tendency to be more easily influenced by these.[45]

---

41 See, for instance, *Branuigh ar chlú ós cloinn Néill*, §27d; *Atáim i gcás eidir dhá chomhairle*, §7c.

42 Mackinnon 1931, p. 20; *OIL*, pp. 265–6.

43 *Is cian 's gur fad' tha mi 'm thàmh*, §§5, 9–12.

44 See above, chapter 5, p. 225.

45 As in the case of the Caimbéal claim to descent from Diarmaid; see above, chapter 4, pp. 155–6. See also pp. 120, 125, and chapter 5, pp. 119–200. For another allusion to Mac Fionghuin descent from Cinéal nGabhráin see Lachlann mac Theàrlaich Òig's

Claims — known through Niall Mac Muireadhaigh's genealogies to have existed[46] — of other Gaelic kindreds' descent from Loarn Mór are not, however, contained in the extant vernacular poetry. What we do find in much of it is the motif of royalism. Many of the elements employed in the formulation of Gaelic royalism as a literary motif can be found scattered through a number of the poems. In *Tha mo chiabhan air glasadh*, a 1716 composition for Eóghan Camshrón, seventeenth chief of Lochiel (†1719), Charles II is defended as the rightful heir, Cromwell's army is represented as *prasgan* ('rabble'), and the defence of the Stiúbhart cause portrayed as a specifically Gaelic concern (§§10d, 14ab, 18d). Those joining the Jacobite forces (for instance Camshrón, Mac an Tóisigh, Mac Fionghuin, or Mac Raith), are praised for their support (and castigated when the poets deem that they have behaved in a cowardly manner), and prayers are said for those who are in exile.[47] Those who, like the Rothaigh and Clann Mhic Aoidh, opposed the royalists are attacked and sometimes virulently satirised.[48] In *'S tearc an-diugh mo chùis ghàire*, a political piece composed in 1716 for Uilliam Mac an Tóisigh (†1743), NicGhillesheathanaich complains of lack of justice and truthfulness, and attacks the *Cuigse*, their deceitfulness, and their banishment of the rightful king. She alludes to the religious conflict, denouncing the manipulation of the true teachings of the Bible by some, and laments, as some poets composing for Clann Ghille Eóin did, the price that those who adhered to the Jacobite cause had come to pay for their loyalty.[49] In a third poem, composed by Iain Lom at the time of the Cromwellian occupation, the enemy are identified as 'luchd nam fallainnean dearga' ('the red-coats') and the Caimbéalaigh placed among their number and attacked.[50] There are several instances of the *mìorùn* motif. Donnchadh nam Pìos refers to the Williamite supporters as 'luchd a mìoruin'.[51] Dòmhnall Bàn

---

Marbhaisg air an t-saoghal chruaidh, §13a.

46 As above, chapter 5, pp. 226, 228.

47 *'S tearc an-diugh mo chùis ghàire*, §12e; *Tha mulad, tha gruaim orm, tha bròn*, §7; *Mhic Coinnich bhon Tràigh*, §§2, 3efgh.

48 *Deoch-slàinte chabair fèidh seo*, §§1klmn, 2–3, 4k, 5cd, 7–10.

49 §§2cdg, 3c, 4ef, 5ab, 15gh. For the Mac Gille Eóin reference see above, chapter 5, p. 221.

50 *Cha b'e tùirneal a' chnatain*, §§5, 10–12, 20b.

51 *Ta 'n saoghal-s' carail*, §2h. For *mìorùn* as a sin to be abandoned see below, p. 259.

— perhaps a MacGhilleathain poet[52] — complains of 'faoin thuaileas luchd mioruin' ('the vain slander of those of ill will'), and uses the related expression 'feachd le droch dhurachd' ('an ill-willed army') to describe the Cromwellian army.[53] In 1719 NicGhillesheathanaich reversed the motif when she stated that the royal usurper — King George — deserved the ill will of the *Gaoidhil*.[54] NicGhillesheathanaich also uses the sin-and-punishment framework, presenting the current evil political circumstances as the atonement required by Divine Justice:

> 'Athair, seall oirnn 'san tim so
> Bhon tha 'n iobairt ud trom.
>
> (Father, have mercy on us at this time,
> for that atonement is heavy).[55]

Finally, she joins the poetic throng who, in the Highlands as well as elsewhere in Britain, from the later seventeenth century were condemning the attack on the true nobility by upstarts:

> Tha na h-urrachan priseil
> Gan cur sios mar am moll.
>
> (The precious nobility
> have been laid down like chaff).[56]

Like NicGhillesheathanaich, Donnchadh nam Pìos (†c.1700) also composed political poems in the strict sense. He was chief of Clann Mhic Raith, born in a family that produced many churchmen and scholars, and the author of the Fernaig Manuscript, which he began to compile in 1688.[57] In *Ta 'n saoghal-s' carail* and *Gur feallta carail an saoghal* he deplored the political lies, complained of the fickleness and deceitfulness of the world,

---

52 See *EB*, pp. lxi–lxii.

53 *Tha mo chiabhan air glasadh*, §§12a, 16e.

54 *'S tearc an-diugh mo chùis ghàire*, §4f.

55 *ibid.*, §ab.

56 *ibid.*, §2ef. For other Gaelic poets on the same see chapter 3, p. 107, and chapter 4, p. 174, and for other poets chapter 1, pp. 19–20.

57 Thompson (ed.) 1994, p. 65.

and availed himself of contemporary Biblical imagery: by seizing the throne William of Orange had behaved as Absolom had against his father David, and the people, like the children of Israel, now could only hope for a miracle.[58] Donnchadh's address to the *Gaoidhil* encouraging them to keep up their support of James connects with the depiction of royalism as a Gaelic concern, and the poet also joins other contemporary authors in portraying the current political evils within a sin-and-punishment context.[59] But while NicGhillesheathanaich merely prays for deliverance, Donnchadh nam Pìos adds to this prayer practical advice. If the current evils are punishment for sin, then sin is to be abandoned: 'farmad ... uabhar ... mìorùn ... fuar chreideamh ... bhi foilleil ... sannt' ('envy ... pride ... ill will ... cold faith ... deceitfulness ... covetousness'), are to be replaced with 'bròn ... trasg' ... ùmhladh ... sìothshaimh ... iochd ... creideamh' ('repentance ... fasting ... humility ... peacefulness ... mercy ... faith'), and with 'fiamh Dè: tús bhi glic' ('fear of God: the beginning of wisdom').[60] This last piece of advice may echo the religious poem *Tùs gliocais eagal Dè*, by Murchadh Mòr MacCoinnich, Donnchadh's slightly earlier contemporary, which in turn may well be an echo of *Tús na heagna omhan Dé* (quoting from the Bible, 'Initium sapientiae timor Domini'),[61] a classical piece by the Irish *file* Aonghus Fionn Ó Dálaigh, composed in the early seventeenth century.

With one exception in Donnchadh's poetry,[62] there are no references to Britain, and *Alba* makes only an occasional appearance. Domhnall Bàn states that *Alba* had yielded to Cromwell under pressure of threats, and NicGhillesheathanaich complains that she rarely finds a reason to smile 'Bhon chaidh Albainn gu strith' ('since Scotland went to war'). The *Goill* are sometimes the Lowlanders; they are described as 'luchd casag is chàb' ('the folk of cassocks and cloaks'), and the cultural Lowlands as 'machair nan Gall' ('the Plain of the *Goill*'). On other occasions the *Goill* are generally those to whom the Jacobite supporters must not yield.[63]

---

58 *Ta 'n saoghal-s' carail*, §1d *Gur feallta carail an saoghal*, §§1, 2efg, 4e, 14ab. See chapters 3, p. 106; 4, p. 146; 5, p. 223.

59 *Ta 'n saoghal-s' carail*, §§16aef, 10cd.

60 *Gur feallta carail an saoghal*, §§14–16.

61 Eccl 1:16.

62 *Gur feallta carail an saoghal*, §10b.

63 *Fhir thèid thar a 'Mhàim*, §5d; *Is cian 's gur fad' tha mi 'm thàmh*, §4a; *Ta 'n saoghal-s' carail*, §6cd.

Despite the appearance of the motif of royalism in a number of the poems considered in this section, most of the extant vernacular verse is concerned with general praise of the subject. In this it adheres to the general pattern of vernacular poetry as studied in previous chapters, and therefore to that of classical panegyric which we have called the later model: the preferred motifs are the individual's nobility and martial prowess, his generosity and hospitality, his love of hunting and feasting, his irresistible appeal to women, and so on.[64] Eóghan Camshrón, seventeenth chief of Lochiel, is, exceptionally, particularly noted as his people's protector.[65] There are instances of the 'friends and allies' and 'kinship connexions' motifs, which sometimes blend into each other, in Mac Fionghuin, Mac Raith, and Mac Neachtain poems.[66] The only allusion to the written word as confirmation of the subject's genealogical or territorial rights can be said to be that made by an anonymous sixteenth-century poet who wishes that Eóghan Beag Camshrón would obtain a written charter for his patrimony.[67] Finally, plant and animal imagery is not frequent in the poetry considered in this section.

Poems for Irish patrons

Although this study is concerned with panegyric composed for Scottish subjects, a brief look at the extant poems composed by Scottish authors for Irish patrons is necessary, if only in order to explore how these compositions may differ, in terms of the rhetoric of authority, or panegyric code, from the former. A number of early-thirteenth-century panegyrics for Donnchadh Ó Briain (†1242), lord of Thomond, and Cathal Ó Conchobhair (the renowned Cathal Croibhdhearg, †1224), lord of Connacht, have been attributed to a poet known as Giolla Brighde Albanach.[68] However, it is not clear whether this author was Irish or Scottish, although he certainly was in Scotland at some point.[69] All we can say is that if he was Scottish then

---

64 See above, chapter 3, p. 113.

65 *Tha mo chiabhan air glasadh*, §§1e, 8abcde, 12g, 19ab.

66 *Is cian 's gur fad' tha mi 'm thàmh*, §§11–12; *'S mi 'g uileag mo leaba*, §§13–16; *'S fhad tha mi ag èisdeachd ri ur dìochuimhn*, §§2–5, 11–12.

67 *B' fheàrr leam gun sgrìbhteadh dhuit fearann*, ll. 2, 8.

68 *Tabhraidh chugam cruit mo ríogh* (for other ascriptions see *BPD*), *Aisling ad-chonnairc o chianaibh*, *Fada dhamh druim re hÉirinn*, and *Tainic an Croibhdhearg go Crúachain*.

69 From internal evidence in the poems ascribed to him (McLeod 2004, p. 95).

his poems fully conform to the 'Irish model'. This includes not only a solid presence of the theme of the patron as the protector of his land and people, but also, in the panegyric for Ó Conchobhair, the employment of the motif of the high-kingship of Ireland — with its associated spouse and Tara motifs — and that of prophecy. The prophetic references are to Bearchán and Marbhán, and therefore to the expulsion of the *Goill* from Ireland.[70] We might add that, in contrast with the genealogical vagueness or even complete blank in some classical poems for Scottish patrons, the subject's ancient noble ancestry is always noted: Ó Briain is from *fine Chais* ('the race of Cas'), Ó Conchobhair is *ó Chréidhe* ('the descendant of Créadh'), *ua Duach Galaigh* ('the descendant of Duí Galach'), *ua Meadhbha* ('the descendant of Meadhbh').[71]

We are on surer footing with later extant poems. Two of them are the work of Giolla Críost Brúilingeach, a Scottish poet who in the earlier fifteenth century visited the courts of Tomaltach Mac Diarmada (†1458), lord of Moylurg, and of Tomás Mág Uidhir (†1480), lord of Fermanagh. We do not know Giolla Críost's surname or affiliations, and there is a view that he was a harper rather than a poet, based, apparently, on the poet's request for the gift of a harp in one of his panegyrics, but this seems unlikely. Harpers did not have the training required to compose in the strict metres used by Giolla Críost, while it is not impossible that a *file*, part of whose training was in music,[72] should have aimed for a harp in payment for his work. There is also evidence that, in Ireland at least, poetic addresses to a chief by anyone who had not achieved the degree of *ollamh* were unacceptable.[73] To judge from one of his poems, *Dá urradh i*

---

70 *Tabhraidh chugam cruit mo ríogh*, §12c; *Fada dhamh druim re hÉirinn*, §20c; *Tainic an Croibhdhearg go Crúachain*, §§2ab, 10a, 29a, 17cd, 33a. For Marbhán see Finan 2002, p. 119.

71 *Tabhraidh chugam cruit mo ríogh*, §6b; *Fada dhamh druim re hÉirinn*, §§7c, 8c, 11d, 12b. *Fine Chais*: Dál gCais, the descendants of Cormac Cas, son of Oilill Ólum, who inhabited Thomond (see, for instance, *FFÉ* iii, pp. 196, 256). For Créadh and Duí Galach see Ó Cuív (ed.) 1969–70, p. 201 nn. 7, 8.

72 Ó Cuív 1973, pp. 4–5. There are many poems reflecting the *filidh's* fondness for music, particularly that of harps. To Gofraidh Fionn Ó Dálaigh the harp was 'aoinleannán na n-eólach' ('the favourite of the learned', *A chláirsioch Chnuic Í Chosgair*, §6a). See also *Tabhraidh chugam cruit mo ríogh*; *Ceolchair sin a chruit an ríogh*; *A Niocláis, nocht an gcláirsigh*.

73 For instance, Giolla Brighde Ó hEódhusa incurred the displeasure of Aodh Ruadh Ó Domhnaill by addressing to him a praise poem when he had only the degree of *ánroth*,

n-iath Éireann, Giolla Críost had severely contrasting experiences in his relationship with the two chiefs. The piece belongs to the category known as *dán leathaoire*, where two individuals are addressed, one to be praised and the other criticised.[74] It may be that Mág Uidhir refused to receive the poet or that his payment for the visitor's work was less than adequate, for he is repeatedly criticised by Giolla Críost who describes him as 'criopal sean gortach' ('and old stingy lameter'), *fear doichleach diúltadhach* ('a grudging man ready of refusal'), and 'daoi dolamh diúltach' ('a boor close-fisted and given to refusal') (§§1c, 3d, 19d).[75] Additionally, there are at least four poems composed by Maol Domhnaigh Ó Muirgheasáin, who belonged to the family of hereditary *filidh* to Mac Leóid of Dunvegan and who visited a number of poetic schools in Ireland in the mid-seventeenth century.[76] No poems addressed by Maol Domhnaigh to a Scottish patron are extant. Leaving aside *Cia feasda as urra don eól*, an elegy for his fellow poet Cú Chonnacht Ó Dálaigh (†1642), we have three eulogies by Maol Domhnaigh for the Munster chiefs Domhnall Ó Donnabháin (†1660), Séafraidh Ó Donnchadha (†1678), and Donnchadh Ó Ceallacháin (†c.1680). It has been noted that Ó Muirgheasáin's eulogies, with their heavy praise of the subject's generosity and fame, are a reflection of the contemporary decline in poetic patronage.[77] At the same time, such una-shamed emphasis is characteristic generally of visiting poets — for, after all, one main purpose of their visit was to obtain reward for a demonstra-tion of their art — and Maol Domhnaigh was indeed a visitor in Ireland.

Despite this emphasis, all poems contain most of the conventional praise motifs, again that of protection of land and people appearing regu-larly in both Giolla Críost's and Maol Domhnaigh's poems.[78] The motif of

as he admits in his poem *Atáim ionchora re hAodh*, §3. For the opinion that Giolla Críost was a harper see, for instance, Thomson 1968, p. 69; *DnS*, pp. 114–15. See also below, n. 75.

74 And perhaps echoes the late-fourteenth-century Irish poem *Námha agus cara dar gceird*; see Dooley 1986.

75 The satirical portions of this poem are very much in a *file*'s style, rather than in that of, for instance, Iain Lom's attacks on the Caimbéalaigh (for which see above, pp. 108, 125–6), adding to the suggestion of Giolla Críost's status as a *file*. For satire as the *file*'s prerogative see Breatnach 2006, p. 63.

76 For less certain ascriptions of other poems see Black (ed.) 1976, pp. 194–5.

77 id., 1981, at p. 300.

78 *Lámh aoinfhir fhóirfeas i nÉirinn*, §§1abd, 3b, 4b, 9b, 17d; *Cia as urra d'ainm an iarthair*,

the foreigners appears sometimes, although always as a passing reference. Mac Diarmada is said to succour 'anbhuain Ghaoidheal is Ghall' ('the distress of *Gaoidhil* and *Goill*'), Ó Donnabháin is claimed to be 'fáth omhuin d' allmhurchaibh' ('the cause of fear of foreigners'), and Mág Uidhir is insulted as being *gallda* ('Saxon of soul').[79] Praise includes, again, allusions to ancient noble lineage. For instance, Eóghan Taidhleach, Fiacha, and Lughaidh are named as Ó Donnabháin's ancestors; Fiacha Muilleathan, Corc, and Oilill Ólum as those of Ó Ceallacháin; and Mac Diarmada, a descendant of Conn Céadchathach through Eochaidh Muighmheadhón, is complimented as 'macaomh tighe Teamhra tréin' ('gallant of Tara's mighty house').[80] Not only do geographical references bind the poems' subjects to their territories, but in the case of Ó Ceallacháin Maol Domhnaigh clearly states that the territory over which he rules is 'seilbh sinnseardha' ('ancestral property'), 'Críoch a shean' ('The land of his ancestors').[81] The mention of the ancestral patrimony, as we noted, is a motif which is absent from the poetry for Scottish nobles whose exact ancestry is obscure.[82] The same idea is expressed in the poet's statement that Ó Donnabháin is 'urra an anma shinnsiordha' ('guardian of the ancestral name').[83] There are two references to the written word as validator of the subject's rights,[84] and a final point of interest is the following remark by Maol Domhnaigh on Ó Donnabháin:

> Gairm shochair na nglún ór ghin
> coiseónaidh d' ais nó d' éigin.
>
> (The favourable reputation of the dynasts from whom he is descended he will maintain by consent or by force).[85]

---

§§12b, 24; *Gnáith féile ag fagháil innmhe*, §33b.

79 *Lámh aoinfhir fhóirfeas i nÉirinn*, §1ab; *Cia as urra d'ainm an iarthair*, §25d; *Dá urradh i n-iath Éireann*, §1c.

80 *Cia as urra d'ainm an iarthair*, §26abc; *Gnáith féile ag fagháil innmhe*, §§8b, 11c, 12b, 13a, 16b, 19c, 20d; *Lámh aoinfhir fhóirfeas i nÉirinn*, §2d. For the identification of these individuals see Black (ed.) 1978, p. 54; id., 1981, pp. 299–300. See also *Ní doirbh go deaghuil na ccarad*, §§2d, 4c, 6b, 7a, 12c, 21a.

81 *Gnáith féile ag fagháil innmhe*, §§18b, 22a.

82 See above, chapter 5, pp. 209, 216, 234, 241.

83 *Cia as urra d'ainm an iarthair*, §5b.

84 *Tainic an Croibhdherg go Crúachain*, §29bd; *Cia as urra d' ainm an iarthair*, §21a.

85 *Cia as urra d'ainm an iarthair*, §6ab.

The poet surely is here using the motif of 'conquest by force' (in the present case by predicting a successful period of rule even if Ó Donnabháin's enemies should oppose him) which has its origins in the ancient Gaelic laws.[86] Again, this motif is virtually non-existent in Scottish classical panegyric. In contrast, upholding the subject's entitlement to be his people's chief, whether on grounds of conquest, heredity, or seniority, and his right to remain in a particular territory on account of long established occupation, are both common themes in classical verse for Irish patrons.[87] One motif absent from the extant poems of both Giolla Críost Brúilingeach and Maol Domhnaigh Ó Muirgheasáin is that of the high-kingship of Ireland. It may be that Scottish poets were not expected to deal in this crucial matter; after all, where we do know the identity of the authors of Mac Domhnaill panegyrics including this particular theme, the poets are always Irish.[88]

The descendants of the *Goill*
Origins and historical background

In the twelfth century and through a good part of the thirteenth a number of Norman lords came to settle in Scotland. During this period the kings of Scots were intent on consolidating their authority and bringing under their sway their neighbours, among whom the kings of Moray, of the royal house of Loarn Mór, represented a particular threat to the continuity of the line of Cinéal nGabhráin on the throne. Lulach, son of Mac Beathadh, was the last of Cinéal Loairn to hold the kingship of *Alba*, but his family, and their allies, would persist in their attempts to overthrow the Cinéal nGabhráin kings for about two centuries after his death in 1058. Relations with England were relatively smooth during that period, and one way the kings of Scots increased their own strength was by granting land within their dominions to their Anglo-Norman allies. Partly because these *Goill* arrived in Scotland by royal invitation, the kingdom of Scots was spared much of the conflict that took place in Ireland as a consequence of Anglo-Norman settlement there, which was of a very different character. While

---

86 For the various grounds for lawful occupation of land see Jaski 2000, p. 209.
87 For a number of examples see Coira 2008a, *passim*.
88 See above, chapter 3, pp. 67, 68.

there was considerable mutual influence between natives and settlers,[89] the greater part of Scotland was still predominantly Gaelic in speech and custom, and many of the descendants of the Norman settlers of Scotland, like their counterparts in Ireland, adjusted to their new cultural medium, adopting the Gaelic language and a number of Gaelic customs. That of raiding perhaps comes to mind immediately, but another was fosterage. For instance, Sím Friseal, third Lord Lovat (*fl.*1307), had his eldest son Aodh fostered with Mac Raith.[90] Also, the education of these Gaelicised nobles of Norman origin was at least partly Gaelic: Eóin, a Grannd chief who lived in the later fifteenth century, was known as An Bard Ruadh,[91] a designation which implies that he was knowledgeable in the art of poetic composition. In a well-known anecdote included in his historical narrative, 'Hugh of Sleat' depicted Alasdair Stiúbhart, Earl of Mar (†1435), composing verse in Gaelic.[92] If the story is true, then Mar may also have had a partly Gaelic education. Finally, the chiefs of the kindreds of *Gall* ancestry adopted Gaelic-style titles, still in use by the early eighteenth century, even if they were also the bearers of royally-conferred honours of more recent creation: the style of the Friseal chief (created Lord Lovat in the mid-fifteenth century) was Mac Shimidh Mór, those of the marquises of Montrose and Atholl, An Grámach Mór and Am Moireach Mór respectively, and so on.[93]

It is, without a doubt, their own Gaelicisation that led many of these kindreds to claim, from a point in time that cannot be specified, a Gaelic origin for themselves. This caused some confusion to professional Irish genealogists. An Dubhaltach Mac Firbhisigh, when speaking of the origin of the Stiúbhairt 'amhuil gebhmid a teaglomaibh saine' ('as we find in various compilations'), first states that they were of the Leamhnaigh, and therefore descendants of Corc mac Lughach. But he immediately cautions the reader: 'gid aderti cineadh do bheth do thír iar ttuinidhe gur minic nar duthchus genealaigh dho an té o sloinnfi an tir' ('although it used to be

---

89 For the Anglo-Norman impact see Barrow 1980, especially at pp. 30–60, 199–203. For the lasting Gaelic influence on the Anglo-Norman settlers see generally 'The lost Gàidhealtachd', in id. 1992, pp. 105–26.

90 Macfarlane 1900, ii, p. 90.

91 *ibid.*, p. 109.

92 *HP* i, p. 43.

93 Macfarlane 1900, ii, p. 151.

said that a people is identified with a country through possession [of it], it is often the case that the person from whom the country is named is not genealogically native to it'), and appears sceptical about this genealogical claim 'do bhrigh nach ffaght*har* inar senleabhruibh an slondadh Sdiobhart' ('since the surname Stuart is not found in our old books').[94] The Stiúbhart genealogical claim of Gaelic origin, like similar claims by other kindreds, such as the Granndaigh, who are known to be of Norman ancestry, is probably explained by intermarriage, Gaelic descent coming to these kin groups through the female line. In fact Mac Firbhisigh himself notes that there are some errors in the sources in his possession since they contain a mixture of male and female succession.[95] To further complicate the matter, he quotes from 'aroile sliocht' ('a certain tract') which he believed to have been brought to Ireland from Scotland by An Fear Dorcha (*fl.c.*1560), an earlier member of his own family of historians. According to this tract, the Stiúbhairt were descendants of Brian Bóroimhe, and therefore ultimately of Éibhear, rather than of Éireamhón like most Scottish kindreds.[96] Mac Firbhisigh, however, remains non-committal, if not unconvinced; since his various sources disagree, he closes by leaving the matter to the reader's discretion: 'Breathnaigheadh an leughthoir m*a*dh ail' ('Let the reader examine [this], if he wishes').[97] His diction similarly reflects his lack of conviction: the claim of Stiúbhart Irish origins, 'mar shaoilid aroile' ('as some think'), comes from 'aroile sliocht', 'nuaishliocht eile' ('another new recension'), all of these being formulaic expressions indicating a source which seems less than credible to the author.[98]

The poetry is rather unhelpful in this respect. Only *Cóir feitheamh ar uaislibh Alban*, one of the two surviving classical poems for *Gall* kindreds, both apparently composed for Eóin Stiúbhart of Garth (†1475), makes any reference to an early ancestor. The poet addresses Eóin as 'a shíl shlat ó chathach Chonn' ('thou scion of the princes of warrior Conn's race', §16d), a claim that could only be possible through an earlier Stiúbhart marriage to

94 *LMG* ii, §§410.5–410.6.

95 *ibid.*, §413.6.

96 *ibid.*, §413.2. For An Fear Dorcha see Ó Muraíle 1996, pp. 49–60. See also below, chapter 7, p. 286.

97 *LMG* ii, §§410.6, 413.5.

98 *ibid.*, §§408A.4, 411.1. For this type of expression see Toner 2005, pp. 68–70, 73–4.

a female descendant of Conn Céadchathach. The lineage of the Stiùbhart cadet branch of Garth can be traced back to Robert I through Alasdair Mór mac an Rígh, 'the Wolf of Badenoch' (†1405). King Robert's wife was 'Marjorie' (probably Mairghréad), countess of Carrick. The ancestry of the earls or *mormhaoir* of Carrick in turn leads back to the lords of Galloway, who were ethnically *Gall-Ghaoidhil*: here we find the possibility of a Conn connexion, although again through the female line.[99] The only other reference to an ancient royal ancestor in poetry for subjects of *Gall* origin is found in an early eighteenth-century vernacular poem by Iain Dubh MacDhòmhnaill, who notes the marriage of Sím Friseal, thirteenth chief of Lovat (†1747), to a descendant of Ailpín, father of King Cionaoth I. Sím's wife was from the Granndaigh, who by this later period were claiming to share with Clann Mhic Fhionghuin and Clann Ghriogóir a common descent from Ailpín.[100] That the Gaelicised descendants of the *Goill* counted themselves among the numbers of the *Gaoidhil* is not only manifest from their genealogical claims. In *Cóir feitheamh ar uaislibh Alban*, for instance, we find an insistence on the identification of Eóin Stiùbhart of Garth as a *Gaoidheal* reminiscent of the Caimbéal near-obsession with their own depiction as *Gaoidhil*.[101] The rhetoric of royalism in the poetry for these kindreds, as we will see presently, conveys the same message.

From the later eleventh century the kingdom of Scots underwent a process of feudalisation, particularly marked by David I's (†1153) 'Revolution' which also included the implementation of the ideals of the Gregorian Reform, the foundation of monasteries, the creation of burghs, and the Anglo-Normanisation of governmental administration.[102] Already familiar with the feudal system, the *Gall* settlers who arrived in Scotland during the period were a key factor in the extension of feudal-style government through the kingdom.[103] The general pattern which the Friseal, Gordan, Grannd, Grám, Moireach, and other families present in their relations with the Scottish kings is one of support of the crown in all

---

99 *Cóir feitheamh ar uaislibh Alban*, §§4a, 5b, 7b, 9c, 13b, 15d. But for the obscurity of the ancestry of the lords of Galloway see Oram 2000, pp. 51–4.
100 *An deicheamh là de thùs a' Mhàirt*, §15ab; *ID*, p. 64. See above, p. 245.
101 See above, chapter 4, pp. 119, 132–5, and below, p. 270.
102 Barrow 2003, pp. 250–74; 'David I of Scotland: the balance of new and old', in id. 1992, pp. 45–65; Lynch 1991, p. 80.
103 See Grant and Cheape 1987, pp. 34–62.

major conflicts, such as the Wars of Independence and later. Some, like the Grámaigh and the Gordanaigh, appear more closely linked to royal government, not only attending its parliaments but also as ambassadors and witnesses of royal charters; this, however, may be simply due to their closer physical proximity to the king's court.[104] The combined facts that the royal army confronting Clann Domhnaill at Harlaw was largely made up of individuals of *Gall* origin, that its main leader was Alasdair Stiúbhart, earl of Mar (†1435), and that the lead-up to the battle was the refusal by duke Murchadh Stiúbhart of Mac Domhnaill's legitimate right to Ross, probably go a long way to explain the annalistic depiction — and a widespread modern popular view — of events as a conflict between *Gaoidhil* and *Goill*.[105] As was the case with the Gaelic kindreds, the descendants of the *Goill* sometimes had their frictions with royal government;[106] indeed many of the major troubles of the Brús and Stiúbhart kings stemmed from this ethnic group, sometimes in collaboration with the English enemy: Robert I and David II both had to contend with serious Balliol opposition, while James I and Mary faced serious threat from within their own kindred, and James III met his death while fighting rebels who were in collusion with his own son, the future James IV.[107]

For the later period the overall pattern for the *Gall* kindreds is not always one of steady support of the house of Stiúbhart, for a number of them joined the king's enemies. Séamas Grám, first Marquis of Montrose (†1650), was

---

104 Macfarlane 1900, ii, pp. 91, 92, and Mackenzie 1896, pp. 33–4, 36–41, 43, 53, 56, 59, 64–5, 71 (on the Friseal family); Macfarlane 1900, ii, pp. 409–20, at pp. 411–2, 413, 416–17 (Gordan); *ibid.*, pp. 103–17, at pp. 106–8, 110–11, 113, and Græme 1903, pp. xx, xxiii–xxvi, xxxi, xxxiii, xxxvi–xxxix (Grannd); Stewart-Murray 1908, 5, pp. 7, 15, 16, 21, 22, 28–9, 30 (Moireach). The Moireich took the Balliol side (*ibid.*, p. 4).

105 See above, chapter 3, p. 71 and n. 89.

106 Even the Gordan chiefs, who were earls of Huntly since 1449 and held important posts in both the military defence and the administration of the kingdom, came to mischief when the fourth earl, Seoras (†1562), opposed Queen Mary after she transferred the earldom of Moray, which was in Huntly's possession, to her half-brother James. Huntly's son and successor, also named Seoras, was attainted and sentenced for treason and would not be restored until 1567; see Dunlop 1965, pp. 16–17.

107 The main enemies of James I were the Albany Stiúbhairt, whom he had executed, and the same monarch's assassination was part of an attempt to usurp power by Uaitéar Stiúbhart, first Earl of Atholl (†1437); Séamas Stiúbhart, first Earl of Moray (†1570), was the leader of the 'Chaseabout Raid', a 1565 rebellion against Queen Mary. See Brown 1994, pp. 60–7, 172–92; Donaldson 1965, pp. 118–19; and Macdougall 1982, pp. 256–63, for events leading to the death of James III.

initially a covenanter, but soon became a staunch royal supporter, and one of the main royalist leaders of the mid seventeenth-century civil wars. The Friseal chiefs too were initially covenanters, subsequently presenting a steady pattern of Stiúbhart support, although they were divided at Sheriffmuir. The Granndaigh were also covenanters and opposed the royal army at Inverlochy (1645). After this they became royalists until 1689 when they transferred their allegiance to the house of Orange, although the battle of Sheriffmuir (1715) found the clan members divided and fighting on both sides.[108] On occasion politics caused unusual disorder in the clan system: Eóin Moireach, second Marquis of Atholl (†1703), transferred his support to William of Orange, but he was on his own: his clan continued to fight, as his successors did, for the Jacobite cause. The Catholic Gordan chiefs, who ran into difficulties with the crown on account of the introduction of religious changes in Scotland and of their own submission to William of Orange in 1689, generally remained loyal to the Stiúbhart line, although they refused to support Montrose. The bestowal of the titles of Marquis in 1599, Duke in 1684 and Knight of the Thistle in 1703 were rewards of the Stiúbhart kings for their loyalty. Alasdair, second Duke of Gordon (†1728) supported the Jacobites at Sheriffmuir, although part of his clan, as in the case of the Frisealaigh, Granndaigh, and others, fought on the opposite side.[109]

The poetry

Both extant Stiúbhart classical poems are anonymous and seem to have been addressed, as noted, to Eóin mac Roibéird of Garth. *Beannuigh do theaghlach, a Thríonóid*, which laments the devastation caused by wolves and encourages Eóin to help destroy them, contains little of the panegyric code, with the exception of some conventional descriptions of the subject, such as '[mac] Roibeirt na ruag dte' ('Robert's son, hot of pursuit'), 'a Eóin Stiúbhairt na stéad mbras' ('thou John Stewart of swift steeds').[110] *Cóir feitheamh ar uaislibh Alban*, in contrast, does contain many of the expected praise terms. Eóin is celebrated for his warrior skills, his physical beauty,

---

108 Macfarlane 1900, i, pp. 114–16; Mackenzie 1896, pp. 160–344.

109 Dunlop 1965, pp. 18–25; *DNB*, Vol. 39, pp. 947, 949.

110 §§11b, 15b. See also §16a, and *SVBDL*, pp. 293–4 for the historical background of the poem.

generosity, good judgement and his patronage of *filidh*.[111] Despite several references to the foreign founder of the kindred, Walter fitz Alan (†1177), first hereditary Steward of Scotland and father of Robert II (§§4a, 10a, 17b), there is much insistence on the depiction of Eóin as a *Gaoidheal*: he is 'Gaoidheal do chloinn Ghaltair' ('a Gael of Walter's family'), 'lámh thréan na nGaoidheal soinnimh' ('mighty hand of the eager Gael'), '[triath] shlat na nGaoidheal ngrinn' ('lord of the princes of the goodly Gael'), and he is addressed as 'A Chú Chulainn cloinne Ghaltair' ('Cú Chulainn of Walter's children').[112] But references to his identity as an *Albanach* are equally abundant: he is an *Albanach*, of 'uaislibh Alban' ('the nobles of Alba'), and '[taca] mhaithean Alban' ('the buttress of the nobles of Alba').[113] The aim of the piece, however, is in fact to intimidate the subject and force him to make amends (and therefore the insistence on Eóin being a *Gaoidheal* may aim at shaming him for behaving in a manner so atypical of the *Gaoidhil*), for he had offended the poet. The offence seems to have been Eóin's failure, or refusal, to pay the poet for his art, for the author states his displeasure 'do thaobh séad' ('in regard to jewels', §18b), and further clues are scattered through the poem:

> gé tá mise ar dál ó a bhronnadh,
>> 's ciste dámh is ollamh é …
>
> Más í do chomhairle bhunaidh
>> bheith 'gam eiteach …
>
> a mheic Ghaltair …
>> nach d'éar file romhainn riamh.

(though I am separated from his bounty, he is a treasury of poet-bands and learned men …

If it be thy fixed intent to make me refusal …

son of Walter … who never before us didst make refusal to a poet) (§§4cd, 9ab, 17bd).

---

111 §§4, 5c, 6bc, 7c, 9bc, 13b, 17bd, 18cd, 19c.
112 §§4a, 9c, 10a, 15d. See also §§5b, 7b, 9c, 13b, 15d.
113 §§1a, 4a, 7a, 9c, 10a, 15d. See also §§5b, 7b, 13b.

The poet would rather make peace, but should Eóin choose to fight him, then he will fight back, and his weapons are his words: the current poem is 'laoidh mholta agus bagar' ('a poem of praise and a threat', §5d) and a reminder that 'nimh na n-aoir ní an cogaidh soirbh' ('the venom of satires is no light warfare', §14b), for satire is 'an t-saighead ghéar ghreanta gháidh' ('the sharp, polished, deadly shaft', §11d). The expression 'cliar chogaidh' ('a band of war', §8d) is a well-known reference to the representation of satire as a warrior-band made up of six powerful combatants who fill fight the poet's cause. A late sixteenth-century crosántacht, *Rannam le chéile, a chlann Uilliam*, a warning poem addressed by Tadhg mac Dáire Mhic Bhruaideadha to the sons of Riocard Sasanach, names them as 'On 7 Ainimh 7 Aithis 7 Gríos 7 Glámh 7 Goirt-Bhriathra' ('Disfigurement, Blemish, Reproach, Incitement, Deadly Satire, and Bitter Words').[114]

A further item of interest in this poem is the employment of legal terminology, frequently found in this type of composition where the problem leading to the breakdown of the poet-patron relationship is presented as a lawsuit: the poet speaks of his *agra, tagra* ('suing, prosecution, claim, plea', §2a, 3a).[115] It is also reasonable to conclude that, whoever the author of our poem was, he was certainly a professional *file*: vernacular poets, including the noble amateurs with various degrees of skill in syllabic verse, might request patronage or complain of its lack, but this type of confident threat of satire came only from the *filidh*, on the basis that, as the successors of the ancient druids, they were endowed with supernatural powers. One final point to be made is the failure of the poet to note his subject's mixed *Gall-Ghaoidheal* descent. This is a motif frequent in classical poems for Irish nobles of Anglo-Norman origin, and it is always complimentary, poets sometimes noting the separate qualities coming to his subject through each separate lineage.[116]

---

114 In the poem's prose section, at p. 382. See also Cathbhaidh's warning in Breatnach (ed.) 1980, p. 14.

115 See Coira 2008a, for a case study in the poetic use of legal terminology generally.

116 For instance, Séamas Buitléar, third Earl of Ormond (†1452) and his family are described in *Aoidhe i n-Éirinn an t-iarla* as 'Goill Banbha' ('the *Goill* of Ireland', §30a; see also §§31b, 32b); Éamann Búrc, Mac Uilliam Íochtair (†1458), is noted in *Do briseadh riaghail rígh Sacsann*, to descend from the Búrc and the Ó Conchobhair families (§§43, 45).

As for the extant vernacular verse composed for descendants of *Gall* settlers, the rhetoric generally conforms to the pattern found in the poems for Gaelic patrons: the emphasis is on the individual as a warrior, his nobility, generosity, hospitality and love of feasting and music, and the kinship connexions and friends and allies motifs are equally common.[117] One difference is the scarcity of the praise motif of the subject's generous poetic patronage, perhaps an indication that such practice, if ever maintained by the chiefs of *Gall* descent, was no longer observed by them. If so, then the lords of Lovat seem to have been one exception, for Murchadh MacMhathain describes the house of Sím Friseal, thirteenth chief, as 'talla nan clarsach 's nan cliar' ('the hall of the harps and the poet-bands').[118] Indeed it is not certain that any of the chiefs considered in this section had any particular *aos-dàna* or *bàrd* attached to them in the way that, for instance, Eachann Bacach was attached to Mac Gille Eóin or Murchadh MacMhathain to Mac Coinnigh. Where we know the authors these tend to be of the surname of the chief's clan, although we have also pieces by a Seumas MacGriogair, by Murchadh MacMhathain himself, and by several MacDhòmhnaill authors, as well as a poem ascribed to the Rev. Robert Kirk of Aberfoyle, a learner of Gaelic. Apart from general praise in the usual style, the poetry also contains the theme of royalism. It is present in poems for Friseal, Gordan, Grám, and Moireach chiefs, and it features the themes and strands we are already familiar with — unsurprisingly, for the authors of the extant political poems for these *Gall* chiefs are always (with the one possible exception of the anonymous *Tha mi fo leann-dubh is fo bhròn*) from Clann Domhnaill: Iain Lom, Sìleas na Ceapaich, and Iain Dubh. Thus we find complaints of political lies and lack of justice, attacks on the Caimbéalaigh as enemies of the Stiúbhart cause, and the motif

---

117 See, for instance, *Mo thriall a sìos air firichean*, §§2e, 3d, 10a, 12; *An deicheamh là de thùs a' Mhàirt*, §§4, 18a, 6–8, 9–10, 11–14, 19a; *Gur h-uasal am macan*, §§1a, 2h, 3, 4, 5dh, 6efgh, 8f; *Mhuire 's muladach a tha mi*, §§2–7; *Mi ag amharc Srath Chuaiche*, §§1f, 3, 4, 6gh; *Iain mhòir bu mhath cumadh*, *passim*; *Lìon mulad mi fhèin*, §§2c, 3cde, 4–5, 6–8, 9abc; *Mo bheud mòr 's mo throm-luighe*, §§2be, rd, 5ab, 6, 7–9; *Soraidh do' n Ghràmach*, §§4, 5–8; *Tional nan sluagh chum na seilg*, §§4g, 37a, 38ab, 39ab, 46, *passim* for friends and allies; *'S mithich dhomh-sa bhith 'g èirigh*, §§2cdgh, 8d, 10; *Slàn a chì mi thu, Mharcuis*, §§1bc, 25a, 3–5, 7–8, 16–17, 25a.

118 *Gur h-uasal am macan*, §3b. There seems to be an indication of Moireach poetic patronage in *Tional nan sluagh chum na seilg*, §38a where he is connected with 'ceòl is dàimh' ('music and poets').

of the wheel of fortune.[119] After the execution of Séamas Grám, Earl of Montrose, in 1650, Iain Lom employs the image of the children of Israel in bondage to describe the royalist plight:

> Mar bha Cloinn Israéil
> Fo bhruid aig Rìgh na h-Eiphit,
> Tha sinn' air a' chor cheudna.

(As the Children of Israel were held in bondage by the King of Egypt, we are in the same plight).[120]

He presents the current political evils within a sin-and-punishment framework:

> Gun ghabh ar n-Athair fearg ruinn,
> Gur dearmad dhuinn 's gur bochd.

(Surely our Father is angered with us; we are neglected and ours is a piteous case).[121]

A similar idea, adding the need for repentance, is implied in another poem as Iain Lom concludes it with a prayer:

> 'S maith as cóir dhuinn do ghrìosadh,
> Fhir as mìorbhailtich feartan,
> 'S a bhith dol air ar glùinean
> Dhèanamh ùrnaigh is trasgadh,
> Dhèanamh aifreann neo-chalgach.

(Well ought we to make supplication unto Thee whose powers are most wonder-working, and to kneel in prayer and fasting, to celebrate Mass without deceit).[122]

---

119 *Mi ag amharc Srath Chuaiche*, §§6, 11cdgh, 14a; *Lìon mulad mi fhèin*, §2d; *Slàn a chì mi thu, Mharcuis*, §§10–16.
120 *Mi gabhail Srath Dhruim-Uachdair*, §5abc.
121 *ibid.*, §4cd.
122 *Mi ag amharc Srath Chuaiche*, §15abcde.

The same poet refers twice to the prophecy of Thomas the Rhymer, and to Montrose as the one who could be instrumental in its fulfilling:

> Nan tigeadh Montròs'
>> Ann ar còmhdhail a dh'Eirinn ...
>
> Le'm brataichibh sròil
>> Agus òrdugh Rìgh Seurlas,
>
> Thug an fhàistinn ud beò sinn
>> Mar dh'òrdaich Tom Reumhair.

(Were Montrose to come to Ireland to join forces with us ... with banners of satin and with King Charles' command, the fulfilment of that prophecy would bring us to life, as Thomas the Rhymer foretold).[123]

Although praised for their support of the Stiúbhart cause, the same individuals are castigated by poets like Sìleas na Ceapaich and the anonymous author of *Tha mi fo leann-dubh is fo bhròn*, when, in their estimation, they have behaved in a cowardly manner.[124] And royalism as a fundamentally Gaelic affair is reflected in Iain Lom's depiction of Eóin Grám, Viscount Dundee, addressing the troops, just before the battle of Killiecrankie (1689), as 'A chlanna nan Gàidheal' ('Oh progenies of the Gaels').[125]

There is little emphasis on *Alba*. Although Iain Lom commented on the capture of Seoras Gordan, second marquis of Huntly, in 1647, as 'bochd ... naidheachd an Albainn' ('sad news that they have in Scotland'), he was fully aware of the contemporary conflict as involving the whole of Britain, as well as Ireland: after Huntly's execution he lamented the dire predicament of the nobility of Charles II's *rìoghachd*.[126] Another reference to *Alba* is in *Mi ag amharc Srath Chuaiche* (§3), where Iain Lom apparently complains about the extortionate costs forced on the Scots towards the upkeep

---

123 *Soraidh do' n Ghràmach*, §2abefgh. For the second reference see *Mi ag amharc Srath Chuaiche*, §8.
124 *Mhic Coinnich bhon Tràigh*, §§1, 3–5; *Tha mi fo leann-dubh is fo bhròn*, §9.
125 *Is mithich dhuinn màrsadh as an tìr*, §5b.
126 *Mhuire's muladach thà mi*, §8a; *Mi ag amharc Srath Chuaiche*, §10a.

of the Cromwellian garrisons.[127] The only other instance of an allusion to *Alba* is found in an early eighteenth-century eulogy for Sím Friseal, first Lord Lovat (†1747), who is complimented as 'torc an drip air Albainn' ('sovereign lord of combat over Scotland').[128]

The royalists' enemies are identified in a general fashion as 'luchd Beurla', and at the time of the Cromwellian invasion of Scotland as 'murtairean Shasainn' ('English murderers'). Around 1716 Murchadh MacMhathain expressed his concern for the safety of Sím, thirteenth chief and Lord Lovat, in 'Sasainn nan cleoc' ('England of the cloaks').[129] *Gall* references are rare. We find one in a eulogy for Séamas Grannd, seventh chief of Freuchie (†1663), which uses general conventional vernacular praise rhetoric and portrays the subject as victorious ' 'N Eilginn nan Gall' ('In Elgin of the *Goill*').[130] More interesting is another *Gall* allusion which appears linked with the *miorùn* motif in an anonymous poem as early as *c.*1630. The author expresses his concern for Eóin Moireach, first Earl of Atholl (†1642), who has been sent to Perth on a certain royal commission:

> 'S mor m' eagal 's mo churam
> Mu do thaghall 's an du-mhachair mhin,
> Aig a cheist thug an Crun duit …
> Gu bheil Gaill an mio-ruin duit,
> Gun tairg iad do chuis a chuir sios.
>
> (Great is my fear and my anxiety
> concerning your visit to the smooth Black Plain [i.e., the Lowlands]
> on the matter entrusted to you by the crown …
> For ill-willed *Goill* are after you,
> proposing to frustrate your business).[131]

Given the context of royal service, while this and other allusions (for instance, the Tay valley, Perth, §§1d, 6h) clearly indicate the geographical

---

127 *OIL*, p. 258.

128 *Mo thriall a sìos air firichean*, §9gh (literally 'a boar [or hero] of combat').

129 *Soraidh do' n Ghràmach*, §4h; *Mi ag amharc Srath Chuaiche*, §14f; *Gur h-uasal am macan*, §5f.

130 *Lìon mulad mi fhèin*, §7a.

131 *'S mithich dhomh-sa bhith 'g èirigh*, §8abcef.

Lowlands, the *Goill* here seem to be the enemies of the monarchy.

It is very noticeable that subjects of *Gall* origin are nowhere identified as *Goill*; just like the Caimbéalaigh and the Stiúbhairt in classical verse,[132] they are incorporated into the ranks of the Gaels, perhaps most strikingly in royalist poems. Thus the depiction of Viscount Dundee addressing the troops before Killiecrankie[133] is one in which *Gaoidhil* and *Goill* are a seamless continuum, and all united under the command of a leader of *Gall* origin. What we have here is a concept, well beyond the more local and much cherished one of Gaeldom, of belonging to the wider kingdom of Britain, and of a duty to defend its true monarchy. It is this same concept that makes it possible to adopt no less than a Lowland prophet, Thomas the Rhymer, as the guarantor of the Gaelic success of the struggle, and to portray Montrose, another *Gall*, as the one who will fulfil the prophecy.[134] Surely it is for the same reason that in political poetry the term *Goill* so often is used to denote the enemies of the house of Stiúbhart generally.[135]

Only Moireach and Stiúbhart subjects are noted to be connected with royalty. Eóin, first Earl of Atholl, is said to be 'Boinne uasal d'fhuil righ' ('a noble drop of royal blood'), no doubt on account of his mother being a Stiúbhart, and Dubhghall Óg Stiúbhart of Appin (*b.*1445) is similarly connected 'Do 'n Righ tha againn air a chrùn' ('to the crowned king we have').[136] Although Mac Firbhisigh states, from his alternative 'new recension', that the earls of Atholl, Mar (a title which over time oscillated between the Stiúbhart and Erskine families) and Caithness (of the Stiúbhart family from the fourteenth century until the mid-fifteenth, the title then passing to the Sinclairs) and the Grannd chiefs were descendants of Éireamhón,[137] claims in this respect are not found in the extant vernacular poetry. Royalty seems to be exclusively related to kinship connexions with the Stiúbhart royal house: any marriage links with ancient noble Gaelic or *Gall* families have lost their prominence, and are ignored.

Among a few more loose items of interest is the 'prophetic poem'

---

132 See above, chapter 4, pp. 132–5, and this chapter, pp. 267, 270.
133 See above, p. 274.
134 See above, p. 274.
135 See above, chapters 3, pp. 92–3; 4, pp. 171–3; 5, pp. 221, 237.
136 *'S mithich dhomh-sa bhith 'g èirigh*, §5b; *An latha dh' fhàg thu taobh Loch Eir*, §3b.
137 *LMG* ii, §§411.3, 413.4.

Clann Ghilleathain on Dreòllainn, attributed to Domhnall Ó Conchobhair (*fl.c.*1634–60), of the hereditary family of physicians to Clann Dubhghaill.[138] It was probably the troubled political conditions of the mid-seventeenth century that caused the author's mood; he foresees the downfall of a number of clans of the Lorn and Mull areas where the Ó Conchobhair family operated, including that of Mac Eóin Stiúbhairt (§3a), this being the Gaelic title of Stiúbhart of Appin.[139] To be noted also is the 'deoch slàinte' motif in an early-sixteenth-century poem for Eóin Óg Friseal of Faraldine (†1546), perhaps the earliest attested use of this motif, while the depiction of the subject as 'ursainn chatha' ('a pillar of combat'), common in classical panegyric, is applied to Brigadier Alasdair Grannd (†1719).[140] Finally, in the celebration of the feasting customary in the house of Sím Friseal, thirteenth chief of Lovat, the drinking of beer ('beoir'), as well as of wine, is noted.[141] Beer-drinking seems to have been unknown as a motif of classical panegyric, where fine wines are typically favoured by the subject praised.[142]

Conclusions

This chapter concluded the overview of the extant poetry concerned with Gaelic (including Irish) kindreds, and examined the surviving poems concerned with subjects of *Gall* origin. Although we have only a few classical survivals, and therefore our conclusions can only be tentative, by and large the poetic rhetoric found in them is generally the same for Gaelic subjects, whether Scottish or Irish, and for those of *Gall* origin. One main difference in the classical poems for Scottish patrons is the absence of the closely-related motifs of the high-kingship and of prophecy in its Irish format, that is the depiction of the individual as the one who will banish foreigners; both motifs, as we have seen, in classical panegyric of Scotland are only present in compositions for the lords of the Isles and for

---

138 For the author see *GC*, p. 265; Bannerman 1986, pp. 146–7.

139 From Eóin Stiúbhart of Innermeath, who married one of the co-heiresses of the Mac Dubhghaill lordship after the death of Eóin Mac Dubhghaill in 1316; see above, chapter 3, p. 75 and n. 104.

140 *Slàint Iain òig mhic Alasdair*, §§1a, 2a; *Mo bheud mór 's mo throm-luighe*, §4d.

141 *Gur h-uasal am macan*, §3d.

142 See above, chapter 5, p. 224 and n. 191.

members of the Mac Domhnaill branch of Islay and Antrim.[143] They do appear in the extant poems of Giolla Brighde Albanach, which are all for Irish patrons, but we cannot be certain that this early thirteenth-century author was a Scot. Where we do a have a certainty of the poet's Scottish origin (as in the cases of Giolla Críost Brúilingeach and Maol Domhnaigh Ó Muirgheasáin), both motifs are absent. It might be that tactfulness, or even convention, precluded Scottish authors from engaging in this topic. If such was the case, then it is almost certain that Giolla Brighde Albanach was an Irish poet.

The extant classical poetry presents the subject addressed as *Albanach*, but also as a *Gaoidheal*, even if he is of *Gall* origin: those who have become Gaelicised are subsumed into Gaeldom, just as Clann Leóid, originally Norse, and Clann Duibhne, originally British, were too. Thus the Stiúbhairt are celebrated as the descendants of Conn Céadchathach, a claim, however, which could only be realistically made on the basis of female descent. Given the *filidh*'s refusal to accept 'new' claims without foundation, it is almost certain that such a kinship connexion did exist. The genealogical claims in the Mac Fionghuin poem, on the other hand, are consistent with the pedigrees, whether the Scottish 'MS 1467' or the genealogical collection compiled by the Irish scholar An Dubhaltach Mac Firbhisigh. The lack of classical pieces for other Scottish nobles of Gaelic origin makes it impossible to know whether, if any poems there were at all, they might have contained genealogical claims similarly in accordance with 'MS 1467', where many clans are said to descend from the royal line of Loarn. Strangely, there are no references at all to Conaire, even though we know, from evidence in Mac Leóid poetry, that the descendants of Loarn Mór, as well as those of Fearghus Mór, were known as Síol Conaire.[144] Worthy of note is the poets' failure to describe their subjects of *Gall* origin as *Goill*, or as of mixed *Gall-Ghaoidhil* ethnicity, in line with Irish practice.

The rhetoric of surviving vernacular poetry for the Scottish kindreds considered in this chapter is chiefly the same as that found in Mac Griogóir and Mac Coinnigh verse. The focus is on martial prowess, nobility, generosity, hospitality, feasting and music, and the allies and kinship connexions motifs are similarly frequent. Also in common we find a lack of references

143 See above, chapter 3, pp. 82, 83–4, 85–7.
144 See above, chapter 4, p. 164, and p. 152 for evidence from genealogies.

to ancient noble ancestors, with the exception of the Mac Fionghuin claim
of descent, shared with Clann Ghriogóir, from Ailpín, and therefore from
Cinéal nGabhráin rather than Cinéal Loairn, thus diverging from the
Gaelic genealogies and from the one extant classical poem for a member
of Clann Fhionghuin. The clans of *Gall* origin are presented as included
within the general body of the *Gaoidhil*, and never identified as *Goill*. This
term is used in the poems for Gaelic nobles to denote the Lowlanders as
well as the enemies of the house of Stiúbhart generally, and it seems to
have the same meaning in *'S mithich dhomh-sa bhith 'g èirigh*, where the
poet expresses his concern for the safety of Eóin Moireach, Earl of Atholl,
on account of the *mìorùn* that the *Goill* feel for him.[145] This allusion to
'mìorùn nan Gall' is interesting in that it seems to be the earliest attested
usage of the idiom. Otherwise, the enemies of the Stiúbhart kings are
described as English speakers or cloaked folk. NicGhillesheathanaich's
view that King George deserves the ill will of the *Gaoidhil* is an interest-
ing, and probably unique, reversal of the *mìorùn* motif. Royalism includes
many of the features present in the rest of the vernacular poetry, including
an awareness of its British dimension and an integration of the *Goill* who
support the Stiúbhart cause into the ranks of the Gaels, and, in common
with Mac Gille Eóin poetry, bitterness on account of the price paid by the
royalists for their loyalty.[146]

Of interest is also the rare employment of the motif of the subject as a
generous patron of poets, which may reflect the decline of Gaelic ways by
the seventeenth century, but might also indicate that poetic patronage was
not necessarily the practice of all nobles of *Gall* origin. Of these, the only
ones to be classed as royal are members of the Stiúbhart and Moireach kin-
dreds. However, the reference is not to ancient royal ancestors, *Gaidheal*
or *Gall*, but to the contemporary ruling monarchy, the Stiúbhairt, of much
later establishment. This silence with respect to ancient progenitors is
also manifest in vernacular panegyric for subjects of Gaelic origin, with
the exception of the seventeenth-century allusions to Mac Fionghuin
descent from Cinéal nGabhráin, rather than from Cinéal Loairn. Other
clans adjusted their pedigrees in a similar manner, an adjustment which
allowed them, while preserving a Gaelic origin, to boast affinity with the

---

145 See above, p. 275.
146 See above, p. 257 and n. 49.

contemporary royal line.[147] Such adjustments, however, were not accepted by the hereditary men of learning, or at most they were given with a caution, as they necessitated information not in their ancient books — for all the fundamentally oral character of Gaelic literature, ultimately it was the written record that was paramount. Finally, there is an early instance of the 'deoch slàinte' motif in a Friseal poem composed in the first half of the sixteenth century, and by the early eighteenth century the consumption of beer, as well as of the more traditionally expected wine, is added on as a praise motif, also in a Friseal panegyric.

147 See above, pp. 245–9, 256.

Chapter 7

From the Dál Riada chiefs to the royal Stiúbhairt: the kings of Scotland and Britain

Origins and ancestry

We now come to the final section in our survey of Scottish Gaelic panegyric, in which we will consider the extant poetry concerned with the monarchs of Scotland and of Britain. Most extant Gaelic genealogies record three separate royal pedigrees among the early *Gaoidhil* of Scotland. Cinéal nGabhráin — the progeny of Fearghus Mór mac Eirc — split into two rival branches after the death of Cionaoth mac Ailpín, the succession subsequently alternating between the descendants of Cionaoth's sons, Cabhsaintín and Aodh. The third royal line stemmed from Loarn Mór, whose offspring were known as Cinéal Loairn. All sources make Loarn Mór another son of Earc, something rejected by modern scholars.[1] The line of Aodh mac Cionaotha was eliminated from the royal succession at the close of the tenth century, and Cinéal Loairn's last king was Lulach, who died in 1058. Maol Coluim III then assumed the kingship, which from that date onwards remained with the descendants of Cabhsaintín.[2] The origins of all three royal lines, through their claimed common descent from Earc, are traced in the genealogies back to Conaire Caomh mac Mogha Lámha, from whom they became known as Síol Conaire. Their pedigree is taken further back, in the Scottish 'MS 1467' as in Irish sources, to Aonghus Tuirbheach Teamhrach, king of Ireland and a great-grandson of Éireamhón, through his son, Fiacha Fear Mara, born of an

---

1 See above, chapter 1, p. 6 and n. 23. For Loarn Mór as the ancestor of Cinéal nEachdhach, a separate group from Corca Riada (Dál Riada), see Woolf 2007, p. 28. Fraser 2009, p. 146 and n. 70; id. 2010, especially at pp. 139–46.

2 *CGH*, pp. 328–30; *Collectanea*, p. 50; *FFÉ* iv, pp. 67–9; *LMG* ii, §§403.10–404.3; Skene 1876–80, iii, p. 476 n. 33.

incestuous relationship.[3] But there seems to be one known hitch in the pedigree. According to An Dubhaltach Mac Firbhisigh:

> baoi dalta ag Fiachaidh Fear Mara .i. Oilill Earonn mac Oilealla Laobhchoraigh, do Chloind Iotha mc Breoghain, agus tug Fiacha Fear Mara a bheandachtain for a dhalta ... (uair as aige baoí an chlannmhaicne), ima-rádha gurbo mac do fén.

> (Fiachaidh Fear Mara had a fosterson, i.e. Oilill Éarann s. Oilill Laobhchorach, and Fiacha Fear Mara gave his blessing to his foster-son ... (for it was he who had the progeny), mentioning that he was his own son).[4]

Thus, he adds, the Munster kindreds stemming from Fiachaidh Fear Mara were in fact the descendants of Íoth (son of Breóghan, ultimate ancestor of Oilill Éarann), rather than of Éireamhón, son of Míl, as would appear at first sight and as was generally believed (see Table 7.1). Niall Mac Muireadhaigh's history certainly preserved this erroneous belief, as did Céitinn's, both influenced by earlier material.[5] References to Míl are not frequent in the poetry of Scotland; apart from some attested in panegyrics for Clann Domhnaill — quite legitimate, since they did stem from Míl through Colla Uais —one is given in a Caimbéal classical verse, and a couple more in Mac Gille Eóin vernacular poems.[6] The original misconstruction may have been deliberate, for although there are other examples of chiefs making their foster-sons their successors, such a move tended to involve conflict and violence.[7]

---

3 For the story of the birth of Fiachaidh Fear Mara see *FFÉ* ii, pp. 178–80. The earliest source for the pedigree is from the eleventh century; see *CGH*, 9. 129.

4 *LMG* ii, §368.2.

5 'sliochd Eir(e)moin o' fuil *Conacht*uidh 7 Laighnigh 7 an rioghrigh albanach' ('the race of Éireamhón from whom are the Connachtmen, the Leinstermen and the Scottish kings', *RC* ii, p. 148). See also *FFÉ* ii, p. 228. For some earlier examples see *CGH*, pp. 322, 329; 'MS 1467', no. 1.

6 *Maith an chairt ceannas na nGaoidheal*, §3a; *Tha mi am chadal 's gur tim dhomh dùsgadh*, §4; *Tha iongnadh air an Dreòllain*, §6a.

7 See, for instance, the inauguration of Feidhlimidh mac Aodha, foster-son of Maol Ruanaidh Mac Diarmada, quoted in full from the 'Annals of Connacht' in Clancy 2003, p. 85.

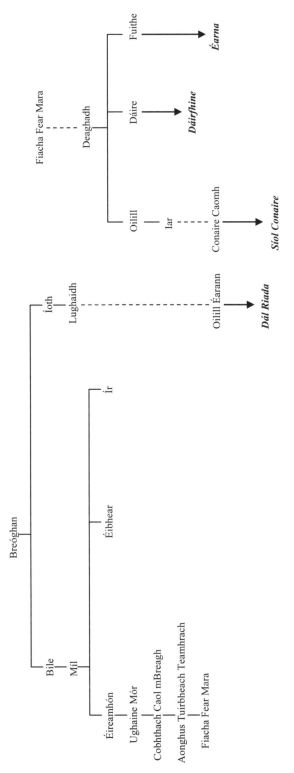

Table 7.1 The origins of the Scottish kings according to Mac Firbhisigh.
Source: *LMG* ii, §368.2.

Table 7.2 Clanna Deaghaidh.
Source: *LMG* ii, §§368.6, 380.6–380.8, 382.3.

Síol Conaire were not the only descendants of Oilill Éarann, foster-son of Fiacha Fear Mara. They were one of three kindreds collectively known as Clanna Deaghaidh, the other main two being the Éarna and the Dáirfhine. The last two were for a long time 'i ccoimhrighe' ('in joint-kingship'), or alternating the kingship of Munster with Éibhear's descend-ants (see Tables 7.1 and 7.2).[8] Síol Conaire descended from Deaghadh's son Oilill.

Of this line were Eidirscéal, his son Conaire Mór and their later descendant Conaire Caomh, all of whom were kings of Ireland. Conaire Caomh's sons, known as the three Cairbres, are said to have taken over the Munster inheritance of the Éarna, and the extent of the territory that fell to Cairbre Riada (whose real name was apparently Eochaidh) is given as 'an tír i ttáid Ciarruighe Luachra agus Orbraighe Droma Iomnocht' ('the land in which are Ciarraighe of Luachair and Orbraighe of Druim Iomnocht').[9] The descendants of Cairbre Riada, according to *seanchas*, left Munster for the north at a time of great famine, some of them subsequently establish-ing themselves in western Scotland, initially as part of the kingdom of Dál Riada in Ulster.[10] As noted, *seanchas* also maintains that they had a *taoise-ach* for their leader until Fearghus mac Eirc took on the title *rí Dál Riada*.[11]

For some unknown reason, the purely Gaelic pedigrees are nowhere — not even in the Scottish 'MS 1467' — brought down any further than King David I (†1153). Mac Firbhisigh does record the pedigree of later mon-archs, but gives it as 'Sliocht seanchadh n-eac<h>trann' ('The version of foreign historians').[12] Yet, royal genealogical records were certainly main-tained in Scotland at least until the reign of Alexander III — from 1249 until 1286 — since this king's genealogy was recited at his inauguration.[13] This king may be considered the last of the original line. The later royal families of Bailliol, Brús, and Stiúbhart monarchs stemmed from families of Anglo-Norman origin. Their respective accessions to the kingship were

---

8 *LMG* ii, §368.2.
9 *ibid*, §387.5.See *Onomasticon, s.v.* ciarraige luachra, druim imnocht. For the real names of the three Cairbres see *LMG* ii, §380.5. For the various versions of their coming to Munster see *ibid*. §§384.1–392.3.
10 *LMG* ii, §407.7. For some earlier accounts see Dumville 2002, p. 188.
11 See above, chapter 1, p. 6.
12 *LMG* ii, §§407.9–408.3.
13 See above, chapter 1, p. 8 and n. 31.

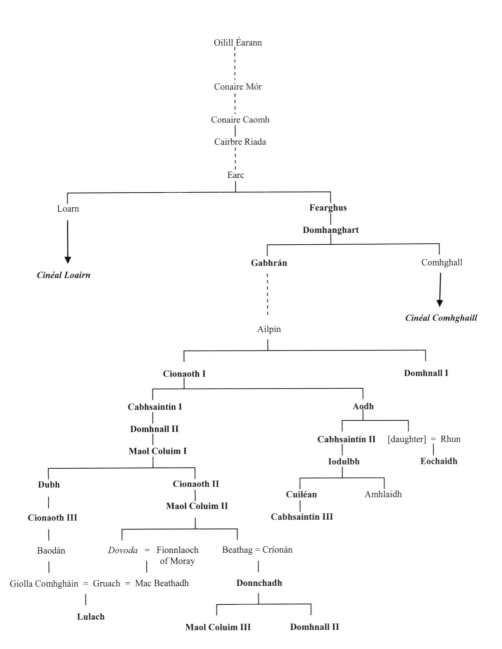

Table 7.3 The Cinéal nGabhráin royal lines (kings in bold).
Sources: 'MS 1467'; *LMG* ii, §§400.1–405.7; Hudson 1994

made possible, as An Dubhaltach Mac Firbhisigh noted, 'do edhreacht bhanda' ('through female inheritance'), for all three families had at various points earlier married into the royal line of Cinéal nGabhráin.[14]

An Dubhaltach was puzzled by what seems to be a certain Scottish tradition, perhaps first taken to Ireland by An Fear Dorcha Mac Firbhisigh about the mid sixteenth century. According to this tradition the Stiúbhairt were of the Leamhnaigh and therefore descendants of Corc mac Lughach. An Dubhaltach was reluctant to accept this claim, as we noted, since the name Stiúbhart was not found in the records of Ireland.[15] Well might he wonder, for what became a surname was initially the name of the office of High Steward held by the head of the family at the royal court. In his confusion he went as far as to suggest that the Leamhnaigh might simply have adopted the country's name after conquering it, rather than giving their name to it, thus implying that they were not in fact the original Gaelic inhabitants of the Lennox district, but that others, among whom were the Stiúbhairt, were.[16] Mac Firbhisigh was aware of Queen Mary's marriage to Henry, Lord Darnley, son of Matthew, fourth Earl of Lennox (+1571), and of the Stiúbhart kinship with the ancient kings of Munster (through James IV's marriage to Margaret Tudor, who descended from the Mortimer earls of March), as shown in the section where he notes the family's affinities, through the female line, with various Irish royal families.[17] The pedigree he gives connecting the Stiúbhart kindred to the Munster kings, 'mar shaoilid aroile' ('as some think'),[18] only goes as far as a certain Banchú, 'Tán ... Locha Abair in Albain' ('Thane ... of Lochaber in Scotland'). At a certain point this Banchú was grafted onto the pedigree of the earls of Lennox of first creation. This was almost certainly a deliberate manipulation by the Stiúbhairt themselves who, as we have seen, appear to be promoting their image as Gaels by at least the mid fifteenth century.[19]

This genealogical concoction was clearly not accepted by fifteenth-century learned men. 'MS 1467' gives no connexion between the early

14 *LMG* ii, §§409.2–410.2, 410.4.
15 See above, chapter 6, p. 266.
16 See above, pp. 265–6; also *LMG* ii, §411.4.
17 *LMG* ii, §§407.9, 408A.1–408A.4; iii, §1165.2.
18 *ibid.* ii, §408.4.
19 See above, chapter 6, pp. 266, 270.

mormhaoir of Lennox and the Stiúbhairt: the formers' pedigree is traced, through Maine son of Corc, up to Mogh Nuadhat after whom Leath Mogha, the Southern Half of Ireland, was named, while the Stiúbhairt are, interestingly, glaringly absent from the compilation[20]. Yet the concoction making the Stiúbhairt the descendants of Éibhear was broadcast through Scotland and also through Ireland, where it had arrived at least by the mid sixteenth century,[21] and apparently gained the acceptance of a good number of poets and historians at least by the early seventeenth.[22] If a connexion was ever formed between the Stiúbhairt and Éibhear, however, it could only be explained, like the connexion with the descendants of Fearghus Mór, through the female line. Yet Mac Firbhisigh remained reluctant to accept a Stiúbhart Irish origin. Clearly, what counted with him was agnatic descent, for throughout his lengthy discussion of the starting points of the various royal lines from the death of Alexander III onwards, he almost obsessively notes that they all involved female succession at least at one point.[23] In the end, unconvinced but still professionally respectful (for his source for the claim of Stiúbhart Irish origin seems to have been no less than the renowned Hector Boece, co-founder and principal of the University of Aberdeen), he leaves it to the reader to make up his mind on the matter.[24]

Mac Firbhisigh's preoccupation with female succession is perhaps not surprising, since this was alien to the Gaelic system. As a fundamentally conservative class and the guardians of tradition, the Gaelic professional learned men may have taken a dim view of succession through the female line. There may also be a hint of disapproval, which may be connected with female succession or with other circumstances, in Mac Firbhisigh's statement that 'gabuis Roibeard Brús coroin Alban air fén' ('Robert Bruce took the crown of Scotland for himself'). This expression, which he uses again when referring to John Balliol's accession to the kingship, seems to imply

---

20 *LMG* iii, §§1159 [B57], 1162.3; Black, *Catalogue*, p. 24. As noted, the pedigree ends with Donnchadh, eighth earl (see above, chapter 5, p. 187 n. 17).

21 See above, chapter 6, p. 266.

22 See Ó Buachalla 1983, pp. 125–6.

23 *LMG* ii, §§407.9, 408.A1, 408.3, 408B.2, 409.2, 410.4, 412A.2–4.

24 See above, chapter 6, p. 266. For Boece as Mac Firbhisigh's source for the pedigree claiming a Stiúbhart connexion with the kings of Munster, see *LMG* ii, §408A.4.

irregularity in some way.[25] We may compare it with the Four Masters' statement that Riocard Búrc an Iarainn (†1583), an individual whose accession and form of rule did not meet with the annalists' approval, had seized the chiefship of Northern Connacht 'dia oirdneadh fein' ('by installing himself').[26] Despite the various changes — particularly those of the Norman period — which gradually moved the kingship of *Alba*, and generally Gaelic society there, away from its original Irish model, by the seventeenth century the Irish men of learning still retained an interest in a people who had originated in their own country and a large part of whom continued to share culturally so much with Gaelic Ireland. Their interest is shown by the recording by historians, down to Céitinn and Mac Firbhisigh in the seventeenth century, of Scottish genealogies, regnal lists, and historical chronicles; to the Irish Franciscan theologian Aodh Mac Cathmhaoil (†1626), Scotland was Ireland's 'inghean ionmhuin' ('dear daughter').[27] An Dubhaltach not only recorded, as earlier Irish historians had, the arrival of the Gaels in Scotland, but also some later developments, with particular attention to the wars of independence and to the Stiúbhart royal line down to the date (1666) when he was writing.[28] Although he writes most confidently on the strength of his Irish sources, Mac Firbhisigh also resorts to the writings of 'seanchaidhe eachtrainn' ('foreign historians'), to supplement, to reinforce, and sometimes to show divergence from the Gaelic record. Bede, Marianus Scotus, Blind Harry, and the German Ubbo Emmius (†1625), as well as Boece, are all mentioned by him as his sources for Scottish history.[29] An Dubhaltach was just as much at home in Latin as he was in Gaelic, and he enhanced his chronicle with a Latin history of the origins and early history of Scotland down to the foundation of the Saxon kingdom of England in the ninth century.[30]

This enduring Irish interest in Scotland, and not only in the progressively diminishing Scottish *Gàidhealtachd*, was not solely confined to

---

25 *ibid*, §§412A.4, 412A.5.
26 Literally 'of his own inauguration' (*ARÉ* v, p. 1724). For some discussion see Dewar 2006, pp. 217–18.
27 Quoted in Ó Mainnín 1999, p. 41.
28 *LMG* ii, §§400.1–422.2; iii, §§1155.5–1166.3. Mac Firbhisigh states 1666 to be the date he is writing in *LMG* iii, §1166.3.
29 *ibid*. ii, §§408.2, 412A.2, 419.2.
30 *ibid*, §§418.1–422.2.

scholarly matters. A sense of a natural, *dualchasach* alliance persisted which was reflected perhaps most dramatically in the offer of the high-kingship of Ireland to Edward, brother of Robert I, in 1315.[31] The continued demand for *gallóglaigh* and later for 'redshanks' is another instance of this sense of alliance, which also manifested itself in schemes to transfer Irish sovereignty to the Scottish king as late as the early sixteenth century.[32] Resort to political alliance is unlikely to have been based merely on physical proximity. Mac Firbhisigh's satisfied note that on his accession to the English and Irish crowns in 1603 James VI of Scotland had been crowned on *Lia Fáil*, the inauguration stone of the Gaelic kings of *Alba*, three hundred years after its stealing by the English, similarly connects with the same sense of shared origins and *dualchas*.[33]

Earlier poetry

It seems quite extraordinary, and it illustrates the progressive devaluation and decline of Gaelic culture in Scotland, that within the whole extant corpus of classical poetry only a few scraps are to be found which are known with certainty to have been composed for a king descending from Fearghus Mór. This excludes the two seventeenth-century eulogies addressed to James VI and I, whose descent from the royal line of Cinéal nGabhráin, being through the female line, is qualified.[34] Although *filidh* were still maintained by the kings of Scots until the mid thirteenth century at least,[35] their work has been lost forever: the extant fragments are all chance survivals, preserved mostly in annalistic and metrical tracts. The earliest of them consists of a couple of quatrains commemorating the drowning at sea of Conaing mac Aodháin (+622). Conaing is described as 'bile Torten' ('the [sacred] tree of Tortan'), and his death as caused by nature, here portrayed as a woman with a crooked smile shaking her mane at him.[36]

---

31 Edward was proclaimed high-king of Ireland, according to *AC*, p. 230. *Annales Hiberniae*, p. 64, states that Edward 'coronatus est' ('was crowned'), probably a Latin rendering of the Gaelic *oirdneadh* ('ordaining, appointing', that is 'inauguration').

32 See Ellis 1998, pp. 148–9.

33 *LMG*, ii, §§412A.6, 421.1.

34 See above, p. 287. For the poems see below, pp. 303–9.

35 See above, chapter 1, p. 8.

36 Greene and O'Connor 1967, pp. 108–9; Clancy (ed.) 1998, p. 113 (translation only). Tortan: the site of a sacred tree near Ardbreccan, Co. Meath (*ibid.*, p. 356).

The next extant piece for a Scottish king is a single quatrain preserved in an Irish annalistic compilation.[37] It may well be an excerpt from a longer piece lamenting the death, in 858, of Cionaoth mac Ailpín, called in the annals 'rex Pictorum' in celebration of his victory over the Picts:[38]

Nad mair Cionaodh go lion sgor
fo déra gol i n-gach taigh;
áoinrí a logha fo nimh
go bruinne Rómha ní bhfail.

(That Cinaed with his hosts is no more
brings weeping to every home:
no king of his worth under heaven
is there, to the bounds of Rome).

This quatrain tells us little of the poetic motifs in use in ninth-century Scotland (if indeed it was composed then), apart from the general grief following the death of a great warrior king,

Walter Bower, writing in the early fifteenth century, included in his historical narrative a poetic address to Maol Coluim III (†1093) which he ascribed to Mac Duibh, *mormhaor* of Fife. The actual date of composition is unknown, but it is thought to be at some point between Mac Duibh's own time and the time when Bower was writing.[39] The poem is, however, presented as composed by Mac Duibh as an exhortation to Maol Coluim, who was in exile in England, to return north and wrest the Scottish crown from Mac Beathadh. One difficulty is that Bower gives the poem in Latin, which may indeed be the language of composition of the original poem; if so, then the piece is likely to be the work of a monk. Whichever the case, its contents would not have been out of place in a Gaelic incitement poem: Maol Coluim is portrayed as the one who can become the defender of the oppressed people (ll. 1–4) and give them relief (l. 6, a theme reminiscent of the liberation from *anbhuain* in Gaelic panegyric),[40] while his right to the throne is argued on the basis of his descent from an ancient royal line:

---

37 Radner (ed.) 1978, pp. 112–13.

38 *AU* i, p. 366.

39 Clancy (ed.) 1998, p. 177.

40 See above, chapter 2, pp. 29–30, for an apparent survival of this motif in an early fifteenth-century poem in Scots.

Scotus et es genitus priscorum cespite regum;

    prospere procedens regna patris subies.

Regni, promitto, pocieries jure corona.

(You are a Scot, and are sprung from a line of ancient kings.

In triumphant progress you will approach your father's kingdom.

You will gain the crown of the kingdom by right, I promise).[41]

Because the poem cannot be accurately dated, the identification of Maol Coluim as *Scotus* must be read with caution. But it is worth noting that in this king's reign, and probably well before his time, the *Gaoidhil* of *Alba* were identified as *Albanaigh* (*Scoti* in Latin) by the Gaelic men of learning.[42] The rest of the poem gives the addressee advice concerning battle: he must never rush into it, but all the same he is to ensure that he will be the first at the battlefield (ll. 14–18).

A further poetic survival is another single quatrain, again possibly a fragment from a longer composition, which was preserved in a fourteenth-century Irish metrical tract. In this quatrain, quoted in the first chapter of this work,[43] the poet criticises Dáibhidh mac Maol Choluim, the future David I, for his threat to obtain Lothian by force in 1113.[44] The poet is concerned about internal division within the kingdom, *Alba* (also so named in other twelfth-century sources).[45] This concern tends to appear in Gaelic poetry at times of actual historical threat, whether internal or external, when it is often more fully developed rather than given only as a passing reference. It is common, for instance, in Irish classical poetry of the later sixteenth century, when unity among the Irish was strongly advised by the poets against advancing Tudor conquest.[46] In classical verse of Scotland we encountered the same concern in the incitement poem composed before

---

41 *Si servare velis insontes quosque fideles*, ll. 9–11.

42 See below, pp. 296 n. 61, 302 n. 86.

43 See above, chapter 1, p. 1.

44 Clancy 2000a, pp. 91–4.

45 See Broun 1998, p. 6. At this time *Alba* comprised the area north of the Forth, south of Moray and east of the central Highlands.

46 See, for instance, *Déanaidh comhaonta, a Chlann Éibhir*, §1; *Máthair chogaidh críoch Bhanbha*, §§10–11; *Síon choitcheann cumha Ghaedheal*, §53. For an example from historical narrative see *BAR* i, §§148, 185.

the battle of Flodden and in poetry belonging to the seventeenth-century civil wars' period. In vernacular verse we noted the same theme in poems composed during the reigns of William of Orange and George of Hanover, both foreign kings who brought about a political polarisation of the whole Britain, that is, in the early Jacobite period.[47]

Between the early twelfth century and the early seventeenth there is a poetic gap as far as the kings of Scots are concerned. Nevertheless, we have a prophetic-historical poem in which *Alba* and her kings feature prominently. Like the quatrains for Cionaoth and for Dáibhidh mac Maol Choluim, this piece has survived only in Irish sources, but unlike them it throws considerable light on the poetic rhetoric of leadership just a little before the arrival of the classical period. This is *Airis biuc a mheic big báin*, purported to have been originally composed by the fifth-century Irish abbot Bearchán and commonly known as 'The Prophecy of Bearchán'. It seems to be the work of three different authors composing at three different times, and a strong case has been put forward for the last two being eleventh-century Scots.[48] There are several parts to the poem, the main two being lists of Irish (§§15–98) and Scottish (§§116–206) kings. The author of these lists seems to have lived during the reign of Maol Coluim III (†1093);[49] indeed he may well have composed most of this section for Maol Coluim, and it is not impossible that he was the king's own *ollamh* in poetry or in *seanchas*. The final quatrains seem to have been added by a slightly later poet.[50] The list of Scottish monarchs is what interests us here. Each king named receives some comment, not always favourable, and sometimes praise and criticism are combined as appropriate (§§173–6, 181–8). Praise and denunciation of the various kings are both made through many of the literary motifs preserved in panegyric of the classical period. Praise is given through the celebration of the warrior and his martial deeds, particularly his ability to keep foreign threat at bay; of his generosity, physical beauty, his capacity to exact tribute, his love of feasting and music.[51] The motif of the right ruler as the one who can unite

47 See above, chapter 3, pp. 89–90, 106 and n. 249, 109; chapter 4, p. 142.
48 Hudson 1996, pp. 116–21.
49 *ibid.*, p. 15.
50 *ibid.*, pp. 19, 119.
51 See, for instance, §§121d, 151–2, 177a, 181b, 193d, 194, 197, 202cd.

From the Dál Riada chiefs to the royal Stiúbhairt

his people is applied by 'Bearchán' to Giric mac Dúngail (†888?) where he states that he is the one 'shúaithfes for Albain d'aon-fhlaith' ('who will knead Scotland into one kingdom', §136b). The motif of prophecy, which in classical poetry of Scotland is only found in panegyric for Clann Domhnaill (if we except the one, vague pasing reference in a Caimbéal poem),[52] appears in the quatrains for Cabhsaintín I (†876):

Mochen mochen maiseadh é
fada ata a ttairngire
rí no rígh ní rádh mbáisi.

(Welcome, welcome, if it is he who has long been prophesied; a king of kings—it is no foolish saying) (§150abc).

Additionally, the successful ruler receives the sanction of nature, by her becoming lavishly fertile, and he is depicted as bringing fortune and prosperity to his people (§§151a, 152, 194c, 197c). For those who receive poetic disapproval the most common accusation is their being excessively violent and warlike (§§144, 146cd, 158, 181d), but also their failure to take hostages, their plundering and oppression of their own, and that, when leading in battle, they led into defeat (§§146a, 171c, 175c, 187a).[53] Additionally, criticism is expressed by means of negative soubriquets: Dubh is 'dubh na tri ndubhrún' ('the black of the three dark secrets'), Maol Coluim II is 'an forránach' ('the violent'), Cionaoth II is 'an fingalach' ('the fratricide') (§§166d, 181d, 169b).

Most of all, the Scottish section of 'The Prophecy of Bearchán' can be said to be all about the *Gaoidhil* of *Alba* as an independent people. It opens praising Cabhsaintín mac Fearghusa (†820) for his determination to shake off Pictish domination (§§116–20), and goes on to celebrate Cionaoth mac Ailpín as finally achieving this goal, becoming:

---

52 See above, chapters 3, pp. 85–6; 4, p. 141.

53 For a warning against excessive violence in princely-advice literature see, for instance, *Audacht Morainn*, §29. For examples of criticism by poets and annalists of excessive violence and belligerence see *Mór iongabháil anma ríogh*, for Riocard Óg Búrc (†1585), at §2; *ARÉ* v, p. 1804.

> ... cédrí ghéabus toir
> d'feraib Érenn i nAlbain.

> (the first king from the men of Ireland in Scotland who will take
> kingship in the east) (§122ab).

The *Gaoidhil* are here referred to as 'fir Éireann', and as *Éireannaigh* in
the quatrains for Cabhsaintín mac Fearghusa (§116d) but, as we will see
presently, they become *Albanaigh* once they expand into and take over
Pictish territory. Elsewhere the term *Gaoidhil* is pervasive, and the kings'
following claimed to be made up of the whole of the *Gaoidhil* of *Alba*
(§§184d, 199c). The *Gaoidhil* as a group also are shown to be the pro-
tagonists of united action against those rulers criticised by the author: they
turn against an unjust king (§§147a, 179d), they shout around his grave
(§§159d, 172c). Place-names are employed to firmly attach them to their
Scottish kingdom: they are 'fir Fortreann' ('the men of Fortriu', §§139d,
140d), the occupiers of 'Magh Fortreann' ('the Plain of Fortriu', §166b),
their king is 'fíalrí Fortrenn' ('the generous king of Fortriu', §193d). *Alba*
is their *cóigeadh* ('province', §162c), to which Iodulbh (†961) has the
honour of adding a portion of foreign territory (§162cd). The reference is
to the annexation of Edinburgh,[54] and the poet notes the addition of this
portion of land 'ar éiccin' ('by force', §162d), one of the various legitimate
ways to obtain lordship of a territory and one which, as noted, is virtually
absent from the poetry of Scotland of the classical period.[55]

Just as plentiful are the references to *Alba*, explicitly attaching the
Gaoidhil to this new land. The representation of the descendants of Colla
Uais as temporary exiles, along with the invitation to return to Ireland,
remained a common praise motif in poetry of Irish authorship,[56] but the
vision of *Airis biuc a mheic big báin* is unequivocally different. Here there
is no looking back at Ireland, no sense of temporary exile: instead, we find
an insistence on the reality of a young but solid Gaelic kingdom of *Alba*.

---

54 Hudson 1996, p. 88 n. 97.

55 See above, chapter 3, p. 73. For some Irish examples of the use of this motif see, for
instance, *Cia adeir nár mealladh Maghnus* (§29ab); *Diomdhach Éire d' fhuil Conuill*,
(§44d); *Fearann cloidhimh críoch Bhanbha* (§§1–9).

56 See above, chapter 2, p. 33; chapter 3, pp. 68–9, 80–3.

Poetic confidence is expressed not only in the proclamation and celebration of Gaelic overlordship of the Picts but in two additional ways. Firstly, the term *airdríghe* [*na hAlban*] is employed liberally in the poem (§§114b, 124b, 135d, 138d, 155d, 163b, 171b, 179b, 185d, 191d, 195b, 199c), indicating supreme dominion of one ruler over all the inhabitants of *Alba* as well as his independent status, not subject to an ultimate overlord: he is the overlord. The leader of the descendants of Conaire who settled in Scotland had progressed in his lordly style from 'taoiseach Dál Riada' to 'rí Dál Riada', and eventually, from the time of Cionaoth mac Ailpín (§124b) onwards as far as the author of *Airis biuc a mheic big báin* was concerned, to 'airdrí na hAlban'. Similarly, in our poem there is an illuminating progression in the identification of the population group: Conaire's descendants, the *Éireannaigh* of the early times and early stanzas, later in the poem are always *Albanaigh*, 'fir Alban' (§§161c, 199d, 204d).

The second way in which the poem reflects the reality of a Gaelic kingdom of *Alba* is through a profuse employment of the motif of the ruler as the protector and defender of his territory and people against foreign threat. The various kings are portrayed as maintaining successful resistance against *Gall* threat (the *Goill* being at this time the Scandinavian invaders) as well as against their neighbours, the Picts, the Britons, and the English. Again and again we come across statements such as this about Iondulbh:

> Bretain Saxain maircc fria linn
> fria ré in ionnsaighthigh airmghrinn.
>
> (Woe to Britons and Saxons during his time, during the reign of the champion of fine weapons) (§161ab).

Or the prophetic vision that during Giric's rule:

> biaidh daora leis ina thigh
> Saxain Gaill agus Brethnaigh.
>
> (he will have slaves with him in his house: English, Vikings, and Britons' (§138cd).[57]

---

57 For other examples see §§124cd, 128, 136cd, 146d, 158d, 183c, 193c.

This representation of the *Gaoidhil* of Scotland as the new *Albanaigh* is bolstered by territorial references associating them with their new possessions. There are numerous place-names throughout the poem, very few of which remain unidentified, and those most frequently given are Fortriu, which we noted above, and Scone (§§123d, 139d, 166b,174d, 195c). This is not without significance, for both Scone and Fortriu had been main centres of Pictish power: the poet wishes his audience to be left in no doubt about who are the new lords of the Pictish territories. There are also allusions to Dunottar, a coastal fort south of Stonehaven first on record in 681,[58] and the Earn is mentioned several times: this river runs eastwards across Strathearn and then south-east south of Perth to join the Tay at Abernethy, another important political — and religious — Pictish seat (§§119d, 124d, 139b, 147b, 180d). The use of place-names in eastern Scotland and the neglect of those in the west (for instance, there is no mention of Dunadd, an earlier seat and the inaugural venue of the kings of Dál Riada) reflects both the Gaelic eastward expansion and the accompanying shift of the centres of royal power.[59] 'Scottishness' is further reinforced by a complete lack (with the exception of a note on the Irish origin of Maol Coluim II's mother, §§183a, 184) of allusions to Irish place-names or ancestry.

In sum, it may be argued that the 'simple and self-contained Scottish identity as a country and a people defined by the kingdom itself' shown to have been in place by the mid thirteenth century[60] can be traced back, in most key elements, to the later eleventh, when the Scottish section of 'The Prophecy of Bearchán' was composed, if not earlier.[61] Broun's proposal is based on the key features of the perception and defence of Scotland as a sovereign realm with the authenticity of a distant and continuous past and with particular laws and customs, and viewed within the framework of relations with England,[62] and it remains valid for the thirteenth century as far as its premises are concerned. But the vision of *Alba* as an independent

---

58 Anderson (ed.) 1900, p. 142; Watson 2004, p. 510.

59 The earlier power centres seem in fact to have been abandoned by the eleventh century (Woolf 2007, p. 313).

60 See above, chapter 2, p. 48 and n. 112.

61 *Alba* and *Albanaigh* begin to replace 'Pictland' and 'Picts' in the sources in the early tenth century; see Broun 1998, pp. 7, 9; Herbert 2000, p. 69.

62 Broun 2007, p. 7.

kingdom is very much manifest in *Airis biuc a mheic big báin*, one main difference between this and the thirteenth-century view being the lack of a distant past in our poem: what operates here is the Gaelic legal principle of possession through sword-conquest ('ar éigin') rather than that other highlighted by the thirteenth century, long established occupation. It is no coincidence that the Pictish origins of the kingdom of *Alba* are given in this poem (§§116–22), just as they are given in other contemporary works, such as *Lebor Bretnach*[63] or the poem *A éolcha Alban uile*, which we will consider below. The next logical step was the presentation of the kings of the *Albanaigh* as the successors of the Pictish kings. This took place in the thirteenth century, when the earlier concept of independence was simply reworked and expanded upon, to reflect territorial expansion, more recent dynastic connexions, and the new (English) enemy threat.[64] While *Airis biuc a mheic big báin* does recall that the Scottish *Gaoidhil* were originally *Éireannaigh*, the poem's emphasis is on their current identification as *Albanaigh* and on the independence of their kingdom of *Alba*. Unsurprisingly, there is manifest hostility towards Eochaidh ap Rhun, a Briton who became king of the *Albanaigh* in the late ninth century but whose connexion with the Gaelic kings was through the female line,[65] and who is dubbed 'in tuilti' ('the usurper', §134b).

One more point remains to be made about this poem. The last king given is Domhnall Bán, who was deposed in 1097. The comment on him, as well as that on the four previous monarchs, seems to have been added by a third author composing during Domhnall Bán's reign.[66] This author has nothing good to say of his subject, merely making two negative remarks, seemingly connected with each other, about him. First:

> is fria ré tíagaid anall
> fir Alban dochum nÉirenn.

---

63 Broun 2007, pp. 55, 57–8.

64 Broun notes (Broun 2007, pp. 49, 195–8), as some important thirteenth-century developments, the focus on Maol Coluim III and his wife, St Margaret, as dynastic founders; the addition of a Pictish king-list to the Scottish origin legend, which would provide venerable antiquity; and the promotion of Scotland, rather than Ireland, as the homeland of the *Gaoidhil* of Scotland.

65 For this king see Hudson 1994, pp. 55–7, and 1996, pp. 205–6.

66 Hudson 1996, pp. 18–19.

(in his time the men of Scotland will go yonder, to Ireland) (§204cd).

Then he adds that Domhnall Bán is the one who 'fagbas Albain do Gheinntibh' ('leaves Scotland to Vikings', §205d, *Geinnte* — literally 'heathens' — being another name for the Vikings). The author seems to be presaging an imminent Viking takeover of Scotland which will force the *Gaoidhil* to flee to Ireland. We might interpret the comment on Domhnall Bán as some enemy's ultimate insult in a poem that is all about the glory and the autonomy of the Gaelic kingdom of *Alba*, whose rulers had, until Domhnall Bán's time, succeeded in keeping at bay the *Goill* as well as the *Breatain* and the *Saxain*. This emphasis on successful defence against foreign threat, incidentally, is absent from the Irish section of the piece which indeed, as Ben Hudson noted, contains praise of two Viking rulers of Ireland (§§23–26, 27–30) and applauds the Viking part played in the downfall of an unrighteous Irish ruler (§57).[67] Yet a different interpretation of the poet's words on Domhnall Bán is possible: the poet might be in earnest in §205d, rather than merely insulting a ruler he disliked. According to Walter Bower, and later chroniclers after him, Domhnall Bán had obtained the throne, after his brother Maol Coluim's death, with the assistance of Magnus III ('Bareleg'), king of Norway. Buchanan certainly was unambiguous that Domhnall Bán 'eas regi Noruegiae cessit, ut eius opera in regno Scotorum adversus ius fasque occupandum adiuvaretur' ('ceded them [the Isles] to the king of Norway, in order to obtain his assistance in his unjust usurpation of the Scottish crown').[68] This view was rejected by William Skene, apparently only on the evidence of the saga of Magnus Bareleg (repeated in a later saga), according to which it was Maol Coluim III who had ceded the Isles to the Norse king.[69]

It is difficult to see why Skene chose to follow the (foreign) saga version, in which he himself in fact noted one important error,[70] and

---

67 *Airis biuc a mheic big báin*, §§23–30; Hudson 1996, p. 17.

68 Buchanan 1582, Vol. i, Bk. i, fo. 8v; trsl. id. 1827, p. 39.

69 Skene 1876–80, i, p. 442 and n. 19.

70 The confusion of Magnus's two expeditions into one (*ibid.*). Maol Coluim and Domhnall Bán reigned in succession; the author of the saga might well have confused the king's names. For the difficulties in using the sagas as historical sources see Woolf 2007, pp. 277–85.

dismiss centuries of home tradition. But in connexion with all this we may note Fordun's statement that after Mac Beathadh's slaying of Donnchadh I in 1040 the latter's son, Domhnall Bán, took refuge in the Western Isles, while his other son, the future Maol Coluim III, fled to Cumbria.[71] It is not impossible that during his exile in the Isles — at the time still under Norse overlordship — Domhnall Bán forged alliances that paved the way towards a later agreement, after Maol Coluim's death, with Magnus, which would include Domhnall Bán's acceptance of Norse (i.e. *Gall*) overlordship in exchange for Magnus's support. Interestingly, Giolla Brighde, Somhairle's father, whose patrimony lay in the west, seems to have supported Domhnall Bán in his claim to the throne in 1093.[72] Such an alliance could have been used later by Magnus III to pressure King Edgar (+1107) into formalising in 1098, the year after Domhnall Bán's death, the treaty — if ever there was one — by which he ceded the Isles to the Norse king.[73] It certainly would explain the poet's accusation in *Airis biuc a mheic big báin* which, it is important to remember, is contemporary evidence. Whatever the case, the naming and shaming of Domhnall Bán as the one who lost the sovereignty of *Alba* to the *Goill* is a fitting completion to the poem, which had started off with Bearchán's sombre prediction of the complete conquest of Ireland by the *Goill*. The twist in the tale is that, in the end, it is Scotland, not Ireland, that is portrayed as about to succumb — according to the author's 'prophetic' words — to the threat of Viking domination, while Ireland would become the place of refuge for the Scottish *Gaoidhil*.

Two more poems, both apparently of Irish authorship and pre-classical in composition, are of Scottish interest. In the first chapter we noted the late eleventh-century *A éolcha Alban uile*, which it has been suggested might have been a mere teaching aid rather than a panegyric composed for Maol Coluim III, who reigned at the time of its composition.[74] Very much in the fashion of current Irish literature,[75] this is a historical poem which gives the history of *Alba* down to contemporary times (§§1–8), followed

---

71 Skene (ed.) 1993, i, p. 180; *Scotichronicon* ii, pp. 426 and 507 n. 13.

72 Gregory 1881, pp. 11–12.

73 Beuermann 2007 suggests that such treaty did not exist, but was a late twelfth- or early thirteenth-century fabrication aimed at justifying Norwegian claims to the Isles (Richard Oram, from a personal communication, 18 August 2009).

74 See above, chapter 2, p. 32 and n. 31.

75 Zumbuhl 2006, pp. 13–21.

by the regnal list of the descendants of Earc down to Maol Coluim himself (§§9–27). One point of interest in the historical section is its probably deliberate 'invasion-waves' format, highly reminiscent of the framework commonly given to Irish history, in poetry as in historical narrative.[76] The author, following the Gaelic translation of *Historia Britonum*, a historical tract probably compiled in Scotland,[77] gives four separate *gabhála* ('takings' or 'invasions'), beginning with that of Albanus — brother of Bríotus who gave his name to Britain — (§§1–3), followed by the arrival of Neimheadh (§4) and then by that of the Picts (§§5–6).[78] The poet closes this section by relating the final conquest of *Alba* by the *Gaoidhil*, although he mentions only 'clanna Conaire' ('the descendants of Conaire', §7c), leaving out other groups, such as the Scottish progenies of Corc and of Niall: this approach he considers sufficient for the purposes of his poem, and indeed he gives all the credit for what he describes as a military conquest to the sons of Earc, ignoring the achievements of Earc's ancestors who had preceded him in the settlement of western Scotland (§§7–8). This might suggest that the poem was in fact composed for Maol Coluim III, a descendant of Earc, rather than as a teaching aid for use in the poetic schools. A further point of interest is the insertion of Loarn mac Eirc 'i ffhlaitheas oirir Alban' ('in sovereignty over the territory of *Alba*'), in fact as her first Gaelic king. Kenneth Jackson noted that such a claim seems to be unique to this poem, but some Irish sources also claim that Loarn had been 'rí Alban'.[79] It may be that Loarn — a leader of Cinéal Loarn, which modern scholars esteem to have been a separate group of Corca Riada, to whom Fearghus Mór belonged[80] — was ruler of Scottish Dál Riada, perhaps the last *taoiseach*, before Fearghus became the first *rí*; the title *rí Alban* is given to him anachronistically in later sources anyway. Loarn's insertion, at any rate, would justify the historical alternating rule of Cinéal Fearghusa (Maol Coluim's

---

76 See, for instance, *Fearann cloidhimh críoch Bhanbha*, §§5–19, especially §9; *Ó Dhia dealbhthar gach óige*, §58c. *Lebor Gabála* is one example from historical narrative. Another is the Irish history by Céitinn, who used headings such as 'Do'n cheud ghabháil ... Do'n dara gabháil ...' ('Of the first conquest ... Of the second conquest ...', *FFÉ* i, pp. 154, 172) and so on.

77 van Hamel (ed.) 1932; Jackson 1957, p. 134; Clancy 2000b.

78 Bríotus: Briotán Maol, for whom see above, chapter 4, pp. 118, 151.

79 See Jackson 1957, p. 136, and above, chapter 3, p. 80 n. 117.

80 Fraser 2009, p. 146.

own line) and Cinéal Loairn (which produced renowned kings such as Fearadhach Fionn, Fearchar Fada, or the later Mac Beathadh).

A éolcha Alban uile is fundamentally a regnal list, but its numerous little chevilles illustrate the panegyric motifs in use at the time, such as nobility, martial deeds, raiding, fame, and so on. *Alba*, as expected, makes a strong presence, and the 'division' motif appears twice. Conall mac Comhghaill is said to have reigned 'trí bliadhna fo chúig gan roinn' ('for fifteen years without division', §11c), and Aodhán mac Gabhráin (†c.608) is dubbed 'Aodhán na n-iolrann' ('Aodhán of the many divisions', §12b). Like *Airis biuc a mheic big báin*, this poem both acknowledges the Irish origin of the Gaels of Scotland (§7) and clearly refers to the kingship, or high-kingship, of *Alba* (§§9b, 17d, 23d, 25d). We begin, then, to see a suggestion of the poetic development of the motif of the high-kingship of *Alba* (reflected by historians in the annals),[81] which in *Airis biuc a mheic big báin*, as we have seen, is reinforced through the employment of the related motif of prophecy.[82] The immediate question is whether an associated motif depicting *Alba* as her king's spouse also developed. It is tempting to see an indication of such a development in two Mac Domhnaill panegyrics. In *Domhnall mac Raghnaill rosg mall* (c.1220–50), the poet urges Ireland to bring the eponym of Clann Domhnaill back from *Alba*, to be her husband or, in other words, her high-king.[83] In *Meisde nach éadmhar Éire* (a.1502) Ireland is again portrayed as unmarried because Clann Domhnaill, 'na géaga a hoirear Éireann' ('the boughs from the land of Ireland', §6d), have been planted 'san fhiodhbhaidh Albanaigh' ('in the Scottish wood', §6b). In both poems it is very much as if two women were contending over the same man. The difficulty is, of course, that the kingship of *Alba* is mentioned in neither. On the other hand, it may be that a spouse motif never developed at all for *Alba*, perhaps simply because there had never been among the Pictish kings, her previous lords, a concept of *Alba* as the sovereignty goddess, as there was in Ireland.

The last of the poems of Scottish interest for the earlier period is *Ro bátar láeich do Laigneib*, preserved in a twelfth-century Irish manuscript.[84]

---

81 See, for instance, *AI*, §995.4; *AU* iii, §§1058.2, 1058.6, 1093.5, 1165.8.
82 See above, p. 293.
83 See above, chapter 3, p. 68.
84 O'Brien (ed.) 1952, p. 159.

It relates a story according to which the Dál Riada king Aodhán mac Gabhráin was not really Gabhrán's son, but Brandubh's twin brother and therefore the son of Eochaidh mac Muireadhaigh, of the royal family of Uí Cheinnsealaigh of Leinster. While Eochaidh was enjoying Gabhrán's hospitality, his wife Feidheilm gave birth to two boys. Gabhrán's wife, who had at the same time given birth to twin girls, persuaded Feidheilm to exchange one of the boys (Aodhán) for one her girls, so that Gabhrán too might have a son. The claim of Eochaidh's paternity of Aodhán is found also in Irish genealogies, and the story, which has additionally survived in tale form, was reproduced by Céitinn in his history of Ireland.[85] The poem contains a number of the motifs familiar to us in panegyric of the classical period: Gabhrán is praised for his hospitality, his generous gift-giving, his raiding exploits, and his capacity to 'snaidm rīge' ('unite kingdoms') (§§16, 21ac, 31b). He is presented as a Gael, 'ria ngasraid Goīdel' ('at the head of his band of Gaels') and as the one 'ro gab giallo Gall' ('who has taken hostages of the Goill') (§§21b, 42a). Gabhrán is given the titles 'rīg nAlban' and 'rīg Monaid', quite anachronistically, for he had been only king of Dál Riada (§§18b, 34b).[86] Aodhán receives the territorial designations 'Āedān Arann' ('Aodhán of Arran'), 'Āedān nĪle' ('Aodhán of Islay'), both territorial styles, and 'rī Forthe' ('king of Forth'), reflecting his campaigns in the Forth area (§§42b, 44b, 49b).[87] While, like his father, Aodhán is thus associated with Scotland, his purported Irish ancestry is also noted: he is of the Gāliān (Leinstermen), of Uí Cheinnsealaigh, his father a descendant of Cathaoir, and his mother of Dá Thí (§§37c, 43bd, 52bd).[88] The Gall motif appears once, as noted above, and similarly prophecy, which here, however, is not concerned with the high-kingship of Ireland and the banishment of foreigners. The prophets mentioned, Cormac and Brighid, had promised to Feidheilm's father that both her sons would be kings, one of

---

85 ibid., pp. 157, 160; FFÉ ii, pp. 408–10. For the lack of basis to the tradition see Bannerman 1974, pp. 89–90. For differing genealogies of Feidheilm, nonetheless always going back to Eochaidh Muighmheadhón, see O'Brien (ed.) 1952, p. 157, and LMG ii, §§4005, 404.5.

86 The title rí Alban denoting a Gaelic king is first applied in the annals to Cionaoth mac Ailpín's grandsons, Domhnall II (r.c.889–900) and Cabhsaintín II (r.900–c.943) (AU i, p. 414; Anderson (ed.) 1990, i, p. 395).

87 For the Forth reference see Watson 2004, p. 53.

88 Cathaoir and Dá Thí: two ancient kings of Ireland (see, for instance, FFÉ ii, pp. 258, 260, 412).

Alba and the other of Leinster; it is in order that this prophecy might be fulfilled that the swapping of babies must take place (§28).[89]

Later poetry

The centuries-long poetic gap closed, quite bizarrely, when some of the Irish *filidh* burst into celebration of a monarch who had a profound hatred of the Gaels. Towards the end of the reign of the English queen Elizabeth there was much cogitation, in Scotland as well as in England, on the likelihood of her being succeeded by her cousin, the Scottish king James VI.[90] Two extant classical panegyrics have been thought to reflect the hope and optimism that such a prospect arose among the *filidh* in Ireland, although as we will see this interpretation is not without difficulties.[91] Since Elizabeth's father, Henry VIII, had taken upon himself the title of King of Ireland in 1541, the Tudor monarchs had embarked upon a reforming campaign which aimed to bring 'civility' to Ireland. Political submission was only part of the campaign's objective; more ominously, the centralisation of government, the abolition of native institutions, and the imposition of the Reformed religion and of English law, speech, and even dress, caused severe disruption and unrest. An increasingly heavy hand, which included militarisation, plantation, and religious iconoclasm, provoked a major rebellion, initiated and led by the main northern lords and joined by chiefs throughout Ireland, known as the Nine Years' War (1594–1603). It may have been at some time during this period, or perhaps as early as 1581 when he visited Scotland, that Fearghal Óg Mac an Bhaird composed his eulogy *Trí gcoróna i gcairt Shéamais*.[92] In this poem Mac an Bhaird celebrated James VI's triple claim to the crowns of Scotland, England, and Ireland, confidently foreseeing that:

> cuirfid*h*ior coróin Sagsan ...
> um ríg*h* n-oirb*h*eartac*h* n-Alban.

---

89 O'Brien (ed.) 1952, p. 157.
90 As early as 1559 Elizabeth declared to the Commons: 'And, in the end, this shall be for me sufficient, that a marble stone shall declare that a queen, having reigned such a time, lived and died a virgin', and in 1599 she stated that 'all my husbands [are] my good people' (Haigh 1998, pp. 23, 24).
91 See below, pp. 304 and n. 93, 308–9.
92 Ó Macháin 1988, i, p. 56.

(the Saxons' crown shall be placed on the powerful king of Alba) (§4bd).

James did indeed obtain the crown of England, and with it the kingship of Ireland, in 1603 and this was celebrated, around that date, by another Irish poet, Eochaidh Ó hEódhusa, in *Mór theasda dh'obair Óivid*, where he anticipated an improvement in the conditions and fortunes of the Irish (§§14–16). It has been argued that the Irish learned classes were encouraged by the fact that James was a Stiúbhart and therefore a *Gaidheal* — according to the tradition which at least An Dubhaltach Mac Firbhisigh would later question — an optimism that was short-lived.[93] Although James seems to have rewarded both poets for their compositions for him,[94] the anticipated improvement never came to Ireland. As for Scotland, we have no extant evidence of poetic celebration, whether classical or vernacular, of James. The Scottish *Gaoidhil*'s experience of government under this king until 1603 had hardly been a pleasant one, and after that date, particularly with the promulgation of the 'Statutes of Iona' and similar subsequent legislation, Scottish Gaelic poets would have had precious little to celebrate about their king.

The most outstanding feature in both syllabic poems for James VI is that they contain those elements that are otherwise elusive in classical poetry of Scotland, albeit sometimes in a slightly modified form. For instance, the prophecy motif is used by Fearghal Óg Mac an Bhaird when arguing for James's right to the kingdoms of Scotland, England, and Ireland. Yet prophecy here refers not to the ruler who will banish the *Goill* from Ireland, but to the advent of a king who would reign over the three kingdoms. Mac an Bhaird does not name any prophets, but such a statement can only refer according to the predictions attributed to Merlin and to Thomas the Rhymer. Merlin's prophecy was recalled in Scotland as well as in England at the time of James's crowning as king of England.[95] Mac Firbhisigh also saw James's accession to the English throne as the

93 *Trí gcoróna i gcairt Shéamais*, 5b; Ó Buachalla 1983, pp. 86, 125–6; Caball 1998, pp. 83–4. For other examples of poetic optimism in Ireland see *ibid.*, pp. 90–3, and pp. 93–113 for the change in mood (though attacking James's subordinates in government rather than the king himself) after the Flight of the Earls in 1607.

94 Bannerman 1990, p. 10. Mac an Bhaird's 'payment' was a grant of lands at the time of the Ulster Plantation (Breatnach (ed.) 1977–8, p. 169).

95 MacInnes 2006d, pp. 18–19; Marshall 2000, pp. 34–5.

fulfilment of prophecy, in this instance in relation to 'Marmar-Chloch na Cinneamhna' ('the Marble Stone of Destiny'), the inauguration stone of the kings of Scots, which had been stolen by Edward I of England: '[baoí] tairrngire ag radh gibe dú a mberthear an *chathaoir* sin go mbia ceannus na criche sin ag na Sgotuibh' ('there was a prophecy saying that wherever that chair was brought, the Scots would have hegemony of that territory').[96] At the time this prophecy had apparently been in circulation in verse, which Mac Firbhisigh quoted in translation in his Latin chronicle:

> Nempe Scotis fatum
> (res mira) ubicunque locatum,
> inveniunt lapidem
> regnare tenentur ibidem.
>
> (Truly an utterance to the Scots
> (a wonderful thing): wherever it be located,
> they find the stone;
> they are regarded as reigning on that spot) (*ibid.* §420.4).

Closely associated with prophecy are the interconnected motifs of the Irish high-kingship and of Ireland (and Ireland only — not Scotland or England or Britain) as her high-king's spouse, both of which Mac an Bhaird included in his poem:

> I gcúirt *Sh*agsan na sreab*h* seang
> a-tá ard*ch*oróin Éireann ...
>
> Fada a-tá i dtairngire *dh*uit
> crí*ch* Sagsan — is iul orrd*h*ruic;
> duit is dú Éire sam*h*laid*h*;
> is tú a céile ar *ch*omhardhaibh.
>
> (In the Court of fair-streamed England is placed Éire's noble crown ...
>
> The Saxon's land has been long —'tis well known — prophesied for thee; so too is Éire due to thee; thou art her spouse by all signs).[97]

---

96 *LMG* ii, §412A.6.
97 *Trí gcoróna i gcairt Shéamais*, §§21ab, 22.

The second of the two quatrains quoted, then, relates to two separate prophecies, both connected with the high-kingship: first that uttered by Merlin and Thomas, then the conventional one regarding the high-kingship of Ireland.

It may be strict conservatism that prevented the author from referring to the high-kingship of England or of Britain; this, as a panegyric-code motif, never existed, its unique appearance — in the guise of the related motif, as in the present poem, of the ruler as his territory's spouse — in the Caimbéal poem *Mó iná ainm Iarrla Gaoidheal* being a late innovation and an anomaly.[98] More difficult to explain is the lack of reference by Mac an Bhaird to the high-kingship of *Alba* which, as we have seen, did form part of the poetic stock-in-trade at least in the eleventh century.[99] Could this lack reflect the changes in the character and style of kingship that resulted from Normanisation particularly from the twelfth century onwards?

James, too, depicted himself as his territory's spouse, but his notion of the king's marriage to his territory was very different from that found in Gaelic tradition. In a 1603–4 speech to parliament he portrayed himself as married to Britain (noting the indissoluble character of marriage), but his depiction, along with further imagery, was borrowed from the Bible, where Christ and his church are portrayed as husband and wife, as the head and the body, and as the shepherd and his flock:

> What God hath conjoined then, let no man separate. I am the husband, and the whole isle is my lawful wife: I am the head, and it is my body: I am the shepherd, and it is my flock.[100]

Mac an Bhaird resorts to heredity to justify James's claim to both the Scottish and English crowns. His genealogy of James, which in fact reads more like a 'réim ríoghraidh' ('regnal list') and only goes back to the first Stiúbhart king, notes that his claim to the throne of England comes

---

98 See above, chapter 4, pp. 138–9.
99 See above, p. 295.
100 Tanner 1961, p. 26. See Mt. 19: 6; Eph. 5: 23; Col. 1: 18. For shepherd references see, for instance, Mt. 9: 36, 25: 32; Jn. 10: 14. Enright 1976 suggests that James may have borrowed the idea from the Gaelic concept of the mystical marriage of the ruler to his territory. He notes, however (pp. 29–30), that similar imagery can be found in medieval Europe.

through his descent from Margaret Tudor, daughter of Henry VII and wife of James IV of Scotland (§§9–14). The kingship of Scotland he has not only on grounds of heredity, but also by divine right (§3), and his claim to the crowns of all three kingdoms is confirmed 'i seinleabhraibh' ('in ancient books', §§2c, 12d, 17d 19d, 20d). Eochaidh Ó hEódhusa in addition portrays James as protector and defender, and as the one who can unite his people.[101] Both poets praise James's wisdom, Mac an Bhaird comparing it to Solomon's.[102] Additionally, both present James as the prince who will bring justice and peace, and whose rule is sanctioned by nature.[103] The nature motif is re-worked by Ó hEódhusa by giving it a Latin twist:

> Atá Seireis — as sé a shuim —
> ag treabhadh thulach ndíoghuinn,
> ag buain fhala d'arm Marsa.
>
> (In sum, Ceres ploughs fruitful hillocks, wiping blood off the sword of Mars).[104]

Another classical reference is provided by Ó hEódhusa's claim that James's accession to the crowns of the three kingdoms will bring about a (political) transformation which Ovid, had he been alive, would have added to his *Metamorphoses*.[105] The poet also uses his knowledge of the classics to re-work the motif of 'tréidhe tighearna'. He presents Fortune and Nature debating the reason why the king has come to assume command of the three kingdoms; the former argues for a twist of fate, and the latter, who eventually wins the debate, for James's personal natural qualities (*airrdhibh*, §24d) along with the lessons that Nature herself has taught him.[106] But Fortune's feeble character — for she regularly turns her Wheel — is very much on the mind of the poet, who closes his panegyric expressing his hope that:

---

101 *Mór theasda dh'obair Óivid*, §§10d, 12a, 16c, 19cd, 20a.
102 *Trí gcoróna i gcairt Shéamais*, §§28c, 29ab; *Mór theasda dh'obair Óivid*, §4a.
103 *Trí gcoróna i gcairt Shéamais*, §§7d, 29cd; *Mór theasda dh'obair Óivid*, §§4d, 5c, 7–8, 9, 18a, 21.
104 *Mór theasda dh'obair Óivid*, §9abc.
105 *ibid.*, §§1–2.
106 *ibid.*, §§22–32.

nā tí d'*fh*illtighe an Fhortún
ar n-athchruthadh go hullamh.

(from reversal of Fortune may no second change come for us
soon again).[107]

Alba is mentioned several times in *Trí gcoróna i gcairt Shéamais*. This
poem was composed by Mac an Bhaird before James VI became also
James I of England, and therefore the poet speaks of 'rígh Alban' and 'rígh
... Monaidh' (§§2c, 8c, 25d). In *Mór theasda dh'obair Óivid*, on the other
hand, *Alba* receives no explicit mention but James is celebrated as ruling
over the three kingdoms which Ó hEódhusa compares to three fierce,
mischievous women, or three furious serpents that finally live together
in peace (§§7, 8). The *Gall* motif appears twice in Mac an Bhaird's
poem. The poet praises James for possessing the bravery of the *Goill*
and describes him as 'rígh slóigh Gall is Gaoidheal' ('king of the host of
Goill and *Gaoidhil*'). The former of these two *Gall* allusions seems to be a
reference to the English blood in his veins, and the latter, although often
a mere praise term without reference to actual circumstances, in this case
accurately proclaims James as reigning over both Gaels and non-Gaels.
The *Goill* are, therefore, in both cases the English, the allusion being of
the type that carries no negative connotations. Finally, neither Mac an
Bhaird nor Ó hEódhusa mentions any ancient noble ancestors or their
early territories: James's genealogy, as noted, stops at Robert II, the first
Stiúbhart king.[108]

Lastly, it may be noted that nowhere do the poets celebrate this king
as a *Gaoidheal*. That the Scottish tradition of a Stiúbhart Irish origin had
become widespread in Ireland is certain,[109] and yet the poets make no
reference to any of James's supposed ancient Irish progenitors. The poets'
silence on James VI's Gaelic ancestry is interesting. Were they aware of
James's dislike of the *Gaoidhil*? Or did they perhaps, like Mac Firbhisigh,
question the Stiúbhart claim of Gaelic ancestry? Whatever the answer
may be, the poets' failure to address James as a Gael poses a question

---

107 *ibid.*,§34bc.
108 See above, p. 308.
109 See above, pp. 266, 286.

on the interpretation that the learned classes' optimism on his acces-
sion to the kingship of Ireland, through that of England, stemmed from
their viewing him as a Gael. If that were the case, one would expect it to
be so indicated in the poems, but instead we find in them a taste for the
Latin classics, including the re-working of some of the traditional Gaelic
panegyric motifs to connect them with the Latin tradition, which was
appreciated by the king.[110] Perhaps we should search for other reasons
for the composition of these eulogies. For Mac an Bhaird it may simply
have been a matter of courtesy or diplomacy at the time when he visited
Scotland. Ó hEódhusa's reasons for composing his panegyric for James
may have similarly been a diplomatic tactic. His vision of better times
coming to Ireland under James's rule should perhaps be seen as a sugges-
tion or a plea to the king, rather than as confident anticipation that such
would be the case. In this context it is well to remember that the rhetoric
of panegyric is all about the depiction of what the subject, as the fitting,
'right' ruler, is capable of doing, rather than a statement of actual facts.
What is very likely to have caused hope and optimism in the Irish learned
classes was, in the first place, that the rule of the Tudor dynasty had finally
come to an end. But also that James was a Scot, and that even in the not
so distant past moves had been made by major Irish lords to transfer
Ireland's sovereignty to Scotland: in other words, they were hoping that
there might be left in James VI and I some vestige of a sense of *dualchas*.[111]

The rest of the extant poetry addressed to or commenting on mon-
archs of Scotland and Britain belongs to the vernacular genre. We may
include within this corpus *I n-ainm an áird-mhic do-ní grása*, by an
anonymous Irish author, addressed to Elizabeth, queen of England. In all
likelihood this is a mock-eulogy. It does display a number of the motifs
normally found in Gaelic panegyric: Elizabeth is praised for her generos-
ity, her noble ancestry, her beauty, her sway not only over England but far
beyond. Yet we can hardly take the author seriously. For instance, the sub-
ject's physical beauty is generally given in poetry in the form of brief and
stereotyped clauses, often aimed to act as fillers within lines and to fulfil
metrical requisites. In this poem, however, Elizabeth's physical attributes

---

110 See above, p. 308. For James's taste for Latin, as well as Greek and French, writing see,
for instance, Ó Buachalla 1983, p. 87.
111 See above, p. 289.

are reviewed in a long, verbose litany spanning no less than three stanzas, twenty-five lines in total, an almost nauseating exercise in alliteration. Secondly, in a section which might be treated as the equivalent of a *caithréim*, we find some absurd claims, as in the author's assertion that Elizabeth receives 'Cíos na Fraince, íonm*h*us Alban ... | Cìos na cruinne' ('the tribute of France, the wealth of Scotland ... | the tribute of the world', §8ac). There is also the poet's statement, verging on blasphemy, that 'Atáid riam*h* buid*h*each dí Dia 'gus daoine' ('God and men are ever grateful to her', §13a). On the other hand, no other important conventional motifs — such as the queen as her people and territory's protector, prophecy, nature's sanction, and so on — are present in the poem. It is also, of course, almost impossible to imagine that any Irish poet might at all wish to praise Elizabeth, whose Irish policies were so heavy-handed.

There are in the extant corpus no other vernacular poems addressed directly to a monarch. What we do have is a considerable body of political verse (as well as the classical Colonsay poems and some input in *Dá chúis ag milleadh ar meanma*) concerned with the defence of the royal house of Stiúbhart. This has come to light in the previous chapters where vernacular verse for the various kindreds was reviewed, and therefore we will give here only a brief summary.[112] Most of what has survived is the work of Mac Domhnaill poets, but other authors also have left witness of the same political ideology. The execution of Charles I and the exile of Charles II, the seizing of the throne by William and Mary, and the accession of George I all provoked a loyal royalist response in the *Gaoidhil* and their poets, all intent in restoring 'an rìgh dleasdanach' ('the rightful king').[113] Divine right and heredity are put forward as the principal bases for their demands. Religious denomination is a secondary factor in that, while the defence of the true faith is associated with the defence of the Stiúbhart monarchy by Catholic poets, yet Protestant authors do not find their own creed incompatible with Stiúbhart support. The Orange and Hanover monarchs are rejected as foreigners and accused, with their adherents, of lying and of attaining to the crown through bribes. They are mere upstarts and the subverters of traditional values. Thus far, then, all

---

112 See above, chapters 3, pp. 102–9; 4, pp. 173–5; 5, pp. 218–21, 234–5; 6, pp. 257–9, 272–6. For the classical poems see chapter 3, pp. 84–5, 89, 93–5.
113 *Sèid na builg sin, ghille, dhom*, §4c.

the themes in the royalist poetry of the *Gaoidhil* are the same as those found in the poetry of royalist Englishmen or Scots.[114]

But additionally Gaelic royalism had its own themes and strands. The struggle for the return of the Stiúbhart monarchs is presented as a Gaelic affair, although there is a manifest awareness that the conflict involves the whole of Britain. Hope and self-confidence are maintained by evoking the prophecy of Thomas the Rhymer that the *Gaoidhil* will triumph in the end. Only rarely do we find gloom or despair in this type of poetry, even though there are a number of complaints about the changeability and deceitfulness of the world. While some authors interpret current affairs within a sin-and-punishment framework, generally we find an unremitting confidence that God will turn the wheel of fortune and justice will be restored. The enemy are identified as *Goill*, English speakers, and cloaked-folk, this terminology sometimes indicating the Lowlanders, but also generally the enemies of the Stiúbhart kings. Bible imagery conjures up images of the plight of the exiled children of Israel to reflect the contemporary political evils, and of David and Absolom to describe William of Orange's turning against his uncle and father-in-law, James VII. Other imagery includes the application of names of ignoble animals, like the pig, the buzzard, or the wolf, to the foreigners occupying the throne. The poets' attacks on the Caimbéalaigh for siding with the enemy are another facet of Gaelic royalism. It is difficult to accept that poor inter-clan relations were what informed political choices, or in other words, that those who supported the house of Stiúbhart — most of the *Gaoidhil* but also a good number of clans of *Gall* origin — were merely taking the opportunity of squaring differences, although this is characteristic of any war. There is enough in the extant poetry, particularly in the themes shared with contemporary royalist poetry elsewhere in Britain, to suggest a genuine sense of preoccupation with the defence of the Stiúbhart monarchy and the preservation of traditional social and political values. This is perhaps most strongly indicated by the general abandonment, in these political poems, of individual praise and of the traditional poetic praise motifs, to focus instead on direct engagement with actual social and political affairs.

---

114 See above, chapter 1, pp. 28–22.

Conclusions

The rhetoric of extant classical poetry composed for or about the kings of Scotland and Stiúbhart kings of Britain displays an amalgam of continuity and innovation. The earlier corpus, composed down to the late eleventh century, whether by Scottish authors as was probably the case of *Airis biuc a mheic big báin* (or rather the section in it of Scottish interest), or Irish as in *Ro bátar láeich do Laigneib*, preserves many of those motifs which later became elusive in, or completely disappeared from, classical Gaelic poetry of Scotland: an emphasis on the depiction of the subject as the one who can unite and lead his people, as their protector and the defender of his territory against *Goill*, and references to prophecy, to the taking of territory 'ar éigin' and to the high-kingship. The fact that the high-kingship in question is that of *Alba* indicates a strong sense of 'Scottishness', that is, of permanent settlement in *Alba* and independence from Ireland, in place at least by the later eleventh century. It is likely that this had been in place for some time, perhaps even since the reign of Domhnall II, who is the first to be recorded in the annals as 'rí Alban'.[115] This is reinforced in *Airis biuc a mheic big báin* through numerous references to places in eastern Scotland, something that also reflects both the self-confidence of the Scottish *Gaoidhil* in their acquisition and settlement of Pictish territory and the eastward shift of their centres of royal power. *Ro bátar láeich do Laigneib*, composed *c.*1100, does include allusions to places in western Scotland, where the Scottish *Gaoidhil's* power centres still were at the time of the events narrated, five centuries earlier. Further reinforcement is achieved by the identification of these settlers of *Alba*, originally *Éireannaigh*, as *Albanaigh* in the eleventh-century poems. Apart from their designation as 'clanna Conaire' on one occasion, there are no allusions to ancient ancestors or territories, again suggesting a deliberate severance from Ireland. The pervasive use of allusions to the high-kingship of *Alba* in *Airis biuc a mheic big báin* suggests that this literary expression may well have been part of the stock-in-trade of the *filidh* both before and after the reign of Maol Coluim III. The overall impression is that the rhetoric of courtly panegyric of Scotland was not always as firmly rooted in Irish tradition, with little or no attempt made at reinterpreting or remoulding it to suit a Scottish context, as has been

---

115 See above, p. 302 n. 86.

thought.[116] The birth of *Alba* as an independent Gaelic kingdom seems to have set in motion such a reinterpretation, which is nevertheless absent from the poetry for other kindreds, a suggestion that the changed, feudal style of kingship in Scotland was accepted by the latter, who never appear in competition with the kings of Scots.

We have no other classical or vernacular verse composed for Scottish kings in the five centuries or so after *c.*1100. Two eulogies for James VI, both of Irish authorship, are the next and last poetic survival as far as classical panegyric for a monarch is concerned. The poems addressed to James VI are of great interest in several ways. Firstly, they show not only a conservative adherence to the rhetoric of classical panegyric, but also a return to those motifs rare in the poetry of Scotland: James is celebrated as protector and defender, as the one who can unite his people, and as a high-king. Yet, although he is clearly noted as ruling over the three kingdoms of Scotland, England, and Ireland, it is only with reference to the kingship of Ireland that we find the high-kingship in its traditional format, including the depiction of James as Ireland's spouse. This may well represent an effort by the poet to elicit some sympathy from James and coax him to soften his Irish policies. It is unlikely that what prompted the two Irish *filidh* to compose their eulogies for James VI was the Scottish tradition of Stiúbhart Gaelic origin. We have evidence that such a claim was questioned at least by An Dubhaltach Mac Firbhisigh, a slightly later contemporary of James. Moreover, nowhere in these poems is James celebrated as a *Gaoidheal*, or a descendant of one: his genealogy is only taken back to the first king of the Stiúbhart dynasty. Secondly, some motifs, such as that of prophecy, are modified to fit in with the circumstances. Because James reigned over *Gaoidhil* and *Goill*, the classical depiction of the subject as the defender against *Gall* attack was inappropriate; instead the reference is to the prophecies of Merlin and Thomas the Rhymer, circulating in Britain generally at the time, concerning the advent of a king who would rule over three kingdoms.[117] But these prophecies were not part of the conventional praise motifs of the classical panegyric code (although they are common in vernacular verse), and neither were the high-kingship of England or of Britain. The lack of reference to the

---

116 See, for instance, Ó Mainnín 1999, pp. 31, 50; McLeod 2004, pp. 113–26, 136–55.
117 See above, p. 304.

high-kingship of Scotland is more difficult to explain. It may well be that it disappeared as a praise motif as Normanisation, particularly from the twelfth century onwards, led to important changes in the character and style of kingship in Scotland — including the removal from office of the royal *filidh*, perhaps by the Brús monarchs.[118] Other traditional motifs are modified by flavouring them with classical Latin references: nature's sanction includes a vision of Ceres ploughing the fields, and James's lordly traits ('tréidhe tighearna') are shown, in a dialogue between Fortune and Nature, to be what led to his high status as ruler of a tripartite kingdom. *Alba* is present in the poem composed before 1603, but vanishes (being alluded to, along with England and Ireland, only metaphorically) in the poem celebrating the Union of Crowns.[119] The *Goill* are mentioned without any negative connotations, because they now form part of James's kingdom, and because of the *Gall* blood in James's own veins. Continuity, then, in the panegyric code is broken in the later poetry, as in the earlier, by innovation through the re-working of some motifs in order to adapt them to changed circumstances.

There is no extant vernacular verse addressed to a Scottish or British monarch in the form of individual eulogy. The surviving poetry containing comment on the monarchy is political in the sense best known to us, and its contents — support for the house of Stiúbhart and attack of its enemies — and rhetoric have been gradually appearing in chapters 1–5 and the first half of the present one. Along with the abandonment of individual eulogy we find an almost total lack of use of the traditional praise motifs. Instead, poets advise, incite, or condemn as appropriate, and review the reasons why the Stiúbhart monarchy is that of 'the right rulers'. Its key arguments are the same as those found in contemporary poetry composed by non-Gaelic authors. Heredity is one of them, as is also in the classical verse for James VI and as was indeed, primogeniture aside, in traditional Gaelic society; another is divine right, which is present also in its Gaelic fashion in earlier classical panegyric. The Orange and Hanover monarchs are rejected not only because they are of foreign extraction, but also because they have been placed on the throne by an upstart rabble, the subverters of the traditional order. At the same time, along with these

118 See above, chapter 1, p. 13.
119 See above, p. 308.

shared themes, Gaelic vernacular verse displays a very distinctive form of royalism. Support of the Stiúbhart monarchy is presented as a Gaelic concern, the royal line's claimed Gaelic ancestry is linked to Thomas the Rhymer's predictions of a Gaelic comeback (thus almost always imbuing the poetry with a single-minded sense of optimism), and the term *Goill* is employed to denote the Stiúbhairt's enemies: the overall effect is the depiction of the contemporary political conflict within the old familiar framework of the conflict between *Gaoidheal* and *Gall*. These uniquely Gaelic aspects of royalism are so finely interwoven with the themes shared with royalists elsewhere in Britain as to be inseparable from them. Thus the subversion of traditional values which the Whig cause represents, with its attacks on the noble class, is not detached from poems which are also a complaint on the decline of poetic patronage.[120] Similarly the enemies of the Stiúbhairt, the *Goill*, are identified as speaking a different language, English, and as dressing differently from the *Gaoidhil*. As kindreds like Clann Ghriogóir, Clann Ghille Eóin, or Clann Domhnaill of Islay were destroyed, and as seventeenth-century legislation dictated on language, place and form of education, size of retinue, and the entertainment of 'baird, nor profest pleisant pretending libertie to baird and flatter',[121] some poets wonder whether royalism was worth it at all. The emergence of the 'poet poverty' motif[122] is directly linked to all these events, which were a major factor in the decline of poetic patronage as well as in the crumbling of the wider traditional Gaelic order.

---

120 See, for instance, chapter 4, pp. 193–6; chapter 5, pp. 238–9.

121 *RPC* ix, p. 29 ('Statutes of Iona').

122 See above, chapters 4, pp. 195–7; 5, pp. 255–6.

Chapter 8

By poetic authority:
the language of authority in Scottish Gaelic poetry

Our survey of the extant corpus of Gaelic poetry of Scotland from earliest times until the early eighteenth century has focused first and foremost on the 'language of authority', the codified diction by which poets presented their subject as the ideal ruler, sending out a powerful message which, by sanctioning a chief's rule, aimed to preserve the order and cohesion of society. This was an essential duty of the *file*, and was carried out at ruling-élite level. The vernacular poets, while themselves members of the nobility, transmitted a similar message. Some of them — the *bàird*, *aois-dàna*, and amateurs from the nobility — did so in imitation of the syllabic metres of the *filidh*, but generally using simpler metrical forms and rarely, if ever, attaining the more complex *dán díreach*. The rest — those whom we have called strictly vernacular poets[1] — composed in accentual verse and did so in the everyday language, thus reaching a much larger audience and facilitating transmission beyond aristocratic circles. Additionally, they engaged in topics which were outwith the conventional remit of the *filidh* (most notably politics in the sense best understood by the modern mind), and which the latter, with rare exceptions, left well alone. One of these exceptions is the anonymous *Mór mo mholadh ar mhac Colla* (1647), which in themes and rhetoric reads much like a vernacular royalist poem, and another *Dá chúis ag milleadh ar meanma* (?1719), where Niall Mac Muireadhaigh, if indeed he was the author, devotes some space to contemporary Scottish and British politics.[2]

As well as themes and rhetoric, our survey has shed some light on matters of historical and cultural import, leading us to revisit questions

---

1   See above, chapter 2, pp. 42–3.
2   See above, chapter 3, pp. 84, 89, 93–5.

such as: how Gaelic, or otherwise, did the Gaels and the Gaelicised kin-dreds feel over the passage of time, as they first became members of the kingdom of Scots, and later of the kingdom of Britain? Where were their loyalties — how positive or negative was the impact of their enduring cultural and military links with Ireland on their loyalty to their king and country of Scotland? In particular, what was the Mac Domhnaill position *vis-à-vis* the crown? These are all questions which we can tackle only once we have learned how to read and interpret the codified diction of the poets, studied the patterns emerging from it, and applied them to the cultural environment in which the poetry flourished. This environment did not remain static. In the earliest times it was formed by a number of colonies of *Éireannaigh* who inhabited a socio-politically fragmented isle of Britain along with Picts, Britons, and Saxons, and later with Norse Vikings, not always at war against each other, but to a degree culturally compromising, for instance through intermarriage and through poetic addresses by the *filidh* to non-Gaelic nobles.[3] By perhaps the late ninth century one of these Irish colonies perceived itself as the new lords of the kingdom of *Alba*, still co-existing with other kingdoms.[4] Among these was the Norse kingdom of the Isles, which Somhairle mac Gille Brighde seized in the twelfth century. Despite the subsequent loss of Man, this kingdom flourished, under Norse overlordship, until 1266, when it came under the jurisdiction of the kings of *Alba*. Over time *Alba* indeed brought under its control the rest of the mainland and island areas that came to shape modern Scotland. After centuries of mostly uneasy relations with England, both the Scottish and English crowns were united in 1603 in the person of James VI and I, now king of Britain and Ireland. Gaelic identities and loyalties as perceived from the poetry must, therefore, be considered bearing in mind the circumstances of particular historical periods.

The Scottish panegyric codes
The rhetoric of the filidh
The first fact established by this study is that it is not possible to speak of one single, uniform panegyric code in court poetry of Scotland. As a general rule we can speak of two broad types, which have been called here

---

3   See above, chapter 1, p. 7; chapter 2, pp. 32, 48. See also Clancy (ed.) 1998, pp. 114–15.
4   See above, chapter 7, pp. 296 n. 61, 302 n. 86.

the earlier and the later models, but even within these two we find that in some cases — notably those of Clann Duibhne and Clann Leóid verse — the rhetoric of praise has its own particular flavour.[5] A second significant fact is that neither of the two main models, nor their variants (again as found for instance in Clann Duibhne or Clann Leóid panegyric), corresponds exactly to the Irish original model which, though not altogether the 'flat table-land' proposed by Eleanor Knott, is one of remarkable continuity.[6] The departures in the poetry of Scotland from the original code of the Irish schools can almost entirely be explained in the light of the specific social and political developments surrounding the *Gaoidhil* in Scotland. This is particularly true of the motif of the high-kingship and the related conceits of prophecy, the territory as spouse, and the *Goill*.[7]

The earlier Scottish poetic model is closer to the Irish one in that it keeps most of the poetic motifs customarily found in poems by Irish authors for Irish patrons. Within this group we find the poetry composed for the lords of the Isles and for the Clann Domhnaill cadet branch of Clann Eóin Mhóir, as well as the panegyric composed for Clann Dubhghaill, Clann Duibhne, and Clann Ghriogóir, and the few extant poems for the descendants of Corc and of Niall. In this same group can be included what little survives composed for or about the kings of *Alba* and for James VI and I, king of Britain.[8] However, there are some differences in the choice of motifs employed in the poetry for the various kindreds classified under this model. Only Clann Domhnaill poetry of Irish authorship includes the motifs of prophecy and of the high-kingship in their Irish format: the subject praised is portrayed as suitable to become high-king and as the one who according to prophecy will become Ireland's spouse. Consequently, it is only Clann Domhnaill subjects who are regularly connected with Tara, although this connexion appears also in a poem for Amhlaoíbh of Lennox, as a descendant of Corc.[9] Prophecy in surviving Clann Duibhne verse occurs only once, and then as a vague passing allusion, while the

---

5   See above, chapters 3, pp. 112–15; 4, pp. 148–50, 180–1.

6   *TD* i, p. li. See below, pp. 326–30, for the patterns of continuity with and departure from the Irish model.

7   See below, pp. 320–1, 326–8, 339, 340–2.

8   See above, chapters 3, pp. 66–91; 4, pp. 122–42; 5, pp. 184–94, 203–4; 7, pp. 303–9.

9   See above, chapters 3, p. 65 and n. 57; 5, p. 189.

spouse motif appears in one solitary instance, where a Caimbéal chief is portrayed as the lover of Britain. This unique representation is something of an aberration, a manipulation of the traditional motif of the high-king-ship, here linking the subject with his ancient noble ancestor, King Artúr. Additionally, *Saor do leannán, a Leamhain*, similarly gives a twist to the motif of the ruler as his territory's spouse by presenting Alún Mór, first earl of Lennox, as the spouse of the river Lennox in his patrimonial land. The high-kingship in its Irish format, however, is absent from the poems concerned with the early kings of *Alba*. Instead, there is a suggestion that the motif of the high-kingship of *Alba* was added to the poetic rhetoric at some point after Cionaoth mac Ailpín united Picts and Gaels, probably in the late ninth or early tenth century, when the annals first begin to speak of kings of *Alba* rather than of kings of the Picts.[10] But the motif of the high-kingship of *Alba* disappeared at some point during the classical period, probably as a consequence of changes in the form of kingship as it moved away from the original Gaelic style and took on many Norman elements. In all likelihood the high-kingship of *Alba* as a poetic motif was lost in the early fourteenth century, when the Brús dynasty introduced a European-style coronation.[11] Finally, Scottish authors composing for Irish patrons, while conforming generally to the Irish model as one would expect, do not engage, in the poems we have extant, in the topic of the high-kingship. This lack may be due simply to tactfulness, or perhaps to some established convention.[12]

Despite the presence of the motif of the high-kingship of Ireland in Mac Domhnaill poetry of this earlier model, and of the depiction of Clann Domhnaill as being in *Alba* only on a military campaign, the subjects praised are always identified as *Albanaigh* and as stalwart supporters of the kingdom of *Alba*. This identification of the subject as a Scot is shared with subjects belonging to other Scottish kindreds, whether their origin be Gaelic, British, Norse, or Anglo-Norman. In the case of Clann Duibhne, however, there is additionally a marked, nearly obsessive insistence on the depiction of the Caimbéalaigh as Gaels, as if this kindred felt the need to

---

10 See above, chapter 7, pp. 294–6, 299–301, 312–13.
11 See above, chapter 1, pp. 12–13; 7, p. 301.
12 See above, chapter 6, pp. 264, 278.

assert their place in the Gaelic world.[13] One notable absence from the pan-egyric composed for the later lords of the Isles is that of the *Gall* motif. In poems composed for the earlier lords the subject is described as *Gall*, but here meaning Hebridean rather than the foreign enemy which is meant by the Irish poetic motif. In this Irish format the *Goill* are found sometimes in the poetry for Clann Duibhne and Clann Ghriogóir, but generally as a mere complimentary motif portraying the subject as capable of keeping a foreign enemy at bay. It is only in the two Caimbéal poems concerned with the battle of Flodden that the Irish-format *Gall* motif is applied to actual contemporary circumstances.[14] In Clann Eóin Mhóir verse the *Goill* also appear normally as a complimentary motif, with only two exceptions, both of Scottish authorship: the mid-seventeenth-century political poems *Saoth liom do chor, a Cholla* and *Mór mo mholadh ar mhac Colla*, for Coll Mac Domhnaill of Colonsay and his son Alasdair, where they are, instead, the Lowland enemies of the house of Stiúbhart, an adaptation of the con-ventional motif probably borrowed from vernacular usage.[15]

The later Scottish poetic model presents some departures, such as the abandonment of the motifs of the high-kingship and the depiction of the subject as his territory's spouse.[16] To this model conforms the poetry composed for all Clann Domhnaill cadet branches other than Clann Eóin Mhóir, and for the rest of the Scottish kindreds generally. Here the poetry focuses on the motifs of martial prowess, generosity, hospitality, poetic patronage, education, character qualities, feasting, hunting and gaming. As in the early model, the subject is always an *Albanach* but also a *Gaoidheal*, even if his ultimate ancestry is not Gaelic: cultural Gaelicisation seems to be all that was required. The extant Stiúbhart poems, like those for Clann Duibhne, seem to reflect a particular desire by this kindred to be placed within the Gaelic milieu.[17] Mac Leóid poetry has its own peculiarities. It lacks any references to the kindred's ancient Gaelic ancestors, always focus-ing on their female-line royal Norse descent. Similarly, it makes no mention of ancient patrimonial lands attached to the early Gaelic ancestors: place-

---

13 See above, chapter 4, pp. 132–5.
14 See below, p. 327.
15 See above, chapter 3, p. 84.
16 See above, chapter 3, pp. 91–2.
17 See above, chapter 6, p. 270.

names are consistently local, linking the kindred to their current territories, with only occassional references to places in Norway, the homeland of their maternal ancestors. This lack is also registered in poetry for other kindreds, and the likely implication, when this silence is considered alongside poetic gaps in respect of ancient noble ancestry, is suggested below.[18] Mac Leóid poetry gives a very localised, self-contained impression, further augmented by a scarcity of allusions to *Alba*. Additionally, there is little in the way of *seanchas* or of classical Latin or Greek references, and royalism is totally absent.

The later Scottish poetic model also includes some poems which either rework traditional motifs or introduce fresh ones. In the Colonsay poems *Goill* is used to mean the Lowland enemies of the Stiúbhart kings, and the Sleat piece *Éireochthar fós le Clainn gColla*, whose concern is also the events of the mid seventeenth-century Wars of the Three Kingdoms, refers to the same enemies as 'fir Alban'.[19] This new persona of the *Goill* is to be seen as connected with one of the new motifs introduced, that of royalism, meaning support for the royal house of Stiúbhart. Royalism is very much a concern of the vernacular poets, and although passing references to a subject's support for the house of Stiúbhart are not uncommon in the poetry of the *filidh*, this theme only is developed at any length in two classical pieces: *Éireóchthar fós le clainn gColla*, and the Clann Raghnaill poem *Dá chúis ag milleadh ar meanma*.[20] Some references to religion may be given as part of the repertoire of motifs connected with the broader motif of royalism, within which, however, the connexion between religion and politics is not fully developed. Another characteristic of the later poetic model is its limited allusions to *Alba*, while by referring to *Breatain* the poets show an awareness of and a preoccupation with the island-wide scope of the conflict. In all this, royalism in classical poetry goes hand in hand with royalism in vernacular verse, but there is one difference: the *filidh*, while presenting the Caimbéalaigh as enemies of the house of Stiúbhart, never launch vicious attacks on them as the vernacular poets do.[21]

---

18 See below, p. 333.
19 See above, chapter 3, pp. 84, 93.
20 See above, chapter 3, pp. 93–5.
21 See above, chapter 4, pp. 125–6.

Within the extant corpus classed as the later model it is quite notice-able that only Mac Domhnaill and Mac Fionghuin poetry contains any references to ancient Gaelic ancestors. It is true that very few classical poems for other kindreds remain extant, and therefore we have little to go by. For Clann Ghille Eóin, for instance, we have only one fragment from a classical piece. When looking for genealogical claims we must instead, in these cases, turn to the genealogies, and here we encounter a problem: the Irish pedigrees and chronicles only record the ancestry of a small number of Scottish Gaelic kindreds (the royal lines of Dál Riada and *Alba*, Clann Domhnaill, Clann Ghille Eóin, Clann Leóid, and three families descend-ing from Cormac mac Airbheartaigh: Clann Mhic Fhionghuin, Clann Ghuaire, and Clann Mhic Ghiolla Mhaoil), and moreover they ques-tion the later claims of Irish descent of some of the others, including the Stiúbhairt.[22] On the Scottish side our earliest source for those not included in, or questioned by, the Irish records is 'MS 1467', which unfortunately stands alone as regards the multiplicity of offspring of Loarn it proposes. Many genealogical claims emerging by the seventeenth century (or earlier, as attested for Clann Ghriogóir), under the influence of Lowland writers and changing fashions, are at variance with 'MS 1467', and therefore are not helpful at all.[23] To the questions of genealogy and ancient noble origins, and what we can learn from the silence of some sources and the changing claims, we return below.[24]

The rhetoric of the vernacular poets

The later model of Scottish classical poetic rhetoric applies almost entirely to vernacular poetry: the focus is on the subject as a skilful warrior, and on his generosity, hospitality, education, character qualities, and his love of feasting, hunting, and gaming. Patronage of learning does not normally (Friseal poetry is one exception)[25] feature in the poems for subjects of Anglo-Norman ancestry, perhaps suggesting a limited extent to their involvement in Gaelic cultural support. There are two distinct types of vernacular verse. One is in the form of eulogy or elegy addressed to an

22 See Tables 6.1 and 6.2, and above, chapter 6, pp. 245–50.
23 See above, chapters 4, pp. 119–20; 5, pp. 199–200, 206–9, 226–8; 6, p. 245–6.
24 See below, pp. 330–5.
25 See above, chapter 6, p. 272.

individual or to a group of individuals, and the other in the form of political poetry in the sense most familiar to us. Amateur poets from the nobility composing in 'semi-classical' style tend to confine themselves to the first type, only some of them (like Murchadh Mòr MacCoinnich)[26] occasionally fully engaging in contemporary politics.

The main and most frequent theme of strictly vernacular poetry is royalism, and this may appear both in panegyric addressed to an individual and, more frequently and with fuller development, in poems in the form of political comment or discussion. The rhetoric of royalism shares very much the same themes and motifs found in poetry composed by English, Welsh, and Lowland Scots authors also supporting the house of Stiúbhart: dynastic continuity and rejection of foreign lines, divine right, condemnation of political and social upstarts subverting the traditional order and, in the case of Catholic poets, the presentation of Catholic belief as the true faith.[27] Sometimes the contemporary evils are set within a sin-and-punishment framework, but on the whole poets express hope and a single-minded determination that the Stiúbhart cause will eventually triumph. This connects with some other elements in the rhetoric of royalism which are unique to Gaelic poetry: the depiction of the royalist struggle as a Gaelic concern (although its British scope is clearly understood from the poems),[28] the confidence that the wheel of fortune will eventually turn,[29] the comparison of the plight of the Stiúbhart supporters to that of the children of Israel, and prayers that God will send a new Moses to help the royalists overcome their enemies.[30] Prophecy is prominent, but not in its classical Irish format (uttered by ancient Gaelic saints and heroes and heralding the coming of the one who will defeat and banish the *Goill*); instead, poets evoke the words of Thomas the Rhymer in connexion with an eventual comeback of the Gaels and the recovery of their original territory.[31] Lowland royalists are incorporated and become indistinguishable from the Gaels, and the Caimbéalaigh are

---

26 See above, chapter 5, p. 235.

27 See above, chapters 1, pp. 13–22; 3, pp. 102–8.

28 See above, chapters 3, pp. 108–9; 4, p. 175; 5, p. 223; 6, p. 274; 7, p. 311.

29 See above, chapters 3, p. 106; 4, pp. 174–5; 5, p. 219; 6, p. 273; 7, p. 311.

30 See above, chapters 3, pp. 105–6; 5, p. 223; 6, pp. 259, 273; 7, p. 311.

31 See above, chapters 3, pp. 102, 109; 5, pp. 219; 6, pp. 274, 294–5; 7, p. 311. The motif of prophecy is not attested in extant Mac Leóid vernacular poetry; see chapter 4, p. 175.

viciously attacked for taking the opposite side. On the other hand, some-times there is also disenchantment, when some poets lament the price that Jacobites had come to pay for their loyalty, and wonder if it had been worth it.[32] Towards the end of our period national politics are connected with the general decline of Gaelic ways, giving origin to the new motif of 'poet poverty' often found in poems complaining about the decay of hos-pitality, the lack of poetic patronage, the adoption of the English language and dress, and so on.[33]

While the vernacular poems share much, in terms of themes and of praise rhetoric, with the classical poetry which we classify as the later model, one important exception is that of 'ceannas na nGaoidheal'. The 'headship of the Gaels', originally a motif of Clann Domhnaill classical verse but contested in that composed for Clann Duibhne, seems to have been a purely academic debate which was exclusively the concern of the *filidh*. As for the *Goill*, they are no longer the English enemies of the *Gaoidhil* as in the classical poetry motif, but the Lowlanders and gener-ally the enemies of the house of Stiùbhart, whether Scottish or English.[34] In vernacular poetry dealing with political conflict or Gaelic decline they are consistently referred to as English speakers, cloaked-folk, and generally described in contemptuous terms. Occasionally, however, in simple praise poems where politics are not a concern, the word *Gall* has no negative con-notations, but is used to emphasise the subject's sway or popularity in the main Lowland towns. The term *Gall* is never applied to patrons of Anglo-Norman origin, perhaps to avoid confusion between an ethnic or cultural marker and a label for an enemy of the Stiùbhart cause.

Among the motifs unique to vernacular poetry we have that of *deoch-slàinte*, the poet's toast to his patron. It is frequent in, but not unique to, Mac Coinnigh poetry, and it is attested as early as 1546 in a Friseal poem.[35] Beer-drinking — along with the more conventionally expected drinking of wine — appears in an early eighteenth-century poem for a Friseal chief.[36] By the mid-seventeenth-century we begin to find references to payments

---

32 See above, chapters 5, p. 221; 6, pp. 257, 279.
33 See above, chapters 4, pp. 177–80; 5, pp. 238–9.
34 See above, chapters 3, pp. 101–2; 4, p. 172; 5, pp. 221, 254–5; 6, pp. 259, 275; 7, p. 311.
35 See above, chapters 5, pp. 239–40; 6, p. 277.
36 See above, chapter 6, p. 277.

of *mál* ('rent'), a witness to a changed society where the chief had become a landlord to his people.[37] As for the theme of 'mìorùn nan Gall', which would become widespread in the eighteenth century, there is a number of instances of it already in the seventeenth, the earliest seemingly being that found in a poem composed for Eóin Moireach, first Earl of Atholl, around 1630.[38] While this motif normally refers to the ill will of the Lowlanders towards the Highlanders, we have one instance of its reversal in NicGhillesheathanaich's 1719 statement that King George deserved the ill will of the *Gaoidhil*.[39]

Continuity and innovation in the classical rhetoric of panegyric of Scotland

Both the early and the late Scottish models into which the classical poetry of Scotland as a whole can be roughly divided preserve a number of the praise motifs of the schools of Ireland, but both have lost some of them and introduced some new ones or reworked existent ones. There is, therefore, continuity as well as innovation in the Scottish classical panegyric codes. One instance is the kingship of Ireland, which is absent with two exceptions: the poetry composed for the lords of the Isles and Clann Eóin Mhóir, and Fearghal Óg Mac an Bhaird's eulogy *Trí gcoróna i gcairt Shéamais*, for James VI and I. The kingship, or high-kingship, of *Alba*, on the other hand, probably originated in the late ninth or early tenth century, when it is first attested in the annals, although our only poetic witnesses are two eleventh-century poems, *A éolcha Alban uile* and, above all, *Airis biuc a mheic big báin*.[40] Its birth is, then, pre-classical, and its death, a likely effect of the Normanisation of kingship, took place at some point in the classical period, perhaps during the rule of the Brús dynasty — a dynasty of *Gall* origin. The kingship of *Alba* is likely to have featured also in poems composed for the subjects from the royal line of Loarn until this line was permanently ousted from the succession in 1130.[41] It never appears in poems composed for nobles who were not descendants of Earc, just as

---

37 See above, chapters 5, p. 225; 6, p. 256.
38 See above, chapter 6, p. 275.
39 See above, chapter 6, p. 258.
40 See above, chapter 7, pp. 295, 301, 302 n. 86.
41 See above, chapter 5, p. 197.

the kingship of Ireland is never connected with Scottish nobles other than the descendants of Colla Uais. James VI and I was, exceptionally, the only king of Scotland acclaimed as king of Ireland, matching historical fact. A 'Scottish spouse motif' (*Alba* as her king's spouse) may have developed along with the motif of the high-kingship but, if it did, no instances have survived aside from, perhaps, an inconclusive suggestion of such a concept in a couple of Mac Domhnaill poems.[42]

Prophecy also shows both continuity and innovation. In its Irish format — the banishment of the foreigners, so closely connected with the high-kingship — it is not attested in the extant poems for the lords of the Isles, but survives in verse composed for Clann Eóin Mhóir. Prophecy is also found in early poetry for the kings of *Alba*, but here it relates to the young kingdom of *Alba*, rather than to Ireland.[43] Prophecy in the Irish format was reworked in the seventeenth century by Fearghal Óg Mac an Bhaird who, as well as portraying James VI as Ireland's prophesied high-king, presented him as the one destined to reign over all of Britain; the allusion, therefore, is not to the prophecies of ancient sages, saints or heroes, but to those of Thomas the Rhymer (a motif borrowed from vernacular tradition) and by Merlin (reproducing a prophecy current in England at the time of James's coronation as king of Britain).[44] As for the *Gall* motif, its scarcity in classical poetry of Scotland is almost certainly due to the mostly non-confrontational nature of Norman settlement in Scotland.[45] When it does appear it is normally given as a passing reference, sometimes to portray the subject as the one capable of keeping foreign enemies at bay, and on other occasions to depict him as the best of all, Gaels and non-Gaels. It remained, therefore, simply one more among of the conventional complimentary sketches that formed part of the panegyric code. The only exception to this pattern is that of the two Caimbéal poems connected with the battle of Flodden, where the *Goill* are the English enemies, as in the Irish model, and *athardha*, *athroinn*, and *fuidheall* are similarly used to frame the current circumstances within the traditional Irish historical and literary framework of the struggle of

---

42 See above, chapter 7, p. 301.
43 See above, chapter 7, p. 293.
44 *ibid.*, p. 304 and n. 95.
45 See above, chapter 3, pp. 69–70.

Gaoidhil against *Goill*.[46] The *Gall* motif, as noted, does not appear in the extant poetry for the lords of the Isles, excepting some early poems, where it is used to note the Norse kinship connexions of the subject: it lacks any negative connotations and it serves to indicate ethnicity and Scandinavian royal ancestry.

'Ceannas na nGaoidheal' first appears in poetry for the lords of the Isles, reflecting their late medieval sway over numerous Highland and Isles kindreds. It remained a motif in the poetry for later Clann Domhnaill cadet branches, and was disputed by the earls of Argyll after the downfall, at the end of the fifteenth century, of the Mac Domhnaill lordship, from which Clann Duibhne so much profited. The 'Red Hand' and the 'house and a half of Scotland' are also Mac Domhnaill themes, while the reference to psalm-reading, and therefore possibly to the Protestant religion, in *Mór an bróinsgél bás í Dhuibhne* (*c*.1631) may suggest an important innovation in the panegyric code make-up of the ideal ruler in poems for Caimbéal subjects. Yet this isolated poetic reference is inconclusive, as a Gaelic taste for psalms is also attested elsewhere.[47] Further references to psalm-reading in Caimbéal vernacular verse, and Carsuel's dedicatory epistle in *Foirm na nUrrnuidheadh*, might, however, lend weight to the postulation of the depiction of the ideal ruler as Protestant as a panegyric code innovation, at least among vernacular authors. But if the reference in the Caimbéal classical poem is indeed to Protestantism, then it would be interesting to know whether the composer had also embraced the Reformed religion, and if so how many Scottish *filidh* did the same. In Ireland the *filidh* generally adhered to the pre-Reformation religion even if their patrons did not.[48] We know that the Mac Muireadhaigh family remained Catholic, but otherwise the religious denomination, or denominations, of the *filidh* of Scotland after Reformation remains a blank. In classical poetry of Ireland the defence of the Catholic faith became, towards the end of our period, linked to the defence of the country against English conquest and to notions of national identity, but this never happened in the classical poetry of Scotland, where it was never fully developed as a motif: it remained

46 See above, chapter 4, pp. 139–41, 142.

47 See above, chapter 4, p. 32 and n. 72.

48 For instance, Tadhg mac Dáire Mhic Bhruaideadha, whose patron, the fourth earl of Thomond, was a Protestant; see Dewar 2006, pp. 316, 321–2.

limited to some allusions to the patron's piety or to his patronage of the Church. Finally, royalism is yet another innovation in classical panegyric of Scotland, although only occasionally is it fully developed in the way it often is in vernacular verse.[49]

In everything else the rhetoric of panegyric of Scotland adheres to that of Ireland, but the adherence is one of quantitative degrees. For instance, references to Irish place-names are most plentiful in poetry of the early model, and particularly in Mac Domhnaill verse of any time. *Apalóga* and references to *seanchas* similarly tend to appear in poems in the earlier model. The Scottish section of the pre-classical *Airis biuc a mheic big báin*, in contrast, abounds in place-names of eastern and southern Scotland, reflecting Gaelic takeover of Pictish territory and asserting the reality of the new Gaelic kingdom of *Alba*, and while acknowledging the Irish origin of the conquering Gaels, it emphasises their new identity as *Albanaigh*.[50] It is very likely that rhetoric to the same effect (including the high-kingship of *Alba* and prophecy motifs)[51] would have been found in other poems, now lost, composed for subsequent Gaelic kings of *Alba* and until Normanisation changed the style of kingship, leading to the underdevelopment or even outright demise of several motifs — not least that of the *Goill* — and eventually to the dismissal of the royal court poets. In other words, the suggestion is that a reinterpretation or remoulding of the inherited Irish tradition to suit the Scottish context did in fact take place, lasting perhaps until the fourteenth century.[52] Classical panegyric of Scotland in general also uses considerably fewer comparisons of the subject to great Gaelic heroes of the past — the few references being principally to Cú Chulainn and Guaire — while Caimbéal verse adds a number of classical Latin and Greek references. Where such similes are found, little is told about those heroes' great deeds or the particular characteristics which gave them their renown (for instance, lavish generosity in Guaire). Neither are the subjects of the classical poems of Scotland often related back to their ancient progenitors (Clann Domhnaill again being the exception, as well as Clann Duibhne, and Clann Mhic Fhionghuin to an extent).[53] Equally rare is the recitation

---

49 See above, p. 317.
50 See above, chapter 7, pp. 294–5.
51 See above, chapter 7, pp. 293, 295, and this chapter, pp. 320, 326–7.
52 See above, chapter 7, pp. 312–13, and this chapter, pp. 320–1.
53 See below, pp. 330–1, 333.

of the patron's *caithréim*, the theme of territorial conquest by force, and the motif *fuidheall áir* ('a remnant of the slaughter'); the contexts for existing instances of these conceits and the significance of their limited presence in Scottish poetry are considered below.[54]

It may be significant that certain forms of diction (such as *cogar, guaille, rún*) reflecting the special relationship between poet and patron seem to have survived only in Clann Domhnaill verse, and that it is also for a Mac Domhnaill that the only extant poem fully developing the motif of the poet as his patron's lover was composed.[55] Some of these terms, however, especially *muirn*, the special affection between patron and poet, appear to have been preserved in vernacular verse, despite the very different relationship between the vernacular poets and their patrons, which did not entail the particular privileges that were the prerogative of the *filidh*.[56] In this context we may note that it is only for the lords of the Isles and some of the Mac Domhnaill branches (Clann Raghnaill and Clann Eóin Mhóir) that we can ascertain the patronage of hereditary poetic families in full traditional style, which included the poets' free holding of land. There is evidence, for instance, that the *filidh* attached to the earls of Argyll did not occupy their lands for free, but as a feu,[57] while by the early eighteenth century, if we are to believe Martin Martin, the old poetic privileges had generally disappeared and the *filidh* received only a small cash payment.[58]

Ancient families and upstarts

It has been noted that 'Linkage to venerable progenitors … was perhaps the single most important source of prestige for a Gaelic ruler'.[59] Allusions to ancient noble ancestors are certainly used in this way in both classical and vernacular poetry of Scotland, but in the poetry for the majority of the Scottish kindreds the general effect is rather lacklustre in comparison with the poetry composed for Irish subjects. This is the case even when we take together both classical and vernacular poems. Thus, for all the pride in Mac Leóid royal Norse ancestry, there is no mention of one

---

54 See below, pp. 340–1.
55 See above, chapter 3, p. 96.
56 See above, chapter 5, p. 238.
57 See above, chapter 4, p. 124 and n. 35.
58 See above, chapter 2, p. 41.
59 McLeod 2004, p. 118.

single ancient Gaelic progenitor of the kindred. Mac Gille Eóin poetry is totally lacking in allusions to either an eponym or some other illustrious ancestor of old. Mac Coinnigh panegyric presents a similar case, as do the poems for Clann Ghriogóir. In the case of the latter the exception is *Aithris fhréimhe ruanaidh Eoin*, whose author, Donnchadh MacGriogair, brother of the Dean of Lismore, was not a *file* and, like some other vernacular poets, appears influenced by the speculations of Lowland historians, in his case by making Clann Ghriogóir the descendants of Fearghus mac Eirc.[60] We find the same pattern in the extant poetry composed for members of most of the rest of the Scottish kindreds of Gaelic origin, with only occasional references to Míl, early ancestor of all the Gaels, or Éireamhón, from whom most Scottish Gaels stemmed. The same lack of allusions to ancient noble forbears is characteristic of poems for subjects of non-Gaelic origin, with the exceptions of Clann Duibhne, consistently celebrated as descendants of King Artúr, and Clann Leóid, praised for their lineal — albeit female-line — descent from Leód and from Olbhar. Nevertheless these originally non-Gaelic kindreds are portrayed as Gaels, notably in the case of the two that became foremost in Scotland, the Stiúbhairt and the Caimbéalaigh, both of whom additionally attempted to concoct a Gaelic ancestry for themselves in the seventeenth century.[61]

Filidh and *seanchaidhe* dismissed, or at least questioned, the later genealogical claims made by many kindreds, and generally any claims that could not be checked against the ancient records preserved by Gaelic hereditary men of learning. Caimbéal claims of descent from Diarmaid were ignored by the classical poets, Mac Firbhisigh had reservations about those of the Stiúbhairt arguing for an Irish origin, and Niall Mac Muireadhaigh put a question mark on the claims of descent from Loarn Mór made by such a suspiciously large number of kindreds.[62] It is perhaps Mac Muireadhaigh's reservation that might be problematic, for he would seem to be questioning the veracity of the Scottish Gaelic historians' own records: most of the clans that he cites as claiming such ancestry are given the same origin in the fifteenth-century 'MS 1467', written by

60 See above, chapter 5, pp. 199–200.
61 See above, chapters 4, pp. 117–18, 119, 132; 6, pp. 265, 270; 7, p. 286.
62 See above, chapters 4, pp. 120, 126–7; 5, pp. 226, 228; 6, pp. 265–6; 7, pp. 286–7.

Dubhghall Albanach, probably one of Niall's own ancestors.[63] On the other hand, Niall's reservation may not concern all of the kindreds he names, but rather those among them whose claims of royal descent from Loarn were being voiced in his own time and are likely to have arisen late: Clann Chatáin, Clann Néill, and the Morgannaigh (Clann Mhic Aoidh of Strathnaver).[64] The Morgannaigh are said by tradition to be of Irish origin but their ancestry remains obscure, but as for Clann Chatáin and Clann Néill we find a clear shift in genealogical claims. Clann Chatáin seem to have come originally from Connacht, but merged with the Mac an Tóisigh kindred in the fourteenth century,[65] perhaps beginning to claim a common descent with the latter from about that time or soon afterwards. The Mac Néill claim of royal descent from Cinéal Loairn is definitely very late, for even sixteenth-century genealogical tradition still attached the family to the eleventh-century Irish noble Anradhán (of whom, incidentally, there is no mention in poetry).[66] It is probably these novel claims that Mac Muireadhaigh was querying.

Where poets are silent with respect of ancient lineage, they seem to attempt to compensate by recalling more recent ancestors. For instance, Eachann Ruadh of Harlaw is proudly remembered in Mac Gille Eóin verse, and Griogór of the Golden Bridles in Clann Ghriogóir panegyric. Additionally, poets fill the vacuum by resorting to the friends and allies motif: they name their praised subjects' various supporters — actual or possible — and the kinship connexions they have established with noble families. This is particularly true of, but not unique to, vernacular authors, some of whom also appear to have been more easily influenced by contemporary or near-contemporary Lowland historians who attempted to link some of the Highland clans to the line of Fearghus Mór.[67] The Highland authors compiling the genealogical histories in English and Scots in the seventeenth century were similarly influenced, but we must remember that, although they were educated gentlemen, they did not belong to the hereditary families of historians, who adhered to ancient Gaelic records as persistently as

---

63 See Table 6.2.
64 *RC* ii, p. 300.
65 'De Origine et Incremento Makintoshiorum Epitome', MacFarlane 1900, pp. 163, 172.
66 See above, chapter 5, pp. 184, 190, and Table 5.2.
67 See above, chapters 5, pp. 199 and n. 68, 216; 6, pp. 245, 256.

the *filidh* did.[68] Additionally, and directly linked to this silence in respect of venerable ancient lineage, we find in the poetry a lack of references to an ancestral patrimony: clearly, if there was no knowledge of progenitors, neither would there be knowledge of their homeland or the territories they had originally held. One more thing that this particular group of kindreds has in common is that they all achieved prominence relatively late, rarely coming into light in the historical record before the fourteenth century, and in the literary — poetic — record never before the fifteenth. They probably had not been in a position to patronise hereditary men of learning until then, and therefore their history and ancestry had never been recorded, and were unknown. This would explain the silence of the poets in respect of these kindreds' early progenitors and original territories.

None of this is true for Clann Domhnaill, who are exceptional in the preservation of their ancient pedigree, in the lack of introduction of novel genealogical claims over time, and in the frequent allusions to both ancient noble ancestors and their patrimonial lands in the poetry. The consistency of their later genealogies with the earlier ones and with those produced in Ireland is quite remarkable. This consistency is maintained in the poetry, not only that composed by *filidh*, who naturally would reproduce the Gaelic historians' records faithfully, but also in vernacular verse: it is never the case that a vernacular poet, seduced by the changing fashions of the seventeenth century, attempts to link Mac Domhnaill descent to some non-Gaelic figure of the past, or to the line of Fearghus Mór. To a lesser degree — but admittedly we have very little material to go by — consistency in genealogical claims is also a feature of Clann Mhic Fhionghuin, Clann Ghuaire, and Clann Mhic Ghiolla Mhaoil. It is true that a tradition of Clann Ghuaire descent from Cinéal nGabhráin had come to develop by the seventeenth century, and that the extant vernacular Mac Fionghuin poem, by making his subject a descendant of Fearghus mac Eirc, similarly betrays an author influenced by contemporary tastes and fashions.[69] Yet the Gaelic men of learning's genealogical records for these three kindreds show no variations over time and are the same for Scotland and Ireland.[70] They are, moreover, supported by the

---

68 See above, chapter 6, pp. 245–6.
69 See above, chapter 6, p. 256.
70 See above, chapter 6, pp. 245–6 and n. 3, 246–50, and Tables 6.1 and 6.2.

anecdote related by 'Hugh of Sleat' concerning the Mac Domhnaill feast at Aros. When Eóin Mac Domhnaill, tutor of Moydart, proceeds to order the guests to be seated, he begins with Mac Domhnaill of Ardnamurchan, immediately followed by Mac Fionghuin and Mac Guaire, and then by Mac Beathadh, the *ollamh* in medicine, and Mac Muireadhaigh, the *ollamh* in poetry. The guests whom he then offends are named as Mac Gille Eóin, Mac Leóid of Lewis, Mac Leóid of Dunvegan, and Mac Néill of Barra: all of these certainly came to prominence at a relatively late time, and their genealogies all present some kind of problem or grey area at a crucial point: in Clann Leóid's case this is their agnatic connexion into a Gaelic lineage, and in the case of the others, the grafting of their pedigrees into that of the Scottish royal lines.[71]

Whether the Aros feast story is true or not is irrelevant. For our purposes it receives the same treatment as the poetic panegyric code and the genealogies: we look for the message they intended to convey to the audience. And the message we receive here is that certain families were — certainly in the writer's time, but probably much earlier too — presented as being of ancient, venerable, and well-established lineage, and others as having achieved prominence only recently, and therefore as upstarts. The question we may ask here is whether this depiction represented general consensus or whether it reflected Mac Domhnaill resentment that others outwith their own kindred had come to share key positions — such as that of councillors to the lords of the Isles — with the heads of the Clann Domhnaill cadet branches. In all probability there was a mixture of both. That the insulted families had no knowledge of their line of descent is suggested by the silence of the Irish records, against which 'MS 1467' contrasts starkly and suspiciously by supplying links to Loarn Mór for all these families.[72] There is still much research to be done on the 'MS 1467' genealogies, not least concerning the writer's sources and the purpose of their compilation. For the time being we may note that even their very lay-out itself might convey a message or hold a key: the genealogies of the families which are also recorded in Irish sources are all grouped together

---

71 *HP* i, pp. 45–6. See above, chapters 4, pp. 151–2 and n. 3, 246–50; 5, pp. 184 n. 4, 206, 209. Mac Domhnaill (or Mac Eóin) of Ardnamurchan descended from Eóin Sprangach, son of Aonghus Mór, fifth lord of the Isles; see Table 3.3.

72 See above, chapter 6, p. 248.

on the same page, neatly separated from the rest, many of which are those of the kindreds for which we have no early genealogical information in Gaelic poetry, annals, or chronicles.[73]

It is also a matter of interest why Loarn was generally so appealing, as an ancestor, for so long. It is quite striking that only the kings of Scotland — including the houses of Brús and Stiúbhart, albeit through the female line — are given descent from Fearghus Mór. It would have made sense, even before the influence of Lowland writers crept in from Boece's time on, that at least a number of kindreds would have attempted to link their pedigrees with that of the royal descendants of Fearghus. Instead, ancient royal descent from Loarn is what was consistently claimed. There may be a hint of the same trend in the learned historical literature of Ireland: Clann Aodha Bhuidhe are often said to stem from the marriage of their ancestor Muireadhach to Earc, daughter of Loarn, and Corc mac Lughach to have married Moingfhionn, daughter of Fearadhach Fionn, a descendant of Loarn.[74] Loarn's appeal remains difficult to explain. It may be due simply to the fact that links with this royal dynasty, permanently removed from the kingship in the twelfth century, would have been harder to disprove than links with the current Scottish monarchs, who preserved zealously their own genealogical records. Any attempts at fabrications by other families might have been readily and authoritatively contested by the royal *filidh* and *seanchaidhe*.

Kingdoms, identities and loyalties

'The Highland problem' is an idiom which originated in the view of the lords of the Isles, and generally the Highland and Island lords, many of whom came to be their vassals, as particularly and persistently difficult and unruly in their relationship with the crown. Some modern historians have to a point vindicated the Highlanders, and in this study we have sought further illumination by exploring the literary sources, particularly the poetry of the *filidh* as a powerful and authoritative contemporary political instrument. Seventeenth-century poetry, as well as the historical writing of Niall Mac Muireadhaigh and 'Hugh of Sleat', consistently presents Clann Domhnaill generally as loyal supporters of the house of Stiúbhart

---

73 See 'MS 1467', under 'map' link, and above, chapter 6, pp. 246–50.
74 See above, chapters 3, p. 80 and nn 116, 117; 5, p. 185.

through the centuries. But is this a deliberately coloured view which aimed to portray contemporary Mac Domhnaill royalism as a political stance unchanged since the lordship of the Isles came under Scottish jurisdiction in 1266? What to make of major Mac Domhnaill conflicts with the government, such as Harlaw (1411) or the Treaty of Ardtornish (1462)? Were the lords of the Isles ever a threat to the Scottish crown?

We must in the first place make a clear separation between the lords of the Isles, their status, identity and loyalties before and after the 1266 Treaty of Perth, by which the Isles were given up by the Norwegian kings and annexed to the Scottish crown. And we must at all times keep in mind the difference between 'kingdom' as lordship or dominion, and 'kingdom' in the more modern sense, with crown and anointment as well as many features of government characteristic of feudal kingship. The first meaning of 'kingdom' is what applies to the early Gaelic kingdom of *Alba*, born in the later ninth century, and to kingdoms contemporary with it for some three centuries. That of the Isles was in the ninth century a Norse kingdom under overlordship of the king of Norway, and it may have been around this time that Somhairle's ancestors were, if Gaelic *seanchas* has it correctly, displaced from their patrimony by the Norse invaders.[75] In the twelfth century Somhairle with his father and their kin from Ireland recovered their lands in western Scotland, and Somhairle himself eventually took possession of Man, and with it the title of king of the Isles. As such, however, he remained a vassal of the king of Norway. He was of mixed Gaelic and Norse ancestry, and it is impossible to know whether he considered himself more a Gael, as later Gaelic tradition portrays him; all that we know is that his Gaelic roots remained strong if, as *seanchas* has it, he resorted to his relatives in Ireland for assistance to regain his patrimony.[76] Two generations later, however, his grandson Domhnall mac Raghnaill, the eponym of Clann Domhnaill, is identified as Ó Colla, the use of this title suggesting a sense of continuity of the ancient Gaelic lordship of Colla's descendants. The implication has to be that Ó Colla was also the title inherited and used by Somhairle.[77] Domhnall's son Aonghus Mór

---

75 Gregory 1881, p. 12.

76 See above, chapter 3, p. 57. The impression from the sagas seems to be that Somhairle was not a Norseman (Gregory 1881, p. 11).

77 See above, chapter 3, pp. 58, 62.

already is known in the poetry as Mac Domhnaill, a style that remained from then on with the heads of the kindred. Despite the loss of Man, Mac Domhnaill chiefs kept for themselves the title of king (or lord) of the Isles. Their territorial expansion is further shown in the poetry by the use of place-names throughout the Western Isles.[78]

The relations between these early 'Scottish' lords of the Isles and the kings of *Alba* were like those between any neighbouring medieval kingdoms, sometimes of mutual support and sometimes of a conflictive nature. This was the pattern of the period of rule of Somhairle himself, and indeed he was killed when he invaded Lowland Scotland as far as Renfrew.[79] Yet Somhairle's friction with the kings of Scots had begun on account of his support of the rebellion of Maol Coluim Mac Aodha, who was connected with Cinéal Loairn of Moray[80] — the real enemies of the kings of *Alba*. The significance of this is that Somhairle's ancestors seem to have been Uí Mhac Uais, a sept which by the seventh and eighth centuries was in a subordinate position to Cinéal Loairn, involving military support to the latter.[81] Admittedly, a few centuries had passed, but it is not impossible that the sense of an expectation of mutual support may have endured. What would certainly have inclined Somhairle to back the rebellion would have been his own sister's marriage to Maol Coluim Mac Aodha.[82]

Somhairle, then, ruled by right independently from the kings of *Alba*. He was lord, or king, of the territories that had been his inheritance, and of others which he had annexed by conquest. He, and after him his successors, could also produce genealogical credentials comparable to those of the kings of *Alba*, something that, as we have seen, most other Highland and Island kindreds could not do. Moreover, if we look a little further back into the pedigrees than just to Colla Uais on the Mac Domhnaill side and to Conaire on the side of the kings of *Alba*, we will find that both lineages converge at Aonghus Tuirbheach Teamhrach, through his sons, Éanna Aighneach and Fiacha Fear Mara respectively:

---

78 See above, chapter 3, p. 63, and further *Ceannaigh duain t'athar, a Aonghas*, §§4b, 10c, 23a.

79 See, for instance, Clancy (ed.) 1998, p. 212.

80 McDonald 1997, p. 49; id.(ed.) 2002, pp. 95, 100.

81 See above, chapter 3, p. 58, n. 22.

82 For this marriage see McDonald 1997, p. 45.

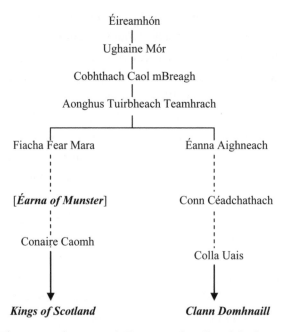

Table 8.1 The ancient lineages of Clann Domhnaill and the kings of *Alba*.
Sources: 'MS 1467', nos. 1 and 35; *RC* ii, 148–50; *LMG* ii, §418.1.

At first sight both sons of Aonghus Tuirbheach Teamhrach appear of the same status. Yet there were differences in their births and in their achievements. Éanna Aighneach was Aonghus's son by his wedded wife, while Fiacha Fear Mara was, according to *seanchas*, the product of an incestuous relationship; and Éanna came to hold the kingship of Ireland, whereas Fiacha never did.[83] There is also the question of the break in true blood-descent in the pedigree of the kings of Scotland, who stemmed not from a son of Fiacha, but from a foster-son, Oilill Éarann.[84] All in all, the Clann Domhnaill pedigree appears the more accurate and reputable of the two. As for the later royal dynasties of Scotland, Brús and Stiúbhart, Gaelic historians note their succession through the female line, but nowhere do we find any objection to them: clearly the *seanchaidhe* accepted that kingship had changed in Scotland, including female succession through the maternal line and even the validity of female sovereignty, as in the case of Mary Queen of Scots.[85]

83 See above, chapter 7, pp. 281–2 and n. 3.
84 *LMG* ii, §368.2.
85 See above, chapter 7, pp. 284, 286–7.

When we turn to the poetry we find no evidence of rivalry or antago-
nism of Somhairle's descendants towards the kings of *Alba*. In the early
poems the subjects praised are placed within their Hebridean possessions.
In the extant poetry composed in the period of rule of the Norman dynas-
ties, when the Isles were already part of the kingdom of Scotland, the sub-
jects are identified as *Albanaigh* (Norse references, understandably, losing
their emphasis) and portrayed as staunch supporters of the kingdom of
Alba, and the *Gall* motif (that is, the non-Gael as a foreign threat) is absent
from the extant poetry composed throughout the time of existence of the
lordship of the Isles. It is equally telling that the lords of the Isles are never
depicted as contenders for the kingship of *Alba*, but are rather consistently
shown as subordinate to and supportive of the kingdom of *Alba*. The same
approach is found after the downfall of Eóin mac Alasdair, tenth lord of
the Isles (†1502), when poets do not even express resentment towards
the crown for its harsh treatment of Clann Domhnaill.[86] In the panegyric
composed for members of Clann Domhnaill generally, in fact, their iden-
tification as *Albanaigh* is even stronger than in verse for other Scottish
kindreds, including the Caimbéalaigh. This pattern of support of *Alba* and
her kings finds a natural continuation in the later development of the motif
of royalism.

As well as *Albanaigh*, Clann Domhnaill are identified as *Gaoidhil*. It is
as such, and on the basis of their descent from ancestors who had held the
kingship of Ireland, that they are claimed as suitable to become Irish kings.
Of these royal ancestors the poets particularly favour Colla Uais, for he had
lived in exile in Scotland, thus explaining how his descendants had come
to settle there. The big question is why it is to Clann Domhnaill only that
this motif is applied. The answer may lie in the creation of the independent
kingdom of *Alba* and the introduction of the motif of the high-kingship of
Alba into the panegyric code, which may have been understood as replac-
ing the high-kingship of Ireland. The Gaels of the kingdom of *Alba* would
be from then on perceived as having broken away from Ireland on a perma-
nent basis — as indeed they had — and it is significant that, unlike Clann
Domhnaill, they are never portrayed as in temporary exile. The Ó Colla
chiefs remained for several centuries outwith the kingdom of *Alba*, and the

---

86 See above, chapter 3, p. 70.

poets could pretend in their eulogies that they lived in hope of their return to Ireland after their 'military expedition', a motif that would continue to be preserved in the poetry composed long after the annexation of the Isles to the Scottish crown in 1266.

If Clann Domhnall are never portrayed as contenders for the kingship of *Alba*, neither are other kindreds. The kingship, it seems well understood, belongs to the line of Fearghus, of Gabhrán, and of Maol Coluim III; all others are these monarchs' vassals. In relation to this, it is worth noting the absence of the motif of the taking of territory by force ('ar éigin'). Although it appears in the Scottish section of *Airis biuc a mheic big báin* in connexion with Dál Riada expansion,[87] it is not found in the later poetry composed for any of those kindreds that became vassals of the kings of *Alba*. It seems to have had no relevance in Scotland almost certainly because it did not apply, perhaps yet another consequence of the feudalisation of kingship and society. The related term 'cairt chloidhimh' ('sword-land') is another great absentee in the court poetry of Scotland, probably for the same reason. The two solitary instances in the Colonsay poems simply reinforce the concept of every chief as a loyal servant of the monarchy, for the sword-conquest is carried out in support of the king of Britain.[88] Even the almost complete lack of the *caithréim* motif may be yet another result of socio-political change in Scotland: we have only three instances of it and they both deal with the subject's martial prowess either within his own territories or in Ireland, never with military action against *Alba*.[89] Yet another motif which is rare in our corpus is that of 'fuidheall áir', representing the remnant of Gaels surviving foreign slaughter. In Irish poetry this often appears in the context of actual struggle against English domination, particularly from the later sixteenth century onwards, when Tudor monarchs were tightening their control.[90] In classical poetry of Scotland we find this motif in two elegies, one for Tormod Mac Leóid of Berneray and the other for Eóin Óg Mac Fionghuin. In the first, musing on the deaths in quick succession of several Mac Leóid chiefs, the poet depicts Clann Leóid as

87 See above, chapter 7, p. 294.
88 See above, chapter 3, pp. 72–3.
89 See above, chapter 3, pp. 64, 86; 4, p. 165.
90 See above, chapter 4, p. 142 and n. 110.

the remnant of Olbhar's race.[91] In the second, Clann Mhic Fhionghuin are said to be a remnant of Fearadhach Fionn's blood.[92] In both cases, then, the motif seems to have been used merely for the purpose of imagery, enhancing the poignancy of the elegies. The only instance where it is found referring to actual conflict against the English is in *Ar sliocht Gaoidheal ó Ghort Gréag* where, along with other motifs common in incitement poems, it is used to encourage the Scots forces about to meet the English army.[93] It is interesting also that the few extant incitement poems are never against the government itself: they are encouragements either to defend Scotland against the English, or to support the rightful royal line against foreign usurpers. The dearth of the motifs 'ar éigin', 'cairt chloidhimh', and *caithréim*, considered jointly with the scarcity of the *Gall* motif and the lack of incitement against royal government, would point to the success of the late-medieval kings of *Alba* not only in feudalising their kingdom but in doing so without provoking major or lasting antagonisms through the introduction of Norman families. The scarcity of the motif 'fuidheall áir', again taken jointly with the scarcity of *Gall*, would indicate that, unlike in Ireland, the Gaels of Scotland never felt under Norman threat.

All in all, the poetry offers no sign of Gaelic opposition to the crown, and no perception of the later Scottish monarchs as foreigners, despite their Norman origins. The Gaelic and Gaelicised kindreds conceive themselves as culturally Gaelic, but as members and loyal supporters of the kingdom of Scotland. The literature shows no animosity towards kindreds of Norman ancestry who, while *Goill* on account of their ethnic origins, for most of our period are not the *Goill* enemy of the panegyric code motif. This changed by the seventeenth century, when some classical poets began to use, as vernacular authors did, the word *Goill* to represent the enemies of the house of Stiúbhart generally, including the English ones. This shift in meaning is closely connected with the development of the motif of royalism. Here the poets, by giving so much emphasis to the representation of Stiúbhart support as a Gaelic concern, found in the *Goill* motif the ideal label for the enemies of the Stiúbhairt: this framed the contemporary circumstances within the centuries-old panegyric code

---

91 See above, chapter 4, p. 166.

92 See above, chapter 6, p. 255.

93 See above, chapter 4, p. 142.

motif of the struggle between *Gaoidhil* and *Goill*, lending powerful reso-
nances that would greatly add to the incitement or the political comment
in their poems. Where *Gall* refers to Lowland persons or affairs, it is often
in connexion with concern for the decline of Gaelic society and traditional
ways which, ironically, had so much to do with attacks on the Gaels by the
Stiúbhart monarchs themselves.

The fact that not even in *A chlanna Chuinn, cuimhnichibh*, the incite-
ment poem traditionally associated with the battle of Harlaw, is the enemy
identified as *Goill* is surely of significance, as must be the fact that what
led to the encounter was not Clann Domhnaill opposition to the crown,
but their resistance, and their allies', to the greedy schemes of a regent
who ignored Mac Domhnaill's legitimate claim to the earldom of Ross.[94]
Significant must be also that throughout the late medieval and early
modern period the government generally tended to turn its attention to
the Highlands and Isles only when conflict flared up, producing the impres-
sion that what history we obtain of the relations between the crown and
their subjects in the north and west was one of sustained friction. Perhaps
less consideration has been given to the fact that the Gaelic and Gaelicised
kindreds regularly appear supporting the kings of Scots in their various
military enterprises, including major battles.[95] In this context, the incite-
ment poem related to the battle of Flodden — of 'fierce national spirit',
of 'pan-Gaelic solidarity against the English enemy ... with the entire
Scottish nation, Lowland as well as Highland'[96] — makes perfect sense; as
suggested by W. J. Watson,[97] there may well have been other poems, now
lost, whose authors abandoned the customary Gaelic in-house outlook,
transferring and adapting its themes to embrace the wider national cause.
Seventeenth-century royalism, historical and literary, might be seen as a
continuation or natural development of this pattern of royal support. As
regards military alliances with Ireland, most of these involved assistance by
redshanks (temporary mercenaries) to the Irish in their conflicts, among
themselves or with the English king — but then again the Scottish kings

---

94 See above, chapter 3, pp. 71–2.
95 See above, chapters 3, p. 58 and n. 21; 4, pp. 156, 158; 5, pp. 202, 211, 212, 228–9; 6, pp.
    251–2, 267–8.
96 *SVBDL*, p. 90; *DnS*, p. 241.
97 *SVBDL*, p. 290.

themselves participated in Irish politics sometimes, particularly through the provision of artillery and weapons.[98] The reverse, the recruitment of Irish soldiers by Scottish Gaels, was far more rare, one exception taking place during the mid seventeenth-century Wars of the Three Kingdoms, when the Gaels were backing the royal cause, not opposing it.

Indeed the alliance of Eóin mac Alasdair, tenth lord of the Isles, with the English king through the 1462 treaty of Ardtornish stands alone as the one clear instance of deliberate threat to the kingdom of Scots, and therefore it deserves particular attention. We know that Eóin was not a good leader, that his lordship had by his time grown to a size difficult to handle and that his period of rule became plagued by internal division. Could Eóin's pact with the English king, which eventually led to his own ruin, be one last desperate attempt by a poor leader to save his lordship from collapse?[99] There is certainly further work for historians to do here, particularly given the fact that in his historical narrative Niall Mac Muireadhaigh, who regularly praises other lords of the Isles and notes their achievements, has little to say about Eóin.[100] He certainly skirts over the joint Mac Domhnaill-England scheme to invade Scotland, perhaps considering it an embarrrasment in the history of a kindred whom otherwise he is at pains to present as loyal supporters of the Scottish crown rather than its potential rivals. There is really nothing to suggest that Mac Domhnaill chiefs viewed themselves as anything other than vassals of the Scottish king. Even their burials at Iona seem to support this acknowledgment of their own place within the hierarchy. Dean Monro tells us that in the graveyard at Iona there were 'three tombs of stanes formit like little chapellis'. In the middle one were buried the ancient 'Scottish' kings, while the one to its south side contained the mortal remains of some Irish kings, and the one to its north side those of several kings of Norway. Whatever accuracy there may be in these lines, what interests us is the tradition that the lords of the Isles — as well as members of the Mac Gille Eóin, Mac Fionghuin, and Mac Guaire families — were also buried in the same graveyard, but not within any of the

---

98 See, for instance, Bradshaw 1979, at pp. 21–2, 33–4; Boardman 2012. For a brief overview of redshank phenomenon see McLeod 2004, pp. 49–52. See also above, chapter 5, pp. 212, 213.

99 A similar desperate measure was taken by Domhnall Dubh in 1545; see above, chapter 3, p. 62 n. 38.

100 *RC* ii, p. 162.

three royal mausolea.[101] This suggests an acknowledgement of hierarchy and of the various individuals' place and standing, clearly leaving Clann Domhnaill outside royalty and on a par, it would seem, with other vassals of the real kings.

The picture emerging from Gaelic poetry is then, above all, one of well-adjusted affinity, one that blurs rather than unveils the differences,[102] contrary to what one might expect in the culturally strong and conservative group that traditional Gaelic society — at least at élite level — has always been recognised to be. Despite the overall unchanging make-up of the language of authority obtained from the schools, the poets were capable, through the silencing of some motifs and the adaptation of others, of applying it as changing circumstances required. In this way, for instance, the high-kingship of *Alba* was born, the *Gaoidheal-Gall* barrier skirted over — but brought in, and reworked if necessary, when appropriate — and unswervingly loyal service to the king made to replace the motif of suitability for the high-kingship. Neither is there any question in the poetry, classical as well as vernacular, of where loyalties lie when Scotland becomes part of the kingdom of Britain: this can be nowhere but with the true king, he who is entitled to the throne by God-given right and by his lineage. Here all the weight previously placed on the Gaelic chief's loyalty to the king of Scotland is thrown in support of the Stiúbhart kings of Britain, so that royalism is presented as a fundamentally Gaelic affair. The poets' ability to accommodate all this within the traditional panegyric code of the schools' curriculum, which in the main reflected very different socio-political conditions in Ireland, is a remarkable achievement. It is also a testimony to the success of a largely non-confrontational Normanisation process of the kingdom of Scots: to the acceptance of change to the degree that change itself is incorporated into the values of traditional Gaelic society and made its own.

So we have it from poetic authority.

---

101 *Monro*, pp. 62–3.

102 The most striking examples are the assimilation of the Gaelicised *Goill*, and of the Stiúbhart supporters generally, into the ranks of the Gaels, and the adoption of the Lowland prophet Thomas the Rhymer as the guarantor of the success of both the Gaels and the Stiúbhairt.

Appendix 1

Námha an cheird nach taithighthear

The poem below is edited from NLS 72.1.48 (fo. 31), a seventeenth-century manuscript almost certainly produced by the Mac Muireadhaigh family of hereditary poets to Clann Raghnaill. The name of the scribe of our poem is unknown, although he was a contemporary of Niall Mac Muireadhaigh (*c*.1639–*c*.1726).[1] Neither do we know the author's name, but several Scotticisms in the text (§§6d, 8d) give away his Scottish origin. What we know for certain is that he was a *file* and that in this piece he satirises the untrained poets who in his time were seeking, and obtaining, noble patronage, thus beginning to displace the *filidh*. Similar poetic complaints are well attested in contemporary Ireland, while further Scottish instances are Cathal Mac Muireadhaigh's §§28–9 in *Éireochthar fós le Clainn gColla*, and his kinsman Niall's *Nár lém choisnes tu clú Chuinn*, an attack on the Irish poet Eóghan Ó Donnghaile, and *T'aire riut, a Ghiolla-easbuig*, on some unknown untrained poet.[2] Sometimes, as in our poem (§1cd), we find embedded criticism of the patrons themselves for their support of upstart, uneducated poets.

There is a hint of the same in *Sona do cheird, a Chalbhaigh* (§§10, 12), and other similarities between the this poem and *Námha an cheird nach taithighthear*, in terms of topic, mood, and style, suggest that Cathal may well have been also the author of the present piece. In both poems ignorant poets are noted for their greed-driven aim to obtain a place in the noble house- holds — when, according to their station, they should be occupied in the work of a peasant (§7)[3] — and satirised for their performance (in more than

---

1 See Mackinnon 1912, p. 98; Mackechnie 1973, p. 205; and Black, *Catalogue*, p. 351 for the most recent description.

2 See Black 1976–8, pp. 336–7, and above, chapter 3, pp. 40 and n. 74, 100. There seems to be a similar complaint of declining patronage of *filidh* in another poem by Cathal, *Cionnas mhaireas mé am aonar*; see Thomson 1977, pp. 239–40.

3 For the same criticism in vernacular poetry see above, chapter 4, pp. 75–6.

one way) there. In *Sona do cheird, a Chalbhaigh* Cathal decries not only such a poet's poor versification skills, but also his inordinate appetite, abuse of drink, and deplorable table manners – telling, sure-fire signs of his humbler and uneducated origin.[4] In our poem the author ridicules the upstart poets' adoption of the nobility's form of dress (§§3–5) and, apparently, their transposition, and consequent debasement, of the mystical concept of the poet as his patron's lover into another form of inordinate appetite – sexual in this instance (see §§3, 6, 7 and notes). Pointing also to the suggested authorship of this piece is the presence an English loan-word (*geimhsean*, §5b), almost certainly a deliberate usage of the sort noted by Black in *Sona do cheird, a Chalbhaigh*.[5] There is little doubt that the noted Scotticisms are similarly calculated: resort to the vernacular language is part of the apparatus of satire in this type of poem,[6] the implication being that an untrained poet, unable to master the classical language, can only be – and only deserves to be – addressed in this manner.

If Cathal Mac Muireadhaigh is the author of our piece, then we can date it to this poet's *floruit* (*c*.1600–1650). The metre is *ógláchas* of *ae freislighe*, $7^3 + 7^2$, with metrical irregularities at §§4abcd, 6b and 7c (see notes). Punctuation, lenition and length marks have been supplied and contractions expanded silently where required by standardisation. The last word in §1a and the second in §6a have been tentatively reconstructed as *taithighthear* and *feirrde*. Words in brackets are not in the manuscript. The spelling has been regularised and classical forms restored as required by the metre. I am indebted to Colm Ó Baoill and Ronald Black for criticising a previous draft of this edition and providing many useful suggestions and corrections. For any errors that remain I alone am responsible.

---

4 *Sona do cheird, a Chalbhaigh*, §§4–8; *Éireochthar fós le Clainn gColla*, §28.
5 See Black 1976–8, pp. 337–8. See also above, chapter 3, p. 100.
6 Black 1976–8, p. 338.

Text and translation

1   Námha an cheird nach taithighthear,
    aithnim ar dhaoinibh éigin.
    An éigse ó nach aithnighthear
    ní anann-se i n-éintigh.

The unpractised craft is an enemy, I
know it from certain persons. Because
learning is not known, it does not stay
in any house.

2   Díoth eolais na healadhna
    tug a fuath ar na daoithibh
    acht beagán, dom bhreathnachadh,
    nach nochtfa dona daoinibh.

Lack of knowledge of art has made
the churls hate it, with the exception
of a few people — in my judgement
— who will not come forward.

3   Buidhean mhómhar mhóirléantach —
    mór an t-ochain don tsuirigh.
    Ní chaithead acht cróichéadach.
    Mo thruaighe, beart na buidhne!

A pompous, large-shirted band —
great is the sighing of the wooing.
They wear only a saffron garment.
Alas, the band's apparel!

4   I gcruth aois ealadhna
    bíd ag siubhal gacha críche:
    i n-éadach da n-eascaraid
    minic bhias an mac tíre.

They travel every district in the guise
of learned men: the wolf often is in
the clothes of its enemy.

1   Namha an chird nach < >dher
    aithnim ar dhaoinuibh egin
    a neigsi onach aithnuidhther
    ní anansi a eintoigh
2   Dioth eolus na healahdna
    tug afuath air na daoithibh
    acht began dom brenachadh
    nach nochdfa dona daoinibh
3   Buidhen mhomur mhor lentach
    mor an tochuin don tsuiridh
    ni chaithead acht crochedach
    mo thruaighe bert na buidhne
4   A cruth aois ealadhna
    bid ag suibhal gacha criche
    an dach da nescaraid
    minic a bhias an mac tire

5   Lucht leabhar do nemhfhéachuin:
    cróch is geimhsean dá léintibh.
    gá miste a mbeadh deaghéadaigh
    's go mbí síoda insna béistibh?

[They are] people who never look at
books, who apply saffron and gentian
to their shirts – what harm would fine
clothes be when there is silk on beasts?

6   Ní feirrde na fíorbhodaigh
    a bheith lán do leabhraibh maithe:
    re gearrán an tsíorshodair
    cuirear srian an eich aice.

Real churls are not the better for being
full of good books: to the ever-trotting
nag is fitted her steed's bridle.

7   Dar éis eirghe ón ealadhain
    ní tráth dá dhéanamh dhoibh-sin,
    ní chuireann acht fear mearaidh
    a lámh i gceann bó maoile.

After rising from poetry-making, they
have no time to do it: only a farmer [?]
puts his hand to the head of a hornless
cow.

8   Agra shalach shuisleannach
    an dámh do-ní go dána.
    Do chobhair na cuideachta
    ní chuir mise acht námha.

The poet-band boldly make
a dirty, arrogant claim.
To assist the company
I will just send an enemy.

                    Námha an cheird

                              The craft is an enemy

5   Lucht leabur do nemhfhechuin
    croch is geimhsun da lentibh
    ga miste ambheadh degh eaduidh
    is go mbi sida annsna beisdibh
6   Ni fer<   > fior bhodidh
    a bheith lan do leabhruibh maith
    re gerran a tsior thsodair
    cuirar srian a neich aice
7   Dar eis eirghe o nealadhuin
    ni trath da dhenamh dhoibhsin
    ni chuiran acht fer meruidh
    alamh acenn bo maoile
8   Agra shalach shuislinnach
    an damh do ni go dana
    do chobhuir na cuidechta
    ni chuir misi acht namha
    namh an chird

Notes

1   *a* The beginning of the last word in this line is missing, as the manuscript is badly worn here. Mackinnon 1912, perhaps having seen the full word before the manuscript further deteriorated, gives *tathuidher* as the last word in this line, as does Mackechnie 1973. Black, *Catalogue* gives *[caithf]idher*. I propose the present passive of *taithigid / tathaigid* 'frequenting, resorting; practising, observing' (*DIL* T 56: 76, 86). The future *caithfid-hear*, rather than the present *caithtear*, does provide a thee-syllable word as required by the metre, but does not represent classical use.

3   *c Léine chróich*, worn by the noble warrior class, both in Gaelic Scotland an Ireland; see, for instance, Grant and Cheape 1987, pp. 48–9, 126–7.
     This quatrain might seem to refer to the convention of the poet as his patron's lover. But while this is all about true love and tender feelings, here we have a picture of the debasement of that mystical relationship. The ignorant poet is depicted as merely looking for sex: loud sighing or groaning (*ochain*) is what is on his mind, and in preparation all he wears is a shirt.

4   *a* and *c* are one syllable too short, while *b* and *d* have one extra syllable each. I suggest *i n-éadach* to obtain the correct syllabic count in *c*. In the case of *d* I have, to the same effect, removed the word *a*, a particle characteristic of the Scottish vernacular relative future.
     The second couplet may be inspired by the wolf clad in a sheep's skin in Aesop's well-known fable, but alternatively might be a biblical reference: 'Beware of false prophets, who come to you in sheep's clothing, but inwardly they are ravening wolves' (Mt 7: 15).

5   *b* Again, an allusion to the ignorant poets pretentiously replicating the dress of the warrior nobility.
     geimhsean 'gentian': I am indebted to Ronald Black for this rendering.
     cd The meaning is unclear. It might be that the author is comparing the pretentious unlearned poets in their fine clothing to fine-furred animals. But perhaps the poet is encouraging his fellow professionals not to be discouraged by the pathetic efforts of ignorants and to press on with true art.

6   *b maithe* required, but gives an extra syllable to this line.
     d There are two Scotticisms in this line: *cuirear*, for *cuirthear*, and *aice*, used to express possession only in vernacular Scottish Gaelic.
     cd The meaning seems to be that the steed is the *file*, the nag the untrained poet, and the bridle the books with which the latter equips himself in imitation of the true professional. But Ronald Black brings to my attention that we may have further sexual imagery here, *sodar* having a second meaning, 'copulating', in Scottish Gaelic.

7   *ab* Here it is possible to detect a mocking sexual innuendo once again: bad poetry, like sex, is made in a horizontal position, good poetry in a vertical one. This sense may also be confirmed by the lenition in *dhéamah*, implying that 'it' is a masculine, while both *eirghe* and *ealadha* are feminine words.
     c fear mearaidh is obscure. It is tempting to take this as *fearmaraigh*, for 'farmers', which would give the required three-syllable word, although the rime is poor. While we do have *feirmeoirí* in modern Irish (Dinneen 1927 and Ó Dónaill 1977, *s.v. feirmeoir*,

nothing of the kind is attested in the earlier forms of the language, although *fermērecht* is attested (*DIL* F, 92: 42–4). Perhaps we could read *fear mearaghaidh* (from *merugad / merachad*, 'wandering, going astray; erring; confusion, error', *DIL* M, 109: 25–6, 39; 'derangement... confusion, mental aberration', Dinneen 1927 and Ó Dónaill 1977, *s.vv. mearadh* and *mearú*). This would give the line an extra syllable, but improve the rime.

An alternative rendering might be: 'Only a deranged person puts his hand to the head of a hornless cow [i.e., becomes involved in the tending of cattle] after rising on account of art – it is no time for them to do it', that is, once they have succeeded in finding patronage for their poetry, they would be mad to return to a churl's occupation.

8 *a shuisleannach*: seems a derivative of *soisle* 'haughtiness, arrogance' (*DIL* S, 333: 34). Cf. Dwelly 1977: *soislean* 'firm or bold standing'.
   d ní chuir: a Scotticism, for *ní chuirfead*, possibly deliberate (see above, p. 375)
   cd The enemy the poet intends to send seems to be his own 'unpractised craft' (as defined in §1a) which he has now turned into this satire.

Appendix 2

Panegyric code motifs: selected glossary

The following list is given as a tool to facilitate understanding of medieval and early modern Gaelic poetry generally, but is the product of a search for those motifs more specifically concerned with the sanction of political leadership. It is therefore not complete. Much could be added to it, especially kennings and stylistic devices, for some more of which see *TD* i: li–lxii, Watson 1914–19, pp. 209–16, McCaughey 1989, Ní Suaird 1999, McLeod 2002b, 2003, 2004, and *Lasair*, pp. xix–xxvii, 525–7.

absent patron	the poet may note the subject's absence as a reason for decline in his territory (internal dissension, inclement weather, poor harvests, etc). He may complain of his lover's absence (see **poet, subject's lover**), or criticise the subject if he absents himself frequently
adage	the poet quotes a proverb or adage to illustrate or argue his point
Anglicisation	a complaint of or attack on an individual's (patron, another poet, or other) adoption of non-Gaelic language, dress or custom; see also **Gaelic ways**
airdrí	'high-king', but merely a complimentary term rather than expressing actual high-kingship; see also **high-kingship**
Alba	a reference to Scotland
Albanaigh	'Scots'. In late Irish poetry, often the Scots planters in Ireland
allies / friends	the poet names those willing to support his subject; see also **following**
anbhuain	'trouble', 'distress', often in the depiction of Ireland as a woman in distress, and of the subject as the one who can rescue her
animal	the subject, if praised, is portrayed as or compared to a noble animal (e.g., lion, hawk, bear, salmon); if satirised, he is portrayed as or compared to an ignoble animal (wolf, pig, hen)

apalóg [**pl.** *apalóga*]   the poet narrates a story from Gaelic, classical Latin or
  see also **Biblical, Latin,**   Greek, continental, Biblical or other traditions to illustrate
  Greek, Arthurian,   or argue his point
  continental, *seanchas*

apologue
  see *apalóg*

ar éigin   'by force', a reference to the acquisition of territory by
  conquest

art, death of   the subject's death is said to herald the end of art /
  learning

Arthurian   a reference to Arthurian tradition, comparing the subject
  to one of its heroes; see also *apalóg*

athardha   'fatherland', 'patria', a reference to the subject's homeland,
  frequently meaning Gaelic territory, and in later Irish
  poetry the whole of Ireland

athroinn [**pl.** *athronna*]   'new division', a reference, based on the various territorial
  divisions of Ireland, to yet a fresh division, normally
  within a context of struggle

baile is leath Alban
  see *taigh is leath Alban*

banner   a motif closely connected with the **warrior** motif. In
  eulogies the poet may refer to the subject's banners on the
  battlefield, in elegies to their inactive, unused condition.

bard [**pl.** *baird*]   a reference to a poet of a category inferior to that of *file*,
  and who formed part of a *file*'s retinue

battle-roll
  see *caithréim*

beauty   a reference to the subject's pleasant appearance through
  established conventions such as 'white palm', 'soft hair',
  'blue eyes', etc

beloved of poets   the subject is said to be the 'darling of poets' (often
  leannán fileadh, leannán na sgol) on account of his
  generous patronage of the *filidh*

Biblical   a reference to a Biblical character to whom the subject is
  compared; see also *apalóg*

boats / seafaring   praise of the subject's magnificent boats and / or seafaring
  skills

brath
  see **expectation**

Breatainn   a reference to Britain

Britain
  see *Breatainn*

Caimbéal attack	within the context of **royalism**, an expression of hostility towards the Caimbéalaigh as enemies of the house of Stiúbhart as well as of the Gaels
cairt	reference to a charter to justify a particular claim or right. *Cf. **cairt chloidhimh**, **cairt chinnidh***
cairt [chinnidh]	'charter-right', a reference to entitlement to a territory by written charter; a sub-class of the **written word** motif. see also ***seinleabhair***
cairt chloidhimh	'sword-right', a reference to entitlement to a territory through military conquest
caithréim	'battle-roll', recitation of the subject's military victories
candle	the subject is compared to a candle or torch; in elegies, he is usually depicted as an extinguished candle
ceannas Gaoidheal*	'the headship of the Gaels', a reference to the subject's leadership of, or suitability to lead, the Gaels
celestial	the subject is compared to the sun, the moon or the stars
character qualities	the subject is praised for his character qualities, e.g., kindness, nobility, mercy, justice
Children of Israel	within the context of **royalism**, a comparison of the plight of the Stiúbhart supporters to that of the biblical Children of Israel in exile in the desert; see also **Moses**
Church	a reference to the subject's patronage of the Church
— **attacks not**	during his military activities the subject will spare ecclesiastical property
— **patron / protector**	a reference to the subject's generous patronage of the Church, including protection, endowments and repairs to buildings
— see also **religion**	
churls see **upstarts, social**	
cniocht	'knight', normally denoting a foreign warrior
cogar see *rún*	
continental	a reference to a historical or tale hero from continental tradition, to whom the subject is compared; see also *apalóg*
courtier	a reference to the subject's presence at the royal court; see also *cúirt* and **royal favour**
creideamh agus athardha	a political ideology, emerging in Ireland in the later sixteenth century and mostly found in seventeenth century poetry and prose, defining Irishness as having been born in Ireland, having the Gaelic language, and being a Catholic

cúirt — 'court', a reference to the subject's presence at the (English, Scottish or British) royal court, usually as a recipient of royal favour

Danar [pl. *Danair*]
    see also *Dubhghall*,
    Gall
— originally 'a Dane', but in the classical period normally synonymous with *Gall* and *Dubhghall* and denoting 'an Englishman'

dancing — a reference to the dancing at the subject's feasts; closely connected with the motifs of **feasting**, **hospitality** and **liberality**

darling of poets
    see **beloved of poets**

defender
    see **protector**

divine right — defence of the subject's entitlement to rule as a God-given right and duty; see also **Providence**, **Providentialism**

division

— among Gaels — poetic warning against internal divisions among the Gaels when they are opposing foreign threat

— of territory
    see *athroinn*

drinking — a reference to the patron's and his guests' lavish drinking, closely connected with the motifs of **feasting**, **hospitality** and **liberality**

Dubhghall [pl. *Dubhghaill*] — originally a Danish invader, but in the classical period normally synonymous with *Gall* and *Dubhghall* and denoting 'an Englishman'

education — a reference to the subject's high standard of education

exemplum
    see *apalóg*

exile — within the context of **royalism**, a reference to the subject's imposed exile abroad on account of his loyalty to the true king

expectation — (*brath, súil*), often in expressions such 'expectation of combat', 'expectation of prosperity', and so on, describing the subject

exposed to attack — the depiction of people and territory as exposed to enemy attack due to the subject's absence; a motif common in elegies, but found also in poems complaining of the subject's absence for other reasons

faith and fatherland
    see *creideamh agus athardha*

faithche green or lawn in front of the subject's fort or residence; often referred to as within the venue of social occasions, in connexion with the motif of **hospitality**

fatherland
    see *athardha*

fame a reference to the subject's current fame, or that which he will achieve through poetic praise, for martial exploits, liberality, etc

feabhas 'excellence', a reference to the subject's pre-eminence in qualities, state and actions, normally as qualifying him to be his people's leader

feasting a reference to the patron's love of feasting, closely connected with the motifs of **hospitality** and **liberality**

file [**pl.** *filidh*] a qualified poet trained in the professional schools

fir Alban 'the men of Scotland'; in the later period often having a negative connotation, in Ireland meaning the Scottish planters, and in Scotland the Lowland enemies, often of the house of Stiúbhart

fire, smouldering often in incitement poems, where the subject is described as smouldering flame about to burst into flames and destroy the enemy

five provinces a reference to the **high-kingship** of Ireland, formerly divided in to five districts

fleadh '[drinking-]feast'; see **drinking** and **feasting**

following a reference to the military support that the subject has or may expect; see also **allies / friends**

foreigners
    see *Gall*

fortune
    see **rath**

friends and allies
    see **allies / friends**

fuidheall [sometimes *iarsma*] 'a remnant', often in incitement poems to indicate the patron and his people, or the Gaels generally who, having been severely decimated by foreign enemies, are now about to make a comeback

Gaedheal [**pl.** *Gaedhil*]
    see *Gaoidheal*

Gael
    see *Gaoidheal*

Gaelic ways a reference to traditional Gaelic language, culture and society, normally in poems condemning Anglicisation and / or threat to the native system; see also **poet poverty**

Gall [pl. *Gaill*, *Goill*]	a non-Gael, a foreigner. In Irish poetry generally denoting the English enemies, but indicating ethnicity, without any negative connotations, if the subject is of mixed Anglo-Irish ethnicity. In Scottish poetry this reference is rare and tends to be a mere motif depicting the subject as the defender of his territory and enemy against foreign threat.
Galldacht	'foreignness', indicating English connection, fashion, ways, always with a negative connotation
gaming	a reference to the playing of board games on social occasions, closely connected with the motifs of **feasting** and **hospitality**
Gaoidheal [pl. *Gaoidhil*]	'a Gael'
Gaoidheal is Gall	'a Gael and a non-Gael', usually to compliment the subject by depicting him as above all generally. Sometimes factual in the description of the subject's command of both Gaels and non-Gaels
genealogy	recitation of the subject's genealogy, to proclaim his prestige, to prove his claim, or both
generosity	a reference to the subject's unfailing bounty
— to poets	a reference to the subject's generosity to the poet class
— to strangers	a reference to the subject's generosity to travellers and strangers
— to the Church	a reference to the subject's generosity to the Church; see also **Church**
— to the poor	a reference to the subject's generosity to widows, orphans and the poor generally
Greek	a reference to a hero from classical Greek tradition, comparing the subject to one of its heroes; see also *apalóg*
grian	'sun', often *grian na nGaoidheal* ('the sun[light] of the Gaels',), a complimentary description of the subject praised
grief	
— beyond Gaels' region	general grief after the subject's death not confined to the Gaelic milieu
— general	a reference to general grief after the subject's death
— poet's see **poet's grief**	
guaille	another form for *guala*
guala	'shoulder', a reference to the poet's right to sit by the chief at drinking time
headship of the Gaels see *ceannas Gaoidheal*	

high-kinship	originally a reference to the subject's suitability to become high-king of Ireland (see also **five provinces, prophecy, Tara**). The motif of the high-kingship of *Alba* seems to have been in place by at least the eleventh century and to have been abandoned during the classical period, perhaps in the early fourteenth century
historical reference	a brief reference (as opposed to a fully developed *apalóg*) to a famous character or event of the past. The subject praised is often compared to ancient heroes, whether from Gaelic or other traditions. See also **Arthurian, Biblical, classical Greek, classical Latin, continental,** *seanchas*
hospitality	a reference to the subject's lavish hospitality
hostages	a reference to the subject's capability to obtain hostages
house	praise of the subject's magnigicent mansion/s
house and a half of Scotland see *taigh is leath Alban*	
hunting	a reference to the subject's love for and skills in hunting
hunting rights	a metaphor by which a subject's territorial sway is described as his hunting rights
imagery see **animal, plant, celestial**	
iuchair	'a guide', often *iuchair na nGaoidheal* ('the guide of the Gaels'), a complimentary description of the subject praised
joy	a reference to the subject as his people's and the poets' joy
judgement	a reference to the subject's capacity for good judgement
kind and harsh	a reference portraying the subject as kind to his friends but harsh to enemies and evildoers
kinship connections	a reference to the subject's noble blood connections, who are sometimes named
knight see *cniocht*	
justice	a reference to the chief as fulfilling his duty of ensuring justice to his people
Lámh Dhearg	'Red Hand', a motif which in poetry of Scotland claims such right for Clann Domhnaill. An early-seventeenth-century Irish poetic debate about this claim was joined by Niall Mac Muireadhaigh
Latin	a reference to a hero from classical Latin tradition, comparing the subject to one of its heroes; see also *apalóg*

law and order	a reference to the chief as fulfilling his duty of maintaining law and order within his territory. A motif closely connected to **marauders and evildoers**
law-abiding	a reference to the subject as law-abiding
legal	the use by the poet of legal terminology and / or argument in defence of his case
lordly traits see *tréidhe tighearna*	
lorg a shinnsear	'[in] his ancestors' footsteps', the poetic claim that the subject reciprocates, in personal qualities and gallant deeds, his noble forbears
marauders and evildoers	a reference to the chief duty to punish evildoers. A motif closely connected to **law and order**
mìorùn	'ill will', a motif of Scottish vernacular poetry representing the *Goill* as hostile to the *Gaoidhil*
Monadh	a poetic name for Scotland
Moses	within the context of **royalism**, an invocation of the biblical Moses in connexion with his leadership of the **Children of Israel**
muirn	the special 'favour' or 'esteem' due to an *ollamh* from his chief
music	a reference to the playing of music at the subject's residence, closely connected with the motifs of **feasting** and **hospitality**
nature	the 'pathetic fallacy', a depiction of good weather and nature as lavish under the right ruler, and of inclement weather and nature as barren upon his death or in satire
nobility	a reference to the subject's noble blood
— of character see **character qualities**	
patria see *athardha*	
learning	
— patron of	a reference to the subject's patronage of learning
— subject's see **education**	
Ó Maol Chiaráin	the poet compares his own grief after the death of his subject to that of the poet Ó Maol Chiarán after his son's death
Oisein	the poet compares his own grief to that of Oisein after the passing of the Fianna
omen	(often *mana*, *séan*, *tuar*), the depiction of the subject as an omen of prosperity, peace, martial victories, and so on

peace	a reference to the subject's duty and capacity to bring about and maintain peace in his territory
plant	the praised subject is portrayed as or compared to a noble plant or tree (e.g., oak, hazel, apple-tree) or its fruit (e.g. acorn, apple, berry)
poet	
— **grief: poet must leave**	the poet's grief upon his subject's death is such that he will leave the territory
— **grief: poet weakened**	the poet is physically and mentally weakened by grief for his dead subject
— **in subject's company**	a reference to the patronage and friendship given by the subject to the poet
— **subject's lover**	a motif portraying the poet as his subject's lover
poet poverty	a motif by which the poet portrays himself as living in abject hardship as a consequence of lack of noble patronage; see also **Gaelic ways**
prophecy	originally the depiction of the subject as the prophesied one who will defeat and banish the *Goill* from Ireland and become her high-king. The prophet may be an Irish saint or a hero from historical or tale tradition; see also **five provinces**, **high-kingship**, **Tara**. But prophecy in Scottish vernacular poetry see **Thomas the Rhymer**
prosperity see *rath*	
protector	
— **of land's honour**	a reference to the subject as the protector of the honour of the land
— **of people**	a reference to the subject as his people's protector
— **of poet**	a reference to the subject as the protector of the poet, and of learned men generally
— **of true faith** see **religion**	
proverb see **adage**	
Providence	a reference to Divine Providence as the regulator of human affairs; see also **divine right**, and *cf.* **Providentialism**
Providentialism	a later motif which presented the current political conditions as brought about by evil, and their improvement subject to repentance and moral behaviour. See also **sin and punishment**
raiding	a reference to the patron as a successful raider
rath	'fortune', a motif, common in Scottish poems, which praises the subject for his great wealth

Red Hand
    see *Lámh Dhearg*

religion

— **Heaven earned**   a motif which claims that the subject's devoutness and general righteous behaviour has already earned him Heaven

— **piety**   a reference to the subject's devoutness

— **true faith**   the representation of the subject as the defender of the true faith, typically the Catholic religion

rights and duties   a reference to the rights and duties entered by poet and patron through their contractual relationship

rí   'king' but, unless referring to a king of Scotland, England, France, and so on, with the sense of 'lord', 'ruler' rather than indicating kingship in contemporary western-European style. Often merely a compliment or a term of affection

roads and bridges   a reference to the legal obligation of the chief to build and repair land communication systems

roinn
    see *athroinn*

royal
    see **nobility**

royal favour   a motif presenting the subject as the recipient of royal favour, often implying his frequent presence at the royal court; see also **courtier**

royalism   from the seventeenth century onwards, support for the house of Stiúbhart against monarchs of foreign extraction; see also **divine right**, *fir Alban*, **wheel of fortune**

rún   'secret', a reference to the poet's right to right to share the chief's secret or confidence; sometimes *cogar*, 'whisper'

Sasainn   England

Sasanach [pl. *Sasanaigh*]   English

seanchas   a reference to Gaelic history or pseudo-history, comparing the subject to one of its heroes; see also *apalóg*

seinleabhair   'ancient books', often cited in poetry to justify a claim; a sub-class of the **written word** motif; see also *cairt [chinnidh]*

shower   a representation, common in elegies, of the subject's death as the darkness brought upon the earth by a rain shower

sin and punishment   a later motif which presented the current political conditions as punishment for sin; see also **Providentialism**

slat na ríghe   'the wand of sovereignty', an allusion to the white rod received by a chief at the inauguration ceremony

spouse	a motif portraying the subject as suitable to become his territory's lover or spouse. When the territory is equated with the whole of the isle of Ireland the motif is a reference to the **high-kingship**
submission	see *umhla*
súil	see **expectation**
sword	depicted as abandoned in a rack and inactive after the subject's death; *cf.* **banner**
taigh is leath Alban	'a house and a half', a motif which claims for Clann Domhnaill 'a house and half' of Scotland
Tara	the reference may be to the subject's descent from a high-king of Ireland, or to his suitability to become Ireland's high-king; see also **five provinces, high-kingship, prophecy**
tax	a reference to the subject's capability to obtain the tax due to him. Often in the expression *cíos is cáin* ('tax and tribute'). See also **tribute**
Thomas the Rhymer	a reference to Thomas the Rhymer's prophecy concerning the eventual comeback of the Gaels; often in connextion with **royalism**
traitors	in vernacular poetry, a reference to those who have betrayed the cause of the house of Stiúbhart
tréidhe tighearna	'lordly traits', a reference to the qualities expected in the right ruler
tribute	a reference to the subject's capability to obtain tribute. Often in the expression *cíos is cáin* ('tax and tribute'). See also *tax*
umhla	'submission', a reference to the subject's capacity to obtain his enemies' submission
unites	a reference to the subject's capacity and suitability to unite and lead his people
upstarts	
— **social**	an attack on those of low birth, often denoted as **churls**, who currently occupy the nobility's patrimony
— **poetic**	an attack on untrained amateurs seeking patronage from those who traditionally patronised *filidh*
war, just	the upholding of war as undertaken for a just cause
warrior	a reference to the subject's warrior skills and military prowess
wealth	see *rath*

weapons a motif which describes and praises the subject's weapons and armoury

wheel of fortune a reference to the changeability of circumstances (often, but not always, within the context of **royalism**) generally to express hope that good fortune will in the end be restored

wisdom a reference to the subject's wisdom and good **judgement**.

women a motif depicting the subject's appeal to women

written word a reference to old written documents as containing proof of the case argued by the poet; see *cairt [chinnidh]* and *seinleabhair*

youth no impediment a motif arguing that the subject's youth is no impediment to his attainment of his people's leadership

Appendix 3

List of poems by subject, with sources

The list below is by no means the total of the poetic sources consulted, but only of those quoted in this study. Ó Baoill and MacAulay 2001 lists the extant corpus of Scottish vernacular poetry to *c*.1730 (with the exceptions noted ibid., p. 1) with all their known sources. Nothing of the kind exists yet for the syllabic poetry of Scotland, although most of it is included in *BPD*. The rest can be tracked in Mackechnie 1973 and Black, *Catalogue*, both, unfortunately, unindexed.

References below are, with some exceptions, to the most recent edition. In the case of unpublished poems extant in more than one manuscript, the reference is to the copy (normally the earliest but in some cases the most easily legible one) consulted by the author.

KEY:

?	before a personal names indicates possible subject
[?]	following a first line indicates possibly for a member or members of that kindred
17E, -M, -L	(for instance), indicates early, mid-, late seventeenth century

Roman numerals indicate either volume number or journal issue number, and are followed by page number.

Caimbéal of Argyll

Ar sliocht Gaoidheal ó Ghort Gréag (1513), Gilleasbaig, 2nd Earl of Argyll (†1513), *SVBDL* 158

Créad í an long-sa ar Loch Inse [?] (15L/16E), *SVBDL* 218

Dual ollamh triall le toisg (*c*.1595), Gilleasbaig (†1638), 7th Earl of Argyll, NLS Adv. 72.2.2, fos. 8v, 10, 11r

Gur h-e sgeul an Iarl' Aora so (1694), Eóin Ruadh, 2nd Duke of Argyll (†1743), *Gaidheal* v 104

Is maith mo leaba, is olc mo shuain (1685), Gilleasbaig, 9th Earl of Argyll (†1685), *LF* 211

Maith an chairt ceannas na nGaoidheal (?c.1580), Gilleasbaig, 4th, 5th or 7th Earl of Argyll, *TGSI* XXIX 217

Mó iná ainm Iarrla Gaoidheal (?a.1641), Gilleasbaig (†1661), 8th Earl & Marquis of Argyll, TCD 1362a, fo.1 (Formerly in TCD 1298 (H.2.7) (see Gwynn and Abbot 1921, p. 459; Black, *Catalogue*, p. 460).

Rug eadrain ar iath nAlban (c.1640), Gilleasbaig (†1661), 8th Earl & Marquis of Argyll, *SGS* iii 153

'S truagh m' imtheachd o chùirt Mhic Cailéin (?1685), Gilleasbaig, 9th Earl of Argyll (†1685), *RC* ii: 321

Tánaig long ar Loch Raithneach [?] (15L), *SVBDL* 224

Tha sgeul agam dhuibh ri innseadh (c.1685), Gilleasbaig, 9th Earl of Argyll (†1685), *BG* 172

Triallaidh mi lem dhuanaig ullaimh [A] (c.1528), Cailéan Meallach,, 3rd Earl of Argyll (†1529), *DnS* 374

Triallaidh mi lem dhuanaig ullaimh [B] (c.1555), Gilleasbaig Ruadh, 4th Earl of Argyll (†1558), *DnS* 380

Triath na nGaoidheal Giolla-Easbuig (c.1640), Gilleasbaig (†1661), 8th Earl & Marquis of Argyll, *SGS* iii 142

Caimbéal of Auchinbreck (Mac Donnchaidh Ghlinne Faochain)

Hò, gur mi tha air mo leònadh (1645), Donnchadh, 2nd Baronet Auchinbreck (†1645), *SRE* 205

O 's uaigneach a nochd Clàr Ghiorra (c.1642), Dubhghall Óg, 1st Baronet Auchinbreck (†1642), *RC* ii: 322

'S uaigneach a-nochd cathair Dhubhghaill (c.1642), Dubhghall Óg, 1st Baronet Auchinbreck (†1642), *TGSI* xxii 189

Turas mo chreiche thug mi Chola (c.1645), Donnchadh, 2nd Baronet Auchinbreck (†1645), *GnC* 112

Caimbéal of Glenorchy

Mór an bróinsgél bás i Dhuibhne (c.1631), Donnchadh (†1631), *Deo-Gréine* xii 132

Caimbéal of Lawers

Fhuaras rogha na n-óg mbríoghmhor (a.1542), Séamas(†1561/2) of Lawers, *SVBDL* 106

Camshrón

B' fheàrr leam gun sgrìbhteadh dhuit fearann (?a.1550), Eóghan Beag, 15th chief (fl.c.1550), *TGSI* xii 212

Cha b'e tùirneal a' chnatain (?1685), Eóghan, 17th chief (†1719), *OIL* 178

Tha mo chiabhan air glasadh (1719), Eóghan, 17th chief (†1719), *E* 273

Friseal

An deicheamh là de thùs a' Mhàirt (?1717), Sím, 13th chief (†1747), *ID* 36

Gur h-uasal am macan (p.1716), Sím, 13th chief (†1747), *GB2* 47

Mo thriall a sìos air fìrichean (?p.1716), Sím, 13th chief (†1747), *TGSI* xlv 192

Slàint Iain òig mhic Alasdair (?16M), Eóin Óg (†1546), *TGSI* xxvi 202

Gordan

Mhuire 's muladach a tha mi (?c.1720), Seoras, 2nd Marquis of Huntly (†1649), *OIL* 44

Mi ag amharc Srath Chuaiche (17M), Seoras, 2nd Marquis of Huntly (†1649), *OIL* 48

Grám

Is mithich dhuinn màrsadh as an tìr (1689), Eóin, Viscount Dundee (†1689), *OIL* 184
Mi gabhail Srath Dhruim-Uachdair (1650), Séamas, Marquis of Montrose (†1650), *OIL* 56
Soraidh do'n Ghràmach (1647), Séamas, Marquis of Montrose (†1650), *OIL* 28

Grannd

Iain mhòir bu mhath cumadh (*a*.1637), Eóin Mór a' Chaisteal (†1637), *MT* viii 352
Lìon mulad mi fhèin (*c*.1650), Séamas, 7th chief of Freuchie (†1663), *GnC* 124
Mo bheud mòr 's mo throm-luighe (1719), ? Alasdair (†1719), *SGS* xiv (2) 39

Lennox, earls of

Mairg thréigios inn, a Amhlaoíbh (13E), Amhlaoibh, s. or grs. of the Earl of Lennox (*fl*.13E), *Celtic Studies* 92
Saor do leannán, a Leamhain (*c*.1200), Alún Mór, 1st Earl of Lennox (†*c*.1200), *ADD* i: 173; *LMG* ii: 168

Lhuyd

Ar teachd on Spáin do shliochd an Gháoidhil ghlais (*c*.1705), Edward (†1709), *EB* 100
Ordheirc an gniomh saor bhur comhluin (*c*.1705), Edward (†1709), *EB* 76

Lyon

Sgeul a thàinig an dràsda oirnn (1715), John, 5th Earl of Strathmore & Kinghorne (†1715), *BSC* 26

Mac an Tóisigh

Fada dhomh an laighe-se (15L/16E), Alasdair (*fl*.15L/16E), *SVBDL* 194
'S tearc an-diugh mo chùis ghàire (1716), Uilliam (†1743) of Borlum, *GC* 375

Mac Beathadh

Mun sgeul so chualas (?18M), Eóin (*fl*. 18M), *BL* 96

Mac Coinnigh of Applecross

An taobh tuath ud cha tèid mi (*c*.1685), Eóin Molach, 2nd chief (†*c*.1685), *GnC* 174
Mo chridhe-sa ta fo chràdh (*c*.1685), Eóin Molach, 2nd chief (†*c*.1685), *LSMR* 156
'S math b' aithne dhomh-sa t' armachd (*c*.1650), Eóin Molach, 2nd chief (†*c*.1685), *TGSI* liv 447
Tha mise ar leaghadh le bròn (*c*.1646), Ruaidhrí, 1st chief (†1646), *GSMM* 14

Mac Coinnigh of Gairloch

An-diugh do Gheàrrloch cha tèid mi (1669), Coinneach, 6th chief (†1669), *MC* 153

Mac Coinnigh of Kintail

A Sheónóid méadaigh meanma (*c*.1635–40), Seónóid (*fl*.1640), *GnC* 94
Creach as truime na gach creach (17M/L), Coinneach (†1678) or Coinneach (†1701), *LSMR* 148
Deoch slàinte an Iarla Thuathaich (1719), Uilliam Dubh, 5th Earl of Seaforth (†1740), *SO* 83

Deoch-slàinte chabair fèidh seo (*c*.1716), Uilliam Dubh, 5th Earl of Seaforth (†1740), *Lasair* 110

Fada ta mis an-dèidh càich (?*c*.1626–30), Cailéan Ruadh, 13th chief, 1st Earl of Seaforth (†1633), *GnC* 80

Gum beannaicheadh mo Dhia dùileach (1726), Uilliam Dubh, 5th Earl of Seaforth (†1740), *TGSI* xlv 188

Gur tric teachdair bhon eug (?1633), Cailéan Ruadh, 13th chief, 1st Earl of Seaforth (†1633), *GC* 365

Mhic Coinnigh bhon Tràigh (*c*.1715), Uilliam Dubh, 5th Earl of Seaforth (†1740), *BSC* 32

Raoir a chunnaic mi bruadar (1719), Uilliam Dubh, 5th Earl of Seaforth (†1740), *TGSI* xlv 186

Tha Uilleam cliuiteach an diugh fo chàs (1715), Uilliam Dubh, 5th Earl of Seaforth (†1740), *TGSI* viii 118

Treun am Mac a thug ar leòn (?1629), Cailéan Ruadh, 13th chief, 1st Earl of Seaforth (†1633), *GnC* 78

Mac Coinnigh of Suddie
Tha mulad, tha sgìos orm (1688), *MC* 156

Mac Domhnaill lords of the Isles
A chinn Diarmaid Uí Chairbre (*c*.1490), Aonghus Óg (†1490), *SVBDL* 96

A Chlanna Chuinn, cuimhnichibh (1513), Domhnall, 8th lord of the Isles (†1423), *Celtic Studies* 147

Ceannaigh duain t'athar, a Aonghas (?*c*.1250), Aonghus Mór, 5th lord of the Isles (†1292/6), *IBP* 169

Ceannas Ghaoidheal do chlainn Colla (*a*.1503), Eóin, 10th lord of the Isles (†1503), *RC* ii: 208

Domhnall mac Raghnaill rosg mall (13E/M), Domhnall, 4th lord of the Isles (?†1247), *DnS* 76

Fíor mo mholadh ar Mhac Domhnaill (*a*.1503), Eóin, 10th lord of the Isles (†1503), *RC* ii: 264

Fuaras aisgidh gan iarraidh (*a*.1448), Alasdair, 9th lord of the Isles (†1449), *ADD* i: 115

Meisde nach éadmhar Éire (*a*.1503), Eóin, 10th lord of the Isles (†1503), *FMUB* 415

Mór an feidhm freagairt na bhfaighdheach (*c*.1476–80), Eóin, 10th lord of the Isles (†1503), *SVBDL* 272

Mór an léan-sa ar aicme Íle (?*c*.1550), Mac Domhnaill family, *RC* i: 134

Ní h-éibhneas gan chlainn Domhnaill (*c*.1500), Mac Domhnaill family, *SVBDL* 90

Thánaig adhbhar mo thuirse (*c*.1490), Aonghus Óg (†1490), *SVBDL* 82

Mac Domhnaill of Antrim
Ainmnigh ria ccách ceann a ccionn (*p*.1644), Raghnall Óg, 2nd Earl & Marquis of Antrim (†1683), *Celtica* x 151

Beid mar do bhádar roimhe (*c*.1644), Raghnall Óg, 2nd Earl & Marquis of Antrim (†1683), *SGS* i 113

Díon tíre dá thighearna (*c*.1620), Raghnall, 1st Earl of Antrim (†1636) and Raghnall Óg, 2nd Earl & Marquis of Antrim (†1683), RIA 744 (A/v/2), fo. 63a

Do bheirim barr buadha is áigh (?*c*.1610), ? Raghnall Óg, 2nd Earl & Marquis of Antrim (†1683), NLS 14901

Do-dhéan craobhsgaoileadh na cColla (?1618), Raghnall, 1st Earl of Antrim (†1636), RIA 785 (23 G 8), fo. 52

Éireannaigh féin Fionn-Lochlannaigh (1620), Raghnall, 1st Earl of Antrim (†1636), *DD* 291

Fada cóir Fhódla ar Albain (16L), Somhairle Buidhe (†1590), *TD* i: 173

Fàilt' a Mharcuis a dh' Alba (1644), Raghnall Óg, 2nd Earl & Marquis of Antrim (†1683), *SGS* i 113

Is in Eachroim an áir atáid ina gcónaí (c.1691), Somhairle (†1691), *Mac Cuarta* 63

Mealladh iomlaoide ar Éirinn (?a.1582), Máire (d. Conn Ó Néill), wife of Somhairle Buidhe (†1590), *LCC* xxiv 77

Taisdil mhionca ór siabradh sionn (c.1639–42), Raghnall Óg, 2nd Earl & Marquis of Antrim (†1683), *SGS* xiii 302

Mac Domhnaill of Clanranald

Alba gan díon an diaigh Ailéin (c.1514), Ailéan, 4th chief (†1505) and Raghnall, 5th (†1509), *RC* ii: 216

Bliadhna leuma d'ar milleadh (1716), Ailéan Dearg, 14th chief (†1715), *Lasair* 54

Cóir fáilte re fear do sgéil (c.1641–5), Domhnall, 12th chief (†1686), *RC* ii: 240; *Laoide* 34

Cumha ceathrair do mheasg mé (c.1636), Raghnall, 1st of Benbecula (†1636) *et al.*, *RC* ii: 232

Dá chúis ag milleadh ar meamna (?1719), Raghnall, 15th chief (†1725), *RC* ii: 280

Deireadh do aoibhneas Innse Gall (c.1686), Domhnall, 13th chief (†1686), *RC* ii: 244

Do ttuirlinn seasuimh síol cCuinn (17), Ailéan Dearg, 14th chief (†1715), *RC* ii: 249

Fáilte d' ar n-Ailín na Raghnallach (c.1696), Ailéan Dearg, 14th chief (†1715), *RC* ii: 286

Gur è naidheachd na Ciadain (1715), Ailéan Dearg, 14th chief (†1715), *Lasair* 50

Maith an sgéal do sgaoil 'nar measg (c.1696), Ailéan Dearg, 14th chief (†1715), NLS Adv. 72.2.2, fo. 12

Moch 's a mhaduinn 's mi 'g èiridh (c.1618), Domhnall, 11th chief (†1618), *MC* 26

Tapadh leat, a Dhomh'aill mhic Fhionnlaigh (?18E/M), Domhnall mac Fhionnlaigh (fl.18E/M), *BG* 71

Theast aon diabhal na nGaoidheal (?15L), Ailéan, 4th chief (†1505), *SVBDL* 134

Mac Domhnaill of Colonsay

Mór mo mholadh ar mhac Colla (1645), Alasdair (†1647), *SGS* ii 75

Saoth liom do chor, a Cholla (c.1623–4), Colla (†1647), *Celtica* x 193

Mac Domhnaill of Glengarry

Ach a nis on a liath mi (1680), Aonghus Óg, 9th chief, Lord MacDonnell (†1680), *OIL* 158

Alasdair a Gleanna Garadh (?1724), Alasdair Dubh, 11th chief (†1721/4), *BSC* 70

Bíodh an uigheam-sa triall (?c.1675), Aonghus Óg, 9th chief, Lord MacDonnell (†1680), *OIL* 132

Cha d' fhuair mi an-raoir cadal (1689), Domhnall Gorm, *tánaiste* (†1689), *TGSI* xxii 168

Fhuair mi sgeul moch Di-ciadain (1721), Alasdair Dubh, 11th chief (†1721/4), *SO* 84

Gura fada mi am chadal (1721), Alasdair Dubh, 11th chief (†1721/4), *MC* 86

Ho ró, gur fada | 's cian fada gu leòr (c.1680), Aonghus Óg, 9th chief, Lord MacDonnell (†1680), *OIL* 152

Is e mo chion an t–óg meanmnach (p.1663), Aonghus Óg, 9th chief, Lord MacDonnell (†1680), *OIL* 94

Mi 'g éiridh sa mhadainn (?1724), Alasdair Dubh, 11th chief (†1721/4), *SO* 55

Appendix 3

Níor ghlac cliath colg no gunna (?*c*.1670), Aonghus Óg, 9th chief, Lord MacDonnell (†1680), *TGSI* xxix 222

Tuar doimheanma dul Raghnaill (1705), Raghnall, 10th chief (†1705), NLS Adv. 72.2.2, fo. 14

Mac Domhnaill of Islay

An síth do rogha, a rígh Fionnghall (?*c*.1590), Aonghus s. Séamas (†1614), *Gaidheal* xix 36

Bí ad mhosgaladh, a mheic Aonghais (*c*.1600), Séamas (†1626), *IBP* 36

Do loiscceadh meisi sa Mhuaidh (*c*.1586), Domhnall Gorm & Alasdair Carrach (both †1586), *Éigse* v 149

Treisi an eagla ioná andsacht (*a*.1585), Domhnall Gorm (†1586), *Irish Chiefs* 72

? Mac Domhnaill of Largie

Clú oirbhirt úaislighes nech (*c*.1590–6) [?], Gilleasbaig, 8th chief (*fl.c*.1597–1605), NLS Adv. 72.2.2, fo. 6

O! 's tuisleach an nochd a taim (?*c*.1649), Aonghus, 9th chief (†1661), *MC* 59

Mac Domhnaill of Lochaber (Keppoch)

Deoch slàinte Mhic 'ic Raonuill (*p*.1715), Coll, 16th chief (*fl*.1715), *MC* 71

Mac Domhnaill of Sleat

A bhean, leasaich an stòp dhuinn (?*c*.1678–80), Domhnall, 10th chief (†1695), *OIL* 144

A Dhomhnaill an Dùin (*a*.1643), Domhnall Gorm Óg, 8th chief & 1st Baronet Sleat (†1643), *GnC* 100

An Nollaig air 'm bu ghreadhnach fion (1678), Séamas Mór, 9th chief & 2nd Baronet Sleat (†1678), *BG* 179

Deimhin do shíol Ádhaimh éag (*c*.1635–40), ? Mairghréad, d. Domhnall Gorm Óg, 8th chief, *Éigse* xi 10

Éireochthar fós le Clainn gColla (*c*.1640), Domhnall Gorm Óg, 8th chief & 1st Baronet Sleat (†1643), RIA 744 (A v 2), fo. 73 v

Fuaras cara ar sgáth na sgéile, Séamas Mór, 9th chief & 2nd Baronet Sleat (†1678), *RC* ii: 132

Is coma leam fhèin na co-dhiù sin (1720), Séamas, 13th chief & 6th Baronet Sleat (†1720), *BSC* 64

Leasg linn gabháil go Gearrloch (*c*.1635–40), Caitirfhíona (†1635), *TGSI* xxix 224

Mo-chean do-chonnarc a réir (*a*.1643), Domhnall Gorm Óg, 8th chief & 1st Baronet Sleat (†1643), *Éigse* xi 1

Sgeula leat, a ghaoth a-deas (1643), Domhnall Gorm Óg, 8th chief & 1st Baronet Sleat (†1643), *BG* 221

Tha ulaidh orm an uamharrachd (?*p*.1695), Domhnall, 11th chief & 4th Baronet Sleat (†1718), *GSMM* 76

Mac Dubhghaill

A Mheic Dhubhghaill, tuar acáin (?16E), Donnchadh Carrach, *SVBDL* 180

Do athruigh séan ar síol gCuinn (?*c*.1512), Eóin Ciar s. Ailéin (†1512), *SVBDL* 166

Mac Fionghuin

Adhbhur tuirsi ag fuil Fhionnghuin (*c*.1682), Eóin Óg (†1682), NLS Adv. 72.2.2, fo. 33r

Is cian 's gur fad' tha mi 'm thàmh (*c*.1660), Lachlann, 16th chief (*b*. 1628), *OIL* 72

Mac Gille Eóin of Brolas

An tùs an t-samhraidh seo bhà (1725), Domhnall, 3rd chief (†1725), *EB* 82

Mo rùn an t-Ailein (*a.*1723), Ailean (*fl.*1723), *MNL* 96

Mac Gille Eóin of Coll

Marbhaisg air an t-saoghal chruaidh (1687), Lachlann, 9th chief (†1687), *EB* 48

'S ann Di-Satharn a chualas (1687), Lachlann, 9th chief (†1687), *DC* 11

Soraidh gu Breacachadh bhuam (*c.*1716–29), Domhnall, 10th chief (†1729), *DC* 32

Mac Gille Eóin of Duart

A Lachainn Òig gun innsinn ort (?*c.*1650), ? Lachlann Óg, 16th chief, 1st Baronet Morvern (†1649), *EB* 26

Ach ga grianach an latha (1651), Eachann Ruadh, 17th chief, 2nd Baronet Morvern (†1651), *BL* 266

Cha choma leam fhèin no co-dhiù sin (*c.*1700), Eóin, 19th chief, 4th Baronet Morvern (†1716), *GnC* 212

Clann Ghille Eóin na mbratach badhbha (?16E/M), ? Eachann Mór, 11th chief (†1568), *SGS* IX 90

Cuid de adhbhar mo ghearain (1647), Lachlann, 16th chief, 1st Baronet Morvern (†1649), *OIL* 40

'Dheagh Mhic-Coinnigh a Brathainn (1691), Eóin, 19th chief, 4th Baronet Morvern (†1716), *BL* 261

Fhuair mi sgeul 's chan àicheam e (*c.*1703–4), Eóin, 19th chief, 4th Baronet Morvern (†1716), *GB2* 86

Ge de stoc mi an dèidh 'n crìonaidh (*c.*1692), Eóin, 19th chief, 4th Baronet Morvern (†1716), *BL* 191

Ge grianach an latha (*c.*1702), Eóin, 19th chief, 4th Baronet Morvern (†1716), *EB* 90

Gur bochd nàidheachd do dhùthcha (*c.*1651), Eachann Ruadh, 17th chief, 2nd Baronet Morvern (†1651), *EB* 44

Gur cràiteach an othail (*c.*1705), Alasdair (†1705) (br. Anndra mac an Easbaig), *EB* 72

Gura h-oil leam an sgeul seo (1651), Eachann Ruadh, 17th chief, 2nd Baronet Morvern (†1651), *EB* 34

Iomchair mo bheannachd (1716), Eóin, 19th chief, 4th Baronet Morvern (†1716), *GB* 186

Is beag adhbhar mo shùgraidh (?1647), Lachlann, 16th chief, 1st Baronet Morvern (†1649), *EB* 10

Is goirt leam gaoir nam ban Muileach (?*c.*1716), Eóin, 19th chief, 4th Baronet Morvern (†1716), *Lasair* 60

Mhic Móire na gréine (?*c.*1635), Lachlann, 16th chief, 1st Baronet of Morvern (†1649), *EB* 6

Mo cheist an Leathanach mòdhar (*c.*1691–1703), Eóin, 19th chief, 4th Baronet Morvern (†1716), *MNL* 40

Mun sgeul-sa tha aca (1703), Eóin, 19th chief, 4th Baronet Morvern (†1716), *BL* 103

Mur bhith 'n abhainn air fàs oirnn (1678), Eóin, 19th chief, 4th Baronet Morvern (†1716), *OIL* 142

Nam faicinn gum b' fhìor (?1704), Eóin, 19th chief, 4th Baronet Morvern (†1716), *BL* 98

Nan tiocfadh, nan tiocfadh, nan tiocfadh do sgeul (*c.*1703), Eóin, 19th chief, 4th Baronet Morvern (†1716), *BL* 100

'*S ann Di-ciadain an là* (*c*.1631–49), Lachlann, 16th chief, 1st Baronet of Morvern (†1649), *EB* 2

'*S mi gun chadal aig smaointean* (*c*.1714–15), Eóin, 19th chief, 4th Baronet Morvern (†1716), *MNL* 60

Tha iongnadh air an Dreòllain (*c*.1695), ? *c*.1695, *EB* 311

Tha mi am chadal 's gur tìm dhomh dùsgadh (*c*.1692), Eachann, 20th chief, 5th Baronet Morvern (†1750), *GB* 180

Thoir fios bhuam gu Anndra (?*c*.1710), Eóin, 19th chief, 4th Baronet Morvern (†1716), *BL* 107

Thriall bhur bunadh gu Phàro (*c*.1649), Lachlann, 16th chief, 1st Baronet of Morvern (†1649), *EB* 14

Uam-s' tha ràitinn (?*c*.1680), Ailéan, 18th chief, 3rd Baronet Morvern (†1674), *EB* 60

Mac Gille Eóin of Knock

Beir an t-soraidh-sa uam-s' (?18E), Anndra (*fl*.1703), *EB* 307

Mac Gille Eóin of Otter

'*S bochd an sgeula seo thàinig* (*c*.1705), Alasdair (†1705), *EB* 68

Mac Griogóir

A mhic an fhir ruaidh (?*c*.1600), *GnC* 68
Aithris fhréimhe ruanaidh Eoin (*a*.1519), Eóin (†1519), *SVBDL* 212
An saoil sibh féin nach foghainnteach (?*c*.1605), Griogór Odhar (*fl.c*.1605), *SGS* XX 157
Buaidh thighearna ar thóiseachaibh (*c*.1415), Maol Coluim (†1440), *SVBDL* 26
Fada atáim gan bhogha (*a*.1519), Eóin (†1519), *SVBDL* 144
Fhuaras mo rogha theach mhór (*a*.1519), Eóin (†1519), *SVBDL* 148
Gabh rém chomraigh, a mheic Ghriogoir ((*a*.1519), Eóin (†1519), *SVBDL* 126
Gealladh gach saoi don each odhar ((*a*.1519), Eóin (†1519), *SVBDL* 140
Is beag mo mhulad 's mi am fràmh (?*c*.1605), *TGSI* xxii 176
Moch madainn air latha Lùnast (?1570), Griogór Ruadh (†1571), *EMWP* 71
Parrthas toraidh an Díseart (?1518), Donnchadh (†1518), *SVBDL* 196
Ríoghacht ghaisgidh oighreacht Eoin (*a*.1519), Eóin (†1519), *SVBDL* 204

Mac Leóid of Berneray

Ar ttriall bhus ésguidh go Uilleam (*c*.1705), Uilliam (*fl.c*.1705), *TGSI* xxix 42
Do ttuirn aoibhneas Innsi Gall (1705), Tormod (†1705), *RC* ii: 264
Gur muladach thà mi (?*c*.1700), Tormod (†1705), *GSMM* 20
Is mi am shuidhe air an tulaich (*p*.1666), Tormod (†1705), *GSMM* 36
Mo chràdhghal bhochd (1705), Tormod (†1705), *GSMM* 96
Ri fuaim an taibh (*p*.1666), Tormod (†1705), *GSMM* 44
Rug an fheibhe a terme as teach (1705), Tormod (†1705), *GSMM* 102
Théid mi le m'dheoin (*p*.1666), Tormod (†1705), *GSMM* 72

Mac Leóid of Dunvegan

A theachtaire téid i ccéin go talamh Mhic Leóid (?*c*.1650), ? Ruaidhrí Mear, seventeenth chief (†1664), *TCD* 1375 (H.5.3), 4, 22 (for other sources see McLeod 2004, p. 98 n. 144)
An naidheachd so an dé (?17L), Tormod, 20th chief (†1706), *GSMM* 60
Cha sùrd cadail (?1706), Tormod, 20th chief (†1706), *GSMM* 88

Creach Gaoidheal i reilig Rois (1626), Ruaidhrí Mór, 15th chief (†1626), *SGS* viii 30

Do ísligh onóir Gaoidheal (*c.*1649), Eóin Mór, 16th chief (†1649), *FEMN* 167

Dual freasdal ar feirg flatha (*c.*1693), Eóin Breac, 18th chief (†1693), NLS Adv. 72.1.39, fo. 31

Gur e an naidheachd so fhuair mi (1699), Ruaidhrí Óg, 19th chief (†1699) & br. Tormod, *GSMM* 52

Is i so iorram na truaighe (1649), Eóin Breac, 17th chief (†1649), *BG* 201

Is muladach mì, hì ó (?17E), Ruaidhrí Mór, 15th chief (†1626), *GSMM* 32

Miad a' mhulaid tha 'm thadhal (1694), Ruaidhrí Óg, 19th chief (†1699), *BH* 58

Mór a n-ainm a n-iath eile [?Eilge)] (*c.*1699), Eóin Breac, 18th chief (†1693) & s. Ruaidhrí, NLS Adv. 72.2.2, fo. 43b

Sé h-oidhche dhamhsa san Dún (?*c.*1613), Ruaidhrí Mór, 15th chief (†1626), 16th chief, *TGSI* xlix 12

Shìl Olaghair gun ainnis (?18E), *GC* 70

Soraidh no dhá le dùrachd uam (17E), Ruaidhrí Mór, 15th chief (†1626), *TGSI* xxvi 235

Tha móran móran mulaid (*c.*1693), Eóin Breac, 18th chief (†1693), *BH* 4

Tha mulad, tha mulad (*c.*1693), Eóin Breac, 18th chief (†1693), *BH* 46

Mac Leóid of Lewis

Fhuaras mac mar an t-athair (?*c.*1500), Torcul, 8th chief (†*c.*1511), *SVBDL* 100

Mac Leóid of Luskintyre

Cubhuidh ttriall ar air tturus (?*c.*1690), Uilliam, 1st chief (*fl.c.*1690), NLS Adv. 72.2.2, fo. 51r

Mac Leóid of Raasay

Mo bheud is mo chràdh (*c.*1671), Eóin Garbh, 6th chief (†1671), *GSMM* 26

Seall a-mach an e an latha e (1671), Eóin Garbh, 6th chief (†1671), *GnC* 156

Tha do mhìolchoin air iallain (1671), Eóin Garbh, 6th chief (†1671), *TGSI* xlix 385

Mac Leóid of Talisker

A Choinnnich, cuiream le chéile (?*c.*1700), Eóin, 2nd chief (†1700), *BH* 74

Air sgiath na maidne as luaithe (?*c.*1720), Domhnall, 3rd chief (†*c.*1743), *BL* 128

Mac Neachtain

'S fhad tha mi ag èisdeachd ri ur dìochuimhn (?*c.*1680–5), ?Alasdair (†*c.*1685), *GnC* 166

Mac Néill

A phaidrín do dhúisg mo dhéar (*c.*1455–70), Niall Óg (*fl.*1455), *SVBDL* 60

Mac Raith

Fhir thèid thar a 'Mhàim (17M/L), Donnchadh nam Pìos (†*c.*1700), *TGSI* xlv 163

'S mi 'g uileag mo leaba (?1670), Domhnall (*fl.*1670), *TGSI* xii 190

Mac Suibhne

Dál chabhlaigh ar Chaistéal Suibhne (*c.*1310), Eóin (*fl.*1310), *CMCS* xxxiv 33

Moireach

'S mithich dhomh-sa bhith 'g èirigh (?*c.*1630), Eóin, Earl of Atholl (†1642), *HMo* ii: 490

Slàn a chì mi thu, Mharcuis (1685), Eóin, Marquis of Atholl (†1703), *OIL* 166

Tional nan sluagh chum na seilg (1682), Eóin, Marquis of Atholl (†1703), EUL La. iii 529: 88

Stiúbhart of Appin

An latha dh' fhàg thu taobh Loch Eir (?1463), Dubhghall (b.1445), Stewart 1880: 75

Stiúbhart of Rannoch

Cóir feitheamh ar uaislibh Alban (15M/L), Eóin (?†1475), *SVBDL* 185
Beannuigh do theaghlach a Thrionóid (15M/L), ? Eóin (?†1475), *SVBDL* 176

Poems for or about monarchs

A éolcha Alban uile (*c.*1058–93), ? Maol Coluim III (†1093), *LMG* ii: 162

Airis biuc a mheic big báin (?*c.*1090), ? Maol Coluim III (†1093) and Domhnall III (dep. 1097), *Berchán* 21

An diugh chuala mi naidheachd (*c.*1692), William of Orange (†1702) and Mary (†1694), *OIL* 202

Cha labhair mi táireil (*c.*1689), William of Orange (†1702), ML 227, fo. 1 *insert*

I n-ainm an áird-mhic do-ní grása (*c.*1589), Elizabeth I (†1603), *Gaelic Journal* iv 14

Mi 'n so air m' uilinn (1660), Charles II (†1685), *OIL* 76

Mór theasda dh'obair Óivid (*c.*1603), James VI and I (†1625), *Éigse* xvii 169

Nad mair Cionaodh go lion sgor (?*c.*858), Cionaoth mac Ailpín (†858), *Fr. Annals*, 112

Ro bátar láeich do Laigneib (*c.*1100), Aodhán mac Gabhráin (†*c.*608), *Ériu* xvi 157

'S binn an sgeul so tha 'd ag ràdhainn (?1714), James VIII (†1766), *BSC* 16

Si servare velis insontes quosque fideles (11L), Maol Coluim III (†1093), *Scotichronicon* iii: 14

Trí gcoróna i gcairt Shéamais (16L/17E), James VI and I (†1625), *ADD* i: 177

Poems for other subjects

Buitléar, Séamas, 4th Earl of Ormond (†1452), *Aoidhe i n-Éirinn an t-iarla* (15M), *ADD* i: 139

—— Séamas, 9th Earl of Ormond (†1546), *Mó iná iarla ainm Séamais* (16M), *PB* 82

Búrc, Éamann (†1458), *Do briseadh riaghail rígh Sacsann* (15M), *ADD* i: 152

—— Riocard (†1585), *Mór iongabháil anma ríogh* (16L), *TD* i: 141

—— Seaán (†1580), *Fearann cloidhimh críoch Bhanbha* (16L), *TD* i: 120

—— —— *Ó Dhia dealbhthar gach óige* (a.1580), *FFCh* 147

—— Teabóid na Long (†1629), *Máthair chogaidh críoch Bhanbha* (17E), *FFCh* 269

—— Uaitéar (†1440), *Toghaidh Dia neach 'n-a naoidhin* (15E/M), *ADD* i: 146

—— Uilleag (†1601) and Seaán (†1583), *Rannam le chéile, a chlann Uilliam* (16L), *DD* 370

Clifford, Tomás (*fl.c.*1395), and Mac Briain Cuanach, Toirdhealbhach (*fl.c.*1392), *Námha agus ccara dar gceird*, (14L), *Celtica* xviii 138

Dáibhidh mac Maoil Choluim [future King of Scotland] (†1153), *Olc a n[dearna] mac Mael Colaim* (*c.*1113), *Ériu* xvii suppl. 269

Mac Cárrthaigh, Domhnall (?†1391), *Beir eolas dúinn, a Dhomhnuill* (14M), *DD* 228

Mac Diarmada, Tomaltach (†1458), *Lámh aoinfhir fhóirfeas i nÉirinn* (a.1458), *SVBDL* 32

—— —— and Mág Uidhir, Tomás (†1480), *Dá urradh i n-iath Éireann* (?15M), *SVBDL* 46

Mac Domhnaill (?Ulster) (?1620), *Cuimhnigh sochar síol gColla* (?1620), TCD 1340 (H.3.19), fo. 35r [p. 64]

Mac Dubhghaill of Connacht, Feidhlim (†1643), *Iad féin mhoras Clann Cholla* (17E), RIA 540c (C/iv/1), fo. 179r

Mac Gearailt, Muiris, 3rd Earl of Desmond (†1356), *A Ghearóid, déana mo dháil* (14M), *DD* 201

Mac Marcuis of Knocknacloy (*fl.*1588), *Éisd re seanchas síol gColla* (1588), TCD 1340 (H.3.19), fo. 36v [p. 65]

Mág Eochagáin, Diarmaid (*fl.*14L), *A chláirsioch Chnuic Í Chosgair*, IBP 66

Mág Uidhir, Aodh (†1600), *Atáim i gcás eidir dhá chomhairle* (16L), DD 215

—— —— *Connradh do cheanglas re hAodh* (16L), *Éigse* xxvii 59

—— Cú Chonnacht (†1589), *Daoine saora síol gColla* (16L), TD i: 57

Ó Briain, Conchobhar, 3rd Earl of Thomond (†1581), *Ceolchair sin a chruit an ríogh*, *Gleanings* 111

—— —— *Lá dá rabha ós ráith Luimnigh* (?1558), ADD i: 105

—— —— *Ní dual gan chuimhne air cheart rígh* (?16M), RIA 490 (23/N/15), fo. 203

—— Donnchadh and Murchadh, *Maith ré sírleanmhain síol mBriain* (*c.*1524–8), RIA 11 (E/iv/3), fo. 200

—— Donnchadh, 4th Earl of Thomond (†1624), *Eascar Gaoidheal éag aoinfhir* (*c.*1624), *Celtica* xvi 87

—— Donnchadh Cairbreach (†1242), *Aisling ad-chonnairc o chianaibh* (13E), *Éigse* vii 80

—— —— *Tabhraidh chugam cruit mo ríogh* (13E/M), *Gleanings* 113

—— Tadhg na nGlaodh Mór (†1444), *Dá bhrághaid uaim i nInis* (*c.*1444), ADD i: 51

Ó Broin, Fiachaidh (†1597), *Branuigh ar chlú ós cloinn Néill* (16L), LB 78

—— —— *Fuath gach fir fuidheall a thuaighe* (16L), LB 147

—— —— *Mairg atá tar éis Fhiacha* (*c.*1597), LB 163

—— —— *Mithigh cuairt a gceann Fhiacha* (16L), LB 83

—— —— *Mór cóir cháich ar chrích Laighion*, LB 90

Ó Ceallacháin, Donnchadh (†*c.*1680), *Gnáith féile ag fagháil innmhe* (*a.*1650), SGS xiii (2): 289

Ó Cearbhaill, Maolruanaidh (?†1443), *Déanaidh comhaonta, a Chlann Éibhir* (15E/M), ADD i: 100

Ó Conchobhair, Brian (†1440), *Do bhriseas bearnaidh ar Bhrian* (15E), DD 261

—— Cathal Croibhdhearg (†1224), *Fada dhamh druim re hÉirinn* (13E), *Éigse* xiii 80

—— —— *Tainic an Croibhdhearg go Crúachain* (12L/13E), *Misc. K. Meyer* 167

Ó Conchobhair Ciarraighe, Conchobhar (*fl.*15E/M), *Fada ó Ultaibh a n-oidhre* (15E/M), ADD i: 28

Ó Conchobhair Failghe, An Calbhagh (†1458), *Briathra cogaid con cath Laighneach* (15M), IBP 154

Ó Conchobhair Sligeach, Donnchadh (†1609), *Síon choitcheann cumha Ghaedheal* (*c.*1609), FFCh 257

Ó Dálaigh, Cú Chonnacht (†1642), *Cia feasda as urra don eól* (17M), RIA3 (23/L/17), fo. 106

Ó Domhnaill, Aodh (†1600), *Biaidh athroinn ar Inis Fáil* (16L), *Celtica* xii 125

—— Aodh Ruadh (†1602), *Atáim ionchora re hAodh* (16L), DnBM 23

—— —— *Leanam croinic clann nDálaigh* (1600), NLI G 167, fo. 239 [This and other MSS are available for consultation on ISOS, http://www.isos.dias.ie]

—— —— *Teasda Éire san Easbáinn* (*c.*1602), *Éigse* XVI 31

—— Maghnus (†1563), *Cia adeir nár mealladh Maghnus* (16E), *Irish Texts* ii: 57

—— —— *Cia ré gcuirfinn séd suirghe* (16M), *Celtica* xvi: 67

—— —— *Diomdhach Éire d'fhuil Conuill* (*a.*1535), *Irish Texts* ii: 57

Ó Domhnaill, Neachtan (†1626), *Mairg as bhráighe ar mhacraidh Murbhaigh* (17E), ADD i: 97

Ó Donnabháin, Domhnall (1660), *Cia as urra d'ainm an iarthair* (17M), SGS xiii (2): 46

Ó Donnchadha, Séafraidh (†1678), *Ní doirbh go deaghuil na ccarad* (*c.*1642/3), *JKHAS* 50

Ó Gairmleadhaigh, Niall (†1261), *A-tá sunn seanchas Mu-Áin* (13M), *DD* 217

Ó Maol Chiaráin, Fearchar (*a.*1500), *Tugadh oirne easbhuidh mhór* (*a.*1500), *Éigse* iii 165

Ó Mórdha, Rudhraighe (†1546), *Mairidh teine i dteallach Gaoidheal*, RIA 1 (23/D/14), fo. 31

—— Uaithne (†1600), *Maith bhur bhfíor catha, a Chlann Róigh* (*c.*1600), RIA 11 (E/iv/3), fo. 65

Ó Néill, Seaán (†1567) or Seaán (†1691), *Ceisd ar eólchuibh iath Banba* (17L), *Irish Nation* ii, no. 2

—— of Clandeboy, Aodh Buidhe (†1444), *Ní leis fhéin a bhfaghann Aodh* (a.1444), RIA 743 (A/iv/3), fo. 691

—— —— *A theachtaire théid bhu thuaidh* (15M), LCAB 65

Ó Súilleabháin Béara, Domhnall (†1618), *San Sbáinn do toirneadh Teamhair* (*c.*1618), *Éigse* xvii 162

Pierse, Nioclás Dall (†1653), *A Niocláis, nocht an gcláirsigh*, *IBP*, 112

Raghnall mac Godhfhraidh, King of Man (†1229), *Baile suthach síth Emhna* (13E), *Éigse* viii 288

Other poems quoted

A' cheud Di-luain de'n ràithe (*c.*1688–93), *BH* 32

A cholann chugat an bás (16M/L), religious, *DD* 7

A chomhachag bhog na Sròine (?*c.*1585), Menzies 2001

A mhic na meabhraigh éigse (17E), Gaelic decline [poetry], O'Grady, I: 392

A rìgh 's diombach mi 'n iomairt (?1715), political, *BSC* 44

An ainm an àigh nì mi tùs (*c.*1689), political (Killiecrankie), *OIL* 190

Aonar dhamhsa eidir dhaoinibh (17E), Gaelic decline [poetry], *IBP* 159

Beir mise leat, a mhic Dè (?17E), religious, *GnC* 82

Ciallach duine fíoruasal (?15L), satire, *SVBDL* 236

Cionnas mhaireas mé am aonar, elegy for a fellow poet, *RC* i: 192

Clann Ghilleathain on Dreòllainn (?17M), prophetic, *GC*, 265, 392

Dá lámh sínte le síoth nDé (16L), religious, RIA 744 (A/v/2), fo. 61

Dh'innsinn sgeula dhuibh le reusan (18E), political (Sheriffmuir), *BSC* 38

Duanaire na Sracaire (?16E), *SVBDL* 2

Flaitheas saor le saoghal sean (1701), address to the Synod of Argyll (1701), *SGS* xii 190

Ge bè dh'èireadh 'san lasair (*c.*1707), political, *OIL* 222

Gluais romhad, a leabhráin bhig (1567), religious, *Foirm* 13

Gu bheil mulad air m' inntinn (1722), various Clann Domhnaill families, *ID* 39

Gur feallta carail an saoghal (1688), religious/political, *LSMR* 170

Is deas duinn cobhair Mhic Dhé (1648), political, Davidson 1998: 475

Is mairg nár chrean le maitheas saoghalta (?*c.*1674), Gaelic decline, *Dispossessed* 120

Labhradh Trían Chonguil go ciúin (*c.*1690), 'Red Hand' contention, *RC* ii: 295

Làmh Dhè leinn, a shaoghail (1692), political (Glencoe), *GnC* 192

Mairg chaomhnas a cholann (17M), religious, *Éigse* X 270

Mairg duine do chaill a ghuth (15L/16E), satire, *SVBDL* 248

Marbhfhaisg air a' mhulad sin (?17L), Gaelic decline, *Lasair* 28

Mi am leabaidh air m' aon taobh (1688), political, *LSMR* 188

Mo-chean duit a Cholaim cháidh (*c.*1394), defence of poetry , RIA 1225 (D/ii/1), fo. 68 (125) v

'N àm dhol sìos (?1691), political, *GnC* 184

'N cuala sibh-se an tionndadh duineil (1645), political (Inverlochy), *OIL* 20

'N Raon Ruairidh seo bha ann (1689), political, *GB* 110

Nach faic sibh, a dhaoine (1693), political, *LSMR* 238

Námha an cheird nach taithighthear (?c.1650), Gaelic decline [poetry], NLS Adv. 72.1.48, fo. 31r

Nár lém choisnes tu clú Chuinn (c.1690), 'Red Hand' contention, *RC* ii: 297

Olc an t-adhbhar uabhair (1648), political, Davidson 1998: 473

'S e latha Raon Ruairidh (c.1689), political (Killiecrankie), *MC* 74

'S mi am shuidhe air a' chnocan (1692), political, *MTT* 33, 95

Seacht saighde atá ar mo thí (16M/L), religious, *SVBDL* 252

Sèid na builg sin, ghille, dhomh (1689), political, *BH* 20

Seo an aimsir 'n do dhearbhadh an targainteachd (1715), political, *Lasair* 38

Slán don droing da ndiongnainn dán (17M/L), Gaelic decline [poetry], *Éigse* i 247

Sona do cheird, a Chalbhaigh (17M), Gaelic decline [poetry], *GnC* 90

T'aire riut, a Ghiolla-easbuig (17L/18E), Gaelic decline [poetry], NLS Adv. 72.1.48, fo. 10v

Ta 'n saoghal-s' carail (1688), political, *LSMR* 175

Tairnig éigse fhuinn Ghaoidheal (17E), Gaelic decline [poetry], *DD* 398

Tha mi fo leann-dubh is fo bhròn (1716), political, *TGSI* xx 20

Tha mulad cinnteach trom air m'inntinn (?1692), political, *LSMR* 212

Tha mulad, tha gruaim orm, tha bròn (1715), political, *BSC* 20

Thàinig fath bròin air ar cridhe (1630), religious / other, *GnC* 84

Tuirseach dhúinne ri port (a.1636–42), political, Davidson 1998: 20

Tùs gliocais eagal Dè (17M/L), religious, *LSMR* 128

Tús na heagna omhan Dé (17E), religious, *AFOD* 50

Bibliography

Alcock, L. (1993) *The Neighbours of the Picts: Angles, Britons and Scots at War and at Home*, Rosemarkie: Groam House Museum Trust

Anderson, A. O. (ed.) (1990, first pub. 1922, Edinburgh: Oliver & Boyd) *Early Sources of Scottish History A.D. 500 to 1286*, Stamford, Lincolnshire: Paul Watkins

Anderson, M. O. (1980 [1973, 1980]) *Kings and Kingship in Early Scotland*, Edinburgh: Scottish Academic Press

Bannerman, J. (1971a) 'Senchus Fer nAlban. Part II', *Celtica*, Vol. 9, pp. 217–65

—— (1971b) 'The Scots of Dalriada', in Menzies, G. (ed.) 1971, pp. 66–79

—— (1974) *Studies in the History of Dalriada*, Edinburgh: Scottish Academic Press

—— (1977) 'The lordship of the Isles', in Brown (ed.) (1977), pp. 209–40

—— (1983) 'Literacy in the Highlands', in Cowan, I. B. and Shaw, D. (eds) (1983), pp. 214–35

—— (1986) *The Beatons: A Medical Kindred in the Classical Gaelic Tradition*, Edinburgh: John Donald

—— (1989) 'The king's poet and the inauguration of Alexander III', *SHR*, Vol. 68, pp. 120–49

—— (1990) 'The Scots language and the kin-based society', in Thomson (ed.) (1990), pp. 1–19

—— (1996) 'The residence of the king's poet', *SGS*, Vol. 17, pp. 24–35

Barrow, G. W. S.(1980) *The Anglo-Norman Era in Scottish History*, Oxford: Clarendon

—— (1992) *Scotland and its Neighbours*, London: Hambledon

—— (2003, first pub. 1973, London: Edward Arnold) *The Kingdom of the Scots*, Edinburgh: Edinburgh University Press

Bateman, V. M. (1990) 'The themes and images of classical Gaelic religious poetry', unpublished PhD thesis, University of Aberdeen

Beaton, A. J. (1882–3) 'Notes on the antiquities of the Black Isles, Ross-shire, with plans and sections', *Proceedings of the Society of Antiquaries of Scotland*, Vol. 17, pp. 477–92

Bennett, J . A. W. and Trevor-Roper, H. R (eds) (1955)*The Poems of Richard Corbett*, Oxford: Clarendon

Bergin, O. (1955) 'Irish grammatical tracts', Supplement to *Ériu*, Vol. 17, pp. 259–93

—— (1970) *Irish Bardic Poetry: Texts and Translations together with an Introductory Lecture*, ed. D. Greene and F. Kelly, Dublin: Dublin Institute for Advanced Studies

Beuermann, I. (2007) 'Masters of the narrow sea: forgotten challenges to Norwegian rule in Man and the Isles, 1079–1266', unpublished PhD thesis, University of Oslo

Black, G. F.,(1993, first pub. 1946, New York: New York Public Library) *The Surnames of Scotland*, Edinburgh: Birlinn

Black, R. I. (ed.) (1976) 'Poems by Maol Domhnaigh Ó Muirgheasáin (I)', *SGS*, Vol. 12, Pt. 2, pp. 194–202

—— (ed.) (1978) 'Poems by Maol Domhnaigh Ó Muirgheasáin (II)', *SGS*, Vol. 13, Pt. 1, pp. 46–55

—— (1976–8) 'The genius of Cathal MacMhuirich', *TGSI*, Vol. 50, pp. 327–66

—— (ed.) (1981) 'Poems by Maol Domhnaigh Ó Muirgheasáin (III)', *SGS*, Vol. 13, Pt. 2, pp. 289–301

—— (ed.) (2001) *An Lasair: Anthology of 18th-Century Gaelic Verse*, Edinburgh: Birlinn

—— *Catalogue of Gaelic Manuscripts in the National Library of Scotland*, 2 Vols [unpublished draft catalogue]

Boardman, S. (2006) *The Campbells, 1250–1513*, Edinburgh: John Donald

—— (2012) 'Highland Scots and Anglo-Scottish warfare c.1300-1513', in King, A. and Simpkin, D. (eds) *England and Scotland at War, c.1296–c.1513*, Brill

—— and Ross, Alasdair (eds) (2003) *The Exercise of Power in Medieval Scotland, c.1200–1500*, Dublin: Four Courts

Bradshaw, B. (1979) ' "Manus the Magnificent": O'Donnell as a Renaissance prince', in Cosgrove, A. and McCartney, D. (eds), *Studies in Irish History Presented to R. Dudley Edwards*, Dublin: University College Dublin, pp. 15–36

Breatnach, L. (ed.) (1980) 'Tochmarc Luaine ocus Aided Athairne', *Celtica*, Vol. 13, pp. 1–31

—— (2006) 'Satire, praise and the early Irish poet', *Ériu*, Vol. 56, pp. 63–84

Breatnach, P. A. (ed.) (1977–8), 'Metamorphosis 1603: dán le hEochaidh Ó hEódhasa', *Éigse*, Vol. 17, pp. 169–80

—— (1983) 'The chief's poet', *PRIA*, Vol. 83, pp. 37–79

Broun, D. (1998) 'Defining Scotland and the Scots before the wars of independence', in Broun, Finlay and Lynch (eds) (1998), pp. 4–17

—— (1999) 'Anglo-French acculturation and the Irish element in Scottish identity', in Smith, B. (ed.) *Britain and Ireland, 900–1300: Insular Responses to Medieval European Change*, Cambridge: Cambridge University Press, pp. 135–53

—— (2007) *Scottish Independence and the Idea of Britain: From the Picts to Alexander III*, Edinburgh: Edinburgh University Press

—— (2009), 'Attitudes of *Gall* to *Gaedhel* in Scotland before John of Fordun', in Broun and MacGregor (eds) (2009), pp. 49–82

——, Finlay, R. J., and Lynch, M. (eds) (1998) *Image and Identity: The Making and Re-making of Scotland through the Ages*, Edinburgh: John Donald

—— and MacGregor, Martin (eds) (2009) *Mìorun Mòr nan Gall, 'The Great Ill-Will of the Lowlander?': Lowland Perceptions of the Highlands, Medieval and Modern*, Glasgow: Centre for Scottish and Celtic Studies, University of Glasgow

Brown, I. *et al.* (eds) (2007) *The Edinburgh History of Scottish Literature*, Vol. 1, Edinburgh: Edinburgh University Press

Brown, J. M. (ed.) (1977) *Scottish Society in the Fifteenth Century*, London: Arnold

Brown, K. M. (1998) 'Scottish identity in the seventeenth century', in Bradshaw, B. and Roberts, P. (eds), *British Consciousness and Identity: The Making of Britain, 1533–1707*, Cambridge: Cambridge University Press, pp. 236–58

Brown, M. (1994) *James I*, Edinburgh: Canongate

—— (2003) 'Earldom and kindred: the Lennox and its earls, 1200–1458', in Boardman and Ross (eds) (2003), pp. 201–24

Brown, P. H. (1891) *Early Travellers in Scotland*, Edinburgh: Douglas

Buchanan, G. (1579) *De Iure Regni apud Scotos*, Edinburgh

—— (1582) *Rerum Scoticarum Historia*, Edimbvrgi

—— (1827) *The History of Scotland*, trsl. James Aikman, Edinburgh

Burns, J. H. (1996) *The True Law of Kingship: Concepts of Monarchy in Early Modern*

Scotland, Oxford: Clarendon

Burton, J. H. *et al.* (1877–) *Register of the Privy Council*, Edinburgh

Byrne, F. J. (2001, first pub. 1973, London: Batsford)*Irish Kings and High-kings*, Dublin: Four Courts

Byrne, M. (ed.) (2000) *Collected Poems and Songs of George Campbell Hay*, Vol. 1, Edinburgh: Edinburgh University Press

Caball, M. (1994) 'Providence and exile in seventeenth-century Ireland', *Irish Historical Studies*, Vol. 29: 114, pp. 174–88

—— (1998) *Poets and Politics: Continuity and Reaction in Irish Poetry, 1558–1625*, Cork: CorkUniversity Press

Calder, G. (ed.) (1917) *Auraicept na n-Éces: The Scholar's Primer*, Edinburgh: John Grant

Campbell, E. (2001) 'Were the Scots Irish?', *Antiquity*, Vol. 75, pp. 285–92

—— (1961) 'The beginning of Mac Vurich's panegyrick on the Macleans', *SGS*, Vol. 9, pp. 90–1

Campbell, H. (ed.) (1926) 'The Genealogical and Historicall Account of the Family of Craignish', in *Miscellany of the Scottish History Society*, Vol. 4, pp. 187–299

Campbell, J. F. (ed.) (1872) *Leabhar na Féinne*, London: Spottiswoode

Campbell, J. L. (ed.) (1984, first pub. 1933, Edinburgh: Grant) *Highland Songs of the Forty-Five*, Edinburgh: Scottish Academic Press

—— (ed.) (1990) *Songs Remembered in Exile: Traditional Gaelic Songs form Nova Scotia Recorded in Cape Breton and Antigonish County in 1937, with an Account of the Causes of Hebridean Emigration, 1790–1835*, Aberdeen: Aberdeen University Press

—— and Thomson, D.(1963) *Edward Lhuyd in the Scottish Highlands, 1699–1700*, Oxford: Clarendon

Campbell of Airds, A.(2000–2) *A History of Clan Campbell*, 3 Vols, Edinburgh: Polygon [Vol. 1] and Edinburgh: Edinburgh University Press [Vols 2 and 3]

Carlton, C. (1983) *Charles I: The Personal Monarch*, London: Routledge & Kegan Paul

Carney, J.(ed.) (1945) *Poems on the Butlers of Ormond, Cahir, and Dunboyne (A.D. 1400-1650)*, Dublin: Dublin Institute for Advanced Studies

—— (1967) *The Irish Bardic Poet*, Dublin: Dolmen

—— and Greene, D. (eds) (1968)*Celtic Studies: Essays in Memory of Angus Matheson, 1912–1962*, London: Routledge & K. Paul

Carrier, Irene (1998)*James VI and I, King of Great Britain*, Cambridge: CambridgeUniversity Press

Céitinn, S. (1990, first pub. 1851, London: Hodges and Smith) *Annála Ríoghachta Éireann: Annals of the Kingdom of Ireland, from the Earliest Period to the Year 1606*, ed. J. O'Donovan, with an introduction by Kenneth Nicholls,Dublin: de Búrca

Clancy, T. O. (ed.) (1998) *The Triumph Tree: Scotland's Earliest Poetry, AD 550–1350*, Edinburgh: Canongate

——(2000a) 'A polemic Gaelic quatrain from the reign of Alexander I, *ca.* 1113', *SGS*, Vol. 20, pp. 88–96

—— (2000b) 'Scotland, the "Nennian" recension of Historia Brittonum and Lebor Bretnach', in Taylor, S. (ed.) (2000), pp. 87–107

—— (2003) 'King-making and images of kingship in medieval Gaelic literature', in Welander, R., Breeze, D. J. and Clancy, T. O. (eds), *The Stone of Destiny: Artefact and Icon*, Edinburgh: Society of Antiquaries of Scotland

—— and Kidd, S. (eds) (2006), *Litreachas & Eachdraidh. Rannsachadh na Gàidhlig 2, Glaschu 2002*, Glaschu: Roinn na Ceiltis, Oilthigh Ghlaschu

—— and Márkus, Gilbert (eds) (1995) *Iona: The Earliest Poetry of a Celtic Monastery*, Edinburgh University Press

Coira, M. P. (2008a) 'Law and the rhetoric of sovereignty in the poetry of Tadhg Óg Ó hUiginn', *Éigse*, Vol. 36, pp. 195–214

—— (2008b) 'The Earl of Argyll and the *Goill*: the "Flodden poem" revisited', *SGS*, Vol. 24, pp. 137–68

—— (2011, forthcoming) 'The high-kingship of Alba, the *Goill* and Scottish independence: some thoughts on pre-classical and classical poetry of Scotland, *SGS*, Vol. 28 [see also Dewar, P.]

Connolly, M. (ed.) (1992) '*The Dethe of the Kynge of Scotis*: a new edition', *SHR*, Vol. 71, pp. 46–69

Cowan, E. J. (1997) *Montrose – for Covenant and King*, London: Weidenfeld and Nicolson

Cowan, I. and Easson, D. (eds) (1976) *Medieval Religious Houses: Scotland*, London: Longman

Cox, R. A. V. and Ó Baoill, C. (eds) (2005) *Ri Linn nan Linntean: Taghadh de Rosg Gàidhlig*, Ceann Drochaid, Perthshire: Clann Tuirc

Cranstoun, J. (ed.) (1887) *Poems of Alexander Montgomerie*, Edinburgh: Scottish Text Society [1st ser], Vols 9–11

—— (ed.) (1891–3) *Satirical Poems of the Time of the Reformation*, 4 Vols, Edinburgh: Scottish Text Society [1st ser], Vols 20, 24, 28, 30

Cunningham, B., and Gillespie, R. (2003) *Stories from Gaelic Ireland: Microhistories from the Sixteenth-Century Irish Annals*, Dublin: Four Courts

Davidson, P. (ed.) (1998) *Poetry and Revolution: An Anthology of British and Irish Verse 1625–1660*, Oxford: Clarendon Press

Davis, L. (1998) *Acts of Union: Scotland and the Literary Negotiation of the British Nation, 1707–1830*, Stanford, CA: Stanford University Press

Dawson, Jane (1988), 'The fifth earl of Argyle, Gaelic lordship and political power in sixteenth-century Scotland', *SHR*, Vol. 67, pp. 1–27

—— (1999) 'Clan, kin and kirk: the Campbells and the Scottish Reformation', in Amos, S. Pettegree, A. and van Nierop, H. (eds), *The Education of a Christian Society: Humanism and Reformation in Britain and the Netherlands*, Aldershot: Ashgate, pp. 211–42

Dewar, P. (2006a) 'Kingship imagery in classical Gaelic panegyric for Scottish chiefs', in *McLeod, Fraser and Gunderloch* (eds) (2006), pp. 39–55

—— (2006b) 'Perceptions and expressions of leadership in Gaelic sources: Ireland, *c.*1400 – *c.*1600', unpublished PhD thesis, University of Aberdeen
[see also Coira, M. P.]

Dinneen, P. (1927) *Foclóir Gaedilge agus Béarla: An Irish-English Dictionary*, Dublin: Educational Company of Ireland

Dodgshon, R. A. (1998) *From Chiefs to Landlords: Social and Economic Change in the Western Highlands and Islands, c. 1493–1820*, Edinburgh: Edinburgh University Press

Donaldson, G. (1965) *Scotland: James V to James VII*, Edinburgh: Oliver & Boyd

Dooley, A. (1986) '*Námha agus cara dar gceird*: a *dán leathaoire*', *Celtica*, Vol. 18, pp. 125–49

Dumville, D. (2002) 'Ireland and north Britain in the earlier middle ages: contexts for *Míniugud senchasa fher nAlban*', in Ó Baoill, C. and McGuire, N. (eds) (2002), pp. 185–211

Duncan, A. M. M. (2002) *The Kingship of the Scots, 842–1292: Succession and Independence*, Edinburgh: Edinburgh University Press

Dunlop, J. (1965 [1955]) *The Clan Gordon*, Edinburgh: Johnston and Bacon

Dwelly, E. (1977, first pub. 1918, Fleet, Hants.: E. Dwelly) *The Illustrated Gaelic Dictionary*, Glasgow: Gairm

Edington, C. (1998) 'Paragons and patriots: national identity and chivalric ideal in late-medieval Scotland', in Broun, Finlay and Lynch (eds) (1998), pp. 69–81

Ellis, S. G. (1998) *Ireland in the Age of the Tudors 1447–1603: English Expansion and the End of Gaelic Rule*, London: Addison Wesley Longman

Enright, M. J., (1976) 'King James and his island: an archaic kingship belief?', *SHR*, Vol. 55, pp. 29–40

Finan, T. (2002) 'Prophecies of the expected deliverer in thirteenth- and fourteenth-century Irish bardic poetry', *New Hibernia Review*, Vol. 6: 3, pp. 113–24

Findlay, D. (2002) 'Divine right and early modern Gaelic society', in Ó Baoill, C. and McGuire, N. (eds) (2002), pp. 243–55

Forsyth, K. (2000) 'Evidence of a lost Pictish source in the *Historia Regum Anglorum* of Symeon of Durham', in Taylor (ed.) (2000), pp. 19–32

Fox, R. L. (ed.) (1978 [1975]) *Alexander the Great*, London: Futura

Fraser, J. E. (2006) '*Dux Reuda* and the Corcu Réti', in McLeod, W., Fraser, J. E., and Gunderloch, A. (eds) (2006), pp. 1–9

—— (2007) 'St Columba and the convention at Druimm Cete: peace and politics at seventh-century Iona', *Early Medieval Europe*, Vol. 15, pp. 315–34

—— (2009) *From Caledonia to Pictland: Scotland to 795*, The New Edinburgh History of Scotland, Vol. 1, Edinburgh: Edinburgh University Press

—— (2010) 'The three thirds of Cenél Loairn, 678–733', in McLeod *et al.* (eds) 2010, pp. 135–66

Fraser of Reelig, C. I. (1954) *The Clan Munro*, Edinburgh: Johnston & Bacon

Freeman, A. M. (ed.) (1944) *Annála Connacht: The Annals of Connacht (A.D. 1224–1544)*, Dublin: Dublin Institute for Advanced Studies

Gatherer, W. A. (trsl. and ed.) (1958) *The Tyrannous Reign of Mary Stewart: George Buchanan's Account*, Edinburgh: Edinburgh University Press

Gillies, W. (1976–8) 'Some aspects of Campbell history', *TGSI*, Vol. 50, pp. 256–95

—— (ed.) (1978) 'The Gaelic poems of Sir Duncan Campbell of Glenorchy (i)', *SGS*, Vol. 13: 1, pp. 18–45

—— (ed.) (1981) 'The Gaelic poems of Sir Duncan Campbell of Glenorchy (ii)', *SGS*, Vol. 13: 2, pp. 108–20

—— (1982) 'Arthur in Gaelic tradition. Part II: romances and learned lore', *CMCS*, Vol. 3, pp. 41–75

—— (1986) 'The classical Irish poetic tradition', in Evans, D. E., Griffith, J. G. and Jope, E. M. (eds), *Proceedings of the Seventh International Congress of Celtic Studies Held at Oxford, from 10th to 15th July, 1983*, Oxford: Oxbow, pp. 108–20

—— (1987) 'Heroes and ancestors', in Almqvist, B., Ó Catháin, S. and Ó Héalaí, P. (eds), *The Heroic Process: Form, Function and Fantasy in Folk Epic*, Dún Laoghaire: Glendale, pp. 57–73

—— (ed.) (1989) *Gaelic and Scotland: Alba agus a' Ghàidhlig*, Edinburgh: Edinburgh University Press)

—— (2006) 'On the study of Gaelic literature', in Clancy & Kidd (eds) (2006), pp. 1–32

—— (2010) 'Clan Donald bards and scholars', in Munro, G. and Cox, R. A. V. (eds), *Cànan & Cultar / Language & Culture: Rannsachadh na Gàidhlig 4*, Edinburgh: Dunedin, pp. 91–108

Goldie, M. (1997) 'Restoration political thought', in Glassey, L. K. J. (ed.) *The Reigns of*

Charles II and James VII & II, New York: St Martin's Press, pp. 12–35

Gordon, C. A. (1958) 'Letter to John Aubrey from Professor James Garden', *SGS*, Vol. 8, pp. 18–26

Gordon of Gordonstoun, R. (1813) *A Genealogical History of the Earldom of Sutherland, from its Origin to the Year 1630. With a Continuation to the Year 1651*, Edinburgh: Constable

Grace, J. (1842) *Annales Hiberniae*, ed. R. Butler, Dublin: Dublin University Press

Græme, L. G. (1903) *Or and Sable: A Book of the Græmes and Grahams*, Edinburgh: William Brown

Grant, A. (1988) ' Scotland's "Celtic fringe" in the late middle ages', in Davies, R. R. (ed.), *The British Isles, 1100–1500: Comparisons, Contrasts, and Connections*, Edinburgh: J. Donald, pp. 118–41

Grant, I. F. (1959) *The MacLeods: The History of a Clan, 1200–1956*, London: Faber & Faber

—— and Cheape, H. (1987) *Periods in Highland History*, London: Shepheard-Walwyn

Gray, E. (ed.) (1982) *Cath Maige Tuired: The Second Battle of Mag Tuired*, Irish Texts Society: Publications, 52, London: Irish Texts Society

Greene, D.(1961) 'The professional poets', in Ó Cuív, b. (ed.), *Seven Centuries of Irish Learning, 1000–1700*, Dublin: Oifig an tSoláthair, pp 38–49

—— and O'Connor, F. (1967) *A Golden Treasury of Irish Poetry, AD 600–1200*, London: Macmillan

Gregory, D. (1831) *Historical Notices of the Clan Gregor*, Edinburgh

—— (1881, first pub. 1836, Edinburgh: Tait) *History of the Western Isles and Highlands of Scotland, from A.D. 1493 to A.D.1625*, London: Hamilton

—— and Skene, W. F. (eds) (1847) *Collectanea de Rebus Albanicis*, Edinburgh: Iona Club

Gwynn, E. J., and Abbott, T. K. (1921) *Catalogue of the Irish Manuscripts in the Library of Trinity College, Dublin*, Dublin: Hodges, Figgis

Haigh, C. (1998) *Elizabeth* I, 2nd edn, London: Longman

Hayes-McCoy, G. A. (1937) *Scots Mercenary Forces in Ireland (1565–1603)*, Dublin: Burns, Oates & Washbourne

Hennessy, W. M., and Mac Carthy, B. (eds) (1998, first pub. 1829–89, Dublin) *Annála Uladh: The Annals of Ulster, from the Earliest Times to the Year 1541*, 4 Vols, Blackrock: Éamonn de Búrca

Herbert, M. (1992) 'Goddess and king: the sacred marriage in early Ireland', in Fradenburg, O. L. (ed.), *Women and Sovereignty*, Edinburgh: Edinburgh University Press, pp. 264–75

—— (2000) 'Rí Éirenn, Rí Alban: kingship and identity in the ninth and tenth centuries', in Taylor, S. (ed.) (2000), pp. 62–72

Hill, J. M. (1993) 'The rift within Clan Ian Mor: the Antrim and Dunyveg MacDonnells, 1590–1603', *Sixteenth Century Journal* Vol. 24: 4, pp. 865–79

—— (1993) *Fire and Sword: Sorley Boy MacDonnell and the Rise of Clan Ian Mor, 1538–1590*, London: Athlone

Hogan, E, (1910) *Onomasticon Goedelicum Locorum et Tribuum Hiberniae et Scotiae*, Dublin: Hodges, Figgis & Co.

Holland, R. (1897) 'The Buke of the Howlat', in Amours, F. J. (ed.), *Scottish Alliterative Poems in Riming Stanzas*, Edinburgh: Scottish Texts Society, pp. 74–75

Hudson, B. T. (1991) 'Historical literature of early Scotland', *Studies in Scottish Literature*, Vol. 26, pp. 141–55

—— (1994) *Kings of Celtic Scotland*, Westport, CT: Greenwood

—— (1996) *Prophecy of Berchán: Irish and Scottish High-kings of the Early Middle Ages*, Westport, CT: Greenwood

Hughes, A.J. (1990) 'The seventeenth-century Ulster/Scottish contention of the Red Hand: background and significance', in Thomson, D. S. (ed.) (1990), pp. 78–94

Innes, C. (ed.) (1855) *The Black Book of Taymouth*, Edinburgh: Bannatyne

Jackson, K. (1957) 'The Duan Albanach', *SHR*, Vol. 36, pp. 125–37

Jaski, B. (2000) *Early Irish Kingship and Succession*, Dublin: Four Courts

Kelly, F. (ed.) (1976) *Audacht Morainn*, Dublin: Dublin Institute for Advanced Studies

Knott, E. (ed.) (1922–6) *A bhFuil aguinn dar Chum Tadhg Dall Ó Huiginn (1550–1591)*, 2 Vols, Irish Texts Society: Publications, 22, 23, London: Simpkin

—— (ed.) (1957, first publ. 1934, Cork: Cork University Press) *An Introduction to Irish Syllabic Poetry of the Period 1200–1600*, 2nd edn, Dublin: Dublin Institute for Advanced Studies

—— (1960) *Irish Classical Poetry, Commonly Called Bardic Poetry*, 2nd edn, Dublin: Three Candles

Knox, J. (1878) *The First Blast of the Trumpet against the Monstrous Regiment of Women*, ed. Edward Arber, London: Constable

Kratzmann, G. (1991) 'Political satire and the Scottish Reformation', *Studies in Scottish Literature*, 26, pp. 423–37

Laoide, S. (1914) *Alasdair mac Colla: Sain-eolus ar a Ghníomharthaibh Gaisge*, Baile Átha Cliath: Códhanna Teo.

Lennon, C. (1994) *Sixteenth-Century Ireland: The Incomplete Conquest* (Dublin: Gill & Macmillan

Leslie, J. (1970 [1569]) *A Defence of the Honour of the Most High, Mighty and Noble Princess Marie Quene of Scotlande, 1569*, Menston: Scolar

Lynch, M. (1991) *Scotland: A New History*, Edinburgh: Pimlico

—— (1994) 'National identity in Ireland and Scotland, 1500–1640', in Claus Bjørn, Alexander Grant, and Keith J. Stringer (eds.), *Nations, Nationalism and Patriotism in the European Past*, Copenhagen: Academic Press, pp. 109–136

—— (1998) 'A nation born again? Scottish identity in the sixteenth and seventeenth centuries', in Broun, Finlay and Lynch (eds) (1998), pp. 82–104

—— (2000) 'James VI and the "Highland problem" ', in Goodare, J. and Lynch, M. (eds), *The Reign of James VI*, East Linton: Tuckwell, pp. 208–27

Mac Airt, S. (ed.) (1944) *Leabhar Branach: The Book of the O'Byrnes*, Dublin: Dublin Institute for Advanced Studies

MacAonghuis, I. (2006) 'Baird is bleidirean', in. Newton (ed.) (2006), pp. 340–56

[see also MacInnes, J.]

Mac Bain, A. and Kennedy, J. (eds) (1892–4) *Reliquiae Celticae: Texts, Papers and Studies in Gaelic Literature and Philology Left by the Late Rev. Alexander Cameron, LL.D.*, 2 Vols, Inverness: Northern Chronicle

Mac Cana, P. (1969) 'Irish literary tradition', in Ó Cuív (ed.) (1969), pp. 35–46

—— (1974) 'The rise of the later schools of *filidheacht*', *Ériu*, Vol. 25, pp. 126–46

—— (1980) *The Learned Tales of Medieval Ireland*, Dublin: Dublin Institute for Advanced Studies

McCaughey, T. (1989) 'Bards, beasts and men', in Ó Corráin, D., McCone, K., and Breatnach, L. (eds) (1989), pp. 102–21

Mac Cionnaith, L. (ed.) (1938) *Dioghluim Dána*, Dublin: Oifig an tSoláthair

[see also M'Kenna, L., McKenna, L.]

MacCoinnich, A. (2003) ' "Kingis rabellis" to Cuidich 'n' Rìgh; the Emergence of Clann Choinnich, c.1475-1508' (pp. 175-200) in Boardman, Ross (eds) (2003), pp. 175–200

—— (2006), 'Mar Phòr san Uisge? Ìomhaigh Sìol Torcail an Eachdraidh', in Clancy & Kidd (eds) (2006), pp. 214-231

—— (2008) 'Sìol Torcail and their lordship in the sixteenth century',<http://eprints.gla. ac.uk/4622/1/MacCoinnichMinchChapter.pdf> (last accessed 2 March 2011); first pub 2008. in Crossing the Minch. Exploring the Links Between Skye and the Outer Hebrides, Port of Ness, Isle of Lewis: Islands Book Trust, pp. 7–32

Mac Craith, M. (1996) 'Creideamh agus athartha: idé-eolaíocht pholaitíochta agus aos léinn na Gaeilge i dtús an seachtú haois déag,' in Ní Dhonnchadha, Máirín (ed.), Nua-Léamha: Gnéithe de Chultúr, Stair agus Polaitíocht na hÉireann, c.1600–c.1900, Baile Átha Cliath: An Clóchomhar, pp. 7–19

Mac Craith, M., and Ó hÉalaí, P. (2007) Féilscríbhinn Mháirtín Uí Bhriain, Galway: Cló Iar-Chonnachta

Macdomhnuill, Raonuill (1776) Comh-chruinneachidh Orannaigh Gaidhealach, Vol. 1, Duneidiunn: Walter Ruddiman

MacDonald, A. A. (1996) 'William Stewart and the court poetry of the reign of James V', in Williams, J. H. (ed.) (1996), pp. 179–200

MacDonald, A. J., and MacDonald, A. (1896–1904) The Clan Donald, 3 Vols, Inverness: Northern Counties

—— (eds) (1911) The Macdonald Collection of Gaelic Poetry, Inverness: Northern Counties

MacDonald, K. D. (1984–6) 'The MacKenzie lairds of Applecross', TGSI, Vol. 54, pp. 411–74

McDonald, R. A. (1997) The Kingdom of the Isles: Scotland's Western Seaboard in the Central Middle Ages, c.1100–c.1336, East Linton: Tuckwell

—— (1999) 'Coming in from the margins: the descendants of Somerled and cultural accommodation in the Hebrides, 1164–1317', in Brendan Smith (ed.), Britain and Ireland, 900–1300. Insular Responses to Medieval European Change, Cambridge: Cambridge University Press, pp. 179–98

—— (2002) ' "Soldiers most unfortunate": Gaelic and Scoto-Norse opponents of the Canmore dynasty, c. 1100–c. 1230', in McDonald, R. A. (ed.), History, Literature and Music in Scotland 700–1560, Toronto; London: University of Toronto Press, pp. 93–119

Macdougall, N. (1982) James III: A Political Study, Edinburgh: J. Donald

—— (1997, first pub. 1989, Edinburgh: John Donald) James IV, 2nd edn, East Linton: Tuckwell Press

Macfarlane, W. (1900) Genealogical Collections Concerning Families in Scotland, 1750–51, 2 Vols, ed. J. T. Clark, Edinburgh

Mac Firbhisigh, D. (comp.) (2003–4) Leabhar Mór na nGenealach: The Great Book of Irish Genealogies, ed. N. Ó Muraíle, 5 Vols, Dublin: de Búrca

McGinnis, P. J., and Williamson, A. H. (eds) (1995) George Buchanan: The Political Poetry, Edinburgh: Scottish History Society

Mac Giolla Léith, C. (ed.) (1993) Oidheadh Chloinne hUisneach: The Violent Death of the Children of Uisneach, Irish Texts Society: Publications, 56, London: Irish Texts Society

McGladdery, C. (1990) James II, Edinburgh: John Donald

McGrath, C. (1943-4) 'Materials for a history of Clann Bhruaideadha', Éigse, Vol. 4, pp. 48–66

Macgregor, A. (1898–1901) History of Clan Gregor, 2 Vols, Edinburgh

MacGregor, M. D. W. (1989) 'A political history of the MacGregors before 1571', unpublished PhD thesis, University of Edinburgh

—— (1999)' "Surely one of the greatest poems ever made in Britain": the lament for Griogair Ruadh MacGregor of Glen Strae and its historical background', in Cowan, E. J. and Gifford, D. (eds), *The Polar Twins*, Edinburgh: John Donald, pp. 114–53

—— (2000) 'Genealogies of the clans: contributions to the study of MS 1467', *Innes Review*, Vol 51: 2, pp. 131–46

—— (2002) 'The genealogical histories of Gaelic Scotland', in Fox, A. & Wolf, D. (eds), *The Spoken Word: Oral Culture in Britain, 1500–1850*, Manchester: Manchester University Press, pp. 196–239

—— (2006) 'The view from Fortingall: the worlds of the *Book of the Dean of Lismore*', SGS, Vol. 22, pp. 35–85

—— (2008) 'Writing the history of Gaelic Scotland: a provisional checklist of "Gaelic" genealogical histories', *SGS*, Vol. 24, pp. 357–79

—— (2009) 'Gaelic barbarity and Scottish identity in the later middle ages', in Broun and MacGregor (eds) (2009), pp. 7–48

—— (2010) '*Ar sliocht Gaodhal ó Ghort Gréag*: an dàn "Flodden" ann an Leabhar Deadhan Lios-mòir', in Munro, G. and Cox, Richard A. V. (eds), *Cànan & Cultar / Language & Culture: Rannsachadh na Gàidhlig 4*, Edinburgh: Dunedin 2010, pp. 23–35

MacInnes, J. (1975) 'Gaelic poetry', unpublished PhD thesis, University of Edinburgh

—— (2006a, first pub.1968, *Scottish Studies*, Vol. 12, pp. 29–44) 'The oral tradition in Scottish Gaelic poetry', in Newton, M. (ed.) (2006), pp. 230–47

—— (2006b, first pub. 1976–8,*TGSI*, Vol. 50, pp. 435–98) 'The panegyric code in Gaelic poetry and its historical background', inNewton, M. (ed.) (2006), pp. 265–319

—— (2006c, first pub. Gillies, W. (ed.) (1989), pp. 89–100) 'The Gaelic perception of the Lowlands', inNewton, M. (ed.) (2006), pp. 34–47

—— (2006d, first pub. in Maclean, L. (ed.) (1981), pp. 142–61) 'Gaelic poetry and historical tradition', in Newton, M. (ed.) (2006), pp. 3–33

—— (2006e, first pub. 1976 in *Scottish Literature in the Secondary School*, Edinburgh: HMSO, pp. 56–67) 'The Gaelic literary tradition', in Newton, M. (ed.) (2006), pp. 163–89

—— (2006f, first pub. 1992 in Price, G. (ed.), *The Celtic Connection*, Gerrards Cross: Colin Smythe, pp. 101–30) 'The Scottish Gaelic language', in Newton, M. (ed.) (2006), pp. 92–119

[see also MacAonghuis, I.]

Mackay, A. (1906) *The Book of Mackay*, Edinburgh

Mackay, R. (1829) *A History of the Clan and House of Mackay*, Edinburgh

Mackechnie, J. (ed.) (1951) 'Treaty between Argyll and O'Donnell', *SGS*, Vol. 7, pp. 94–102

—— (1973) *Catalogue of Gaelic Manuscripts in Selected Libraries in Great Britain and Ireland*, Vol. 1, Boston, Mass.: Hall

M'Kenna, L. (ed.) (1919) *Dánta do Chum Aonghus Fionn Ó Dálaigh*, Dublin: Maunsel

McKenna, L. (ed.) (1922) *Dán Dé: The Poems of Donnchadh Mór Ó Dálaigh, and the Religious Poems in the Duanaire of the Yellow Book of Lecan*, Dublin: Educational Co.

—— (ed.) (1939-40) *Aithdioghluim Dána*, 2 Vols, Irish Texts Society: Publications, 37, 40, Dublin: Educational Company of Ireland

[see also M'Kenna, L., Mac Cionnaith, L.]

Mackenzie, A. (1884) *History of the Camerons, with Genealogies of the Principal Families of the Name*, Inverness: Mackenzie

—— (1894) *History of the Mackenzies with Genealogies of the Principal Families of the Name*, Inverness: A. & W. Mackenzie

—— (1896) *History of the Frasers of Lovat*, Inverness: A. & W. Mackenzie

MacKenzie, A. M. (ed.) (1964) *Orain Iain Luim: Songs of John MacDonald, Bard of Keppoch*, Scottish Gaelic Texts, 8, Edinburgh: Oliver and Boyd

Mackenzie, J. (ed.) (1904, first pub. 1841, Glasgow: Macgregor, Polson & Co.) *Sàr-obair nam Bàrd Gaelach*, Edinburgh: N. Macleod

Mackenzie, W. C. (1964) *History of the Outer Hebrides*, Edinburgh: Thin

MacKillop, J. (1998) *A Dictionary of Celtic Mythology*, Oxford: OxfordUniversity Press

MacKinnon, D. (1931) *The Chiefs and Chiefship of Clan MacKinnon*, Oban: Oban Times

Mackinnon, D. (1912) *A Descriptive Catalogue of Gaelic Manuscripts in the Advocates' Library Edinburgh and Elsewhere*, Edinburgh: Brown

M'Lauchlan, T. (ed.) (1862) *The Dean of Lismore's Book: A Selection of Ancient Gaelic Poetry*, Edinburgh: Edmonston and Douglas

Maclean, L. (ed.) (1981) *The Middle Ages in the Highlands*, Inverness: Inverness Field Club

Maclean, S. (1951–2) 'Alasdair mac Mhurchaidh', *TGSI*, Vol. 41, pp. 132–54

Maclean-Bristol, N. (1988) 'The Macleans from 1560–1707: a re-appraisal', in Inverness Field Club, *The Seventeenth Century in the Highlands*, Inverness: Inverness Field Club, pp. 70–88

—— (1995) *Warriors and Priests: The History of the Clan Maclean, 1300–1570*, East Linton: Tuckwell

McLeod, W. (2002a) 'Rí Innsi Gall, Rí Fionnghall, Ceannas nan Gàidheal: sovereignty and rhetoric in the late medieval Hebrides', *CMCS*, Vol. 43, pp. 25–48

—— (2002b) 'Anshocair nam Fionnghall: ainmeachadh agus ath-ainmeachadh Gàidhealtachd na h-Albann', in Ó Baoill, C. and McGuire, N. (eds) (2002), pp. 13–23

—— (2003) 'Réidh agus aimhréidh: súil air cruth na tíre ann am bàrdachd nan sgol', in McLeod, W. agus Ní Annracháin, M. (eds), *Cruth na Tíre*, Baile Átha Cliath: Johnswood Press, pp. 90–120

—— (2004) *Divided Gaels: Gaelic Cultural Identities in Scotland and Ireland, c.1200 – c.1650*, Oxford: Oxford University Press

—— (2010) 'Am filidh ann am bàrdachd dhùthchasach na Gàidhlig', in McLeod *et al.* (eds) 2010, pp. 237–44

—— and Bateman, M. (2007) *Duanaire na Sracaire / Songbook of thePillagers: Anthology of Gaelic Verse to 1600*, Edinburgh: Birlinn

—— *et al.* (eds) (2010) *Bile ós Chrannaibh: A Festschrift for William Gillies*, Ceann Drochaid, Perthshire: Clann Tuirc

——, Fraser, J. E., and Gunderloch, A. (eds) (2006) *Cànan & Cultar / Language & Culture. Rannsachadh na Gàidhlig 3*, Edinburgh: Dunedin

McManus, D. (2004) 'The bardic poet as teacher, student and critic: a context for the grammatical tracts', in Ó Háinle, C. G., and Meek, D. E. (eds), *Unity in Diversity: Studies in Irish and Scottish Gaelic Language, Literature and History*, Dublin: School of Irish, Trinity College

Macphail, J. R. N. (ed.) (1914–34) *Highland Papers*, Scottish History Society, 2nd series, Vols 5, 12, 20; 3rd series, Vol. 22, Edinburgh

Mac Phàrlain, C. (ed.) (1923) *Làimh-sgrìobhainn Mhic Rath*, Dun-de: MacLeod

Macrae, A. (1884) *History of the Camerons; with Genealogies of the Principal Families of the Name*, Inverness: A. & W. Mackenzie

—— (1899) *History of the Clan Macrae, with Genealogies*, Dingwall: A. M. Ross

Mag Craith, C. (ed.) (1980) *Dán na mBráthar Mionúr*, 2 Vols, Dublin Institute for Advanced Studies

Mair, J. (1892 [1521]) *A History of Greater Britain*, ed. and trsl. Archibald Constable, Scottish History Society, Publications: 10, Edinburgh

Mapstone, S. L. (1986) 'The advice to princes tradition in Scottish literature, 1450–1500', unpublished PhD thesis, University of Oxford

Marshall, T. (2000) *Theatre and Empire: Great Britain on the London Stages under James VI and I*, Manchester: Manchester University Press

Mason, R. A. (1983) 'Covenant and commonweal: the language of politics in Reformation Scotland', in Macdougal, N. (ed.), *Church, Politics and Society: Scotland, 1418–1929*, Edinburgh: J. Donald, pp. 97–126

—— (1998) *Political Thought and the Commonweal: Political Thought in Renaissance and Reformation Scotland*, East Linton: Tuckwell Press

Matheson, Angus (1953–9) 'Bishop Carswell', *TGSI*, Vol. 62, pp. 182–205

Matheson, W. (ed.) (1938) *The Songs of John MacCodrum*, Scottish Gaelic Texts, 2, Edinburgh: Oliver & Boyd)

—— (1942–50) 'Traditions of the MacKenzies', *TGSI*, Vol. 39–40, pp. 193–224

—— (ed.) (1970) *The Blind Harper: The Songs of Roderick Morison and his Music*, Edinburgh: Scottish Gaelic Texts Society

—— (1976–8) 'The Morisons of Ness', *TGSI*, Vol. 50, pp. 60–80

—— (1978) 'Replies: The O'Muirgheasain bardic family', *Notes & Queries of the Society of West Highland and Island Historical Research*, Vol. 7, p. 24

—— (1978–80a) 'The Ancestry of the MacLeods', *TGSI*, Vol. 51, pp. 68–80

—— (1978–80b) 'The MacLeods of Lewis', *TGSI*, Vol. 51, pp. 320–37

Meek, D. E. (1982) 'The corpus of heroic verse in the Book of the Dean of Lismore', unpublished PhD thesis, University of Galsgow

—— (1996) 'The Scots-Gaelic scribes of late medieval Perthshire: an overview of the orthography and contents of The Book of the Dean of Lismore', in Williams (ed.) (1996a), pp. 254–72

—— (ed.) (1997) ' "Norsemen and noble stewards": the MacSween poem in the Book of the Dean of Lismore', *CMCS*, Vol. 34, pp. 1–49

—— (1998) 'The Reformation and Gaelic culture: perspectives on patronage, language and literature in John Carswell's translation of "The Book of Common Order" ', in Kirk, J. (ed.), *The Church in the Highlands*, Edinburgh: Scottish Church History Society, pp. 37–62

Menzies, G. (ed.) (1971) *Who Are the Scots?*, London: BBC

Meyer, K. (ed.) (1909) *The Instructions of King Cormac Mac Airt*, Royal Irish Academy: Todd Lecture Series, 15, Dublin: Hodges, Figgis

—— (ed.) (1917) *Miscellanea Hibernica*, Urbana: University of Illinois

Morgan, H. (1995) 'Faith and fatherland in sixteenth-century Ireland', *History Ireland*, Vol. 3: 2, pp. 13–20

Munro, J. and R. W. (eds) (1968) *Acts of the Lords of the Isles, 1336–1493*, Edinburgh: Scottish History Society

Munro, R. W. (ed.) (1961) *Monro's Western Isles of Scotland*, Edinburgh: Oliver and Boyd

Murphy, G. (1940) 'Bards and filidh', *Éigse*, Vol. 2, pp. 200–207

Neville, C. J. (2005) *Native Lordship in Medieval Scotland: The Earldoms of Strathearn and Lennox, c.1140–1365*, Dublin: Four Courts

Newton, M. (ed.) (2006) *Dùthchas nan Gàidheal: Selected Essays of John MacInnes*, Edinburgh: Birlinn

—— (2010), 'Prophecy and cultural conflict in Gaelic tradition', *Scottish Studies*, Vol. 35, pp. 144–73

Ní Annracháin, M. (2007) 'Metaphor and metonymy in the poetry of Màiri nighean Alasdair Ruaidh', in Arbuthnot, S. and Hollo, K. (eds), *Fil súil nglais: A Grey Eye Looks Back. A Festschrift in Honour of Colm Ó Baoill*, Ceann Drochaid, Perthshire: Clann Tuirc, pp. 163–74

Ní Suaird, D. (1999) 'Jacobite rhetoric and terminology in the political poems of the Fernaig MS (1688–1693)', *SGS*, Vol. 19, pp. 93–140

Nicholls, K. W. (1975) 'The Irish genealogies: their value and defects', *The Irish Genealogist*, Vol. 5, pp. 256–61

—— (1991) 'Notes on the genealogy of Clann Eoin Mhoir', *West Highland Notes & Queries*, Ser. 2, Vol. 8, pp. 11–24

—— (2003, first pub. 1972 by Gill & Macmillan) *Gaelic and Gaelicised Ireland in the Middle Ages*, Dublin: Lilliput

Nicholson, R. (1974) *Scotland: The Later Middle Ages*, Edinburgh: Oliver & Boyd

Nieke, M.R., and Duncan, H. B. (1988) 'Dalriada: the establishment and maintenance of an early historic kingdom in northern Britain', in Driscoll, S. T. and. Nieke, M. R (eds), *Power and Politics in Early Medieval Britain and Ireland*, Edinburgh: Edinburgh University Press, pp. 6–21

Ó Baoill, C. (ed.) (1970) *Eachann Bacach and Other Maclean Poets*, Edinburgh: Scottish Academic Press

—— (ed.) (1972) *Bàrdachd Shìlis na Ceapaich: Poems and Songs by Sìleas MacDonald c.1660–c.1729*, Edinburgh: Scottish Academic Press

—— (1972–4) 'Scotland in early Gaelic literature', *TGSI*, Vol. 48, pp. 382–94

—— (1976) 'Domhnall Mac Mharcuis', *SGS*, Vol. 12:2, pp. 183–93

—— (1988) 'Scotticisms in a manuscript of 1467', *SGS*, Vol. 15, pp. 122–39

—— (1990) 'Bàs Iain Luim, *SGS*, Vol. 16, pp. 91–94

—— (ed.) (1994) *Iain Dubh: Òrain a Rinn Iain Dubh mac Iain mhic Ailein (c.1665–c.1725)*, Obar Dheathain: An Clò Gàidhealach

—— (ed.) (1997) *Duanaire Colach, 1537–1757*, Obar Dheathain: An Clò Gàidhealach

—— (ed.) (2009) *Mairghread Nighean Lachlainn: Song-maker of Mull*, Scottish Gaelic Texts, 19, Llandysul: Gwasg Gomer

—— and Bateman, M. (eds) (1994) *Gàir nan Clàrsach: The Harps' Cry*, Edinburgh: Birlinn

—— and MacAulay, D. (comps) (2001 [1988]) *Scottish Vernacular Verse to 1730: A Checklist*, Aberdeen: Aberdeen University Department of Celtic

—— and McGuire, N. (eds) (2002) *Rannsachadh na Gàidhlig 2000: Papers Read at the Conference Scottish Gaelic Studies 2000 Held at the University of Aberdeen 2–4 August 2000*, An Clò Gaidhealach: Obar Dheathain

Ó Briain, M. (2002) 'Snaithín san uige: "Loisc agus léig a luaith le sruth" ', in Ó Briain and Ó hÉalaí (eds) (2002), pp. 245–72

—— and Ó hÉalaí (eds) (2002) *Téada Dúchais: Aistí in Ómós don Ollamh Breadán Ó Madagáin*, Indreabhán, Conamara: Cló Iar-Chonnachta

O'Brien, M. A. (ed.) (1952) 'A Middle-Irish poem on the birth of Āedān mac Gabrāin and Brandub mac Echach', *Ériu*, Vol. 16, pp. 157–170

—— (1976) *Corpus Genealogiarum Hiberniae*, Vol. 1, Dublin: Dublin Institute for Advanced Studies

Ó Buachalla, B. (1983), 'Na Stíobhartaigh agus an t-aos léinn: Cing Séamas', *PRIA* 83 C: pp. 81–134

—— (1989) 'Aodh Eanghach and the Irish king-hero', in Ó Corráin, D., McCone, K., and Breatnach, L. (eds.) (1989), pp. 200–32

—— (1996) *Aislig Ghéar: Na Stíobhartaigh agus an tAos Léinn, 1603–1788*, Baile Átha Cliath: An Clóchomhar

Ó Cléirigh, L. (comp.) (1948-57) *Beatha Aodha Ruaidh Uí Dhomhnaill: The Life of Aodh Ruadh Ó Domhnaill*, ed. Paul Walsh, 2 pts, Irish Texts Society: Publications, 42, 45, Dublin: Educational Company of Ireland

Ó Corráin, D., McCone, K., and Breatnach, L. (eds.) (1989) *Sages, Saints and Storytellers: Celtic Studies in Honour of Professor James Carney*, Maynooth: An Sagart

Ó Cuív, B. (1963) 'Literary creation and Irish historical tradition', Sir John Rhys Memorial Lecture, *PBA*, Vol. 49, pp. 233–62

—— (ed.) (1968) 'A poem attributed to Muireadhach Ó Dálaigh', in Carney and Greene (eds) (1968), pp. 92–8

—— (ed.) (1969) *A View of the Irish Language*, Dublin: Stationery Office

—— (ed.) (1969–70) 'A poem for Cathal Croibhdhearg Ó Conchubhair', *Éigse*, Vol. 13, pp. 95–202

—— (1973) *The Linguistic Training of the Mediaeval Irish Poet*, Dublin: Dublin Institute for Advanced Studies

—— (ed.) (1984a) 'An elegy on Donnchadh Ó Briain, Fourth Earl of Thomond', *Celtica*, Vol. 16, pp. 87–105

—— (1984b) 'Some Irish items relating to the McDonnells of Antrim', *Celtica*, 16, pp. 139–56

O'Curry, E. (1873) *Manners and Customs of the Ancient Irish*, 3 Vols, London

Ó Dónaill, N. (1977) *Foclóir Gaeilge-Béarla*, Baile Átha Cliath: Oifig an tSoláthair

Ó Donnchadha, T. (ed.) (1931) *Leabhar Cloinne Aodha Buidhe*, Baile Átha Cliath: Oifig an tSoláthair

Ó Gallchóir, S. (ed.) (1971) *Séamas Dall Mac Cuarta: Dánta*, Baile Átha Cliath: An Clóchomhar

O'Grady, S. H. (1926–53) *Catalogue of Irish Manuscripts in the British Museum*, 3 Vols, London: BritishMuseum

O'Grady, S. H. (ed.) (1988 [1929]) *Caithréim Thoirdhealbhaigh: The Wars of Turlough*, Irish Texts Society: Publications, 26, 27, London: Marshall

Ó Macháin, P. (1988) 'Poems by Fearghal Óg Mac an Bhaird', 2 Vols, unpublished PhD thesis, University of Edinburgh

Ó Mainnín, M. (1999) ' "The same in origin and blood": bardic windows on the relationship between Irish and Scottish Gaels, c.1200–1650', *CMCS*, Vol. 38, pp. 1–51

—— (2002) 'Gnéithe de chúlra Leabhar Dhéan Leasa Mhóir', in Ó Briain and Ó hÉalaí (eds) (2002), pp. 395–422

—— (ed.) (2007) "Dán Molta ar Eoin Mac Domhnaill, 'Tiarna na nOileán' (†1503)", in Mac Craith, N. and Ó hÉalaí, P. (eds), *Féilscríbhinn Mháirtín Uí Bhriain*, Galway: Cló Iar-Chonnachta, pp. 415–35

Ó Muraíle, N. (1996) *The Celebrated Antiquary Dubhaltach Mac Fhirbhisigh, c.1600–1671: His Lineage, Life, and Learning*, Maynooth: An Sagart

Ó Murchú, L. P. (2001) 'Is mairg nár chrean re maitheas saoghalta', in Riggs, P. (ed.), *Dáibhí Ó Bruadair: his Historical and Literary Context*, Irish Texts Society: Subsidiary Series, 11, London: Irish Texts Society

Ó Raghallaigh, T. (ed.) (1938) *Filí agus Filidheacht Chonnacht*, Baile Átha Cliath: Oifig an tSoláthair

Ó Riain, P. (1973–4) 'The "*crech ríg*" or "regal prey" ', *Éigse*, Vol. 15, pp. 24–30

O Riordan, M. (2007) *Irish Bardic Poetry and Rhetorical Reality*, Cork: Cork University Press

Ó Tuama, S. and Kinsella, T. (eds) (1981) *An Duanaire, 1600–1900: Poems of the Dispossessed*, Mountrath, Portlaoise: Dolmen

Oram, R. (2000) *The Lordship of Galloway*, Edinburgh: John Donald

—— (2004) *David I: the King who Made Scotland*, Stroud: Tempus

Pearse, P. H. (ed.) (1908) *Bruidhean Chaorthainn: Sgéal Fiannaidheachta*, Baile Átha Cliath: Connradh na Gaedhilge

Pine, L. G. (ed.) (1952) *Burke's Genealogical and Heraldic History of the Landed Gentry*, 17th ed., London: Burke's Peerage

Quiggin, E. C. (1911) 'Prolegomena to the Study of the Later Irish Bards 1200–1500', *PBA*, Vol. 5, pp. 89–143

Quin, E. G. (ed.) (1983) *Dictionary of the Irish Language: Based Mainly on Old and Middle Irish Materials. Compact Edition*, Dublin: Royal Irish Academy

Radner, J. N. (ed.) (1978) *Fragmentary Annals of Ireland*, Dublin: Dublin Institute for Advanced Studies

Rhodes, N., Richards, J., and Marshall, J. (eds) (2003) *King James VI and I: Selected Writings*, Ashgate: Aldershot

Robson, M. (ed.) (2003) *Curiosities of Art and Nature: The New Annotated and Illustrated Edition of Martin Martin's Classic* A Description of the Western Islands of Scotland, Port of Ness, Isle of Lewis: Islands Book Trust

Rogers, P. (2005) *Pope and the Destiny of the Stuarts: History, Politics, and Mythology in the Age of Queen Anne*, Oxford: Oxford University Press

Ryan, J. (ed.) (1940) *Féil-sgríbhinn Eoin Mhic Néill: Essays and Studies Presented to Professor Eoin MacNeill, D.Litt., on the Occasion of his Seventieth Birthday*, Dublin: Three Candles

Sellar, W. D. H. (1966) 'The origins and ancestry of Somerled', *SHR*, Vol. 45, pp. 123–42

—— (1971) 'Family origins in Cowal and Kanapdale', *Scottish Studies*, Vol. 15, pp. 21–37

—— (1973) 'The earliest Campbells – Norman, Briton or Gael?', *Scottish Studies*, Vol. 17, pp. 109–25

—— (1981) 'Highland family origins – pedigree making and pedigree faking', in MacLean (ed.) (1981), pp. 103–116

—— (1989) 'Celtic law and Scots law: survival and integration', O'Donnell Lecture 1985, *SGS*, Vol. 29, pp. 1–27

—— (1997–8) 'The ancestry of the MacLeods reconsidered', *TGSI*, Vol. 55, pp. 233–58

—— (2000) 'Hebridean sea-kings: the successors of Somerled, 1164–1316', in Cowan, E. J. and McDonald, R. A. (eds), *Alba: Celtic Scotland in the Middle Ages*, East Linton: Tuckwell, pp. 187–218

Sharpe, R. (ed.) (1995) *Adomnán of Iona: Life of St Columba*, Harmondsworth: Penguin

Simms, K. (1987) 'Bardic poetry as a historical source', in Dunne, T. (ed.), *The Writer as a Witness: Literature as Historical Evidence*, Historical Studies, 16, Cork: Cork University Press, pp. 58–75

—— (2000 [1987]) *From Kings to Warlords: The Changing Political Structure of Gaelic Ireland in the Later Middle Ages*, Studies in Celtic History, 7, Woodbridge: Boydell

—— (2007), 'Muireadhach Albanach Ó Dálaigh and the classical revolution', in Brown, I. et al. (eds) *The Edinburgh History of Scottish Literature, Volume 1: From Columba to the Union*, Edinburgh: Edinburgh University Press, pp. 83–90

—— (comp.) *Bardic Poetry Database*, <http://bardic.celt.dias.ie/> (last accessed 1

September 2010)

Sinclair, A. M. (ed.) *The Gaelic Bards from 1411 to 1715*, Charlottetown P. E. I. : Haszard & Moore, 1890

—— (ed.) *The Gaelic Bards from 1715 to 1765*, Charlottetown: Haszard & Moore., 1890

—— (ed.) (1898–1900) *Na Bàird Leathanach: The Maclean Bards*, Charlottetown: Haszard & Moore

—— (ed.) (1901) *Mactalla nan Tùr*, Sydney: Mac-Talla Pub. Co.

Skene, F. J. H. (ed.) (1880) *Liber Pluscardensis*, 2 Vols, Historians of Scotland, Vol. 10, Edinburgh: William Paterson

Skene, W. F. (1876–80) *Celtic Scotland: A History of Ancient Alban*, 3 Vols, Edinburgh: D. Douglas

—— (1902, first pub. 1837, London: Murray) *The Highlanders of Scotland*, 2nd edn, Stirling: E. Mackay

—— (ed.) (1993, first pub. 1872, Edinburgh) *John of Fordun's Chronicle of the Scottish Nation*, 2 Vols, Lampeter, Dyfed

Skretkowicz, V. *et al.*, *Dictionary of the Scots Language: Dictionar o the Scots Leid*, <http://www.dsl.ac.uk/> (last accessed 1 September 2010)

Smith, R. M. (ed.) (1928) 'The *Senbríathra Fíthail* and related texts', *Revue Celtique*, Vol. 45, pp. 1–92

Sproule, David (1984) 'Origins of the Éoganachta', *Ériu*, Vol. 35, pp. 30–7

—— (1985) 'Politics and pure narrative in the stories about Corc of Cashel', *Ériu*, Vol. 36, pp. 11–28

Steer, K.A., and Bannerman, J.W.M. (1977) *Late Medieval Monumental Sculpture in the West Highlands*, Edinburgh: Royal Commission on the Ancient and Historical Monuments of Scotland

Stevenson, J. and Davidson, P. (2001) *Early Modern Women Poets (1520–1700): An Anthology* Oxford: Oxford University Press

Stewart, J. H. J. (1880) *The Stewarts of Appin*, Glasgow: Maclachlan and Stewart

Stewart-Murray, J. (1908) *Chronicles of the Atholl and Tullibardine Families*, 5 Vols, Edinburgh: Ballantyne

Stokes, W. (ed.) (1877) *Three Middle-Irish Homilies on the Lives of Saints Patrick, Brigit and Columba*, Calcutta

—— (ed.) (1891) 'The Second Battle of Moytura', *Revue Celtique*, Vol. 12, pp. 52–130

Stringer, K. and Grant, A. (1995) 'Scottish foundations', in Grant, A. and Stringer, K. (eds), *Uniting the Kingdom? The Making of British History*, London: Routledge, pp. 85–108

Tanner, R. (1961 [1930]) *Constitutional Documents of the Reign of James I, 1603–1625*, Cambridge: Cambridge University Press

Taylor, S. (ed.) (2000) *Kings, Clerics and Chronicles in Scotland, 500–1297: Essays in Honour of Marjorie Ogilvie Anderson on the Occasion of her Ninetieth Birthday*, Dublin: Four Courts

Thomas, K. (1991 [1984], first pub. 1971, London: Weidenfeld & Nicolson) *Religion and the Decline of Magic: Studies in Popular Beliefs in Sixteenth- and Seventeenth-Century England*, Penguin

Thomson, D. S. (1958) 'Scottish Gaelic folk-poetry ante 1650', *SGS*, Vol. 8, pp. 1–17

—— (1960–3) 'The MacMhuirich bardic family', *TGSI*, Vol. 43, pp. 276–304

—— (1968) 'Gaelic learned orders and literati in medieval Scotland', *Scottish Studies*, Vol. 12, pp. 57–78

—— (ed.) (1968) 'The Harlaw Brosnachadh: an early fifteenth-century literary curio', in

Carney, J. and Greene, D. (eds) (1968),pp. 147–69

—— (1969–70) 'The poetry of Niall MacMhuirich', *TGSI*, Vol. 46, pp. 281–307

—— (1977) 'Three seventeenth-century bardic poets', in Aitken, A. J., Diarmaid, M. P., and Thomson, D. S. (eds), *Bards and Makars*, Glasgow: Glasgow University Press, pp. 221–46

—— 'The poetic tradition in Gaelic Scotland', *Proceedings of the Seventh International Congress of Celtic Studies* (Oxford, 1986), pp. 121–32

—— (1990, first pub. 1974, London, Gollancz) *An Introduction to Gaelic Poetry*, 2nd edn, Edinburgh: Edinburgh University Press

—— (ed.) (1990) *Gaelic and Scots in Harmony: Proceedings of the Second International Conference on the Languages of Scotland, University of Glasgow, 1988*, Glasgow: Dept. of Celtic, University of Glasgow

—— (ed.) (1994, first pub. 1983, 1987, Oxford: Blackwell,) *The Companion to Gaelic Scotland*, Glasgow: Gairm

Thomson, R. L. (ed.) (1970) *Foirm na n-Urrnuidheadh: John Carswell's Gaelic Translation of the Book of Common Order*, Edinburgh: Oliver and Boyd

Thomson, T. and Innes, C. (eds) (1814–75) *The Acts of the Parliaments of Scotland*, 12 Vols, Edinburgh

Todd, J. H. (ed.) (1848) *Leabhar Breathnach Annso Sis: The Irish Version of the Historia Britonum of Nennius*, Dublin: Irish Archaeological Society

Toner, G. (2005) 'Authority, verse and the transmission of *senchas*', *Ériu*, Vol. 55, pp. 59–84

van Hamel, A. G. (ed.) (1932) *Lebor Bretnach: The Irish Version of the Historia Britonum Ascribed to Nennius*, Baile Átha Cliath: Oifig an tSoláthair

Walsh, P. (ed.) (1920) *Leabhar Chlainne Suibhne: An Account of the MacSweeney Families in Ireland, with Pedigrees*, Dublin: Dollard

—— (ed.) (1933) *Gleanings from Irish Manuscripts*, Dublin: Three Candles

—— (1960) *Irish Chiefs and Leaders*, ed C. Ó Lochlainn, Dublin: Three Candles

Watson, F. 'The enigmatic lion: Scotland, kingship and national identity in the wars of independence', in Broun, D., Finlay, R. J., and Lynch, M. (eds) (1998), pp.18–37

Watson, J. C. (ed.) (1940) 'Cathal Mac Muireadhaigh cecinit', in Ryan, J. (ed.), *Féil-sgríbhinn Eoin Mhic Néill: Essays and Studies Presented to Professor Eoin MacNeill, D.LITT., on the Occasion of his Seventieth Birthday*, Dublin: Three Candles, pp. 167–79

—— (ed.) (1965, first pub. 1934, London; Glasgow: Blackie and son) *Gaelic Songs of Mary McLeod: Òrain agus Luinneagan Gàidhlig le Màiri nighean Alasdair Ruaidh*, Scottish Gaelic Texts, 9, Edinburgh: Oliver and Boyd

Watson, W. J. (1914–19) 'Classic Gaelic poetry of panegyric in Scotland', *TGSI*, Vol. 29, pp. 194–235

—— (ed.) (1927) 'Unpublished Gaelic poetry — III.', *SGS*, Vol. 2, pp. 75–91

—— (ed.) (1932, first pub. 1918, Inverness: Northern Counties) *Bàrdachd Ghàidhlig: Specimens of Gaelic Poetry 1550–1900*, Stirling: Learmonth

—— (ed.) (1937) *Scottish Verse from the Book of the Dean of Lismore*, Scottish Gaelic Texts, Vol. 1, Edinburgh: Oliver and Boyd

—— (2004, first pub. 1926, Edinburgh: Blackwood) *The Celtic Place-Names of Scotland*, Edinburgh: Birlinn

Watt, D. E. R. (ed.) (1987–) *Scotichronicon: New Edition in Latin and English with Notes and Indexes*, Aberdeen: Aberdeen University Press

Weiss, R. (ed.) (1937) 'The earliest account of the murder of James I of Scotland', *The English Historical Review*, Vol. 52: 207, pp. 479–491

Williams, J. H. (ed.) (1996a) *Stewart Style 1513–1542: Essays on the Court of James V*, East Linton: Tuckwell Press

—— (1996b) 'David Lyndsay and the making of King James V', in Wiliams, J. H. (ed.) (1996a), pp. 201–226

Woolf, A. (2005) 'The origins and ancestry of Somerled', *Mediaeval Scandinavia*, Vol. 15, pp. 199–213

—— (2007) *From Pictland to Alba 789–1070*, The New Edinburgh History of Scotland, Vol. 2, Edinburgh: Edinburgh University Press

Worden, B. (1985) 'Providence and politics in Cromwellian England', *Past & Present*, Vol. 109, pp. 55–99

Zumbuhl, Mark (2006) 'Contextualising the *Duan Albanach*', in McLeod, W., Fraser, J. E., and Gunderloch, A. (eds), pp. 11–24

Index of Poems

General Index